Mostly Theatre

A History of Speech and Theatre
at Muskingum College
1837–2000

Donald P. Hill, Ph.D.

Mostly Theatre
A History of Speech and Theatre at Muskingum College: 1837-2000

©2002 Donald P. Hill, Ph.D.

First Edition

Library of Congress Card Number: 2002100785
ISBN 1-887932-76-3

Printed in the United States of America

Designed and Produced by

New Concord Press

P. O. Box 8016
Zanesville, Ohio 43702-8016

http://www.newconcordpress.com

Dedication

I dedicate this book to my mother and father, who unknowingly started it all, and to my teachers, colleagues, Muskingum Players, and all those people who, at some time, participated somehow, and in some way, in a theatrical production.

apologia

I cannot explain the public's fascination for certain plays. No one can. If there exists a formula for discovering what audiences will accept or reject, commercial producers would have a bonanza. Nevertheless, the play-going public is willing to accept the idea that the same play produced by different people is not the same play. When the human element of production differs the results are different.

The same is not true for the reader: repetition is repetition. I apologize to the reader for repeating productions of the same play. My excuse is twofold: in recording history one discovers that history repeats itself, and as an old play director I have the habit of <u>seeing</u> plays, never really <u>reading</u> them.

The Alumni Gymnasium • 1900

The Alumni Gymnasium was built in 1900. In 1938, it was converted to a theatre workshop. In 1939, alumni renovated it for use as a theatre, which was dedicated to Dr. and Mrs. Layton. *Known thereafter as the Little Theatre, it became the center for departmental theatre productions for the next forty years. Theatre file photo courtesy Muskingum College Public Relations Office.*

Preface
by Dr. Lorle Porter

Mostly Theatre is the result of a decade of meticulous research during which [Dr.] Donald Hill mined the Muskingum College archives, its publications, and the memory of its people to reconstruct the history of Speech and Theatre at the college.

Anyone who has ever settled into a seat in the Little Theatre, or Layton Theatre, or any other venue commandeered for a theatrical performance at Muskingum College, is in for a nostalgic and informative trip when they open this book.

On one level, it is autobiographical, for theatre has been Don's life. We are treated to tales of his training as an actor; his interaction with personalities such as Stella Adler and Mercedes McCambridge, and teachers and colleagues in New York, California, and Iowa. We begin to appreciate the basis for his wonderful knowledge of the literature of the theatre (the core of his success as a teacher) and the development of his fundamental creed: good theatre comes only through hard work and through respect for the book. When you "do theatre" you leave the world outside–for the theatre is a special world, a world where life's meaning–the human condition–is explored.

Mostly Theatre is also a tribute to his colleagues of the past five decades and to the students whose work and commitment made his life's work meaningful. The book is his gift to them. It features at its core a veritable ode to the legendary Laytons, who brought Muskingum College to national attention through their work in Speech and Theatre.

Don Hill was "well-taught' and he taught well. *Mostly Theatre* is the curtain call of his teaching. Well done, "Snoopy."

Lorle Porter, Ph.D.

Foreword
by Dr. Jerry Martin

Muskingum College, like most other private liberal arts institutions founded in the early part of the nineteenth century, finds its strongest foothold for the future in its roots. Tradition is very important for those who attended such a college and who, now, look at the experience in retrospect. Conversely, for those who are beginning study at a liberal arts institution, understanding institutional tradition and heritage is as much a part of the educational process as is the contemporary course work.

The Speech Communication and Theatre Department at Muskingum experienced a traditional development, finding its roots in the liberal traditions of rhetoric and public address from Aristotle and Horace. The study of rhetoric and public address evolved into communication studies. As the disciplines developed, many colleges established a theatre department, separating it from its classical roots. Muskingum has stayed true to liberal arts traditions, however, and theatre has remained as a vital part of the academic life.

Mostly Theatre takes a look at the development of the theatre program at Muskingum through the eyes of an alumnus, long-serving faculty, and an emeritus faculty member. By being involved with the theatre program development at the college for more than half a century, Don Hill brings the perspective that few have of an academic institution. Through the examination of the history and tradition of the Speech Communication and Theatre Department, Don Hill has given us a look at Muskingum College's heritage.

Table of Contents

Author's Preface

In the fall of 1945, I enrolled as a freshman at Muskingum College. For the next fifty years, the college and its theatre were central to my life and career. After graduating in 1949, with a major in both Speech and English, plus a teacher's certification, I taught in the public schools until the fall of 1959, then I received an appointment as Assistant Professor of Speech and Director of Theatre at Muskingum College, a post which I held for the next thirty-six years.

In the spring of 1995, I retired with the intention of writing, something I'd never had time to do while I was actively teaching and directing. I did publish the *Muskingum Theatre Handbook* (1970), a "how to" book on play production, which became an effective teaching tool for me and for some of my students who also became teachers. However, it does not represent much of the history and information I would like to record. Some of that history is encompassed in this book which proposes to be a partial history of speech, but mostly theatre. The reader will find that one point of emphasis is upon the early history of speech and theatre at Muskingum as they evolved from the beginning (1837) into a modern department (1914-1958). A second point of emphasis is upon the history of theatre as I experienced it as a student and teacher from 1945 to 1959 and, later, as Director of Theatre at my *alma mater* from 1959 until 1995.

I have tried to limit my subject to the theatre; however, at Muskingum, the theatre grew out of the elocutionary movement which later appeared as speech and theatre. The two are almost inseparable. That came as no surprise to me, but the research and recording of history always reveals surprises large and small. Perhaps the biggest surprise for me was the significant role which elocution played in the nineteenth-century history of the college and later, in the twentieth century, under the auspices of both presidents J. Knox Montgomery, Sr.* and his son, Robert N. Montgomery.

In eighteenth-century England, the demands of the ministerial office gave rise to a movement to reform the speaking habits of ministers and, at their own bidding, the result was the elocutionary movement. The same movement was repeated in America during the nineteenth century.

In 1837, Muskingum College was founded by ministers and devout congregations for the purpose of educating ministers. Every president of the college in the nineteenth century was a minister. The same trend continued in the twentieth century and ended when Robert N. Montgomery retired in 1962.

---

* The extent to which President J. Knox Montgomery, Sr. was committed to a strong speech program may be seen in a special "Forensic Edition" of the Muskingum College Bulletin dated June 8, 1925. On the front of the magazine is a picture of President Montgomery which bears the title "Father of Oratory at Muskingum."

Inside, on the first page, is a picture of Dean Charles R. Layton captioned "Head of the Department of Oratory," followed by a short history of oratory at Muskingum. Part of that history has Muskingum winning recognition in twenty-one oratorical contests. The college won first place in the National Intercollegiate Oratorical contest in 1913, ten first's in the state and interstate contests, seven second's, and four third's.

The next page shows a picture of Professor Ermy H. Jackson, the 1925 Debate Coach. (Both Dr. and Mrs. Layton were on leave, studying at the University of Michigan.) The debate record is equally impressive. Since the beginning of intercollegiate debating in 1907, Muskingum had lost only three home debates. Since 1920, Muskingum had won twenty-three out of twenty-six intercollegiate debates. The college was recognized as the undisputed champion of the Ohio Intercollegiate Debate Conference. In 1923, Muskingum won twelve out of twelve intercollegiate debates. The final two pages of the Bulletin show pictures and records of the 1924 and 1925 winning debate teams: Harry B. Crytzer, Robert Secrest, James Leitch, John Smith, William Finley, Lewis Brown, William Nichol, Melton Boyd, Harold Finney, and Benjamin Hazen.

The presence of a minister at the head of a college is nothing new to education in America. The earliest college was Harvard, founded in 1636 for the purpose of supplying colonials with moral guidance and an orderly environment. The task of ministering to any community requires a learned command of language and the ability to speak it well. Harvard's success made it a model for nearly every other college in America.

The discovery of the close relationship of the ministry and elocution, combined with the Scotch-Irish love of education, made clear the love-hate relationship between the Presbyterians and the theatre. The church's complaint against the theatre was about the tawdry moral character of the professional theatre and its practitioners. Theatre for educational purposes in schools was an entirely different matter. (After all, there were precedents for good relationships, such as the classical Greek theatre that was central to Greek culture and spiritual life, and the Medieval theatre that church clerics used as a teaching tool.)

Early oratory departments used elocution as a means of improving the delivery of student speeches. Modern speech departments grew out of oratory, and theatre grew along with it. At Muskingum, this transition from oratory to speech was shepherded by Dr. Charles Rush and Mrs. Ferne Parsons Layton. When they retired, the transition of theatre into a discipline (which was initiated by Mrs. Layton) was carried forward by Mary Elizabeth Johnson and Martha Moore. I was hired to continue the advancement of theatre toward an academic discipline.

If there is meaning to be found in this book (in my life!), it must be found in the history of theatre in education and in the public performance of plays by teachers and students. Plays keep theatre alive: Broadway successes and flops, the great works of major playwrights and the lesser works of minor playwrights, published and unpublished works of student playwrights all are fuel for the theatre. Plays keep the audiences coming and going with the eternal ebb and flow of their constant search for truth and knowledge, excitement, and emotional fulfillment.

Acknowledgements

The groundwork for the early history of speech and theatre (1837-1944) was established by Dr. William Fisk and Thomas Berkshire in their separate histories of the college. Muriel Bain's history of the department supplied important pertinent information. On a more specific note are the theatre histories written by former students and alumni, Cheryl D. Swiss, William Laing, and Kathleen O'Brien. Most of the information contained in the sections on theatre from the 1960's through the 1990's and the Index, "A Production History," came from my personal collection of play programs, pictures, and publicity materials.

The Muskingum College Library and its archives provided general and specific details relating to the college theatre. The library staff—especially the Reference Librarian, Marie Jones, Associate Librarian Barbara Fischer, and Head Librarian, Robin Hanson—were models of cooperation, as was Janalyn Moss, the archivist.

I gratefully acknowledge Helen Coleclaser and the staff of the Delmont Public Library (PA) for supplying me with background information on speech education; the Pittsburgh Carnegie Library Reference Staff for sending me information on Stella Adler, Angna Enters, and several Off-Broadway productions; and Michael Westbrook of the Illinois College Library for confirming the spelling of S. S. Hamill's name.

The following college offices, officers, and staffs were equally responsive to my requests for information and guidance: Academic Affairs, Margaret C. Adams; Alumni, Ronald Mazeroski; Development, J. Ransom Clark and Susan Dannemann; President Anne C. Steele; Public Relations, Janice Tucker McCloud, Rod Lang, and Sharon Walker; the Registrar; and Student Life. I owe a special debt to Ronald Mazeroski, Director of Alumni Relations, for assisting me in organizing and presenting the program of speech recitals for the "Forty-Niners'" Fiftieth Reunion, and for providing me with a "bully" pulpit for the workshop presentation on the history of speech and theatre at Muskingum, during the 2000 Alumni Reunion.

Crucial information was supplied by college and student publications, such as the *Black and Magenta, Muscoljuan, McWeek,* the *Alumni Bulletin,* the *Annual College Catalog,* and a variety of newsletters and calendars of events. Issues of the Muskingum Players' magazine, *Cue,* supplied me with a significant number of details.

I would like to thank Virginia Massenberg ('87) for research she did on speech and theatre during the time she was an Agnes Moorehead Scholar, Mary Ann Spitznagel DeVolld ('73) for her excellent record keeping, Dr. Jack Peterson for the information he supplied on *A Little Night Music,* and Gail Modica, the secretary for the Art, Music, and Theatre Departments, who was always ready to lend a helping hand.

I am grateful for the support and assistance of Dr. Jerry Martin, Chairman of Speech Communication and Theatre, and to the members of that department. I especially wish to thank Dr. Diane Rao Harman for contributing the section on theatre in 2000.

Photographs in this book came from a variety of sources and were donated by the Muskingum College Library Archives. Dr. Coleman Knight took pictures for many years for college publications and the theatre. Without his commitment to the general welfare of the college, many events would have lacked illustrative support. Dr. Knight took most of the theatre photographs throughout the '40s, '50s, and '60s. I wish to thank Ronald N. Lauck, Technical Director of Theatre, for lending pictures from the late '80s through the '90s, and Sharon Walker for helping me find pictures of past productions. William Blakesley and Chab Guthrie are duly honored in the section on the Little Theatre Gallery for their contribution of art work to the Muskingum College Theatre.

My deepest appreciation goes to Larry R. Bell, B.S.Ed. for the hours he spent helping me with the original manuscript and for keeping it within the bounds of recognizable English syntax and punctuation; to Toni M. Leland, professional publicist, who led me through the labyrinth of formatting, indexing, proof-reading, and other esoteric elements of preparing a book for publication; and to my friend and colleague, Dr. Lorle Porter, who, from a distance, urged me ever onward and upward, and along the way, refreshed my memory with important moments of mutual delight and glee.

Presidents of Muskingum College

Rev. Benjamin Waddle, D.D.	1837-1838
Rev. Samuel Wilson	1838-1846
Rev. David A. Wallace, D.D., L.L.D.	1846-1848
Rev. John Milligan	1848-1849
Rev. Samuel G. Irvine, D.D.	1849-1851
Rev. Samuel McArthur	1851-1855
Rev. Benjamin Waddle, D.D.	1855-1858
Rev. J. P. Lytle, D.D. *(pro tem)*	1858-1859
Rev. H. P. McClurkin, D.D. *(pro tem)*	1859-1861
Rev. L. B. W. Shryock	1861-1864
Rev. David Paul, D.D.	1865-1879
Rev. F. M. Spencer, D.D.	1879-1886
Thomas Hosack Paden, Ph.D. *(pro tem)*	1886-1887
Rev. John D. Irons, D.D.	1887-1892
Rev. D. K. McKnight *(pro tem)*	1892-1893
Rev. Jesse Johnson, A.M., D.D.	1893-1902
Chester J. Marshall, A.M. *(pro tem)*	1902-1903
Leonard J. Graham, A.M. *(pro tem)*	1903-1904
Rev. J. Knox Montgomery, D.D., L.L.D.	1904-1931
J. Knox Montgomery, Jr., L.L.D. (Acting President)	1931-1932
Rev. Robert N. Montgomery, B.A., M.Th., D.D., L.L.D.	1932-1962
Glen Lowery McConagha, Ph.D.	1962-1964
William P. Miller, B.A., B.S., M.Ed., Ed.D. (Acting)	1964-1965
Harry S. Manley, B.A., L.L.B., Ph.D.	1965-1970
William P. Miller (Acting President)	1970-1971
William P. Miller	1971-1975
John A. Brown, L.L.D., L.H.D., Litt.D.	1975-1978
Rev. Russell S. Hutchison, B.S., D.D., B.D., M.Th., Ph.D. (Acting)	1978
Arthur J. DeJong, B.A., B.D., M.Th., S.T.D.	1978-1987
Samuel W. Speck, Jr., B.A., M.A., Ph.D. (Interim)	1987-1988
Samuel W. Speck, Jr.	1988-1999
David Skeen, B.S., M.A., Ph.D. (Interim President)	1999-2000
Anne C. Steele, B.A., M.S., Ed.D.	2000 -

(Sources: *Annual Catalogue of Muskingum College,* 1896, p. 62, and *Muskingum College 1996 Alumni Directory* (White Plains, New York: Bernard C. Harris Publishing Company, Inc., 1996, vi.)

The Early Years: 1837–1914

The present Muskingum College Speech Communication and Theatre Department is the result of a gradual development over the years. Three of the many influences on that development were: 1) early rhetorical practices, 2) student literary societies, and 3) elocution.

Early Rhetorical Practices

Although speech as we know it today did not appear until the twentieth century, it was present in many forms early in the nation's schools. Daily classroom activities required recitations, oral readings, and oral reports even at the elementary (common-school) level. Such activities were the staple of the *McGuffey Readers*.

William Holmes McGuffey (1800–1873) was a teacher and educator who wrote and published six readers between 1835 and 1857. They were compilations of essays, short stories, and poetry, with themes of self-improvement, patriotism, and moral instruction. They became so popular they were used as textbooks throughout the Midwest and the South.[1]

McGuffey followed the elocutionary principles recommended by John Walker, the English author of *Elements of Elocution* (1781), a popular source book for elocutionary training in higher education and in professional schools. McGuffey was not alone in fostering speech activities in the lower grades. William Russell, who was the editor of the *American Journal of Education* from 1826 to 1829, encouraged interest in elocution in the elementary schools.[2]

The Latin grammar school, which prepared boys for college, taught the classical curriculum that grew out of the Renaissance tradition. Boys learned to speak and write Greek and Latin. They also learned oratory, declamation, and forensics. Academies superseded the Latin grammar school at the end of the eighteenth century, with classes in both written and spoken composition (rhetoric) and with some emphasis on conversation and discussion. The secondary schools (high schools) which replaced the academies had public speaking, public reading, and recitation. Plays, debates, declamations, spell-downs, and dialogues were extracurricular. At mid-nineteenth century, the high schools had courses in elocution and declamation; rhetoric meant elocution, but leaned more and more toward written composition.[3]

In addition to lectures, professors of higher education used the Socratic method, which required student response. Formal reports, disputations, declamations, dramatic dialogues, essays, and poems were read aloud. Students spoke to single classes and in assembly on certain days of the week. Some courses ended with a final oral examination. Public holidays and ceremonies, such as commencement, offered suitable occasions for plays, orations, and oral readings which climaxed the many rehearsals that took place over the year.[4]

If students entering Muskingum College had not already experienced some of the activities mentioned, they were readily available to them when Muskingum opened its doors in 1837. If they were not available, they would be added soon to the eclectic mix of oral activities befitting the era of Jacksonian frontier democracy.

The two-year Preparatory Course (which the College required of students lacking in background) consisted of an intensive study in Latin, Greek, English Grammar, Math, Geography, and Algebra. The students were then ready for the rigors of the Classical Course, which included the following:

Freshman Year: Virgil, Xenophon, Greek Testament, History of Greece, Horace's *Odes*, Livy, History of Rome, Geometry, and Higher Algebra.

Sophomore Year: Trigonometry, Horace's *Satires*, Physiology, Herodotus, Homer, Thucydides, Rhetoric,[5] Botany, and History of Modern Europe.

Junior Year: Tacitus, Thucydides, Conic Sections, Euripides, Logic, History of English Literature, Natural Philosophy, Juvenal, Analytical Geometry, Differential Calculus, and History of the United States.

Senior Year: Cicero's *De Oratore*, Chemistry, Butler's *Analogy*, Hebrew (optional), Evidences of Christianity, Astronomy, Geology, Political Economy, Demosthenes' *De Corona*, and Mental Philosophy.[6]

Oratory and the study of drama had long been part of the classical curricula, traceable to the Medieval and Renaissance scholastic traditions. The presence of Greek and Roman antiquities in the curricula made possible the study of tragedies by Sophocles, Euripides, and Seneca, as well as the comedies of Aristophanes, Plautus, and Terence. The philosophies and theories of Plato, Aristotle, Cicero, and Quintillian explained the relationship between the orator and the actor.[7]

In Colonial America, there were laws against play performances in every state except Maryland and Virginia.[8] Even in those two states, professional actors performed at their own risk. The paucity of theatre was explained by two facts: the Puritans considered play-acting idolatrous, and the early settlers were too busy, clearing the land and making a home out of a wilderness, to be concerned with stage plays.[9]

However, everyone was concerned about education and there was no strong feeling against educational theatre. The first attempt to establish a Latin grammar school was in Boston in 1635. The chief purpose was to prepare boys for Harvard, which was founded a year later.[10] At that time, there was an interest in theatre among members of the student body, but it found an outlet in oral reading or dialogues " . . . used in the classroom to develop habits of good speech, clear thinking, and poise in front of an audience—certainly not for entertainment."[11]

As the eighteenth century wore on and people became settled, play performances in colleges persisted under claims of educational value. Scenes from plays by Seneca, Terence, Plautus, and Greek authors were acted out in classes, and there were performances of original plays on anniversaries and at holiday celebrations.[12]

The Continental Congress outlawed plays during the Revolutionary War; however, both British and American troops entertained themselves with original farces, parodies of the enemy, and even classics, such as Sheridan's *The Rivals* and Addison's *Cato*.[13]

After the Revolutionary War and during the nineteenth century, religious objection to the professional theatre dwindled. College students who were interested in theatre no longer disguised it as "moral dialogues" or lectures.[14]

Between 1800 and 1861, there were 168 colleges founded. Only eighteen were state institutions; 150 were denominational for the express purpose of educating ministers.[15] The Old Northwest was more prolific in starting new colleges than any other part of the country. Ohio founded over twelve; Muskingum College was one of them. Of the colleges surrounding the Great Lakes region, Samuel Morison remarked that these poorly-endowed, religiously-inspired colleges "...educated the whole man and maintained a standard of excellence in the liberal arts that has seldom been attained in wealthy tax-supported state universities."[16]

Burnet Hobgood stated that people expected that there would be more theatre in government-supported colleges than in church-related schools. Such is not the case

> ... in the states surrounding the Great Lakes, a higher percentage of church-related schools offer theatre programs than do colleges supported either by private or government means.[17]

After the Civil War, the liberating influence continued. Extracurricular activities increased with renewed energies: athletics, glee clubs, social fraternities, and play production. Foreign language departments presented plays in the original languages. In 1881, Harvard presented *Oedipus Tyrannus,* and German and French departments sponsored plays by Schiller and Racine. The plays were tied to the curricula and helped the establishment of curricular drama presentation.[18]

At Muskingum, the Classical Course led the way to the study of drama as literature. As part of the junior class work, Euripides was studied in 1867, and again in 1873. In 1877, the *Alcestis*, a difficult tragi-comedy by Euripides, was a course in itself. In 1887, and again in 1894, a Greek Tragedy was the generic title of the course, wherein "The Greek stage is studied in connection with the reading of a Greek Tragedy."[19]

Toward the end of the century (1894), the Department of Modern Languages offered second- and third-year German courses in Schiller's *Wilhelm Tell*, Lessings's *Minna von Barnhelm*, and Goethe's *Faust*. The French language area featured a third-year course in Moliere's *Misanthrope* and Corneille's *Le Cid*.[20] The English Department taught Dramatic Art, a reading course in Shakespeare's plays.[21]

Although the emphasis of this history is on theatre, it is also very much about the entire field of speech. Speech and theatre have been companions since classical Greece. Actors of fifth century B.C. theatre used the art of oratory in the performance of plays. Playwrights utilized elements of rhetoric (oral and written) in the composition of plays, which consisted mainly of long speeches by three principal actors. In fact, sections of the plays were based upon techniques of argumentation and debate. Originally, the play was the thing and the actors orated or recited the speeches.

As indicated earlier, rhetorical practices were part of the everyday classroom activities. In one of the first catalogs published by the college (1846-47), there is a description of the Collegiate Course (Classical Course) of study, after which is stated, "Compositions and declamations attended to throughout the course." The "course" referred to the entire curricula of four years, not to just one course.[22] In another catalog, under "Work of the Departments," the Psychology Department declared, "The Senior class recites in this branch five times a week during the Fall and Winter terms."[23]

Muriel Bain writes,

> Other than these, the first evidences of requirements in public speaking are to be found in the records of a meeting of the Board of Trustees of the College, held September 3, 1856, when the following motion, among others, was passed: "Resolved: That the faculty be authorized to require the students in alphabetical order, to deliver speeches in the Hall, immediately after morning prayers, no speech to be shorter than two minutes, nor longer than fifteen." Also, "Resolved: That the faculty be authorized to give no diplomas to students who refuse to perform in public as assigned."[24]

Pedagogical traditions dictated daily recitations in Latin and Greek, as in other language courses, and students often stood for oral examinations at the end of each term.[25] Juniors in the Classical Course read and discussed Hugh Blair's *Lectures on Rhetoric and Belles Lettres* (1783) and Richard Whately's *Elements of Rhetoric* (1826). Both books were standard texts on the subject.[26]

The administration gave students opportunities to exhibit their dramatic and speaking skills in public. Commencement was a popular choice for such public presentations. At Commencement on September 21, 1854 H. L. McKee gave the Salutatory Address in Greek and English. On the afternoon of the 1856 Commencement, there was a discussion by the graduates on the topic, "Is the Profession of Divinity worthy of more honor than the Profession of Teaching?" J. H. Buchanan spoke for the "Affirmative" and B. F. Peairs for the "Negative." At the 1878 Commencement on June 27, there were orations in Latin, Greek, and Hebrew.[27]

The Commencement of 1902 was front-page news in the *Zanesville Evening Signal*. The entire program was given in detail, under the headline "End of a Gay Week At Old Muskingum, Commencement Exercises Are Attended by Great Number of Visitors, Diplomas Presented to a Large Class." Commencement week began on Sunday, June 15, with a forenoon address in the town hall by Reverend Robert K. Porter (Ph.D.) of Minneapolis. His topic was "Culture for Young Men and Young Women." That evening in the College Chapel, President Jesse Johnson delivered the Baccalaureate Sermon.

On Monday evening the Literary Societies awarded diplomas to their graduating seniors and listened to an address entitled "A Young Man's Value in Society," delivered by Reverend Charles H. Robinson (D.D.) of Wheeling, West Virginia. On Tuesday, guests were entertained by a double-header baseball game between Muskingum College and a Byesville team. That evening, separate oratory contests were held for men and women; Mr. J. M. Brown of Wheeling, West Virginia, awarded first place prizes to each of the winning orators. Wednesday was a day of meetings. In the morning, the Board of Trustees met with the president and, in the afternoon, the Alumni Association held an open meeting in the chapel. That evening, "Alumni Night" included a program of music and an address by Reverend W. K. Fulton ('89) of Union Station, Pennsylvania.

Thursday, June 19, was Commencement Day. The morning was dedicated to "Class Day Exercises," during which the fourteen members of the graduating class presented "An Hour with Shakespeare." The program consisted of an introductory synopsis of *The Merchant of Venice*, a reading of the "Court Scene" from the play, two orations on

Shakespearean subjects, presentation of the "Key of Knowledge," and a Response. In the afternoon, diplomas were awarded. That evening, Anna Catherine R. Walter, teacher of elocution, read "The Black Horse and His Rider" (Sheppard), and the Annual Concert concluded the eventful Commencement Week.[28]

A later chapter shows how the dynamic Student Literary Societies energized the early rhetorical practices of classical studies which were conveyed by traditional education teaching methods and supported by a conservative administration.

REFERENCES

1   William Holmes McGuffey was born in western Pennsylvania near Claysville. When he was two years old, his Scotch-Irish parents moved to the Ohio Territory north of Youngstown. He began teaching in the subscription schools of rural Ohio at the age of thirteen. During eleven years of teaching in Ohio and Kentucky, he continued his own education through tutors at Greensburg Academy and Washington College, where he received his A.B. with honors in 1826. He was a professor of languages at Miami University in Oxford, Ohio, for eleven years, during which time he also assisted elementary school teachers, and established his own model school with neighborhood children.
     From 1836 to 1839, McGuffey was president of Cincinnati College; from 1839 to 1843, he was president of Ohio University. He helped found the common school system of Ohio. In 1845, he was elected to the Chair of Mental and Moral Philosophy at the University of Virginia, Charlottesville, where he served until his death in 1873.
     The *McGuffey Readers* have sold 122,000,000 copies, and continue to be reprinted. (*Encyclopaedia Britannica*, Vol. 14, first published in 1768 by a Society of Gentlemen in Scotland, (Chicago: Encyclopaedia Britannica, Inc., William Benton, Publisher, 1970), p. 515.

2   Mary Margaret Robb, "The Elocutionary Movement and Its Chief Figures," in *A History of Speech Education In America: Background Studies*. Edited by Karl R. Wallace. (New York: Appleton-Century-Crofts, Inc., 1954), p. 180.

3   Gladys L. Borchers and Lillian R. Wagner, "Speech Education in Nineteenth-Century Schools." in *A History of Speech Education in America: Background Studies*, pp. 289-294.

4   George V. Bohman, "Rhetorical Practice in Colonial America," in *A History of Speech Education in America: Background Studies*. pp. 60-61.

5   The course in rhetoric used Blair and Whately as textbooks for the course. See note #26 for further details.

6   *First Annual Circular and Catalogue of the Officers and Students of Muskingum College, New Concord, Ohio: 1846–1847* (Zanesville, Ohio: Parke and Bennett, Printers, Gazette Office, 1847), pp. 10-11. Also see subsequent *Catalogues*, 1867–1868, pp. 10-11; 1873–1874, p. 11.

7   Edwin Duerr, *The Length and Depth of Acting*,(New York: Holt, Rinehart and Winston, 1962), pp. 30-31.

8   Garff B. Wilson, *Three Hundred Years of American Drama and Theatre: From Ye Bear and Ye Cubb to Hair* (New Jersey, Englewood Cliffs: Prentice-Hall, Inc., 1973), pp. 12-13.

9   Ibid., pp. 18-19. See also Barnard Hewitt, *Theatre U.S.A.: 1665–1957* (New York: McGraw-Hill Book Company, 1959), pp. 1-2.

10   Edgar W. Knight, *Education in the United States*, Third Revised Edition (New York: Greenwood Press Publishers, 1969), p. 113.

11   Hewitt, p. 2.

12   John L. Clark, "Educational Dramatics in Nineteenth-Century Colleges," in *A History of Speech Education in America: Background Studies*, pp. 525-526.

13   Hewitt, pp. 30-32.

14   Clark, p. 537.

15   Clark, p. 534.

16   Samuel Eliot Morison, *The Oxford History of the American People* (New York: Oxford University Press, 1965), p. 533.

17   Burnet Hobgood, "Theatre in U.S. Higher Education: Emerging Patterns and Problems," *Educational Theatre Journal*, XVI (May, 1964), p. 144.

18   Clark, pp. 541-543.

19   *Annual Catalogue of Muskingum College: 1894*, p. 30.

20   *Annual Catalogue of Muskingum College: 1891*, p. 20.

21   *Annual Catalogue of Muskingum College: 1905*, p. 28.

22   *Annual Catalogue of Muskingum College: 1847*, p. 12.

23   *Annual Catalogue of Muskingum College: 1903*, p. 27.

24   Muriel Bain, "History of Speech Department, Muskingum college, Compiled 1937," (unpublished paper), Library Archives: Muskingum College, p. 1.

25   Fisk, William L., *A History of Muskingum College*. (Muskingum College, New Concord, Ohio, 1978), pp. 35, 40.

26   Clarence W. Edney, "English Sources of Rhetorical Theory in Nineteenth-Century America," in *A History of Speech Education in America: Background Studies*, pp: 82-83.

27   Commencement Programs for 1854, 1856, 1878, Muskingum College Archives.

28   *Zanesville Evening Signal*, June 19, 1902, p. 1.

A Hymn to McGuffey's Readers
and
A Portrait of Grandmother Grove

Grandma and Grandpa in the following account refer to my mother's parents. Rosa Bell Sellers Grove was born in 1877 and died in 1958. Enoch Elwood Grove was born in 1874 and died in 1959. The time of the following account was the early Thirties and it takes place in rural Bremen, Ohio.

The Grove family on the porch of the Park Hotel in Bremen, Ohio. Enoch Elwood, the builder and owner of the hotel, is at left and Rosa Bell Sellers is at right. They flank their daughter and son, Madaline and Casel. The author's mother Madaline (Madge) was born in 1898, and her brother, Casel, was born in 1902. *Grove Family Album.*

One of the most unforgettable characters I ever met was my grandmother Grove. Her approach to life was extremely practical. To the mind of a small young boy, there were few things she could not do, from baking the best melt-away lemon cookies, planting a garden, milking the cows, or killing snakes, to facing the fury of a nest of bumble bees with a tea kettle of boiling water in one hand and a broom in the other.

All this practicality and versatility were combined with an exuberance for life that, considering the amount of work she did each day, was astonishing. These qualities were enough to make visiting Grandma and Grandpa on the farm a welcome relief for a small town kid.

Add to these qualities the ability that Grandma had for communicating ideas with wit and charm; she possessed the talent for making the most mundane events attractive and humorous.

For example: working on the farm was lonely work; there were few strangers who came along to interrupt the daily routine of chores. People who did happen along were friends, neighbors, or relatives. Why worry about wardrobe? Even so, my grandmother was known for her peculiarities of dress. To her own stock of everyday garb, she added bits and pieces of clothing that Mother would give her for quilting or making rugs. On one particular day, I recall her running to greet us. She had on her usual apron, under the top of which was visible an old worn-out sweater of one of my brothers, below which was one of her own tattered calico print skirts. Her stockings were a knee-length woolen pair that one of us boys had worn with knickers. She was laughing as she came toward us. "I'm not crazy," she said, "It's just the way they dress me."

Every Saturday, rain or shine, we took a trip from the farm into Bremen. We got all dressed up to do this because the trip was an occasion. One trip a week for supplies and a haircut (if needed) was all the traveling we did. As we all got seated comfortably in the one and only seat of the old Model T Ford, as soon as the door banged shut, came Grandmother's prologue to the venture: "Heel and toe and away we go."

The first snowflake of winter did not bring fear of the cold or sorrow for the hard weather ahead, it merely brought from Grandmother, "'It snows!' cried the school boy and his shout rang through parlor and hall."[1]

Now where in the world did she get all of these qualities? What was it about her generation that seemed to make these qualities a part of their point of view and the way in which they lived? I have a suspicion that schooling and family rearing had a big influence. I remember my grandmother telling me that she had to walk a mile to school; she carried her own books and even her own chair! I also remember that I would look up at her sometimes after some funny or knowledgeable remark rang new and true on my ears, and I would ask, "Grandma, where did that come from?" Grandmother would reply, "Why, *McGuffey's Reader*, of course."

The *McGuffey Readers* will continue to be published as long as the 'Three R's' are fundamental to the education of the young, and as long as basic universal values such as truth, integrity, hard work, common sense, and morality are honored by civility.[2]

REFERENCES

1. William Holmes McGuffey, *McGuffey's Fifth Eclectic Reader,* Revised Edition (Cincinnati: American Book Company, 1920), p. 57.
    (The actual wording of Mrs. Sarah Joseph Hale's first line of "It Snows" is, "It snows! Cries the schoolboy, "Hurrah" and his shout is ringing through parlor and hall." Personally, I like Grandmother's paraphrase because it is more rhythmic and it is hers.)
2. Besides the section on prose and poetry and the illustrations that accompany it, the *"Readers"* contain "Introductory Matter" which includes: "I. Preliminary Remarks, II. Articulation, III. Inflections, IV. Accent, V. Emphasis, VI. Modulation, VII. Poetic Pauses, (and) Exercises. *McGuffeys Fifth Eclectic Reader.*

Campus Buildings Used for Speech and Theatre Activities

These campus buildings, while not built primarily for speech or theatre activities, were, at one time or another, used for public performances.

Paul Hall • 1873

Paul Hall is the oldest building on campus, and was named for President David Paul. It had several large rooms and an auditorium that was used by the campus literary societies for public speeches, debates, and dramatic readings. *Photo courtesy M.C. Public Relations Office.*

Johnson Hall • 1899

Johnson Hall, named for President Jesse Johnson, also housed the literary societies and their programs. The building was maintained as a college chapel, which was renovated into a platform stage in 1978, and dedicated in honor of Dr. and Mrs. Layton. *Photo courtesy M.C. Public Relations Office.*

The Literary Societies: 1836–1923

In the early history of the college, literary societies were a major influence on the development of speech and theatre on campus.

These societies were popular in the nineteenth century, when people delighted in forums that served as an outlet for discussion and debate of current events, as well as for the reading and interpreting of literature. Besides providing intellectual stimulation, they also satisfied the desire for friendly companionship that develops community culture.

Students will come together because they have much in common. No matter how strict the codes of behavior, no matter how difficult class assignments, students will find a way to circumnavigate the first, and accomplish the latter. In so doing, they come together and talk to each other, alternating agreement with disagreement, and approval with disapproval. They learn as they teach each other in an enthusiastic manner seldom seen or seldom possible in a formal classroom.

As a group, students represent the present generation, inevitably opposed to the older generation, in terms of philosophy, fashion, and finance. They also often differ in the way they view the past, live the present, and see the future. The two generations are destined to clash. In *A History of Muskingum College*, Dr. William Fisk records some of the irrepressible pranks, hi-jinks, and peccadilloes of the societies, some of them harmful, but most of them harmless.[1] If weighed in the scales against present-day student behavior, the activities of students in the nineteenth and early twentieth centuries created far less havoc and concern.

In the early years, there were few activities to occupy the spare time of students. The many single and group extracurricular activities we have today did not exist. Libraries had little printed matter for casual reading, and there were no organized athletics. Left to themselves, with little faculty supervision, they organized debates, gave orations, recited declamations, created literature, and devised dramatic productions for themselves, the faculty, and the general public. Debating was the most popular of their activities. They invented the extempore debate, and their inter-society debate contests led to inter-collegiate debating.[2]

The Union Literary Society in New Concord was formed in 1836, one year before the founding of the college. In fact, some of the first students enrolled in the college were members of that society.[3] There were two literary societies for men–the Union and the Philomathean. When the college became co-educational in the1850's, the Erodelphian Literary Society was formed for women.[4] In the 1880's, the Erodelphian Society was regrouped and named the Aretean.[5] Again, in 1910, the Erodelphian Society was reformed to give the college two women's societies.[6]

These societies are mentioned in the early catalogs of the institution, as existing alongside the curriculum for the valuable means of supplementing course work and socializing. At first, membership was voluntary; however, as time passed, their contribution to the cultural climate of the college resulted in the administration's requirement that every student join one. Neglect of literary society work was regarded as neglect of required academic work.[7] (See Section Note on society "halls" or rooms.)

The December issue of *The Black and Magenta* for 1902 (that paper's first year of publication) gives the reader some idea of the work of the student literary societies. Under the title "Literary Notes" is reported the order of business for each society. The Aretean Society was called to order and, after the usual reading of the Scriptures followed by a prayer, there was a debate on the question, Resolved: "That the Good Results of Labor Unions Are Greater than the Evil Results." The debate was followed by three extemporaneous speeches. A short recess was held, after which five members of the essay class performed on such subjects as "The Study of Music," "The Druids," and "A Visit to Mt. Vesuvius." Next came the orations by three members of the oratory class, and then there were four declamations. A musical interlude by the college quartette occurred after the first of the declamations listed above. After the final declamation, the society decided on assignments of performances for the next meeting, before adjourning with a prayer.[8]

A recounting of the Union and Philomathean Societies followed a similar pattern. Their programs consisted of debates on matters of national importance, extemporaneous speeches, orations, and performances by the essay and declamation class members. Musical interludes were judiciously spaced throughout the meetings, and they all adjourned with a prayer.[9]

Besides performing for themselves, the societies provided programs for the public, one of the most notable being the annual Commencement Exercise. They were given one evening called "Literary Diploma Night," during which diplomas were distributed to their respective seniors and at, the end of which, they were greeted by an address from a visiting speaker.[10]

The student annual, the *Muscoljuan*, began publication in 1907. The extent of student enthusiasm for oratory and debate can be seen in the glowing way in which every oratorical and debating event was chronicled. Pictures of orators and of debate teams filled the pages devoted to "Oratory and Debate." Literary society affiliations were made part of the coverage.

In the 1911 *Muscoljuan* is found the following:

> The oratorical and debating interests of Muskingum are in the hands of the students themselves, . . . The Oratorical Association is made up of the entire student body and faculty.
>
> Credit is given to the instruction received from the Department of Oratory, but student support in true "oratorical spirit" drives individuals into the work if they have any ability whatever.[11]

Again, the 1912 *Muscoljuan* reported:

> Of all forms of student activity, Oratory and Debate call out about the greatest interest at Muskingum College.
>
> But beside these more spectacular exhibitions of platform work, there is a little world of work going on in classes, silently but surely giving Muskingum students the power of expression. And not only the Lecture and Recital platform, the Bench and the Bar and the Pulpit will claim our finished product; the shop, the office, the parlor will here and there be blessed with those who have learned to give clear and pleasing expression to their thoughts.[12]

Definitely, a high point of student interest in the oratory and debating prowess of Muskingum was the year 1913. This was the year in which Albert Benjamin Cunningham, a "Philo" (Philomathean Literary Society member), was captain of the First Debate Team, winner of the Brown Oratorical Contest, winner of the State Oratorical Contest, winner of the "Tri-State Oratorical Association Contest,* and winner of the Inter-State Oratorical Association Contest.** No orator from Muskingum had ever achieved such an amazing number of "firsts"; and no orator from Ohio had ever won the Inter-State contest.[13]

In 1915, a student, appearing to be in a near-state of frenzy, close to that of a cheerleader during the final minutes of a conference title football game, recorded the details of a Muskingum delegation train trip to Wooster to cheer A. B. Cunningham on to victory for Muskingum and Ohio.[14]

In the same edition of the *Muscoljuan* is an article entitled "Inter-Society Contests." After explaining that the literary societies have, as their function, the training of student members in speech and literature, the author comments on the quality of training:

> Ever since the foundation of the literary societies in Muskingum the work done in the Society Halls has been of the highest order.
> As an evidence of the quality of the work done you need only observe what our debaters and orators have been and are doing.[15]

The author then announces that the literary societies are organizing a series of Inter-Society Debate, Essay, and Declamation contests. The purpose is to encourage more students to try out for Inter-Collegiate contests. The final paragraph of the article is worth quoting for the zeal shown by the author as he warms to his task.

> The preliminary for the debate teams has been held and if this can be taken as a fit criterion from which to judge we certainly can look forward to great things. If you are a REAL Muskingum man or woman get behind this thing and "BOOST."[16]

The literary societies were also interested in dramatics, but it was an interest that grew slowly, and held a different kind of excitement than that elicited by contest-driven oratory and debate. Students were used to the study of plays; as an academic exercise, the reading of scenes or plays in class was common. The production of the same plays was complex, expensive, and time-consuming. It was much more practical to have one person interpret a scene or present a recital of a play, or to have a group reading of the play for the public. The oral reading or oral interpretation of literature was very popular in the nineteenth century as a form of entertainment in schools. There were also many professional actors who performed and toured the lecture circuit with programs of oral interpretation.[17] The public performance of literature and plays became a permanent part of the elocutionary movement.

The literary societies presented an organized voice in favor of elocutionary training, and since they had the stamp of administrative approval, they carried some weight in the hiring of teachers of elocution. Teachers of elocution were more interested in oral reading than public speaking, but the interest in voice and movement served as

---

*Member colleges were from Ohio, West Virginia, and Pennsylvania.
**Member colleges were from Ohio, Iowa, Nebraska, Kansas, Indiana, Illinois, Michigan, Minnesota, Missouri, and Wisconsin.

common ground that connected the two areas.

It is not surprising that teachers of elocution were also performers, and that recitations such as "The Merrimac and the Monitor"[18] appeared on commencement programs, along with orations and debates. In 1900, a teacher of elocution, Miss Maud Hollingsworth Bethel, recited "The Royal Bowman" on June 21 at Commencement.[19]

Student interest in play presentation was encouraged by the popularity of oral reading and by the itinerant teachers of elocution who taught at Muskingum in the late nineteenth century. Elocution courses used drama in exercises, and departments of oratory and expression became interested in producing plays in English.[20] Clifford Hamar, in "College and University Theatre Instruction in the Early Twentieth Century," reported:

> Henry Fink of Hamilton College in 1892 complained that oratory was being used for the training of dramatic readers. Theatre courses often entered the curriculum through schools of oratory and elocution.[21]

Literary societies at the University of Illinois are credited with the first American college production of Shakespeare in 1875. The Aretean Society produced *The Spinster's Return* in 1905, the first staged presentation of a play at Muskingum .[22]

The literary societies continued to perform well past the turn of the century. They continued to garner their share of space in the *Muscoljuan. H*owever, the growth of courses in oratory and expression, and the extracurricular theatrical activities of the junior and senior classes began to absorb the forensic and dramatic ambitions of the societies.

Fortunately for the literary societies and the Department of Oratory and Expression, when Professor Charles R. Layton assumed his duties in the fall of 1914, President Montgomery also appointed him as supervisor of the societies.[23] Although this was an added burden to an already busy person, it had its advantages. The appointment gave Professor Layton some control over the societies' activities in oratory, debate, and drama, which co-existed with those of the department.

Previous chairmen of the department, such as Elbert Moses and Ray Immel, had already established a working relationship with the societies by permitting a healthy exchange of interest, energy, and knowledge that led to mutually satisfying results. The task of Professor Layton, whether he knew it or not, was to oversee the phasing-out of the societies, or the amalgamation of certain activities of the societies with those of the department. By 1923, the societies ceased to exist. The purpose of the societies as academic assistants to the curriculum had been served. Their duties had been absorbed by new departments and cultural clubs, and the students in the societies were looking for organizations that were more personally and socially satisfying. This transition period could not have fallen into more astutely capable and diplomatic hands than those of Professor Layton.

The student literary societies that kept the faculty and administration of the college ever-vigilant to any trespass of proper conduct also kept the college alive to change. There were, after all, some very good minds at work in the student body; they replenished the ministry with some outstanding clerics and supplied the schools with a steady stream of qualified teachers. Then, too, Muskingum liked to think of itself as the "Mother of College Presidents,"[24] claiming William Rainey Harper, the first president of the University of Chicago, and William Oxley Thompson, president of the Ohio State University, as two of its honored graduates.

The abundant enthusiasm and youthful energy displayed by the literary societies supplied the momentum for curricular, extracurricular, social, and even administrative change. If the societies could be harnessed and channeled, they would be even more effective and beneficial to everyone. They needed direction.

History answered the need for direction in three ways: 1) the elocutionary movement arrived in America and, toward the end of the nineteenth century, received impetus from Francois Delsarte's theories of speech and system of oratory; 2) higher education, invigorated by a series of discoveries in the natural and social sciences, founded modern departments to control the influx of knowledge that created new disciplines and courses of instruction; and 3) a college president, in the person of Reverend J. Knox Montgomery (himself, an excellent orator),[25] who had the fortitude and vision to preside over a period of change for Muskingum as it entered a new century.

Section Notes
Literary Society Plays

Below is a partial list of plays produced by the various literary societies.

1905 In the spring of 1905, the Aretean Society produced *The Spinster's Return*. This play may well have been the first full production of a play at Muskingum. (Cheri Swiss, "A History of Theatre at Muskingum College," p. 17.)

1917 On March 3, 1917, an unidentified organization, probably one of the literary societies, produced *The Gentleman from Indiana*. (Swiss, p. 17.) In December 1917, the Areteans produced "Rebecca's Triumph." (*Muscoljuan, 1919), p. 133.)

1919 On May 13, 1919, the Areteans produced "Leave It to Polly." (Virginia Massenburg quoting from the college calendar of the *Muscoljuan, 1921*: "The stars of the Aretean Literary Society present 'Leave It to Polly' to a crowded house.")

1920 On April 23, 1920, the Areteans presented *Miss Fearless and Company*. (*Muscoljuan, 1922*, "Dramatics," n.p.; Swiss, p. 23.)

1920 On November 20, 1920, the Erodelphian Literary Society produced an Irish fantasy, "The Twig of Thorn," in which Agnes Moorehead made her debut at Muskingum in the role of the poet, Aileel. (*Muscoljuan, 1922*, "Dramatics," n.p.; Swiss, p. 23.)

1920 The Aretean and Philomathean Literary Societies joined forces to produce "Madame Butterfly" and "The Man Who Married a Dumb Wife." (*Muscoljuan, 1922,* "Dramatics," n.d., n.p.)

1922 In February, the Philomathean Literary Society produced *The Arrival of Kitty,* a play based on Shakespeare's *As You Like It. (Muscoljuan, 1923,* "Dramatics," p. 175; Swiss, pp. 23-24.)

1922 The Erodelphian and Union Literary Societies produced three one-act plays: "The Work House Ward," "The Slave with Two Faces," and "Nevertheless." (*Muscoljuan, 1923*, "Dramatics," n.d., p. 176.)

Section Note
Literary Society "Halls" or Rooms

Since the college made it a requirement that all students join a society of their choice, the college felt obligated to provide rooms for their weekly meetings and programs. In his *A History of Muskingum College*, Dr. Fisk points out that in the first college building (1838) " . . . the college chapel or hall and library [occupied] the ground floor." On the second floor, a "Corridor divided the Union Literary Society Room on the east from three recitation rooms on the west side. The attic was left unfinished, but it soon became the hall of the Philomathean Literary Society."[1]

The first building burned down in 1851 and a second one was hastily erected. It was replaced in 1873 by a new and more stable main college building, Paul Hall. Spaces, again, were provided for the societies. In 1899, when Johnson Hall was built, the published diagrams of the second floor identified halls for the Union, Philomathean, and Aretean Literary Societies, as well as a "Recitation Room."[2]

SECTION NOTE REFERENCES
1   William L. Fisk, *A History of Muskingum College* (New Concord, Ohio: Muskingum College, 1978), p. 51.
2   *Annual Catalogue of Muskingum College: 1899* (Columbus, Ohio: Nitschke Bros. Press, 1899), p. 57.

REFERENCES
1   William L. Fisk, *A History of Muskingum College*, (Muskingum College, New Concord, Ohio, 1978). Literary societies are discussed at various places throughout Chapters 2 and 3.
2   David Potter, "The Literary Society," in *A History of Speech Education in America: Background Studies.* Edited by Karl R. Wallace (New York: Appleton-Century-Crofts, Inc., 1954), pp. 238-245.
3   Fisk, p. 65.
4   Ibid., p. 66.
5   Ibid., p. 85.
6   Ibid., p. 131.
7   *Annual Catalogue of Muskingum College*, Muskingum College,(New Concord, Ohio, 1903), p. 12.
8   *Black and Magenta*, December 1902, pp. 17-18.
9   Ibid., pp. 18-19.
10   Commencement Programs, 1900-1917. Muskingum College, (New Concord, Ohio, 1900–1917), pp. 3 or 4 for the different *Catalogue* years.
11   *Muscoljuan*, 1911 (Published by the Junior Class, New Concord, Ohio: Muskingum College, 1911), p. 77.
12   *Muscoljuan*, 1912, p. 100.
13   *Muscoljuan*, 1915, pp. 90-91.
14   Ibid., pp. 170-171.
15   Ibid., p. 97
16   Ibid.
17   John D. Clark, "Educational Dramatics in Nineteenth Century Colleges," in *A History of Speech Education in America: Background Studies*, p. 546.
18   Commencement Program for June 25, 1885, Muskingum College, New Concord, Ohio.
19   Commencement Program for June 21, 1900.
20   John D. Clark, p. 546.
21   Clifford Eugene Hamar, "College and University Theatre Instruction in the Early Twentieth Century," in *A History of Speech Education in America: Background Studies*, p. 572.
22   Cheryl D. Swiss, "A History of Theatre at Muskingum College," (Unpublished Master's Thesis, Athens, Ohio: Ohio University, 1972), pp. 3, 7.
23   Fisk, p. 121.
24   *Muscoljuan*, 1911, p. 142.
25   Fisk, p. 107.

Elocution
The Movement: 1750–1914

Elocution, along with invention, arrangement, memory, and delivery, was considered one of the five elements of rhetorical theory. To Cicero in *De Inventione*, it meant "expression" or "style."[1]

From 1750 to 1800, the English considered that elocution referred to the way a public speaker used the voice and the body to express ideas and emotions. Prominent writers on the subject were Thomas Sheridan *(Lectures on Elocution,* 1762), Joshua Steele *(Prosodia Rationalis,* 1775–1779), and John Walker *(Elements of Elocution,* 1781).[2] Thomas Sheridan defined elocution as ". . . the just and graceful management of the voice, countenance, and gesture in speaking."[3]

Led by ministers, the elocutionary movement became a criticism of the way in which their fellow clergymen, orators, and public officials addressed audiences. The land of Shakespeare in the 1750's was also the age of Garrick, England's greatest actor, known for his vocal and gestural talents. The English public wanted their tradition of excellence to continue and demanded better than what they were getting from the pulpit, the Bar, and the Parliament. Although elocutionists were more interested in oral reading than public speaking, they taught professionals and others how to transfer the techniques of voice and action from reading to speaking.[4]

Teachers of elocution developed four areas for instruction: 1) vocal production, which included a study of speech organs and how they formed sounds; 2) pronunciation, which dealt with syllabication and correct stress; 3) voice management, which drew attention to inflection, emphasis, pitch, volume, rhythm, rate, and pause; and 4) bodily action, which included all forms of visual communication and the effects of emotional expression on physical activity.[5]

In their teaching, elocutionists used the principles of ancient rhetoric and the practices of the stage. The voice, the body, and the text were central to their study. To the older traditions of rhetoric and oratory, they added new scientific techniques of observing, recording, and reproducing sounds of the English language.[6]

The elocutionary movement spread to America early in the nineteenth century, mainly for the same reason it had swept England in the eighteenth century. However, there were some noticeable differences. To the Americans, elocution was an art and a science. As an art, it involved oral interpretation of literature; as a performance area, it attracted many professional actors, such as Edwin Forrest and Edwin Booth.[7] Toward the end of the century, when the Delsarte system of aesthetics was introduced into this country, the artistic element of elocution became very complicated. The scientific element received much early attention, and it was readily accepted for the new knowledge it shed upon the vocal anatomy and the correction of speech defects. The connecting link between the artistic side and the scientific side of elocution was known to the Americans as "delivery." The vocal drills for improving the voice and the physical exercises that led to a form of physical culture were also readily accepted, especially when they proved beneficial to the entire area of oratory and speech.

Americans, like the English, complained about the quality of speech delivered by ministers, lawyers, and public officials. Although the average American might not be able to speak well himself, he was quick to detect faulty speech and a lack of physical response to the text on the part of those who spoke in public.

Education also received criticism. College graduates displayed poor vocal management and unconvincing gestures. Student speakers who engaged in debates, gave declamations at public exhibitions, or presented orations at commencements, proved so unskilled that their performances " . . . would not have been tolerated in a village school."[8]

One cause of the problem in higher education was that the emphasis in courses of rhetoric was on writing, instead of on speaking. Since oratory began with a written composition, English departments laid claim to oratory as oral English. Orations depended more and more on the written word and, in many instances, were read instead of spoken. With the help of elocutionists, the classic approach to oratory was separated from rhetoric, which was concerned almost solely with *belles lettres* (pure literature).[9] The classical approach continued with the usual studies in Cicero, Demosthenes, and Quintillian. Elocution added the necessary aid of delivery to the equation: it activated the voice and body response to the written text.

Early in the nineteenth century, Americans used the writings of Sheridan, Steele, and Walker as textbooks. Then, in 1811, the Reverend Ebenezer Porter, Bartlett Professor of Pulpit Eloquence at Andover Seminary, published his *Lectures on the Analysis of Vocal Inflection*, followed in 1827 by *An Analysis of the Principles of Rhetorical Delivery*. In 1831, his *Rhetorical Reader* became the most popular text in colleges.[10]

An Englishman, Dr. Jonathan Barbour, came to America in 1823 and, a few years later, was teaching at Yale, then at Harvard in 1830. He based his form of scientific elocution on *The Philosophy of the Human Voice* (1827) by Dr. James Rush. In this book, medical science and speech came together to explain how the anatomy of the human voice functions. Dr. Barbour also used his own *Grammar of Elocution* (1830). By mid-century, elocution was a required subject in most colleges.[11]

Porter, Rush, and Barbour were all interested in the scientific basis for voice training in the light of physiology and anatomy.[12] They were the pioneers in disciplines later known as speech correction, speech therapy, and phonics.[13]

Professional schools of elocution and oratory were established in large cities to satisfy the public's desire for entertainment and education in the excellence of the spoken word. Some of the schools were privately owned; some were attached to universities. In 1844, William Russell, an educator and author, and James E. Murdoch, an actor, founded the School of Practical Rhetoric and Oratory in Boston. It was one of the first privately-endowed schools. Three of its students became prominent educators: S. S. Hamill who became a professor of elocution at Illinois College, Thomas C. Trueblood who founded the Department of Elocution and Oratory at the University of Michigan, and Robert I. Fulton who founded the School of Oratory at Ohio Wesleyan University.[14] Fulton and Trueblood wrote their own text, *Practical Elocution* in 1893; it is dedicated to James E. Murdoch. In the introduction to that book, they define the two-fold nature of elocution: "Elocution is the science and art of expression by voice and action."[15]

Steele MacKaye, actor, director, inventor, and playwright, had been to Paris, where he studied movement and voice under Francois Delsarte. He became so proficient in the Delsarte system that the originator urged him to teach some of his classes. In 1871 the Franco-Prussian War broke out, and Delsarte suspended his lectures and fled Paris. MacKaye returned to America and established an acting school to teach the Delsarte system at the St. James Theatre. When the school closed, he continued to lecture, then opened another school in 1877 on Union Square. After it also closed, he opened a third school at the Lyceum Theatre in 1884. He later turned the management of the school over to Franklin Sargent, a Harvard graduate whom MacKaye had won as a Delsarte convert. Under Sargent's leadership, the school became the American Academy of Dramatic Art.[16]

The Delsarte system of expression was the most popular method of speech training in the country from 1870–1900. Teaching the method had its impetus from MacKaye and came directly from Delsarte. Delsarte was not a speech teacher; he was a teacher of vocal music and an operatic acting coach in Paris from 1839 to 1871. In all that time, he never published, and no formulation of his principles and practices was ever made. [A few of his articles were translated by Abby L. Alger and published by Edgar S. Werner in *Delsarte System of Oratory,* Part V, "The Literary Remains of Francois Delsarte."] Teachers and actors were free to write, teach, and promote his system as they interpreted it. As a result, many debates occurred over what the true Delsarte system implied.[17]

MacKaye, as the chief advocate of Delsarte, conveyed the central Delsartian philosophy of the triune nature of all things. In his theory, Delsarte, a devout Roman Catholic, followed the Holy Trinity: Father, Son, and Holy Spirit. Objects have height, width, thickness; time is past, present, and future; man is divided into life, mind, and soul. Vocal sounds express life; words express mind, and movement expresses soul. Delsarte explained, through diagrams and pictures, how the voice and body were rhythmically connected, as they responded to ideas and emotions. To help explain Delsarte's theories, MacKaye developed a series of physical exercises similar to a course in physical culture.[18]

E. T. Kirby, a professor of theatre at the State University of New York at Brockport, explains the Delsarte influence in his article, "The Delsarte Method: 3 Frontiers of Actor Training." According to Kirby, Delsarte's emphasis on rhythmic movement was central to the work of dancers, Ruth St. Denis and Isadora Duncan; it influenced the system of Eurythmics developed by Jacques Dalcroze in the early 1900's. The same continuous movement sequence relates to the Chinese T'ai Chi Ch'uan in use today as physical therapy. Delsarte's insistence that the body responds in standard ways to emotions, makes him a pioneer in the field of body language or kinesics. His development of vocal and physical signs into a system also makes him a pioneer in the science of signs: semiology.[19]

One could almost say the same of Quintillian and other rhetoricians who, through the ages, promoted similar illustrations to explain how the voice and body respond to ideas and emotions. Nevertheless, Delsarte was clearly ahead of his time.

Two other MacKaye students were Lewis Baxter Monroe and Samuel Silas Curry.

Lewis B. Monroe (Snow Professor of Oratory) founded the Boston University School of Oratory in 1872. The School of Expression was established by two of Monroe's students: Anna Bright Curry and S. S. Curry during the period of 1879–1883. Samuel Curry did not like the many connotations clinging to the term, "elocution"; therefore, he preferred to use "expression" in the title of his school. The Emerson College of Oratory opened in 1880, under the auspices of Charles Wesley Emerson, another student of Monroe. The Leland Powers School of the Spoken Word, founded by Leland Powers, another Monroe student, was also a student of Curry, and fellow classmate of Emerson. Powers wanted to develop artistic platform readers. He was one of the most popular readers of his day; he taught at both the Emerson and Curry schools.[20] All the afore-mentioned schools were in Boston.

One of the most prominent professional schools was in Philadelphia. It was founded by J. W. Shoemaker in 1873. The National School of Oratory offered a two-year course, ending with an examination and thesis for a Bachelor of Oratory degree, and a three-year course, which resulted in a Master of Elocution degree.[21] The Delsartian "trinity" is explained in the text of *Practical Elocution*: man receives impressions through the physical phase; man interprets them in the spiritual phase; man communicates them through the voice and action.[22]

Mary Blood and Ida Rile, two Emerson graduates, moved to Chicago and began the Columbia School of Oratory, Physical Culture, and Dramatic Art. The Phillips School of Oratory was also located in Chicago, as was the nearby School of Speech at Northwestern University, founded by Robert McLean Cumnock. Also of note was the Byron King School of Oratory in Pittsburgh, founded in 1888.[23]

All of these schools were located in large urban centers, to which people flocked for business, entertainment, and culture. They were all in some way affected by the Delsarte system of oratory and aesthetic theories or interpretations thereof. They trained actors, as well as readers, orators, and teachers.

Many teachers and directors of dramatic art–of amateur groups, in particular, and of professionally-oriented organizations, as well–were graduates of the schools of expression. Professional theatre training became an important, and even a major, aim of their programs.[24] All of these schools favored a natural delivery in which the speaker was free of personal and obtrusive habits. They avoided mechanical and artificial vocal patterns and stereotyped postures. They preferred simplicity and directness.[25]

The graduates of these schools were trained teachers of elocution and oratory who served as catalysts for the early rhetorical practices and speech activities of the student literary societies. The early history of speech and theatre at Muskingum is found with the teachers of elocution. In twenty-nine years, there were eleven of them; the average length of stay was two years. In reality, three of them stayed for one year, and one teacher had a tenure of five years. In spite of the rapid turnover in personnel, the courses they taught had a similarity of content and coverage of the different areas of speech: Principles of Elocution, Argumentation and Debate, Interpretive Reading and Dramatic Expression (a combination of acting and play production), and Advanced Public Speaking.[26]

At Muskingum, the teachers of elocution set up their own classes of instruction under various titles: "Courses in Elocution," "Department of Oratory and Elocution," or "School of Expression." The variety of titles indicates the tentative standing occupied by these teachers and their subject in the traditional academic community. At this time in history, there were no real departments as we think of them today. There existed only a series of classes in one field of knowledge, taught by one instructor. The various disciplines found identity as part of a specific course leading to a certain degree. At Muskingum, there was a two-year Preparatory Course, which qualified a student to enter the Collegiate Course (Classical Course), leading to the B.A. degree. There was also a Scientific Course, leading to the B.S. degree and, later, a Literary Course, leading to a B.L. degree. The Literary Course was later changed to a Philosophy Course, which offered a B.Ph. degree. There was also a special Pedagogy Course for those students who desired teaching certification.[27]

REFERENCES

1   Wilbur Samuel Howell, "English Backgrounds of Rhetoric," in *A History of Speech Education in America: Background Studies*. Edited by Karl R. Wallace (New York: Appleton-Century-Crofts, Inc., 1954), p. 5.

2   Frederick W. Haberman, "English Sources of American Elocution," in *A History of Speech Education in America: Background Studies*, pp. 115-117.

3   Thomas Sheridan, *A Course of Lectures on Elocution, Together with Two Dissertations on Language and Some Other Tracts Relative to Those Subjects* (London, 1762, Revised by Benjamin Blom, Inc., New York, 1968), p. 19.

4   Haberman, pp. 105-109.

5   Ibid., pp. 110-111.

6   Ibid., pp. 109-110.

7   Mary Margaret Robb, "The Elocutionary Movement and Its Chief Figures," in *A History of Speech Education in America: Background Studies*, p. 180.

8   Marie Hochmuth and Richard Murphy, "Rhetorical and Elocutionary Training in Nineteenth Century Colleges," in *A History of Speech Education in America: Background Studies*, p. 159.

9   Ibid., pp. 161-164.

10   Ibid., p. 162.

11   Ibid., p. 163.

12   Robb, p. 181.

13   Ibid., pp. 185-186; Haberman, pp. 109-110.

14   Robb, p. 200; Hochmuth and Murphy, p. 171.

15   Robert I. Fulton and Thomas C. Trueblood, *Practical Elocution* (New York: Ginn & Company, 1893), p. 1.

16   Francis Hodge, "The Private Theatre Schools in the Late Nineteenth Century," in *A History of Speech Education in America: Background Studies*, pp. 560-561.

17   Claude L. Shaver, "Steele MacKaye and the Delsartian Tradition," in *A History of Speech Education in America: Background Studies*, p. 202.

18   Ibid., pp. 204-205.

19   E. T. Kirby, "The Delsarte Method: 3 Frontiers of Actor Training," *The Drama Review: Acting: Some New Approaches* (March 1972), pp. 55-69.

20   Edyth Renshaw, "Five Private Schools of Speech," in *A History of Speech Education in America: Background Studies*, pp. 302-307.

21   Ibid., p. 301.

22   Ibid., p. 311.

23   Robb, p. 199.

24   Fred C. Blanchard, "Professional Theatre Schools of the Early Twentieth Century," in *A History of Speech Education in America: Background Studies*, p. 624.

25   Renshaw, pp. 309-310.

26   *Annual Catalogues of Muskingum College: 1846–1914*, Muskingum College Library Archives, New Concord, Ohio.

27   *Annual Catalogues of Muskingum College: 1846–1910*, Muskingum College Library Archives, New Concord, Ohio.

The Teachers: 1837–1914

In the early history of the college, elocution was taught as a part of classical rhetoric classes, just as it had been since the days of Cicero. A specific course in elocution was identified in 1857-58 as being taught in the Pedagogical Course of study.[1] Ministers and teachers found such a course particularly pertinent in their roles as public speakers.

Although there was no faculty member designated as a teacher of Elocution until 1885-86, it is possible that a professor of rhetoric or languages taught the subject as an integral part of another course. Such a practice was common at a time when the college faculty was small, and professors taught multiple disciplines, even though they were listed only in their areas of expertise.

As the century wore on, elocution became increasingly recognized as a proper subject, and teachers who had training in the subject became more plentiful. The students of Muskingum College were fortunate, indeed, to have some of the best instructors in elocution (or expression) in the country. At various times, they were taught by nationally and internationally known authorities in the field. One such time occurred early in the history of the college.

According to the *Zanesville Courier* for August 29, 1863,

> . . . we are informed that the students of Muskingum College have been enjoying the instructions for the past two weeks of Prof. S. S. Hamill in Elocution and vocal culture. This gentleman has taught this subject in a very large number of the first colleges in the country both east and west, and in many of the Theological Seminaries. He is very successful as a teacher and thoroughly up to the times. Hereafter this subject is to receive special attention at this institution.[2]

The incomplete records of the college make it difficult to report further on the matter, other than to note the often-made statement that compositions and declamations were required throughout the course.

Mary Margaret Robb identifies S. S. Hamill, Thomas C. Trueblood, Robert I. Fulton, and John R. Schott as students of James E. Murdoch and William Russell. Russell, a former Harvard professor, believed that elocutionary training should begin in the lower schools. Murdoch was an actor who was concerned with training public entertainers, readers, and actors. These two teachers and their students

> . . . . agreed that art rested upon the science of the voice and worked to develop a delivery that could reveal thought and emotion. Many of their theories, methods and exercises are found in modern textbooks.[3]

As for S. S. Hamill, who taught Muskingum students in 1863, Marie Hochmuth and Richard Murphy recall,

> Speech programs were becoming formalized toward the end of the 19th century. Elocutionary training from itinerant teachers similarly became affixed to curricula which was stabilizing. At Illinois College in 1877 William Jennings Bryan was a student of S. S. Hamill, who instructed in elocution. In the summer of 1878, Hamill attracted two students who were later to carry on his work and establish departments and schools of oratory: Thomas C. Trueblood and Robert I. Fulton, who also trained with Murdoch.[4]

William Jennings Bryan (holding umbrella) is shown here leaving Brown Chapel with Dr. Charles Layton on October 9, 1919. Bryan had just delivered a chapel address in which he praised Prohibition (an era that lasted from 1920-1933) and congratulated the Muskingum audience on its fight against booze. *Photo courtesy M.C. Public Relations Office.*

The influence that these famous teachers of oratory and elocution had upon Muskingum students, together with S. S. Curry and Leland Powers, will be discussed later in the order in which that influence occurred. The chronological order of teachers after Hamill is not clear. It is quite possible that before Hamill left Muskingum, he sowed the seeds which later led students to demand more classes in elocution. Berkshire reports that, in May of 1870, the Board of Trustees appointed Mr. O. H. Roberts as Professor of Languages. [5]

The *Zanesville Courier,* in an account of the 1870 Commencement exercises, reported:

> On the evening of the Commencement an entertainment consisting of Comedies, Recitations, Poetry, Declamations, etc., will be given by the Elocutionary Class under the direction of Prof. O. H. Roberts, whose reputation as an elocutionist is well-known.[6]

According to Berkshire, further information on O. H. Roberts is supplied by a Miss Smith, who was a member of the graduation class of 1871:

> Before the beginning of my last year, Professor Marshall had removed to another field and his place was taken by Professor Roberts, who was regarded as an outstanding orator and ready linguist.[7]

The *Argus*, a short-lived student publication of the time, provides interesting information about elocution in the same year as Miss Smith's recollection. The article is an evaluation of orations and recitations exhibited at the 1871 commencement. The names of the speakers are withheld because the interest is in the criticism embodied in the piece. It resembles the criticism which was leveled against Harvard graduates in similar circumstances between 1819 and 1850. It is a sign that Muskingum students had advanced enough in their knowledge of elocutionary delivery to offer intelligent criticism of their classmates.

> The first oration . . . was followed by an excellent essay, excellently read . . . enunciation was superior. The next two orations . . . were not well delivered. The first was preached, and the last was killed by a machine-like movement of the hands and arms, which was independent of the ideas and feeling as if each had been rendered by separate persons. This gentleman might profit by an article in the Argus for June on elocution.[8]

The 1885–86 *Annual Catalogue of Muskingum College* listed Mr. R. K. Porter on the Faculty as Instructor of Elocution. Mr. Porter was the first known faculty member to be so designated; and, with the exception of Hamill, he was the first professionally-trained teacher of elocution at Muskingum.[9] At a board meeting on June 24, 1885, the Board made the following request:

> $50 be paid to Mr. Robert K. Porter for instruction to be given in elocution during the fall term of 1885; and that each student taking lessons be required to pay a fee of $2.00, providing one lesson a day was taken. Mr. Porter to teach as many classes as may be necessary.[10]

Two pages of the *Catalogue* for 1885–86 described the courses Mr. Porter taught, and emphasized the fact that he came to Muskingum from J. W. Shoemaker's National School of Elocution and Oratory in Philadelphia. He had indicated that he would use that school's text, *Practical Elocution,* for appropriate classes. Mr. Porter taught a Graduating Course that met the demand for practical experience in speaking and reading " . . . our mother tongue." Another course, Voice Culture, was described as " . . . the first step in the study of elocution. . . . The different qualities and colors of voice to express the different sentiments and passions of the soul will receive special attention."[11]

The first curriculum in elocution also included Orthoepy (Pronunciation) which embraced the " . . . principles of articulation, accent and phonics." In connection with the course in Gesture, calisthenics were taught " . . . to develop chest capacity, and give grace to movement." Expressive Reading was the aim of elocutionary training and the guidelines stated that, in this course, the speaker " . . . blends all his power of voice, articulate speech, and gesture . . . Here art is lost in the simplicity of nature." Public Rehearsals gave students the experience of working in front of an audience. A Juvenile Class, which met the needs of children nine to sixteen years of age, was formed because " . . . persons who have not formed incorrect habits make better readers than older ones." After completion of one year of the prescribed course of study, students received a diploma in the Science and Art of Elocution.[12] (See Section Note D of "The Layton Years" for a history of diplomas in Oratory and Speech.)

Mr. Porter taught over ninety students, both privately and in classes, during his first year. This number was exceptionally good, because the combined enrollment for the freshmen, sophomore, junior, and senior classes of the main college never totaled over one hundred students, until 1904.

The number of students enrolled in a course, or in a college, is very important because it often reflects the effectiveness of a course, or the health of an institution. In some cases, enrollment may determine the survival of either one or the other. This fact is painfully true for privately-endowed schools whose main source of income is from tuition, or the kindness of individuals. Enrollment problems have plagued Muskingum College at various times throughout its history. Berkshire and Fisk are especially sensitive to the importance of this problem in their respective histories of the college. (See Section Note A for complete enrollment figures.)

Mr. Porter left after one year. His reasons for leaving are not known, but they could not have been for lack of popularity or enrollment in his classes.

It was five years before the appointment of Josephine (Jose or Josie) E. Martin, B.S. as Teacher of Elocution. A native of New Concord, Miss Martin graduated from Muskingum in 1888. She had probably been a student of Mr. Porter.[13] Under the title "Elocution," Miss Martin explained that the work of the area " . . . will always be of practical use, without restricting [it] to any fixed system. Imitation is studiously avoided." Since she used Professor King's *Practice of Speech* as a text, she may have studied in Pittsburgh at the Byron King School of Oratory.[14] Miss Martin's appointment was prompted by the following explanation: "Elocution being justly demanded by the students, a teacher has been secured, and those desiring to study this art can now be accommodated."[15] Student demand in 1891 totaled twenty-three.[16] In 1892, five more students were added to Miss Martin's roster.[17] The number of students taking elocution was still significant; it amounted to about one-quarter of the total college attendance.

When Miss Martin left at the end of two years, there was no waiting for a replacement this time. In 1893, Mrs. Viola Doudna-Romans took over from Miss Martin. She also taught Physical Culture for women, the first teacher in that subject.[18]

According to Mrs. Romans, elocution as a study was justified because an educated man needed to know how to convey his knowledge to the world. She said, "Correct Elocutionary training can best furnish this means."[19] (See Section Note B on Mrs. Romans and the history of Muskingum's school colors.)

Mrs. Romans was forced to resign during 1895–96 academic year because of ill health, and Miss Elizabeth Marshall was appointed as Director of the Departments of Music and Elocution. Her description of the elocution area is a curious blend of oral and written rhetoric, mixed with Delsarte: "The importance of being able to express . . . one's thoughts in precise and beautiful terms with fitting warmth, energy, and gesture is a primary requisite to success in any line of professional life."[20]

The following courses composed a two-year course of study in Elocution:

First Year: Physical Culture, Vocal Technique, Mental Technique, Economy of Breath, Methods of Delivery, Inflection, Emphasis, Pitch, Gesticulation, Physical Expression, Readings and Recitations from Best Authors, Dramatic, Pathetic, Declamatory, Humorous, etc.

Second Year: Analysis of Shakespeare's Plays, Study of the Classic Writers, Range and Strength in Delivery, Light and Shade Effects in Tone, Cultivation of the Imagination, Facial Expression, Physical Culture and Expression, and Application of Gesture. Graduates in Elocution had to pass the examination on the course in English Literature.[21]

The course in Physical Culture that Miss Marshall inherited from Mrs. Romans was designed to preserve health and develop the body, not to produce muscle, so much as to enable the body to respond at will to the demands of music and elocution.[22]

Up to this point, all the teachers of elocution had recognized the importance of the subject to vocations in life. They had all emphasized voice and physical training in order to enable students to become good readers and articulate speakers. Elizabeth Marshall was a departure from the other teachers, because her curriculum was a blend of music, and oral and written rhetoric. Although she resigned after one year, her courses must have had an effect on the administration because shortly thereafter, a new course in Literary Studies, leading to a Bachelor of Literature degree, was instituted. The course required the student to enroll in the Scientific Course for the first two years, and in Modern Languages, Music, and Elocution during the final two years.[23]

Frank S. Fox, A.M. became the teacher of Elocution and Oratory in 1896–97 for a term of two-and-one-half years. Fox stated, "Every person can be trained to be a Speaker, if not an orator." According to Fox, the work of the department " . . . will be broad and scientific, embracing all the studies necessary for liberal training in Speech Arts. Sore Throat, Lisping, Stammering, Stuttering, cured." The course involved two years of training.[24]

The first sentence in Fox's description of elocution was, "Poets are born, but orators are made . . . ." Then followed the practical nature of training in speech culture, expression, and eloquence: "Noble thoughts and sentiments, uttered by the combined power of voice and bodily gesture."[25] An outline of the work that Professor Fox prepared for the department had ten steps: 1) Breathings, 2) Vocal Calisthenics, 3) Vocality Drill, 4) Articulation, 5) Pitch and Force of Vocality, 6) Subvocality and Aspiration, 7) Accentuation for words, 8) Time, Respiration, and Pause, 9) Inflection, Waves, and Slides, and 10) Concentration of Tone.[26]

Although no mention was made of Physical Culture in 1896–97, a class was formed each term in 1897–98 for women and men.[27]

Maude Hollingsworth Bethel joined Professor Fox in the 1898-99 school year. Fox taught the first term only; when he did not return, Bethel took his classes in the spring term. The next year, she continued teaching Elocution and Physical Culture for ladies, while E. A. Peterson became the first full-time director of men's Physical Culture.[28]

Miss Bethel became Principal of the Department of Elocution, having earned her B.S. degree at Franklin College in 1894. She had also completed courses of study at King's School of Oratory in Pittsburgh, Pennsylvania, and the Capitol School of Oratory in Columbus, Ohio.[29]

Miss Bethel believed that elocution trained the mind, intellect, will, and emotion. It was very useful in every occupation. Outlined briefly, the course consisted of three areas: Voice Culture, Physical Exercises, and Development of Thought and Feeling. The work extended over a period of two years.

First year. One private lesson per week and the following class work: Physical Culture and Delsarte, Theory of Elocution, Composition and Rhetoric, Literature.

Second Year. One private lesson per week. Class lessons, Delsarte and Pantomime, Theory of Elocution, Study of words, Shakespeare.
Upon completion, a diploma was granted.[30]

With Miss Bethel in charge from 1899 to 1901, Oratory was dropped from the departmental title. Miss Bethel remained at Muskingum through the 1900–01 school year and was succeeded in 1901–02 by Anna Catharine R. Walter, B.A. The title "Department of Elocution and Oratory" made its reappearance under Miss Walter. She kept the same courses and structure as her predecessor.[31]

Mary Alice Carothers, B.E. succeeded Miss Walter in 1902–03. She was a graduate of J. W. Shoemaker's National School of Oratory in Philadelphia, and she had taken private lessons from Mme. Bertha Kunz-Baker of New York. She remained at Muskingum for three years and kept the same curriculum as that of Walter and Bethel. As a teacher of Expression " . . . she LEADS OUT what is in the student, allowing him to retain his individuality; [she excels] as a reader and impersonator . . . a second and third engagement with the same audience is not uncommon."[32] Miss Carothers was admirably suited to her position and rather popular with students.

President J. Knox Montgomery, who took office at Muskingum in 1904, was very interested in speech, debate, oratory, oral reading, and the formation of a Gospel Team. With the departure of Miss Carothers in 1905, he searched for another suitable candidate with exceptional training and experience. He hired Elbert Raymond Moses to head the Department of Oratory, Public Speaking, and Interpretive Reading, and to be the Physical Director for Ladies.

Mr. Moses received his early training in the public schools of Mapleton, Minnesota, and completed the sophomore year at Wooster. He graduated from the Dixon College of Oratory and from the Cumnock School of Oratory at Northwestern. He was an instructor in Oratory and Reading in the Wooster Summer School for five years.[33] He was mentioned in Hochmuth and Murphy's "Rhetorical and Elocutionary Training in Nineteenth Century Colleges," as director of the Department of Oratory and Physical Culture at Huron College, South Dakota, at the end of the century. He taught " . . . club swinging, fencing, walking, and calisthenics as part of the program."[34]

Additional information concerning Moses can be gleaned from Berkshire. Moses came to Muskingum in the fall of 1905 and, in 1907, he was made "director" of the Muskingum College of Expression. "Interest in Oratory and Public Speaking became so great during 1906–1907 that a full-fledged department was a necessity." Among his recommendations was one from the Director of the Wooster Summer School (the largest of its kind in the state) where Moses spent the last five summers as instructor of Oratory and Reading. It declares Moses to be

> . . . a man well prepared by both nature and study for his work, a Christian
> gentleman, a teacher of unusual ability and enthusiasm in instructing, a man of
> great energy and executive ability. His work has been satisfactory to the highest
> degree, both to the school and to the patrons. He has a pleasing personality and is
> possessed of those nameless graces of character which will make him a valuable
> man to any institution with which he may cast his lot.[35]

Such a man would have taken great joy to know that his son, soon to be born, would walk in his father's shoes.

Under Moses, the Department of Oratory, Public Speaking, and Interpretive Reading (1905–06) was also known as the Department of Elocution and Oration, to which he added a School of Speech Arts (1906–07), subdivided into a Department of Oratory and a School of Expression. In 1907–08, the Departments of Elocution, Oratory, and Argumentation were working in conjunction with the School of Speech Arts. The final two years of Moses' term of office were spent in the Departments of Elocution, Oratory, and Argumentation. Courses were listed under the traditional Department of Oratory and School of Expression.[36]

Moses's 1905-06 introduction to the work of the department explained the philosophy so well that it was used under the School of Speech Arts for the next two years, and under the School of Expression for the final two years of his career at Muskingum (1909–10). In that introduction, Mr. Moses showed a sensitivity to the prevailing importance of speech communication in the world. He explained how training in speech helped students become successful in the world. In his phrase " . . . [in] the symmetrical man—the man with a keen intellect, a pleasing voice and an impressive body, . . . " are seen the classic ideals of balance, harmony, and unity, as well as the American ideal of success through self-improvement. He ended with a quote from Gladstone: "Many a professional man now in obscurity might rise to the highest rank if he were farseeing enough to train his voice and body as well as his mind."[37]

Noteworthy in the course work is the connection of theory to practice, the learning of fundamentals by requiring participation in speech activities, the importance of class size, the adherence to a sequence of courses for developing skills, and the need for rigid attendance policies. Inherent in the course work itself was a very modern curriculum: voice and diction, body movement and mime, speech composition, argumentation and debate, persuasion, literary analysis and interpretation of literature, oral reading, all the forms of public address, dramatic literature, history and criticism, and play production.[38]

The School of Speech Arts specified many elements that related to modern speech and theatre departments. There was little, if any, mention of Delsarte, but vocal and physical exercises were still used. The terms Elocution and Expression seemed to be used interchangeably.[39]

The Department of Oratory required three years of work. Actual course listings were: I. Analytic Expression, II. Written and Vocal Oratic Expression, and III. Argumentation and Debate. These courses were to be taken in the sophomore year. Six more courses, evenly divided and sequenced by number, were to be taken in the junior and senior years. They were listed in the curriculum for the School of Expression.[40]

The School of Expression had a two-year course that contained Rhetoric, Literature, Elocution, Oratory, and Physical Education. Specific course titles were IV. Bible and Psalm Reading, V. Practical Public Speaking, VI. Extemporaneous Speaking, VII. Essentials of Elocution, VIII. Interpretive Reading, and IX. Dramatic Expression.[41]

Mr. Moses was active in all areas of the department. In 1907, he coached the

Muskingum debate team against Wooster in the first inter-collegiate debate held on campus. That same year, he founded the Dramatic Club, and, on a personal note, he earned a Bachelor of Literature degree from Muskingum.[42] In 1908–09, the debate team won all three debate competitions entered against Mt. Union, Ohio Northern, and Cedarville. The next year (1909–10), the debaters lost one decision to Geneva, but won from Mt. Union and Hiram.[43] Oratory also did well. In 1908–09, R. A. Pollock won the State Oratorical Contest. The next year, Earl Lewis came in second in the State Contest and W. J. Giffen won the Tri-state Oratorical Contest.[44]

During Moses's tenure at Muskingum, the School of Expression awarded what were probably the first diplomas and degrees in Oratory and Elocution:

1907	*Bachelor of Elocution*
	Anna Kennedy
1909	*Bachelor of Oratory*
	Margaret Faith McCall
	Alva Lee Yarnelle
1910	*Expression Diploma*
	Edna Amanda Gallogly
	Carrie Mabel Henderson [45]

When members of the junior class received permission to present a play at the 1906 Commencement, Moses supported them by directing *The Private Secretary,* by Hawtrey, on June 11, thereby beginning a tradition that continued into the 1940's. The play was given at the Opera House, an " . . . elegant name for the Auditorium or Town

The Town Hall and Opera House, circa 1880. When the town built the Town Hall, it was made available to the college for commencements and class rooms. *Photo courtesy M.C. Public Relations Office.*

Hall."[46] (See Section Note on Opera House.) The following plays were the direct result of Moses's involvement, or the desire to emulate his success.

> *Niobe*, Junior Play, directed by Moses for Commencement
> on June 10, 1907
>
> *She Stoops to Conquer*, Junior Play, directed by Moses for
> Commencement on June 8, 1908
>
> School of Expression Commencement, with Grace Emily Makepeace in
> Recital: "The Man Who Would Be King" (Kipling)
>
> *The Professor's Predicament*, Junior Play, directed by Moses for
> Commencement, June 14, 1909
>
> *The Rivals*, produced by the Dramatic Club and directed by Moses,
> December 2, 1909
>
> *A Happy Mistake*, presented by the sophomore class
> on February 17, 1910
>
> *Julius Caesar*, presented by the Christian Associations at Norwich
> on March 12, 1910
>
> *Julius Caesar*, repeated for the college on March 18, 1910
>
> *For Old Eli*, Junior Play, directed by Mrs. Mary Alice McConagha
> for Commencement, June 13, 1910
>
> *A Midsummer Night's Dream*, presented by the Dramatic Club and
> directed by Moses for Commencement, June 15, 1910 [47]

Mr. Moses came to Muskingum with more experience than most of the previous teachers of elocution and oratory, and with the active support of President Montgomery. He made sweeping changes in the department, offering more courses than ever before, and altering the title of the area at least three times. He was ambitious, energetic, and very popular with students.

Although the title of the department changed several times during Mr. Moses' stay in office, the School of Expression retained that name from its inception in 1906. In fact, that title did not leave the catalog until 1921. The nine courses also remained the same, until Mr. Moses left in 1910 to head the Department of Oratory at Westminster College in Pennsylvania.[48]

Another former member of the faculty, Mary Alice Carothers-McConagha, returned to Muskingum in 1909. She had been the head of the Department of Elocution and Oratory for three years, from 1902 until 1905. She was a native of western Pennsylvania, a graduate of Slippery Rock State Normal College, and of the J. W. Shoemaker's National School of Elocution and Oratory in Philadelphia. She began her career as a teacher in the public schools of Pitcairn, Pennsylvania. After leaving Muskingum in 1905, she married John E. McConagha, an alumnus. During the winter of 1908–09, she directed a private studio in San Jose, California. On the death of her husband, she returned to Muskingum as Dean of Women and as an assistant in the Departments of English and Elocution.[49]

Mrs. McConagha worked closely with Mr. Moses in the department, and directed the junior class production of *For Old Eli* in 1910.[50] She also worked with Professor Immel, Moses's successor, and taught elocution in the summer schools from

1910 to 1911.[51] In 1913, she directed the senior class production of *As You Like It*, the first play to be staged in Brown Chapel.[52] As the chairmanship changed from Moses to Immel, and from Immel to Dennis (1912), Mrs. McConagha served as an important link, and maintained continuity for the department and the students.

Professor Ray Kessler Immel replaced Mr. Moses in the Department of Elocution and Oratory and School of Expression in the 1910–11 school year. Professor Immel was born in Gilead, Michigan. He attended Coldwater High School, where he was an honor debater. He matriculated to Albion College and transferred to the University of Michigan, where he received the B.A. in 1910. He was a student of Thomas C. Trueblood, an Assistant in Oratory, and a member of Phi Beta Kappa.[53]

Under Professor Immel, the aim of the Department of Elocution and Oratory was to give the student knowledge in theories of speaking and expression, and to provide practice in applying them. Courses offered were Practical Public Speaking, Argumentation and Debate, and Oratory.[54]

The forensic record indicates that in 1910–11, Muskingum lost to Mt. Union in debate, but won from Otterbein and Hiram. The College Orator, Earl Lewis, won the State Oratorical Contest and took second place in the Inter-State Contest. In 1911–12, Muskingum lost again to Mt. Union in debate, but won a second debate from them, also defeating Geneva and Ohio University. In the 1911–12 oratorical contests, Fred Myers took third place in the State Oratorical Contest, and H. J. Giffen won second place in the Tri-State Contest.[55]

In the School of Expression, the aim was to complete work begun in Oratory and educate capable readers of the best literature. Courses offered included Advanced Public Speaking, Practical Elocution, Interpretive Reading, Dramatic Reading, Bible Reading, Declamation, The Occasional Speech, and Private Work.[56]

While Immel was in charge, the following plays were produced:

> *The School for Scandal* was presented by the Dramatic Club, February 24, 1911.
>
> *What Happened to Jones* was produced by the junior class for Commencement, June 12, 1911.
>
> *The Prince and the Pauper* was staged by the junior Expression class, October 6, 1911.
>
> *Fanny and the Servant Problem* was produced by the Oratory Department, March 2, 1912.
>
> *The Servant of the House* was offered as a Faculty Play, March 5, 1912.
>
> *Brown of Harvard* was the Junior Play presented at Commencement, June 10, 1912.
>
> *The Servant of the House* was repeated by Faculty for Commencement, June 12, 1912.[57]

Just as Music Faculty gave recitals, it was not unusual to find performances by professors in the School of Expression. Maude Bethel, Mrs. McConagha, and Elbert Moses performed often, and Professor Immel was no exception. When Lois Caldwell gave her graduating recital of *Macbeth*, Immel played Macbeth to Caldwell's Lady

Macbeth.[58] Since Immel was a Trueblood student, he must also have had a hand in luring that public reader to Muskingum for a performance ". . . well worth hearing . . . ."

> On Friday evening, April fifth the students and town people had a grand chance to hear a recital of "Ingomar, the Barbarian." The speaker was Prof. Thomas C. Trueblood of the University of Michigan. Prof. Trueblood is one of the greatest teachers of Oratory in the United States, and indeed the world. He has given this recital around the world, and in most of the largest colleges of this country.
> 'Ingomar' . . . in the hands of such an artist as Prof. Trueblood proved an exceptional entertainment.
> Prof. Trueblood years ago read to the poet Whittier the great poet's poem "Rivermouth Rocks" and Mr. Whittier said, "Why, friend, that makes me like the poem better than when I wrote it."[59]

During Immel's tenure, the following students received degrees or diplomas:

1911	*Bachelor of Oratory*
	Sylvester Christoph Britton
	Jessie Eva Snodgrass
	Bessie Mary Summers
	Master of Elocution
	James Larmor Graham
	Earl Ramage Lewis
	Expression Diploma
	Neva Call
1912	*Bachelor of Oratory*
	Lois Margaret Caldwell
	Adam Raymond Gilliland
	Robert Spencer McClure
	Daniel Crane McCoy
	Master of Elocution
	John Paul Jones Harkness[60]

Although the Master of Elocution had not been mentioned in the *Catalogue* as a possible degree since 1911, it was not discontinued until after the 1913 commencement.

After teaching for two years at Muskingum, Professor Immel was elected to the faculty of the University of Michigan, where he returned to teach and to complete more degree work. He eventually became Dean of Oratory at the University of Southern California.[61]

Wilbur Cookman Dennis replaced Immel in 1912 as the chairman of the Department of Oratory and Expression. Professor Dennis had an M.A. from Ohio Wesleyan School of Oratory and graduated from Northwestern University School of Oratory. He had taught at three other universities in Iowa, Illinois, and Ohio over a ten-year period. Dean Robert I. Fulton of the School of Oratory at Ohio Wesleyan gave him the following recommendation:

> He is doing excellent work with his students here and is much liked by them. I

wish I could have him another year myself as assistant.

> We are sure that the splendid record which Muskingum has made in Oratory and Argumentation will be furthered by Professor Dennis as he takes up his work next fall. Those who heard him on the 75th anniversary program were much pleased with his reading and interpretation. . . . Two other institutions wanted him but Muskingum won.[62]

The goals of the department that Professor Dennis headed were similar to those previously set: the art of public speaking was mastered through voice and action techniques, which were learned by doing. This was the first year that courses were designated by a series of numbers.

Professor Dennis' first year (1912–13) was a memorable year for Oratory. A. B. Cunningham won the State, Inter-State, Tri-State Oratorical Contests. Fred Myers took third place in the Peace Contest.[63] The debate record for 1912–13 saw Muskingum winning from Geneva, Wittenberg, and Mt. Union, and losing to Heidelberg and Otterbein. In 1913–14, debaters again won three and lost two: they beat Geneva, Mt. Union, and Ohio Northern, but lost to Otterbein and Heidelberg.[64]

While Dennis was chairman, the following plays and recitals were performed:

> *As You Like It*, first play performed by the senior class, first play performed in Brown Chapel, February 20, 1913. (Until this time, plays had been staged in the town's Opera House.) [65]
>
> *The College Widow*, presented by the junior class for Commencement, June 9, 1913
>
> *Thank Goodness, the Table Is Set*, produced by the German Club, March 19, 1914
>
> *Strongheart*, a Junior Class Play performed in Cambridge at the Colonial Theatre, on June 3, 1914
>
> Graduation Recital, School of Expression, by Miss Marie Loughry, June 3, 1914
>
> *Strongheart*, repeated by the junior class for Commencement, June 8, 1914[66]
>
> *The Belle of Richmond,* presented by the senior class, May 19, 1915 (as noted by Virginia Massenburg from the *Muscoljuan, 1916,* "Calendar," n.p.)

The following students received degrees and diplomas under the tutelage of Professor Dennis:

1913	*Master of Elocution*	
	Adam Raymond Gilliland	
1914	*Oratory Diploma*	
	Marie Elizabeth Loughry [67]	

After two years, Professor Dennis left Muskingum to continue more graduate study, and to eventually assume the post of Professor of Oratory at Northwestern University.[68]

The frequent turn-over of personnel in oratory, elocution, and expression kept those areas in a state of flux. While the atmosphere was unsettling because of changes in personalities, teaching styles, and teacher expectations of students, it was far from chaotic.

There were a number of stabilizing factors that assured continued growth and popularity. The professors were well qualified for their assignments. Even early teachers of elocution held diplomas from professional schools in The East or degrees from universities. More often, they held both. As the twentieth century wore on, the quality of training increased as programs were perfected and curriculum solidified. Competition among schools helped the drive toward excellence.

There were certain agreements also on matters of philosophy and curriculum. The basic philosophy of teachers bore a striking similarity to one another by expressing the practical and useful nature of speaking, and agreeing that it could be elevated to an art form in oratory and interpretation of literature. The curriculum had, as its basis, courses in fundamentals or principles of speech, argumentation and debate, extemporaneous speaking, interpretive reading, oratory or public speaking, and dramatic expression, or play production.

True, there was some quibbling over what the term "elocution" meant. S. S. Curry helped resolve the problem when he set up his School of Expression in Boston. Curry avoided the term *"elocution"* because too many of its proponents emphasized the mechanical and artificial methods of training the voice and body. Curry praised Delsarte for training the whole body to be receptive to the demands of the material, but condemned the tendency of the Delsarte system to place artificial pre-conceived ideas upon nature. Curry believed that training began with the mind, which must control the voice and the body. The voice and body must be flexible to express the mind and soul of the speaker.[69]

Few teachers of elocution would argue for the mechanical, as opposed to the natural, interpretation of literature. The term *"expression"* was favored over *"elocution"*; it became popular and the one most generally acceptable. As Robb indicates, most educators in the profession were " . . . sincere in the desire to improve the speaking and reading of Americans."[70]

There were other stabilizing forces in the traditional rhetorical practices inherited from the Latin grammar school and the classical training required of ministers, teachers, and lawyers. The literary societies provided firm student support and gave continuity to the discipline—the same discipline that was slowly supplanting the societies with teachers, curricula, and departmental activities.

The administration established ancillary support through Christian associations (YMCA & YWCA), the Gospel Team, and a Lecture Series which brought professional speakers and performers to the campus.

Under the auspices of the administration, contest prizes were established in Oratory, Debate, and Bible Rendition. The Brown Oratory Prizes for the best orations by men and women were offered by J. M. Brown of Wheeling; the Garvin Prizes for those making the first debate team were offered by the Hon. T. M. Garvin of Wheeling; and, the Hanna Prizes for Bible Reading were offered by Rev. A. J. Hanna of Piper City, Illinois.[71]

To those prizes were added the Orr Medal, for the best declaimer in the

Declamation Contest, offered by the Reverend W.W. Orr (D.D.) of Charlotte, North Carolina, and the Weaver Bible Prizes and Weaver Declamation Prizes, offered by Mr. J. Riddle Weaver of Cannonsburgh, Pennsylvania.[72]

Oratory in the United States became very popular during the nineteenth century, a popularity that continued through the first half of the twentieth century. At Muskingum, the Brown prizes for oratory and the Weaver prizes for declamation continued through most of the 1970's. Public speaking styles that were affected by new technological inventions such as the radio, public address systems, and television were forced to change drastically. Nevertheless, early in the twentieth century, Oratory combined the best of composition with the best of delivery. What elocution lost in popularity it gained back in respect, because it was a necessary training tool to students taking part in intercollegiate debates and oratorical contests which sprang up all over the country.[73]

Muskingum belonged to at least four oratorical associations by the 1912–13 school year: the Inter-Collegiate Association, the Tri-State Inter-Collegiate Association, the Prohibition Inter-Collegiate League, and the Peace Oratorical League. Through these associations, the college competed with the leading educational institutions of eleven states. A local association was organized for the purpose of promoting Oratory and Argumentation and had charge of the preliminary contest for the choice of representatives in the Inter-Collegiate meets.[74]

The Department of Elocution, Oratory, and Expression was strengthened in 1911 with the installation of the first sub-chapter in Ohio of Tau Kappa Alpha, the National Fraternity to Honor Men in Oratory and Debate—the highest honor given in those areas at Muskingum. "The gold key of the fraternity has a national significance and the fraternity numbers among its members such men as W. J. Bryan, Senator Beveridge, Governor Buchtel, and others."[75]

Debate was even more popular than oratory. The following paragraph from the *College Catalogue* attested to that fact:

Muskingum College is attaining high rank among the colleges of Ohio in Argumentation. During the past five years twelve Inter-Collegiate debates have been won by Muskingum. Five teams represented the college last year winning

Presidents J. Knox Montgomery, Jr. (left) and Robert N. Montgomery (right) stand before the portrait of their father, President J. Knox Montgomery. *Photo courtesy M.C. Public Relations Office.*

over Mt. Union, Geneva, and Ohio University. A marked interest has been awakened among the students, both ladies and gentlemen taking part in these debates.[76]

President J. Knox Montgomery, Sr. was known as a skilled and forceful public speaker. Dr. Fisk points out how important speech and Bible training were to Montgomery.[77] They were central to the education of ministers and, after all, the education of ministers was the original reason for establishing almost every private denominational college since the founding of Harvard in 1636. President Montgomery put his weight of office and personal interest behind the speech areas; the hiring of good teachers of oratory and expression were vital to his cause.

The President wanted a strong speech department and there was avid student support for a quality of excellence in that area. This was a desire that Reverend Montgomery brought with him to Muskingum, and it was a desire that grew with the years. In his search for instructors to help maintain a strong program of continued growth, he found the Laytons. Together, they built and strengthened one of the best Oratory, Debate, and Dramatic Expression programs in the country.

The consistently steadfast presence of the Laytons for the next half-century ended the period of itinerant professors.

Section Note A
Enrollment Figures

Enrollment figures differ depending upon the type of figures under discussion. Here are enrollment figures for the Department of Elocution (and at times, the class in Physical Culture). The college enrollment refers to the students in the four classes, Freshmen through seniors working toward a degree. Total enrollment in the entire college refers to students, both degree and non-degree, enrolled in various sections and classes of the college, such as the Preparatory Department, Commercial Department, Music students (exclusive of Chorus and those in Chorus not counted elsewhere), students in Art, Elocution, Physical Culture, and Music.

School Year	Teacher in Elocution	Enrollment in Elocution	Enrollment in College	Total Enrollment in College
1885-1886	R. K. Porter	90		
1890-1891	Josephine Martin	23		
1891-1892	Josephine Martin	28		107
1892-1893	Viola D. Romans	39		92
1893-1894	Viola D. Romans	29		131
1894-1895	Viola D. Romans	25		111
1895-1896	Elizabeth Marshall	14		143
1896-1897	Frank S. Fox	48	83	208
1897-1898	Frank S. Fox	37	85	203
1898-1899	Fox & Bethel	24	75	183
1899-1900	Maude H. Bethel	28	89	231
1900-1901	Maude H. Bethel	21	96	215
1901-1902	Anna C. Walter	26	99	214
1902-1903	Mary A. Carothers	51	95	274

School Year	Teacher in Elocution	Enrollment in Elocution	Enrollment in College	Total Enrollment in College
1903-1904	Mary A. Carothers	31	103	270
1904-1905	Mary A. Carothers	28	143	293
1905-1906	E. A. Moses	25	131	294
1906-1907	E. A. Moses	27	129	295
1907-1908	E. A. Moses	69	121	365
1908-1909	E. A. Moses	132	141	470
1909-1910	E. A. Moses	106	147	475
1910-1911	R. K. Immel	133	176	610
1911-1912	R. K. Immel	166	200	561
1912-1913	W. C. Dennis	10	220	607
1913-1914	W. C. Dennis	?	259	700

Sources: 1885-1886 & 1890-1891, see ACMC, pp. 23 & 37.
1891-1896, see Thomas Berkshire, A History of Muskingum College, "Chapter 1887-1904" (unpublished manuscript), for the total enrollments of different years, pp. 21, 45, 38, 47.
1891-1896, ACMC, for the enrollments in elocution in different years, see pp. 30-31, 13, 18, 14-15.
1897-1914, ACMC, for all enrollments for the successive school years, see pp. 17-19, 68, 67-68, 69-72, 64-66, 57-60, 65-67, 64-66, 73-75, 89-91, 87-89, 106-111, 106-109, 120-125, 117-122, 114-120, 96, 107.

Section Note B
Mrs. Romans and the School Colors

Cheryl D. Swiss, in "A History of Theatre at Muskingum College" (p. 6), recounts the part which Mrs. Romans accidentally played in the history of the school colors. The *Alumni Bulletin* for June, 1931 carried the story that a freshman committee charged with deciding on school colors admired a black hat, trimmed with black and magenta, worn by Mrs. Romans. The freshmen who admired not only the hat, but also Mrs. Romans, decided that black and magenta would make excellent school colors. And so it came to pass . . .

Section Note C
The Opera House

The commencement program was the most auspicious occasion for which the societies performed. The audience was so large that the college halls could not handle the traffic. As a result, the college obtained permission to use the Opera House, a large auditorium on the second floor of the village Town Hall.[1] The college continued to use the Opera House for plays and concerts at commencement until 1912, when Brown Chapel was built. The chapel could accommodate seven hundred people, and has been arranged to serve over a thousand audience members at times.

1. Cheryl D. Swiss, "A History of Theatre at Muskingum College," (An unpublished thesis presented to the faculty of the Graduate College of Ohio University, in partial fulfillment of the requirements for the degree of Master of Arts, 1972), p. 10.

REFERENCES

(The following abbreviations are used: ACMC = Annual Catalogue of Muskingum College; B&M = Black and Magenta.)

1   *ACMC: 1857–1858* (Zanesville, Ohio: W. H. Hurd, Printer, Excelsior Book & Job Office, 1858), n.p.; *ACMC: 1867–1868* (Zanesville, Ohio: Zanesville Courier, 1868), p. 13.

2   Thomas Berkshire, *History of Muskingum College*, "Chapter 1857–1867," (unpublished manuscript), p. 86.

3   Mary Margaret Robb, "The Elocutionary Movement and Its Chief Figures," in *A History of Speech Education in America: Background Studies*. Edited by Karl R. Wallace (New York: Appleton-Century-Crofts, Inc., 1954), p. 200.

4   Marie Hochmuth and Richard Murphy, "Rhetorical and Elocutionary Training in Nineteenth Century Colleges," *A History of Speech Education in America*, p. 171.

5   Berkshire, "Chapter 1867–1877," pp. 8-9.

6   Ibid., "Muskingum in the News in 1870 and in 1873-4," p. 1.

7   Ibid., pp. 10-11.

8   Ibid., "Additional Data Concerning the Commencements of 1870 and 1871," p. 3.

9   *ACMC: 1885–1886*, no page reference except "Faculty" title page.

10   Berkshire, "Chapter 1877–1887," p. 46.

11   *ACMC: 1885–1886*, p. 22.

12   Ibid., pp. 22-23.

13   *ACMC: 1890–1891*, p. 6; Berkshire, "Chapter 1887–1904," p. 24.

14   *ACMC: 1891–1892*, p. 30.

15   *ACMC: 1890–1891*, p. 36.

16   Ibid., p. 37.

17   *ACMC: 1891–1892*, pp. 30-31.

18   *ACMC: 1892–1893*, p. 6.

19   *ACMC: 1893–1894*, p. 39.

20   *ACMC: 1895–1896*, pp. 33-34.

21   Ibid., p. 34.

22   Ibid., p. 35.

23   *ACMC: 1897–1898* (Pittsburgh, Pennsylvania: Murdoch-Kerr Press, 1898), pp. 26-29.

24   Ibid., pp. 37-38.

25   Ibid., pp. 47-48.

26   Ibid., p.48.

27   Ibid., p. 49.

28   Berkshire, "Athletics at Muskingum, 1887–1904," in "Chapter 1887–1904," pp. 14-15; *ACMC: 1898-1899* (Columbus, Ohio: Nitschke Bros. Press, 1899), p. 7.

29   *Circular of Information, Muskingum College: 1900* (Zanesville, Ohio: George Lilienthal, 1900), p. 16.

30   ACMC: 1899–1900, pp. 54-56.

31   ACMC: 1901–1902, pp. 48-49.

32   ACMC: 1909–1910, p. 7; 1910–1911, p. 89.

33   Muscoljuan, 1910, p. 18.

34   Hochmuth and Murphy, p. 172.

35   Berkshire, "Chapter 1904–1939," pp. 17-18.

36   *ACMC: 1905–1906* (New Concord, Ohio: Enterprise Print, 1906), pp. 69-70; *1906–1907*, pp. 45,64-69; *1907–1908*, pp. 73-78; *1908–1909*, pp. 48-49, 72–76; *1909–1910*, pp. 56-57, 86-90.

37   *ACMC: 1905–1906*, p. 69.

38   *ACMC: 1907–1908*, pp. 73-78.

39   Ibid., p. 73.

40   Ibid, pp. 74-75.

41   Ibid., pp. 75-77.

42   *Muskingum College Bulletin*, "Forensic Edition," June 5, 1925, n.p.; Swiss, p. 10; Berkshire, "Chapter 1904–1939," p. 18.

43   *Muscoljuan*, 1923, p. 170.

44   Ibid., p. 170.

45   Commencement Programs for the years indicated were found in The Archives of the Muskingum College Library; also in the *ACMC*, degrees were listed at the end of each catalogue. An outline of Commencement activities could be found in the early pages of each *ACMC*. (At least, this was true of the catalogs from 1900–1915.)

46   Berkshire, "Chapter 1904-1939," p. 13.

47   Commencement Programs for the years indicated and the *ACMC*s in The Archives.

48   *Muskingum College Bulletin*, "Forensic Edition," June 5, 1925, n.p.

49   *Muscoljuan*, 1913, p. 36; *ACMC: 1909–1910*, pp. 6-7.

50   Swiss, p. 11.
51   *ACMC: 1909–1910*, pp. 6-7; 1910–1911, p. 89.
52   Swiss p. 13.
53   *Muscoljuan*, 1913, p. 34.
54   *ACMC: 1910–1911*, pp. 56-57.
55   *Muscoljuan*, 1923, p. 170.
56   *ACMC: 1910–1911*, pp. 83-86.
57   Commencement Programs for the years indicated, Archives.
58   *B&M*, June 1912, p. 15.
59   *B&M*, "Great Recital," April 1912, pp. 13-14.
60   Commencement Programs for the years indicated, Archives.
61   *Muskingum College Bulletin*, "Forensic Edition," June 5, 1925, n.p.
62   *B&M*, April 1912, p. 14.
63   *Muscoljuan*, 1923, p. 170.
64   Ibid.
65   Swiss, pp. 12-13.
66   Commencement Programs for the years indicated, Archives.
67   Commencement Programs for the years indicated, Archives.
68   *Muskingum College Bulletin*, "Forensic Edition," June 5, 1915, n.p.
69   Robb, pp. 193-197.
70   Ibid., p. 181.
71   *ACMC: 1905–1906,* pp. 26-27.
72   *ACMC: 1908–1909*, pp. 20-21; *1911–1912*, pp. 22-23.
73   Hochmuth and Murphy, pp. 165-169.
74   *ACMC: 1912–1913*, p. 20.
75   *ACMC: 1911–1912*, p. 23.
76   Ibid., p. 22.
77   William L. Fisk, *A History of Muskingum College*, Muskingum College (New Concord, Ohio, 1978), pp. 107 & 121.

The Layton Years: 1914–1958
The Teachers

Professors Charles Rush Layton and Ferne Parsons Layton founded the present Muskingum College Department of Speech Communication and Theatre, " . . . the first department in the college to win a national reputation."[1] The husband and wife team came to Muskingum in the fall of 1914 with the blessing of President J. Knox Montgomery, who wanted the pre-ministerial students to have expert training in speech. This fact, combined with traditions already established by the literary societies, training from previous professors of oratory and elocution, and the curriculum, together with student enthusiasm for the subject, provided a friendly climate for the Laytons.

As the Laytons commenced their joint careers at Muskingum (careers that were to span five decades), they not only proved capable, but also exceeded all expectations. For forty-four years, the Laytons devoted their talents and undiminishing capacity for work to teaching students, directing plays, and coaching intercollegiate debate teams. Although a team themselves in every respect, Dr. Layton (who headed the department) concentrated his expertise in the areas of debate and oratory, while Mrs. Layton plied her skills in the fields of interpretation and theatre. The Layton insistence upon honesty, sincerity, simplicity of expression, reliability, thorough research, energy, and unstinting loyalty to the task at hand inspired even mediocre talents and average intellects to give skillful performances and maintain above-average grades.

The 1953 Muskingum College Debate Team coach, Dr. C. R. Layton, presents the National Debate Winners Plaque to President Robert N. Montgomery. Surrounding the dignitaries are the team: (from left to right) W. Fischer, D. Fee, R. Marmaduke, R. Larson, R. Hershberger, and J. Borton. *Photo courtesy M.C. Library Archives and Public Relations Office. Caption courtesy William Fischer and Ronald Marmaduke.*

Where the Laytons led, the students followed. The debating prowess of Muskingum College grew in the state and the region, and finally, the small southeastern Ohio college became nationally famous for the consistently fine performance of its debaters and orators. Programs in interpretation and theatre drew audiences not only from students and alumni, but also from neighboring communities. Of special note were the senior speech recitals directed by Mrs. Layton—individual performances by students of poetry and drama, similar in format to the one-man shows still seen today on the professional stage.

As the reputation of the department and the Laytons grew, so did the enrollment in speech courses. The effect on other teachers and departments in the college was at once stimulating and debilitating. Dr. William Fisk, in *A History of Muskingum College,* writes: "The standards they [the Laytons] upheld became an embarrassment to some of their more easygoing colleagues, one of whom honestly admitted that the rising standards of academic performance and the pace set by Professor Layton made him too uncomfortable to stay longer at Muskingum." [2]

Peer pressure exerted influence on students in a like manner. The Laytons would not tolerate a "slacker" in the classroom or on the platform. They didn't have to, because competition among students to achieve excellence drove the lazy ones away. I experienced this competitiveness in 1945 when I was a freshman at Muskingum. To me, it seemed, and probably was, a part of the academic climate by that time.

There was a saying at Muskingum that a "Muskingum 'B' was worth an 'A' at any other school." One of my fellow students challenged me by saying that I would not be able to make such good grades if I were in a larger school, where there were more students and assumptively higher intellects at work. I accepted the challenge, and the first semester of my sophomore year, I transferred to Ohio University. (Another reason for transferring was the belief that a state school would cost less. My colleague and I both were wrong in our assumptions.) Ohio University, in the fall of 1946, was larger than Muskingum by at least 3,000 students. The professors and the courses of instruction I had were of excellent quality; however, I received straight "A's," with the exception of one "B", a record better than my average at Muskingum. The small private school also proved, mysteriously, to be less expensive than the state-supported school. I returned to Muskingum for the spring term.

The competition at Muskingum was greater; furthermore, if a student wanted to work for an "A" in a Layton course, he must do what was known as "creative scholarship." This meant that a student must not only have an "A" average on the required work for the course, but also he must contract for extra work, and do it equally well. I concluded that this system of grading prevailed, not just in Layton courses; it was college-wide. The Muskingum "B" was no myth.

The Layton teaching style, which resulted from their personality and character traits, had a lasting influence on the lives of their students. Another factor of equal importance was their educational background which informed the Layton theory and content.

Charles Rush Layton received his B.A. from Otterbein College in 1913, his M.A. from the University of Michigan in 1917, and his Ph.D. from the same school in

Charles Rush Layton, A.M. 1924
Photo from Muscoljuan, 1924.

1952. Ferne Parsons Layton received a Bachelor of Oratory from Mount Union-Scio College in 1909, her B.A. from the University of Michigan in 1923, and her M.A. from Michigan in 1925.[3]

Both professors taught previously before coming to Muskingum. Dr. Layton taught history and public speaking in high school from 1913 to 1914. He was hired as a Professor of Speech in 1914, and, except for the title "Dean of

Ferne Parsons Layton, B.O.
Photo from Muscoljuan, 1924.

Speech" conferred on him in 1920, his status continued as such until his retirement in 1958. Mrs. Layton taught oratory at Scio College during the summer of 1910; she was the Instructor in Physical Training at Otterbein College (1912–13); she continued as an instructor in Physical Training at Muskingum College from 1914 to 1919, concurrent with her work in speech. She became an Assistant Professor in 1920, and a Professor of Speech in 1925.[4]

An interview with the Laytons in the spring of 1968 revealed the substance behind their degrees and training. Upon receiving their appointments to Muskingum in the spring of 1914, husband and wife studied that summer with Thomas C. Trueblood at the University of Michigan. According to Dr. Layton, the University of Michigan was outstanding at that time in the study of speech, the reason largely being the presence of Trueblood, who was considered, in Dr. Layton's words, " . . . one of the masters, academic masters anyway . . . " of speech in the country.[5]

Giles Wilkinson Gray traces the career of Trueblood in his article, "Some Teachers and the Transition to Twentieth Century Speech Education." Trueblood, a product of Earlham College, studied with S. S. Hamill, James E. Murdoch, and the Amherst rhetorician, Genung. He formed lasting friendships with William Jennings Bryan and Robert I. Fulton. With Fulton, Trueblood wrote books, traveled as an itinerant teacher of elocution, and formed a school of oratory at Kansas City. In 1892, he was appointed chairman of the new Department of Elocution and Oratory at the University of Michigan.[6] According to Mrs. Layton, it was the law school students who brought speech into the curriculum at Michigan, starting with requests for short courses and summer school study that eventually evolved into a permanent course of study, and then into a department.[7]

The Laytons returned to Michigan often after that first summer, and spent their sabbatical of 1922–23 working on advanced degrees. Gray concludes that Trueblood made two major contributions to the teaching of speech. First, he explained the difference between elocution as a matter of delivery and elocution as an art form. In the first instance, elocution meant the use of voice and body in speaking, while in the latter, elocution referred to the elocutionist who, as a professional reader, performed in an exaggerated, mechanical manner because of a misunderstanding of Delsarte. Second, Trueblood insisted that speech teachers should urge students to get as much liberal education as possible, raise requirements for admission, and strengthen courses for graduation.[8]

Layton students heard much about Trueblood, and the concepts mentioned above were re-interpreted and reiterated by the Laytons. They insisted that students practice, practice, practice, in order to be skilled in the use of voice and gesture. The student needed such drill to free himself of technique that became second nature to him. Only then could the student concentrate on meaning and content. Technique meant nothing without content and meaning, but unskilled gestures and an inexpressive voice could ruin the best ideas.

The high academic standard upheld by the Laytons has already been addressed; that they also were generalists, who believed in a broad liberal arts education, is indicated by the fact that they urged students to take courses in as many other departments of the college as possible. Courses in history, political science, and English were valuable in supplying substance and content to a student's communication and education.

The Laytons' interdisciplinary approach to learning was manifested within the department as well. The beginning speech course became a survey of the many disciplines encompassed by the area of speech: fundamentals, public speaking, interpretation, broadcasting, and theatre. At times, students in the class even produced a one-act play.[9] Majors were encouraged and required to take courses in all the different aspects of speech: debaters took acting and actors took argumentation. [10]

Teaching colleagues were not exempt from the interdisciplinary-multidisciplinary approach. As teaching staff were added over the years, the Layton student with a B.A. from Muskingum dominated the appointments. Although this practice is frowned upon by some as "academic in-breeding," it was a tradition among professional schools to hire talented graduates in order to assure quality of performance.[11] The Laytons could be generalists even in the structuring of teaching assignments. With the exception of advanced courses and certain areas that demanded special expertise for the sake of teaching standards, the Laytons felt that a teacher should be knowledgeable in most areas covered by the curriculum. The ideal teaching staff would be one that could teach across the curriculum; most important, however, was avoidance of a specialization that led to imbalance in the curriculum, fragmentation, or the establishing of separate "pet" territories.

It was the Layton tradition that all members of the department teach—or be able to teach—the beginning speech course. This practice kept the teachers familiar with theories and practices fundamental to all speech courses, and it served to introduce all teachers in the department to the student body.

Another University of Michigan professor who had a lasting influence on the Laytons, and consequently on their students, was R. D. T. Hollister. The Hollister book on interpretive reading is still considered the best text, because of its combination of theory and choice of selections made readily available for student practice. The influence of both Trueblood and Hollister was felt in the emphasis that Mrs. Layton placed on Tennyson and Browning in her oral reading courses.

Soloman Henry Clark of the University of Chicago was another "master" teacher and performer with whom the Laytons studied. It is interesting to note that William Rainey Harper (first president of the University of Chicago, and a Muskingum graduate) was in Chautauqua, New York, in 1891, when he met Clark, who was just beginning his career as a teacher and reader. Harper was searching for a faculty to start a new university and he was impressed by Clark. When the University of Chicago opened in 1892, Clark was head of the Department of Public Speaking.[12] It was also in Chautauqua, although at a later time (as well as at the University of Chicago), that the Laytons studied with Clark.[13]

S. H. Clark was known as one of the best teachers of interpretation and " . . . one of the ten best readers in America."[14] Although it is difficult to tell the extent of Clark's influence on the Laytons, some of his most prominent principles may be seen as part of the Layton program. They were one with Clark in believing that the reader 1) should have a good education, especially in literature; 2) must be able to analyze and understand selections; 3) needs a knowledge of the psychology of the mind (the Laytons taught a course "Psychology of Vocal Expression"); 4) must subordinate technique to thought; and 5) should feel, as closely as possible, the emotion to be portrayed.[15]

The Laytons would agree with Clark, that reading or interpretation is a re-creative art, suggestive rather than impersonative, in order to distinguish it from acting. Like Clark, they encouraged use of the reading stand and a script;[16] however, the student had to know the selection so well that such items were not crutches—they were present to keep the reader from acting and the audience from expecting him to act. Dr. Layton believed that Clark's book, *The Interpretation of the Printed Page,* had few equals. [17]

The third "master" with whom the Laytons studied was the famous S. S. Curry, founder of the School of Expression in Boston in 1883. Curry had been a student of Lewis Baxter Monroe, the first head of the Boston University School of Oratory. Monroe was a teacher and performer of public readings, known for his insistence on the importance of ideas as opposed to a mere display of technique. He held theories similar to those of Delsarte, and Samuel Silas Curry held theories similar to his teacher, Monroe.[18] One summer, Curry took his entire faculty to Pittsburgh for a session, and the Laytons traveled there to take classes. Curry placed emphasis on the imagination and the creation of images in the mind, and he accepted Delsarte's principles of body training, which freed the interpreter of repression.[19] Mrs. Layton used Curry's book, *The Province of Expression,* in her interpretation classes. In her recital work, Mrs. Layton put the student on a bare stage with nothing but his imaginative response to the memorized literature. Dr. Layton felt that Curry had much to offer students, especially in his books, which he believed should be rewritten for a modern audience.[20]

Of the great masters of the time, Leland Powers was one with whom the Laytons did not get to study. However, they brought Powers to Muskingum for a recital in March of 1915 and, again, in March of 1920, so that students might witness first-hand one of the great readers of literature.[21] Mrs. Layton also used Powers' book, *The Fundamentals of Expression,* as supplementary reading. Powers' philosophy, "To do is to Know," was compatible with the Laytons' coupling of practice with theory.[22] All speech activities were connected in some way with the curriculum. Knowledge and theory were essential for practice, and practice made theory clear. They liked the hands-on experience that increased student knowledge and skill, and also gave students a challenge. One such course was Play Production which met twice a week through the year. Producing a play was a requisite, and classes were so large that usually two plays were performed. "The Acting," said the Laytons, "was not always the best because some students were more talented than others, but the learning experience was the most important factor."[23]

The Laytons studied with the great teacher-performers in order to increase their knowledge and skill in speech and, therefore, make themselves rich in experience. The great teachers of the day did not always agree, but the Laytons were able to take what they considered the best from each, and harmonize the various points of view to benefit the student.[24]

The Laytons were teachers who also practiced what they taught. They presented many programs to various college and civic organizations. Their students took a special pleasure in watching the Laytons perform the skills they taught, for they were expert and gracious entertainers.[25] However, the demand was always greater than the supply, because the Laytons were first of all teachers, and it was into their teaching that the Laytons preferred to put all their time and energies.

REFERENCES

1   William L. Fisk, *A History of Muskingum College* (New Concord, Ohio: Muskingum College, 1978), p. 122.
2   Ibid.
3   *Muskingum College Catalogue: 1952–1953* (New Concord, Ohio: Muskingum College, 1953), p. 8.
4   Ibid., p. 11.
5   Donald P. Hill, "An Interview with the Laytons." Audio Tape (New Concord, Ohio, spring, 1968).
6   Giles Wilkinson Gray, "Some Teachers and the Transition to Twentieth-Century Speech Education," In *A History of Speech Education in America: Background Studies*, Ed. Karl R. Wallace (New York: Appleton-Century-Crofts, Inc., 1954), p. 425.
7   Hill, "An Interview with the Laytons."
8   Gray, pp. 426–427.
9   Hill.
10 James L. Golden, "The Rhetorical Thrust of the Laytons," *Muskingum College Bulletin* (New Concord, Ohio: Muskingum College, summer, 1970), p. 14.
11 Edyth Renshaw, "Five Private Schools of Speech," In *A History of Speech Education in America: Background Studies*, Ed. Karl R. Wallace (New York: Appleton-Century-Crofts, Inc., 1954) p. 307.
12 Gray, p. 431.
13 Hill.
14 Gray, p. 431.
15 Ibid., pp. 431–432.
16 Ibid., p. 431.
17 Hill.
18 Renshaw, pp. 302, 306.
19 Ibid., p. 316.
20 Hill.
21 *Muscoljuan, 1915 & 1920, VIII* (New Concord, Ohio: Muskingum College).
22 Renshaw, p. 319.
23 Hill.
24 Ibid.
25 Charles Rush Layton and Ferne Parsons Layton, "National Collegiate Players Initiation Program," (New Concord, Ohio, 1948).

The Department

In 1914, the Laytons inherited the Department of Oratory and Expression from Professor Wilbur C. Dennis. The parameters of the department were limited to Public Speaking and Reading. In 1917, the title was changed to Department of Oratory and School of Expression. In 1922, it became the Department of Public Speaking and School of Oratory. In 1930, it was known as the Department of Speech and School of Oratory. Whatever the title of the department, the parameters of Public Speaking and Reading remained paramount until 1930, when Acting was added to the fields of exploration and practice. Finally, in 1931, it was called the Speech Department, a name that was retained for the next forty years.

Just as the title of the department changed, so did the philosophy of the department, as stated in the paragraphs preceding course descriptions. These changes were expected as the Laytons progressed in their teaching careers, and as the particular emphases in the field of speech responded to the changing world pressures in politics, society, psychology, and economics.

From the beginning of their tenure in 1914, and throughout the 1920's, the Laytons maintained that the object of oratory and expression was to "stimulate clear and orderly thinking, cultivate the imagination, and develop the emotional nature." They wanted the student to know the subject well and to express his thoughts on the subject with a quality of ease and naturalness that came from solid, thorough research and was communicated by a well-developed voice and body.[1]

Theory was proven through practice, and practice came first; therefore, the student could clearly see how the theory was confirmed. The Layton philosophy contradicted every facet of what F. Scott Fitzgerald called the "Jazz Age," which was characterized by a carefree, careless, unthinking hedonism. There was only a hint of self-indulgence in the introduction to the curriculum: "The cultivation of the artistic in expression is an ideal of the department."[2] The Laytons denied the artistic as an end in itself, but they encouraged the traits of the genuine artist: truth, honesty, and sincerity. Later, they openly admitted that they were not interested in "producing professional performers."[3]

Emphasizing this credo, the Laytons fashioned a series of courses that lasted through the Great Depression, World War II, and the beginning of the Cold War. The curriculum was not just a series of courses; each course was part of a well-defined structure that was informed by their philosophy of academic excellence and unshakeable faith in human kind. Like stepping-stones, one course led to another; to ensure a student's safe passage and course continuity, there were prerequisites for entering a course and suggestions for a destination, as the student exited the course.

There are many examples of how the Laytons sequenced their studies in speech and expression. The course in Public Speaking 1 was a fundamental course, about which the Laytons stated, "The course is a prerequisite for all other courses in the department. It is suggested that those who are particularly interested in public speaking take this course in their freshman year. This course should be followed by Course 2, the second semester of the same year." At the end of the description for Course 2 was the following suggestion:

> Incidentally, this course lays the foundation for more intensive work of advanced studies in Public Speaking; but primarily, it aims to develop the ability to think and talk well. Those who expect to try out for debating or oratorical contests should take this course in the Freshman year.[4]

The Laytons restricted Junior Play Production to juniors only. Oratory and Orators-Rhetoric had a prerequisite of two semesters of the fundamentals course; also: "Students are not eligible to take intercollegiate oratory unless they have taken or are taking this course." Debating Seminar was "Open only to those who make the intercollegiate debating teams." Advanced Oratory was "Open only to intercollegiate orators." Advanced Public Speaking was "Open only to students who have shown ability in speaking and reading, and who receive permission or invitation."[5] Advanced Interpretive Reading was a continuation of Interpretive Reading, and Literary Analysis and Interpretation was a Junior level course with the prerequisite of "permission."[6]

There are various ways of looking at departments that establish a curriculum with many prerequisites. One way is to believe that learning is a progression in knowledge and skill, which means that, once a person possesses a unit of information, it is easier for him to understand the next phase. The same may be said of a skill: learning to do the most simple action enables one to move on to the next and more complex activity. Speech is, at once, a reservoir of knowledge and a showcase of skill. Since the Laytons took their subject area and their teaching seriously, they used prerequisites as guideposts by which they could monitor their students' success and ability to take the next step. Their students regarded the completion of the prerequisites as signs of achievement and as indicators that they were ready for the next challenge.

The atmosphere of the department was serious and business-like. Students knew that they could do well if they had instruction. They accepted the Layton *dicta* that, if one wanted to be a debater, he took a course in debate; if he wanted to be in a play, he took a course in play production.[7]

The educational continuity provided by the long tenure of the Laytons resulted in a central core of courses that experienced few changes over the years. Some courses by previous professors, inherited by the Laytons, never made it to the 1920's. Parliamentary Usage was dropped from the curriculum after 1914, but it was reintroduced as Parliamentary Law and Practice in 1931. Bible Reading was incorporated into the Interpretation courses after 1917; and Dramatic Reading was phased out after 1916, in favor of the Play Production courses. Private Work was translated into Interpretation Seminar, with the same tutorial mode of operation that resulted in a graduation recital or public performance. The Literary Analysis and Interpretation course became a junior level course with another public recital as a goal. The course, Theory of Expression, was introduced in 1917–18 for one year only. It was a theory-type course which explained the history and various theories behind the art of expression; it was advertised as being very helpful to teachers of the subject.

Some courses were dropped from the curriculum in the 1930's. The Psychology of Expression, which was a study of the how and why of elocution, was gradually phased out of the course work in the 1930's. Shakespearean Reading fell victim to the suggestion that students take the Shakespeare course offered in the English Department. Advanced Public Speaking was dropped in the same decade.

Courses added in the 1930's were Radio Speech (later titled Principles and Practices of Radio Broadcasting), Speech Correction (later called Principles of Speech Re-education, with a one-hour laboratory included,) and How We Think, a course based on John Dewey's book of the same title, which was also the text for the course. It explained the scientific method of reasoning and was a prelude to the Argumentation and Debate course. Elements of Play Production was added in 1932; it covered all the areas of Scenography; John Gassner's *Play Production* was the all-encompassing text.

During the final decade of the Laytons' tenure, there were few changes. Production, Direction, and Performance of Radio Shows was added to the list of courses in 1949. Introduction to Theatre was also added in 1949, in order to give freshmen and sophomores a one-act play production course to complement the play production course open only to juniors and seniors. Television was added to both of the Radio courses in 1958, and Methods of Teaching Speech was phased out in the 1950's, with the suggestion that the student take an equivalent methods course offered in the Education Department.

Courses which spanned the Laytons' teaching careers from 1914 through 1958 were Principles of Elocution, later re-named Public Speaking and, finally, just Speech. In 1943, it became part of a composite General Education Core course titled Communication. It combined Speech with English and met three times a week. Two more class days were devoted to laboratories dealing with orientation materials, such as "How to Study," and ancillary speech topics, such as listening. The labs were sometimes taught by two professors sharing different points of view on selected topics. The course was offered throughout the year for four credit hours each semester.

Communication ran concurrent with the original Fundamentals of Speech course, which was never taken off the books because it was still being taught in the summer school. Communication ended in 1959, and the Fundamentals of Speech course (worth three credit hours) was re-instituted as part of the core education program.

Over a dozen more courses became permanent members of the curriculum. Interpretative Reading was a standard survivor; Advanced Interpretive Reading remained under the name of Literary Analysis and Interpretation; and the Acting Drama (later called Modern Drama) was the main dramatic literature course that remained in the curriculum through 1958. (It was maintained in the theatre curriculum through 1995.) Junior Play Production and Senior Play Production eventually became a single course, Play Production, which withstood the test of time. Other courses that survived were Extempore Speaking, Oratory and Orators-Survey, Oratory and Orators-Rhetoric, Argumentation and Debate (later titled Reasoning and Discussion), Debate Seminar, Advanced Oratory, Oratory Seminar (later titled Speech Seminar), and Parliamentary Law and Practice.

When the Laytons began teaching at Muskingum in 1914, the curriculum was composed of eleven courses, totaling a possible twenty-three to twenty-seven hours, all of which were taught by them. When they retired forty-four years later, there were five professors teaching twenty-one courses, totaling a possible eighty-four hours.

Charles and Ferne Layton at their retirement ceremony. The husband-wife teaching team was credited with putting the Muskingum College speech department on the map nationally. *Photo from Muskingum College Alumni Bulletin, 1970, Courtesy Public Relations Office.*

The faculty teaching the carefully-designed and time-tested curriculum were just as important as the courses themselves. It was important to maintain a faculty that understood the philosophy of the department and teachers who worked together to steer students through the sequence of courses. As in most professional schools, the Laytons never hesitated to hire former students as their teaching colleagues. It was an easy and almost fool-proof way of preserving their philosophy of speech. The appended list of speech faculty uses asterisks to indicate Muskingum graduates.

Because the discipline of speech is an area of theory and knowledge combined with skill and performance, the quantity of its productivity and, to some extent, the quality of its productivity is traceable through records of performance. To that end, the reader will find appended to this chapter some of the records of debate and oratory contests, a list of departmental plays performed, and the names of the recipients of diplomas in oratory and/or speech.

REFERENCES

1   *Annual Catalogue of Muskingum College: 1915-1916*, p. 52.
2   Ibid.
3   *ACMC: 1930-1931*, p. 125.
4   *ACMC: 1920-1921*, pp. 76-77.
5   Ibid., pp. 77-81.
6   *ACMC: 1929-1930*, p. 120.
7   Cheryl D. Swiss, "A History of Theatre at Muskingum College," (unpublished Master of Arts Thesis, Athens, Ohio: Ohio University, June 1972), p. 16.

Section Notes A
Departmental Faculty: 1914–1958

Years	Department Title	Faculty
1914-1917	Oratory and Expression	Prof. C. R. Layton and Asst: Mrs. Layton (part-time, she was also Physical Director for Ladies)

("The School of Expression has in view two departments: Public Speaking and Reading.")

Years	Department Title	Faculty
1917-1919	Oratory and School of Expression	Prof. C. R. Layton; Asst: Mrs. Layton (p.t.)
1919-1920	No change in title	Prof. C. R. Layton; Asst: Mrs. Layton (She is now full-time.)
1920-1921	No change in title	Prof. C. R. Layton is named Dean of Oratory; Asst: Mrs. Layton.
1921-1922	Public Speaking & School of Oratory	Prof. C. R. Layton; Assoc. Mrs. Layton; *Miss Pearl M'liss Rice
1922-1923	Public Speaking & School of Oratory	Prof. C. R. Layton; Mrs. Layton; *Mr. Ermy Jackson
1923-1924	Public Speaking & School of Oratory	The Laytons; *Gibson Reid Johnson, *Mr. Ermy Jackson, *Miss Virginia Gibbon, Mr. McCarty
1924-1925	No change in title	The Laytons; *Miss Virginia Gibbon, Mr. McCarty

(There is a change in the aim of the department: "The School of Oratory has in view three activities: Public Speaking, Reading, and Acting.")

Years	Department Title	Faculty
1925-1926	No change in title	The Laytons; *Mr. Ermy Jackson, *Miss Virginia Gibbon, *Miss Mildred Keboch, *Mr. T. C. Pollock
1926-1928	No change in title	The Laytons; *Miss Virginia Gibbon, *Miss Mildred Keboch
1928-1929	No change in title	The Laytons; *Miss Virginia Gibbon, *Mr. John Ballantyne
1929-1930	No change in title	The Laytons; *Miss Virginia Gibbon, Mr. William H. Ewing, *Miss Sara McFadden
1930-1931	Speech & School of Oratory	The Laytons; *Miss Virginia Gibbon, Mr. William H. Ewing
1931-1932	Speech	The Laytons; *Miss Virginia Gibbon, Mr. William H. Ewing
1932-1937	No change in title	The Laytons; Mr. William H. Ewing

Years	Department Title	Faculty
1937-1940	No change in title	The Laytons; Mr. William H. Ewing, *Mrs. Muriel Bain
1940-1941	No change in title	The Laytons; Mr. William H. Ewing, Miss Lucile M. Brady, *Mr. Chester B. McKirahan
1941-1943	No change in title	The Laytons; Mr. William H. Ewing, *Mr. Chester B. McKirahan, *Mr. Wallace Fotheringham
1943-1944	No change in title	The Laytons; *Mr. Wallace B. Fotheringham
1944-1947	No change in title	The Laytons; *Mr. Wallace B. Fotheringham, *Miss Mary Elizabeth Johnson
1947-1948	No change in title	The Laytons; *Mr. Wallace B. Fotheringham, *Miss Mary Elizabeth Johnson, *Miss Martha Moore
1948-1949	No change in title	The Laytons; *Miss Mary Elizabeth Johnson, *Miss Martha Moore, *Mrs. Dorothy Myers Gage, Mr. Ralph Arnold
1949-1951	No change in title	The Laytons; *Miss Mary Elizabeth Johnson, *Miss Martha Moore, Mr. Ralph Arnold, *Mr. Pressley McCoy
1951-1952	No change in title	The Laytons; *Miss Mary Elizabeth Johnson, *Miss Martha Moore, Mr. Theodore J. Huesemann
1952-1953	No change in title	The Laytons; *Miss Mary Elizabeth Johnson, *Miss Martha Moore, Mr. Darrell C. Holmes
1953-1954	No change in title	The Laytons; *Miss Mary Elizabeth Johnson, *Miss Martha Moore, *Mr. David Lorimer
1954-1955	No change in title	The Laytons; *Miss Mary Elizabeth Johnson, *Miss Martha Moore, Mr. G. Shanley
1955-1957	No change in title	The Laytons; *Miss Mary Elizabeth Johnson, *Miss Martha Moore, Mr. Arthur Schreiber
1957-1958	No change in title	Prof. C. R. Layton; *Miss Mary Elizabeth Johnson, *Miss Martha Moore, Mr. Arthur Schreiber, *Miss Gail Joseph

Source: *ACMC* for the appropriate year.

Forensic Oratory Record: 1908–1922

Year	Orator	State Contest	Eastern Div. Interstate Contest	Interstate Contest	TriState Contest	Peace Contest
1908-1909	R. A. Pollock	1				
1909-1910	Earl Lewis	2				
	W. J. Giffen				1	
1910-1911	Earl Lewis	1		2		
1911-1912	Fred Myers	3				
	H. J. Giffen				2	
1912-1913	A. B. Cunningham	1		1	1	
	Ralph Martin					6
	Fred Myers					3
1913-1914	Wallace Collins					
	William Wishart					
1914-1915	Hodge Eagleson	2				
	J. B. Sturgeon				3	
1915-1916	G. R. Johnson				2	
1916-1917	Richard Johnson					
1917-1919	(War-time Recess)					
1919-1920	Gerald Melone	1	1	2		
1920-1921	Virgil Baker	2			1	
1921-1922	J. C. Ballantyne	1			1	

Forensic Debate Record: 1908–1922

Year	Won From	Lost To	Ranking in Ohio Conference *(formed in 1916-1917)*
1908-1909	Mt. Union Ohio Northern Cedarville		
1909-1910	Mt. Union Hiram	Geneva	(Muskingum won first place in the Hiram-Baldwin-Wallace-Muskingum and Mt. Union-Denison-Muskingum triangles.)
1910-1911	Otterbein Hiram	Mt. Union	
1911-1912	Geneva Mt. Union Ohio University	Mt. Union	
1912-1913	Geneva Wittenberg Mt. Union	Heidelberg Otterbein	
1913-1914	Geneva Mt. Union Ohio Northern	Otterbein Heidelberg	
1914-1915	Otterbein (2 debates) Mt. Union		

Year	Won From	Lost To	Ranking in Ohio Conference
	Ohio Northern		
1915-1916	Otterbein	Otterbein	
	Mt. Union		
1916-1917	Otterbein	Heidelberg	
	Hiram	Wittenberg	
1917-1918	Heidelberg	Otterbein	
	Mt. Union	Hiram	
1918-1919	Heidelberg	Wooster	
	Mt. Union	Geneva	1
1919-1920	Hiram	Heidelberg	
	Otterbein	Geneva	1
		Bethany	
		Mt. Union	
1920-1921	Hiram	Otterbein	
	Hiram (2 debates)		2
1921-1922	Hiram	Denison	
	Baldwin-Wallace		
	Mt. Union		

Source: *Muscoljuan*, 1923, p. 170.

In her "History of the Speech Department," Muriel Bain reports the following information:

"The first records we have been able to find of College Orators are in connection with the Class Day Programs held, either as a part of Commencement Exercises or during Commencement Week."

1870   William Rainey Harper, Salutatorian, Address given in Hebrew
1879   J. A. Lawrence, Orator
1880   H. T. Jackson, Orator
1881   C. P. Taylor, Orator
          M. J. Sebright, Poet
1882   Bryl Tracy, Orator
          W. R. Scott, Poet
          Frank Murch, Salutatorian
1883   W. R. Hutchinson, Orator
          C. E. White, Orator
1884   S. A. Dixon, Orator
          J. B. Tannehill, Orator
          Eula Anderson, Salutatorian, this marks the first time that a woman was so honored.
1885   A. H. McCulloch, Orator
          J. P. Hutchison, Orator
          J. W. Shepherd, Salutatorian
          J. H. Martin, Valedictorian
1886   J. M. Work, Jr., Salutatorian
          W. W. Maxwell, Valedictorian
1887   E. E. Fife, Orator
          J. Johnson, Orator
          Bessie Brown, Salutatorian

J. E. McGee, Special Semi-Centennial Speaker

L. J. Graham, Special Semi-Centennial Speaker

After this time, the plans were altered and the diplomas were presented according to the Literary Society membership, a presentation and acceptance speech being made for each of the three (or at times four) societies.

In connection with the list of commencement speakers, it is of interest to note that, in 1896, Dr. J. Knox Montgomery was the orator. This appearance on Muskingum's Campus preceded his acceptance of the presidency of the college by eight years.

At this point, Muriel reports the oratory standings listed in the *Muscoljuan,* then continues the history through 1937.

Year	Orator	State Contest	Eastern Division Inter-State Contest	Inter-State Contest	Tri-State Contest	Peace Contest
1923	Cary Graham	2				
1924	Richard McLeery	2				
1925	Martin Giffen	5				
1926	Melton Boyd	6				
1927	Harry Crytzer	3				
1928	William Timmons	4				
1929	John Galloway	6				
1930	John Galloway	1				
1931	Harrison Rose	2				
1932	Bruce Maguire	4				
1933	Albert Capuder	4				
1934	Charles Woods	2				
1935	Charles L. Moore	2				
1936	Alex Fleming	2				
1937	Joseph McCabe	7				

Using the *Muscoljuan* as my main source, I tried to complete the list of orators. Their ranking in the various contests was not readily available. As the century progressed, the listing of orators gradually faded from the annual.

1938	Harry Sweitzer
1939	Richard Cooper
1940	Jack Mullens
1941	Lowell McCoy took first honors in the divisional Ohio Conference Oratorical Contest held at Muskingum (page 90). "Professor Layton is a national president of the Tau Kappa Alpha fraternity having succeeded Lowell Thomas to the position last year." (page 91)
1942	Ed Eshelman
1943-1945	During the war years, all forensic activities were abandoned.
1946	There is no listing of college orators for this year.
1947	Robert Huestis. During this year the Forensic Club was revitalized. After four years of inactivity, in celebration, the new members dunked their advisors, Professors C. R. Layton and Ralph Arnold, in the pond with the swans.
1948	Frank Erwin
1949	Boyd Martin

| 1950 | Larry McMaster, College Orator, and Bill Phillippe, Peace Orator |
| 1951 | There was no identification of a College Orator this year; however, a picture of Bruce Brackenridge is featured on the page dedicated to the Tau Kappa Alpha honorary fraternity in forensics. |

From this point on, the listing of orators in the *Muscoljuan* becomes erratic. What little information I found was by accident, in a variety of sources.

1958	Bill McIntyre (*Muscoljuan, 1958*, p. 77.)
1959	Sam Speck won the Annual Ohio Intercollegiate Oratory Contest. (*Black and Magenta,* March 25, 1959, p. 1.)
1960	Ken Vaux won the State Oratorical Contest. (*Muscoljuan, 1960*, p. 100.)
1960	Charles Dause won the State Interpretive Reading Contest (*Muscoljuan, 1960,* p. 100)
1961	Charles Dause, Charles Hast, and Joel Swabb won first place in Original Oratory at the Ohio State Sweepstakes Men's Speech Competition. (*Muscoljuan,* 1961, p. 148.)

There is a set of trophies in the display case in Cambridge Hall that acknowledges Muskingum College orators. Nationwide Insurance of Columbus, Ohio, sponsored a trophy for excellence in Ohio Men's Intercollegiate Oratory which was awarded to Muskingum in 1956, 1957, 1958, 1959, 1960, and 1961.

Another First Place trophy for the National Intercollegiate Oratory Championship identifies the following winners: 1913—Albert B. Cunningham, 1963—Joel Swabb, 1965—David L. Jamison, and 1967—Larry Bryan. A fine trophy was awarded to Lawrence Bryan for taking First Place in the National Intercollegiate Peace Oratory Contest in 1966, and another was awarded to Joel D. Wingard for taking Second Place in the same contest in 1967.

Tim Halverson took first place in persuasive speaking at the National Conference of Delta Sigma Rho-Tau Kappa Alpha, held at the University of Alabama. (*Black and Magenta,* April 10, 1970, p. 1,) Tim also won first place in the Men's Division of the Ohio Speech Tournament, held at Ohio Northern University on April 10-11. (*Black and Magenta,* April 24, 1970, p. 6.)

Another trophy shows that, in 1985, Muskingum won first place in Persuasive Speaking at the Wilcox International Contest.

The *Muscoljuan* reports the following debate achievements:

1923-1924	The Muskingum College Debate Team won the Ohio Debating Conference Championship.
1924-1925	The Debate Team won the Ohio State Championship for the third consecutive year.
1925-1926	The Conference Championship was a tie between Muskingum, Bluffton, and Heidelberg.
1926-1927	Muskingum won the Championship again, as they did in 1924 and 1925.
1936-1937	During the twelve years of the existence of the Ohio Debating Conference, Muskingum's team won eight conference victories.
1939-1940	December 9, 1940, Muskingum shares the Ohio Conference Championship with Kenyon.
1943-1946	Because of the war, debate activities were halted temporarily.

1947-1948	The debaters came back this year under the coaching of Professor Ralph Arnold. Dr. Layton became Dean of Faculties and held that office through 1949. He then went on sabbatical to the University of Michigan, where he completed his studies for a doctorate.
	This year the debate team took second place in the Ohio Conference Debates held in Columbus.
1951-1952	Dr. Layton returned to coach debate this year. The team won second place in the Ohio State Tournament.
	They took first honors in the National Tau Kappa Alpha Debate Tournament.
1952-1953	Muskingum College debaters, for the second straight year, won first place in the National Tau Kappa Alpha Debate Tournament held in Denver, Colorado.

The trophy case in Cambridge Hall holds several trophies for debate achievements.

1939	There is a scroll trophy for winning First Place in the Midwestern Convention Debate Tournament.
1953	A Wachtel Award plaque is on display for Outstanding Achievement in the Tau Kappa Alpha Conference Debate.
1955	Another First Place trophy exists for winning the 1955 Intercollegiate Men's Debate.
1959	Still another plaque indicates that Muskingum College took third place in the TKA Ohio-Kentucky Regional Debate.
1961	Muskingum debate teams won the Intercollegiate Debate Championship: Affirmative Team was Charles Horner and Fred Bonkowsky; Negative Team was Charles Hast and Joel Swabb.

Section Notes C
Departmental Major Play Productions: 1914–1958

Note: All play productions, whether they were major full-length plays or one-act plays, were connected to, and then came out of, classes in the speech curriculum. As the first grouping indicates, all the plays from 1914-1950 were the result of work done by students enrolled in Senior and Junior Play Production Classes (and it was so printed on each of the programs for the plays). From 1950-1954, the play programs listed Muskingum Players as the sponsoring organization. The classes in Play Production were still admitting only juniors and seniors, and the plays still originated from those classes. However, to designate Muskingum Players as the presenter of the plays was an indication that curriculum changes were about to occur. The change came in 1954, when "senior" and "junior" were dropped from the course titles. Play Production classes no longer had class pre-requisites. The only requirement was that students must have already taken the beginning speech course in Communication, which was four credit hours, through the year, during the freshman year. It was a college core requirement anyway.

With noted exceptions, the Play Production classes usually produced at least one senior play and one junior play each school year. Although there were some deviations, the seniors presented their plays during the winter months, leaving the juniors to produce during the spring. From 1923 to 1941, classes were so large that each of the two classes added an extra play, making a total of four major productions in a school year. The war years (World War II, 1941-1946) played havoc with enrollment, and the production schedule became erratic. In 1946, events stabilized and the play schedule settled down to two full-length major productions, one each semester during the school year.

An attempt has been made to list each of the plays in the chronological order in which they were presented. Sources for the following play index were the *Muscoljuan*, the *Black and Magenta*, Cheri Swiss's "History of Theatre at Muskingum College," Muriel Bain's "History of the Speech Department, Muskingum College, Compiled 1937," and the author's *Muskingum Theatre Handbook*.

(I have used the standard abbreviations of "Sr." for Senior Play and "Jr." for Junior Play, to indicate how each new grouping was classified, and when deviations occurred during the war years.)

Senior and Junior Play Class Presentations

1914-1915
Twelfth Night (Sr.)
The Hunchback (Jr.)

1915-1916
Ingomar
The Man From Home

1916-1917
Secret Service
Alias Jimmy Valentine

1917-1918
The Lion and The Mouse
The Melting Pot

1918-1919
Pillars of Society
Within the Law

1919-1920
Much Ado About Nothing
Disraeli

1920-1921
The Country Cousin
The Admirable Crichton

1921-1922
As You Like It
The Aristocrat

1922-1923
Friend Hannah
Lady Windermere's Fan

1923-1924
The Cassils Engagement (Sr.)
The Merchant of Venice (Sr.)
Icebound (Jr.)
False Gods (Jr.)

Friend Hannah, 1923. The senior class play in which Agnes Moorehead appeared as Margaret Lightfoot. *Muscoljuan, 1924; M.C. Library Archives.*

1924-1925
The Importance of Being Earnest
What Every Woman Knows
The Rivals
The Great Adventure

1926-1927
Romeo and Juliet
The Lady From the Sea
You and I
The Lamp and The Bell

1928-1929
The Great Divide
Pillars of Society
The Ivory Door
The Yellow Jacket

1930-1931
Hotel Universe
Pygmalion
The Mob
Ayuli

1932-1933
Giants in the Earth
Berkeley Square
Beggar on Horseback
The Admirable Crichton

1934-1935
Distant Drums
Both Your Houses
Craig's Wife
The Three Musketeers

1936-1937
Brittle Heaven
Much Ado About Nothing
Pride and Prejudice
Having Set Their Hands

1938-1939
Gold in the Hills
The Old Maid
You Can't Take it With You
Julius Caesar

1925-1926
The Goose Hangs High
The Taming of the Shrew
Old Man Minick
She Stoops to Conquer

1927-1928
Disraeli
Caponsacchi
Milestones
Sherwood

1929-1930
The Vikings
A Midsummer Night's Dream
Right You Are, If You Think You Are
The Swan

1931-1932
Death Takes a Holiday
Twelfth Night
Three One-Acts:
"The Traveling Man"
"The Twelve Pound Look
"'Op-O'-Me Thumb"
Once in a Lifetime

1933-1934
The Good Hope
The Lamp and The Bell
Ladies of the Jury
Elizabeth The Queen

1935-1936
Moorborn
The Merchant of Venice
Cradle Song
Pickwick

1937-1938
Accent on Youth
Daughters of Atreus
Stage Door
The Late Christopher Bean

1939-1940
She Stoops to Conquer
Our Town
Wingless Victory
Knickerbocker Holiday

1940-1941
Night of January 16th
Mary of Scotland
Two On An Island
Family Portrait

1941-1942
George Washington Slept Here (Sr.)
Flight to the West (Sr.)
Brother Rat (Jr.)

1942-1943
Jane Eyre (Jr.)

1943-1944
The Old Maid (Sr.)
The Man Who Came To Dinner (Jr.)

1944-1945
Ladies in Retirement(Sr.)
Quality Street (Jr.)

1945-1946
Strangers at Home (Jr.)

1946-1947
Deep Are The Roots (Sr.)
Idiot's Delight (Jr.)

1947-1948
The Little Foxes
Berkeley Square

1948-1949
The Great Big Doorstep
Dark Victory

1949-1950
Children of the Moon
The Young Idea

The Great Big Doorstep, 1949. Commodore (D. Bradley), Mrs. Crochet (H. Reskovac), Topal Crochet (D. Chapman), Mr. Topin (A. Stanley), Arthur Crochet (T. Swan) Evvie Crochet (H. Baird). *Courtesy M. E. Johnson theatre files.*

Muskingum Players' Presentations

1950-1951
Papa Is All
The Late Christopher Bean

1951-1952
The Silver Whistle
Harvey

1952-1953
All My Sons
Blithe Spirit

1953-1954
Cry Havoc!
Death Takes a Holiday

Play Production Class Presentations

<u>1954-1955</u>
Guest in the House
The Rivals

<u>1955-1956</u>
Goodbye, My Fancy
The Shrike

<u>1956-1957</u>
The Crucible
The Torch Bearers

<u>1957-1958</u>
The Madwoman of Chaillot
Berkeley Square

The Crucible, 1957. A montage of scenes. *Courtesy M. E. Johnson theatre files.*

After Dr. Layton retired, Dr. James Golden became chairman of the department. The Play Production Class presented two full-length plays that school year:

<u>1958-1959</u>
The Skin of Our Teeth
Night Must Fall

Section Notes D

A History of the Oratory/Speech Diploma and Recipients: 1914-1958

A diploma in elocution, oratory, or speech was a means by which the college recognized excellence of achievement in the discipline. The diploma is not to be confused with a degree, or even a certificate, although educational institutions may present to a deserving student, any or all three of those documents.

A person may receive a certificate from any number of institutions for completing some course or a particular task. For example, certificates are given to students for reading all the designated books in a summer reading program; certificates may be given to those who complete a course in first aid; a school of trade, a government agency, or a school of music may issue certificates of accomplishments.

A diploma is a kind of certificate that is classified as an official document, granted by an educational institution upon the completion of a course of study regulated or approved by a government agency.

A degree may come with the diploma and is an academic title (i.e., B.A., B.S.) conferred by educational institutions, recognizing the completion of a course of study, or as an honorary recognition of achievement. Degrees are regulated by state agencies which require different regulations for granting different degrees.

The history of the diploma in elocution, oratory, or speech began at Muskingum in 1885-86 with Mr. R. K. Porter, one of our first itinerant teachers of elocution. Mr. Porter was a graduate of J. W. Shoemaker's National School of Elocution and Oratory (founded in 1873 in Philadelphia). The school offered a two-year course ending with a diploma, after examinations and a thesis. By 1878, a Bachelor's of Oratory was available; later, a three-year course produced a master's degree. Chartered by the state in 1875, the school operated until 1943, when World War II depleted the enrollment.[1]

In the *1885-1886 College Catalogue*, Mr. Porter described six courses in elocution, and stated that the prescribed course could be completed in one year, at which time the student graduating in the Science and Art of Elocution could receive a diploma.[2]

Mr. Porter left after one year. It seems likely that, since most of the professional schools in the East were offering diplomas and degrees for prescribed courses of study in the relatively new discipline of elocution, graduates of those schools would continue the practice, if possible. Five years passed before instruction in elocution was again offered at Muskingum, this time by Josephine Martin, a Muskingum graduate and a student of R. K. Porter.[3] However, there was no mention of a diploma until 1900-01, when Maude Hollingsworth Bethel became head of the area. She described a two-year course of studies which, upon satisfactory completion, was rewarded with a diploma.[4]

The structure of courses that Bethel described which led to a diploma, lasted until 1906-07, when Elbert Raymond Moses, in his second year, offered a two-year course of study that led to both a diploma and accompanying degree. Upon completion of a two-year course of study, a diploma was awarded, regardless of whether or not the student held a college degree. Besides course work, graduation also required a public recital once every term, and 140 private lessons.[5] Although it is not specifically mentioned, one of the public recitals must have included a senior performance. Commencement programs from 1907 through 1914 list "School of Oratory Recitals," "School of Expression Commencements," and "School of Expression Recitals."[6]

In 1910, under the professorship of Ray K. Immel, requirements for degrees and diplomas changed. No diplomas could be given to anyone who was not a graduate of an approved secondary school. The student had to complete twenty-seven hours of class work in the Department of Oratory and School of Expression, and had to have at least sixty private lessons. The Bachelor of Oratory was awarded to those who did all the work, as stated above, and who held, or who were currently receiving, the B.A. degree.[7]

From 1912 to 1914, the department was in the charge of Professor Wilbur C. Dennis. More changes occurred. This time, students wishing to graduate from the School of Expression were required to take all of the listed courses (20 hours, or 8 courses) and one private lesson per week. They were exempt from taking Advanced Debate. The students had to prepare two full public programs and an original adapta-

tion of one standard work of fiction for a graduating recital. No student would be granted a diploma from the department who did not have a bachelor's degree or equivalent.[8] There was no mention of any kind of degree, be it a Master of Elocution or Bachelor of Oratory. After 1913, only the diploma was awarded.

Upon their arrival at Muskingum, in the fall of 1914, Professor Charles Rush Layton and Mrs. Ferne Parsons Layton kept the existing diploma requirements. In 1915, they added the requirement of an original thesis of not less than three-thousand words, on a theme relevant to the work of the department, to be submitted not less than one month prior to graduation.[9]

The requirements for the diploma remained essentially the same during the tenure of the Laytons at Muskingum, which ended with their retirement in 1957 and 1958. There were minor changes in the requirements, such as the number of courses taken and the usual exemption

1948 Junior Speech Recitalists: (left column back to front) Director, Mrs. Ferne Parsons Layton, D. Chapman, H. Baird; (right column back to front) D. Hill, J. Birbeck, E. McMichael, C. Boyd, and B. Jane McWilliams. (Not pictured: H. Reskovac, D. Lorimer). *Courtesy Dr. Donald Hill personal files.*

of students from Advanced Debate and Intercollegiate Oratory. At times, a clarification was inserted, as in the *1917-1918 College Catalogue:* "The graduation recital may consist of selected readings, or an original adaptation of one standard work of fiction, or a lecture recital of a standard play (preferably Shakespearean), or an extended address.[10]

In 1928, a reorganization of the curriculum resulted in dropping one public recital. Heretofore, the diploma had required two public recitals and a graduation recital. After the reorganization, the diploma required that one recital come from the junior level course, Literary Analysis and Interpretation. This recital became known as the Junior Speech Recital and was given in concert by the entire class, with some solo readings, usually in the second semester. The second recital came from the Interpretation Seminar. It became known as the Senior Speech Recital and was given usually in April before graduation exercises. It was performed by an individual and represented work that began after the junior recital, continued through the summer as individual study on the student's own recognizance, and did not end until a public performance in the final semester of the senior year. It was largely tutorial in nature, requiring considerable research and background study, and adherence to a strenuous rehearsal schedule. A recital notebook replaced the thesis.[11]

From 1920 to 1954, the required course work for a diploma represented thirty-six credit hours. From 1954 to 1958, the number of credit hours was increased to forty.[12]

The diploma was dropped as an option from the curriculum after 1958. The recital existed as an option under the course title of Speech Seminar throughout the 1960's, and as Individual Study in the 1970's. It is probably still a valid area for student investigation under the present courses, Seminar in Research and Seminar in Performance. However, the magnitude of the task and the commitment of time required for the project presents a formidable obstacle to the modern student.

Diplomas in Oratory/Speech
Diploma in Oratory

1916	Gibson Reid Johnson		
1918	Jean Gladys Caldwell		Thomas Clark Pollock
	Mary Katherine Caldwell	1923	Mildred Miriam Keboch
	Mary Mildred Kirkpatrick		Hazel Lititia Miller
	Alice Adaline Teener	1924	Dorothy Edgar
1920	Lillian Ray Baker		Margaret Lois Timmons
	Susannah Sill Bebout	1925	William Martin Giffen
	Cora Lena Culbertson		Elizabeth Reid McMaster
	Dora Eunice Giffen		Eva Charlotte Maxwell
	Leila Gertrude Knipe		John Coventry Smith
	Marie Fern McKelvey		Ruth Irene Trimble
	Pearl M'liss Rice	1926	Ruth Mabel Borland
1921	Margaret Ethel Aikin		Mary Elizabeth Johnson
	John Stanley Gray		Thelma Auriel Rush
	Helen Hoyle		Helen Kathryn Smith
	Frances Katherine Martin		Gladys Olive Stephenson
1922	Nancy Jemima Ford	1927	Earl Edwin Curtis
	Virginia Lee Gibbon		Martha McConnell
	Margaret Hunter Miller		Sara Margaret McFadden
	Velma Catherwood Moss		Faye Juanita Turner
		1928	Mary Jeannette Duncan

Anna Louise Ferguson
Lois Mae Leeper
Allene Dorothy Montgomery
Edith Isabelle Ross
Lucille Ruth Willerton

1929 Mary Elizabeth Borton
Dorothy Lillian Hall
Winifred Thompson
Mildred Lucile Wilson

1930 Nancy Power Bowman
Thalia Eleanor Haley
Margaret Elizabeth McMaster
Margaret Agatha Woodburn

1931 Olive Elizabeth Endler
Ruth Elizabeth Mehaffey
Genevieve Patton
Ivy Gertrude Young

1932 Elizabeth Lucille McCutcheon
Elsie Kirk McGeorge
Agnes Maybeh McRoberts
Jo Clude Sturm

Diploma in Speech

1933 Nelda Evans Brown
1934 Helen Louise Armstrong
Albert L. Capuder
Louise Haag
Mary L. McWilliams
Emerson R. Ray

1935 Grace Elizabeth Cottrell
Wallace Croft Fotheringham
Margaret Monica Hall
Harry B. Poppe, Jr.
Helen Lee Richardson

1936 Margaret Elizabeth Henderson
Jennie McCandlish
Chester Bryce McKirahan

1937 Robert Arwood Byler
Elizabeth Cashdollar
V. Linza Mason
Emogene Roberts

1938 Mary Elizabeth Claudy
Sara Lucile Keck
Harry P. Sweitzer
Millicent Caroline Pearson

1939 Betty J. Bartlett
Clark Richard Cooper
Sara Louise Kunkle

1940 Ethel Jane Thomas
1941 Betty Jane Burris
Sara Frances Crothers
Richard F. Dunlap
Anna Mae Schofield
Minerva Whittier Pearson

1942 Elizabeth R. Bowers

Paul Huber
Anna Jane Mull
Robert Edward Sweitzer
Mary Virginia White

1943 Margaret Lois Birch
1944 Dorothy Eleanor Myers
Ruth Ann Hutchens

1945 Martha Isabel Mansfield
Joan Elizabeth Patton

1946 Mary Anna Bode
Helen Louise Huntley

1947 Ruth Hamilton
Judith L. Hill
Hope Caroline Johnson
Renee Lee Joseph
Betty Joye Wright

1948 Marian Ausherman
Dorothy Jane Bichsel
Suzanne Fitzwater
LaVonne Hartman
Evelyn Louis McCarty
Pressley Crane McCoy
Thomas Graham Mansell

1949 Helen Louise Baird
Constance Boyd
Dorothy Lucile Chapman
Donald Phillip Hill
Mary Helen Reskovac

1950 John Dickson Bolton
Margaret Amanda Dias
Mary Jane Ready
Doris Jane Williams

1951 Shirley Ann Emhoff
Kenneth Edward Grice
Mildred Ann Merrick

1952 Lemoyne Ray Myers
Shirley Hellen Price
Barbara Jane Wieand
Joyce Williams
William Walter Worstall
Daniel James Yolton

1954 Lois Ann Cheney
Georgia Gail Joseph
Nancy Louise Lannert
Elizabeth Annette Monroe
Nancy Elizabeth Nolin

1956 Joretta Kay Brown
Roberta Lee Dietrich
Lois Eileen Miller
B. Bruce Wagener

1957 Patricia Ann Harmon
Mary Jane Wilson

1958 Barbara Jean Sittig[13]

REFERENCES

1   Edyth Renshaw, "Five Private Schools of Speech," *A History of Speech Education in America: Background Studies,* edited by Karl R. Wallace (New York: Appleton-Century-Crofts, Inc., 1954), p. 301.

2   *Annual Catalogue of Muskingum College: 1885-1886,* (Zanesville, Ohio: Courier Book and Job Printing House), pp. 22-23.

3   *ACMC: 1890-1891,* p. 6; Thomas Berkshire, *History of Muskingum College*, "Chapter 1887-1904," (unpublished manuscript in College Library Archives), p. 24.

4   *ACMC: 1900-1901,* pp. 50-51.

5   *ACMC: 1906-1907,* pp. 64-69.

6   Commencement programs for the years indicated: 1907-1914, in *Annual Catalogues of Muskingum College.*

7   *ACMC: 1910-1911,* pp. 56-57, 83-86.

8   *ACMC: 1912-1913,* pp. 45-47.

9   *ACMC: 1915-1916,* p. 77.

10   *ACMC: 1917-1918,* p. 85.

11   *ACMC: 1928-1929,* pp. 107-108.

12   See appropriate *Catalogues* for the years indicated.

13   Names of the recipients were found in the commencement programs for the corresponding years.

A Decade of Decision: 1949-1959

After graduating from Muskingum, I entered a period of learning about the teaching profession in what has been called the *best* school: the school of experience. I also began learning more about the content fields in which I had always been interested: English, Speech, and Theatre.

Over a period of ten years, this sojourn as a teacher in the public schools led me to four universities, and professional studios in New York City.

Whether I knew it or not (mostly *not*), I was constantly making decisions that would ultimately influence my career. Curiously enough, I ended where I started: Muskingum College. The lives of many people are like that; they seem circular in nature. This notion often leaves them with the self-defeating feeling that if they had just stood still, the result would have been the same. That conclusion is impossible. Rather than circular in nature, life is more like a spiral which seems circular, but it is always advancing. No matter what a person does or how he does it, he learns something in life. Doesn't he?

Saginaw High School

The pattern of behavior which began as early as the primary grades (that of dividing my attention between theatre and education) continued throughout high school and college. At some time, a decision would have to be made as to which of three careers I was to pursue. Would I direct plays, act in plays, or teach? As it turned out, I did a little of each.

The Laytons had supplied the general educational background in public speaking and interpretation; now, I was to apply knowledge and skills to life situations.

Saginaw High School in Saginaw, Michigan, needed a teacher of English and a director of plays. I applied and was accepted; my duties began in the fall of 1949. Principal S. H. Lyttle and his friendly staff helped acclimate me to classroom management and organization, and a seasoned staff of teachers made me feel welcome and at ease.

As a result, my first year of teaching was a success. I am sure that I learned more than my students did, and there were no distracting disciplinary problems. Besides teaching English, my two years at Saginaw High included directing a set of one-act plays and a major production each semester.

Because I was a relatively young and inexperienced director dealing with younger and inexperienced actors, I chose plays that were not emotionally or intellectually difficult; yet, they did present situations universal to life's experiences. Major productions the first year were *Little Women* and *Uncle Fred Flits By*; the second year, we produced *We Shook the Family Tree* and *Our Miss Brooks*.

The plays were easily understood and there were no difficult emotional scenes.

Little Women, 1950. Presented by the Senior Class of Saginaw High School; front row (left to right): Jo (J. Robbins), Beth (D. Sagasser); middle row (left to right): Meg (B. Woolever), Marmee (M. Matthews), Aunt March (J. Mandelstamm), Amy (W. Scott); back row (left to right): Father, Mr. March (D. Severance), Professor Bhaer (M. Garcia), Laurie (A. Socha), and Mr. Brooke (H. Soddt). *Courtesy Dr. Donald Hill personal files.*

The challenge was for the students to act the plays in a believable manner and, at the same time, learn the fundamentals of theatre.

I quickly discovered that students of high school age–at least at that time–lived life on the surface. They seldom delved into the depths of an experience unless forced to do so by circumstances beyond their control.

With the help of Stanley Schubert, a much more experienced director, who held a position similar to mine at Arthur Hill High School, I learned how and when to take students aside and explain a situation to them in terms which would elicit the emotion that was required.

Nevertheless, I never hesitated to act out a scene for the students, after deciding that they were not going to give it the required emotion and believability necessary for the audience's understanding and appreciation of the play. Such blatant illustrating was usually self-defeating, because the student's response was likely to be, "Well, I can't do that!" or, what was worse, "That's hammy!" That response introduced another element of acting "exaggeration," or making gestures and emotions so that they were big enough for the theatre. Students needed help, but whatever their age, they had great imaginative powers when stimulated in ways that inspired creativity: improvisation was one of them.

I also learned that students are lazy about learning lines. They will take just about as long as they are given. If lines are required to be memorized in two weeks, they will take two weeks, and even push for a little more time. Professional actors can learn a considerably lengthy part in twenty-four hours. If lines are required in one week, most actors, experienced or not, will have them in one week.

One experiment with line memorization proved very interesting, but nerve-wracking to the actors. After the first reading of the play, when the actors were familiar with the story and their characters, and after they had recorded movements (blocking) in their books (approximately three meetings) I banned books from the stage. Although I had announced beforehand that they could not carry their books on stage, after one rehearsal, it was obvious who had studied their parts and who had not. The actors who had not studied apologized to their fellow actors for a tedious and lengthy rehearsal. From that moment on, there were very few problems with lines. I was able to devote rehearsals to more important matters, such as interpretation, and the prompter lived a rather carefree existence.

After my first year of teaching, there was time for me to work in two other areas of theatre. One area was the all-city musicals, and that meant meeting Marian Newberry. Marian Newberry had studied in New York and Europe before appearing in Broadway musicals, and singing with name bands on radio and television. She had studied with Eva Le Gallienne in New York, and became known for her work as an entertainer with the Theatre Wing and U.S.O. Since 1948, she had staged benefits for the Quota Club and St. Luke's Hospital Guild in Saginaw.[1] Her productions were always well-organized, well-directed, and well-attended.

When Miss Newberry advertised try-outs in the fall of 1950 for a "Showboat" Revue, I tried out and won a spot as a song-and-dance man. The cast was announced in the paper, and the next day one of the young secretaries in the principal's office remarked, "I hope you have better luck than the last faculty member." When I asked what had happened, the only response came on a forbidding note: "Disaster!" With that bit of encouragement, I set about developing a routine for an old Eddie Cantor number, "Ida." Singing and dancing was what I wanted to do; I was always doing it around the house, but never in public. Let the chips fall where they may, here was a chance for me to have fun doing what I liked to do.

Since I was a child of the Depression, I grew up with Astaire and Rogers, Bill Robinson, and Shirley Temple. These stars and their movies helped everyone through the hard times of the '30s. Like so many mothers, mine sent me off to tap-dance class to join the craze that swept a nation. Years later at Muskingum, I took voice lessons from Professor Bloom at the Music Conservatory. (I did not achieve the level of "Ida" in my voice lessons, but I did receive a passing grade for such *lieder* as "None But The Lonely Heart" and "Three Grenadiers."

My accompanist worked wonders with the song, and I rehearsed the dance, which I choreographed from the few steps I had learned twenty years ago. From my own wardrobe, I commandeered a pair of light gray slacks, a white shirt, a maroon bow tie, and a maroon blazer. I still had my old tap-shoes, and I took them to the cobbler to be refurbished. To these items, I added a straw "boater." (I have no idea where it came from, but I still have it.) I then rehearsed, rehearsed, rehearsed wherever I could find a space and whenever I could find the time.

Dress rehearsal came and Marian said that I was a "natural." I went home and rehearsed some more. Opening night at the Civic Auditorium, I did my number. The audience applauded and nobody threw anything. Before the first class bell rang the next day at school, the young secretary said, "You ought to be in pictures." No greater compliment could be paid to a Depression Kid. Later that day, the *Saginaw News* came out with the information that the third annual Quota Club "Showboat" had offered forty-two numbers within two hours. My name was among those who had won audience approval. The reviewer wrote: "Top number in the show was a song-and-dance act by Don Hill, who did "Ida" in a way that the ghosts of the old minstrel men in the wings must have applauded vigorously."[2] Savor the moment! It would be a long time before I would get such kudos again. The experience made me a believer: if the three requisites of real estate are location, location, location, it is equally true that the three requisites of performing are rehearsal, rehearsal, rehearsal!

Community theatre was another kind of theatre I had yet to experience. Pit and Balcony was a well-established community theatre in Saginaw. The members had developed a strong following over the years, a theatre of their own, a board of directors sympathetic and devoted to good plays, and a treasury to hire a professional director.

When Pit and Balcony advertised try-outs for J. B. Priestley's *An Inspector Calls,* I responded. Luckily, I found a place in the cast as Eric Birling, the son of a wealthy family and a bit of a wastrel. Typical of J. B. Priestley's plays, *An Inspector Calls* is a mystery-morality drama with several layers of meaning. The director of the play was Gordon Hatfield, and the technical director was Fred Schuller. Both were from the Cleveland Play House.[3]

An Inspector Calls, 1951. Arthur Birling (B. Davis) keeps his son, Eric (D. Hill), from attacking his mother, Sybil (V. Kearful); the daughter, Sheila (M. Bassett) protests. Courtesy Pit and Balcony.

The drama presented two distinct problems: 1) For the actors, the play was a challenge in character portrayal; 2) for the cast and the director, the play required a mood of suspense in an unhealthy atmosphere. Under expert direction, the play was an ensemble production that proved highly successful. Over 2,500 people attended. As a result, the seven-day run was extended for two more days. At that time, it was the longest run of any play in the history of Pit and Balcony.[4] The box office people were ecstatic!

A month later, I appeared as the male lead, John Kent, in Marian Newberry's production of *Roberta,* by Jerome Kern. The *Saginaw News* reviewer was indeed kind to me with the following: "Rosalie Nagel Stevens will take the part Tamara made famous. Don Hill, who showed his musical deftness in an absolutely perfect song-and-dance act in the last "Showboat" of the Quota Club and his dramatic ability in "An Inspector Calls," Pit and Balcony's last presentation, plays opposite her."[5] The musical was a benefit for the St. Luke's Hospital Guild. The Civic Auditorium was packed and the reviews were favorable.[6] I concluded the year of performing with another song and dance routine to Al Jolson's "Swanee" as a part of Saginaw High School's *Bandrama* entertainment.

From the cast and crew members of these various productions, I learned about B. Iden Payne and his reputation as a director and scholar of Shakespeare. I discovered that he, along with Lucy Barton, (author of the definitive book on stage costume) and E. P. Conkle (playwright), were all on the faculty of the University of Texas.

The desire to leave teaching, at least temporarily, in favor of more formal instruction in theatre became overwhelming. After two years at Saginaw High, I embarked on a journey to the University of Texas. It was a hasty and ill-timed venture that did not turn out well—not well at all.

REFERENCES

1   Program for *Roberta*, April 27, 1951, p. 3.
2   Our Drama Reviewer, "Tuneful 'Showboat' Performance Has An Appreciative Audience," *Saginaw News,* November 1950.
3   Program for *An Inspector Calls*, March 13-21, 1951, p. 4.
4   "Saginaw Drama," *Saginaw News,* March 25, 1951.
5   "Saginaw Drama," "'Roberta' to Feature New Faces," *Saginaw News,* April 15, 1951.
6   Our Drama Reviewer, "Well-Loved Songs of Jerome Kern, Performances Score at 'Roberta'," *Saginaw News,* April 28, 1951.

Deep in the Heart of Texas

The summer session was just beginning when I arrived at the University of Texas in Austin. However excellent, the theatre staff was minuscule, compared to that of the regular school year. The professors I wanted were away at various conferences and seminars. Only then did I realize that even Texans leave Texas in the summer because of the unbearable heat. I registered for two courses: High School Play Directing and Shakespeare, and waited for the fall semester to begin.

During the summer of 1951, there was a heat wave that reached 114 degrees Fahrenheit. People were packed in ice in the Dallas hospitals – a frequent way in which Texans spend their summers. My room was in air-conditioned Roberts Hall, but when I stepped outside, it was like entering a sauna. My clothes were drenched with perspiration within a few minutes. Hot sand was everywhere. As I walked to class, small lizards slithered off the sidewalk out of my way. The cockroaches at the local eatery were more bold; real or imagined, there was always one ready to challenge me over a sandwich or bowl of chili.

There was also a plague of crickets that summer. The unfortunate insects were attracted to the lights in downtown store windows, where they carpeted the sidewalks. Moving through the shopping district was like walking on popcorn, as the unavoidable black bodies of the crickets snapped, crackled, and popped underfoot.

To the local residents, my Mid-West accent identified me as a "Damn Yankee." Nevertheless, their bred-in-the-bone hospitality was indomitable; their attentiveness and courtesy were unassailable. Store clerks followed me to the door of their establishments and sent me off with an invitation to return: "You-all come back now, ya hear!"

By the time the fall semester began, I felt completely at home, but somewhat shop-worn and bedraggled. I registered for Payne's Play Analysis class, Barton's History of Costume course, and Conkle's Playwriting. Payne's class was everything I had hoped for: informative, scholarly, and interesting. One of my most vivid memories was the way in which he called the class role precisely after the class bell rang. Every name was given added significance by his precise and clipped British accent; when he came to my name, he gave it added emphasis by holding onto the final "L's." It was as if I had never heard my name pronounced before: the difference between English enunciation and American articulation was striking.

Simultaneously with registration, FOOTBALL season arrived! There is always a ripple of excitement in the air at registration: students getting adjusted to new quarters, roommates, classmates, professors, and courses. Add the football season to this mix and there is even more tension. In the Midwest, the clear, cool autumn air always provides a lot of free electricity. In the Southwest, the hot heavy air creates tension that is positively stifling.

I have never experienced anything like a Texas Longhorn football game. The stadium was packed. Under the unflinching glare of the Texas noonday sun, the fans in short sleeves and Stetson hats packed the stadium; each fan invariably carried a thermos bottle of something cool to drink. The lightly clad, but heavily padded,

Longhorns clashed with the University of North Carolina Tarheels that Saturday afternoon in October 1951.[1] In the shimmering haze of heat, it seemed as if every fan in the stadium felt, individually, the violent collision of bodies, the clash and smash of flesh upon flesh, and the grinding and pounding of bone upon bone. The fans screamed, groaned, and "ahh-ed" themselves into an empathic frenzy, driven not only by the gladiators in the arena, but also by the sustenance they received from whatever they were sucking out of those thermos bottles – which I suspect contained more than orange juice or lemonade.

All of this was just too much for this intrepid son of West Virginia pioneers and southeast Ohio farmers. One week later, I landed in the University Infirmary with a fever of over a hundred degrees and a classic case of dysentery (AKA "Montezuma's Revenge"). As I lay feckless and flummoxed on my bed of pain, through the fog of my fever, a bizarre Kafka-esque scene played over and over: giant cockroaches were fighting nimble-footed crickets, while long-tongued lizards slurped my bowl of chili. Through it all Ben Iden Payne was calling my name: "Hilllllll."

After two weeks, I returned to classes, fully recovered and in possession of my senses. My morale took a nose dive when I realized how far behind I was in my course work. Added to this fact was the extremely low status of my personal exchequer. I had the choice of dropping half my classes and going to work, or leaving the field to fight another day. I chose retreat, packed my trunk, and headed for home.

The Texas climate had done me in!

REFERENCES

1   "North Carolina vs. Texas," (Austin, Texas: Published by Athletic Council, University of Texas, Memorial Stadium, October 6, 1951).

University of Colorado

I caught up with Ben Iden Payne in the summer of 1953 at the University of Colorado in Boulder. He was a visiting professor, teaching a course in Shakespeare and directing *Twelfth Night.* I registered for his course and two others: Advanced Oral Interpretation and Physical Education.

The climate of Colorado in the summer was much more amenable than that of Texas. Instead of having the sun drain every bit of energy out of me, the air of Boulder and nearby Denver was exhilarating. (Some people are affected adversely by the rarity of the atmosphere. Every year some students have to leave because they don't have the energy to comb their hair, much less walk to class or do sustained study.) The altitude had one ill effect on me: it caused a blood vessel to burst in my nose. It was a minor injury which incapacitated me for one day. I spent a day in the doctor's office, while he cauterized the offending vessel.

The course in Shakespeare met all of my expectations. It fed my desire for more knowledge of the man, the plays, and the Elizabethan theatre. I was especially invigorated by the way in which Payne connected the literature to the practical production of Shakespeare's plays. I had never directed a Shakespearean play; in fact, I was afraid to tackle what seemed to me an insurmountable job. But the more I learned from Payne, the more I began to see the possibility of actually producing Shakespeare.

Payne's production of *Twelfth Night* was performed on August 13, 14 and 15 in the Mary Rippon Amphitheatre, as part of the annual Shakespeare Festival at the University. The Mary Rippon Theatre was especially designed by the noted stage historian, George R. Reynolds, for outdoor productions of Shakespeare's plays. The theatre is a beautifully designed open air structure, with high hedges to protect the entrances on either side of the stage, and with steps leading to different levels. The movement flowed easily and quickly from one scene to another (an absolute requirement of any Shakespearean play). The lighting towers, well out of sight of the audience, held spots that illuminated the players, dressed in their Elizabethan costumes. In the Colorado dusk, the play took on a special luminous quality that furthered the fantasy element and softened some of the low-comedy of the play. Every aspect of the play was honest and true. Payne made Shakespearean production look deceptively easy. I wanted, more than ever, to direct Shakespeare.

That summer in Boulder went so smoothly that I returned for the second session of the 1954 summer session. This time, there was an unexpected bonus served up by the university. Glenn Miller and his wife had both attended the University of Colorado. The production company for *The Glenn Miller Story* was on campus, filming some scenes for the film that was to be released that same year. As luck would have it, I was carrying my camera one day while walking across campus. I noticed a crowd forming outside one of the buildings and, as I approached, I heard the names Jimmy Stewart and June Allyson mentioned. On the outer rim of the crowd, there was no way I could get the height needed for a good shot. I held my camera high and clicked; the result was minimal, but I got enough of Jimmy Stewart to recognize him, and to show June's profile and her lovely golden hair.

Section Notes
Ben Iden Payne: A Brief Biography

Ben Iden Payne was born in Newcastle-on-Tyne, England, in 1881. Early in his life, he became fascinated by the stage and began his professional career at the age of eighteen, when he joined the famous Frank Benson Shakespeare Touring Company. After leaving Benson's company, he toured extensively in England with a variety of repertory companies and, during this time, he honed his acting skills and learned the fundamentals of producing. (Americans call it directing.)[1]

In 1907, William Butler Yeats hired Payne as a director for the Abbey Theatre in Dublin, Ireland; there, he witnessed the famous "Playboy Riots" and directed the Abbey company for its first London appearance.[2]

Miss A. E. Horniman, who supported the Abbey Theatre, brought Payne to Manchester to manage her repertory company. The company prospered under Payne's direction, and Miss Horniman bought the old Gaiety Theatre, refurbished it, and put Payne in charge. The Gaiety Theatre became famous for its influence on the founding of repertory theatre in England. Payne developed a company of actors that included Dame Rebecca West, Clarence Derwent, and Sybil Thorndike. Payne championed the new dramatists, as well as Shakespeare, and produced the plays of Galsworthy and Shaw.[3]

While at the Gaiety, Payne convinced William Poel, of the Elizabethan Stage Society, to direct a production of *Measure for Measure.* He became intrigued with Poel's ideas of producing Shakespeare's plays on a simple architectural stage, similar to that of Shakespeare's Globe where the plays were originally performed.[4]

Payne was no antiquarian, but he later adopted and pursued some of Poel's ideas. Invoking his own imagination, he developed a modified Elizabethan stage which permitted the action to flow quickly and without interruption, in order to preserve the "melodic line of the play."[5]

An invitation in the first quarter of the twentieth century brought Payne to America, where he directed plays for Frohman, the Schuberts, Ziegfeld, and the Theatre Guild. These directing chores brought him in contact with Broadway stars such as John and Ethel Barrymore, William Gillette, Helen Hayes, Otis Skinner, John Drew, and Billie Burke.[6]

While in America, Thomas Wood Stevens requested Payne's help with the founding of a professional actor's training program at Carnegie Tech in Pittsburgh. Payne obliged and, for sixteen years, he improved his modified staging by directing Shakespearean plays at Carnegie when he was not busy on Broadway. When Stevens left his position at Carnegie Tech, Payne became chairman of the drama department.[7]

In 1935, Payne accepted a position as managing director of the Shakespeare Memorial Theatre at Stratford-on-Avon. During the eight years at the English festival, Payne was able to produce only a few plays in the style that he had developed.[8]

Disappointed, Payne resigned his post and returned to America, where he continued his career in educational theatre. He found that working with students was much easier and more productive than working with professionals. Like Poel, Payne found that professional actors had little knowledge of, or faith in, new ideas. He taught at many universities, including Iowa, Colorado, Michigan, San Diego State College, and Washington University; however, he found a home at the University of Texas. He taught there for twenty-three years until his retirement at the age of eighty-one.[9]

In 1958, on Shakespeare's birthday, the American Shakespeare Festival Theatre and Academy honored B. Iden Payne " . . . for continued service to the works of Shakespeare–actor, director, teacher–an inspiration for generations of theatre people.[10]

Shortly before his death, Payne learned that his memoir would be published, and that a new theatre at the University of Texas would be named in his honor. An emissary from Queen Elizabeth II presented him with the Order of the British Empire. Ben Iden Payne died in 1976 at the age of ninety-five.[11]

REFERENCES

1   Ben Iden Payne, *A Life in a Wooden O: Memoirs of the Theatre* (New Haven & London: Yale University Press, 1977), pp. 8-11.
2   Ibid., pp. 65-77.
3   Ibid., pp. 75-112.
4   Ibid.
5   Ibid., pp. 157-172.
6   Ibid., pp. 128-149.
7   Ibid., pp. 120-124, 150-156, 157-172.
8   Ibid., pp. 183-186.
9   Ibid., pp. 187-194.
10 John Houseman and Jack Landau, *The American Shakespeare Festival: The Birth of a Theatre,* "ASFTA Annual Shakespeare Awards," (New York: Simon and Schuster, 1959), p. 94.
11 Ben Iden Payne, "Publisher's Preface," *A Life in a Wooden O: Memoirs of the Theatre* (New Haven & London: Yale University Press, 1977), xiii.
Note: More information on Payne may be found in *Who's Who in the Theatre,* London, and *Who's Who in the American Theatre,* New York.

Heights Haven & Western Reserve University

During the spring semester of 1954, I began my duties as Director of Assemblies and Teacher of English at Roosevelt Junior High School in Cleveland Heights, Ohio. The school was well organized, efficiently run, and a model of discipline. The atmosphere was conducive to teaching and learning; student morale was enthusiastic, but controlled.

The students were more than usually respectful toward education; they were determined to learn. Nowhere was this attitude demonstrated more clearly than toward their heritage. In the 1950's, the population of Cleveland Heights was at least 95% Jewish. At the end of the school day, the students left the public schools and immediately went to a parochial school for lessons in Hebrew culture.

The position of Director of Assemblies was a manager of events, rather than an actual director of them. There was no season of plays, although short skits or one-acts were possible. Assemblies were mainly determined by tradition and sanctioned by the administration. All-inclusive activities central to the school were the norm, such as scholarship awards, cultural club events, music and sports programs, holiday celebrations, and guest speakers.

On the other hand, Heights High School had a thriving drama program which had been developed by Dina Rees Evans. Her Heights Players and an appreciative audience were concerned with plays considerably more advanced and challenging than the usual high school fare. In December of 1954, she directed the Players in an excellent production of *The Taming of the Shrew,* which would have done any college proud. As Payne would have it, she included the Prologue with Sly; she kept a spot on Sly, and Players spoke asides to him, some even sitting with him during the performance.

Of special interest to me was Western Reserve University, which was just a short bus ride away from where I taught and lived. Western Reserve, along with Carnegie Tech, was one of the first colleges in the country to have a professionally oriented theatre program, with an MFA as a terminal degree.

Classes at Western Reserve were arranged for working people who wanted advanced degrees and who could attend in the late afternoon and evening. In the spring of 1954 I began work on my master's degree in theatre. Barclay Leathem, who originated the theatre program, taught directing; Nadine Miles, a former member of the Theatre Guild in New York, taught acting and directed main stage productions; and Henry Kurth, an excellent designer, together with William McCollom, who taught dramatic theory and literature, were all on the staff. In addition, Professor White of the English Department taught History of Theatre and an excellent course in Restoration and Eighteenth Century Drama. Western Reserve also had a cooperative arrangement with the Cleveland Play House which enabled Frederic McConnell, its founding Director, and members of his staff to instruct in certain graduate courses.

It was almost impossible to take classes at Reserve without becoming involved in productions–not only student shows, but also main stage performances. As a professional training ground, the program was aimed at production. The first year found me as Count Villardieu in an MFA production of Anouilh's *Ardele* and, after that, in *All at Sea*, a bizarre and convoluted comedy by Osbert and Sacheverall Sitwell (brothers of the Gothic temple goddess of modern poetry, Edith). *All at Sea* was a perfectly titled comedy; nobody, especially the critics, had any idea where dry land was from the moment the curtain parted to the time it closed. I was one-half of a team listed in

All at Sea, 1954. This scene is in the lounge of an ocean liner; (standing) Mr. Jameson (F. Cover) talks and listens to the sophisticated passengers. *Photo courtesy Western Reserve University Theatre.*

the play program as "The Silent Couple." We were so named because we had no lines. (This is important, considering what was to happen on opening night.) We sat at a table in the lounge, on board an ocean liner. The set was designed in the shape of a triangle, with my partner and me sitting upstage at the apex. On opening night, during our big scene, Frances Stridinger (my partner) and I began to notice that something was wrong. In a well-rehearsed play (and Nadine never put anything on stage that wasn't), it is difficult to say just what it is that first alerts the cast that something is not right. It is probably the rhythm or tempo of the production that sends an inconspicuous flutter through the cast and alerts them. At this particular time, Frank Cover and Ray Smith were down stage at middle right, talking. Then I noticed that they had stopped talking. I could not resist taking my eyes off my partner and looking downstage. I was horrified to see that both Frank and Ray were looking up at our table. It was only then that I realized that they must have run out of ad-lib lines because someone had missed an entrance. When the tardy actor finally entered, the play proceeded without having to launch a lifeboat.

That was not the end of the episode; the best was yet to come. After the play was over, the dressing rooms were cleared of a congratulatory audience, and we were taking off our make-up. Cover began to laugh. He then blatantly suckered me into a negative response when he asked, "Don, do you know what I heard an audience member say as he was leaving the theatre?"

"No," I replied.

Cover continued, "Wasn't it too bad that the couple upstage had only one line in the whole play and they forgot that!"

It's a great story, not because it was true, but because it shows the power of *direct focus* on stage. This same direct focus, which Cover and Smith used so effectively on stage, can be used in life: just stop on any busy street and look up. You will be surprised at how many people start looking up with you. (I was not unhappy at being the butt of a joke that really did help cover a missed entrance. Oh, yeah!)

My first year in theatre at Western Reserve was marred by "line problems." I insisted on learning a part "word-perfect"; I did not want even an article of the text to be out of place. As a result of this silly line fetish, I developed a psychological block. When I spoke a line differently than the way in which the author had written it, I tried to move on from the mistake, but my mind split in two. Half of it registered the imperfect rendering and went to war against the other half, which tried to proceed with the text. Eventually I would "dry up," unable to continue.

I had not yet learned that all lines are not of equal importance. In fact, some lines are "throw-aways" because they add nothing to the meaning, character, plot, or atmosphere of the play. Cue lines–which are sign posts for fellow actors to begin speaking– are important and should be delivered as closely as possible to the written text. If an actor does not receive his cue to speak or if his cue to speak, is so garbled that he doesn't recognize it, there can be some awkward silences on stage.

The significance of words and the value of their meaning are important, especially when the text is poetic. However, a play is not literature. A play is a script for action, and words should not be so important as to stop an actor from acting. No actor can be word-perfect or speech-perfect every night; some mistakes are inevitable. Once the curtain rises, the play must move forward. The actor must concentrate not only on words, but also on his character, the situation, the action, and the story being told. It is best not to hold any post-mortems on accidents or mistakes until after the final curtain, if at all.

I refused to surrender to the psychological block and I kept fighting against it. I continued to be cast and I continued to act. I appreciated the help of classmates who knew what I was going through, because they had faced similar problems. When the summer of 1955 rolled around, I decided to find a summer theatre to continue my training.

San Diego Shakespeare Festival

In the summer of 1955, I was accepted as a member of the repertory company of the Old Globe Theatre in San Diego. The Old Globe was a simplified Elizabethan stage, a descendant of the one designed by Thomas Wood Stevens for the Chicago World's Fair in 1934. During that fair season, Ben Iden Payne directed a series of one-act versions of Shakespeare's plays, edited by T. W. Stevens. The same theatre was rebuilt at the Pacific National Exposition in San Diego (1935), and Payne directed the same abbreviated plays there for two years. The plays were so popular that the Old Globe Theatre became the center for the San Diego Community Theatre in 1937, and the resultant San Diego National Shakespeare Festival.[1]

Since the Old Globe Theatre in San Diego's Balboa Park was a community theatre, most of the sixty-five members of the 1955 Shakespearean Repertory Company came from San Diego and surrounding communities. There were twenty-six members of the company who received scholarships; nine of these were from San Diego, San Diego State, and San Jose State. There were at least seventeen members from universities representing various states of the union.[2]

Plays chosen for the sixth season of the festival included *Measure for Measure* (directed by B. Iden Payne, who was on staff at the University of Texas); *The Taming of the Shrew* (directed by Craig Noel, who was the resident director for the San Diego Community Theatre); and *Hamlet* (directed by Allen Fletcher, who was on staff at Carnegie Institute of Technology). Beginning on July 22, and ending on September 4, the plays were scheduled to run for six weeks on alternate nights. Rehearsals began on June 16 and continued for a five-week period.

In order to insure the success of the productions, common sense dictated that some tentative pre-casting (tricky though it may be) had to be done. (Only three members of the company came from the University of Texas, and five came from Carnegie Tech.) After interviews and try-outs, cast lists were posted. I was cast for a Gentleman and Warden in *Measure for Measure,* for six small roles in *The Taming of the Shrew,* and for the choice role of Rosencrantz in *Hamlet.* The competition was so good, I would have been happy with much less.

Shortly after casting, I was awarded a George A. Scott Scholarship. Although I had some money of my own, the scholarship guaranteed sufficient funds for the summer run.

Rehearsals began in earnest on June 16. During rehearsals, any actors not on immediate call deployed themselves around the nearest entrance to the stage, so that they might hear the stage manager's call. The California sun was always available for relaxation, but most of the company had books in hand, memorizing lines.

The San Diego Zoo was within walking distance in the park. As a reminder of this fact, several in-house peacocks strutted around the grounds. During one break in rehearsals, Tommy Riggs (Polonius) could not resist the proud strut and feathered magnificence of one bird. He followed it behind the Tavern. Shortly thereafter, we heard the sudden, indignant scream of the bird. Holding one tail feather of the bird aloft, Tommy proudly reappeared.

There was much to explore in San Diego and its surrounding territory. Although there was little free time for exploration while the company was in rehearsal, once performances started, we could use some of our free time as we desired. Members of the company were entertained at various family homes, and sight seeing tours were arranged. One particularly memorable event was a visit to the La Jolla Playhouse. The entire company were guests at a matinee performance of *Billy Budd,* which featured Vincent Price, Charles Nolte, and Sean McCrory. Also memorable was a trip that a few cast members took across the border to Tijuana, Mexico, in order to see a bull-fight. In reality there was not just one bullfight on that sunny Sunday afternoon—I counted eight! The fights had a predictable effect on me: I felt sorry for the bull, and I admired the bravery and finesse of the matador. Much of my free time was spent watching movies at Sparkles, which was open twenty-four hours a day. However, as with other members of the company, most of my time was spent on stage and in rehearsals.

Payne was meticulous and confident in his direction, and he showed great concern for his actors. When blocking the action of any scene, he watched the actors carefully. If any actor looked somewhat dubious about his position, Payne interjected, "Don't worry. You will be lit."

One afternoon at dress rehearsal, I developed an insidious itch on my right knee. I was in a down-stage-right position, which meant that the offending leg was clearly visible to the seats in the auditorium. I tried to ignore the itch, but it would not go away; I reached down with my right hand and scratched. After the scene was over, Payne said quietly, "Hill, you can't scratch when you're wearing tights."

Payne's meticulous attention to detail is demonstrated in the following stories.

While he was directing *A Midsummer Night's Dream* at the University of Texas, a gel slipped off a spotlight during one of the performances, and the beauty of the dream-like atmosphere was shattered by a shaft of harsh white light. Payne, who was in the back of the theatre at the time, raced so quickly into the back stage area that he was half-way up the light bridge before he met the stage manager, who was also on his way to adjust the offending light.

In *Measure for Measure,* as the warden of the prison where Angelo was confined, it was my responsibility to hook into place the parapet on the inner above as I exited. One night, I forgot the crenellated structure, and I received a written reminder from the stage manager with Payne's name on it. After the show had been in production several weeks and Payne had left town, he wired the following message to the stage manager: "Tell Hill not to forget the parapet."

Rehearsals for *Hamlet* went well. Director Allen Fletcher cut several of my long speeches. That was fine with me; however, at the last rehearsal before opening night he told me to completely restore one speech that he had excised. I had so successfully forgotten the cut portion of the speech that I couldn't possibly reinstate it without several rehearsals, something that was not possible. In spite of the danger, I was determined to follow the director's wishes. I explained to Claude Jenkins (the King), who had lines immediately after my speech, that I would not be able to restore the cut portion completely. I kept adding lines each night. He watched me closely and when he saw that I was about to "dry-up" he came in immediately. One night I dried up, but he didn't come in. Rather than be stuck on stage with egg on my face, I began to speak in Sid Caesar's fake French. The King hurriedly broke in. In the meantime, there were some puzzled expressions on several actors' faces, as well as on some members of the audience whom I caught looking at me, as if to say, "What was that!" Eventually, I had the complete speech solid in my memory, but I would not want to repeat the anxiety of those moments.

Hamlet, 1955. Elsinore Castle throne room. Guildenstern (B. Howard) and Rosenkrantz (D. Hill) are briefed by Queen Gertrude (J. Galbraith) on the status of Hamlet; (up center) Polonius (T. Riggs) discusses an article with King Claudius (C. Jenkins). Courtesy San Diego Shakespeare Festival.

In *The Taming of the Shrew*, I played six different roles, each of which had so few lines that I could have done them in mime. I was a Huntsman, a Musician, a Servant to Baptista, Joseph (servant to Petruchio), an Officer, and a Servant to Lucentio. I could have suffered from multiple personality disorder, but because of adequate rehearsals, I was able to develop a different make-up for each part. This, and the fact that I had a different costume for each character, gave me the necessary confidence required for changes in character. Nevertheless, I'm sure I didn't hide my true identity from the audience. I spent more time backstage changing make-up and costume than I ever spent on stage!

In the *San Diego Evening Tribune* for Monday, July 25, drama critic, Bruno Ussher, expressed his pleasure over the summer season:

> . . . the Shakespeare statue in Balboa Park wore a smile last night. It seems a pleased smile now that the Current National Shakespeare Festival had run successfully in its first round: *Measure for Measure*, on Friday, *Hamlet* on Saturday and yesterday, *The Taming of the Shrew*.
>
> But even one less experienced than Master Will will recognize standards that were higher than last year. The best was better even now.[3]

Ussher went on to specifically praise the Hamlet that Bill Ball created. He described him as "a flaming rather than melancholy prince." He also praised Craig Noel's direction of *the Taming of the Shrew* as a "Potpourri of boisterous and mincing humor."[4]

The San Diego National Shakespeare Festival was a pleasant experience. I felt as though I had regained some of my old confidence. I had no trouble at all with lines, except for the unusual experience with the one speech in *Hamlet*.

I was ready to return to my teaching duties at Roosevelt Junior High School, and to my final year of classes at Western Reserve.

REFERENCES

1   B. Iden Payne, *Life in a Wooden O: Memoirs of the Theatre* (New Haven: Yale University Press, 1977), p. 187.
2   "The San Diego National Shakespeare Festival Sixth Annual Summer Season, 1955, Presents *Measure for Measure, Hamlet, Prince of Denmark, The Taming of the Shrew* Nightly in Repertory, July 22 to September 4, *"The Old Globe Shakespeare Festival Program, Magazine San Diego"* (San Diego, California: Magazine San Diego Publishing Company, August, 1955), centerfold between pp. 36-37.
3   *Curtain Call,* "Bruno Ussher Views Music-Drama Scene," *San Diego Evening Tribune,* (San Diego, California, Monday July 25, 1955), p. a-14.
4   Ibid.

Western Reserve University Conclusion

In November of 1955, I was cast as Oberon in *A Midsummer Night's Dream,* directed by Nadine Miles. Shakespeare's comedy-fantasy of a tangled tale of love denied and then fulfilled was beautifully enhanced by designer Henry Kurth's touch. He fashioned a wonderful and austere architectural setting, with delightfully vivid Japanese Kabuki costuming and make-up, all under silvery-blue lighting. A modified Kabuki stage was executed in redwood lumber, and fitted into the architectural stage of the Eldred Hall Theatre. The Kurth style is characterized by simplicity of line, clarity of color, and a blue cyclorama that hints of influences from Appia and Craig. I cannot be objective, since I was in the play, but the elegant costuming supplied the scenic splendor which Shakespeare's plays require, when there is no overt scenic display. The costuming also engendered a statuesque posture and formal delivery of lines, in order for the poetry to receive due emphasis, in keeping with the director's plan. It was a beautiful and exciting production. Backstage was memorable for the contest I had with Sarah Schilling (Titania) over make-up. I glued silver glitter to the black lines of my Kabuki make-up. Sarah added glitter to her hair and lashes. I found some dressmakers little half-moon mirrors to add to the end of the French curves painted on my cheeks; they reflected the lights prismatically. When Sarah added glitter to her long fingernails (which she managed to show-off with her flowing gestures), I admitted defeat; my arms and hands were encased in huge squares of black and white material, stiffened with cardboard.

In December came a Strindberg drama of mental pain and spiritual anguish: *Easter.* I played Elis, a schoolmaster troubled by family debt and family pride, as well as a lack of will to improve his situation. Just before being cast in this play, my principal at Roosevelt Junior High School suggested that I was spending too much time on stage for a full-time teacher. The irony of the situation was that I, as myself, suffered along with Elis each night I was on stage. I tried to turn the reality of my life situation to advantage in the part, but it didn't quite work. As a result, my theatrical activity on main stage was kept to a minimum.

In March, Miss Miles directed John Millington Synge's famous *Playboy of the Western World.* I played Shawn Keogh, a timid and bashful wooer to the female lead, Pegeen Mike. My character was totally eclipsed by Christy Mahon, the Playboy. The play was a delightful and enjoyable experience, but perhaps I emphasized the comedy of Shawn too much. One reviewer of the opening night performance wrote that I resembled the old vaudeville duo, Weber and Fields. After that comparison, I thought I had better subdue the comedy a little. On the second night, I featured the humanity of Shawn. After the final curtain, there was a knock on the dressing room door. When I responded, I heard Miss Miles's voice cautioning, "Don't change the way you played Shawn opening night." After that, I didn't pay too much attention to critics or reviewers. I remembered what William Gillette had said about never reading reviews. This famous actor, who had written *Secret Service* and created the original role of Sherlock Holmes, had learned not to trust reviews or pay too much attention to critics. I learned my lesson, and the next night the Shawn that Miss Miles had directed was back on stage.

The Playboy of the Western World was an excellent play in which to end my career at Western Reserve. I received a Master of Arts degree in Dramatic Art in June of 1956.

Cain Park Creative Youtheatre
1956 & 1959

I spent the summer of 1956 teaching at Cain Park Creative Youtheatre in Cleveland Heights.

Dina Rees Evans has written her own history of Cain Park Community Theatre. My knowledge of the founding of that remarkable institution is mainly oral in nature. From what I have heard, Dina Rees Evans was a pioneer in affecting the founding of that organization, one of the earliest community theatres to be municipally owned as a non-profit institution. Built like a Roman amphitheater, Cain Park Theatre seats about three thousand people. [1]

In 1956, the open-air theatre presented such musicals as *Paint Your Wagon, Of Thee I Sing, Sing Out, Sweet Land,* and *Finian's Rainbow*. The managing director was Ray Smith and the production director was William Walton.[2] Three years later, the same theatre was the venue for celebrities who traveled with their own shows: Bob Hope (a Clevelander), Johnny Mathis, Frankie Avalon, Sammy Davis, Jr., Harry Belafonte, and Jerry Lewis.[3]

For educators interested in theatre, Cain Park Creative Youtheatre and its school of arts were the jewels in the crown of Cain Park. Since I was on the teaching staff in 1956 and 1959, I can speak with a little more authority on the founding of this important children's theatre institution. Dina Rees Evans was the moving force behind the Creative Youtheatre. It began as a by-product of the community theatre, when adults in rehearsal needed a care center for their children. Since Mom and Dad were engrossed in theatre, it seemed a natural activity in which their children should be similarly employed. Hence, Cain Park created a children's theatre and school staffed by teachers from major universities all over the country.

My first summer there saw the Dina Rees Evans persona evident in the managing director, Edith Underwood, a very capable successor to the founder. Mrs. Underwood was very low-key, very kind, gentle, and firm (not authoritative), but very much in control and very efficient. All of these characteristics endeared her to the children participating in the classes and plays, and to the teaching staff, most of which was composed of graduate students who were interested in learning more about children's theatre.

The Creative Youtheatre was divided into three levels of learning: Junior (grades 2-6), Intermediate (grades 7-9), and Senior (grades 10-12). In the Junior Division, training was in creative dramatics, combined with classes in allied arts: music, dance, pictorial art, and puppetry. Two outstanding artists were on the faculty: Louis Penfield, an excellent artist and teacher, who was in charge of technical theatre, and George Latshaw, the well-known puppeteer. The Intermediate and Senior Divisions merged at certain points, in order to emphasize the more formal aspects of theatre. This was not a professional program; it was based on the premise that the "arts offer unique potentialities for the creative growth and development of youth."[4]

During my first summer at the Creative Youtheatre, four shows were produced in July: *Snow White and Rose Red, King Midas, Jr., Tom Sawyer,* and *A Midsummer*

Night's Dream, in which I played Theseus. Shakespeare's comedy-fantasy seemed ideally suited to the aims of the school and to the students' pursuit of the creative aspects of the arts. Once the script was combined with action during rehearsals, the unfamiliar language and its poetic expression was not a barrier. When the script was translated into action, it stimulated the students' understanding of the text, and challenged their imaginative response to the literature.

On my return to Cain Park Creative Youtheatre in 1959, Dina Rees Evans was Director Emeritus and Edith Underwood was the Director. Courses being offered that year in the Junior Division were Art, Music, Creative Dramatics (required), Dance, Puppetry, Spanish, Production, Passport to Adventure, Art of Animation, and Mask and Mime; in the Intermediate and Senior Divisions, the classes consisted of Acting, Oral Interpretation, Theatre Speech, Makeup and Stagecraft, Instrumental Music, Theatre Chorus, Directing, Mime and Chamber Theatre, Dance, and Art,

The story of the play I chose to produce was the familiar *Rip Van Winkle.* In order to challenge the students' creative resources, I pulled it out of New England and set it in Texas. With very little re-writing, the play adapted itself to the Texas landscape, which provided the production with very colorful costumes and a lively historical setting.

My production notes of 1959 reveal my production idea and director's rationale for *Rip Van Winkle:*

> There is a saying in show business that if you don't know what to do with a show, give it a Texas setting and let it rip. (No pun intended). It would have been easy to give the usual performance of Washington Irving's classic tale, "Rip Van Winkle." However, I found the whole production idea much more stimulating and exciting if I placed the story in Texas in the year 1846, just ten years after the battle of the Alamo. With this setting, instead of Henrik Hudson and sailors, I could use the ghost of Davy Crockett and his Tennessee Volunteers. According to history, they came to the defense of the Alamo and died there. The thunder in the original story, caused by the bowling of ninepins, was easily explained as the cannon of Santa Ana, pounding away at the thick walls of the old historic mission. The color of the Texas landscape and the glamour of the cowboy costumes had dramatic possibilities that encouraged my idea. I believed that children would find participation as actors, and also as spectators, greatly entertaining because the production idea matched the rash of television westerns in vogue.

I was not disappointed with the seven performances.

After the Cain Park season closed, I moved south to New Concord, Ohio, where I began my tenure as Director of Theatre at Muskingum College.

REFERENCES

1   Cain Park Theatre; "Program for the First Week of 1956 Season" (City of Cleveland Heights, Ohio, 1956), n.p.
2   Ibid.
3   Cain Park Theatre "Program for the 1959 Season" (City of Cleveland Heights, Ohio, 1959) n.p.
4   "Cain Park Creative Youtheatre Important Notice To All Parents and Students," (Cain Park Youtheatre: Cleveland Heights, Ohio, 1956) p.1.

New York! New York!

Perhaps the single most important year of my life was the self-determined sabbatical I took in the fall of 1958 through the spring of 1959 in New York City. New York City was the theatre capitol of the world, and when I decided to spend a year there, I planned on taking advantage of as many theatrical events as possible.

I took a job as a waiter at Schraft's Restaurant on Times Square, to assure myself of one good meal a day; I attended as many Broadway and Off-Broadway shows as possible; and, I enrolled in as many classes in a variety of professional theatre studios and schools as time would permit.

Of the many Broadway shows I saw, I must limit my list to the most memorable: *The Ages of Man,* by John Gielgud, and *Rashomon,* by Fay and Michael Kanin. Touring companies supplied the remaining memorable productions. The Theatre National Populaire, under the direction of Jean Vilar, produced *Lorenzaccio* (Musset), *Don Juan* (Moliére), *Marie Tudor* (Hugo), and *Le Cid* (Corneille). Outstanding performances by Jean Vilar, Gerard Philipe, Philippe Noiret, Maria Casares, and Genevieve Page contributed to the excellence of the productions. The Old Vic Company produced Shakespeare's *Hamlet, Twelfth Night,* and *Henry V,* with such luminaries as John Neville, Barbara Jefford, Laurence Harvey, and Judi Dench (then little known) .

When I look back on that year, the number of classes I managed to take was amazing. I took a class in voice from Marian Rich at the Herbert Berghof Studio, and a Workshop for Young Directors at the Curt Conway Studio. Since I was not a member of Equity, I could not enroll in Morris Carnovsky's class in Shakespeare Scene Study, offered at the American Shakespeare Festival Theatre and Academy, but when I agreed to be class secretary, I was permitted to audit the course. I enrolled at Columbia University and, as a registered student, took Mark Van Doren's class in the Art of Poetry and Maurice Valency's Main Currents of Drama. Of all the classes I took, the most influential were the courses in acting and mime taught by Stella Adler and Angna Enters, respectively, at the Stella Adler Theatre Studio.

Employing a habit I had developed during my school days, I kept a daily journal of all classes. The journals contain a record of the teachers' lectures and class activities. Together, all of these journals comprise what I call "The New York Notebooks" and remain, as do so many such student class notes, unpublished.

A Lesson From Stella

In the fall of 1958, following a high school dream I had failed to fulfill, I found my way to New York City. I had all the teaching experience and all the university training I needed for the time being. I was excited and anxious to learn everything and anything about acting and the theatre from the professionals. I was not disappointed.

Bruce Williamson, a classmate from South High School in Grand Rapids, Michigan, who had been in New York since the late 1940's, pointed me toward Stella Adler's Theatre Studio. I subsequently registered for Miss Adler's beginning acting class, and she became one of the most important influences in my life and work. (See Section Note on Williamson.)

Stella Adler's classes convinced me that all my previous training and experience were good and true, but that I had developed some bad habits–too much reverence for the text was one of them. Most of all, Stella's classes gave me new and exciting insights into the theatre. There was a whole new world to be explored and I was learning how to explore it!

After my first class at the Stella Adler Theatre Studio, I wrote the following remarks concerning her teaching method.

Stella Adler at the Stella Adler Theatre Studio in New York, 1959. *Photo by the author.*

> She was ALIVE! She was intense! She was enthusiastic. She was honest. She hated sham of any kind. She would not tolerate pretense. These [sham and pretense] were merely cover-ups for insecurity. She made us understand that we were to ask questions before or after class, because the only one interested in the answer was the person who asked the question. Teaching was her work–the word teaching was mine, not hers, because she claimed she was not a teacher–and she indicated that no one liked to have his work interrupted. Her effect upon me and upon the class was electric. I was under her spell from the moment I met her at the interview, and from the moment she joined the class; I had the feeling of being in the presence of a rare personality, a magnetic individual.[1]

I was no stranger to Stanislavsky. I had read Elizabeth R. Hapgood's translations of *An Actor Prepares* and *Building a Character,* and Christine Edwards' history of *The Stanislavsky Heritage.* I thought I understood Stanislavsky's message and his importance in the history of theatre. However, Stella Adler quickly shattered that idea. She had worked with the Group Theatre, had applied Stanislavsky techniques to acting for over twenty years, and had studied with The Master one summer in Paris. She made Stanislavsky not only plain and clear, but also plainly and clearly obvious. She made the technique useful and practical for the stage. I realized that I only knew Stanislavsky intellectually; Miss Adler made him a three dimensional presence.

I know of no better way to explain what I learned from Stella Adler than to present, for the reader, a few excerpts from the notes which I took during class. I kept a journal for every lesson. After class, I rushed home, sat down at my typewriter, and filled them out as close as possible to what she said during class. At the end of the term, I gave her a copy of the journal so that she would have a record of that particular class at that particular time.

Through her teaching, Stella Adler taught many principles of acting, filtered through Stanislavsky's and her own experiences. She made very clear the cause of some of the bad habits I had developed over the years. Some of the worst were: 1) setting a performance and doing it the same way every night, 2) being too conscious of myself on stage, 3) failing to concentrate on the part, 4) relying too much on the text, and, 5) losing focus on the action.

Below are a few of the notes which I culled from the journal from Lesson 1 on October 6, 1958 through Lesson 42 on January 15, 1959. They all refer to my weaknesses as an actor.

> Don't set the way you say things. Keep it fresh. Don't set things; it will paralyze you . . . . You must be responsible for your action; you must know when you are too conscious of you . . . . Don't be a literary actor; they are boring. They have everything in their minds and nothing in their eyes . . . You are too respectful. Make it your own first; don't take anything that is not your own . . . Even stronger than the fear of being in front of an audience are the hours you have put in. Respect them both . . . Don't become a victim of the author. Paraphrase his words so that the ideas become your own . . . . When you are rehearsing on stage, there are fifty layers of distraction, but your concentration must be so great that you don't notice them. Yet, you must never lose yourself in your part; you must always be able to stop at the command of the director and go back and start over again without losing the mood or the action. [2]

One day in class, Stella made me conscious of several of my bad habits, especially my reliance on the text, which had caused the many problems I had at Western Reserve.

I was doing a speech from a play that was to show a specific action. An imaginary partner sat across a table from me. Suddenly, Stella, who had been watching, listening, and sipping coffee from a mug, sat down in the imaginary partner's place. Here was a real person listening to me and reacting to what I was saying. The addition of a live partner made little difference to me, since I was concentrating on the words. Then without warning, Stella smashed her coffee cup against the wall of the studio and coffee streamed toward the floor. Oblivious to the reactions of my partner, I continued as if I were in a straight jacket.

Stella made it very clear that I was giving her yesterday's performance, that I had *set* the speech. I was not paying attention to the action of the character. I was not living or acting in the moment, the immediate NOW. If I had been, I would have reacted to my partner's behavior and still been able to complete the action. The words of the author would have been there, but the way in which I said them would have reflected what was happening at the time.

Stella had warned us before that some of us had developed bad habits, and that it would take a derrick to pull them out of us. She was right, at least in my case.

LESSON EARNED. LESSON LEARNED.

REFERENCES

1   Donald Hill, "Stella Adler Principles of Acting: Lesson 1," (New York City: unpublished class notes, October 6, 1958) p. 2.
2   Stella Adler, quoted by the author, "Stella Adler Principles of Acting: Lesson 1 thru Lesson 42," (New York City: unpublished class notes, October 6, 1958 through January 15, 1959) n.p.

Section Notes

Bruce Williamson progressed from being the editor of the *South High Tattler* to a theatre and movie critic in New York City. A short biography can be found in *Twentieth Century Writers/Authors*.

Stella Adler: A Brief Biography

"The source of acting is imagination, and the key to its problems is truth, truth in the circumstances of the play."

— *Stella Adler via Stanislavsky*

Stella Adler came from a theatrical family. Her father, Jacob Adler, and her mother, Sara, were the foremost tragedians of the Yiddish stage. Jacob Adler owned his own theatre and was known as the Jewish Henry Irving.

Stella made her stage debut at the age of four in 1906 and, for the next eleven years, toured with her parents here and abroad.

Stella made her first Broadway appearance in Karel Capek's *The Insect Comedy* in the 1922-23 season. She attended New York University and the American Laboratory Theatre, where she studied with Stanislavsky disciples, Maria Ouspenskaya and Richard Boleslavski. From 1927 through 1931, Stella toured Latin America, Western Europe, and the United States. She returned home to play a series of leading roles in her father's company.

In 1931, Stella joined the Group Theatre, which modeled itself on the theories of Stanislavsky and the Moscow Art Theatre, a socially-conscious theatre as opposed to the commercial theatre of Broadway.

When Stella began having problems with acting, she went on leave from the Group for a vacation in Europe. While in Paris, she was introduced to Stanislavsky. In five weeks, he was able to resolve the problems she was having with the excessive attention that Lee Strasberg (also of the Group Theatre) gave to "affective memory."

Stella stayed with the Group Theatre until 1935, when she left for Hollywood and film acting. Having little success in film, she returned to New York to teach at the New School for Social Research and to direct for the Group Theatre. She directed the acclaimed touring production of Odet's *Golden Boy*, which received stunning reviews in London and Paris in 1938-1939.

In 1941, Stella returned to Hollywood. She made *The Shadow of the Thin Man* for MGM, and became an associate producer to Arthur Freed on such films as *DuBarry Was a Lady*, *Madame Curie*, and *For Me and My Gal.*

Stella returned to Broadway in 1943 as Catherine Canrick in Max Reinhardt's *Sons and Soldiers*. In 1956, she directed the anti-war musical, *Johnny Johnson*. She performed in *Pretty Little Parlor* in 1944, and played Zinadia the Lion Tamer in a Theatre Guild revival of Leonid Andreyev's *He Who Gets Slapped*. Her final stage appearance was in London, in 1961, as Madame Rosepetal in Arthur Kopit's *Oh Dad, Poor Dad, Mama's Hung You in the Closet and I'm Feelin' So Sad*. Her acting career spanned more than two hundred productions.

Since Stella always felt an inclination to teach acting, in 1949 she opened the Stella Adler Acting Studio. However, her interests were not limited to her own school. She also served as adjunct professor of acting at Yale University's School of Drama (1966-67) and, for a long time, she was associated with New York University in a similar capacity.

In 1960, Stella's studio was renamed the Stella Adler Conservatory for Acting. The school had grown to include more than a dozen faculty members. In 1986, she began the Stella Adler Conservatory for Acting West in Los Angeles. It was there, in 1992, that she ended her final days at the age of ninety-one.

REFERENCES

Fearnow, Mark. "Stella Adler," *American National Biography, Vol. 1.*(American Council of Learned Societies), John A. Garraty and Mark C. Carnes, ed., (New York: Oxford University Press, 1999), pp. 167-168.

Gilbert, Irene. "Biography of Stella Adler," *The Technique of Acting by Stella Adler*, foreword by Marlon Brando (New York: Bantam Books, 1988), pp. 127-132.

Graham, Judith, ed. *Current Biography Yearbook, 1993*, Obituaries, "Stella Adler," (New York: The H. W. Wilson Company, 1993), p. 619.

Moritz, Charles, ed. *Current Biography Yearbook, 1985*, "Stella Adler," (New York: The H. W. Wilson Company, 1985), pp. 6-9.

Lessons in Mime
from
Angna

Angna Enters's influence on my life and work was equal to that of Stella Adler. Angna was a mime of extraordinary gifts, a genuine genius who had won international acclaim, not only as a mime, but also as an author, dancer, painter, sculptor, director, and designer.

Shortly before I enrolled, Stella Adler had convinced Angna to teach classes in mime at her studio. I was, indeed, fortunate to have arrived when both of these talented women were on the same teaching staff. I learned later from Angna's book, *On Mime,* that she felt that mime could not be taught and that she really could not teach mime. Mime is not an easy subject to teach. Mime begins when speech fails, and mime ends when words are found to express an idea or emotion. Mime lives in those expressive silences that speak louder and more clearly than language.

Angna was wrong. It was the naiveté of genius speaking when she said that she couldn't teach mime. Her teaching began the very moment she stepped in front of the class. She taught by example, which is one of the best kinds of teaching. Every gesture and every movement spoke to us in eloquent fashion. There were no gestures without meaning, and no movements without cause.

Angna did not offer us a series of fundamentals for mime. She did the hard thing: she awakened in us the possibilities of what we could accomplish through our own creativity and imaginative responses to reality.

Angna's world of mime existed not in technical displays of movement and gesture, nor in self-conscious exhibitions of clever pyrotechnics. The world of Angna Enters was that of a singular personality wedded to a particular time in a specific place, and totally free of clichés and stereotypes. Each of her characters was a living and breathing individual who came to her through the study and research of those universal characteristics that make the past understood by the present. Although rooted in history, they were not historical characters; they were individuals born from her own imagination which existed outside of herself.

Angna's book, *Artist's Life* (which is largely autobiographical), describes how she created many of her characters. It contains a wealth of information on how her travels, research, and experiences helped develop what James Agate called " . . . a métier entirely her own . . . ,"[1] and led Louis Untermeyer, to reveal, after her London debut:

"You Americans!" said Arnold Bennett as we were leaving–the only sentences he addressed directly to me–"You people have every talent except the ability to recognize your own genius. You lost Whistler and Henry James to us–and I hope you lose this girl who is a little like both these expatriates. She, too, is a painter of portraits."[2]

Angna Enters's book, *Angna Enters On Mime,* relates her experiences as a teacher. One of the many perceptive observations she makes about acting explains the actor's real contribution to the play. Her discourse begins with the playwright who provides the play; next, she moves to the director, who interprets the play to the actor and designs movement; and, finally, she discusses the actor who translates the play into action with technical skill. Then, she adds the following:

> . . . in the end, his [the actor's] creative contribution to the play is as mime. This is the visual image he presents to the audience; in this is embodied all his understanding of the character. It is the behavior of the character by which the audience understands the play visually. The way the character walks, stands, sits, listens–all reveal the meaning of his words. All the nuances of his speech have little meaning unless accompanied by an effective visual portrait. It is here that he becomes a creative collaborator, for here he reveals the character as an individual human being. No small responsibility, for it requires the ability to make the character come to life for the audience, by actions as well as words. Acting is a combination of intelligent reading of lines and MIME! Mime, used with discretion, only to enhance the playwright's words. It is an exacting art.[3]

Every day in Angna's class was a revelation. I will never forget how she explained the relationship of acting to character. Angna observed that the actor must connect the character to class, period, and animals. The actor must be *obsessed* with the character. He must understand that the character behaves with his own mental processes and rhythm. If the actor *says* that the character does *this*, he is lost. The sense of touch with the eye, when it rests on someone, is the eye of the character, not the eye of the actor. As a result, the actor will know when he is out of character, but he will not know when he is in character.[4]

These ideas helped explain my unusual experience in *An Inspector Calls*. In March of 1951, I played the part of Eric Birling in this play at the Pit and Balcony in Saginaw, Michigan. I had the experience of being lost in the character. It was the oddest feeling, because I was not thinking

Angna Enters at the Stella Adler Theatre Studio in New York, 1959. *Photo by the author.*

of the character or the words he uttered; the lines of dialogue seemed to fall from my mouth automatically as reactions to what the other characters were saying. The realization of being myself did not occur until the play was over and I sat in a cold sweat in the dressing room. The other actors looked at me in an odd way and asked, "What happened to you tonight?" I did not know, but I think I know now. As the actor, I was in control. My lines were there and my movements were there, but the character was doing them. My experience can also be explained by the theory of the "dual function" of the actor: the actor is like a split personality. The character takes over and, although the actor is still there, he is very much in the background where he functions as an objective observer. In other words, I had been *obsessed* (or possessed) by the character of Eric.

I wish I could say that I had that experience more times than I have. It has happened to me off and on as I played different parts, but it has never happened so completely. When I am in musicals, singing or dancing, it always happens–perhaps because my entire body and mind are so occupied that my soul naturally follows; therefore, I cannot help but be obsessed. It's a great feeling.

Later, Angna continued her discussion of character. She said that gestures and movement must be made within the mood and rhythm of the character. According to her, the actor must establish the character, become possessed by it, and then intuitively let go. Each move must not be thought out mentally. (The mental work has already been done early in rehearsal.) During the performance, the actor must sit back and let the character go. He should not be continually on top of the character.[5]

The actor must let the character take over; the actor is simply the vessel or shell for the character. Once the actor makes the character possible, the actor must let the character live. This theory is similar to the foundation of many religions: the actor must die so that the character can live. The patient control with the techniques of the art of acting is what makes the performance possible.

When Angna performed at the Phoenix Theatre in 1959, I saw her on stage for the first time. It was a stirring and sterling evening, mixed with the many emotions evoked from the different characters she represented. "Pavana" and "The Boy Cardinal" were quickly my favorites. She exhibited all the various ideas she had taught us in class, especially the theory of being "obsessed" by the character. I recognized her as my teacher, but she had been taken over completely by these other living souls. It was a revelation to watch. I was grateful; and after so many years, I am even more knowingly grateful now, for having known her and her all-encompassing artistry.

On her performance that night, Whitney Bolton wrote:

> I was young and had hair when I first fell under the spell of Angna Enters, and now I am neither young nor have hair and not only am I still under her spell but the years that have damaged me have done nothing at all to her except to increase her glamour and sharpen her art. The lovely proof was on view at the Phoenix Theatre Monday night.[6]

I corresponded with Angna for several years after I left New York. I wanted her to perform for the students at Muskingum in the spring of 1960. For some reason, the dates did not work out and she did not perform for them until the winter of 1963, when I was at the University of Iowa.

In October 1961, she wrote to me:

> I accepted an invitation to be artist-in-residence there [the Dallas Theatre Center] and at Baylor University at Waco for this term, ending January 31st. My doctor thought it might help pull me out of my despondency after the loss of my husband in June. I am teaching the players in Dallas acting as well as the Baylor drama students.[7]

Paul Baker was Chairman of the Theatre Department at Baylor and also Director of the Dallas Theatre Center, which was designed by Frank Lloyd Wright. Professor Baker was developing a professional repertory company for the theatre. Angna continues " . . . it is this company I have in charge. In addition, I have just undertaken to direct a production of *The Mad Woman of Chaillot* for January presentation . . . "[8]

Professor Baker must have read the Whitney Bolton column (which appeared in the Waco paper) in which he announced the arrival of Angna at the Center. He suggested that Mr. Baker

> . . . turn her loose on costume design and setting design. She has ideas that sparkle and are fresh, that make theatrical good sense and they just may draw the attention of the world to your theater.
> Whatever she does, she does well. Whatever she undertakes, she will finish. Whatever she designs for you will have distinction.[9]

In her next letter from Dallas, Angna wrote,

> In a weak moment I agreed to remain for the spring term and now find myself not only involved in complete charge of the players here and at Baylor, but also as consultant in all productions, no matter who the director![10]

Of her work on the production of *Madwoman,* John Rosenfeld reported in the *Dallas Morning News:*

> *Madwoman* enters the Theatre Center's repertory and Miss Enters enters (the many entrances are unavoidable) the ranks of one of the more successful stage directors. Miss Enters shows a consistent instinct of what a stage is for. Why, for the play, of course.[11]

Angna's doctor must have felt good about this. She had become immersed in work again, even though it was not what she had anticipated. It was having a good effect, for she wrote that she was giving a performance in Columbus, Ohio, in April, " . . . the first I've been able to face since the loss of my husband." In the same letter, she informed me that, in 1963, she would be a Fellow at the Center for Advanced Studies at Wesleyan University in Connecticut, where she hoped " . . . to complete writing projects as well as paint and give performances!"[12]

Sam Wilson, in his column, "On the Rialto," wrote after her performance in Columbus,:

> Great is the debt of gratitude owed OSU for having brought back to Columbus that incontestably great and wholly unique artist, Angna Enters.
> Tragedy, comedy . . . drama sweeps across the stage, surges out into the auditorium as this remarkable artist creates a wide variety of character portraits, by pantomimic means alone, probing deeply and subtly into the human soul and mind in a series of vignettes which, more often than not, say as much in a few minutes as the average playwright might say in a full evening of words, words, words.[13]

Angna performed at Muskingum early in 1963. In her letter of February, she wrote,

> Thank you for the letter which arrived a few days before I left for Muskingum. I thought that the show went well and the house was packed although how much those at the back or in the balcony could see because of the rather sketchy lighting, I cannot know! There was no time or equipment for an attempt at light changes so we turned on what was available and hoped for the best! The student crew were

most cooperative and did very well. Mr. McGraw saw to it that I had as much help as possible. I saw him only briefly after the performance as he had to go off for tryouts for a production of J.B. but I did get to know Mr. and Mrs. Kendall of the music department who took us to their home for homemade bread and cheese after the show as we had had no dinner. Naturally we never eat before a show. I had a comfortable room in the new Faculty-Student Center and my accompanist stayed in a motel which he reported was also comfortable . . . I enjoyed the visit to Muskingum and the students and others we met.[14]

When she wrote the above, she was at Wesleyan. She had finished the semester in Dallas and was asked to return the next winter to direct another play. She had been to California and was enjoying life at Wesleyan. She still had not accomplished as much as she had hoped, but she felt " . . . that I am on the road to some kind of recovery." She had already directed her students in two one-acts: an O'Casey and a Chekov that were well received.[15]

In March, Angna gave a performance at Coe College in Cedar Rapids, Iowa. I drove up from Iowa City to see her. She did both the "Pavana" and "The Boy Cardinal," and I was as intrigued with her work as ever. I stopped backstage to see her. As usual, things were hectic after the performance. She was disappointed because her paintings had arrived too late for a showing, and she was packing costumes to leave. She had to return to Wesleyan to complete work she had in progress. In the middle of March, she was suffering from the Asian flu and trying to finish a show for an exhibition in Minnesota. " . . . how I ever got it finished is a mystery to me, what with a fever bordering on delirium at times."[16]

In May, she was working on a paper to be delivered to a panel of top full professors. She was also preparing paintings for the big commencement show at the Davidson Art Center. She had hoped to spend the summer in Europe, but felt that it was impossible because of a book commitment *(On Mime?)* and the performance that she had to prepare for the coming year.[17]

That seems to be the last letter I received from Angna. Our correspondence fell victim to very busy careers. For that I was glad, because she seemed to be fully recovered from her depression and her career was in full swing again.

REFERENCES

1   James Agate, in the *London Sunday Times*, quoted in "The Theatre of Angna Enters," (New York City: a brochure published by the Giesen Management, Audrey Wood, personal representative), n.p.
2   Louis Untermeyer in "From Another World," quoted in "The Theatre of Angna Enters."
3   Angna Enters, *Angna Enters On Mime* (Middletown, Connecticut: Wesleyan University Press, 1965), pp. 42-43.
4   Angna Enters, from her class on Mime as reported in the author's class notes, Stella Adler Theatre Studio, New York City, April 14, 1959.
5   Ibid., May 8.
6   Whitney Bolton, in the *Morning Telegraph*, March 1959, quoted in "The Theatre of Angna Enters."
7   Angna Enters, in a letter to the author, October 26, 1961.
8   Ibid.
9   Whitney Bolton, the *Waco Times-Herald*, Wednesday, September 20, 1961, p. 4.
10   Angna Enters, in a letter to the author, February 23, 1962.
11   John Rosenfield, in the *Dallas Morning News*, January 18, 1962, quoted in "The Theatre of Angna Enters."
12   Angna Enters, in a letter to the author, February 23, 1962.
13   Sam Wilson, in the *Columbus Dispatch*, April 12, 1962, quoted in "The Theatre of Angna Enters."
14   Angna Enters, in a letter to the author, February 15, 1963.
15   Ibid.
16   Angna Enters, in a letter to the author, March 18, 1963.
17   Angna Enters, in a letter to the author, May 8, 1963.

Section Notes
Angna Enters: A Brief Biography

Angna Enters was born in New York City, but she grew up in Milwaukee, Wisconsin. Arriving in New York from Milwaukee, Angna gave her first performance in 1924. She created a type of mime that was entirely unique and different than that of Marcel Marceau, or of the silent film, as exemplified by Charlie Chaplin. She was not interested in displaying a technique or in telling a story. She was interested in creating a person, more than a character, who lived at a particular time in a specific place.

Miss Enters accomplished this task by a careful study of history, autobiographies, journals, and diaries. She filtered this research through her own knowledge of people and, later, her experiences as a world traveler. Slowly, the insubstantial realm of "Imagination" and "Creativity" were fired by the spark of "Inspiration" and a new creation appeared on "Earth." Along with the newborn, she also made and sewed (designed and executed) its clothing (costume), found a home (setting), gave it movement (choreography), and composed a rhythm (music). Then she placed (directed) the new creature in a life situation (scene), in order that she (the Mother of this invention and a casual observer) might watch (along with the audience) it live and react (perform)–all in silence, of course, because it was too young, too smart, and too sophisticated for words!

Angna had it all and did it all. She was an internationally-known mime, a world-class painter, and a recognized author. Her mime theatre was performed innumerable times in theatres and colleges throughout the United States, and over ten London seasons; she also performed in Paris and Berlin. Her paintings had over twenty successive New York exhibitions (two of them Guggenheim Fellowships). Her work is found in one hundred and fifty private collections and is represented at the Metropolitan Museum. Her books include *First Person Plural, Silly Girl, Among the Daughters, Artist's Life,* and *Angna Enters On Mime*. She wrote at least two plays that were produced: *Love Possessed Juana* and *The Unknown Lover*. She worked in films as a consultant and screen writer.[1] At MGM Studios, Angna worked on the screen plays, *Lost Angel* (1944) and *Tenth Avenue Angel* (1948). She wrote the *comedia dell' Arte* episodes and staged them for the film *Scaramouche* (1952).[2]

Angna died in 1989 at the age of ninety-two. Her collected papers were deposited in the Dance Collection of the New York Public Library for the Performing Arts at Lincoln Center.[3]

REFERENCES

1　Factual information contained in the above biographical sketch was collected from the book jackets of *Love Possessed Juana,* (New York: Twice a Year Press, 1939), *Artist's Life,* (New York: Cowan-McCann, 1958), and *Angna Enters On Mime,* (Middletown, Connecticut: Wesleyan University Press, 1965).

2　Jacqueline Maskey, "Agna Enters," *American National Biography* (published under the auspices of the American Council of Learned Societies), Edited by John A. Garraty and Mark C. Carnes, Vol. 7 (New York: Oxford University Press, 1999), pp. 537-538.

3　Ibid.

Theatre in the '60s

The Department: 1958–1965

When Dr. Layton retired in the spring of 1958, a worthy successor was found in Dr. James L. Golden. Dr. Golden held his B.A. from George Washington University, an M.A. from Ohio State University, and a Ph.D. from the University of Florida (1953). He had previous teaching experience at the universities of Maryland and Richmond, and Pasadena College. He had, to his credit, authored a long list of articles published in *Vital Speeches*, the *Quarterly Journal of Speech,* and *Southern Speech Journal*; and he had co-authored *The Rhetoric of Blair, Campbell, and Whately.*[1] More importantly, he possessed managerial skills in relation to curriculum and staff. He was extremely polite–a gentleman's gentleman, tactful, pleasant, and genuine. An experienced scholar in the field of speech, Dr. Golden was well aware of the Layton tradition; indeed, he wrote about that tradition several years later in "The Rhetorical Thrust of the Laytons," an article which appeared in the *Ohio Speech Journal* and the *Muskingum College Alumni Bulletin* of 1970.

The Laytons left a well-organized department and a curriculum that not only suited their generalist approach and the requirements of a small liberal arts college, but also covered the recognized areas of the growing field of speech. J. Jeffrey Auer's, *An Introduction to Research in Speech* (published the same year that Dr. Layton retired), lists seven areas in the field of speech: Fundamentals of Speech, Public Address, Interpretation, Radio and Television, Theatre, Speech and Hearing Disorders, and Speech Education.[2]

Using these areas as guidelines, the Layton curriculum could be classified as follows (number in parenthesis indicates credit hours):

I. Fundamentals of Speech
    A. Communication (8)
    B. Speech Fundamentals, adapted to upper-class levels (4)
    C. Extempore Speaking (2)
II. Public Address
    A. Parliamentary Law and Practice (2)
    B. Oratory and Orators-Survey (3)
    C. Oratory and Orators-Rhetoric (3)
    D. Reasoning and Discussion (2)
    E. Debating Seminar (1–4)
    F. Speech Seminar (1–2)
    G. Advanced Oratory (1–3)
III. Interpretation
    A. Interpretative Reading (4)
    B. Interpretative Reading, adapted to upper-class levels (2–4)
    C. Literary Analysis and Interpretation (2–4)
    D. Interpretation Seminar (4)
IV. Radio and Television
    A. Principles and Practice of Radio Broadcasting (2–4)
    B. Production, Direction, and Performance of Radio Shows (2–4)

V. Theatre
    A. Introduction to the Theatre (1–2)
    B. Elements of Play Production (2–4)
    C. Modern Drama (2–4)
    D. Play Production (2–4)
VI. Speech and Hearing Disorders
    A. Principles of Speech Re-Education (2)
    B. Speech Re-Education Laboratory (2–4)
VII.   Speech Education

(A "Methods" course in teaching speech and English had been taught in the department since 1926. After the school year 1953–54, the course was dropped. It is taught today in the Education Department.) [3]

According to the above classification, the Public Address area seems large, but it is not, considering the amount of knowledge and number of activities it had to cover. The area of Interpretation was strongly represented in the curriculum by four courses amounting to as many as sixteen hours. Speech and Hearing Disorders received little attention, in spite of its importance. For a small liberal arts college it was, and still is, regarded as a specialized area, much too expensive for the college to give more

The 1958-1959 Debate Team and their Coach, Dr. James Golden. Front Row: G. Sulzer, Dr. Golden, S. Mugnani, D. Phillips, R. O'Connor. Back Row: W. Osborne, W. Lammie, M. Smith, R. Brown, F. Bonkowsky. *M.C. Library Archives.*

than meager attention. In fact, this area has dropped in and out of the curriculum several times over the years, depending on available personnel and finances. Speech Education received more attention than is apparent. The only course devoted to that area was taken over formally by the Education Department; however, staff members in Speech also advise and observe students teaching speech and theatre in the high schools. It is also true that many courses have units of study particularly applicable to those interested in teaching; similar units have also been devoted to history of speech and theatre in education. These units of study within other courses amount to a "hidden curriculum" which is difficult to assess.

The Radio and Theatre areas seem small by today's standards. They were small, even then, when compared to what some schools were doing in those disciplines. One reason these areas were not more fully developed is related to the liberal arts attitude toward specialization. Radio and Television and Theatre were looked upon then as special areas. Another very practical reason was money; the special facilities, equipment, and staff necessary to maintain more than a nodding acquaintance with these fields of speech amounted to a considerable investment—more than the college was willing to underwrite. Nevertheless, both of these areas were to expand over the next two decades, in an attempt to stay abreast of the technical and cognitive advances being made, and to maintain the popularity they held with the student body.

The faculty members who taught the courses in the department consisted of Dr. Golden, who continued Dr. Layton's work in debate and oratory. Mary Elizabeth Johnson succeeded Mrs. Layton in the area of Interpretation; she also taught the Speech Re-Education and, later, the Speech Correction courses. Martha Moore taught general speech courses and Interpretation. Gail Joseph, another Layton graduate, was appointed to the staff the year before Dr. Layton's retirement; she married Arthur Sinclair and they both taught speech and theatre courses. Mr. Schreiber, who came to Muskingum in 1955, continued to teach the Radio courses.

At the end of the 1958–59 school year, Mr. Schreiber and the Sinclairs left. Mr. Charles Buzzard was appointed to the position in Radio, and immediately introduced Television into the curriculum. The Theatre position remained open.

During the 1958–59 school year, I had finally made my way to New York City. One day at Columbia University, I renewed my acquaintance with Martha Moore, who had joined the Speech Department staff in 1948, when I was a junior. We were both enrolled in classes taught by Mark Van Doren and Maurice Valency. Martha was on sabbatical, and through her, I learned that Muskingum was searching for a professor of theatre. A permanent appointment had been in the offing for several years. Shortly after I received my degree from Western Reserve in 1956, "Doc" Bob wrote to me concerning a position in theatre, but I was already under contract. I was tempted to apply for the position. I had begun to realize that making my way in the professional theatre would take about ten years of "beating the pavement" to agents' doors, "cattle calls,"* and interviews, with little promise of success. Because I had already been a teacher and director, the educational theatre began to look very appealing to me. I went for an interview.

The spring of 1959 was to be a turning point for me. Lunch was epilogue to the formal interview I had with Dr. Golden; Dr. and Mrs. Layton joined us. I remember all of us sitting around a table in McCall's Chicken House, just east of New Concord. It was the best restaurant in the neighborhood and retained that reputation for some time. (The building stands today, but the restaurant has long since been replaced by a beer drive through.) We were having a very pleasant and convivial time, for I had not

---

*Cattle calls are general, non-selective try-outs in the professional theatre, which result in hundreds of hopefuls showing up, and take up unprecedented amounts of time.

seen the Laytons for several years. They were enjoying their retirements, and seemed relaxed and at ease.

A serious undercurrent ran beneath the surface pleasantries; it was, after all, a working lunch. The Laytons were concerned about the welfare of the theatre. Since 1914, they had been involved in serving the Department of Speech in which debate, interpretation, and theatre had been key areas. Dr. Golden shared their concerns. The department was on sound footing, with Dr. Golden managing the forensic-debate areas, and Miss Johnson and Miss Moore heading up general speech and interpretation. However, they were aware of the increased importance of theatre on college campuses, and they felt the need to find someone to further develop that area.

At any rate, whoever was offered the position of Director of Theatre would be charged with the single task of strengthening that area. When I was offered the position later, I accepted.

With new leadership came changes. Under Dr. Golden, these changes were not abrupt, but gradual; they followed a logical manner consistent with the progress of speech on a national scale. The tendency was toward centrality within the department, its course offerings, and its activities. A pruning and trimming process occurred in some areas; expansion occurred in others. The strong forensic program continued, and the department turned out some very good orators who won state and national honors. Notably, one of them was Sam Speck, our former college president who, as a graduating senior, won the annual Ohio Inter-Collegiate Oratory Contest. The front page of the March 25, 1959 issue of the *Black & Magenta (B&M)* carried a picture of Sam receiving the trophy from Dr. Golden.

The May 19, 1959 *B&M* carried the story of changes that had been made in the new Basic Education program. The eight-hour freshman Communication course (which had been a requirement when I was a freshman) was abandoned; in its place was a Fundamentals of Speech course for three credit-hours.

A Speech major in 1960 consisted of 28 hours, which did not include the required Fundamentals of Speech. These hours did include Interpretative Reading (3), Modern Drama (2–4), Speech Composition and Rhetoric (3), Argumentation and Debate (3) or Group Discussion (3), Introduction to Speech Correction (3), and a Speech Seminar (2–4). Also required were 2 hours from Introduction to Theatre or Play Production.[4]

Absent from the major was the suggestion that 6 hours could be taken in approved courses from other departments, English being the one most commonly chosen. The special Diploma in Speech, which had been granted to qualified students—a tradition extending back to the turn of the century—was dropped after the 1959–60 school year.[5] (See Section Notes for "Recital Seminars" and specific course changes.)

I knew the theatre area needed changes. Other colleges of the same size and type, such as Denison and Marietta, had better facilities, majors in the discipline, and even departments with a faculty of three to five members. Larger colleges and universities had been awarding advanced degrees since the 1920's.

The curriculum and the production program were major concerns. I believed that students in a small liberal arts college should get to know the various aspects entailed in the study of theatre; theatre was more than literature and acting. Just as my predecessors (the Laytons) were generalists, wanting a curriculum that covered the field of speech in all its different facets, I wanted students in theatre to know all of its facets: stagecraft, acting, directing, theatre history, design, costumes, lighting, and make-up. These courses were the basic structure of the discipline. Also important were the many types of theatre: children's theatre, religious theatre, musical theatre, and arena theatre. The burgeoning areas of arts management, and the connections being made with psychology, sociology, and political science were worthy of exploration.

Two changes that were deemed necessary were made the first year. Elements of Play Production was limited to an introduction of technical aspects and entitled Stagecraft. A course in Play Direction was added.

Play Direction was especially important. It was not just a study of directing; it was also a laboratory in which students directed a one-act play. This course was the foundation of a student program in play production that ran concurrently with the usual season of plays directed by theatre and speech staff. Supported by class discussions and lectures, the students selected a play, analyzed it, and made a complete production book to be used as a guide from rehearsals through performance. Then they held try-outs, selected a cast, rehearsed and, finally, performed the plays before an audience. I believe students learn more and better about theatre when they are given first-hand experience. The eventual popularity of the course among speech, theatre, English, and music majors who planned to teach, or who were interested in directing, justified its existence.

Two more professors who served with Dr. Golden during his years at Muskingum were Stanley Schutz, who replaced Mr. Buzzard in the Radio and Television area in 1961, and Mr. Judson Ellertson, who was added to the staff in 1964. Mr. Schutz was working on his doctorate in theatre at Michigan State University, and he had directed plays while at Wooster College. He made a welcome addition to the production program by directing one play each year.

My work in theatre for the first three years consisted not only of teaching and directing, but also designing and doing my own technical work. Too much time was spent trying to make the technical elements equal to the performance aspects of the production. I thought that if I knew more about design and technical production, I could be much more skilled, assured, and efficient in dispatching those necessary elements of any production. I also became fascinated by the design area and the requisites for creating a practical, inexpensive, and aesthetically-pleasing environment for a play.

The search for a good school in design led to Arnold S. Gillette (Director of University Theatre, State University of Iowa) who had a national reputation in design and technical theatre. I also knew of him through his daughter, Jo, with whom I had acted at Western Reserve. The theatre faculty, as well as the speech faculty, was a veritable "Who's Who" in my field. Dr. Clay Harshbarger, Sam Becker, Douglas Ehninger, and John Bowers in speech were complemented by Arnold Gillette, David Thayer, Margaret Hall, and Oscar Brockett in theatre.

With a recommendation from Dr. Layton, who knew Dr. Harshbarger, I applied for a teaching assistantship and was accepted. I left Muskingum for two years of work on the Master of Fine Arts in scene design at Iowa. I had only a verbal agreement with Dean Howard Evans: "If at the end of two years, you want me back, and I want to come back to Muskingum—fine; if either one changes his mind in the meantime—fine."

During my absence from fall of 1962 through spring of 1964, Mr. Rex McGraw replaced me as Director of Theatre.

Section Notes

Although the Speech Diploma was no longer offered, the student interested in interpretation could take the course Speech Seminar, which offered the opportunity for presenting a recital. Following is a list of Recital Seminars given by students after 1958. The information was taken from corresponding issues of the *Black and Magenta* and is not intended as a definitive list.

RECITAL SEMINARS

May 9, 1961	Nancy Penry presented *Mary of Scotland* in recital, in Brown Chapel.
April 24, 1962	Bonnie Mugnani Clemens presented *Pygmalion* in recital, in Brown Chapel.
April 17, 1965	Beth Robinson presented the poetry of Carl Sandburg and *Spoon River Anthology* in recital, in Brown Chapel.
May 1, 1969	Donna Brevak presented Scenes from *Miracle Worker, The Silver Cord, Agamemnon, Atlas Shrugged,* and *The Unsinkable Mollie Brown* in Brown Chapel.
April 17, 1975	Terry McCord presented "Twixt Here and There" in recital, in Brown Chapel. This recital was a combination of oral interpretation and song.

COURSE CHANGES

In 1960, the following courses were added to the curriculum:

Stagecraft (2-4), Argumentation and Debate (3), Group Discussion (3), Introduction to Speech Correction (3), Advanced Speech Correction (2), Introduction to Radio and Television (3), Production, Direction, and Performance in Radio and Television Shows (2), and Play Direction (3).

The following courses were dropped in 1960:

Elements of Play Production (2), Speech adapted to upper-class levels (2-4), Parliamentary Law and Practice (2), Interpretative Reading adapted to upper-class levels (2-4), Advanced Oratory (1-6), Speech Re-Education Laboratory (2-4), and Interpretation Seminar (2-4).

Changes in titles and course equivalencies in 1960 were as follows:

Speech Composition and Rhetoric (2) took the place of Oratory and Orators-Rhetoric (3); Intercollegiate Forensics (1-8) took the place of Debate Seminar (1-8); Advanced Interpretation (2-4) replaced Literary Analysis and Interpretation (2-4); and

History of Public Address (3) filled the position of Oratory and Orators-Survey (3).

(All the foregoing information comes from the *Muskingum College Bulletin*, 1960-1961, pp. 131-134.)

REFERENCES

1   *Directory of American Scholars*, Seventh Edition, Vol. II, English, Speech and Drama, Edited by Jaques Cattell Press, (New York: R. R. Bowker Company, 1978), p. 251.
2   J. Jeffrey Auer, *An Introduction to Research in Speech*, (New York: Harper & Row, Publishers, 1959), pp. 2-7.
3   *Muskingum College Bulletin: 1958–1959*, pp. 136-139.
4   *Muskingum College Bulletin: 1960–1961*, pp. 131-134.
5   Ibid.

My First Theatre Season
1959-1960

The student is the most important element of the educational process. I have been blessed with wonderful students throughout a teaching career that spanned forty-six years. The years spent at Muskingum are especially meaningful to me because the students made it that way.

My first year teaching and directing at Muskingum was enhanced by a cadre of exceptionally talented students who were vitally interested in theatre. The professors who had preceded me had left a group of eager students, ready and willing to enter into a season of plays. Another equally bright and enthusiastic group of freshmen was willing to join the upper classmen in making the theatre season exciting and attractive.

For the first major production in January, I chose one of my favorite plays—an American classic— *The Glass Menagerie,* by Tennessee Williams. I chose *Menagerie* because it has literary and theatrical values. It possesses certain universal ethical values—parental-filial conflicts over paths to the future; it contains acting problems within the range of student actors, providing a good learning experience; it takes a small cast and provides opportunities for ensemble work; it lacks objectionable scenes or language

The Glass Menagerie, 1960. Amanda (M. Wertz), Laura (S. Wolfe), Jim O'Connor (H. Shaver), and Tom (D. McDowell). *Theatre file photo.*

that would pose problems of acceptance for the community; it is inexpensive to stage; and it suits the physical limitations of the Little Theatre.

After studying the play, I began to see each character in my mind's eye, and that made casting easy. The field of talent was awash with first-class minds eager to begin and enough available students to cast the play three times over. I cast Mardie Wertz as Amanda Wingfield; Sandy Wolfe as her daughter, Laura; Dave McDowell as Laura's brother, Tom, and Hal Shaver as Jim O'Connor, The Gentleman Caller. It was, I thought, perfect casting; the actors fell into their characters as if the roles had been tailored for them.

For this production, I wanted to present each character in a favorable light; after all, everyone wants to be liked! I believe this attitude created natural conflicts because each actor/character was driven by natural desires. The depth of these desires did not seem to be scripted and that became an element for our rehearsals to develop.

As my image of the play developed, the jonquil became the key to the color of the set and costumes–a sort of washed-out green, white, and yellow that must look old and worn, as if it were hidden behind marquisette curtains. The texture of the play was soft, like velvet, but light, like nylon chiffon. The music must be like that also; as a result, instead of using the violin music written for the play, I chose to use music from the Paradise Dance Hall across the alley—old sad, nostalgic music of the war years. The black drapes that covered stage left and center were taken down to reveal the crumbling red bricks of the Little Theatre's walls. They were perfectly suited to represent the tenements that surrounded the Wingfield apartment, which was a cut-down set revealing the dining and living rooms.

The setting for the play is St. Louis, Missouri, around 1939. Historically, St. Louis was the gateway to the West—the land of promise and the future, which did not exist for Amanda and Laura. *Menagerie* is not a character play, although the characters are what command the attention and supply the emotion. In *Menagerie,* I saw a strong theme, something to be learned about Southern agrarian culture, and what happens when it meets the Northern industrial complex. St. Louis is neither the "Deep" South," nor the "Far North." It is a middle ground where the two different cultures meet, clash, and founder.

We rehearsed the play according to the Stanislavsky Method. Although it is a memory play, seen through the eyes of Tom, it must first be based in reality, then taken to a level of memory that is close to a dream, with the hard edges of reality smoothed down and filed off. Not one of the characters gets severely seared by the heat generated from the emotional scenes; they simply get hurt. The characters never change or progress; they stand still; they remain inviolably the same to the end of recorded time, just as Tom remembers Amanda and Laura in that last scene. Over and over again in his mind he sees them going through the same motions, like one of those recording tapes glued to form a loop which, when played, keeps repeating itself.

The rehearsals became so intense that we sometimes did not know the hour when we began rehearsal or the hour we ended. As an ensemble, we became so imbued with the spirit of the play that, whenever we met years later, that same aura of sad, tender, nostalgia that we had all worked to create, was still present.

The Glass Menagerie is a favorite of the American repertory. Every student should see it on stage, or be in it if possible. It is a good vehicle from which to learn something about yourself, your friends, and American culture.

My first season of plays at Muskingum College ended in May of 1960, with a major production of *The Playboy of the Western World,* by John Millington Synge. In the program, I gave the audience a few facts about the play, in order to help them understand the importance of what they were about to see and hear. The program gave the following description of the scene: "The action takes place in a public house on a wild coast of Mayo, Ireland, in 1907. The first act passes on an evening of autumn, the other two acts on the following day."

About the Play

The Playboy of the Western World is a satire on hero-worship which the author, Synge, molded around the true story of a Connaught man who killed his father with a spade and fled to an island where he was hidden by the natives, then shipped to America. Synge's hero, Christy Mahon, becomes a village idol when he boasts he killed his bossy father in a far-off potato patch—a romantic crime that enchants the villagers. But when they later see him commit what looks like murder in their own village, they want to hang him.

The Playboy of the Western World was first produced in 1907 at the Abbey Theatre in Dublin, where it incited riots because it twitted Irish character. Two years later when Synge died, the play was revived in his honor and received unstinting praise.[1]

Synge laced his play with language that proved offensive to his fellow countrymen. One word, "shift" (Irish for petticoat), received a noisy objection. Since the words of the play were, to a certain degree, responsible for some of the rioting and criticism of the play, it is appropriate to hear what Synge himself said about the language.

. . . In a good play, every speech should be as fully flavoured as a nut or apple, and such speeches cannot be written by anyone who works among people who have shut their lips on poetry. In Ireland, for a few years more, we have a popular imagination that is fiery and magnificent, and tender; so that those of us who wish to write start with a chance that is not given to writers in places where the springtime of the local life has been forgotten, and the harvest is a memory only, and the straw has been turned into bricks.[2]

For the playboy, Christy Mahon, I was indeed fortunate in having a very sensitive and energetic American Irishman in Jack Wilkins and, for his father, Old Mahon, an equally feisty Dorsey Doddroe. Hal Burlingame made a very robust, if at times tipsy, publican (bar owner), Michael James Flaherty, and Nancy Penry portrayed his excellent feisty daughter, Margaret (Pegeen Mike). Janet Click made a very proud, but shrewd, Widow Quinn, and David Kafer proved to be a very able equivocator, Shawn Keogh, who favored Pegeen Mike, but feared everyone else. The supporting cast was composed of a number of talented actors and actresses who would prove themselves in future productions: Bing Bills (Philly Cullen), Donald Kelm (Jimmy Farrell), Lee Ann Phillips (Sara Tansey), Elsie Marie Patterson (Susan Brady), Sandy Wolfe (Honor Blake), Sally Lu Marquis (Nellie), and David Clark (Bellman).

I congratulated myself on a good first season of plays. They were good plays, theatrically effective, and, with few exceptions, valued literature. What some of the productions may have lacked in technical expertise, I tried to make up for in hard work, good direction, and many rehearsals. I was satisfied that I had given each play tender loving care.

I looked forward to a summer vacation with the proper rest and relaxation and a lot of play reading in order to set the season for next year, interspersed with trips to two Stratfords: the Stratford Ontario Shakespeare Festival and the Stratford Connecticut Shakespeare Festival.

REFERENCES

1   Donald Hill, Original Program, *The Playboy of the Western World,* May 18-21, 1960, Little Theatre, n.p.
2   John Millington Synge, "Preface," *The Playboy of the Western World* in *Five Great Modern Irish Plays* (New York: The Modern Library, 1941), p. 4.

The Plays: 1960–1962

1960-1961

The 1960-1961 Theatre Season opened with Noel Coward's *Private Lives,* a comedy of manners which reflects the scandalous and irresponsible life of the leisure classes during the 1920's.*

The story of *Private Lives* concerns Elyot Chase and Amanda Prynne, who were once married, but are now divorced. By coincidence, they not only marry the second time at the same time (to Sibyl and Victor), but they also select the same place–Deauville on the French Riviera and the same hotel, with adjoining suites, for their honeymoons. When Elyot and Amanda meet, they fall in love again and elope to Paris, leaving the deserted partners to their own devices. Once in Paris, Elyot and Amanda enjoy a few

Private Lives, 1960. (standing) Sibyl Chase (M. Lemley), Victor Prynne (D. Kelm); (on floor) Elyot Chase (B. Bills), Amanda Prynne (N. Penry). *Theatre file photo.*

days of unwedded bliss, but it is short-lived because old jealousies cause new quarrels, and the elopement ends with a fight and the discovery by Sibyl and Victor of their retreat. They agree to the divorces insisted upon by Sibyl and Victor, who get into a fight over the cause of the ruined marriages. Elyot and Amanda, recognizing that a good fight might indicate sincerity and true affection, steal away again.

For the Muskingum production of *Private Lives,* which was to play the Little

---

Private Lives was written as a consolation prize for Coward's good friend, Gertrude Lawrence. She had been his first choice for the lead in his operetta, *Bitter Sweet*; however, when the score was finished, the part proved too strong for her voice. He promised that his next play would be written especially for her. That play turned out to be *Private Lives*, which he conceived on a trip to the Far East. On a December night in the Tokyo Imperial Hotel, he went to bed early and, according to him, the moment he switched out the lights, ". . . Gertie appeared in a white Molyneux dress on a terrace in the south of France, and refused to go again until four a.m., by which time, *Private Lives*, title and all, had constructed itself." Three weeks later (January 1930), while convalescing from influenza in the Shanghai Cathay Hotel, he wrote the script, ". . . propped up in bed with a writing-block and an Eversharp pencil, and completed it, roughly, in four days." (Noel Coward, *Present Indicative, An Autobiography*. New York: A Da Capo Paperback, 1947; pp. 299, 320-322).

Theatre from October 19 through 22, I chose the following cast: Marsha Lemley (Sibyl Chase), Bing Bills (Elyot Chase), Nancy Penry (Amanda Prynne), Donald Kelm (Victor Prynne), and Nancy Munn (Louise). I could not have wanted a better cast. All five players were primed for the rehearsal period and eager to get started on the witty, sophisticated comedy.

The dialogue of Coward's comedies requires special treatment because it is not easily memorized. The speeches are seldom longer than two or three sentences and there are always passages of dialogue that consist of single short sentences that must be delivered in rapid succession. The rhythm and timing of the speeches are crucial for the intended effect. Coward, who not only acted in, but also directed many of his own plays, refused to start rehearsals unless the cast knew their lines. Robert Helpmann explained:

> He's as difficult to learn as Bernard Shaw, because he puts everything so rightly that if you get a word wrong you can't substitute words for Noel's lines. If you dry up you can't substitute—you're lost—even Shakespeare you can substitute, you can sometimes make up a Shakespearean line in rhythm, but you can't Noel—you've got to keep it on the nose.[1]

Coward had a highly personal way with dialogue. He not only perfected it through language, but also he insisted on reading all his plays to the actors. An example of the importance of language in Coward's dialogue occurred during rehearsals for *Hay Fever.* In 1964, Sir Laurence Olivier scheduled the play to open the season of the new National Theatre Company, and he wanted Noel to direct it. The cast was strong. It included Maggie Smith, Robert Stephens, Robert Lang, Lynn Redgrave, and Dame Edith Evans, who was to play the lead, Judith Bliss. Edith Evans was one of the most accomplished commediennes in the English theatre, but she put Coward on edge because she could not remember the exact content of her lines. One line which especially annoyed him was, "On a clear day you can see Marlow."

> Dame Edith gave the line as "On a very clear day you can see Marlow." Coward finally lost patience because she was destroying the rhythm of the line. He stood up in the stalls and called out, "Edith, the line is, 'On a clear day you can see Marlow.' On a very clear day you can see Marlow <u>and</u> Beaumont and Fletcher." (In performance, Dame Edith was word-perfect.)[2]

John Gielgud, who followed Coward in several roles, said,
> Some of Noel's lines are so extraordinarily characteristic that, when once you have heard him deliver them himself, it is almost impossible to speak them without giving a poor imitation of him.[3]

In the educational theatre, lines can be a real stumbling block. Unless the director forces the students to understand the play, the character, and the production, it is possible to spend two weeks out of a four- to five-week rehearsal period, baby-sitting students who agonize over lines that they have only half-memorized. Work on motivation and interpretation is a constant companion to all phases of production. I needn't have worried–there were no problems with this cast. Nancy Penry must have had a photographic memory; she showed up at the second rehearsal with the complete text well in mind. The two sophomore men had been put on notice; from the looks on their faces I imagined their "sub-text" that evening to be, "No girl is going to out-shine me." Before the first weekend, they all knew their lines. From that moment on, rehearsals and performances were a breeze. All of the rehearsal time was devoted to important elements of the play, such as style, timing, and rhythm. The production was a joy to direct and a pleasure to watch. At curtain rise, the play took off and never touched ground until the curtain fell. As a director, I felt useless; the cast had taken the play away from me. I couldn't think of a single thing to do. As a director, I had served my purpose. I was no longer needed. That is the way it should be!

The next major production was *The House of Bernarda Alba*, by Federico Garcia Lorca, scheduled for December 7-10. The Lorca folk-tragedy was quite a change from the sophisticated elegance of Coward's comedy . The cultural climate of late nineteenth century- and early twentieth century-Spain is far removed from anything a modern American ever experienced. It is a world dominated by women, a world of iron clad social codes, and a world with close ties to the history of the Catholic Church.

In my notes "About the Play," I discussed the career of Lorca and the history of his last play.

> Federico Garcia Lorca is ranked with Lope de Vega, Cervantes and Caldron [sic] as one of the great writers of Spain. With the translation of his four major tragedies, *Doña Rosita, Blood Wedding, Yerma,* and *The House of Bernarda Alba*, Lorca took his place among the great playwrights of the world.
> *The House of Bernarda Alba* was completed just two months before Lorca's murder by Spanish Fascists in 1936. Of all his plays it is considered the greatest. It is the lyric expression of an Old Spanish theme: honor. To be more explicit, it deals with the attempts of Bernarda Alba, the personification of Spanish matriarchy, to preserve honor and tradition in the face of sexual instinct as expressed by her five unmarried daughters.
> *The House of Bernarda Alba* was first produced in this country at the American National Theatre and Academy in New York in 1951 with Katina Paxinou and Kim Stanley. It has since become a favorite of Little Theatres all over the country. It will receive two productions in Ohio this year: one at Antioch College and the other at Ohio Wesleyan University.[4]

The husband of Bernarda Alba has just died and left his wife with a wealthy farm and five unmarried daughters. Bernarda commits her daughters to eight years of mourning. They are confined to the house and bound to their daily chores; they are not to speak to any man or engage in any frivolity. The oldest, Angustias, has already been spoken for; the others must sit and wait. In the meantime, there are the duties of the house and their embroidery to console them. Bernarda rules over her daughters with an iron hand, always watching and monitoring their daily lives, their character, and their honor. Adela, the youngest daughter, must be closely watched, for she is believed to have had an assignation with Angustias's betrothed, Pepe. The conflicts that the daughters have with one another and with their mother mirror the conflicts between generations and the strict social code of honor.

What I needed for the play was not just a group of dedicated women; I had that. They were present when I arrived on campus the year before. Now, they had to be employed. The following students formed the cast for the play: Judy Johnson (Servant), Barbara Kurkura (La Poncia), Peggy Young (Beggar Woman), Sherran Reynolds, Eve

Fernengel, and Lorraine Commeret (Women in Mourning), Judith Spillard (Little Girl) Bonnie Mugnani (Magdalena) Marilyn Gleason (Amelia), Nancy Penry (Martirio), Sandy Wolfe (Adela), Elsie Marie Patterson (Angustias) Rebecca Gillis (Bernarda), Elianda Lefkathetou (Maria Jesefa), and Phyllis Knapper (Prudencia).

Lines meant nothing to these students; they were required to learn them quickly and they did it. What I needed was the atmosphere of hate, silence, and foreboding to fill the stage and permeate the entire theatre. How was I to get it? I did not plan what I did, it just happened. One night, the entire group came down the hill to the theatre and I heard them coming. They were young. They were laughing and talking about things that young girls talk and laugh about. When they got to the old double doors of the theatre, the laughter and talk spilled over into the lobby.

I had been at the theatre for some time, preparing for the rehearsal, and I was well into the atmosphere of the drama. All that gaiety hit me the wrong way. I jumped out of my seat and shouted, "Quiet!" There was quiet. Better than that, there was absolute silence. I had never yelled at them before.

"How dare you come into my house that way!" I said. Now they were stunned, and I was a little startled myself.

"When you come to the theatre, you must leave the world outside. You enter into a special world—a world of order. Everything is planned. You know what is going to happen to you. It is different from life—and yet it is lifelike—a different form of life. Now you are in the world of nineteenth century Spain. You are in the house of your mother, Bernarda Alba. I don't want to hear one sound out of any of you, off or on stage, unless it is a line from the play."

Then we rehearsed and after rehearsal was over, I told them how important it was that the tone and atmosphere of the play be present at every rehearsal in order for

The House of Bernarda Alba, 1960. Angustias (E. M. Patterson), Magdalena (B. Mugnani), Amelia (M. Gleason), Adela (S. Wolfe), Bernarda Alba (R. Gillis), and Martirio (N. Penry). *Theatre file photo.*

it to be made part of the performance. Atmosphere, tone, and mood are difficult concepts to grasp because they are intangible, and yet, they are very important elements of drama.

After the night I exploded, the silence grew as rehearsals wore on. The silence intensified; it became a presence that built a wall around each character. The feelings of passion, jealousy, and hate grew as a part of the play and stayed there throughout the remaining rehearsals and throughout the performances. It was what the play needed to survive on the stage.

In this unforgiving tragedy, Adela, in complete frustration, hangs herself in her mother's house. Bernarda hides her broken heart and demands that her daughter be buried in white.

Bing Bills wrote an excellent review of the play. He centered his attention on "acting, mood and setting." He singled out certain players for comment and, in summary, found, "It is sufficient to say that the acting left little to be desired in most cases." He found the setting "striking," drawing "praises from all sides . . . a unique background, well-executed and in harmony with the play."[5] Of most interest to me were his comments on the mood.

> The tragic mood of the drama was inexorable. From the moment the first act began, it was evident that something terrible was about to occur. Throughout the drama, the ominous tones of all the actresses increased the intensity of the horrible suicide of Adela. This mood could only be accomplished by highly intelligent and polished performances on the part of the cast. They caught it, and it was sustained most of the time.[6]

In March, another totally different kind of play was presented as the third major production. *Under Milk Wood* was written by one of the most gifted and most discussed poets of the twentieth century, Dylan Thomas. The Welsh poet died in November of 1953, at the age of thirty-nine; *Under Milk Wood* was completed within a month of his death.[7] Previously, the play had been given try-out performances to admiring audiences and critics in New York City. Thomas directed and played several roles himself. Henry Hewes, the theatre critic of the *Saturday Review*, welcomed it as " . . . probably the richest and certainly the earthiest theatre experience of this season," and the *New York Times* noted that the audience " . . . was treated to a dazzling combination of poetic fireworks and music-hall humor."[8]

The stage production of *Under Milk Wood* was produced as an experiment at the Edinburgh Festival. The overwhelming success of that reception caused it to be taken to London, where it was the surprise success of the season. It was then moved to Broadway, where it was equally well-received.[9] The success of the play was due, largely, to the totally original poetry of Thomas and to the characters of the small Welsh fishing village of Llareggub. The inhabitants of this little town are the most exotic and eccentric group of individuals one is liable to meet in any drama. Thomas introduces us to the village inhabitants who go about their everyday lives as the day moves full circle, from just before dawn to dusk.

The audience at this beautifully poetic verse play understands some of the core idea which Thomas intended, although it is not one that is driven home. There is a contrast between the eccentrics of Llareggub who are "strong in their individuality and freedom, and the sane ones who sacrifice everything to some notion of conformity."[10] Whether an audience comes away from the play with an articulated theme or not, one cannot help but enjoy what Randall Jarrell has written: "It would be hard for any work of art to communicate more directly and funnily and lovingly what it is like to be alive."[11]

I imagined *Under Milk Wood* as an ideal vehicle for a staged reading, with nothing but lights, black drapes, music stands, and stools for the six principals, and a bench upstage for a chorus of women. The cast needed trained and flexible voices and the ability to vocally portray many different characters. For the six principals, I cast three music majors (Karen Cobbett, Lindsay Barr, and David Clark) two speech majors (Donald Kelm and Sandra O'Connell), and myself. The chorus of Neighbor Women and School Girls were portrayed by Pat Koster, Corley Morton, Anne Sindelar, and Peggy Young. Approximately fifty-five to sixty-four different characters were portrayed by the ten member cast.

I was about to learn a valuable lesson. I had unwittingly cast three music majors, all of whom had very heavy schedules of music events. I had made the rehearsal schedule without consulting any of the students' advisors. As the rehearsals progressed, drawing nearer to the critical performance stage, there was a problem with Karen, who had to give her senior voice recital, and had a very strict regimen in order to make her recital date. There were some tense moments until I could get together with Professor John Kendall, head of the Music Department, and work out a compromise schedule. Karen is one of those mercurial, universally-talented people who can do anything and do it well; she eventually ended up in New York at the Met Studio. I wouldn't have, and couldn't have, done the show with anyone else; her Polly Garter was one of the highlights of the show, which was a big success.

Bing Bills again wrote a favorable review of the production. In "Student Gives

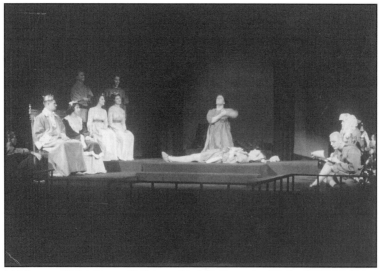

A Midsummer Night's Dream, 1961. (seated far left): Demetrius (W. Sturni), Duke Theseus (T. Fox), Hippolyta (V. Price), Ladies (C. Gibson, M. Caldwell); (behind ladies): Lords (R. Gebhart, S. Price); (center kneeling): Flute (D. Kelm), Bottom (on floor) (A. Dawson); (seated far right): Snug (M. Stewart), Quince (R. Layton), and Snout (P. Alvarez). *Theatre file photo.*

Review of 'Under Milk Wood,'" he praised the play: "The Little Theatre gave its audience an intelligent, sophisticated, and humorous view of the Welsh people as Dylan Thomas had come to love and see them."[12]

In my second year of teaching at Muskingum, I put *A Midsummer Night's Dream* on the schedule of plays. Tryouts supplied me with more than enough student talent to cast the enchanting comedy.

My first directorial experience with Shakespeare was a delight from beginning to end. I had a perfect cast. The directorial image of each character came alive in the student actors' representations. I did not hope for perfection in speech, but the training of the voices in rendering the verse, making it a clear, sustained utterance, was a labor of love. I emphasized the action, the comedy, the mistakes of a night—the moonlit spirit of a cupid run rampant.

Barbara Kukura designed the costumes. They were inspired by the Late Gothic period (1350-1450), otherwise known as Early Renaissance or late Medieval period. They were a hybrid of the Greek loose, flowing garments and the Elizabethan tights, capes, short tunics, and high-waisted gowns.

I designed a free-flowing stage. A short Elizabethan forestage (bordered by a one foot rail) jutted into the audience. There was no inner* above or below, because I wanted swift action flowing from one area to another, and a set of stairs leading to an "above" might impede the movement. A ramp and a raised platform at the back of the stage gave a lift and variety to the staging. A blue ground cloth and blue cyclorama at the back, together with black curtains arranged in circles to simulate columns and trees, gave the feeling of outdoors. Actors carried props and furniture on and off the stage. One intermission of ten minutes assured a playing time of no more than two hours.

The success of the production was encouraging. Students realized that Shakespeare acted much easier than he read, and he was understood better through the combination of visual and aural facets of the stage. I discovered that Shakespeare was easier to direct than I thought. As Stella Adler might have said, "Don't be afraid. Shakespeare is good. He will hold you up!"

My spirits were lifted by the manner in which the students responded to Shakespeare, and by the pleasure and rapt attention exhibited by the audience. The *Black and Magenta* announced, "Shakespearean Comedy Gets Excellent Review."[13]

More than anything else, I cherish a note that President Robert N. Montgomery sent to me. Let me preface the note by saying that this man was a most unusual person. When I was a student in the 1940's, he knew every student on campus by their first name. He regarded each one of us as his personal charge. During my first year of teaching at Muskingum, I fractured my larynx in an automobile accident. I was taken to Bethesda Hospital, where I met my parents before being admitted. I was no sooner in my bed than Dr. Montgomery arrived to see how I was getting along. As busy as he was with the affairs of the college, he was never too busy to care about the welfare of each student and each member of his faculty and staff. He was an amazing person,

---

*A high platform at the back of the stage with stairs leading up to the "inner above," and the open portion under the platform, which is the "inner below." These specific areas gave the Shakespearean stage two more acting areas for the many scenes in the plays of the time.

deservedly blessed for his service to the college and the Lord. His memo to me was dated May 29, 1961.

> Dear Don:
>
> I am writing to say how much we have appreciated the good work that you have done this year and how sorry I am that I had to miss out on seeing the plays. I thought you might be interested to know that I had a very nice letter from Mr. R. J. Kukura of Cleveland, father of Barbara. He was expressing in the highest terms his appreciation for the splendid work that you have done and how fortunate he feels Muskingum is that we have you as a member of our staff. Needless to say, we share in that feeling and I want you to know that there are many who are appreciative of your splendid work.
>
> Best Wishes to you.
>
> Dr. Bob[14]

That summer, I continued my study at the Stratford, Ontario, Shakespeare Festival Seminar, sponsored by the University of Canada and the Stratford Festival. The seminar was organized similar to the Connecticut Festival, with lectures on the plays scheduled that summer–*Love's Labour's Lost, Henry VIII,* and *Coriolanus.* While there were no actor training classes to attend or rehearsals to watch, there was a tour of the theatre, a critics panel, lectures by prominent scholars, a special lecture by Michael Langham on "Directing Shakespeare," and a poetry reading by the actor Paul Schofield. Every day there was a liberal sprinkling of luncheons and teas at the Stratford Golf and Country Club.[15] The atmosphere was very casual and social, but still enlightening.

I came away from the Festival invigorated with the idea of offering two Shakespearean plays in repertory for the spring season of plays at Muskingum. If possible, I could repeat the performance of *A Midsummer Night's Dream,* and by using the same players, add a second play, a tragedy, possibly *Hamlet*. It would mean a lot of work, but it would also provide an excellent learning experience for actors and crew, and an unusual entertainment for the community.

The Cast
Midsummer Night's Dream
(William Shakespeare)

Theseus, Duke of Athens .... Tom Fox
Hippolyta, Theseus's betrothed .... Virginia Price
Philstrate, Chamberlain .... Frank Balantine
Lords and Ladies of the court: .... Robert Gebhart, Stephen Price, Christine Gibson, Miriam Caldwell
Egeus, Father to Hermia .... Jack Wilkins
Hermia, in love with Lysander .... Bonnie Mugnani
Lysander, Gentleman in love with Hermia .... Fred Jenkins
Demetrius, Gentleman in love with Hermia .... Wade Sturni
Helena, in love with Demetrius .... Janet Driggs
Peter Quince, a Carpenter .... Robert Layton
Nick Bottom, a Weaver .... Alan Dawson
Francis Flute, a Bellows-mender .... Don Kelm
Tom Snout, a Tinker .... Paul Alvarez
Snug, a Joiner .... Marion Stewart
Robin Starveling, a Tailor .... Barry Baughman

Oberon, King of the Fairies .... Bing Bills
Titania, Queen of the Fairies .... Lorraine Commeret
Puck, Oberon's Messenger .... Judy Sjoberg
Peaseblossom, Titania's Messenger .... Janice Neill
Voices of the Fairies: .... Janice Neill, Christine Gibson

1961-1962

The official 1961-62 theatre season began with my production of Maxwell Anderson's *Bad Seed*. I thought it would be a good idea, a departure from the past two seasons, to do a melodrama. I chose *Bad Seed*, not so much because it was a thriller, a real shocker, but because Maxwell Anderson had a good reputation as a playwright, and the drama had been successful on Broadway.

Anderson adapted *Bad Seed* from William March's best selling novel. Considering Anderson's usual interest in historical subjects, the content of the novel was a strange choice. At the basis of the story is the theory that the tendency to murder can be inherited. Little Rhoda Penmark, a sweet, charming girl of 10 or 12, is loved by her parents and admired by one and all for her social graces. Contrary to her amenable outward behavior, Rhoda deliberately drowns a boy classmate who won a penmanship medal that she wanted. Her mother begins to have an uneasy feeling about her daughter. She knows the family history and believes that Rhoda has inherited a bad gene. The audience witnesses a scene between Rhoda and Leroy, the naive janitor of their apartment building. When Leroy dies in a fire that has been set in his basement office, the audience knows who is responsible. The tension grows in the play as the mother begins to realize the true nature of her daughter.

Melodrama is a difficult form to act. The actors must plumb the depths of emotion and develop strong motivations, in order to make the plot of the melodrama absolutely believable. The cast never winced at the long and detailed rehearsals required to make the thesis of *Bad Seed* believable. Judy Sjoberg carried the difficult role of Rhoda Penmark; Harold Burlingame played her father, Colonel Kenneth Penmark; Lorraine Commeret portrayed the mother, Christine Penmark; Shirley Nehrenberg played a neighbor, Monica Breedlove; Donald Kelm was Emory Wages; Robert Layton was Leroy, the janitor; Carol McFarland was Miss Fern; James Davis was Reginald Tasker; Sherran Reynolds played the role of Mrs. Daigle, the murdered classmate's mother; Paul Alvarez played Mr. Daigle; and Bing Bills was Richard Bravo. The play was well-received because of the acting ability of the cast.

The first major production of the second semester was directed by Mr. Stanley Schutz, a new member of the Speech Department. Mr. Schutz's first priority was supervision of the College Radio Station, WMCO. However, at Wooster College, his previous place of employment, he had directed plays. It was my good fortune that he was amenable to direct one play a year, thereby giving me a welcome break from my duties, and supplying the students with the experience of working with another director.

Mr. Schutz chose to direct *Inherit the Wind*, by Jerome Lawrence and

Robert E. Lee. It was scheduled for March 7-10 at the Little Theatre; I served as technical director. The Lawrence and Lee collaboration produced a particularly tense drama concerning an historical incident in a small Tennessee town. A young biology teacher, John Thomas Scopes, was brought to trial in 1925 for teaching the Darwinian theory of evolution. In the end, he was nominally fined, but the incident produced some of the most exciting courtroom drama in history. Two of America's greatest speakers went head to head in the courtroom: William Jennings Bryan (a political leader who ran for President of the United States three times) was the State prosecutor and Clarence Darrow, a famous Chicago attorney, defended Scopes.

Director Schutz explains further in his "Program Notes" for the play:

> The authors of the play have stated, "*Inherit the Wind* is not history. The events which took place in Dayton, Tennessee, during the scorching July of 1925 are clearly the genesis of this play. It has . . . an exodus entirely its own . . . . Some of the characters of the play are related to the colorful figures in the battle of giants ('the Scopes Monkey Trial'); but they have a life and language of their own . . . . It is theatre. It is not 1925. The stage directions set the time as 'Not too long ago.' It might have been yesterday. It could be tomorrow."[16]

In her review of the drama for the *Black and Magenta*, Sandra O'Connell wrote,

> *Inherit the Wind* proved to be a moving drama packed with controversy, powerful dialogue, small town characters, and a problem of justice, for Cates [Scopes] had broken the law. The combination was an effective one, with a few scenes in particular highlighting the evening.[17]

Repertory company for *A Midsummer Night's Dream* and *Hamlet*, May 1962. Pictured are thirty members of a company of seventy-five who produced the plays. (left to right, first row seated on steps): L. Commeret, J. Neil, S. Reynolds, N. McQueen; second row: A. Barnum, D. Irwin, J. Driggs; third row: J. Morton, D. Loynachan, T. Hudgin; fourth row: R. Rodabaugh, J. Parmeter, E. Saviers. (standing by left rail of steps, top to bottom): W. Snyder, R. Greenwald, K. Swiss, J. Sjoberg, V. Price; (standing or sitting by right rail, top to bottom: W. Sturni, B. Bills, D. Kelm, A. Dawson. Back row (standing left to right): R. Layton, M. Redfield, P. Alvarez, C. Williams, N. Dowling, B. Baughman, R. French, F. Williams. *Theatre file photo, courtesy M.C. Public Relations Office.*

The final major production for the 1961-62 theatre season consisted of a Shakespearean Repertory which included a revival of last year's *A Midsummer Night's Dream* and a new production of *Hamlet.*

From May 7-12, *A Midsummer Night's Dream* and *Hamlet* were performed in repertory, alternating for three nights and one matinee each.

There was a large carry over in the cast of *Midsummer* from the previous year. Only six parts had to be re-cast due to graduation. Where possible, and with student consent, I tried to cast *Midsummer* actors in *Hamlet,* taking care not to overburden anyone with lines. Out of a cast of 24 in *Midsummer,* 9 did not appear in *Hamlet*; out of a cast of 35 in *Hamlet* (4 actors were cast twice), 17 did not appear in *Midsummer.*

Students who participated in both plays remarked that it was not a burden, since they had learned the parts for one play the year before. In fact, the revival of that one play alone resulted in greater learning by everyone, with reference to understanding the play as a whole, as well as in the individual parts. The playing of two different characters on successive nights was a new experience and an exciting one for the actors. They developed inner and outer techniques of characterization invaluable to an actor and they learned the historical system of repertory.* On the second time around, I was able to add some business that time had not permitted in the first production of *Midsummer;* for example, the bergomask dance of the rustics.

Students and adults in the audience–some of whom had never experienced repertory–enjoyed seeing the same actor in two different roles on successive nights.

Hamlet, 1962. Rehearsing for the duel at the end of the tragedy are W. Sturni (Laertes) and B. Bills (Hamlet). *Theatre file photo, courtesy M.C. Public Relations Office.*

*Repertory theatre is a form of production popular in the last century in both England and America, but more native to England. Repertory differs from the exigencies of the commercial theatre, which demands that a show be run for as long as it can still earn a profit. Repertory theatre usually involves a company of actors who rehears a number of plays and then perform them in nightly rotation. The system offers a number of advantages to both actor and audience. The actors get to appear in a significant number of roles in a short period of time. The plays are usually of literary value and comprise the best of dramatic literature. The audience is provided with a variety of theatrical fare and a large number of plays in a short period of time.

They also got to see two of Shakespeare's greatest plays. They came out of the experience with more appreciation for the play the second time than they had the first time. As a director, I found it most satisfying that the audience had grown with the revival of *Midsummer* as much as the actors had grown. From the learning situation presented by this type of repertory, I concluded that much is to be gained by repeating or reviving the same play over a period of time. [See note from Dr. Golden, (Departmental Chair) at the end of this section.]

The box office also found the repertory a most satisfying experience. In eight performances, these plays played to 1,161 people, which was only 146 fewer than the entire attendance for the 1959-60 season. The box office took in $936 and pulled the Little Theatre out of the red, and put it $84.42 in the black. (Tickets were only $1 for adults and 50¢ for students, with even lower rates for groups from high schools.) Up to that time, no single theatrical activity had drawn a larger audience or made more money at the box office.[18]

For his seminar, senior student Robert Layton directed Bertolt Brecht's one-act play "The Measures Taken." It was presented on Saturday, May 26 in the Little Theatre, to a full house–an appreciative audience composed of adults and students. It was a satisfying conclusion to an exciting and profitable season.

In the summer of 1962, I left for two years of study at the University of Iowa. I was also guest director at the University of Idaho Summer Theatre for the following two years.

> MUSKINGUM COLLEGE MEMORANDUM
> SUBJECT: Shakespeare Festival
> TO: Donald Hill   FROM: J. L. Golden   DATE: May 11, 1962
> Dear Don:
> Once again let me thank you for the outstanding productions which you have presented in the Little Theatre this week. In all, they are among the finest plays I have seen on a college campus. Bing Bills as Hamlet and Lorrie Commeret as Ophelia achieved distinction rarely seen on an undergraduate level. And I think it would not be an exaggeration to say that *Midsummer Night's Dream* was perhaps the best balanced college play I have seen. It is a rare treat to see every part filled by such competent performers. The success of the plays was matched by the brilliant stage designs. It was with pleasure that I heard these words last night: "Midsummer Night's Dream was even better than last year."
> I hope that when you return from Iowa that we will be able to provide you with the facilities necessary for continued excellence in drama at Muskingum.
> Jim Golden

Cast for *Inherit the Wind*
(Jerome Lawrence and Robert E. Lee)

"He that troubleth his own house
Shall inherit the wind."
Proverbs 11:29
* Indicates Guest Artists

Howard	Steve Kendall
Melinda	Lois Bohn
Rachel	Sue Hutchison
Meeker	Tom Hudgin
Bert Cates	Bill Blake
Goodfellow	Paul Schauer
Mrs. Krebs	Pat Koster
Rev. Brown	Rob Wilkinson
Sillers	Jim Mitchell
Phil	Al Tuttle
Cooper	Doug McDonald
Bollinger	Jim Peebles
Dunlap	Drew Irwin
Bannister	Mike Brandt
Mrs. Loomis	Carol Upperman
Mrs. Blair	Sue Wade
Hot Dog Man	Chuck Sproull
Mrs. McLain	Shirley Nehrenberg
E. K. Hornbeck	Fritz Williams
The Hurdy Gurdy Man	*Tony
The Monkey	*Chris
Elijah	Dave Loynachan
Mayor	Jim Measell
Matthew Harrison Brady	Harry Clark
Mrs. Brady	Virginia Price
Davenport	Dave Wright
Harry Esterbrook	Larry Humm
Henry Drummond	Joel Swabb
Judge	Al Dawson
Reuter's Man	Willard White
Dr. Keller	Chuck Welsh
Dr. Page	Dan Castello

Townspeople and Jury .... Gordon Bartells, Tom Kelley, Dan McGrath, John Morton, Tom Swinehart, Jeff Teets, Carter Williams, Carol Link, Marjorie Gabriel

Scene: .... The scene is a small town. It is summer–a summer not too long ago. The story unfolds in the town square and within the courthouse.

Director: .... Stanley Schutz
Technical Director: .... Donald Hill

Cast for *Hamlet*
(William Shakespeare)

Francisco, Officer	Carter Williams
Bernardo, Officer	Robert French
Marcellus, Officer	John Parmeter
Horatio, friend to Hamlet	Fritz Williams

The Ghost of Hamlet's Father ....Kirk Swiss
Claudius, King of Denmark
     and Hamlet's Uncle ....Donald Kelm
Hamlet's mother, Queen Gertrude ....Sherran Reynolds
Hamlet, Prince of Denmark ....Bing Bills
Polonius, Lord Chamberlain ....Drew Irwin
Laertes, son of Polonius ....Wade Sturni
Ophelia, daughter of Polonius ....Lorraine Commeret
Reynaldo, Attendant ....David Loynachan
Rosencrantz, Courtier...................................John Morton
Guildenstern, Courtier ....James Howson
Player, King ....Alan Dawson
Player, Queen ....Carolyn Aiken
Player, Lucianus ....Thomas Hudgin
Player, Prologue ....Ann Barnum
Gentleman ....Neil Dowling
Messenger ....Dan McGrath
Lord ....Roger Greenwald
Osric ....Robert Gebhart
Courtiers ....Neil Dowling, Roger Greenwald, Ronald
     Rodabaugh, Eldred Saviers
Ladies ....Susan Calhoun, Christine Gibson, Janice Neill,
     Judy Sjoberg
Soldiers and Attendants ....David Loynachan, Dan McGrath, John Newell,
     James Peebles, Mark Redfield
Scene: ....The Royal Castle Kronborg at Elsinore, Denmark
Time: ....11th Century
Director: ....Donald Hill
Designer/Technical Director: ......Donald Hill
Lighting Designer: ....Barry Baughman

Cast for *A Midsummer Night's Dream*
(William Shakespeare)

Theseus, Duke of Athens ....Fritz Williams
Hippolyta, Theseus's betrothed ....Virginia Price
Philstrate, Lord Chamberlain ....James Peebles
Lords and Ladies of the Court: ....Robert Conley, Robert Gebhart, Nancy
     McQueen, ChristineGibson
Egeus, Father to Hermia ....David Loynachan
Hermia, in love with Lysander ....Bonnie Mugnani Clemens
Lysander, Gentleman in love
     with Hermia..Fred Jenkins
Demetrius, Gentleman in love
     with Hermia..Wade Sturni
Helena, in love with Demetrius ....Janet Driggs
Peter Quince, a Carpenter ....Robert Layton
Nick Bottom, a Weaver ....Alan Dawson
Francis Flute, a Bellows-mender ....Donald Kelm
Tom Snout, a Tinker ....Paul Alvarez
Snug, a Joiner ....Kirk Swiss
Robin Starveling, a Tailor ....Barry Baughman
Oberon, King of the Fairies ....Bing Bills
Titania, Queen of the Fairies ....Lorraine Commeret
Puck, Oberon's Messenger ....Judy Sjoberg
Peaseblossom, Titania's Messenger ....Janice Neill
Voices of Fairies ....Christine Gibson, Janice Neill

```
Scene: ............................. Athens, and a wood near by
Time: ............................... 15th Century
Director: ........................... Donald Hill
Technical Director: ........... Barry Baughman
```

On Leave

The University of Iowa: 1962–1964

The first year of my special leave at the University of Iowa went better than I expected. Because I had a teaching assistantship in Rhetoric, the number of graduate courses I could take was limited to six hours each semester. Professor Arnold Gillette's course in History and Principles of Scene Design kept me busy doing a design a week, but I managed to squeeze in Professor Oscar Brockett's Seminar in Theatre History, and Professor David Schaal's course in Backgrounds of Modern Theatre Practices.

Studies came first; however, it was impossible for me to stay away from the stage. Professor David Schaal directed *The Importance of Being Earnest,* for which I tried out and I was awarded the part of Merriman, the butler at the John Worthing country estate. The comedy was scheduled for the last of October and the first week in November of 1962.

All went well until Dr. Schaal became ill. Professor Oscar Brockett, an eminent theatre scholar, replaced Dr. Schaal until he returned, and saw the production through to completion. Dr. Brockett proved to be as good a director as he was a scholar.

The Importance of Being Earnest was close to performance when I was hospitalized with "strep throat." Within a few days, I was out of danger and I convinced the doctor at the infirmary that I could still do the part. The contagious stage of the illness was over; and if I left the hospital in the evening, just thirty minutes before curtain, I could do the part and return to my bed immediately following the final curtain. Our director agreed.

Merriman was a small part, but I had worked hard on it. I employed all the techniques of acting that I had learned in New York and I wanted the chance to make them work. Opening night came; I went on stage and did my part. After the final curtain, I returned to the infirmary, as promised. The reviews were favorable; unfortunately my name was misprinted in the program and someone called "Donald Young" got credit for my work. The management caught the error and, after the first night, there was a correction slip inside each program.

In essence, the first reviewer, Walter Keller, wrote, "Mr. Smith and Mr. Young did admirable jobs. I especially enjoyed Merriman–I mean Donald Young. He was beleaguered just to the right degree."[1] Two days later Louis D. Giannetti rectified the error for the reading public when he wrote, "Mr. Donald Hill–curiously re-dubbed Donald Young in the program–illustrated what a fine actor can do with an 'unimportant' role like Merriman."[2]

It is nice to have good reviews, but I haven't changed my opinion that reviews are dangerous. For example, because I got a good review, I was self-conscious about the part and failed to do as well on the second night. The third night, I was back on track for the rest of the run.

At the end of the school year, I received the good news that Professor Gillette had accepted me as a candidate for the MFA degree in scene design. The work would take a second year of study and, during that time, I would have to design the set for a major production. It was a challenge I accepted with some trepidation, because all of my previous work had been in acting and directing. Except for the practical experience I had at Muskingum, I was relatively new to the technical and design areas. However, if Professor Gillette thought I could do it, I was willing to give it my best.

The second year (1963-64) of study at the University of Iowa was more pleasant because I had become accustomed to the surroundings; nevertheless, it was more difficult. Two of the reasons it was more pleasant were two of my former students who had graduated from Muskingum had chosen to attend Iowa. Lorraine Commeret and Bing Bills were both awarded teaching assistantships in the department, and they began working on advanced degrees in theatre. They had been scholarship students at Muskingum and they did no less than excellent work in Iowa's graduate program. I was not only glad to have such good company, but also glad to know that Iowa was (and still is) an excellent school for theatre training. Along with Carnegie Tech and Western Reserve, Iowa was another college that had been in the vanguard of those institutions farsighted enough to develop a professional program in theatre leading to the MFA degree. No less an authority than E. C. Mabie had led the way.

The second year at Iowa was more difficult than the first year because I had to complete all my graduate courses required for the MFA, fulfill my duties as a teaching assistant, design a show for the main stage, and complete the MFA thesis. As it happened, I was able to do all of the above, except complete the thesis. That particular requirement took three more summers.

Rashomon, a fascinating Japanese classic of murder and rape, was scheduled as the University Theatre's opening production for the 1963-64 season. It was based on a short story by Ryunosuke Akutagawa and dramatized by Fay and Michael Kanin. It was to be directed by Professor Larry D. Clark. I had seen the play on Broadway during the 1958-59 season with Noel Willman, Rod Steiger, and Claire Bloom.

The action of *Rashomon* takes place in Kyoto, Japan, over a thousand years ago, at a corner of the Rashomon Gate, a police court, and a nearby forest. The opening scene–the main scene of the play–is the famous Rashomon Gate in Kyoto, which was once the capital of Japan. With the decline of West Kyoto, the gate fell into disrepair " . . . and became a decayed relic with an unsavory reputation, a place which most people bypassed–if they could."[3] A Samurai Husband has been murdered while traveling through the forest with his Wife, who has been raped. An infamous Bandit is suspected, and the only witness is a local Woodcutter. Brought before a court, each of the three main characters and the Woodcutter tell different versions of the crimes. Using flashback techniques, each of the four versions are re-enacted for the audience. In the end, the play expresses a concern for the truth and Man's pride, which sometimes shapes the truth to fit the circumstances. A film on the same story by director Akira Kurosawa won an Academy Award in 1961 for Best Foreign Film.

With my study schedule, I should not have tried out, but the opportunity was too great to pass up. As it turned out, both Bing Bills and I were cast, he as a Buddhist Priest and I as the Woodcutter. I went to work on the Woodcutter in much the same way as I had for Merriman. I studied the historical background, constructed a biography of the character, identified my main action ("to avoid punishment"), and connected it

Rashomon, 1963. At the Rashomon Gate, Kyoto, Japan, the Woodcutter (D. Hill) confesses to the Priest (B. Bills). *Courtesy University of Iowa Theatre.*

to the main action of the play, which I decided was "to find the truth." I compared the above results with the production idea of the director, and applied them in rehearsal.

Externally, I did not try to look Japanese. I made up to suggest the character which was consistent with the style of the other characters in the cast. The costume, designed by the expert hand of Margaret Hall, conformed to the character, time, and place; the scenes, designed by the creative A. S. Gillette, suggested the famous Rashomon Gate and its environs, the forest, and the police court.

In acting the role of the Woodcutter, I realized that he was not a sympathetic character, nor a particularly exciting one. The excitement of the drama was supplied by the Samurai. In the Broadway production, rumor had it that Noel Willman (the Samurai), who was English classically-trained, had to fight for his life each night against Rod Steiger (the Bandit), who was American Stanislavsky-trained. At Iowa, the fight scene was well-rehearsed and controlled, and performed that way each night.

In my mind, the most dramatic scene involved the Medium calling up the Ghost of the Dead Husband to testify. This scene was close to a convention of the Japanese Noh drama, very startling and very gripping. The part of the Medium in the Broadway production originally went to Angna Enters, who would have been terrific, but she gave it to Elsa Freed.

The Iowa production of *Rashomon* received mixed reviews. The play itself was found wanting in the technique employed, when it was compared to the film by Kurosawa.

The set was "adequate," but the design should have been more realistic or stylized. The costumes were appropriate but generally "undistinguished." The lighting by David Thayer was "impeccably right." The acting was uneven and inconsistent. The Wigmaker (D.G. Buckles) gave the most sustained performance, and the Bandit (Ronald Duffy) gave the most exciting performance of the evening. The direction was "efficient," but worthy of praise for an "entertaining, if spotty, production." And so it goes: "There's no business like show business." The reviewers' judgments for this show proved to be as confusing and contradictory as the points of view of the characters in the play.

Besides finishing required courses–Hall's excellent History of Costume Design for the Stage and Thayer's thorough Theory and Practice of Stage Lighting–my second challenge for the final year at Iowa was to design scenery for a main stage production. I wanted to begin the process as soon as possible, but first I had to wait for my advisor and a director to suggest a play. I was told that *A Thurber Carnival* needed a designer. I liked the play and I was especially fond of Thurber's style and his whimsical–but trenchant–content. However, when I discovered that the play would require three turntables, I immediately expressed doubt as to whether my mechanical skills could do justice to the imagination of the director. Fortunately for me, when Professor John Terfloth announced a production of *Oedipus Rex*, my interest was immediately aroused. The design position was mine after a brief interview with both Gillette and Terfloth. I set to work researching architecture of the fifth century BC (the centuries that preceded that of the Classical period) and other world architecture contemporary with the Greek civilization. The study led me to Roman, Mycenaean, Minoan (the island of Crete) and, most surprising of all, Aztecan. The architecture of the Aztecs in central Mexico bore an uncanny similarity to that of the Greeks.

My concentration was focused on one word that Dr. Terfloth had used to describe his vision of the set: primitive. I presented him with several carefully researched sketches before I realized that what <u>he</u> meant by "primitive," and what I meant, were two totally different concepts. He wanted what I called a "classical simplicity." To me, "primitive" meant rough-hewn, heavy, rugged, and craggy. After this initial mistake, I smoothed out the lines of the set that I had designed and we were in business.

Oedipus Rex was scheduled to run from April 9 through April 18. The set was completed well before the opening and the cast had adequate rehearsal time on it. As April 9 drew closer, I developed a sense of foreboding. I realized that I was suffering from a form of stage fright known as "opening night jitters" in a way I had never before experienced. I knew how an actor and director felt on opening night, but I had no idea how to respond as a designer.

Wondering what would happen when the curtain rose and the audience saw the set, I squirmed in my seat on opening night. I was numb with anxiety. I couldn't do anything. I felt trapped! A director could give last minute instructions or words of encouragement; an actor could take instructions, re-run lines and movement in his head. However, as a designer, I could do nothing. I couldn't run backstage and change an element or color of the set. I could only sit and pray. Then the curtain rose. The audience did not laugh; they did not boo. They accepted the setting and waited for the actors to begin the play. Well, that was a relief!

During those moments before the curtain rose, I was thinking only of myself and of the reactions the audience would have to <u>my</u> set. After the curtain rose, I began to feel what I should have been feeling from the start. I remembered what Gillette had told me when I complained that some actors had damaged <u>my</u> set during a rehearsal. Quite simply he said, "It is not <u>your</u> set. It belongs to the play." That was a stern reminder that a play is a production requiring the cooperation of many people from many different areas of the theatre. My set was just one facet of a very complex art form.

In his review of the play, Edward Eriksson thought the tragedy " . . . was staged with a handsome set, attractive costumes, and intelligent lighting,."[4] Brauch Fugate of the *Iowa Defender* went into more detail:

> The curtain rose to reveal Mr. Donald Hill's stunning set–certainly one of the finest seen here in recent years. Not only was the full depth of the stage occupied by the set, it was used during the production. From the opening scene of supplication, the combination of an imposing set, eerie voice-like music, and the rhythmic movements of the chorus maintained the mood of the entire play.[5]

Oedipus Rex, 1964. (center stage) Oedipus (A. K. Gravett). Courtesy University of Iowa Theatre.

All the work and effort I had put into the set design had not been in vain. I had already felt adequately rewarded by Gillette and Terfloth when they accepted my design, and by the approval of the audience on opening night. Such kind reviews made me feel that "my cup runneth over."

After I had finished my course work at Iowa in the spring of 1964, I headed for the beautiful green hills of Moscow, Idaho, where I had signed on as guest director for the third season at University of Idaho Summer Theatre.

I would return to Iowa during the summers of '65, '66, and '67 to finish the thesis. I received the MFA in August of 1967.

REFERENCES

1. Walter Keller, "Hectic Reviewer Takes Full Responsibility," *The Daily Iowan,* Iowa City, Iowa, October 27, 1962, p.1.
2. Louis D. Giannetti, "The Importance of Being Earnest," *Iowa Defender*, Iowa City, Iowa, October 29, 1962, p. 1.
3. *Rashomon*, "Playbill," New York: Playbill Inc., Gilman Kraft, Publisher, May 18, 1959, p. 13.
4. Edward Eriksson, "Oedipus Staged Well," *The Daily Iowan*, Iowa City, Iowa, April 11, 1964, p. 2.
5. Brauch Fugate, "SUI Theatre: Oedipus Rex," *Iowa Defender*, Iowa City, Iowa, April 20, 1964, pp. 1-2.

The University of Idaho Summer Theatre
1962, 1963, 1964

*How did you like Idaho? I thought the University exciting when I played there
some years ago.*
*I was very happy to learn that you are returning to Moscow, Idaho, this summer;
take a good look at those beautiful waving wheat hills for me!*
*. . . I'm delighted about the news that you will go back to Idaho this summer, for,
as I told you, I have a special affection for that University.*
　　　—Angna Enters in letters to the author

Angna was right. The University of Idaho is absolutely beautiful in the sum
mer. Surrounded by national forests and mountains, the University at Moscow is
an island of green; situated in former Nez Perce territory, it is the home of some of the
richest farmland in the country. There are clear running trout streams, scenic drives,
and camping, picnic grounds, and water sports at famous Lake Cour d'Alene, just a
short drive north. It is as perfect a vacation spot in the summer as Sun Valley in the
south is during the winter.

Knowing that I had a free summer ahead of me before I began work on the
master's at Iowa, I applied for a position in the University of Idaho's summer theatre.
I never regretted wiring my acceptance of the offer which came via telegram from
Boyd A. Martin, Dean of the College of Letters and Science: "President Theophilus
has approved your appointment as visiting Instructor in Dramatics and Associate Director of the Summer Theatre at the University of Idaho for this coming summer
school . . . Please wire me acceptance and consider the matter closed."

Theatre at the University of Idaho developed in the English Department, unlike
Muskingum, where theatre was always joined to classical rhetoric and debate. One of
the most prominent theatrical events came in 1899, when President Blanton sponsored a tour to Boise of *The Rivals* and *She Stoops to Conquer*, directed by Miss
Aurelia Henry. In 1919, John H. Cushman organized the first major in dramatics, and
in 1934, Jean Collette became Instructor of Dramatics and English.[1]

Miss Collette received both her bachelor's and master's from the University
and, under her influence, the department grew in popularity and enrollment. In 1954,
Miss Collette, Chairwoman of Dramatics, and Edmund M. Chavez, Technical Director (who received his MFA from the University of Texas) organized a summer theatre.
The purpose of the enterprise was " . . . to create interest in the theatre, in the University, and community."[2] Summer theatre at the University was a model of organization
and efficiency.

From its inception, the Summer Theatre operated during the first seven weeks of the regular eight-week summer session. Five plays were presented during the last five weeks of the session, one each week for a three-night run. Try-outs for the first two shows were held on the opening day of summer school. These two shows went immediately into rehearsal, and the first show opened on the Tuesday night of the third week. Succeeding shows were cast each weekend, which allowed for a little more than two weeks' rehearsal for each play.[3]

The staff for the theatre consisted of three members. Miss Collette managed the administrative duties and directed the first and fourth plays. Edmund Chavez, the Technical Director, was responsible for technical details for each of the five shows, and he directed the third show. A visiting director was in charge of publicity, and he directed the second and fifth shows.[4]

Casts and crews for the five productions came from regularly-enrolled students and members of the community. There were two courses offered for credit: Drama 25, "Summer Theatre," carried one to four credits and was open to lower division students; Drama 125, "Summer Theatre" carried one to eight credits and was open to upper division and graduate students.[5]

The University of Idaho Summer Theatre Company, 1962. (sitting, left to right) N. Harbour, M. Bowlby; First Row (standing): S. Hui, J. Basque, C. Tovey, G. Goodenough, T. Huff, C. Kellog; Second Row: B. Poape, T. Oleson, G. Lewis, J. Wallace, A. Cummings, D. Davidson, L. Prasher, B. Scott, A. Arrien, H. Hosack, G. Farnam; Third Row: J. Merrick, C. Hosack, R. Greening, D. Gardner, K. Gupta, M. Kienzle, D. Bowman, R. Bowman, A. Tozier, and directors Edmund Chavez, Jean Collette, and Donald Hill. *Courtesy University of Idaho Summer Theatre.*

Since there were no regularly scheduled classes, rehearsals were set from 8:00-12:00 in the morning and 1:00-5:00 in the afternoon. If a third play was in rehearsal, there was a 6:30-9:30 evening time available. Weekends were included in the rehearsal period. Dates for the season of plays usually began the final two weeks of June and ended the first week of August.[6]

The theatre designed by Edmund Chavez was completely portable because it had to be set up each summer in the field house and dismantled after each season. It consisted of a series of platforms bolted together to form a 16 x 22-foot rectangle, covered with canvas. Above the stage, the spots for lighting hung from a false ceiling made of pipe and canvas. The stage was surrounded on all sides by risers which held folding chairs for the audience. The theatre could seat as many as 350–later it was enlarged to accommodate 400 people. Both auditorium and stage were walled-in by strips of colored burlap hung from wooden frames.[7]

Other important elements of this theatre were a light booth with a portable control board, a tent-like structure divided in half to serve as dressing areas for cast members, an area for furniture and properties, and a refreshment stand and ticket booth.*[8] Mr. Chavez reported that it took seven days for a crew of six to set up the theatre and make it ready for the coming season. At the end of the season, it took the entire company of players three hours to pack it up and prepare it for storage.[9]

Every member of the production staff received a manual of responsibilities and duties, as a matter of orientation for the work that lay ahead. The manual contained job descriptions of the director, technical director, assistant to the director, and stage manager. An important part of the manual included guidelines for actors during the rehearsal and performance periods. Crew assignments were given in detail for the stage crew, light crew, property crew, costume crew, sound crew, make-up crew, publicity crew, and ushers. Special instructions for the final strike and the operation of the Curtain Booth were also part of the manual.[10] The Curtain Club was a dramatics honorary which supplied scholarships for those members of the company who did the most to make the season a success.[11]

As head of publicity, it was my duty to establish a calendar for the distribution of posters, café cards,** and newspaper articles. I also had to arrange for the times when pictures of the cast or crew of each production were to be taken. Finally, I had to provide the summer supplement of the *Daily Idahoan* with stories about the theatre and emphasize the productions scheduled for that particular summer.[12]

The following plays were scheduled for Summer Theatre '62: *Three Men on a Horse,* written by George Abbott and John C. Holm, and directed by Jean Collette; *Laura*, written by Vera Caspary and George Sklar, and directed by myself; *Beyond the Horizon*, written by Eugene O'Neill, and directed by Edmund Chavez; *Blithe Spirit,* written by Noel Coward, and directed by Jean Collette, and *The Man Who Came to Dinner,* written by George Kaufman and Moss Hart, and directed by myself.

It was a varied bill of tried-and-true plays that promised an enjoyable experience for the cast, crew, and audience. *Three Men on a Horse* was on the honor list of long runs on Broadway. *Laura* is an extremely well-written and original mystery thriller that achieved fame first as a novel, then as a film, and finally as a play. *Beyond the Horizon* won a Pulitzer Prize for O'Neill. It had a special appeal to western audiences because the West was that section of the country offering refuge and a

---

*Tickets cost 75-cents per show or $3 for the season. In '64 they were increased to $1.00 per show.

**Café cards were small 4"x6" white cards on which were printed the title of the play, author, date of performance, curtain time and admission price, together with interesting bits of information about the play. Folded in half, these cards were distributed to all the restaurants in Moscow and to appropriate places on campus where they could be placed on tables.

The Man Who Came to Dinner, 1962. Broadway critic, Sheridan Whiteside (T. Oleson) and movie star, Lorraine Sheldon (A. Cummings) plot the break-up of a love affair between his secretary and a local newspaper editor. A visiting celebrity, Banjo (G. Goodenough, at stage center) enjoys the intrigue. *Photo courtesy University of Idaho Summer Theatre.*

new beginning for those determined to succeed. *Blithe Spirit* is a fantasy farce that complicates the life of a man faced with the mischievous ghosts of his two dead wives. *The Man Who Came to Dinner* is a verbal fun-fest about a New York critic who attracts a variety of famous eccentrics when he is forced to spend time in a Marion, Ohio, household while his broken hip heals.

Three Men on a Horse and *The Man Who Came to Dinner* drew record audiences of over a thousand, which meant packed houses for all three nights of each play's run.

The success of my first season at Idaho was a tribute to the astute organization of the theatre itself, the skillful direction of Jean Collette, and the efficiency of the technical director, Edmund Chavez. They both commanded the respect of students, and attracted loyal alumni and members of the community who wished to participate in the enjoyment of quality plays well presented.

Summer Theatre '63 was equally successful. Again, the selection of shows attracted students and drew interested audiences. *The Great Big Doorstep*, written by Frances Goodrich and Albert Hackett, and directed by Jean Collette, proved a sure-fire hit with its heart-warming story of a Cajun family striving for a better life. Emlyn Williams's thriller, *Night Must Fall,* directed by me, tweaked the natural curiosity that audiences have for the psychopathic killer.

Ladies of the Jury, written by Fred Ballard and directed by Edmund Chavez, was a complete departure from the preceding shows, because of its ingenious display of the complications that ensue when women are solicited for jury duty. Another departure from the usual was *A Member of the Wedding*, written by Carson McCullers and directed by Jean Collette. This award-winning play astounded Broadway in 1950 and

The Matchmaker, 1963. Act I. Horace Vandergelder (M. Alexander) tells his housekeeper, Gertrude (A. Risetter), his Barber (R. Greening), and his niece's fiancée, Ambrose Kemper (C. Tovey) how the world turns and how he is going to help turn it. *Courtesy University of Idaho Summer Theatre.*

captured the hearts of every audience because of the universal quality of its theme: the desire to belong to something that is larger than the smallness of our everyday lives.

The Matchmaker, written by Thornton Wilder and directed by me, was as different as any play on the bill of fare could be. Who would have thought that a widow's prayer for a husband, a miser's search for a wife, and two innocent hardware clerks' desire for adventure would collide and erupt into the fireworks of a carefree farce. *The Daily Idahoan* reported, "Matchmaker Has Audience in Grip," and the Spokane *Spokesman Review* announced, "Top-Rate 'Matchmaker' Pulls Moscow Crowds."[13]

Ladies of the Jury and *The Matchmaker* both ran over the thousand mark in audience attendance.

In Summer Theatre '64, Jean Collette was on leave, and Edmund Chavez directed Philip King's *Pool's Paradise* and *A Majority of One,* written by Leonard Spigelgass, as the first and fourth plays of the season. Edgar Vandevort directed Noel Coward's *Hay Fever* for the third play, and I directed *The Corn is Green,* written by Emlyn Williams, and Moliére's *The Doctor In Spite of Himself* as the second and fifth plays.

Again, the season was very successful. Audiences had fun with the farce of *Pool's Paradise,* and empathized with the triumph of Miss Moffat's educational zeal in *The Corn is Green.* The literate comedy/farce of *Hay Fever* received much deserved praise, while *A Majority of One* captured a sympathetic response for the friendship between Jewish and Japanese cultures. Moliére still got credit for writing a masterful farce, *The Doctor In Spite of Himself,* even though I disguised it with a western setting and costumes. The actors played the slapstick to the hilt. The management, realizing how much an active farce would please the younger generation, arranged a special matinee for the "young fry."[14]

A Doctor in Spite of Himself, 1964. In a Western setting, Samuel, an unlucky woodcutter (A. Tozier) is being beaten so that he can become a Doctor. Ranch Hands, Val (R. Beamer) and Luke (R. Rohrbacher) gladly apply absolution. *Courtesy University of Idaho Summer Theatre.*

It is important that I note here those factors which I believe made the University of Idaho Summer Theatre such a success. I have already mentioned the fine organization and efficiency with which it was managed. In large part, that management was in the hands of Jean Collette and Edmund M. Chavez, who founded it, and whose knowledge of theatre, enthusiasm for quality literature and plays, and good common sense remained the force behind it. In their own direction of plays, they provided excellent examples of how theatre works and how it supplies good entertainment for all.

However, there is another factor in this mix which also deserves recognition: the actors. The actors themselves seemed to understand and agree with management in every respect, from the youngest and least experienced to the oldest and most experienced. Many of the company were teachers or graduate students. They supplied a maturity and unerring sense of good theatre which provided leadership to all the others.

I wrote the following as a tribute to my actors in *The Matchmaker* and *The Doctor In Spite of Himself*, but it could be applied to every person who was in the company during the three summers I served as visiting director.

> The entire cast and crew deserved all the praise which the critics heaped upon them for their performances. They proved true to the concept of the play; and with good high spirits and a keen sense of timing delivered stellar performances. It was a delight to watch them every night of the run.

The three seasons I spent with the University of Idaho Summer Theatre taught me much about directing in general, and about directing in the arena in particular. I would put that knowledge to good use in the decades to come at Muskingum. Knowing that my next three summers would be engaged at the University of Iowa, where I hoped to earn my degree, I found it difficult to leave Idaho that summer in 1964. I also had to prepare for the next level of education which was to begin in the summer of 1968: the doctorate at the University of Minnesota.

In the meantime, it was already fall and I had to rush across the country to resume my duties as Director of Theatre at Muskingum College, where there were classes to teach and another season of plays to present.

In my absence, Rex McGraw and Stanley Schutz had had two very good seasons of plays. Rex, who had his Ph.D. by then from the University of Indiana, moved to Ohio University, which had an excellent theatre program leading to an MFA in theatre. He had great success there with a production of Pinter's *The Birthday Party,* which won entry to the American College Theatre Festival and was performed at the Kennedy Center in Washington, D.C. Sue Cook (Muskingum's dance instructor who often helped with theatrical productions) and I took some students with us and drove to Washington to see the performance and to give our added support to his already successful production.

Over the years, I heard various reports of his activities. After leaving Ohio University, Dr. McGraw taught at the University of Nebraska and, from Nebraska, he moved to Ohio State University, where he was head of the Directing Program. Recently, he retired from OSU ('98). He wrote to me that he was going to remain active in theatre as an actor. In fact, he had already signed for summer theatre engagements.

Dr McGraw was very fond of Muskingum and the friends which he had made there. Our librarian, Robin Hanson, informed me that she had met him at Ohio State and he had told her he wanted to leave his theatre library to the college. On one of my visits to the library, I saw the stacks of books which had arrived at Rex's request.

REFERENCES

1   Jean Collette, "University Drama History Dates Way Back to 1899," *Playtime*, Supplement to the *Daily Idahoan,* Moscow, Friday, June 21, 1963, p. 6.

2   "Summer Theatre Begins Its Ninth Season on U. Campus," *University of Idaho Summer Theatre 1962,* Supplement to the *Daily Idahoan,* Moscow, Tuesday, July 3, 1962, p. 2.

3   Mimeographed Information Sheet, Department of Dramatics, University of Idaho, Summer, 1962.

4   Ibid.

5.   Ibid.

6   "Summer Theatre Rehearsal Schedule," Department of Dramatics, University of Idaho, Summer, 1962.

7.   "Arena Theater for Summer Use Unique Undertaking," *University of Idaho Summer Theatre 1962,* Supplement to the *Daily Idahoan,* Moscow, Tuesday, July 2, 1962, p. 2.

8.   Ibid.

9.   Ibid.

10   "Summer Theatre Production Staff Manual of Responsibilities and Duties," Department of Dramatics, University of Idaho. n.d.

11   "Scholarships Are an Aid," *University of Idaho Summer Theatre 1962,* Supplement to the *Daily Idahoan,* Moscow, Tuesday, July 2, 1962, p.2.

12   "Summer Theatre Production Staff Manual of Responsibilities and Duties," Department of Dramatics, University of Idaho, n.d.

13   Ed Costello, "Drama Review: Top-Rate Matchmaker Pulls Moscow Crowds," *The Spokesman-Review,* Spokane, Washington, Thursday, August 1, 1963. Portions of the review are quoted below:

> . . . visiting faculty member Donald Hill (on leave from Muskingum College, Ohio, to work on his master's at the State University of Iowa and doing his second summer play in as many years at Moscow) is directing what must be one of the funniest American plays ever written .
> . . . Hill has his characters spring to life from a tableau at the beginning of each act and the effect is to catapult the action at the audience every time, for each act is a riot. The farcical

aspect of the vehicle is given further impact by having the characterizations over-exaggerated slightly. This must be finely done or the effect is lost and for the most part Hill's cast copes well with this additional challenge.

. . . This is quality theater from every point of view.

14   Ed Costello, "Idaho Drama Students Play Moliére to the Hilt," *The Spokesman-Review*, Spokane, Washington, Thursday, August 6, 1964. Mr. Costello reported:

The play [*The Doctor In Spite of Himself*] is Moliére at his best, but the adaptation is flavored with the West and the action, being timeless, is in the present. The production as directed by Donald Hill, visiting theater specialist from the University of Iowa (on the Moscow campus for his third consecutive summer) is a unique and delightful blending of the popular theatrical idioms of two different ages.

. . . The adaptation heightens the humor, if anything.

Hill is an excellent craftsman and has his actors affix to their characterizations an overlay of choreographed rhythm, almost, that creates a nice climate for the gentle exaggerations this type of theater calls for.

. . . The most skeletal of sets is employed and the absurdities of the action spill over, when, to musical accompaniment, a strange trio of [clowns] stagehands (some of which show up in the action and one is the director) engage in some useful pantomime that is as entertaining as the play itself.

The Plays: 1962–1965

1962-1963

Stanley Schutz started a tradition when he produced the James Thurber and Elliot Nugent comedy, *The Male Animal,* during Homecoming Week, October 24-27, 1962. Mr. Schutz gives important details concerning the comedy in his "Program Notes."

The Male Animal first appeared in the Cort Theatre on January 9, 1940, and remained for a successful Broadway run. Co-author Nugent played the original role of Tommy Turner.

Thurber and Nugent need no introduction to Ohioans. Born in Columbus and Dover respectively, both attended public schools and graduated from Ohio State University.[19]

Particularly appropriate for its Muskingum premiere, the play is set at a midwestern university during homecoming week, when the home team plays the University of Michigan. Mixed with the typical excitement of the big game are political "red scare" tactics involving the Sacco-Vanzetti case,* questions of academic freedom, and marital jealousies when one of Ellen's (Tommy's wife) old flames arrives for the festivities.

Schutz continues:

The Male Animal represents their best efforts as playwrights and has become a classic of its type. The plea for academic tolerance and independence of thought, the follies of Kellers and Fergusons, the seasonal insanity of the Homecoming football weekend, are as visible today as they were in 1940.[20]

The second major production of the season was directed by Rex McGraw, December 12-15. He chose Archibald MacLeish's retelling of the *Book of Job,* which MacLeish called *J. B.* According to the author, the play concerns two unemployed

*Late in 1919, two payroll messengers in Massachusetts were held up and shot. Two foreign-born laborers, Sacco and Vanzetti, were executed for the crime eight years later.

actors, Mr. Zuss and Mr. Nickles, who are down on their luck. They have been forced to join an ancient circus and travel through all the towns of the earth playing, year after year, the Old Testament story of the sufferings of Job. Finally, the two decide to play it for themselves the way in which they think it should be played. Mr. Zuss casts himself as God and Nickles is cast as Satan. They also take on the wager of the *Book of Job*: Satan's bet that, if God strips Job of everything he has, Job will curse God to His face.[21]

The two actors no sooner begin than the story from the Bible takes over and when Job is due to appear, he comes as a modern American J. B., not Job. The disasters that occur are not the old ones of the Bible, but present ones. At the end of the play, the courage of J. B. and his wife, as in the *Book of Job,* are the center of attention.[22]

In his review of the production, Alan Dawson praised the directing and acting as exemplary.[23]

On March 13-16, Rex McGraw directed Lillian Hellman's *The Little Foxes.* The set design was based on models which Becky Hatcher, Janet Small, and Judy Branzhaf submitted as a special project for Stagecraft. All crews for the production were composed entirely of women.

Mr. McGraw provided the following information concerning the playwright and play in his "Program Notes."

> As a playwright, Lillian Hellman has often been compared to Ibsen in the tight structure and the "well-made" components of her plays.
> *The Little Foxes* is considered the strongest and most closely knit of Miss Hellman's plays. Its obvious virtues of compactness and firmly drawn characterizations are supported by its crackling style.[24]

Judy Sjoberg praised the production in her review, "'The Little Foxes' in Retrospect," which appeared in the *Black and Magenta.*[25]

Shakespeare's *Twelfth Night* or *What You Will* concluded a well-received season of plays. The comedy played four nights (May 8-11) and two matinees (May 10-11) at the Little Theatre. Rex McGraw directed the performances and Donald Kelm designed the setting, while Sherran Reynolds designed the costumes.

The story begins with a shipwreck off the coast of Illyria, during which twins, Viola and Sebastian, are separated. For safety reasons, Viola disguises herself as a boy (Cesario) and finds employment in the service of Duke Orsino. Viola falls in love with Orsino, who is in love with Olivia. Olivia is in mourning for the death of her brother and, encouraged by her Steward, Malvolio, has ordered the entire household to mourn with her. When Orsino sends Cesario to plead his love for Olivia, she refuses, but is taken by the disguised figure of Viola. Meanwhile, Sebastian is not dead, as Viola has supposed, and when he arrives at the court of Olivia, she mistakes him for his disguised sister and immediately orders a priest. The plot complications are easily solved when the twins meet. Orsino marries Viola and Olivia marries Sebastian.

The subplot involves servants in Olivia's household who wish to remove the pompous Malvolio from favor. Maria, Sir Toby Belch, and Sir Andrew Aguecheek achieve their purpose while engaging in some of the best low comedy in all of

Shakespeare.[26]

A favorable review of the production titled, "'Twelfth Night' Revisited," appeared in the *Black and Magenta*.[27]

Cast for *The Male Animal*
(James Thurber & Elliot Nugent)

Maggie	Miffie Fox
Ellen Turner	Susan Wade
Tommy Turner	Robert French
Patricia Stanley	Marilyn McDonald
Dean Damon	Alan Dawson
Michael Barnes	Joel Bixler
Wally Myers	Mike Naas
Mrs. Blanch Damon	Darlene Martin
Joe Ferguson	Mike Brandt
Ed Keller	Frank Ballantine
Myrtle Keller	Susie Young
Nutsy Miller	Robert Wickens
Reporter	Dale Stansbury
Scene:	The home of Professor Thomas Turner, in a Midwestern university town.
Director:	Stanley Schutz
Technical Director:	Rex McGraw

The Cast of *J. B.*
(Archibald MacLeish)

First Maid	Judy Moore
Second Maid	Ann Barnum
First Roustabout	Robert Shinn
Second Roustabout	Michael Naas
Nickles	Bing Bills
Mr. Zuss	Don Kelm
A Distant Voice	Frank Ballantine
J. B.	Wade Sturni
Sarah	Lorraine Commeret
David	Glenn Morckel
Mary	Sue Conine
Ruth	Nancy Wheeley
Jonathan	David Bechlen
Rebecca	Holly Schutz
An Older Woman	Sally McCracken
A Younger Woman	Jan Neill
The Girl	Carol Link
Miss Mabel	Claudia Blumenstock
Mrs. Botticelli	Pat Koster
Mrs. Lesure	Judy Sjoberg
Jolly	Cherie Barcalow
Mrs. Adams	Marilyn McDonald
Mrs. Murphy	Sandy Wilkins
Bildad	Barry Spigener
Eliphaz	Beth Robinson
Zophar	Joe Destein

Scene: .... A traveling circus which has been on the roads of the world for a long time.
Director: .... Rex McGraw
Lighting Designer: .... Barry Baughman

The Cast of *The Little Foxes*
(Lillian Hellman)

Addie .... Ellen Gary
Cal .... Bob McCausland
Birdie Hubbard .... Beth Robinson
Oscar Hubbard .... Frank Ballantine
Leo Hubbard .... Barry Spigener
Regina Giddens .... Sherran Reynolds
William Marshall .... Neil Dowling
Benjamin Hubbard .... Donald Kelm
Alexandra Giddens .... Sara Sprowls
Horace Giddens .... Richard Houghton
Scene: .... The living room of the Giddens house, in a small town in the South
Time: .... Spring, 1900
Director: .... Rex McGraw

The Cast for *Twelfth Night*
(William Shakespeare)

Orsino .... Joe Destein
Sir Toby .... Donald Kelm
Sir Andrew .... Jerry Goodman
Curio .... Anthony Barta
Sebastian .... Douglas McDonald
Antonio .... John Ross
Malvolio .... Mike Brandt
Fabian .... Barry Baughman
Feste .... Bing Bills
Sea Captain .... Ross Marouchoc
Priest .... Alan Dawson
1st Officer .... Dave Loynachan
2nd Officer .... Carl Gottschalk

	May 8 and 10	May 9 and 11
Olivia	Ann Barnum	Sally McCracken
Viola	Marilyn McDonald	Lois Norman
Valentina	Ellen Gary	Carol Springer
Maria	Elinor Hubert	Susie Young
Ladies in Waiting		Nancy Moore, Ronnie Reed, Carol Rogers, Sue Russell

Musicians:
Recorders .... Priscilla Cook, Ann Hess, Mary Larkin
Viola .... Judy Banzhaf
Flute .... Anthony Barta
Triangle .... Carol Rogers
Tambourine .... Beth Robinson
Trumpeters .... Dave Loynachan, Eldred Saviers
Director: .... Rex McGraw
Setting: .... Donald Kelm
Costumes: .... Sherran Reynolds
Lighting Designer: .... Eldred Saviers

1963-1964

For Homecoming Week in October, Rex McGraw presented *The Fantasticks,* "A Parable of Love," with book and lyrics by Tom Jones and music by Harvey Schmidt. Amy Sanders did the choreography; Barry Baughman designed the lighting; Alan Dawson and Ross Marouchoc supplied the music on pianos; Chip Baxter was on drums with Carolyn Clark; and Caroline McBane turned pages.[28]

The Muskingum College "Outlook" announced the play:

> Now in its fourth year Off-Broadway, this play with music utilizes a small cast and a plain wooden platform to create its own world of romance. Quite simply, it is the story of two parents who try to marry off their progeny. Aided by a bandit, two old actors and two mutes, this delicate spoof blends satire with sensation and bright comedy with serious verse.[29]

The cast for the production gave a special preview performance on October 15 and altered the usual 8:15 p.m. curtain time to 9:00 p.m. to perform for the Homecoming audience on Friday, October 18. According to the review in the *Black and Magenta,* "'Fantasticks' in Retrospect," it was a show worth seeing at any time.[30]

On December 11-14, Stanley Schutz directed Arthur Miller's adaptation of *An Enemy of the People,* by Henrik Ibsen.* The setting for the drama was designed by senior speech major, Barry Baughman. The "Outlook" encapsulated the plot: "The new municipal baths are almost ready for tourist trade when young Dr. Stockmann discovers impurities in the water. Ensuing struggles approach mob violence as a town tries to suppress the truth."[31]

The first major production of the second semester was the production of two *Antigone's* presented by Rex McGraw, March 10-14. According to the Muskingum College "Outlook,"

> College theatre is the place to experiment, so the critics say. We are willing to try by performing two *Antigones* in a single evening. Part I will be a presentation of Sophocles' *Antigone*, followed by a staging of Anouilh's modern French adaptation of the Greek legend.[32]

David Jamison chronicled the event of the two *Antigones*** in "Sophocles and

---

* Ibsen's contribution to the theatre is possibly still not fully realized. He is often credited as "the father of modern drama," one of the theatre's first social reformers, the innovator of the thesis play, the founder of modern realism and the greatest playwright since Shakespeare. Among his best known plays are *Hedda Gabler, A Doll's House, The Wild Duck*, and *Ghosts*. The violent public reaction to *Ghosts* (1881), a bleakly realistic shocker about heredity and venereal disease, provoked Ibsen to strike back with *An Enemy of the People* the following year. His attack on the "compact majority" and on individual compromise to society has relevance today. Critic Gassner says no one in the theatre had "struck society so flatly in the face before."

** Of the three great tragedies in the Theban Cycle which Sophocles devoted to Oedipus and his family, *Antigone*, produced in 441 B.C., was the first to be written. Chronologically, however, the play concludes the saga of the Theban dynasty. Although the three plays involve the same legend, they were not conceived with a single purpose, as in the case of Aeschylus' *Oresteia*. Hegel considered *Antigone* to be the ideal example of Greek tragedy, probably because there is a maximum display of ethical tension. Both Creon and Antigone are right in the sense that ethical loyalties are valid. Both characters are wrong in assuming that ethical principle exerts an absolute claim on loyalty. Nevertheless, the reconciliation, as envisaged by Hegel, occurs in the mind of the spectator, not necessarily in the mind of each character. Each age and each country has had its own Antigone. Anouilh's treatment of the Greek legend was written in 1943 in Paris under the stress and indignity of the German occupation. After the first production, Antigone began to Symbolize France herself—a France rejecting the German New Order with its promise of prosperity of happiness, provided the French people would agree to surrender spiritual independence. Yet *Antigone* is not just a French play nor a Greek one. An American analogy could easily be found if the play were about Jefferson Davis and the sister of a Yankee spy. The pertinence of the law of the individual conscience and the central power of the state is a universal question.

Anouilh Plays Show Dramatic Contrast," which appeared in the *Black and Magenta*.[33]

The Muskingum College "Outlook" announced the following production of *The Merry Wives of Windsor* for May 6-9.

> To celebrate the 400th anniversary of the world's greatest playwright, the last play of the season will be a production of Shakespeare's single low comedy. At the focal point of the merriment, Sir John Falstaff becomes the dupe of the merry wives and angry husbands of Windsor. Set in sixteenth century England, it is a play of social intrigue and marital jealousy of middle-class life.[34]

To the original schedule, an extra evening performance was added on May 5, and a matinee on May 8. Rex McGraw directed the comedy, Sally McCracken designed the scenery, and Judy Moore designed the costumes.*

The Merry Wives of Windsor, 1964. Mistress Quickly (E. Huber) and Falstaff (W. McCloskey). *Theatre file photo courtesy M.C. Public Relations Office.*

In its review of *The Merry Wives of Windsor,* "McGraw Scores Another Hit," the *Black and Magenta* sounded the keynote of what had been an excellent series of successes.[35]

At the end of this, his last year of a two-year appointment as Director of the Muskingum College Theatre, Rex McGraw bid a fond farewell to the Muskingum College audiences on the last page of the program for *The Merry Wives of Windsor:*

Merci et adieu . . . Rex McGraw

---

*The Merry Wives of Windsor, both in date and subject, forms a link between the history plays and the so-called "joyous comedies" of Shakespeare's second period. According to Leslie Hotson, the play was first performed on April 23, 1597. Unlike other poetical and romantic Shakespearean comedies, this farce of social intrigue and marital jealousy was apparently written for the gratification and the unsentimental tastes of courtly aristocrats who enjoyed a realistic picture of middle-class life. Some critics say Queen Elizabeth commanded Shakespeare to write another play about Falstaff. In any case, there is an irresistible gaiety about the play that has made it a success on the stage for 367 years.

Cast for *The Fantasticks*
(Tom Jones and Harvey Schmidt)

The Mutes .... Beth Robinson, Barry Spigener
The Narrator .... John Ross
The Girl .... Carol Link
The Boy .... Bob Holcomb
The Boy's Mother .... Suzanne Aultz
The Girl's Mother .... Suzie Young
The Old Actor .... Mike Naas
The Man Who Dies .... Jerry Goodman
At the Pianos .... Alan Dawson, Ross Marouchoc
At the Drums .... Chip Baxter
Those Who Turn Pages .... Carolyn Clark, Caroline McBane

"*The Fantasticks* is based upon *Les Romanesques* by Edmond Rostand, who suggests that 'the action takes place where one pleases, provided the costumes are pretty enough.'" (Original Program)

Director: .... Rex McGraw
Choreographer: .... Amy Sanders

Cast for *An Enemy of the People*
(Henrik Ibsen)
(Adapted for the American Stage by Arthur Miller)

Morten Kiil .... Bob Kinnard
Billing .... Walt Young
Catherine Stockmann .... Jean Moyer
Peter Stockmann .... Al Dawson
Hovstad .... Mark Wise
Dr. Stockmann .... Rich Houghton
Morten .... Richard Duncan
Ejlif... David Schutz
Captain Horster .... Slade Ballantyne
Petra .... Carol Moorhead
Aslaksen .... Jay Harris
The Drunk .... Dave Teufel
Nansen... Bill Stedeford
Edvard .... Will White
Henrik .... John Waltman
George .... Roy Stewart
Hedvig .... Elinor Hubert
Gunnar... Gary Mayes
Paul.. David Loynachan
Knut... Bob McCausland
Tora .... Janie Jenkins
Finn .... Susan Dalva
Scenes: .... Dr. Stockmann's living room, Editorial office of the *People's Daily Messenger*, Captain Horster's house

Director: .... Stanley Schutz
Scene Design: .... Barry Baughman
Technical Director: .... Ellen Gary

Cast for *Antigone*
(Sophocles)

Antigone .... Sally McCracken
Ismene .... Suzanne Laurent
Chorus of Theban Elders: Barbara Drake, Carol Boyer, Elinor Hubert, Carol Moorhead, Mary Jo Thomas, Susan Rau, Sandy Wilkins, Darlene Martin, Audrey Mowitt, Suzy Fontaine, Ann Brown, Pam Staats, Linda Redman, Olinda Gonzalez, Elaine Savage

Creon .... Malcolm Rothman
A Guard .... Bob Childs
Haemon .... Barry Spigener
Teiresias .... Larry Bryan
A Boy .... Cathy Lindsay
A Messenger .... Judy Jacob
Eurydice .... Joyce Conklin
First Maiden .... Connie Gaeth
Second Maiden .... Jean Moyer
Second Guard .... Ray Van Stone
Director: .... Rex McGraw
Costume Design: .... Judy Moore

Cast for *Antigone*
(Jean Anouilh)

Chorus .... Judy Sjoberg
Antigone .... Beth Robinson
Nurse .... Laraine Gagliano
Ismene .... Gracie Hutchman
Haemon .... Heath Simpson
Creon .... Raymond Swope
Page .... Judy Banzhaf
First Guard .... Jerry Goodman
Second Guard .... Gary Mayes
Third Guard .... Doug Shamp
Messenger .... Janet Small
Eurydice .... Judy Dixon
Director: .... Rex McGraw

Cast for *The Merry Wives of Windsor*
(William Shakespeare)

Sir John Falstaff .... Bill McCloskey
Fenton .... Rick Holcomb
Shallow .... Bob Kinnard
Slender .... Jerry McDonald
Ford .... Mike Naas
Page .... Fritz Enstrom
Sir Hugh Evans .... Mark Wise
Doctor Caius .... Rich Telford
Host of the Garter Inn .... Bob Quillen
Bardolph .... Paul Hudson
Pistol .... Clifford Haines
Nym .... Melvin Forbes
Robin .... Suzy Fontaine
Simple .... Beth Bricker
Rugby .... Peg Heimbrook
Mistress Ford .... Laraine Gagliano
Mistress Page .... Nancy Peterson
Anne Page .... Sara Sprowls
Mistress Quickly .... Elinor Hubert
John .... Mike Grunau
Robert .... Lloyd Billman
Director: .... Rex McGraw
Scene Design: .... Sally McCracken
Costume Design: .... Judy Moore

1964-1965

George Bernard Shaw's *Androcles and the Lion* opened the 1964-65 theatre season and provided entertainment for Homecoming Week. Stanley Schutz directed and designed the set, and I supervised the technical production. One unusual technical aspect of the production was the crowd noise from the Roman Coliseum. The requisite sound effects were supplied when WMCO engineers, assisted by Varsity Cheerleaders, recorded the crowd at the Muskingum-Marietta football game.

As for *Androcles and the Lion,* the Roman author Aulus Gellius tells the tale of a Roman slave, Androcles, who lived in the first century, and who removed a thorn from a lion's paw. Later, when Androcles is thrown to the lions in the arena, the lion recognizes him and saves his life.[36] Shaw* seized upon the fable as the basis for his version of *Androcles and the Lion.* The usual Shavian persiflage reveals the silliness of Rome in opposing Christianity. According to Shaw, when Androcles and the lion meet in the arena, the lion licks Androcles' face. Caesar regards this as a miracle and declares all of Rome to be Christian.

The show was a sure-fire hit with the Homecoming audience.[37] I especially enjoyed the scene in which the lion chased Caesar from his private box in the Coliseum!

On my return to Muskingum after a two-year absence, I chose *The Importance of Being Earnest,* by Oscar Wilde, for my first directing assignment, which was scheduled for December 9-12. I was familiar with the play; I felt safe with it; and I thought it would be easy to cast because it required only nine actors to perform.

In spite of some "doubting Thomases," I believe that the Stanislavsky method can be used productively in acting and directing classical and period dramas, as well as modern ones. As was my usual habit, I divided the play into motivational units** which contributed to the main action of each individual player and to the spine of the play. I tried to practice what I taught in my directing classes. I used John Dietrich's *Play Direction,* because he used motivational units as a means of analyzing the play. His text was a perfect supplement to my classes in acting and my trust in the Stanislavsky method.

Once the actor can deal with these elements on a serious level, if the play is a comedy or a farce, the actor has earned the right to treat them lightly, or in a comic manner. With a firm foundation in reality, the actor can lift the play to a lighter level or take it deeper into the realms of melodrama or tragedy.

Wilde called his farce, "A Trivial Comedy for Serious People." If one looks

---

*"G. B. S.," as he became known, was an Irish dramatist, a music critic, and a social reformer. He never wrote plays simply to entertain. He always had some cause which he was promoting and he frequently attached prefaces to his plays to make certain that his message was clearly understood. Shaw lived from 1856-1950, a full ninety-four years, during which he wrote continually and copiously. His complete works have never been, and may never be, published. Although there is an English collection of thirty-six volumes, it does not contain all of his plays, novels, music, and literary criticism, political writings, and letters.

**Characters of a play symbolize universal human drives that motivate their actions: Hamlet is driven by revenge; Macbeth, by ambition. A play may be analyzed by dividing it into unified segments (scenes) that are controlled by desires such as self-preservation, protection of others, hunger, love, sex, hate, social acceptance and recognition, and adventure. Whatever forces human beings to action, moves the play on its course to a climax and resulting conclusion.

closely beneath the surface, the play is anything but trivial. It is really a criticism of Victorian society and its outworn customs and traditions. Lady Bracknell (Barbara Drake) stubbornly blocks the marriage of Jack Worthing (Mark Wise) to her daughter Gwendolyn Fairfax (Linda Weber) because he does not have the right social connections. Unwittingly, Lady Bracknell also blocks the marriage of her nephew, Algernon Moncrieff (Ronald Crouch), because Jack will not permit his ward, Cecily Cardew (Carol Link), to marry Algernon unless he can marry Gwendolyn. A further obstacle presented by the girls is that they cannot marry anyone whose name is not Ernest. Two knowing, but confused butlers, Lane (Tad Lyon) and Merriman (Ronald Grim), help as much as they can. All ends well, however, because the men get christened and Jack turns out to be Algernon's brother. A subplot concerns the courtship of Cecily's tutor, Miss Prism (Beth Bricker), and the Reverend Canon Chasuble, D.D. (Frederick Enstrom). In the end, there are three marriages in the offing. In the process of ending things well, Wilde burlesques English social hierarchy through Lady Bracknell, spoofs christenings, and, of all things, mocks English tea-time!

The Importance of Being Earnest, 1964. (from left) Cecily Cardew (C. Link), Algernon Moncrieff (R. Crouch), Lady Bracknell (B. Drake), Rev. Canon Chasuble (F. Enstrom), Miss Prism (B. Bricker), John Worthing (M. Wise), and Gwendolen Fairfax (L. Weber). *Theatre file photo courtesy M.C. Public Relations Office.*

The production went according to plan. The actors worked hard individually and they played well as an ensemble. The flavor of the 1900's came through; the style of the play glittered; and the wit of the dialogue sparkled. Back stage, after opening night, Art Historian Louis Palmer chortled, "It was piss elegant!" That was all I needed to hear to realize that I had accomplished what I wanted. My judgments in these matters were strictly subjective and, therefore, null and void. My regard for the production and my Iowa training in design found support and solace from an objective source: Bob Kinnard's review in the *Black and Magenta*.

> Oscar Wilde's farcical comedy for serious people was presented in all its delightful atmosphere and brittle dialogue by all concerned; by the director, a topflight cast, and an exceptionally good technical and make-up crew. This was evident from the intelligent laughter of the audience at the scintillating lines, elaborate manners, and deliberately absurd plot.
>
> In giving credits to individuals or groups, I would like to start with Mr. Hill's Introduction to Theatre and Stagecraft classes for their fine sets for Algy's town

house and Jack's place in the country.

In the acting department, there were quite a number of excellent moments provided by a cast noticeably well-integrated and unified in style. All performances showed an understanding and perception of the play and its style, and none exceeded the requirements which Wilde wrote into the piece.[38]

The first major production of the second semester was *Dinny and the Witches*, by William Gibson, who sub-titled it, "A Frolic on Grave Matters." I directed, designed, and supervised the technical work for the play, which was presented March 17-20 at the Little Theatre. Robert Barrows, who was to become an invaluable student assistant, was the lighting supervisor. Other members of the production staff who served loyally throughout the year were Judy Ross, Norma Hall, Ted Cooper, Suzanne Fontaine, Bill McCloskey, Margaret Basnett, Linda Weber, Nancy Wheeley, Sandra Wilkins, Carol Boyer, Marsha Croom, Robert Price, Lillian Kestner, Carol Moorhead, and Barbara Drake.

Dinny and the Witches is a morality play, similar to the plays which monks of the Medieval period used to teach the populace the right and wrong way to live. As such, it is a direct descendant of the famous *Everyman* and Marlowe's *Dr. Faustus*. In the program notes, "About the Play," I wrote:

> William Gibson here portrays modern man's search for values in a nuclear world. It is a heart-breaking search because everything he touches turns to dust; it is a nightmarish search, for through it all he is a mortal under sentence of death. In the end he finally realizes that the object of his search is under his nose: LOVE. His pilgrimage dissolves in the triumph of the world as it is, as long as we have it. As Ben [John Riden in the play] says: " . . . who wouldn't make a love song to the world at its worst, the day it died?"[39]

Dinny and the Witches, 1965. Michael Naas as Dinny (seated up center) seems to be delighted by the diversion presented by the Three Temptations: (left to right) Terry Persohn as Dawn, Sheila Williams as Chloe, and Carol Moorhead as Bubbles. *Theatre file photo courtesy M.C. Public Relations Office.*

The production was designed in the Expressionistic style, in order to convey the idea that life in a nuclear world is like a nightmare. The set was obvious and at strange angles to typify the topsy turvey state of modern values. The props used were oversize or under-size to illustrate the unusual dependence on objects. The costumes and make-up were garish and intrusive to draw attention to the importance of people in the drama. The acting was not without motivation or logic, but it was designed to be loud and exaggerated, in order to continue the style of a nightmare or a dream gone wrong.

The season ended April 9-10, when senior seminar student, Janet Small directed a Children's Theatre version of *Beauty and the Beast*. In this ancient fairy tale, which dates from the early Renaissance (1450), a young maiden, Beauty, is forced to live with the Beast to save the life of her father. The Beast is freed from a spell by Beauty's love and becomes a handsome prince who marries her.[40]

Cast for *Androcles and the Lion*
(George Bernard Shaw)

Our Distinguished Guest (G.B.S.)	Dr. John McKenney
The Lion	Chip Baxter
Megaera	Nancy Peterson
Androcles	Bob Kinnard
Centurion	Doug Bury
Roman Soldiers	Bill Babcock, Jerry Patterson, Jack Robinson, Tom Smead
Christians	Barbara Drake, Tom Fragasse, Gail Jordan, Suzanne Laurent, Darlene Martin, Bob Saunders, Sally Schenck, Don Spurlock, Bill Taggart, Linda Weber
Lavinia	Beth Brown
The Captain	Barry Spigener
Lentulus	Tad Lyon
Metellus	Larry Corbett
Ferrovius	Mike Brandt
Spintho	Dave Jamison
Ox Driver	Chip Baxter
The Call Boy	Gordon Davison
The Editor	John Dietz
The Keeper	Jerry McDonald
Caesar	Mal Rothman
Secutor	Chuck Wallace
Retiarius	Steve Bauman
Scenes: Prologue	A Jungle Path
Act I	Outskirts of Rome
Act II	Behind the Emperor's box at the Coliseum (We also see within the Coliseum briefly.)
Director:	Stanley Schutz
Stage Design:	Stanley Schutz

Cast for *Dinny and the Witches*
(William Gibson)

Dawn	Terry Persohn
Chloe	Sheila Williams
Bubbles	Carol Moorhead
Tom	Denny Thompson
Dick	Ronald Grim
Harry	Tim Connelly
Ben	John Riden
Jake	Jerry Goodman
Stonehenge	Bill McCloskey
Dinny	Michael Naas
Amy	Sally Schenck

Luella ....Jill Friend
Ulga ....Sally Smith
Zenobia...Beth Brown
Scene: ....Central Park, New York City
Time: ....Now and Again
Director and Designer: .....Donald Hill

Cast for *Beauty and the Beast*
(Nora MacAlvay)

Renard ....Rick Schneider
Antionette ....Elinor Hubert
Prince Armand ....Jerry Goodman
Queen ....Lois Norman
Fairy Godmother ....Carol Kreger
Beauty ....Sue Calhoun
Aurelie ....Janice Bopp
Alphonsine ....Saralynn Wingard
Beauvais ....Bob Kinnard
Harlequinn ....Jo Pollock
Page ....Anne Brown
Townspeople ....Gail Jordan, Judie Loughman, Carol Stapf
Scene: ....Prince Armand's Secret Palace
Time: ....Long, long ago
Director: ....Janet Small (senior seminar student)

The Department: 1965–1970

Associate Professor Mary Elizabeth Johnson ('26), senior member of the department, became Acting-Chairperson until a suitable replacement for Dr. Golden was found. Miss Johnson had served the department since 1944. Upon coming to Muskingum, she taught and directed in the theatre area and in general speech. She knew the Laytons well, having been their student and, later, their colleague. Like the Laytons, she received her M.A. at the University of Michigan, and came under the influence of the Trueblood heritage. With Miss Johnson as Chairperson, the department continued at an even and uninterrupted pace. The same concepts regarding content, method, and the interdisciplinary nature of speech, which the Laytons passed to Dr. Golden, continued. A noticeable change was the growing trend to emphasize possible vocations for speech majors. In the 1966-67 *Muskingum College Bulletin*, the second paragraph of the introduction to the speech curriculum specified a few areas of work for which a speech major was prepared:

"He may enter sales personnel, public relations, recreation, and secondary teaching. He is also provided pre-professional background to such fields as broadcasting, Christian education, government service, higher education, law, ministry, speech therapy, and theatre."[1]

After a two-year search, the administration announced the appointment of Dr. Richard K. Curtis as head of the Speech Department. Dr. Curtis held a Bachelor of Theology degree from Northern Baptist Theological Seminary and a Master's and Doctorate from Purdue. He had been chairman of Barrington College in Rhode Island and Bethel College in St. Paul, before becoming Pastor of the Immanual Baptist Church in Kansas City.

Dr. Curtis was interested in language and the moral challenge of the symbolic functions of language. Course work changed complexion. Theory rather than practice was pre-eminent. A major in speech became more general: a student must take the usual twenty-eight hours beyond the fundamentals course. Rather than specify certain courses (as in the past), the major elected at least three hours in each of the five areas of concentration in the department: public speaking and debate, interpretation, radio and television, theatre, and speech correction.[2]

In the meantime, Mr. Schutz had received his doctorate in theatre from Michigan State University and returned to Wooster College. In 1966, Muriel Bain, who had taught in the department in the late '30s, returned to help me shoulder the responsibilities of teaching and directing theatre. Muriel, a Muskingum graduate, held an M.A. from the University of Michigan.

The theatre area had grown from five courses and eighteen hours in 1959, to eight courses and twenty-seven hours in 1969. At the same time, the production program had doubled because of student-directed one-act plays and student-directed seminars. A major in theatre seemed practical and I proposed one; however, the department was not convinced.

In the midst of negotiations for a theatre major, time for a sabbatical arrived. I wanted to increase my knowledge in the area of theatre history, theory, and criticism,

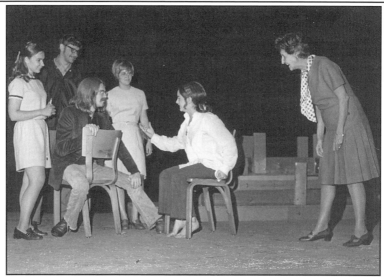

R. Hamilton (seated center) and A. Roberts illustrate a point in acting for rehearsal supervisor Muriel Bain while, at far left, S. Simerka, W. Morrison, and M. Harris observe. 1970. *Theatre file photo courtesy M.C. Public Relations Office.*

and, to that end, I enrolled in the doctorate program at the University of Minnesota.

During my sabbatical, Mrs. J. Herbert (Muriel) Bain and Mrs. Arthur (Elizabeth) Wills directed the theatre season and taught classes. Mrs. Wills had an M.A. from the University of Denver, a well-known school in theatre. Both ladies were more than capable of carrying on the program.

I returned in the fall of 1969, and renewed discussions with the department concerning a theatre major. In my absence, Dr. Curtis had departed and Assistant Professor Judson Ellertson was Acting-Chairman of the department. Members of Muskingum Players, as well as dedicated majors in the department (such as Cheri Swiss), were not only deeply dedicated to theatre, but also very strong-willed and determined. They knew what they wanted and they went after it: a major in theatre. With pressure being exerted from within the department by me, and from without by students, Mr. Ellertson suggested that I write a position paper or proposal for a major. I agreed.

I had already collected substantial information on the practicality and benefits of a major. Certain that my position was tenable and the request reasonable. I soon presented a loose-leaf notebook to the department, Muskingum Players, and the administration. The notebook contained my proposal for an interdisciplinary major in theatre entitled, "Theatre Major Rationale," which was supported by letters from various theatre authorities and theatre alumni, comparative data and statistics from similar colleges, information on teacher accreditation, and pertinent articles from the American Educational Theatre Association.[3]

This loose-leaf collection of materials rendered two important results: 1) it served as a position paper and 2) it led to the publication of the *Muskingum Theatre Handbook.* That document solidified my thinking about the philosophy and purpose of educational theatre, it gave details of the theatre major, and it contained a practical guide on play production.

I considered it my duty as Director of Theatre to present my views on various aspects of theatre and theatrical art in a clear, articulate, and meaningful manner. I have made my views public in *The Muskingum Theatre Handbook* and in a variety of brochures issued by the Muskingum College Theatre over the years.

The Purpose of a Theatre Arts Program

The liberal arts environment is precisely where theatre arts belong; their nature and purpose are closely aligned. The liberal arts college is interested in the development of self-knowledge and an understanding of the world. By its nature, the theatre is not only a "composite art" of literature, music, dance, painting, and acting, but also a culmination of them. Furthermore, the subject matter of theatre not only concerns those permanent qualities of mind and character that are fundamental to the human condition, but also deals directly and immediately with them on stage. Theatre's range of knowledge encompasses that of every other department of learning, as well as of life itself. The recent surge of theatrical activity in our country is the result of a rediscovery that theatre is a sociological, political, therapeutic, and communicative tool, as well as entertainment.

The Objectives of a Theatre Arts Program

The aims and objectives of the theatre arts program include the following: 1) to serve as the cultural center for the college community, by offering a production program both entertaining and enlightening; 2) to offer a program of practical value to all who participate in its activities; 3) to train and prepare students to serve as superior teachers of drama; and 4) to provide the foundation of training for those students who wish to pursue a professional career.

The Practicality of a Theatre Arts Program

Training in theatre is training for life. Quite aside from the artistic values which are inherent in theatrical work, the theatre offers a diversified and practical training, which remains a permanent asset, whether the student becomes a housewife, a mechanic, a business executive, a salesman, a doctor, or a lawyer. In fact, few occupations exist that do not need the poise, good speech, and cooperation supplied by the theatre. The interdisciplinary emphasis given at Muskingum makes such training more apparent and practical.

The Curriculum of a Theatre Arts Program

Muskingum will reflect the new importance of theatre if the faculty passes a theatre major consisting of thirty hours. Besides new courses in acting, history, and dramatic literature, the unique feature of the program is its interdisciplinary nature. Students discover that theatre makes an excellent companion major or minor to any area of knowledge they wish to study.

The Production Schedule of a Theatre Arts Program

An inseparable adjunct to the curriculum is the season of plays that gives students practical training through performance. From three to four full-length productions are directed by faculty members, and five to ten one-act plays directed by students. Seminar students in theatre direct full-length plays as part of their requirements in directing. Each season is designed to give students and the community a variety of plays, according to type and theatrical period. In any one season, comedy, farce, tragedy, and melodrama may be represented. These types come from different historical periods so that, in four years, students have experience with at least one Greek, Medieval, Shakespearean, Restoration, Victorian, or modern play. Past seasons have included such productions as *The Rivals The Crucible, Private Lives, Antigone, Twelfth Night, Mother Courage, Ten Nights in a Bar Room, The Little Foxes, J.B., Inherit the Wind, The Lion in Winter, Hamlet, The Firebugs, Under Milk Wood,* and *The Fantasticks.*

Although these views are nearly a half-century old, they still sound good to me. I tried to keep them in mind whenever I chose a play to produce, and while I was teaching students who were contemplating productions of their own. These views served as a basic philosophy that helped to give individual productions and seasonal programs a focus.

The *Handbook* also contained the original theatre major proposal described herewith.

Interdisciplinary Theatre Major

Students who are candidates for a Bachelor of Arts degree may major in the area of theatre or they may concentrate in theatre while majoring in speech.

I. A major in theatre consists of a total of 30 hours, of which 18 may be elected from theatre courses, and as many as 12 from selected interdisciplinary courses.

II. A concentration in theatre, with a speech major, consists of a total of 28 hours beyond Speech Fundamentals 105. Required courses consist of Individual Study and a minimum of three hours in each of the areas of public address, radio, interpretation, and speech correction.

As a discipline with its own body of knowledge, theatre may be divided into the areas of acting, directing, designing, history-theory, and dramatic literature. Such are the areas which students may emphasize within their major or concentration.

THEATRE COURSES

Course No.	Course Title	Credits
151	Theatre Arts	3
251	Theatre History	3
255	Scenic Arts I	3
	(Stagecraft, scene design, stage lighting)	
256	Scenic Arts II	3
	(Stage make-up, costume design, stage lighting)	
351	Modern Drama	3
355	Acting	3
356	Directing	3
451	World Theatre	3
455	Advanced Acting & Directing	3
495	Individual Study	2
101; 102	Theatre Practicum	1-2
201; 202	*(Theatre majors may take as many as 4-8 hours)*	1-2
301; 302		1-2
401; 402		1-2

In addition to the above courses, which form the core of a theatre major or concentration, there are always one or two interim courses a year which are appropriate to the curriculum.

A major in theatre is free to elect 12 hours above the Basic Education requirements from a variety of courses in other areas and departments. Although these courses may vary as to number and content, a listing of offerings from the *1971 Catalogue* will suffice to give the student an idea of the interdisciplinary nature of theatre.

SPEECH

215	Extemporaneous Speaking	3
241	Oral Interpretation of Literature	3
335	Decision-Making	4
343	Advanced Interpretation	3
363	Radio-TV-Film in Modern Society	3
366	Radio-TV-Film Production	3

ART

101	Drawing	4
278	The Arts	3
329	Arts of Ancient Civilization	2
330	Medieval, Renaissance Art	2
331	European, American Art	2
340	Graphic Art	3

ENGLISH

223	Comedy and Tragedy	3
342	Shakespeare	4
368	Modern Dramatic Literature	3
485	Readings in Lit.(Dramatic)	3

CLASSICAL–MODERN LANGUAGES

For the student proficient in any of the foreign languages, there are various dramatic literature courses within these departments. Some are conducted in English.

MUSIC

101	Applied Music: Voice	1-3
103	Music Theory	4
104	Music Theory	4
241	Intro. to Music	4
423	Music History	3
424	Music History	3

PHYSICAL–HEALTH EDUCATION

102	Fundamental Movement	1
201	Dance	1
202	Fencing	1

PHILOSOPHY

| 370 | Special Studies: Aesthetics | 3[4] |

This was the major that was accepted by the Speech Department and the Division of Humanities. Approved by the Dean and the Curriculum Committee, it became a reality in 1970.

REFERENCES

1   *Muskingum College Bulletin: 1966-1967*, p. 98.
2   *Muskingum College Bulletin: 1969-1970*, p. 121.
3   Donald Hill, "Theatre Major Rationale," (unpublished Theatre Major Proposal, 1969-1970, Muskingum College: New Concord, Ohio), p. 2.
4   Donald Hill, *Muskingum Theatre Handbook,* Illustrated by Chab Guthrie (Cambridge, Ohio: Southeastern Printers, 1971), pp. 8-10.

The Plays: 1965–1970

1965-1966

During Homecoming Week (October 13-16), Arthur Miller's *Death of a Sales man* opened the 1965-66 theatre season. I directed and designed the production, which Arthur Miller called, "Certain private conversations in two acts and a requiem." I took a risk offering a tragedy for Homecoming, when a comedy is more fitting for the festive occasion, but I did not want to under-estimate the critical intelligence of the Muskingum audience. I was glad, because attendance ran high and the S.R.O. sign was put out more than once.

Death of a Salesman, somewhat modeled after Miller's father, is often considered his masterpiece. This tragic story of the last days of a salesman's life also marks the end of an era—that of the traveling salesman. There is another and deeper level of meaning dealing with the values and morals of American society. Failure in America is looked upon as a crime by many people. Being well-liked and knowing the right people do not guarantee success; hard work and talent are also requisites. During the "Requiem" over Willy's grave, the audience commonly experiences guilt feelings because people identify with Willy.

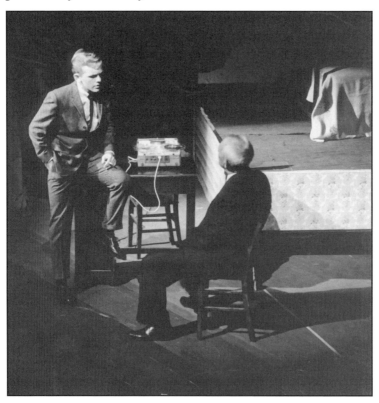

Death of a Salesman, 1965. Howard Wagner (R. Jackson), Willy Loman (Howard Donahoe, Guest-Actor). *Theatre file photo courtesy M.C. Public Relations Office.*

Few people can leave the theatre after a performance of Miller's play without questioning their own sense of values.

Rehearsals for the play were emotionally exhausting. As usual, I rehearsed the play by motivational units, because that is the best way to make each actor's motivation clear to everyone in the play and, hopefully, to the audience. Working through the play in this way was tedious and tiring, but it paid off in the end with some deeply-felt emotional scenes.

Led by Howard A. Donohoe as Willy Loman, the cast gave an outstanding ensemble performance of the Miller play. Howard, as guest actor, did the same role for the Cambridge Community Theatre in 1964. He stepped into the part when Fritz Enstrom, who was originally cast in the lead, developed a bad throat condition. All was not in vain for Fritz. When Miss Johnson requested excerpts from *Salesman* for the Drama and Poetry Conference, Fritz was back on stage in the leading role.

The review in the *Black and Magenta* called the Miller play a "blockbusting production . . . which must certainly rank as one of the outstanding productions of the Little Theatre's history." The review concluded with, "if the other three productions at the Little Theatre are of the same caliber as this one, Muskingum theatre-goers can look forward to one of the best seasons ever."[41]

Stalag 17, written by Donald Bevan and Edmund Trzcinski, was first staged on Broadway in 1951 by Jose Ferer. The authors, who had spent two years in a POW camp in Kerms, Austria, during World War II, used their first-hand knowledge of the war to score a success with their first play. The motion picture that followed earned William Holden an Academy Award for Best Actor.[42]

Directed by Stanley Schutz, *Stalag 17* was performed on December 8-11 at the Little Theatre. The story takes place in a German prison camp and concerns a group of American prisoners. One of the prisoners has sabotaged a train and faces serious punishment, if caught; another prisoner is a stooge for the Germans. The tone of the play is comic, but the suspense surrounding the plot creates and holds serious interest.

In the "Director's Notes" for the play, Mr. Schutz announced:

> On Tuesday, December 14, we will take the play to McConnelsville, Ohio, for a "one-night stand" in the Opera House. This performance will be only the second stage production in approximately thirty years at the seventy-five year old show place. We are grateful for the opportunity to present *Stalag 17* to the theatre patrons of that area.[43]

A review of *Stalag 17* in the *Black and Magenta* was favorable, as indicated by the headline of the article, "War Play Well-Staged."[44]

In *Doña Rosita, The Spinster*, or *The Language of the Flowers*, Federico Garcia Lorca supplied another romantic tragedy for the Muskingum audience. Less violent, but just as tragic as *The House of Bernarda Alba* (1960), the play, according to Lorca, " . . . is life tame on the outside and burning on the inside, of a Granadine maiden who, little by little, is converted into that grotesque and pitiable thing that is a spinster in Spain." Betrothed to her cousin, they are forced to separate; but Doña Rosita dreams of their reunion and marriage, until the passage of years brings the pain of frustration and finality of loss. It is a quiet tragedy of many Spanish women who are defeated, not so much by frustrated love, as by a society which makes such rejection a symbol of shame.[45]

I directed and designed the production, which was performed on March 16-19 at the Little Theatre. The directorial image is easily found in the mutable rose. The play is unified by the symbolism of this rose, a rose which lasts only twenty-four hours. It is red in the morning, pink in the afternoon, and white at night. Rosita is the human counterpart of the rose, as her life follows the simple pattern of its existence through the three acts of the play. Through the life of Rosita, each act symbolizes an aspect of the rose's life: morning, afternoon, and night. The twenty-four years that the drama spans are represented by one day's existence of the flower.[46]

Considerable rehearsal time was devoted to creating the poignant atmosphere required by the drama, and to rendering the poetic language of the dialogue. Another time-consuming job was translating my designs for each of the three different acts. These designs involved the construction of a set of pylons, two feet wide and eight feet high. The pylons were painted a neutral gray and spaced at four foot intervals around the perimeter of the set. Set changes took place by removing and replacing "plugs" between the pylons, in order to suggest different places. The first scene was a room leading to a greenhouse in 1885; the second scene was the garden in 1900; and the third scene was a small living room in 1910. There were three doorways for entrances and exits: one stage right, one stage left, and one up center. Barry Baughman ('64), who was on the technical staff at Kent State University Theatre, created the lighting for the play.

The play drew good reviews for the actors, and the scene design received applause from the opening night audience. It was a very difficult, but very satisfying production. Beth Brown gave an even and consistently-fine performance as Doña Rosita, supported by the equally fine acting of Donna Brevak as the Aunt. Other good performances were turned in by such theatre "steadies" as Linda Weber, Ted Hissam, Fritz Enstrom, Judy Moore, and Rick Jackson. It was also the acting debut of a very reluctant, but talented, Bob Barrows, our veteran and indispensable Production Assistant.

Doña Rosita, 1966. (from left) Second Ayola (J. Horine), First Ayola (S. Williams), Doña (B. Brown), Aunt (D. Brevak), Housekeeper (L. Weber), (seated) Mother of the Spinsters, (J. Moore), Third Spinster (S. Fontaine), Second Spinster (L. Kestner), First Spinster (M. Goldberg). *Theatre file photo courtesy M.C. Public Relations Office.*

The review, "'Doña Rosita' Scores Little Theatre Success," in the *Black and Magenta,* commented on the setting:

> The most successful aspect of the production were the sets designed by Mr. Hill. . . . they captured the mood of the play with their changes with the passage of time . . . . These changing moods were greatly facilitated by the lighting schemes worked out by alumnus, Barry Baughman, '64, who returned from Kent State to set it up. Small wonder that the set drew applause with the curtain rise on opening night.
>
> Overall the effect gained was one of aesthetic satisfaction . . . from effective set design and competent acting. *Doña Rosita* must certainly rank as one of the most artistic productions seen at Muskingum in recent years.[47]

Noel Coward got the idea for *Hay Fever* from true experiences he had with actress Laurette Taylor, her two children, Marguerite and Dwight, and her second husband, the playwright, J. Hartley Manners. This family was in the habit of inviting weekend guests. They would encourage the guests to join in parlor games, which would soon turn into a family argument over the rules. The family would angrily leave the room, forcing the guests to fend for themselves. The family would be found later in the kitchen, amicably enjoying tea. According to Coward, it was only a matter of time before someone put the eccentricities of the Manners's household into a play. He just happened to be the first to do so.[48]

What happens in *Hay Fever* would hardly constitute a plot, but the way in which Coward arranges the arrival of each guest in Act I, the explanation of the rules of a parlor game to the guests in Act II, and the departure of the guests in Act III, makes it seem as though there is a lot of activity.*

A summary of the play, as produced at Muskingum on May 4-7, 1966, follows. A retired actress, Judith Bliss (Barbara Drake, understudied by Linda Weber), lives in the country with her children, Sorel (Carol Moorhead) and Simon (Jim Scott), and her second husband, novelist David Bliss (Michael Naas). Each member of the family, unknown to the others, has invited a guest for the weekend. Judith has invited a young athlete, Sandy Tyrell (Brent Harrell); David has invited a young flapper, Jackie Coryton (Sandra Shaw); Sorel has invited a diplomat, Richard Greatham (John Applegate); and Simon has invited a divorcee, Myra Arundel (Carol Beth Boyer). The much harassed maid, Clara, was played by Beth Bricker. In the evening, they all play a parlor game which ends in a family argument and recriminations, after which, each member of the family pairs off with a guest other than the one he or she invited. In the final act, the guests come down to breakfast; they have a hurried discussion, decide to leave before the family awakens, and rush upstairs to pack. The guests leave while the family is at breakfast.

Seminar student Sally Schenck designed a beautiful and functional setting for the comedy.

---

*Hay Fever was Coward's favorite of all his plays. Its technical symmetry appealed to him: "It's quite extraordinarily well constructed, and as I did the whole thing in three days, I didn't even rewrite. I enjoyed writing it and producing it, and I have frequently enjoyed watching it."
Source: Sheridan Morley, *A Talent to Amuse: A Biography of Noel Coward* (Garden City, New York: Doubleday & Company, Inc., 1969), p. 130.

I'm glad I made the decision to direct *Hay Fever* as part of the 1965-66 theatre season.* The *Black and Magenta* agreed.

> The 1965-1966 season of the Little Theatre was rounded out last week by a highly successful production of Noel Coward's mannered farce, *Hay Fever*, written in 1924 and still going strong.
> Here at the Little theatre under Mr. Hill's direction, the reason for such staying power was obvious. It is a fast, stylish, light-weight comedy of a delicate blend of slapstick, and the traditional English comedy of manners, and so it was presented.[49]

Cast for *Death of a Salesman*
(Arthur Miller)
†Guest Actor

Willy Loman	†Howard Donohoe
Linda	Barbara Drake
Biff	Mike Naas
Happy	Cliff Haines
Bernard	John Applegate
The Woman	Linda Weber
(Understudy)	Carol Moorhead
Charley	Larry Bryan
Uncle Ben	Ted Hissam
Howard Wagner	Rick Jackson
Voice of Howard's Daughter	Loas Gerlach
Voice of His Son	Peter Gerlach
Voice of His Wife	Nancy Wheeley
Jenny	Alma Perry
Stanley	Steve Timmons
A Waiter	Tom Forgrave
Miss Forsythe	Darlene Martin
Operator's Voice	Mary Ellen Matson
Page's Voice	Tom Forgrave
Letta	Daryle Favro

Scene: The action takes place in Willy Loman's house and yard and in various places he visits in the New York and Boston of Today
Director and designer: Donald Hill

Cast for *Stalag 17*
(Donald Bevan and Edmund Trzcinski)

S.S. Guard	Joel Ferree
Stosh	George Lazarides
Harry Shapiro	Bill McCloskey
Price	Lyle Marquardt
Herb Gordon	Robert Bundy

---

* At the time I directed *Hay Fever*, I knew very little about the comic techniques employed by Coward. Four years later (1970), while researching Coward for my dissertation, I discovered that Henri Bergson's theory of the comic explains how Coward achieved his comic effects. Coward's use of repetition in situation, words, and character conveys the feeling of "something mechanical encrusted on the living," which defines Bergson's comic theory: "Wherever there is repetition or complete similarity, we always suspect some mechanism at work behind the living . . . . This reflection of life towards the mechanical is here the cause of laughter." (Henri Bergson, "Laughter," in *Comedy*, Wylie Sypher, ed. (New York: A Doubleday Anchor Book, 1956), p. 82. In 1966, I merely knew that I liked the play, I thought it was funny, and I wanted other people to enjoy it with me. When I discovered at try-outs that I had a cast that felt the same way about the play as I did, I put aside *Blithe Spirit*, which had been scheduled originally, and substituted *Hay Fever*.

Hoffman .... Chuck Wallace
Sefton .... Gary Gardner
Duke .... Bill Taggart
McCarthy .... Ed Neeley
Horney .... Tom Taylor
Marko .... Ted Griffin
Corporal Schultz .... Mal Rothman
Dunbar .... Dave Wray
Reed .... Ted Hissam
Peterson .... Albert Moore
Red-Dog .... Stan Feltz
Witherspoon .... Jim Haddock
McKay .... Jack Taylor
German Captain .... Joe Greene
Geneva Man .... Chuck Baumgartner
Second Guard .... Stephen Watt
Scene: .... A barracks of Stalag 17, somewhere in Germany during World War II.
Director: .... Stanley Schutz

Cast for *Doña Rosita*
(Federico Garcia Lorca)

Housekeeper .... Linda Weber
Aunt .... Donna Brevak
Uncle .... Ted Hissam
Doña Rosita .... Beth Brown
Nephew .... Tom Forgrave
First Manola .... Kathy Miner
Second Manola .... Norma Hall
Third Manola .... Kathie Crouse
Instructor of Political Economy .... Fritz Enstrom
Mother of the Spinsters .... Judy Moore
First Spinster .... Marian Goldberg
Second Spinster .... Lillian Kestner
Third Spinster .... Suzy Fontaine
First Ayola .... Sheila Williams
Second Ayola .... Janey Horine
Don Martin .... Rick Jackson
First Workman .... Gary Gardner
Second Workman .... Brent Harrell
Youth .... Bob Barrows
Scene: .... The home of Doña Rosita, Granada, Spain
Time: .... 1885, 1900, and 1910
Director and Designer: ..... Donald Hill

1966-1967

In 1966, when I wanted a really fun show for Homecoming Week (October 19-22), I chose *A Thurber Carnival* by James Thurber.

In the play program, I mentioned how appropriate it was to present another Thurber play for Homecoming, since the first Homecoming play of the decade (1962) was the Stanley Schutz production of *The Male Animal.* I also mentioned that *Carnival* became a stage success at the insistence of Thurber admirer, Haila Stoddard, who, with staging by Burgess Meredith and music by Don Elliott, produced the show in 1960.* It ran for 224 performances on Broadway, won a special Tony award, and opened in London in 1962.[50]

One of the unique features of *A Thurber Carnival* is the musical score composed by Don Elliott. (Dame Fortune was riding with me on this one.) As it happened, a student, Jim Roberts, had put together a quartet, with himself at the piano, John Ackerman on drums, Dave Flinner on saxophone, and Buff Yount on bass. I featured the quartet by placing them on stage; there, they could view the actors and easily take their cues. They looked good and sounded even better. Their permanent presence served as a unifying scenic element between the relatively short scenes of the performance.

In the program, I saluted the cast members who had made the production possible.

> The director has particularly enjoyed working with the cast of *A Thurber Car-nival* because they are imaginative and talented people. Most of them are newcom-ers to the Little Theatre and to Muskingum. There are only four seniors in the cast: Tom Forgrave, Robert Kinnard, Carol Beth Boyer, and Alma Perry, all of whom have acted before, and all of whom are speech majors, except Bob Kinnard, who has, nevertheless, been in shows here since he was a freshman. The one junior, Charles Clark, is a speech major, but entirely new to our stage. Donna Brevak, Janey Horine, Ted Hissam, Rick Jackson are all sophomores who were last seen in *Doña Rosita.* Brent Harrell and Steve Watt, also sophomores, were last seen in *Hay Fever* and *Stalag 17*, respectively. James Hall, Jr., Lance Roepe, Douglas Snook, Sherri Atkins, and Nancy Gleason have all had some experience in high school, but are completely new to our audiences at Muskingum. It has been a pleasure working with them.[51]

As its contribution to the U.S.A. and Africa Conference at Muskingum College, the Speech Department presented "The Swampdwellers" by Wole Soyinka on No-vember 9, 11 & 12 at the Little Theatre.

> "The Swampdwellers" reflects several current tensions in Nigerian life—for example, the difficulties encountered by the inlander when he faces city life; the emotional conflict he experiences as traditional values are challenged, and the an-tagonisms between the Muslim of the north and the polytheism of the southern Yoruba. Wole Soyinka captures the feelings and tempo of his homeland as no Euro-pean dramatist has done.

---

* Although Thurber's drawings and essays are often funny, Goddard Lieberson perceptively remarked, " . . . the big things of Thurber are the ideas, the concepts, the insights, and they are the result not of his humor, but of his humanity. This he has in such large proportion that no matter how amusing are the things he says, or writes, or draws, no one ever has the effrontery to consider him comical—he is much better than that: he is seriously funny." (Goddard Liberson quoted by Donald Hill, "The Author and the Play," Original Program, *A Thurber Carnival*, October 19-22, 1966, Little Theatre, n.p.

Muriel Bain directed the play and I designed the set, which was a village hut on the coastal plains of Nigeria. The cast members included Danette Abdulah (a first year student from Philadelphia), who played Alu, an older woman; Leonard Mseka (a senior economics major from Mbamba, Likoma Island, Malawi) played Makuri, Alu's husband; Winston Gooden (a first year student from Jamaica, W.I.) played A Beggar, a northerner; Nathan Epenu (a junior biology major from Soroti, Uganda) played Kadiye, a priest; Ted Griffin (a junior from Closter, New Jersey) played Igwezu, son of Alu; and Oliver Warobi (a junior psychology student from Kikuyu, Kenya) played A Drummer.[53]

Because of the international significance of the conference, and because of the unusual nature of the setting and content of the play, "The Swampdwellers" was one of the most interesting and successful productions of the decade.

The second major production of the 1966-67 theatre season was Robinson Jeffers's adaptation of Euripides's *Medea*. The story is well-known as a part of Greek mythology.* Medea, daughter of the king of Colchis, is a sorceress and priestess of Hecate. She falls in love with Jason, betrays her father, and helps Jason with the Golden Fleece. While fleeing the country, she also murders her half-brother in order to delay their pursuers. Jason returns with Medea to Corinth, where she bears him two sons.

Medea, 1966. (left) Medea (B. Brown), The Nurse (C.B. Boyer), Chorus of Corinthian Women (C. Florance, S. Williams, M. Hartman), Attendant (C. Guthrie), and Jason (R. Jackson). *Theatre file photo courtesy M.C. Public Relations Office.*

All goes well until Jason, driven by ambition, deserts Medea to marry Creusa, the daughter of Creon, ruler of Corinth. Mad with jealousy, Medea uses her supernatural powers to kill both Creusa and Creon. Her final act is to kill the sons she bore Jason,

Medea won third prize for Euripides at its first performance in Athens in 431 B.C. Since that time the universality of this Greek tragedy has impelled twenty playwrights and uncounted translators to repeat this protest against woman's status in a man's world. The legend has been treated in six languages as drama, opera, and poetry. But *Medea* achieved its greatest success 2,378 years after its first performance when Robinson Jeffers wrote a version for Judith Anderson who played it for a record 214 nights and toured it for eight years, undoubtedly the longest continuous run a Greek play has ever had anywhere. (Hill) who is devastated by the holocaust he has triggered. Medea flies away in a chariot drawn by two winged serpents.

I directed and designed the production, which played the Little Theatre on December 14-17. Peggy Basnett designed the costumes and Barry Baughman, Guest Designer, created the lighting. (Mr. Baughman had just recently joined the staff of Kent State University Theatre.) The sons of Jason and Medea were played by Eric and Evan Stults, sons of History Professor Taylor Stults and his wife, Jan. They were coached for the occasion by Mrs. J. Herbert (Muriel) Bain.[54]

My interpretation of the play was guided by H. D. F. Kitto who, in his book, *Greek Tragedy*, remarked how the uncontrollable passion of the sorceress Medea from Asia Minor completely mystified the Greeks, whose ideals were reason, logic, and temperance. Western civilization at the end of the twentieth century is experiencing a similar threat from the terrorists of Iraq and Iran, the very countries of Medea's birth and civilization.

Beth Brown and Rick Jackson played the fated lovers of Greek Mythology, and very well, too, I might add. Our Choral Director, Woodrow Pickering, congratulated the cast with what I considered the supreme compliment: "Everyone seems to know exactly what he is doing on stage."

The Amorous Flea, which was presented March 9-11 at the Little Theatre, was never a smash Broadway hit, or even a big success Off-Broadway. However, this small-cast musical has been popular with many amateur groups. Based on Moliere's *The School for Wives*, as adapted by Jerry Devine with music by Bruce Montgomery, it was a production I could not resist.

I had a cast that played Moliere the way in which I saw and felt him. They approached the light level with grace and finesse. Early in rehearsals the play began to float, it took to the air, and eventually never touched the ground. Jim Hall made a perfect Arnolphe, and I played his serious-minded friend, Chrysalde. Carol Beth Boyer was a fine, recalcitrant Agnes, and Jim Scott proved to be her excellent lover, Horace. The two mischievous servants, Alain and Georgette, were played to perfection by Chab Guthrie and Donna Brevak, while Stephen Watt and Ted Hissam rounded out the cast as Oronte and Enrique, the two lost fathers.

The incomparable Al Evans was at the piano and patiently followed the singers wherever they led. Members of the Music Conservatory and Mr. Palmer helped coach the singers, and Barry Baughman helped us borrow many of the costumes for the play. I directed when I wasn't having fun on stage, and I designed the set with a magic wall: swinging one way, it revealed a garden in a private residence; swinging in the opposite direction, it revealed a street in seventeenth century Paris.

The *Black and Magenta* review praised the show:

> Through the design of a colorful and functional set; through the lively staging of the intricate plot; through the happy blending of song and dance; and through the appropriately elegant period costumes, the production was visually on the ball. The energy was not merely business and traffic.[55]

On March 15, senior seminar student, Lillian Kestner, directed Edward Albee's "The Zoo Story" for the New Concord Community Lenten Program at the Methodist

Church in New Concord. Her able cast consisted of Rick Jackson (Peter) and Brent Harrell (Jerry).

March 20-21 saw another seminar by student director Tom Forgrave, who presented a readers theatre production of *The Flies* by Jean-Paul Sartre.

The final major production of the 1966-67 theatre season took place on May 10-13 at the Little Theatre. I directed and designed a special presentation of Samuel Beckett's *Waiting for Godot,* with two Guest Actors: Donald Kelm, a 1963 graduate who played Estragon; and Fritz Enstrom, a 1966 graduate, who played Pozzo. Besides the Guest Actors, the other cast members were Ted Hissam (Vladimir), David Beall (Lucky), and Steve Watt (A Boy).

In spite of the reputation of the play as a classic of its kind, I was never attracted to Beckett or Theatre of the Absurd. I am too much of a traditionalist. However, there were classes in philosophy studying *"Godot"* and the professor believed that, if the Theatre produced the play, the students, upon seeing it acted, might better understand what Beckett was saying.*

In my mind, I saw the play being performed in-the-round. I designed an arena production because the form of the play is a circle; it ends the way it began. The circle is a form of magic; one cannot tell where it begins and where it ends—just like the

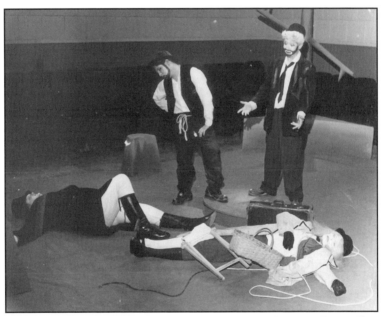

Waiting for Godot, 1967. On the floor, Pozzo (F. Enstrom), Lucky (D. Beall); (standing) Estragon (D. Kelm), Vladimir (T. Hissam). (Enstrom and Kelm Guest Actors). *Theatre file photo courtesy M.C. Public Relations Office.*

play. I tore out the seats in the Little Theatre auditorium and placed some of them on the old stage, and others I arranged around the center of the former basketball court. I placed a bench toward the northwest part of the circle and, behind the bench on which

---

Waiting for Godot is considered a masterpiece of the Theatre of the Absurd. There is no plot or formal structure, other than the situation of waiting. The audience experiences, along with the actors, the action of waiting for someone or something, which the author has given the name of Godot. The characters talk, become frustrated, and commit themselves to meaningless actions. They do everything that we do in life when we are trapped into waiting. The play ends the same way in which it began, with the characters waiting for someone or something that has not yet come.

Estragon and Vladimir would sometimes sit, I created a sterile tree, barren of leaves, but with two limbs arranged at a crazy angle, like a cross gone wrong. As far as the costumes and make-up were concerned, it was a black-and-white production. Vladimir and Estragon were like two Emmett Kelly's. They wore black pants, white shirts, black coats or vests, and maybe derbies. Pozzo wore a black tuxedo, maybe tails, and a top hat; his companion, Lucky, would have a derby and dark trousers covered by a trench coat. Steve Watt as A Boy was dressed in a gray bell-boy outfit with a perky bell-cap's hat. All of the characters wore a base make-up of clown white with black liner to define the features.

Jane Horine wrote a review for the *Black and Magenta*. The title explains the content, "Student Reviews *'Waiting for Godot'* and finds Performance Most Capable."[56] As the professor of philosophy and I suspected, the production helped students understand what reading and discussion could not explain.*

Cast for Medea
(Adapted from Euripides' Medea by Robinson Jeffers)

The Nurse ....Carol Beth Boyer
The Tutor ....Lance Roepe
The Children ....Eric Stults, Evan Stults
Chorus of Corinthian Women ....Sheila Williams, Cheri Florance, Martha Hartman
Medea ....Beth Brown
Creon ....Tim Braaten
Attendants to Creon ....Jim Scott, David Beall
Jason ....Rick Jackson
Attendant to Jason ....Chab Guthrie
Aegeus ....Brent Harrell
Attendant to Aegeus ....Ted Hissam
Attendants to Medea ....Lillian Kestner, Susan Bopp
Scene: ....The entire action of the play occurs before Medea's Palace in Corinth

Director and Designer: ..... Donald Hill
Costume Designs: .... Peggy Basnett
Lighting Design: .... Guest Designer Barry Baughman
Children's Coach: .... Mrs. J. Herbert Bain

Cast for The Flies
(Jean-Paul Sartre)

Narrator ....J. Edward Barrett
Orestes ....David Johnson
Tutor ....James Hall, Jr.
Zeus ....Richard Bovard
Old Woman ....Helen Bartter
Electra ....Nancy Gleason

---

*I wanted to direct *"Godot"* for a personal reason. The play had such a fine reputation that I felt I should like it. Maybe if I directed it, I would learn to like it. I was right. While doing research on the play, I discovered that Beckett was Irish. He was an ex-patriot in Paris just as J. M. Synge had been. Although he wrote the play in French, he translated the English version himself. During rehearsals, I could hear the Irish lilt of the language, and I realized that two old tramps by the side of the road (who were Irish mainstays of many an Abbey Theatre production) were being repeated here in Beckett's play. The language and the characters helped enlarge my imagination into acceptance of the play.

Clytemnestra ....Mrs. Arthur Wills
Aegistheus ....Robert McCreight
High Priest...Bruce Blakeslee
Young Woman ....Carol Bannister
Woman ....Judith Van Kirk
First Soldier...Joel Feree
Second Soldier ....Douglas Snook
First Fury ....Judith Van Kirk
Second Fury ....Carol Bannister
Scenes: ....A public square in Argos, A mountain terrace
near Argos, The throne-room in the palace,
The Temple of Apollo

Director: .... Thomas Forgrave

1967-1968

I had never seen *Little Mary Sunshine*, but I had heard about it, and I had heard the musical score on record. I sent for a reading copy of the play and immediately felt that it would make an excellent offering for Homecoming Week in October. More than anything else, what really appealed to me were the memories it evoked of the old style operetta. I was an avid fan of the Jeanette MacDonald and Nelson Eddy musicals that were made during the 1930's. *Little Mary* revived all the nostalgia of those innocent days. The musical score provided a charming vehicle for the melodramatic plot, and softened, but did not obscure, the character stereotypes. The possibilities of the show caught my imagination and I sent for the book and music for cast and chorus.

Little Mary Sunshine, 1967. Corporal "Billy" Jester (J. Hall, far left) and the Forest Rangers sing, "You've Got to Hand It to Little Mary Sunshine," as each one hands a flower to Mary (K. S. Blunt). *Theatre file photo courtesy M.C. Public Relations Office.*

In the program for the show, I related some of the history behind *Little Mary Sunshine:*

> *Little Mary Sunshine* opened at the Orpheum Theatre on November 18, 1959, and was immediately acclaimed as one of the outstanding successes of the Off-Broadway stage. Rick Besoyan conceived the show as a nostalgic exercise to acquaint the modern generation with a type of musical that possessed a wealth of melodies and moral integrity: the old-fashioned operetta. Although the show pokes gentle fun at the best of Victor Herbert, Rudolf Friml, and Sigmund Romberg, the author cautions us to take the whole thing seriously. Could it be that deep down in our sardonic, realistic souls, we yearn for the adventurous escape into the land of Rose Marie when we go to the theatre, that we are tired of living reality and facing it second-hand when we see a play? At any rate, the old-fashioned operetta had something the modern musical doesn't: charm.[57]

I directed and designed the show as if it were a MacDonald and Eddy musical. With Bob Barrows as production supervisor and Cheri Swiss as costume mistress, we turned the arena into a place in front of a Colorado Inn, high in the Rocky Mountains, during the early 1900's. As a symbol of Little Mary Sunshine, a huge yellow flower was painted in the middle of the arena. The flower provided a suitable place for the Young Ladies from Eastchester Finishing School and the Gentlemen of the United States Forest Rangers to dance, play croquet, sing, and swing in the flower-rope-held swings that were rigged from the ceiling of the Little Theatre. Kerry Sue Blunt, with her sunny disposition and golden hair, played Jeanette MacDonald, and Gerry Lefever played Nelson Eddy. Al Evans played the piano as if he were the New York Philharmonic! Mr. Louis Palmer assisted singers with their vocal scores; Miss Sue Cook provided expert assistance for the dances; and, Sheila Williams helped comedienne, Nancy Trumbull, with her "Mata Hari" number.

After complimenting the entire cast for " . . . one of the most enjoyable pieces of musical fantasy every seen by Muskingum College," Harry Dixon continued:

> The happy ending of *Little Mary Sunshine* promises a happier beginning of the 1967-1968 Little Theater season. The members of the Little Theater will have to work very hard to top this delightful performance. Anyone who missed *Little Mary Sunshine* should be very sorry indeed.[58]

I agreed! It was a wonderful show, and I enjoyed every rehearsal and every performance. The cast who made this joyous occasion possible is listed at the end of this section. I have also included an enthusiastic note on the play from our Department Chairman, Dr. Richard Curtis.

Mother Courage and Her Children, "A Chronicle of the Thirty Years' War," written by Bertolt Brecht and adapted by Eric Bentley, was produced December 6-9, 1967, at the Little Theatre. I directed; Bob Barrows, the production supervisor, designed the set; and Rosa Terranova, guest actress from the Cambridge Community Theatre, played Mother Courage. The musical score by Paul Dessau and Brecht was played by Don Mercer, piano; Joan Esposito, flute; Betty Larrick, flute; and Fran Pavlov, accordion. William Blakesley created magnificent silk-screen posters for the event.

This play gave me problems. *Courage* requires a large cast and I never felt comfortable directing large-cast shows. I cut down on cast members by double- and triple-casting some of the actors. That helped, but there were other problems, as well. The play has a rough texture; there are many scenes which Brecht deliberately butts against one another in a way that draws attention to the butts! There are many scenes in a Shakespearean play, but Shakespeare constructs the scenes so that the action flows easily from one scene to another. Rough or flowing, bumpy or smooth, is fine with me, but one way or another, the play must move. The rehearsal schedule had to be adjusted to allow time to run more continuity rehearsals than was originally planned. Even before continuity, after each rehearsal, I developed the habit of running several scenes in sequence, in order to establish some semblance of movement, progression, and rhythm. I was also intimidated by the fact that ideas, not characters, must dominate the Brechtian stage. The actors must *present* the characters directly to the audience; they must not get lost in their roles and begin to *represent* the characters realistically. In other words, these are Brechtian, not Stanislavskian, characters! I had to re-train some of the actors to talk directly to the audience, instead of naturally to each other. It was important to give some attention to these problems because they were germane to the Brechtian style, what he called "the alienation effect."

In the play program, I discussed the history of the play and some of Brecht's ideas on staging.

Mother Courage and Her Children was written in 1939 by Bertolt Brecht, probably the most outstanding German playwright of the twentieth century. The play was first performed in Zurich in 1941 and by 1954 it was established as one of the authentic masterpieces of the modern stage. It has since been playing before audiences in all of the major capitals of the world; last seen on Broadway in 1963 with Anne Bancroft. It has been played with great success in colleges and universities all over America. *Mother Courage* is the play in which Brecht made his most passionate statement against war, but perhaps Brecht's greatest achievement in the drama lies in the creation of the character Anna Fierling, nicknamed "Mother Courage," the itinerant trader who drags her canteen through the blood and carnage of the Thirty Years' War and whose fatal error is to believe that she can make the war serve her ends. Mother Courage is essentially courageous because she continues her struggle for survival even after she has lost all three of her children.

Mother Courage and Her Children, 1967. Sons Elif (D. Deal) and Swiss Cheese (R. Jackson) pull the war wagon with their sister Kattrin (B. Brown) and Mother Courage (Rosa Terranova, Guest-Actress). *Theatre file photo courtesy M.C. Public Relations Office.*

Opposite this character of cunning, and ingenuity, is her daughter Kattrin who is essentially heroic, who gave up her life to save the children of a village under attack. One of the questions the play poses then is: Which trait is more desirable: Courage or Heroism?

A Note on the Staging: Brecht's theory of theatre held that ideas were more important than any other element of the theatrical situation. He wanted people to THINK not FEEL. To help get his audience in a correct critical attitude he would deliberately make them aware of the staging: lights would be visible, curtains would be burlap on wires, costumes and properties would not always be historically correct, and scene changes occurred in front of the audiences, music to irritate rather than please was introduced. We have tried to live up to his theory of staging, hoping to make the ideas of the play more important than anything else.[59]

In his *Black and Magenta* review, Harry Dixon commented,

In an extremely sensitive and well done performance of *Mother Courage* the players of the Little Theater gave a statement on war.

I would be amiss [sic] if I did not thank the Cambridge Players for the loan of an exceptionally gifted actress in Rosa Terranova. She and all of the rest of the cast gave a performance which could not be equaled in the professional theater. They put across a new idea of war with startling clarity. This was a play which did not allow you to get involved with the characters, but rather made you sit back and look at the action more or less objectively. It made you think. It asked, "why do we make war glamorous?"[60]

On March 6-9, 1968, Mrs. J. Herbert (Muriel) Bain directed Thornton Wilder's *Our Town* in the Little Theatre arena. It was a perfect setting for the play. Muskingum College was a small college, in a small town, and the theatre was a bare arena; the only scenery were the props and the costumes, which the actors brought with them. It was ideal, it was beautiful, and Muriel directed it beautifully.

She had this to say "About the Play,"

"*Our Town*" came from a search by Thornton Wilder for the universal and the eternal. He transformed the commonplaces to be found in daily life into the verities of reality. The emotional climate of the play is warm, yet as dry and spare as the lives of the people of Grover's Corners. It is infused with genuine sentiment, yet avoids sentimentality. The opening in New York in February of 1938 came with tremendous impact derived from the inherent spirit of the play, reinforced by the deliberate absence of stage scenery and properties, planned because Wilder believed "that when you emphasize place in the theatre you drag down and limit and harness time to it." Although this technical device is a heritage from the Greek and Shakespearean drama, as well as traditional Chinese theatre, it

Our Town, 1968. Emily Webb (N. Gleason) and George Gibbs (T. Spengler). *Theatre file photo courtesy M.C. Public Relations Office.*

came to the audiences of 1938 as an innovation. The author did not present *"Our Town"* as a picture of life in a New England village, but as an attempt to find a value above all price for the smallest events in our daily lives, seeking to show us that what is eternal has nothing to do with places, names, earth or even the stars, but has to do with human beings.[61]

In his review of *Our Town*, Harry Dixon paid tribute to the director, the actors and the author: "I don't think that I have ever been more impressed with the acting than I was during *Our Town*." He continued,

> Wilder has a point to make. He sets his play in a rural town and deliberately makes everything seem homey and minor. Then he draws a powerful parallel in the third act. . . .
> Our town has become the world, and we are too busy to know anyone on it. We have become so inflated with being alive that we overlook life, and ourselves."

Then, he draws a moral by referring to a popular song which goes, "Slow down, you move too fast. You've got to make the moment last. . . [62]

Taming of the Shrew, 1968. Petruchio (R. Jackson) hoists Katharine (D. Brevak) aloft to show her how to tame a shrew. *Theatre file photo courtesy M.C. Public Relations Office.*

I directed and designed a production of Shakespeare's *The Taming of the Shrew* on May 8-11, 1968, at the Little Theatre arena. From the beginning, I knew that I was going to cut the introduction with the drunken tinker, Christopher Sly. It was an early and firm decision, because I did not want to deal with more cast members than I had to, and I would have had to design a space for Sly to watch the show, and thereby lose badly-needed audience seating area.

For the main plot (which is the story of Petruchio and Katharine) and the sub-plot (which is the story of Lucentio and Bianca), I designed a replica of the Stratford Ontario stage. It was a modified Elizabethan open stage with stairs leading to the inner above and an inner below, which could be curtained for scene changes. I placed the structure against the wall in which the lobby door led into the main arena, so that the audience must pass through the inner below to get to their seats.

I cast well-trained and talented Rick Jackson and Donna Brevak in the leads; they were supported by an ensemble of experienced players who turned each of their roles into memorable characters. I especially enjoyed coaching the servants of Petruchio who, knowingly or unknowingly, helped tame the shrewish Katharine.

In his review for the *Black and Magenta*, Harry Dixon called the show a "Big Success." He also complimented the actors with such superlatives as "magnificent," "delightful," "charming," and "deserving of commendation." What pleased me was his opinion of the set.

> Special mention must be made of the magnificent set constructed by Mr. Hill and his crew. It was by far the best set that I have ever seen.[63]

As soon as the 1967-68 theatre season was finished, I left on sabbatical for the University of Minnesota to begin work on my doctorate in theatre. I studied straight through the summer of 1968, the regular school year, and the summer of 1969 to complete all my course work. I left the theatre in the capable hands of Muriel Bain and Mrs. Arthur (Elizabeth) Wills.

> Memorandum from Chairman Dr. Curtis
> Wed. 11-1-67
> Don—
> Let me congratulate you and your crew for the very fine piece of work in "Little Mary Sunshine!" It was a delightful spoof!
> Beth and I were amazed at your ingenious improvising of a facility that is, at best, inadequate for drama. We have been accustomed to superb drama at UMKC, where our Dept. Chmn. directed many of the plays. We are not disappointed in coming to Muskingum's theatre.
> Good Work!
> Cordially,
> Dick

Cast for *Little Mary Sunshine*
(Rick Besoyan)

Chief Brown Bear	Joseph K. Hand
Corporal "Billy" Jester	Jim Hall
Captain "Big Jim" Warrington	Gerry Lefever
Little Mary Sunshine	Kerry Sue Blunt
Mme. Ernestine Von Liebedich	Donna Brevak
Nancy Twinkle	Nancy Turnbull
Fleet Foot	Mr. Donald Hill
Yellow Feather	David Beall
General Oscar Fairfax, Retired	Chab Guthrie
Young Ladies from Eastchester Finishing School	
Cora	Kay McCracken
Henrietta	Patricia Finnegan
Gwendolyn	June Sadowski
Blanche	Sally Thompson
Maud	Nancy Gleason
Gentlemen of the United States Forest Rangers	
Pete	Larry Ledford
Slim	Robert Polenz
Tex	Jim Brubaker
Buster	Dennis Deal
Hank	Al Moore

Scene: .... In front of the Colorado Inn, High in the Rocky Mountains
Time: .... Early this Century (1900)
Director: .... Donald Hill
Designer: .... Donald Hill

Cast for *Mother Courage and Her Children*
(Bertolt Brecht adapted by Eric Bentley)
Indicates Guest Artist

Mother Courage .... Rosa Terranova*
Kattrin .... Beth Brown
Eilif .... Dennis Deal
Swiss Cheese .... Rick Jackson
Yvette Pottier .... Sally Uffner
Chaplain .... Ross Black
Cook .... Eric Walter
Recruiting Officer, Old Colonel, Lieutenant .... Bob Adams
Protestant Sergeant, Catholic Sergeant, First Soldier . Bill Smith
Swedish Commander, Old Peasant .... Fritz Enstrom
Off-Stage Voice, Stretcher Bearer, Soldier .... Mike Maslar
Ordnance Officer, Second Soldier .... Bill Barilka
Young Soldier, Second Soldier, Young Peasant .... Bob Bielecki
Man with Bandage, Soldier .... David Beall
Stretcher Bearer, Soldier .... Don Sharp
Regimental Clerk, Young Man .... David McCreight
Old Soldier, Regimental Clerk, Second Soldier .... John Mason
Singing Soldier .... James Hall
Woman .... Linda Clark
Peasant Man .... Steve Watt
Old Woman .... Joan Esposito
Peasant Woman .... Linda Enstrom
Scene: .... Sweden, Poland, Germany
Time: 1624-1636
Director: .... Donald Hill
Scene Design: .... Robert Barrows
Poster Art: .... William Blakesley

Cast for *Our Town*
(Thornton Wilder)

Stage Manager .... Robert Adams
Dr. Gibbs .... Charles W. Clark, Jr.
Mrs. Gibbs .... Jacqueline Dudek
Mrs. Webb .... Jane Ross
Joe Crowell .... David McCreight
Howie Newsome .... Dave Wiles
George Gibbs .... Tim Spengler
Rebecca Gibbs .... Holly Schutz
Emily Webb .... Nancy Gleason
Wally Webb .... Mark Sturtevant
Professor Willard .... Chab Guthrie
Mr. Webb .... Tom Tewell
Simon Stimson .... David McCreight
Mrs. Soames .... Joyce Gallagher
Constable Warren .... Dick Carrier

Si Crowell .... Chad Biegler
A Neighbor Woman .... Sheila Williams
Mrs. Howie Newsome .... Corrine Smyth
Mrs. McCarthy .... Helen Bartter
Joe Stoddard .... Mike Maslar
Sam Craig .... Robert McCreight
Pall-Bearers .... David Boyles, Bruce Farrar, Brian Pope, Gregory Van Atta
Scene: .... The action of the play takes place in Grover's Corners, New Hampshire—along the street, in the Gibbs' and Webb's homes, in Mr. Morgan's drug store, the Congregational Church, and in the cemetery, high on a hill above the village.
Time: .... May, 1901, July, 1904, and Summer, 1913
Director: .... Mrs. J. Herbert Bain
Set Design: .... Mike Maslar
Poster Art: .... William Blakesley

Cast for *The Taming of the Shrew*
(William Shakespeare)

Lucentio .... James Montieth
Tranio .... Robert Polenz
Baptista .... Ted Hissam
Katharine .... Donna Brevak
Bianca .... Janey Horine
Hortensio .... Dennis Deal
Gremio .... Stephen R. Watt
Biondello .... Chab Guthrie
Petruchio .... Rick Jackson
Grumio .... Al Evans
Servant .... Mike Maslar
Curtis .... Bob Bielecki
Sugarsop .... Mike Maslar
Philip .... Lewis Mitchell, Jr.
Joseph .... John Russell
Nathaniel .... Jim Shelton
Pedant .... John B. Mason
Haberdasher .... Fritz Enstrom
Tailor .... Bob Bielecki
Vincentio .... Fritz Enstrom
Widow .... Lynn Crothers
Servant .... John Russell
Officer .... Jim Shelton
Ladies .... Holly Blowers, June Sadowski
Scene: .... The play takes place in and around 16th Century Padua and Verona, Italy.
Designer/Director: .... Donald Hill
Poster Art: .... William Blakesley

 1968-1969

The 1968-69 theatre season opened during Homecoming Week, with Elizabeth Wills's production of *The Glass Menagerie* by Tennessee Williams. The

Little Theatre had been restored to its original configuration of a proscenium theatre, in order to accommodate the season of plays and the design concepts of the directors.

Mrs. Wills's approach to *The Glass Menagerie* may be seen in the *Black and Magenta* article written by Martha Green:

> Written in 1945, this play established Williams' reputation as a writer, for it was his first work to reach Broadway. The play focuses on the characters' inability to emerge from their dream-worlds and face the failures of their own lives. Amanda hides from her pauper world by dreaming of her glamorous childhood. Laura has completely withdrawn from reality, living only in the world of her glass animals (hence the name GLASS MENAGERIE). Even Tom escapes from his dreary warehouse job by dreaming of becoming a poet. This play, which won the Drama Critics Award of 1945, is often considered Tennessee Williams' most successful work.[64]

The play had a fine cast and the Homecoming audience was very appreciative of the production.

For the roles which have now become part of the classic American theatre, Mrs. Wills chose Linda Clark to play The Mother (Amanda Wingfield), James Ware Hall, Jr. to play Her Son (Tom), Catherine Smith to play Her Daughter (Laura), and G. Richard Hamilton, Jr. to play The Gentleman Caller (Jim O'Connor).

The Glass Menagerie, 1968. (foreground standing) The Mother (L. Clark), Her Daughter (C. Smith), Her Son (J. Hall, standing in the background) and The Gentleman Caller (R. Hamilton). *Theatre file photo courtesy M.C. Public Relations Office.*

Immediately following the final performance, the cast reprised scenes from *"Menagerie"* for the Drama and Poetry Reading Conference on October 26.

The year 1968 was the first year of a new calendar called "Interim." The month of January separated the two regular semesters of the school year. During that one month, students could take one course, on or off campus, or they could enjoy a full month of vacation. Miss Johnson's class in Readers' Theatre produced an original program, "Journey into Everyman," on January 29 at the Little Theatre.

On March 19-22, Muriel directed William Goldman's tense melodrama, *The Lion in Winter.* This drama of Henry II, King of England, and his estranged wife, Eleanor of Aquitaine, details a family quarrel that kept England and the Continent on the edges of their collective seats for almost a century.

Muriel cast the production with an experienced ensemble of players that did justice to the rich metaphorical language of the play, and the stormy struggle for power that waged within and without the royal family. Ted Hissam played Henry II, King of England; Donna Brevak played Henry's wife, Eleanor of Aquitaine; Richard Jackson played their eldest son, Richard the Lionheart; Charles W. Clark, Jr. played the middle son, Geoffrey; and Jim Shelton played the youngest son, John. Nancy Gleason was cast as a French Princess, Alais, and David Beall was Philip, King of France.

In her program notes for the play, Muriel wrote,

> Here we encounter the people who wielded the power that controlled the destiny of 12th century Europe and, through their involvement with the Crusades, the Middle East. Playwright Goldman says, "The historical material on Henry's reign is considerable insofar as battles, plots, wars, treaties and alliances are concerned. This play, while simplifying the meeting of the French and English Kings in 1183, is accurately based on the available data and the characters are consistent with that information. Much [sic] of the personal relationships of the people are heavily tinged with comedy, but delving deeper I also found great tragedy in this terrifying family who fought and plotted among themselves, but usually reunited and forgave." It is the tragedy of those who deeply wanted peace but were unable to use their enormous power to that end.[65]

Bob Bielecki, reviewing *Lion in Winter,* complimented the "experienced cast" for an "excellent job in their characterizations." He found "The tempo was forceful but not too fast, the lines were well delivered, and the cast worked well together. The technical work was excellent with especially good costuming. *The Lion in Winter* was a fine piece of theatrical work."[66]

The final production of the season was William Saroyan's *The Time of Your Life,* directed by Elizabeth Wills and performed on May 14-17 at the Little Theatre. Another classic of the American theatre, this play tells the story of Joe's search for happiness. Like so many of Eugene O'Neill's plays, the search takes him to a waterfront saloon and a cast of unique characters, all of whom are searching for the same thing as Joe. The play won both the Drama Critics' Circle Award and the Pulitzer Prize for 1939-1940.

In the program of the play, Mrs. Wills quoted some of Saroyan's philosophy of life, which explained the background for the play.

> In the time of your life, live—so that in good time there shall be no ugliness or death for yourself or for any life your life touches. Seek goodness everywhere, and when it is found, bring it out of its hiding-place and let it be free and unashamed. In the time of your life, live—so that wondrous time you shall not add to the misery and sorrow of the world, but shall smile to the infinite delight and mystery of it.[67]
> —*William Saroyan*

Cast for *The Time of Your Life*
(William Saroyan)

Joe, a loafer .... J. Theodore Williams

Tom, his disciple .... Thomas A. Bonomo
Nick, owner of Nick's Pacific Street
    Saloon, Restaurant, and Entertainment Palace .. Gary C. Gardner
Kitty Duval, a young woman with memories ...... Corinne E. Smyth
Arab, an Eastern philosopher .... Mike Maslar
Newsboy .... Margaret Leta Harris
Dulley, a young man in love .... Jeffrey A. Hillyer
Willie, a marble-game maniac .... James Anderson, Jr.
Harriet, a natural born hoofer .... Rozelle (Rocky) Hill
Wesley, a natural born pianist .... Steve Curtis
McCarthy, a longshoreman .... David Johnson
Krupp, a waterfront cop .... Jeffrey Wade Clark
Kit Carson, an old Indian fighter .... Ken Magill
Elsie, a nurse .... Joan Marie Lacey
Lorene, a life-saver .... Cheryl Thornton
Mary L., a woman of quality .... Susan Willis
Blick, a heel .... Peter Shonkwiler
A street walker .... Helen Bartter
Her side kick .... Amanda Emily Roberts
A Society lady .... Mary Alice Patrick
A Society gentleman .... G. Richard Hamilton
The Drunkard .... Theodore H. Hissam
A Cop .... David Johnson
Sam .... G. Richard Hamilton
Nick's mother .... Mary Alice Patrick
Scene: .... Nick's waterfront Pacific Street Saloon, Restaurant, and Entertainment
                Palace
Time: .... Afternoon and night of a day in October
Director: .... Elizabeth Wills

1969-1970

Homecoming Week (October 1-4) was blessed by one of the Little Theatre's most popular productions of the decade. Two music majors, Al Evans, a senior at Muskingum, and Darryl Bojanowski, a senior at Otterbein, had written an original musical based on William Pratt's nineteenth century temperance melodrama. They had been working on *Ten Nights in a Bar-Room* for two years, rewriting and revising it until they felt that it was ready for production.[68] When they offered it to me, I read it, listened to the music, and immediately began production.

With the help of Al Evans as the musical director and Chab Guthrie as the production designer, I analyzed the script for treatment and style. Since the show was based on an old-fashioned temperance melodrama, the original and main idea was to warn people about the bad effects of alcohol on the human system, the human spirit, and human society in general. The message of the musical was made clear in the opening "Prologue," spoken by Mr. Romaine and taken from the Book of Proverbs, 23:29-38:

> Who has woe? Who has sorrow?
>   Who has strife? Who has complaining?
> Who has wounds without cause?

Who has redness of eyes?
Those who tarry long over wine,
    Those who go to try mixed wine.
Do not look at the wine when it is red,
    When it sparkles in the cup
    And goes down smoothly.
At the last it bites like a serpent
    And stings like an adder.
Your eyes will see strange things,
    And your mind utter perverse things.
You will be like one who lies down in the midst of the sea,
    Like one who lies on the top of a mast.
"They struck me," you will say, "but I was not hurt;
    They beat me, but I did not feel it.
When shall I awake?
    I will seek another drink."[69]

This temperance message is reinforced by Mrs. Tippler's opening song, "Ten Nights in a Bar-Room,"

Ten Nights in a Bar-room
Will lead you to shame.
Numb, dumb, a drunken bum
Whom no one wants to claim.
Ten Nights in a Bar-room
Will lead you to shame.[70]

Darryl Bojanowski (standing) wrote the book, and Al Evans (seated) composed the music and lyrics for *Ten Nights in a Bar Room*, a 1969 original musical melodrama based loosely on a temperance melodrama by William Pratt. *Theatre file photo, M. C. Public Relations Office.*

I could not tamper with the message itself, because it was true–one which young people, especially the "innocent," need to take to heart. The townspeople of New Concord believed in the message, having voted the township dry for the past sixty-odd years of the twentieth century. The basic premise of the play was still good today, but with a difference. That difference was caused by the passage of time, the changing attitudes toward liquor, and the methods of treatment for alcohol abuse, as well as the changing styles of theatre. That the musical was written for entertainment was made clear by the way in which the authors used the time-worn plot lines, the exaggerated stage directions, and the melodramatic dialogue. The authors had fun writing the show and they

Ten Nights in a Bar Room, 1969. Simon Slade, Landlord of the Sickle & Sheaf (P. Greskovich) stops Harvey Green, a Gambler (L. Keffer) from attacking Willie Hammond, a Young Man (J. Hillyer). Drunk No. 2 (C. Smi th) on Green's right and Drunk No. 1 (J. Reed) on Green's left, hold him back. *Photo courtesy M.C. Public Relations Office.*

wanted the audience to have fun watching it.

While I couldn't tamper with the message, I <u>could</u> tamper with the "packaging"– the way in which the message was presented. The script was frankly presentational in the use of a narrator, Mr. Romaine, who was similar to the Stage Manager in *Our Town*. This fact made a less realistic style of staging permissible. Historically, the nineteenth century melodrama carried with it certain stage devices that could be handled in a way that would lighten the message, even give it a sense of humor. For example, the scenery could be painted and two-dimensional instead of three-dimensional as in the realistic theatre. In my mind's eye, the scene in which Mary ascends to Heaven could be done with a harness and wire and angel's wings or, as done in the script, with Mr. Romaine simply bringing on a pair of angel's wings and then taking Mary off the stage. The acting must be convincing, but it also could be broad and exaggerated, true to the style of old-fashioned melodrama.

With few exceptions, the lyrics to the songs were simplistic and platitudinous; they demanded a sincerity and delicate touch that possessed just the right amount of whimsy to keep and hold attention. The music and lyrics were a mixture of styles from a variety of musical forms that spanned three centuries of operetta and musical comedies.

With such a script, there were many possibilities for fun without doing damage to the message of the play. I did what my imagination prompted and, where it failed, I listened to Al Evans, Chab Guthrie, and the cast of players whose imaginations never went dry.

Barbie Benson's review of the production, "Homecoming Play Smash Hit!!!", was enthusiastic and complimentary.

> The first good thing about watching the Little Theatre's production of *Ten Nights in a Bar-Room*, which sold out for all four evenings last weekend, was that it captured your very closest attention, mixing fun with funny, and updating so many of the sticky emotional characteristics of ordinary melodramas. . . ..
>
> Alongside of the acting, clever use of the stage mechanics of the script, such as the twinkling star above the audience, an obstinate curtain for Mrs. Tippler and an "instant forest" from the proscenium, made the play a very memorable occasion. Any hangover produced by *Ten Nights in a Bar-Room* can only be from grinning so hard.[71]

The production of a new play always carries with it some trepidation as to how the audience will react to it. I was pleased with the audience's reception, which, according to the box office and our S.R.O. sign, was enthusiastic in its approval. On the other side of the footlights, the actors and the crew believed in the moral, theatrical, and entertainment values of the musical. They worked assiduously and cooperatively throughout the rehearsal and performance periods. What might have been a difficult and labored production came off with ease and joy.

Following *Ten Nights in a Bar-Room*, students from the class in Play Direction produced a series of one-act plays on December 4-6. One of the plays, "The Whiteshop," was a Midwest premiere for Columbus playwright, Garrett Robinson. Rozell ("Rocky") Hill directed and Muriel Bain was the production supervisor for the series of four one-act plays.

Ms. Sue Cook and I supervised an Interim course called "Theatre of Involvement." The course involved lectures, rehearsals, and performances of a series of *avante garde* theatre pieces, January 13-22 and February 5. The roster of events included Bethany College Touring Company, which performed "The American Dream" and "The Zoo Story" by Edward Albee, a Happening,* a protest theatre piece, several original one-acts, and an Interpersonal Communication Workshop with guest communication consultant, Sandra O'Connell ('62).

On January 28, Miss Johnson directed a class in Readers Theatre in an original performance of "Every Face Tells a Story," at the Little Theatre.

For the second major production of the 1969-70 theatre season, I directed and designed Walter Kerr's adaptation of *The Birds* by Aristophanes (March 18-21). We used Ms. Sue Cook's Modern Dance Club and Tap Dance Club as the singing-dancing choruses, in which Ms. Cook performed, as well as advised. Janet Fittkau supplied the choreography, and Al Evans remained faithfully at the piano throughout the rehearsal and performance periods.

The Birds is a "Utopian" comedy, in which two earthlings search for the ideal place in which to live. They create a city in the clouds (Cuckooland) which is free from all corruption, pollution, unhappiness, and perils of war.[72] Aristophanes makes his serious anti-war theme palatable by overlaying it with topical humor, jokes about politicians, music with choruses of singers and dancers, and sketches bordering on the lewd and suggestive, similar to those of modern burlesque.

Walter Kerr's adaptation maintains the significance of the original, even though

---

*A Happening is an event in which the audience is expected to participate by performing certain actions or complete specific tasks. The audience may be joined by actors in the event, or the audience may be directed by actors in completing their actions.

The Birds, 1970. The finale. (far up center) Prometheus-in-drag (C. Sweigart) appears and, to the tune of "When You Wish Upon a Star," waves his "poof" wand and everyone disappears. Theatre file photo.

he eliminates the topical jokes, which mean little to a twentieth century audience, and substitutes slapstick comedy for the sexual innuendoes. In other words, Kerr cleaned up the comedy of the world's first "dirty old man" of dramatic literature. The students gravitated to the script and added some of their own impromptu gags, which they pulled out of the bag of campus humor. When appropriate, I quickly made the improvisations part of the script.

I designed an Italianate set by using a series of platforms that were faced with ground-rows of painted, contoured clouds, and matched with a series of cloud borders and wings. A runway for the dancers extended from the front of the stage into the auditorium. One piece of antiquated Renaissance machinery was simulated in the chariot that lowered the Rainbow Goddess, Iris ("Rocky" Hill, wearing a multi-colored Ionic himation), from the Little Theatre Heavens to the runway. It was a spectacular entrance!

The costumes were simple Greek chitons and himations for the principals. The bird choruses wore leotards befitting the color of their species: we had black, red, blue, and yellow birds. The birds wore colored hats with pointed bills. Nylon webbing was sewn to the arm and torso of the leotards to simulate wings when the arms were raised. The acting was directed to be believable, but fast-paced, in keeping with the comedy and tempo of the dancers. I exploited every appropriate bird song I could find, from bouncy Broadway rhythm numbers to lyrical love calls.

Everyone had a lot of fun with this show: the director, the actors, the crew, and the audience. I have included President Manley's response to *The Birds*.

April 16-17 brought two one-act plays, directed by senior seminar students Rozelle ("Rocky") Hill and Cheryl D. Swiss. Rocky directed "The Relatives, or The Best Part of Us Is Underground," a new script by student playwright, Sally Stinson.

Cheri Swiss directed "Something Unspoken" by Tennessee Williams.

The final major production of the season was *The Firebugs* by Max Frisch, directed by Muriel Bain and performed May 13-16 at the Little Theatre. The play was typified as an " . . . allegory depicting the intrusion of unwelcome and dangerous forces into the lives of the Biedermans."[73]

Max Frisch, a contemporary Swiss playwright, blends several dramatic forms in this play: the realism of Ibsen, and the epic style of Bertolt Brecht can be seen. There is also a Greek-like Chorus of Firemen who comment on the action. The author sees " . . . his work as a 'Learning Play Without a Lesson,' in which Gottlieb Biederman is Everyman."[74] The subjection of the Biederman family is a symbol of what occurs when people do not act against invasive powers in their lives.

The cast was composed of Chab Guthrie and Margaret Leta Harris as The Biedermans; Mandy Roberts, a Maid; Jack Falcon, Sepp, a wrestler; Robert Bielecki, a Waiter; Ron Wheeler, a Policeman; Jeff Schroeder, a Professor; and Janna Blair, Mrs. Knechtling. James Monteith, Pete Shonkwiler, and Bob Thiele were the Chorus of Firemen.

The play was well-directed, well-acted, and well-received by the campus audience.

The 1969-70 theatre season provided a suitable ending to a decade of successful productions, in a climate conducive to an expanding theatre program. The original musical, *Ten Nights in a Bar-Room,* epitomized the joyful creativity of the pool of student talent that had developed over a ten-year period. In "Theatre of Involvement," that talent felt free to explode in a controlled fashion into various forms of experimental theatre, such as Theatre of the Absurd, Street Theatre, Happenings, and Improvisational Theatrics. *The Birds* continued the celebration with the help of Aristophanes's exuberant vaudevillian extravaganza.

Muriel's production of *The Firebugs* proved a necessary reminder that there was another side to the coin of comedy: a dark side. It served as a warning that happiness is not a permanent life-style; there are incendiaries abroad; the world is a fickle mix of elements, extremely volatile.

Who could have foretold the mixture of joys and sorrows that would engulf our theatre in the next decade.

MUSKINGUM COLLEGE
MEMORANDUM
office of the president [sic]
    March 23, 1970
Mr. Don Hill
Campus
Dear Don:
    Your production of "The Birds" was a real success. The cast seemed to have as much fun during it as the audience had watching it. It seemed to me you took just the right type liberties in infiltrating the presentation with local references and colloquialisms. Please express my thanks and congratulations to each member of the cast and production crew.
    Harry Manley

Cast for *Ten Nights in a Bar-Room*
(An Original Musical Melodrama Based Loosely on a Temperance Melodrama by William Pratt)

Music and Lyrics   Book
Al Evans   Darryl Bojanowski

Mr. Romaine, a Traveller .... Mr. Chab Guthrie
Mrs. Tippler, a Temperance Crusader .... Miss Martha Zebreski
Harvey Greene, a Gambler .... Mr. Larry Keffer
Simon Slade, Landlord of the Sickle & Sheaf .. Mr. Paul Greskovich
Frank Slade, his Son .... Mr. James Monteith
Mehitable Slade, his Daughter .... Miss Mary Ann Spitznagel
Mrs. Slade, his Wife .... Miss Cheri Swiss
Willie Hammond, a Young Man .... Mr. Jeff Hillyer
Joe Morgan, a Drunkard .... Mr. Tim Spengler
Mary Morgan, his Daughter .... Miss Helen Bartter
Mrs. Morgan, his Wife .... Miss Cynthia Crowther
Drunk No. 1 .... Mr. Jeff Reed
Drunk No. 2 .... Mr. Cary Smith
Drunk No. 3 .... Mr. Mike Abood
Barmaid.. Miss Margaret Harris
Another Barmaid .... Miss Rocky Hill
Townsperson .... Miss Priscilla Bentley
At the Piano .... Mr. Al Evans
Scene:In and Outside the Sickle and Sheaf Bar-Room
Director: .... Mr. Donald Hill
Production Designer: .... Mr. Chab Guthrie
Poster Art & Program Cover: .... Mr. Chab Guthrie

Cast for *The Birds*
(Aristophanes)

At the Piano .... Al Evans
Pithataerus, the footloose .... Richard Hamilton
Euelpides, the footsore .... Timothy Spengler
Trochilus, the butlerbird .... Jeff Hillyer
Epops, King of the Birds .... Charles Garner
Procne, the Nightingale, wife to Epops .... Liz Head
Chorus of Birds .... Mary Ann Spitznagel, Mandy Roberts, Julie Howe, Corinne Smyth, Priscilla Bentley, Susan Simerka
The Priest Bird .... Larry Keffer
The Poet .... James Monteith
The Prophet .... Mike Maslar
The Real-Estate Man .... Jeff Clark
The Inspector .... Thomas Purchase
The Lawyer .... Stephen Driscoll
First Messenger .... Jeff Hillyer
Second Messenger .... Thomas Purchase
Iris, the Swift, a small-time goddess .... Rocky Hill
A Herald .... Larry Keffer
Prometheus .... Charles Sweigart
Neptune .... Jeff Clark
Hercules .... R. B. Riley

(Understudy ....Cheri Swiss)	
Barbarian God...Mike Maslar	
Chorus of Red Birds ....Marta Young, Aija Ribens, Sherrie Crawford, Connie Henderson, Lisa Freeman	
Chorus of Yellow Birds....................................Janet Fittkau, Lyn Climo, Debby Barden, Sandy Simmerer, Miss Sue Cook	
Scene: ....Cloud Cuckooland on a high mountain top	
Designer/Director: ....Donald Hill	
Choreographer: ....Janet Fittkau	
Dance Instructor: ....Sue Cook	
Poster and Program Art: ....Chab Guthrie	

REFERENCES (The Plays: 1960–1970)

1   Robert Helpmann quoted by Charles Castle, *Noel* (New York: Doubleday & Company, Inc., 1973), pp. 18-20.
2   Sheridan Morley, *A Talent to Amuse: A Biography of Noel Coward* (Garden City, New York: Doubleday & Company, Inc., 1969), p. 398.
3   John Gielgud, *Early Stages* (New York: The Macmillan Company, 1939), p. 98.
4   Donald Hill, "About the Play," Original Program, *The House of Bernarda Alba, A Drama About Women in the Villages of Spain*, December 7-10, 1960, Little Theatre, n.p.
5   Bing Bills, "*Bernarda Alba* Reviewed," *B&M,* December 13, 1960, p. 1.
6   Ibid.
7   Daniel Jones, "Preface," to *Under Milk Wood, A Play for Voices* by Dylan Thomas (New York: A New Directions Book, published by James Laughlin, 1954), vii.
8   Jacket cover for *Under Milk Wood, A Play for Voices* by Dylan Thomas (New York: New Directions Book).
9   Donald Hill, "About the Play," Original Program, *Under Milk Wood, A Play for Voices*, March 8-11, 1961, Little Theatre, n.p.
10   Daniel Jones, "Preface," ix.
11   Hill, "About the Play," n.p.
12   Bing Bills, "Student Gives Review of *Under Milk Wood*," *Black and Magenta*, March 14, 1961, p. 1.
13   "Shakespearean Comedy Gets Excellent Review," *B&M,* May 16, 1961, pp. 1 & 3.
14   Robert N. Montgomery, in a Memorandum to Donald Hill, Muskingum College, New Concord, Ohio, May 29, 1961.
15   "1961 Stratford Seminar on Shakespeare," a mimeographed information sheet from the Stratford Shakespearean Festival Foundation of Canada, Stratford, Ontario, 1961, n.p.
16   Stanley Schutz, "Program Notes," Original Program, *Inherit the Wind*, March 7-10, 1962, Little Theatre, n.p.
17   Sandy O'Connell, "*Inherit the Wind* Reviewed," *B&M,* March 13, 1962, p. 1.
18   Donald Hill, "Repertory Theatre," Personal File, 1962, pp. 1-3.
19   Stanley Schutz, "Program Notes," Original Program, *The Male Animal*, October 24-27, 1962, Little Theatre, n.p.
20   Ibid.
21   Archibald MacLeish, "Program Notes," (Paraphrased by Donald Hill), Original Program, *J. B.*, December 12-15, 1962, Little Theatre, n.p.
22   Ibid.
23   Alan Dawson, "*J. B.* Reviewed," *B&M,* December 18, 1962, p. 3.
24   Rex McGraw, "Program Notes," Original Program, *The Little Foxes,* March 13-16, 1963, Little Theatre, n.p.
25   Judy Sjoberg, "*The Little Foxes* in Retrospect," *B&M,* March 19, 1963, p. 2.
26   "Twelfth Night," *Benet's Reader's Encyclopedia,* Third Edition, Carol Cohen, Editorial Director (New York: Harper & Row Publishers, 1987), p. 1003.
27   "*Twelfth Night* Revisited," *B&M,* May 24, 1963, p. 2.
28   "*The Fantasticks, A Parable of Love,*" Original Program, October 16-19, 1963, Little Theatre, n.p.
29   "*The Fantasticks,* October 15-19," *Outlook: '63-'64,* Department of Speech, Muskingum College, 1963, n.p.
30   "*Fantasticks* in Retrospect," *B&M,* October 29, 1963, p. 1.
31   "*An Enemy of the People,* December 11-14," *Outlook: '63-'64,* n.p.
32   "*Antigone,* March 11-14," *Outlook: '63-'64,* n.p.
33   Dave Jamison, "Sophocles and Anouilh Plays Show Dramatic Contrast," *Black and Magenta*, March 17, 1964, p. 1.
34   "*The Merry Wives of Windsor,* May 6-9," *Outlook: '63-'64,* n.p.

35   "McGraw Scores Another Hit," *B&M,* May 12, 1964, p. 1.

36   "Androcles," *Benet's Reader's Encyclopedia,* p. 35.

37   "*Androcles and the Lion*: George B. Shaw's Play Is Week End Highlight," *B&M,* October 24, 1964, p. 6.

38   Bob Kinnard, "Hill Leads Wilde Success," *B&M,* December 15, 1964, pp. 1 & 3.

39   Donald Hill, "About the Play," Original Program, *Dinny and the Witches,* March 17-20, 1965, Little Theatre, n.p.

40   "Beauty and the Beast," *Benet's Reader's Encyclopedia,* p. 80.

41   "Hill and Little Theatre Do Miller's Play Justice," *B&M,* November 2, 1965, p. 3.

42   Stanley Schutz, "Director's Notes," Original Program, *Stalag 17,* December 8-11, Little Theatre, n.p.

43   Ibid.

44   "War Play Well-Staged," *B&M,* January 11, 1966, p. 3.

45   Donald Hill, "The Author and the Play," Original Program, *Doña Rosita*, March 16-19, 1966, Little Theatre, n.p.

46   Ibid.

47   "*Doña Rosita* Scores Little Theatre Success," *B&M,* March 29, 1966, p. 5.

48   Noel Coward, *Present Indicative,* pp. 135-136.

49   "Muskies Respond to *Hay Fever, B&M,* May 10, 1966, p. 3.

50   Donald Hill, "The Author and the Play," Original Program, *A Thurber Carnival,* October 19-22, 1966, Little Theatre, n.p.

51   Donald Hill, "A Look at the Cast," Original Program, *A Thurber Carnival,* n.p.

52   Mrs. J. Herbert (Muriel) Bain, "The Play," Original Program, "The Swampdwellers," November 9, 11 & 12, 1966, Little Theatre, n.p.

53   Mrs. Bain, "Cast Notes," Original Program, "The Swampdwellers," n.p.

54   Hill, "Program Notes," Original Program, *Medea,* n.p.

55   "Faculty Play Critique," *B&M,* March 16, 1967, p. 3.

56   Jane Horine, "Student Reviews *Waiting for Godot* and Finds Performance Most Capable," *B&M,* May 18, 1967, p. 3.

57   Donald Hill, "About the Play," Original Program, *Little Mary Sunshine,* October 18-21, 1967, Little Theatre, n.p.

58   Harry Dixon, "Muskie Theatre Cast Voted 3-1/4 Stars for *Little Mary Sunshine* Opening," *B&M,* November 2, 1967, p. 3.

59   Donald Hill, "About the Play and the Playwright," Original Program, *Mother Courage and Her Children: A Chronicle of the 30 Years War,* December 6-9, 1967, Little Theatre, n.p.

60   Harry Dixon, "*Mother Courage* Prompts the Audience to Consider Why We Engage Ourselves in War," *B&M,* December 14, 1967, p. 1.

61   Muriel Bain, "About the Play," Original Program, *Our Town,* March 6-9, 1968, Little Theatre, n.p.

62   Harry Dixon, "Robert Adams Does an Impressive Job as the Lead in Wilder's *Our Town,*" *B&M,* March 14, 1968, p. 4.

63   Harry Dixon, "*Shrew* Production is Big Success," *B&M,* May 16, 1968, p. 3.

64   Martha Green, "Mrs. Wills Directs Homecoming Play," *B&M,* September 26, 1968, p. 1.

65   Muriel Bain, "About the Play," Original Program, *The Lion in Winter,* March 19-22, 1969, Little Theatre, n.p.

66   Bob Bielecki, "*Lion in Winter,*" *B&M,* March 25, 1969, p. 9.

67   William Saroyan, quoted by Mrs. Wills, Original Program, *The Time of Your Life,* May 14-17, 1969, n.p.

68   "Bojanowski Combines Talents to Write Musical, Opening Night–October 1," *The Tan and the Cardinal*, a Student Publication of Otterbein College, Westerville, Ohio, September 26, 1969, p. 3.

69   Al Evans (Music and Lyrics) and Darryl Bojanowski (Book), *Ten Nights in a Bar-Room*, A Musical Entertainment Based Loosely on a Temperance Melodrama by William Pratt, "Prologue," n.p.

70   Ibid., p. 2.

71   Barbie Benson, "Homecoming Play Smash Hit!!!" *B&M,* October 10, 1969, p. 6.

72   Donald Hill, "Director's Note," Original Program, *The Birds,* March 18-21, 1970, Little Theatre, n.p.

73   Mrs. J. Herbert (Muriel) Bain, "About the Play," Original Program, *The Firebugs,* May 13-16, Little Theatre, n.p.

74   Ibid.

Theatre in the '70s
People and Events

The decade of the '70s was so crowded with events that affected the Muskingum College Theatre, both favorably and unfavorably, that for clarity and brevity, it may be best to deal with them chronologically.

1971
Richard Downing

Mr. Richard Downing (M.A., University of Michigan) was appointed as the technical director of the theatre. With this appointment, the theatre staff doubled in size. Now there were two people to share the work load, students could receive more attention and supervision, and the campus could look forward to an expanded program of one-act and full-length plays.

Muriel Bain

With the production of Shakespeare's *Comedy of Errors,* Muriel Bain retired from the directing staff of the theatre. She remained one of the theatre's loved and cherished friends.

1972
Miss Mary Elizabeth Johnson

Miss Mary Elizabeth Johnson, Associate Professor of Speech, announced her retirement in March, after twenty-eight years of service. Miss Johnson received her A.B. in Speech from Muskingum College (1926) and her M.A. in Theatre and Interpretation from the University of Michigan. Her graduate instruction included work with such famous teachers as Thomas Wood Stevens, Valentine Windt, Louis M. Eich, and Frank Rarig. Further work in the area of speech pathology was done at Northwestern University and Ohio State.

In 1944, Miss Johnson began her career at Muskingum College as Instructor of Speech and Director of Theatre. She held the latter position until 1957. When Mrs. Layton retired, Miss Johnson assumed some of the duties in the interpretation area. Miss Johnson's career at Muskingum also saw her as Chairperson of the Drama and Poetry Reading Conference from 1946 until 1968. In that position, she was responsible for bringing hundreds of high school students from the southeastern Ohio area to Muskingum for a day of oral interpretation, play production, and discussions by experts. She also held the position of Chairperson of the Communications Area from 1950 to 1953, and

Mary Elizabeth Johnson ('26). *Theatre file photo courtesy M.C. Public Relations Office.*

she was Acting Chairperson of the Speech Department from 1965-67.[1]

Cheri Swiss

Cheryl D. Swiss, a 1970 Muskingum College theatre graduate, completed her M.A. thesis at Ohio University. Entitled "A History of Theatre at Muskingum College," the work covers theatrical beginnings from 1837 to development of a theatre major (1970-1971). As the only history of its kind, it is extremely valuable, and a copy resides in the Archives of the Muskingum College Library.

Barry Baughman

The theatre was devastated by the news that Barry Baughman ('64) was electrocuted at the Dorset Summer Playhouse in Dorset, Vermont, while backstage serving as that theatre's technical director. During his years at Muskingum, Barry acted in "The Bald Soprano," *A Midsummer Night's Dream,* and *Twelfth Night*; however, he was better known as a permanent member of the theatre's production staff from 1960 to 1963, serving mainly in the capacity of lighting designer. Barry had continued his association with Muskingum after his graduation; he had presented a workshop on lighting for Muskingum Players, and designed lighting for *Dona Rosita* (1966) and *Medea* (1966). He had received his M.A. in technical theatre from Kent State University, and then accepted a position at the University of Kentucky, where he was employed at the time of his death.[2]

1973

Mrs. Ferne Parsons Layton

A sense of grief again enveloped the theatre with the passing of Mrs. Ferne Parsons Layton, long-time teacher and guiding light of the theatre at Muskingum. In 1914, Mrs. Layton and her husband, Dr. Charles R. Layton, laid the foundation for the present Speech Communication and Theatre Department. A graduate of Mount Union-Scio College and the University of Michigan, she became a full professor at Muskingum until her retirement in 1957.

I always regarded Mrs. Layton as the patron saint of theatre at Muskingum; no theatre could have asked for more. She was fond of reciting, on appropriate occasions, the words of Charlotte Cushman, the great American actress:

> I think I love and honor all arts equally, only putting my own just above the others because in it I recognize the union and culmination of them all. It seems to me when God conceived the world, that was poetry; when He formed it, that was sculpture; when He colored it, that was painting; when He peopled it with loving beings, that was the divine, eternal drama.

Mrs. Layton was one of those loving beings, because she loved people and she expressed her love through teaching the great literature that mirrored the lives of people. In the humanness of her spirit, and in her concern for the eternal drama of life, lay her charm and undying influence.[3]

Victor Buono

The Artist-Lecture Series brought the actor, Victor Buono, to the campus for a series of readings. At the December 3 Convocation, he performed Dylan Thomas's play, "A Child's Christmas in Wales." In the evening, he entertained the audience with a program of poetry and drama drawn from such diverse writers as Robert Burns, Emily Dickinson, Mark Twain, Tennessee Williams, and Buono himself.

Mr. Buono brought with him a wealth of experience on stage, television, and film. He became well-known for his villainous roles in *Whatever Happened to Baby Jane* (for which he received an Academy Award nomination) and *Hush, Hush, Sweet Charlotte*. On stage, Mr. Buono was impressive and every inch the artist. Off stage, he was just as impressive, but quite ingenuous and unassuming. He particularly enjoyed talking with students at their coffee hour, and he was delighted to be invited, after his evening performance, to the Little Theatre, where he watched dress rehearsals for one-act plays that were scheduled to be performed that week.[4]

1974
Mercedes McCambridge

Another Artist-Lecture Series event was the appearance of Mercedes McCambridge for two workshops and an evening performance on April 22-23.

Portrait of Mercedes McCambridge "'Anything that happens to you that doesn't kill you will be good for you.'" (from *The Quality of Mercy, An Autobiography* by Mercedes McCambridge. Photo courtesy of American Program Bureau.

"Mercy" (as she liked to be called) won an Academy Award for best supporting actress in her first film, *All the Kings Men* (1949). The prestige of this honor ensured her a film career that resulted in twenty films over the next twenty years. She played opposite Joan Crawford in *Johnny Guitar* (1954), a film in which the two women strapped on six-guns for the required Western shoot-out ending. This gender-bender film became a favorite cult film for fans and film theorists, who likened it to a McCarthy-era allegory or a Freudian exercise.[5] Two years later, she received a second Academy Award nomination for her role in *Giant* (1956), a legendary film based on Edna Ferber's story of cattle and oil in Texas. The film featured Rock Hudson, Elizabeth Taylor, and James Dean who, at the height of popularity, was killed during the making of the film. During the following years, she was cast in *A Farewell to Arms* (1957), *A Touch of Evil* (1958), and *Suddenly Last Summer* (1960).

Then came the horror film, *The Exorcist* (1973), which changed the face of that genre forever.[6] Mercy supplied the Voice of the Demon which inhabited the body of a young girl (Linda Blair). The director of the film, William Friedkin, promised to give her credit for such a significant contribution.

In her autobiography, *The Quality of Mercy*, she tells how she attended the premiere of the film and waited for the credits to appear. When they did begin to roll, there was no mention of her name! She sued Warner Brothers for recognition of her work and won.[7] The film won an Academy Award for Special Effects. Mercy shared the Award, in recognition for her work on the film.

Mercy's films constitute only one-fourth of her career, which includes radio, theatre, and television. Orson Wells called Mercy "the world's greatest living radio actress." She was only a junior at Mundelein College in Chicago when she signed a five-year contract with NBC.[8] She quickly became known as the girl who could breathe life into the most hackneyed script. In her own words, "For a year-and-a-half, I played on every soap opera that came out of Chicago, and in those days, all of them did . . . and I did all of them!"[8] She was heard on "Abie's Irish Rose," "I Love a Mystery," "Inner Sanctum," "One Man's Family," "The Guiding Light," "The Mercury Theatre," and she played Nora Drake on "This is Nora Drake." Her career in radio deeply influenced her training as an actress, and she attributes a large percent of her success to that area. (Witness *The Exorcist.*)[9]

While still a radio actress, Mercy began a stage career. She made her Broadway debut in *A Place of Our Own* (1945). Since that time, she has played leading roles in *The Miracle Worker, Candida, The Little Foxes, The Glass Menagerie, Medea, The Subject was Roses,* and *The Madwoman of Chaillot.* In 1963, Mercy returned to the New York stage to take over Shelley Winters's role in John Carlino's *Cages,* and in 1964, succeeded Uta Hagen as Martha in *Who's Afraid of Virginia Woolf?,* Edward Albee's Broadway hit.[10]

Mercy's careers in radio, film, and theatre quite naturally led to television. She has appeared on most of the nation's prominent TV shows, including "Bonanza," "The Ed Sullivan Show," and "Studio One." She starred in her own series, "Wire Service" and "Defense Attorney."[11]

Mercy spoke with experience and knowledge about her career in the media and about acting. In the two workshops she held at Muskingum, she developed improvisations with students that brought admiration and delight. Her presentations consisted of character portrayals of desperate women she has acted in plays, such as *Who's Afraid of Virginia Woolf?, The Miracle Worker,* and *Macbeth.*

Highlighting the performance was her interpretation of Lady Macbeth's soliloquy, from which she led into the voice of the Devil from the film, The Exorcist . . .

Ms. McCambridge's performance was enthusiastically received by the Brown Chapel audience and the actress was given a spontaneous standing ovation.[12]

Agnes Moorehead

Hardly a week had passed after Mercy's final performance, when the college received news that Agnes Moorehead had succumbed to cancer at Methodist Hospital in Rochester, Minnesota.[13] Miss Moorehead, a 1923 graduate, had become an internationally-renowned actress. She was a student and friend of the Laytons. During her student years, she appeared in a one-act play, "The Twig of Thorn," and two full-length productions, *The Aristocrats* and *Friend Hannah.* After graduating from Muskingum, she attended the University of Wisconsin, taught school in her hometown of Reedsburg, Wisconsin, and went on to study at the American Academy of Dramatic Art. From there, she began a career that embraced radio, theatre, film, and television. She achieved critical acclaim in all branches of entertainment; however, she became most widely known for the role of Endora on the "Bewitched" television series.

Although acclaimed the world over, Agnes never forgot her roots. She spent many happy days on her grandfather's farm in Rix Mills, Ohio. Her father, Reverend John H.

Agnes Moorehead, as she appeared after performing her one woman show, "That Fabulous Redhead," on October 22, 1954. *Theatre file photo courtesy M.C. Public Relations Office.*

Moorehead, was a Presbyterian minister, and it was his influence and closeness of the Rix Mills farm that led Agnes to Muskingum. She frequently returned to visit friends and relatives. She was awarded an honorary Doctor of Literature by her alma mater in 1947, and later became a member of the Board of Trustees. During Homecoming Week in 1954, she performed her one-woman show, *That Fabulous Redhead*, at the college. In the 1960's, she built a beautiful home on the family farm in Rix Mills. Agnes specified that her papers and library be shared by both Muskingum College and the University of Wisconsin, and that a scholarship in her name be awarded to students interested in theatre. From her papers is the following testimony concerning the college:

It would be inaccurate to say that only one fond place in my heart will always be reserved for Muskingum and its beautiful campus among the hills of old New

Concord. The truth is that at least five fond places are held in that chamber of memory and sentiment loosely called the heart.

First, are my unforgettable four years as a student in the college, absorbing as much as I could of the great good that can be gleaned from an education in a small liberal arts institution.

Second, it was at Muskingum that my childhood interest in dramatics was encouraged, and I became a member of Muskingum Players, and acquired some of the rudiments of acting on their stage.

Third, I was done the honor of being invited to serve as vice-president of Muskingum's nine-year Development Program, which began in 1953; and that gave me a sense of active citizenship which is always good for the soul.

Fourth, I was thrilled to receive an honorary degree from my alma mater. Such degrees are not common in this world, and I shall always cherish mine with special pride.

Agnes Moorehead, internationally-acclaimed actress and 1923 graduate of Muskingum College, received an Honorary Doctor of Literature Degree at the 1947 Commencement. She is seen here with President Robert N. Montgomery, a former classmate at Muskingum. Photo by Dr. L. C. Knight; courtesy M.C. Public Relations Office.

Fifth, the many lasting associations I have made in the past and the many happy recollections I have of the college, both of its people and its activities, form a residuum of ineffable warmth and value to me.

Viva Muskingum![14]

1975
President William P. Miller

William P. Miller was succeeded by John Anthony Brown as President of Muskingum College.

Mercedes McCambridge

Mercedes McCambridge returned to Muskingum to guest star in Dylan Thomas's play, *Under Milk Wood*. Mercy's first visit in 1974 had been an unqualified success. At no time could anyone remember the entire campus community accepting a visiting artist with such whole-hearted approval. It was a mutual and instant bonding, as Mercy and the college adopted each other!

It was common to hear students, in workshops or rehearsals, comment, "She made me better than I thought I could be." From faculty and administration alike, she elicited admiration for her friendly attitude, understanding, and thorough professionalism.

Dr. Lorle Porter, Professor of History, wrote, "It is in her enthusiasm for living,

Mercedes McCambridge conducted various acting workshops in 1978, sponsored by the Cultural Events Series. *Theatre file photo courtesy M.C. Public Relations Office.*

for sharing, and for treating every person with deep-felt compassion that she makes the over-used cliches of 'relevant,' 'concerned,' and 'committed' live in the lives of those who touch her." President Miller commented, "Ms. Mercedes McCambridge is a delightful conversationalist. She seems to have a deep and abiding interest to help college students use all their talents to achieve success. Perfection is her goal."

In her art and in her life, Mercedes McCambridge proved to be an inspiration. For these reasons, and her interest in the college, Muskingum Players elected her an honorary member of their organization.[15]

Mercy had no sooner left campus than I began receiving requests to have her back. I began to formulate plans for another appearance. I had wanted a professional guest artist for a production, but the opportunity and right person for the occasion never materialized. Mercy seemed ideal; everyone liked her. She was the kind of actress who could do almost any role in any play. In fact, before she left campus in 1974, I suggested that perhaps someday she could return to be in a play with the students. She said that she would be happy to do just that; all I had to do was let her know what play, what part, and when. With that tentative agreement, I set to work planning the next season.

I thought immediately of *Under Milk Wood.* It had been over a decade since our first production of the play in 1961. The students had enjoyed working on it and the audience had enjoyed listening to it. Originally commissioned by the BBC as a radio script in the early 1930's, Thomas called it "a play for voices." It was the kind of play that might appeal to Mercy because of her background as a radio actress. Working with Mercy on such a script would be an excellent learning experience for student actors.[16]

In some ways, this verse-play is reminiscent of Thornton Wilder's, *Our Town.* There is little plot, only a number of situations created by the characters as they go about their every-day business. The author takes the audience on a twenty-four-hour tour of a small coastal village in Wales. We see into the intimate lives of the inhabitants:

a sea captain dreaming of the dead past, a draper making love, a school teacher waiting for Mr. Right, a lunatic caring for sixty-six clocks, and children playing. Thomas explores their souls in lyrical and earthy prose and song. According to Thomas, the play was written for "the love of Man and in praise of God."[17]

Under Milk Wood, 1975. N. Gartner and Guest-Artist, Mercedes McCambridge. *Theatre file photo courtesy M.C. Public Relations Office.*

For this production, I decided to keep the format the same as that of our first production. I divided the more than sixty characters among eight actors and a chorus of nine. Mercy led the cast: Robert Bartlett, Debbie Davidson, Neil Gartner, Linda Hierholzer, Richard Hill, Mark Preslan, and Myra Stanley. The chorus of townspeople were portrayed by Jennifer Baxter, Debbie Dearing, Jeff Hill, Sue Hitch, Becca Leitch, Sherman Liddell, Becky Mellon, Pam Nicholson, and Bonita Tackett. I enlisted Sue Cook as the co-director; her experience with dance made her a good judge of any vitally-important movement. The simplistic design of the production threw emphasis on the lyrical nature of the language, and the eccentricities of the villagers. To this end, the setting for Brown Chapel, as executed by Jerry Martin, consisted of platforms, stools, and reading stands for the eight actors downstage, and benches for the chorus upstage. There was no realistic costuming and no scenery. The lighting, designed by Bruce Hare, suggested the atmosphere and movement of the day from dawn to dusk.[18] The play was quite successful.

The performance was scheduled for Thursday, May 1, 1975, but Mercy arrived early so that we could get in as many rehearsals as her time would permit. She also did two open acting workshops: one on April 29 and the other on April 30.

1976
Ossie Davis & Ruby Dee

Ossie Davis and Ruby Dee, Ruby Dee and Ossie Davis: which one gets first billing doesn't really matter because they are a husband and wife team of actors—each with enough talent to raise the Titanic. They entertained the Muskingum audience on February 23, 1976, with an evening of drama and poetry that delighted the listeners and awakened their concerns for racial equality.

Ossie Davis and Ruby Dee are both known for their work concerning racial equality.* They belong to the NAACP and CORE. In May of 1970, they were presented with the Frederick Douglass Award by the New York Urban League, for bringing a "sense of fervor and pride to countless millions."

They have recorded "The Poetry of Langston Hughes" for Caedmon Records, and they have toured the United States together, giving recitals of dramatic scenes, poems, and stories.[19] Muskingum was grateful for having the opportunity to experience the talents of two such expert performers.

1977
Ms. E. Sue Cook

When cancer claimed Ms. E. Sue Cook in March of this year, the theatre lost a valuable friend and ally. She came to Muskingum in 1962 to serve as Director of Women's Athletics and Assistant Professor of Physical Education. She resigned her position in 1976 and retired to Florida to engage in business with her sister Sara, a Muskingum graduate.

Ms. Cook held a B.S. degree in Physical Education from Bowling Green State University. She received her Master's degree from Miami University of Ohio in 1968; her thesis subject was "The History of Physical Education at Muskingum."

Ms. Cook's interest in modern dance led her to offer courses in modern dance and tap-dancing, as well as courses in Movement for Performance. She choreographed for the Fine Arts Festival in 1968, and also for the Ohio University Ohio Valley Summer Theatre. Her continuing interest in dance sent her to study with Hanya Holm in 1971 at Colorado College (Colorado Springs) and at a Dance Workshop at Hampshire College. Through dance, she became interested in theatre, and she was frequently asked to help actors at the Little Theatre with movement and choreography. She designed dances for *Little Mary Sunshine* (1967) and *The Birds* (1970), in which she also performed.[20]

Over the years, her participation in dance and theatre increased. During the Interim of 1970, she and I offered a course called "Theatre of Involvement," in which body movement, voice, dance, and acting were combined for the purpose of improving a student's confidence in a variety of performing situations. This course evolved into Movement and Voice, a permanent course in the theatre curriculum, which combines improvisation, dance, movement, and vocal training.

In 1974, Ms. Cook was proud to dance one of the roles in a theatre-dance seminar, "Seven Stimulations," created by her student, Jill Giguere.[21] One of her great joys during her last year at Muskingum was acting the part of Lucy in *You're a Good Man,*

---

* Ruby Dee broke the color line in 1966, when she became the first black actress to take on major roles for the American Shakespeare Festival at Stratford, Connecticut. She played Kate in *The Taming of the Shrew,* and Cordelia in *King Lear.* She again made headlines as Lena, in Athol Fugard's *Boesman and Lena,* when that play was produced at the Circle in the Square in Greenwich Village. (Current Biography.)

Charlie Brown (a faculty play). Whatever Sue did–whether it was teaching, dancing or acting–her dedication to the task was fiercely loyal and total; she was never satisfied with anything but her best. In her brief stay in Florida before her final illness, she had a radio show and was acting in another play.

It was the opinion of those who knew Sue Cook that her vitality, enthusiasm, determination, and constant striving for the best be honored in some way. Dr. Lorle Porter and I made the following proposal to the Student Senate, upon the request of the Student Senate president, Ken Fouts:

> Sue's contribution to the theatre area should be honored in some way. It is such a contribution as Sue has made that insures the continued survival of institutions by putting the stamp of personal commitment on them. Sue wanted, and this college needs, a place for dance. She often bemoaned the fact that there was no suitable rehearsal and performance area for dance. She proposed that dance be included in the Fine Arts Division; and when the multi-million dollar Fine Arts Center was planned some years ago, she designed a dance studio which was to be combined with a theatre rehearsal area in the projected building. That building was never built and now we are engaged in another arts complex in which there is no room for dance. My suggestion is that the Little Theatre be improved and equipped in such a way as to serve as a dance studio where students can rehearse and perform in an atmosphere conducive to creativity. My suggestion is that this be done in her memory and as soon as possible.[22]

The proposal was accepted by the Student Senate and one thousand dollars was appropriated for equipment, such as mirrors and dance bars, which were to be installed at the Little Theatre. The mirrors were installed, but the use of the Little Theatre as a temporary dance studio never materialized. The facility was already over-used for theatre productions. It was used in the daytime for construction of sets, and at night for rehearsals of plays. Furthermore, the renovation of the Little Theatre into a flexible theatre made it physically impossible to clear enough space for dance. Finally, several years after Sue retired, the Physical Education Department eliminated dance from the curriculum; therefore, the practicality of a dance studio became a moot point.

Student L. Overmire observes Nicolas Pennell conducting relaxation exercises at a workshop in the Little Theatre. 1977. *Theatre file photo courtesy M.C. Public Relations Office.*

Nicholas Pennell and Marti Maraden

Nicholas Pennell and Marti Maraden were members of the Stratford, Ontario Shakespeare Festival Acting Company. Both of them were excellent performers whom many of us had seen on stage during our summer trips to the Canadian Festival. We were extremely fortunate to have them included in our Cultural Events for November 7-8, 1977. They conducted workshops at the Little Theatre, and performed an evening of dramatic scenes and poetry, centered on the theme, "Rogues and Vagabonds."

Nicholas Pennell had extensive experience in the British regional theatre, seasons with the Bristol Old Vic and Oxford Playhouse. His previous Festival roles were legion, but a sampling embraces Orlando, in *As You Like It,* Pericles in *Pericles, Prince of Tyre,* Berowne in *Love's Labours Lost*, Antipholus of Syracuse in *The Comedy of Errors,* Jack Worthing in *The Importance of Being Earnest,* Hamlet, Ariel in *The Tempest,* Mercutio in *Romeo and Juliet,* Oswald in *Ghosts,* and Bertram in *All's Well That Ends Well.* For the previous three years, in the Stratford off-season, he had been Guest-Artist-in-Residence at the University of Michigan. He had been most recently touring in the USA in "Rogues and Vagabonds."[23]

Marti Maraden had appeared in Canada at the Vancouver Playhouse, the Frederick Wood, Bastion, and Neptune theatres, and at the Manitoba Theatre Centre. Her Festival roles included Juliet, Regina in *Ghosts,* Jackie Coryton in *Hay Fever,* Ophelia in *Hamlet,* Miranda in *The Tempest,* Irina in *Three Sisters,* and Cecily in *The Importance of Being Earnest*–all of which received critical acclaim. She had been touring with Nicholas Pennell in "Rogues and Vagabonds."[24]

New Ph.D.

On December 14, 1977, the regents of the University of Minnesota awarded Donald Phillip Hill the degree of Doctor of Philosophy, with all its privileges and obligations (there is a catch to everything!). I was exactly 51 years and 2 months old, but I had finally done it. Praise the Lord!

1978
President John Anthony Brown

John Anthony Brown, president of Muskingum College, had barely served three years when he suddenly died of a heart attack. The college community was stunned. When people became aware of the reality of the situation, some of his projects were abandoned or put on hold, until the Board of Trustees made a decision. The completion of the Johnson Hall renovation was turned over to Executive Vice President of Development, Paul Morris. Under his supervision, the East Wing of Johnson Hall was turned into an art gallery, later dedicated to the memory of Louis Palmer. The West Wing became a theatre, which was later dedicated to the memory of Charles and Ferne Layton.

The Layton Theatre

As an "Honored Guest," Mercedes McCambridge spoke at the dedication of the Ferne P. and Charles R. Layton Theatre on March 28, 1978.[25] She remarked, "This room [the Layton Theatre] is the only room where truth can come out."[26]

Mercedes McCambridge

Mercy's conception of truth and lies is very interesting. In her autobiography, *The Quality of Mercy,* she writes, "I have always had a lot more trouble with my truths than with my deceits."[27] Mercy says that she lies a lot! There is no doubt that she means what she says. I wouldn't presume to explain what she means; however, I believe her "lies" are just another way of telling the truth. She is a born spinner of tall tales: it's the Don Quixote influence that she inherited from her imaginary Spanish grandmother, and the Irish blarney she got from her real Irish grandmother.[28]

Anyway, to belabor my point about truth and lies, Harold Clurman prefaces his book of theatre reviews and essays, *Lies Like Truth*, with two quotations. The first is from Picasso, "Art is a lie that makes us realize the truth," and the second is from Shakespeare's *Macbeth* V,v, "I begin . . . to doubt the equivocation of the fiend that lies like truth."[29] Both quotations are apropos to Mercy's "lying." She is simply justifying the truth. When she signed Burgess Meredith's name for an autograph-seeking taxi driver or when she told the Pope that she was just a tourist (while she was making the film, *A Farewell to Arms*), she was telling her audience what they wanted to hear.[30]

Mercy's third visit to Muskingum for the three-day residency was full of activity. Jeff Morgan ('78), Lorle Porter, and Patricia Ellertson prepared an informative souvenir booklet for her visit, with drawings by Galen Wilson ('78). The brochure invited the community to "sample her multi-faceted career 'as a radio and TV performer, by visiting the Library Listening Room where there were tapes from H. Edwin Titus's collection, including Inner Sanctum's "Murder at Midnight," I Love a Mystery's "The Thing That Cried in the Night," Screen Director's Playhouse's "Spellbound," and an episode from "Abie's Irish Rose".'" Visitors were also welcomed to experience her as a teacher by attending workshops on March 28 and 29. A film festival featuring Mercy was held in the Science Center Auditorium on March 27-29. Among the films shown were *Suddenly Last Summer, Giant* (for which she received an Oscar nomination as Best Supporting Actress), *Angel Baby,* and *All the King's Men* (for which she won the Academy Award for Best Supporting Actress in 1949). On the evening of March 29, there was an autograph party in the Top of the Center for those who wished to meet and chat with her. All of these events climaxed on the evening of March 30, when Mercy was seen in performance in Brown Chapel.[31]

The souvenir program also contained a short biography of the star and a list of her credits from radio, theatre, film, and television. This souvenir program was beautifully finished with a front cover that pictures Mercy, as she must have appeared as Martha in *Who's Afraid of Virginia Woolf?* On the back of the last page is another picture of Mercy, looking her beautiful self.[32]

1979
Marilyn and Nancy Gleason

At the end of the decade, the loss of two graduates in the same accident was devastating. Marilyn Gleason ('61) and her sister, Nancy Gleason Gavola ('70), both died as the result of injuries received in a plane crash in January 1979. While at Muskingum, both sisters contributed their talents to major productions. Upon graduation, Marilyn taught Speech and English, and then pursued a professional theatre career. Nancy taught Language Arts and served as drama club sponsor in the Bethel Park School District of Pennsylvania. The Gleason Memorial Fund, a permanently-endowed theatre scholarship, was established by friends of the sisters.[33] We continue to mourn the loss of two such talented young people.

Victor Buono

Victor Buono on his second visit to Muskingum College: always available and always attentive to the needs and desires of the students. *Theatre file photo courtesy M.C. Public Relations Office.*

Muskingum students and faculty remembered well the artistry and personality of Victor Buono. In his first visit (1973), he presented an outstanding convocation with a reading of a "A Child's Christmas in Wales." Then he charmed the evening audience with interpretations from his favorite authors. Students were especially pleased with the manner in which he greeted them and presented himself at their gatherings. It was obvious that Mr. Buono liked what he was doing. I remember one student session in the Top of the Center, when Ted Sofis asked him, "Doesn't it make you nervous to have everyone watching you?" Victor replied, with a chuckle, "No, I like the attention!"

In February 1979, Muskingum had a second opportunity to enjoy Mr. Buono's talents. In a three-day period, he conducted workshops and performed in Brown Chapel.[34] Aside from his usual impeccable performances, as both teacher and entertainer, there was as much memorable activity off-stage as on.

Six years later, after his first visit, Victor's plane arrived in Columbus during a terrible ice storm. Students Mark Wentz and Mark Preslan were going to meet him, when they "totaled" the car. The next morning, I took a college station wagon to pick him up at the airport. (Remembering our first meeting, I made sure that Victor had plenty of room on this trip.) I found him in the airport Concourse Hotel, regaling the staff and guests at his breakfast table.[35]

It was on this visit that he discovered my admiration for Mae West. In the early days of Hollywood, she was one of the few women who managed her own career, in a business dominated by men. (Lillian Gish was another.) She also wrote, produced, and acted in her own plays. When I was looking for a dissertation subject, Mae West was one of my early choices.

Victor remarked that he and Mae shopped at the same supermarket. One day, he recognized her limousine parked a few cars away. In the back seat sat the star, waiting for her chauffeur to return from shopping. He decided that it was a good time to get her autograph. The only paper he had with him was a legal-size pad of yellow ruled paper, which he took to her car. When he tapped on her window, Mae recognized him and rolled the window down just enough to speak to him. He asked for her autograph and, when she acquiesced, he passed the legal pad and a pen through the window. Mae wrote on one small corner of the blank page, tore it off, and handed it back to Victor. On the tiny scrap of paper, Mae had written her name and the message, "Waste not. Want not." Mae kept the legal pad . . . but she did return his pen!

In a phone conversation with Dr. Porter, I learned that Victor had been asked back for a third engagement in the college Cultural Events Series. The possibility of his doing Falstaff had been tentatively discussed. The project was abandoned when Victor Buono died of a heart attack in the early 1980's.[36]

Muriel Bain ('28). *Theatre file photo courtesy M.C. Public Relations Office.*

Mrs. J. Herbert Bain

In 1979, the Muskingum Theatre lost another friend in Mrs. J. Herbert Bain— "Muriel" to those who knew her. She was a Layton student who had graduated in 1928, and taken her Master of Arts at the University of Michigan. She joined the faculty of her alma mater in 1936, and taught speech for three years. During that time, she helped spearhead the movement to renovate the former Alumni Gym into the Little Theatre.[37]

Muriel was married to J. Herbert Bain, M.D., and they had two sons, John and Philip, both of whom are also graduates of Muskingum. Her husband became the College Physician and remained in that position until his death. At that time, the family was grown and Muriel sought a way to be of some service to the community. She expressed a desire to return to teaching and she was particularly interested in theatre. I saw in Muriel a woman whose love of the theatre and expertise could prove valuable in an expanding program. In 1966, she became a director in the theatre, an advisor to Muskingum Players, and a teacher of the Introduction to Theatre course.

Muriel was a pleasant colleague and an experienced teacher. She had raised two boys and, from them, she had learned student psychology. She reminded me of Mrs. Layton because she was so kind, gentle, firm, and very learned in her field. The lesson came first and it was the student's duty to know it. For the same reasons, she was a very good director. I played Dromio of Ephesus in her *The Comedy of Errors*. Her direction was always clear, precise, and knowledgeable.

Muriel was especially effective as the advisor to Muskingum Players. Under her leadership, the Players became an active and effective organization. She encouraged the membership to develop workshops in various phases of technical theatre, and then sent them out to visit various high schools, thereby promoting education and interest in the theatre, and in Muskingum College. Muriel also developed a touring company of players who took the student-directed one-acts to various high schools in the vicinity. She directed scenes from musicals, classics, and Broadway hits; she arranged for several one-act plays in French, Spanish, and German, to tour schools and local clubs.[38] She directed the one-act, "Dust of the Road," for a Christmas convocation, and "The

Diary of Adam and Eve" for area alumni meetings.

It was Muriel who saw the advantages of taking students on a field trip every fall, to see the plays at the Canadian Shakespeare Festival in Stratford, Ontario. Starting in the late Sixties, these trips became very popular with students, and lasted for two decades, until the ticket prices and the cost of travel proved prohibitive.

It was Muriel who made me aware of some very important theatre events that were happening outside the college. (I am known for my "tunnel vision.") She told me that Joanne Woodward was acting in *Hay Fever* at Kenyon College. We immediately got into the car and off we went.

It was also Muriel who alerted me to the fact that Charles Sweigart was acting with Myrna Loy in *Relatively Speaking,* at the Reynoldsburg Country Dinner Playhouse. Charlie loved the theatre, but his parents did not believe it was a good choice for a career. During his two years at Muskingum, he did not take one course in theatre because his parents would see it on his semester grade report. However, he worked backstage, and appeared in *The Birds* (1970) as Prometheus and in *The Comedy of Errors* (1970) as Dromio of Syracuse. After his sophomore year, Charlie went home, had a "heart-to-heart" with his father, and ended up in the professional theatre program at Carnegie Tech. He graduated from there with a BFA in theatre and moved immediately into professional work. Now, he was back in Ohio in October of 1978, touring with Myrna Loy. Muriel and I went to see the play. After the curtain, we went backstage for a visit and Charlie introduced us to Myrna Loy. I had always been in awe of this "Wife of the Thin Man," and was bold enough to ask for her autograph. I also imposed upon Charlie's good nature to come to Muskingum and talk to the students about the professional theatre. He did, and the students loved it; and I have been a Sweigart fan ever since.

When Muriel left us, she was missed by one and all. We still miss her.

Franklin Harold Hill

My own father, Franklin Harold Hill, died in September of 1979. He had been ailing with emphysema for some time. With his passing, I became weary of the whole decade and wished for an end to the carnage. This was not to be. There was one more event that proved to be a fitting climax to these ten years.

A New Department

The climax of the decade came in 1979 when Theatre was separated from Speech Communication, and placed (along with Art and Music) in a new Department of Fine Arts. For an explanation of the separation, the reader is directed to the section "The Department: 1978-1980."

REFERENCES

1   "Mary Elizabeth Johnson Retires," *Cue*, New Concord, Ohio, May 1972, p. 2.
2   "In Memoriam," *Cue*, New Concord, Ohio, April 1973, p. 1.
3   Donald Hill, "In Memoriam," *Cue*, New Concord, Ohio, 1975, p. 2.
4   "Guest Artists Enliven Season," *Cue,* 1975, p. 6.
5   "Johnny Guitar," V*ideo Hound's Golden Movie Retriever,* 1995 (Detroit, Michigan: Visible Ink Press, 1995), p. 533.
6   "The Exorcist," *Video Hound's Golden Movie Retriever,* p. 370.
7   Mercedes McCambridge, *The Quality of Mercy, An Autobiography*, (New York: Times Books, 1981) pp. 89-95.
8   Ibid., p. 84.
9   Ibid., p. 89.
10 "Mercedes McCambridge," *Current Biography, 1964*, (New York: The H. W. Wilson Company, 1964), pp. 262-264.
11 "Mercedes McCambridge," *American Program Bureau All Points Bulletin*, (Boston, Massachusetts, 1974).
12 "Mercedes McCambridge Fills Chapel, Thrills Enthusiastic Audience," *The Black and Magenta*, Muskingum College, New Concord, Ohio, Friday, May 3, 1974, p. 1.
13 "Agnes Moorehead will be buried in Dayton," *The Journal Herald,* Dayton, Ohio, Thursday, May 2, 1974, p. 42.
14 "Agnes Moorehead and Muskingum," *Cue, Sesquicentennial Issue,* Muskingum College, New Concord, Ohio, Fall 1986, p. 2.
15 "Mercedes McCambridge, '75," *Cue,* 1975, p. 1.
16 "Under Milk Wood," *Cue,* 1975, p. 1.
17 "About the Play," Programs for *Under Milk Wood* published by Muskingum Players, New Concord, Ohio, 1961-1962, and by the Muskingum College Artist-Lecture Series, 1975.
18 "Under Milk Wood," *Cue,* 1975, p. 1.
19 "Ruby Dee," *Current Biography, 1970*, (New York: The H. W. Wilson Company, 1970), pp. 107-110.
20 "E. Sue Cook Resigns," *Fine Arts Newsletter from the Old Campus,"* Muskingum College, New Concord, Ohio, April 1976, p. 2.
21 "Seminars '74," *Cue,* 1975, p. 6.
22 "E. Sue Cook Dance-Theatre Studio," *Cue,* Summer 1977, p. 1.
23 "The 1977 Festival Company: The Acting Company," *Stratford Festival, Canada: 1977, 25th Season, June 6 to October 15,* a souvenir magazine by Integrated Graphics Limited, 1977; pages not numbered, but constitute the last 15 pages of the publication.
24 Ibid.
25 "Ferne P. and Charles R. Layton Theatre Dedication," Original program, Muskingum College, New Concord, Ohio, March 28, 1978.
26 William M. Laing, "The History of Theatre at Muskingum College from 1971-1983," (An unpublished seminar presented to the faculty of the Speech Communication and Theatre Department at Muskingum College, May 1983), p. 36.
27 Mercedes McCambridge, *The Quality of Mercy, An Autobiography*, p. 22.
28 Ibid., p. 5.
29 Harold Clurman, *Lies Like Truth*, (New York: The Macmillan Company, 1958), title page.
30 Mercedes McCambridge, *The Quality of Mercy, An Autobiography*, pp. 4, 22.
31 "The Fine Arts Series of Muskingum College Celebrates the Achievements of Miss Mercedes McCambridge in Residency, March 28, 29, 30, 1978," Muskingum College, New Concord, Ohio, with Support of the Ohio Arts Council and the National Endowment for the Arts, 1978, souvenir booklet edited by Jeff Morgan, Lorle Porter, and Patricia Ellertson, drawings by Galen Wilson, pp. 1-2.
32 Ibid., pp. 3-6, cover.
33 "Gleason Memorial Fund," *Cue,* Fall 1984, p. 3.
34 "Victor Buono," *Cultural Events, 1978-1979*, Muskingum College, New Concord, Ohio, p. 1.
35 Lorle Porter, in a letter to the author, postmarked January 20, 2000.
36 Lorle Porter, in a telephone conversation with the author, January 16, 2000.
37 "Memorial Scholarship Funds in Progress," *Cue,* Fall 1980, p. 2.
38 Cheryl D. Swiss, "A History of Theatre at Muskingum College," (An unpublished "Thesis Presented to the Faculty of the Graduate College of Ohio University," June 1972), p. 67.

The Department: 1970–1978

The 1970's brought many changes in the department and in the college. The decade opened with a new chairman, Mr. Judson Ellertson, a new major in Theatre, and a new departmental title: "Speech and Theatre Department." A student majoring in the department now had a choice of two majors (Speech or Theatre) and five concentrations: public address, theatre, radio and television, oral interpretation, and speech correction.

Tim Halverson (right) and his speech instructor, Mr. Judson Ellertson, hold the National Championship Trophy that Tim won for persuasive speaking in 1970. *Theatre file photo courtesy M.C. Public Relations Office.*

A new concentration in speech-communication required thirty hours beyond the basic education course (Fundamentals of Speech) and a total of eighteen hours from the field of speech. With the approval of the chairman, the remaining twelve hours came from the student's major field of study. Departments acceptable were Economics and Business, English, History, Political Science, Psychology, Religion and Philosophy, and Sociology.[1] (See the Section Notes for curricula at the beginning and toward the end of the decade.)

Changes in curriculum that had been taking place gradually over the first part of the decade, came to fruition in 1975. The concentration in speech-communication that was introduced in 1970 grew in popularity until, in 1973, it, too, became a major; and for a time, the department housed three majors: speech, speech-communication, and theatre.[2]

In theory, the interdisciplinary majors (speech-communication and theatre) were good ideas; in practice, they did not prove feasible. The theatre major is an example. Theatre majors planning their schedules could always count on the availability of theatre courses, because they were the core curriculum. However, the twelve hours that were elected from courses in other departments were not always available. Other departments had the autonomy to change courses as they saw fit or necessary, without consulting our department or notifying students on the theatre major track. Consequently, frustration became part of the interdisciplinary phase of the theatre major.

The department did not need the problem of dealing with programs outside the area of its control. A move to centralize both theatre and speech-communication majors within the department was a wise and necessary move. It stabilized the curriculum and it gave students a feeling of security. In 1975, the speech major and speech-communication major were joined under a single title of Communication Major. This major and the Theatre Major were both maintained in the department.[3]

The department was fortunate to have enough courses with the credit hours, in 1975, to house both majors. A third major, designed for teacher certification, emerged in a combination of communication and theatre courses. Such a combination was needed because speech and English teachers in Ohio's public schools were expected to handle theatre classes and productions. In fact, the state of Ohio never had an accreditation for teachers of theatre until the 1980's.[4]

Two further changes occurred in 1975: the Department of Speech and Theatre changed its title to Speech Communication and Theatre Department. (The Speech Association of America had changed its title several years earlier to Speech Communication Association of America.); also, for purposes of clarity and convenience, the course listings in the *College Bulletin* were printed under separate titles of "Speech Communication" and "Theatre."[5]

Other events conspired to make the seventies particularly troubling. In 1970, the entire faculty was thrown into disarray when the North Central Accrediting Association threatened to place the college on academic probation. President Miller succeeded in having the threat removed in 1973, but the emotional ripples from that traumatic shock still lingered.[6]

Equally upsetting were the fluctuations in top-level management. Since the retirement of Dr. Robert N. Montgomery in 1962, there had been a new president every four years: Glenn McConagha, Harry Manley, and William Miller (who had twice been President *pro tem*, once after each of the above resigned). Finally, Miller became a full president in 1971. Now, in 1975, President Miller was due to retire to make way for the new president, John Anthony Brown. Added to these turn-overs in personnel were those that had occurred in our department since the retirement of Dr. Layton (over the five-year period from 1970-1975).[7]

Clay Waite, who was in radio and television at the beginning of the decade, left and was replaced by James Sheldrew in 1971; he left in the spring of 1975. Miss Johnson retired in 1972. Richard Downing, the theatre's first technical director, was appointed in 1971 and left in 1973. Muriel Bain stayed as a part-time instructor through 1973.[8]

The theatre was invigorated with the presence of Jerry Martin, who served as technical director and director in the theatre from 1974-1977. Outside of his regular duties, Mr. Martin engineered "The Auction of the Stars,"[9] which netted the Theatre Contingency Fund over two thousand dollars. He also remodeled the lobby of the Little Theatre into an art gallery. In 1967, I had turned the auditorium of the Little Theatre into a temporary arena. Almost ten years later, Jerry turned the auditorium into a permanent flexible black box, thereby increasing the usefulness of the facility. He also conducted and produced several workshops that attracted surrounding communities and schools.[10]

In 1975, the speech-communication and theatre staff held steady at seven full-time faculty. Jud Ellertson was chairman and forensic coach; his wife, Patricia, taught public address; Dr. James Holm was in communication and general speech; Steve Brown directed the radio and television area; Martha Moore led the interpretation area; and Jerry Martin and I were in theatre.[11] During the last half of the decade, the departmental staff dwindled to five, and then three, full-time faculty members. There was a time when Martha Moore was the only remaining regular in the department.[12]

Section Notes

The following courses were being offered at the beginning of the decade:

151. Theatre Arts
215. Extemporaneous Speaking
241. Oral Interpretation of Literature
255. Scenic Arts
105. Fundamentals of Speech
315. Argumentation and Debate
325. Persuasion: Theory and Practice
335. Decision–Making
343. Advanced Interpretation
351. Modern Drama
355. Acting
356. Directing
363. Broadcasting in Modern Society
366. Radio–TV–Film Production
371. Introduction to Speech Correction
451. World Theatre
495;496. Individual Study
Speech Practicum: 10l;102/ 201;202/ 301;302/ 401;402
(*Muskingum College Bulletin: 1971-1972*, pp. 125-127.)

In 1976, the Speech Communication curriculum consisted of the following courses (Asterisks indicate new additions to the permanent curriculum):

105. Fundamentals of Speech Communication (3)
*210. Radio Programming and Production (3)
*211. Television Programming and Production (3)
*235. Interviewing and Interpersonal Communication (3)

260. Oral Interpretation of Literature (3)

*310. Mass Media (3)

315. Argumentation (3)

*320. Photographic Communication (3)

325. Persuasion: Theory and Practice (3)

335. Decision-Making (4)

360. Advanced Interpretation (3)

370. Introduction to Speech and Hearing Disorders (4)

*444 Communication Theory and Criticism (3)

495;496. Individual Study (2)

Communication Practicum: 101;102/ 201;202/ 301;302/ 401;402 (4)

There were 15 courses totaling 49 credit hours.

The theatre curriculum consisted of the following courses (Asterisks indicate new additions to the permanent curriculum):

151. Theatre Arts (3)

*175. Movement and Voice (3)

*245. Technical Production (3)

*251. Theatre Past (3)

*252. Theatre Present (3)

275. Acting (3)

345. Scenic Arts I (3)

346. Scenic Arts II (3)

351. Modern Drama

*352. Children's Theatre (3)

375. Directing (3)

475. Theatre Styles (3)

497;498. Individual Study (2)

Play Production: 103;104/203;204/303;304/403;404 (4)

There were 14 courses totaling 46 credit hours.

The foregoing curriculum remained unchanged for the next two years.

(Muskingum College Bulletin: 1977–1978, pp. 65-67.)

REFERENCES

1   *Muskingum College Bulletin: 1971–1972*, Muskingum College, (New Concord, Ohio; 1971), p. 125.

2   *Muskingum College Bulletin: 1974–1975*, pp. 128-129.

3   *Muskingum College Bulletin: 1976-1977*, pp. 124-125.

4   Ibid., p. 125.

5   Ibid., pp. 124-127.

6   Dr. William P. Miller, "He Always Had the Time," *The Bill Miller Story: Muskingum College's 16th President* (New Wilmington, Pennsylvania: Son-Rise Publications & Distributing Company, 1993), pp. 53-54.

7   William L. Fisk, *A History of Muskingum College* (New Concord, Ohio: Muskingum College, 1978), p. 257.

8   *Muskingum College Bulletins, 1970-1977.*

9   William M. Laing, "The History of Theatre at Muskingum College from 1971-1983" (An unpublished seminar presented to the faculty of the Speech Communications and Theatre Department at Muskingum College, New Concord, Ohio, May, 1983), p. 26.

10 William M. Laing, pp. 30-31.

11 *Muskingum College Bulletins, 1975-1978.*

12 *Muskingum College Bulletins, 1977-1979.*

The Plays: 1970–1978

1970–1971

The 1970-71 theatre season opened at the Little Theatre with a Viet Nam War drama, *Summertree,* written by Ron Cowen. The play won the Off-Broadway Vernon Rice Award for its ingenuous, if heart-rending, look at family relationships. I designed and directed the play. The action centered around a large tree which, at times, was located in the family's backyard and, at other times, in Viet Nam. Lighting was used to show the shift in time and location, as a young soldier, who lay dying, dreamed about his family and himself.

Mitch Grunat was the Soldier; Bob Thiele played the Soldier before he enlisted; Kent Biegler played him as a young boy. Mary Ann Spitznagel was the Girlfriend; Corinne Smyth played the Mother; and Wayne Morrison, the Father. The cast turned in a moving and tender performance of a sensitive subject for that date in time. The production played during the week of Homecoming, October 8-10, and was performed again for Parents Weekend, October 16-17.[1]

Muriel Bain's production of *The Comedy of Errors* (Shakespeare) had a successful run on March 17-20, during the spring semester of 1971. An early play of Shakespeare, *The Comedy of Errors* is based upon Plautus's *Menaechmi*, which concerns the search of a father for his lost son, who has a twin brother. Shakespeare compounds the plot by adding another set of twins who are servants to the twin brothers. When they all come together in the same city, the play becomes a hilarious farce of mistaken identity.

Rehearsals for the play almost came to a halt, two weeks before performance, when the student who was cast as the servant, Dromio of Ephesus, became ill. I told Muriel that if a replacement could not be found, I would do the part. The following day, she held me to my promise and I found myself onstage opposite Charlie Sweigart, who played Dromio of Syracuse. I had to summon all my reserve energy to match Charlie's youth, and I had to find a wig to match his curly blonde hair.

All went well until opening night, when I committed an infraction of the rules which upset Marypaul Magura, who was playing Adriana, my master's wife. We had a scene together in which she had to slap me when I misbehaved. We rehearsed the business, which was devised to let me receive the slap on the upstage side of my neck, where the audience could not see it, where it would not damage any make-up, and where it would hurt less than on the cheek. On opening night, as Adriana drew back and delivered the blow, I flinched and tried to duck; as a result, her hand hit my cap and wig, and both went tumbling to the stage floor. The audience reacted with a roar of laughter; I said something as a startled ad lib, picked up both items, put them back on my head, and finished the scene.

Off stage, Marypaul was upset. I consoled her with the fact that it was not her fault; I was the one who failed to carry out the business as it had been rehearsed. That helped a little, but she was still upset. My gaffe was probably the only mistake on opening night; in fact, it may have been fortunate, in that it served as an ice-breaker for the audience to "let go" for the rest of the evening and enjoy the farce. That was just what happened. The comedy settled down to a successful and flawless run.

The Comedy of Errors, 1971. (Foreground from left): Dromio of Ephesus (D. Hill), Adriana (M. Magura), Antipholus of Ephesus (R. White), Egeon of Syracuse (J. Schroeder), The Abbess (P. Bentley), Antipholus of Syracuse (W. Morrison), Luciana (D. Cox), Dromio of Syracuse (C. Sweigart). *Theatre file photo courtesy M.C. Public Relations Office.*

Patty Madigan wrote a review of the *Comedy of Errors,* in which she lauded the cast for their " . . . remarkable naturalness . . . . " and their delivery of the verse.[2]

The cast members responsible for the success were, in order of appearance: Tim Schirack (Attendant to the Duke), Ron Richwine (Duke Solinus of Ephesus), Jeff Schroeder (Egeon), Walter Sherman (Jailer), Chuck Spadone (First Merchant, Friend to Antipholus), Wayne Morrison (Antipholus of Syracuse), Charles Sweigart (Dromio of Syracuse), Don Hill (Dromio of Ephesus), Mary Paul Magura (Adriana, Wife of Antipholus of Ephesus), Denise Cox (Luciana, Her Sister), Robert White (Antipholus of Ephesus), Mitch Grunat (Angelo, a Goldsmith), Dennis C. Burkhardt (Balthazar, Friend of Antipholus of Ephesus), Margaret Leta Harris (Luce, a Serving Girl), Mark Weingart (Second Merchant), Bob Good (First Officer), Linda Norlander (Erotium, a Courtesan), Ray Valentine (Pinch, a Conjuror), Chuck Spadone (Second Officer), Walter Sherman (Third Officer), and Priscilla Bentley (The Abbess).

The theatre season was climaxed by three student-directed seminar productions. Susan Simerka directed *Suddenly Last Summer,* by Tennessee Williams, Amanda Roberts directed a version of *The Romancers,* by Edmond Rostand (May 5 and 7), and Richard Hamilton directed *Tiny Alice* by Edward Albee (May 6 and 8).

In *Suddenly Last Summer*, themes of homosexuality, murder, cannibalism, and insanity permeate one of the most unpleasant, but breathtakingly tense plays by Tennessee Williams. The wealthy and powerful Mrs. Venable (Margaret Leta Harris) is determined to have a surgeon, Dr. Cukrowicz (Mark Weingart) perform a lobotomy on her niece, Catharine Holly (Karen Lohr), in order to suppress the story of how her son, Sebastian, died. Other members of the cast were Miss Foxhill (Lindy Norlander), Mrs. Holly (Denise Cox), George Holly (John Barker), and Sister Felicity (Bobbi Roberts).

The Romancers tells of the romance between Sylvette (Mary Ann Spitznagel) and Percinet (Doug Sisterson). Their fathers want them to get married; however, the fathers believe that won't happen unless they pretend to hate each other. Bergamin (Percinet's father (Bob Good) and Pasquinot, Sylvette's father (Dennis Burkhardt) pretend to argue; they even build a wall between their properties. They plan an abduction and hire Straforel, a "bravado" (Ray Valentine), to carry it off. When Percinet arrives, he foils the fake abduction, the lovers are united, and the wall comes down.

Tiny Alice has been described as a "metaphysical dream play." Miss Alice is the richest woman in the world. Through her lawyer, she offers the church one hundred-million dollars a year, for twenty years. A lay brother, Julian, the cardinal's secretary, must go to Miss Alice's castle to complete the details. Julian is a quiet man who has retreated from life and, seemingly, subdued his passions. However, once in Miss Alice's castle, he is seduced to become her lover. His passions are awakened and the mysteries begin to be revealed.

Tiny Alice, 1971. Miss Alice (D. Loesch) seduces Brother Julian (L. Keffer). *Theatre file photo courtesy M.C. Public Relations Office*

The play was judged by Broadway critics to be theatrically rich and intellectually challenging. The cast for the production included Jeff Schroeder, Bob Bielecki, Larry Keffer, Jim Monteith, and Debbie Loesch.[3]

  1971–1972

*T*he Matchmaker, by Thornton Wilder, (as its counterpart, *Hello, Dolly!,* has proved) is a born crowd-pleaser. As part of the Parents Weekend entertainment, it opened the 1971-72 theatre season, and played to packed houses on October 20-23.[4] The

Macbeth, 1972. Macbeth (R. Werner), the usurper king is held at bay by Macduff (B. Thiele). *Theatre file photo courtesy M.C. Public Relations Office.*

center of the play is, as Barnaby says at the end of the comedy, all about "adventure." I used the same directorial approach at Muskingum as I had at the University of Idaho Summer Theatre, and the cast responded just as well. The Idaho ensemble had more experience and maturity, but the Muskingum cast responded to my direction with a youthful energy and enthusiasm that was equally rewarding and fun to watch.[5]

The imaginative settings by the Theatre's first technical director, Richard Downing, promoted the pace of the show.

The January Interim class presented *Spoon River Anthology* by Edgar Lee Masters, which was adapted by Charles Aidman and directed by Richard Downing on January 21-23. Miss Johnson also had a Readers' Theatre Interim entitled, "People Will Be People" (January 26).

The first of two repertories in 1972 was produced in March. Shakespeare's *Macbeth* was teamed with Alfred Jarry's *King Ubu*. Cheri Swiss directed *King Ubu*, which had an unusual number of alumni in its cast (five to be exact), and I directed *Macbeth*. Both of the plays were connected by a similar theme: *Macbeth* was a play concerning the abuse of power, and *King Ubu* was a parody on the same theme, made brutally ridiculous by Jarry's absurdist point of view. *Macbeth* was scheduled for 8:00 p.m. on March 13, 15, 17, and at 1:00 p.m. on March 14, 15, 16, and 17. *King Ubu* played at 8:00 p.m. on March 14, 16, 18, and 2:00 p.m. on March 18.

Rehearsals for *Macbeth* moved along swiftly. Most of my time was devoted to helping students deliver the verse and project the content. I remember that we used quite a few long velour cloaks on almost everyone, as part of the costume design. Mr. Downing made iron swords which were very heavy. The stage combats were rehearsed carefully and often. The combatants grew tired of wielding the weight of the swords. The swords were not sharp, but they were heavy, and actors had to be careful not to mash each other. When Macduff and Macbeth met in battle, there was a glorious series of sparks emanating from the blades of the swords, as they crashed into and onto one another.

Cheri Swiss seemed to have fun directing her cast through the perils of *King Ubu,* as Ma and Pa Ubu fought their way to the top in the Slavic nations. I remember our conference on the scatology Jarry used in the play. I thought there was too much use of the "sh_t" and "f__" words. Cheri did too, and there was some squeamishness on the part of certain actors, when they remembered that their parents would appear in the audience. I think we decided to let a minimum of profanity go uncensored, as long as the actors could say the words naturally–without drawing attention to them in an obviously "smart aleck" way.

The *Black and Magenta* reviewer, David Hall, announced, "Little Theatre Productions Win Reviewer Acclaim,"[6] and Marypaul Magura declared that "Alums Sparkle in Absurd Play."[7]

The theatre season ended with senior seminar student Margaret Harris's direction of *You're a Good Man, Charlie Brown.* Jeff Hillyer designed the show for his seminar, which played May 10-13 at the Little Theatre. It was a delightful production that received three different reviews written by Bob Good,[8] a staff writer,[9] and Nancy Bain[10]—rave notices published in the *Black and Magenta.*

The enthusiastic cast who carried out Margaret Harris's direction were: David Van Dyke (Charlie Brown), Mary Ann Spitznagel (Lucy), Ted Sofis (Linus), Doug Sisterson (Schroeder), Ray Valentine (Snoopy), and Tina Stiles (Patty). Musical accompaniment was supplied by Rob Backstrom on piano, Joyce Wonnacott on flute, and Pete Andrews on drums.

Cast for *The Matchmaker*
(Thornton Wilder)

Horace Vandergelder, a merchant of Yonkers, NY	Bob White
Dolly Levi, a friend	Debbie Loesch
Ermengarde, Vandergelder's niece	Marypaul Magura
Ambrose Kemper, in love with Ermengarde	Rich Werner
Cornelius Hackl, Vandergelder's clerk	Mark Weingart
Barnaby Tucker, junior clerk	Gary Crissman
Mrs. Molloy, a milliner	Denise Cox
Minnie Fay, her assistant	Margaret Harris
Miss Van Huysen, friend of Vendergelder	Pris Bentley
Her cook	Terry Haschke
Malachi Stack, a huckster	Bob Thiele
Joe Scanlon, a barber	Ray Valentine
Gertrude, Vandergelder's housekeeper	Pat Carter
A Cabman	Jeff Schroeder
Rudolf, headwaiter at Harmonia Gardens	Bob Good
August, a waiter	Terry McCord

March 1972 Repertory Cast
Macbeth
(William Shakespeare)

Robert Backstrom	Servant
Bruce Carothers	Donalbain, Young Siward
Jeff Clark	Duncan, Hecate

Gary Crissman	3rd Witch, 3rd Murderer, Mentieth
Harry Eadon	Sergeant, Old Man, 3rd Apparition
Peggy Harris	Lady Macduff
Terry Haschke	Lady Macbeth
Mr. Donald Hill	Porter
Richard Hill	Messenger
Jeff Hillyer	2nd Witch, 2nd Murderer, Doctor
Karen Lohr	Gentlewoman
Terry McCord	Seyton
Robert Russell	Ross
Jeffrey Schroeder	1st Witch, 1st Murderer, Doctor
Mark Scott	Lennox
Ted Sofis	Fleance, Macduff's Son
Robert Thiele	Macduff
David Van Dyke	Malcolm
Mark Weingart	Banquo, Old Siward
Richard Werner	Macbeth
Scene:	Scotland and England
Time:	11th Century
Director:	Mr. Donald Hill
Technical Director:	Mr. Richard Downing

King Ubu
(Alfred Jarry)

Patty Carter	Conscience, People of the Palace, Russian Soldier, Sailor
Debbie Chaffin	Danziger Guard, People of the Palace, Judge Cuckoo
Denise Cox	Tails
Steve Davison	Renski, People of the Palace, Noble, Peasant
Tim Dransfield	M'Nure, Sea Captain
Fritz Enstrom	Pa Ubu
Lyn Enstrom	Ma Ubu
Bob Good	Boleslas, Tzar, Noble, Peasant
Chab Guthrie	Boggerlas
Margaret Leta Harris	Lackey, Noble, Peasant, Bear
Jeff Hillyer	Laski, People of the Palace, Financier, Sailor
Bud Holtgreve	Ancestor, Danziger Guard, Councilor, Russian Cavalry
Pete Hurd	Ladislas, Financier, Peasant, Soldier, Russian Cavalry
Debbie Loesch	Heads
David Lyle	Danziger Guard, People of the Palace, Peasant, Councilor, Soldier
Terry Lee McCord	Wenceslas, Judge, Lackey, Soldier
Debbie Shelton	Queen Rosamund, Noble, Councilor
Jim Shelton	Gyron
Bernice Steinberg	Polish Army
David Taylor	Polish Army
Scene:	The Slavic nations
Time:	Limbo
Director:	Cheri Swiss
Technical Director:	Mr. Richard Downing

Homecoming Week saw the second repertory of 1972. *Antigone* by Sophocles was directed by Richard Downing and I contributed Moliére's *The Misanthrope*. The unlikely combination of a Greek tragedy and a French social satire worked very well. The fifth century classic Greek tragedy and the seventeenth century neo-classic French comedy had similar themes: both dealt with the unhappy repercussions of what happens when Man, acting in the extreme, opposes the prevailing wisdom and code of conduct. The repertory schedule saw *Antigone* playing October 17, 21, 15; October 27; and October 19 and 26. *The Misanthrope* was featured on October 18, 20, 26; October 28; and October 17 and 24.

Technical Director Downing's staging for *Antigone* consisted of a formal set of steps and columns which could be moved easily to make way for *The Misanthrope* set. The Greek costumes and masks were well done. The cast did a superb job with the style of the play and the projection of the theme. Bev Puckett, in her *Black and Magenta* review, wrote, "Anyone who did not see *Antigone* . . . missed a fine show and an excellent portrayal of Creon and Antigone by Mr. Elli and Miss Cox."[11]

Antigone, 1972. Creon (M. Elli) persuades, but Antigone (D. Cox) cannot be swayed. *Theatre file photo courtesy M.C. Public Relations Office.*

The set that I designed for *The Misanthrope* was formal and stylized in the French manner, but the costumes were modern formal attire. The style of acting was also formal–almost presentational in nature–in order to focus attention on the language and theme of the play. Dee Dee Verley, in her *Black and Magenta* review, caught the gist of *The Misanthrope* in her headline, "Expression is Key to Satire." She wrote, "The actors involved in this play display a fine performance through their portrayals of the characters."[12] As was true in the earlier repertory of *Macbeth* and *King Ubu*, attendance was exceptional at regular evening performances and school matinees.

Mr. Downing's January Interim class in Pantomime produced an original play, *The Silence of Life,* January 19-20 at the Little Theatre.

The 1973 spring semester began in February with *Purlie Victorious*, written by Ossie Davis. It was directed by Ray Valentine for the UHURU Black Week celebration, and performed February 7-10. Mr. Richard Downing designed the set. The play was so well done that I felt it was worthy of seminar status, which was awarded to the production.[13]

Mr. Downing designed another beautiful set for my production of Shakespeare's *Twelfth Night,* which was performed on May 11-14. At this point in time, the Little Theatre had collected a devoted nucleus of actors who were fond of the classics, and who had developed a taste for good dramatic fare. Not all of these students were theatre majors, by any means, but they were interested in good theatre. This happy band of players took pride in the fact that Lee Anne Smith, in her review of the production, pronounced "Twelfth Night Superb."[14]

Twelfth Night, 1973. The public disgrace of Malvolio. Countess Olivia (D. Cox, center) disapproves of the cross-gartered Malvolio (M. Elli). (from left) The Public: Valentine (M. Weingart), Duke Orsino (R. Thiele), Viola (B. Sheil), her twin, Sebastian (T. Sofis), Antonio (B. Carothers), Curio (T. Foster), Feste (D. Van Dyke), Fabian (R. Werner), (behind pillars, right) Maria (D. Howes), Ladies (M. Magura and M. Stanley). *Theatre file photo courtesy M.C. Public Relations Office.*

It is always a difficult task for a director to identify certain performances as outstanding; however, perhaps the passage of time (some twenty-seven years!) will dull any damage to egos. Matt Elli's Maivolio was marvelous, one that I will remember always. Bob Russell's Sir Toby Belch was excellent. I knew that Rich Werner could do a comic role when I assigned him the part of Fabian, but he needed to prove it to himself! I could find no fault with Bob Thiele's Orsino, or Denise Cox's Olivia, both solid performances. Dodi Howes always managed to break me up with her Maria. I still admire the persistence of Bobbi Sheil and Ted Sofis; they totally ignored certain elements of their disguise as the twins, Viola and Sebastian, to turn in commendable performances every night.

However, outstanding performances by a select few do not a play make. The rest of the cast also performed admirably. They consistently maintained a fine standard of acting: Tim Foster (Curio), Mark Weingart (Valentine), John Swan and John Pidgeon (Lords), Harry Eadon (Sea Captain), Greg Senf (Sir Andrew Aguecheek), David Van Dyke (Feste), Bruce Carothers (Antonio), Myra Stanley and Marypaul Magura (Ladies), John Pidgeon (Servant), Rick Hill (First Officer), Steve Davison (Second Officer), and Tom Morehouse (A Priest). Ray Zepp's Musicians in The Recorder Consort were David McLellan, Teresa Montgomery, and Beverly Wilson.

The season continued on April 25-28, when Debra Chaffin directed Samual Beckett's *Endgame* for her senior seminar. A portion of her seminar was published in the April 20 issue of the *Black and Magenta,* under the title "Analysis of Beckett's Writing." The article presented some guidelines for viewing *Endgame.* She pointed out that Beckett's theatre is not the conventional nor traditional theatre; he belongs to the theatre of the absurd. Debra explained that Beckett demands an open approach, void of the usual expectations that one has of the traditional theatre. Beckett's concept of theatre is total involvement, which means he appeals to an audience through all the senses: touch, taste, smell, sight, and sound, as well as the emotions and the intellect. It is wrong to focus on only one element of theatre. One should not try to make intellectual sense out of a play, to the exclusion of all the other appeals that theatre offers. Debra wrote,

> . . . For Beckett, the words are only a part of something bigger. Our response is derived from the whole experience, so that the effect is not from what is said, but what experiencing the play does personally to each spectator.

The key word, then, is "experience" or "experiencing," not just thinking and feeling. Debra concluded,

> When you come to see *Endgame* don't expect to view an experience from the author's life, or the affirmation of a general truth. And above all don't expect mere entertainment, or escape. But do prepare to be enlightened.[15]

Absurdist drama is not easy to produce or direct, but Debra had the discriminating intelligence to work her cast into a memorable production. Jeff Schroeder played Hamm; Bob Bielecki, Clov; David Holdridge, Nagg; and Ruth Whittier, Nell.

While *Endgame* was being readied for the stage, Mary Ann Spitznagel was working on her directing seminar. She was helping Betty Ward with a school production of *Carousel,* the popular hit musical by Richard Rodgers and Oscar Hammerstein II. Mary Ann was student-teaching at John Glenn High School where, at the time of this writing, she is on the faculty. She was especially fond of (and good at) musicals, and enjoyed assisting the director, Betty Ward, in making *Carousel* a success. At the same time that *Endgame* was running at the Little Theatre, *Carousel* was being performed in the John Glenn High School Auditorium (April 25-28).

A final set of one-acts, produced by Muskingum Players, took the stage on May 9 at Salt Fork State Lodge. Again, at the same time (May 9-12), the final production of the year opened at the Little Theatre: Mark Weingart's seminar production of *Last of the Red Hot Lovers.*

The play was well-directed and well-acted, and the student audiences especially loved it. A director could not have wanted a better or nicer cast with which to work: David Van Dyke portrayed Barney Cashman; Terry Haschke was Elaine Navazio; Bobbi Sheil was Bobbi Michele; and Karen Lohr was Jeanette Fisher.

October 1972 Repertory Cast
Antigone
(Sophocles)

Ismene, Daughter of Oedipus .... Marypaul Magura
Antigone, Daughter of Oedipus .... Denise Cox
Creon, King of Thebes .... Matthew Elli
Haemon, Son of Creon .... Bruce Carothers
Teiresias, a blind prophet .... David Van Dyke
Guide to Teiresias .... Charlie Stout
A Sentry .... Harry Eadon
A Messenger .... John Pidgeon
Eurydice, wife of Creon .... Debbie Loesch
Chorus .... Patricia Taylor, Marguerite Harman
Guards .... Terry McCord, Dale Gnidovec
Scene: .... The royal palace of Thebes
Director: .... Mr. Richard Downing
Technical Director: .... Mr. Richard Downing

The Misanthrope
(Moliére)

Alceste, an honest man .... Richard Werner
Philinte, his friend .... Bob Thiele
Oronte, a gentleman and poet .... Jeffrey Schroeder
Celimene, a lady of fashion .... Terry Haschke
Basque, her butler .... Terry McCord
Eliante, Celimene's friend and cousin Mary . Ann Spitznagel
Acaste, Man of distinction .... Ted Sofis
Clitandre, Man of distinction .... Greg Senf
An Officer of the Court .... Rick Hill
Arsinoe, a prude in love with Alceste .... Dodi Howes
De Bois, Alceste's valet .... John Pidgeon
Scene: .... A salon in Celimene's Paris Home
Time: .... 17th Century France
Director: .... Mr. Donald Hill
Technical .... Director: Mr. Richard Downing

1973–1974

The 1973-74 theatre season opened with Noel Coward's "improbable farce," *Blithe Spirit.*

Blithe Spirit takes place in the Condomine's living room in Kent, England. Charles Condomine, a novelist, is doing research on the occult. He invites a professional medium, Madame Arcati, for a séance, in order to gain first-hand information for his next book.

> During the séance, the spirit of Elvira, Charles' first wife who died seven years ago, materializes. She and Ruth, Charles' present wife, begin a figurative tug-of-war over his affections. Elvira plans to outwit Ruth by killing Charles so that she might have him to herself on an "astral plane." Unfortunately, Ruth is killed by mistake. When Madame Arcati tries to de-materialize Elvira, Ruth's spirit materializes instead. Edith, the maid, is revealed as a "Natural" whose mischievous subconscious calls up the spirits of both wives. Using Edith as her "control," Madame Arcati is able to de-materialize the two spirits, leaving Charles free to travel and enjoy life.[16]

The subtitle "An Improbable Farce," is well chosen. To the usual comedy of manners, marital intrigue, and witty dialogue, Coward adds a dollop of the occult. The supernatural mixes with the natural to offer the author unlimited scope for devising innumerable antic complications.

Blithe Spirit, 1973. The Seance. (from the left): Charles (R. Werner), Madame Arcati (K. Lohr), Ruth (D. Cox), Dr. Bradman (R. Thiele), Mrs. Bradman (M. Magura). *Theatre file photo courtesy M.C. Public Relations Office.*

I had learned (with *Private Lives* and *Hay Fever*) that a director does not attempt a Noel Coward comedy unless he has certain actors. Such actors must have the ability to memorize lines quickly, must understand the ambiguities of the language, and must be able to jump out of bed at three o'clock in the morning and recite their lines verbatim.

I was sure that I had the right people for the cast, and the production went forward, much to my satisfaction and, according to Becky Englert's review, to the delight of the audience.[17] Richard Werner played Charles Condomine with just the right amount of frustration. Denise Cox was delightfully provoking as Charles' second wife, Ruth alive; and as Ruth's ghost, she was ingenuously acerbic. Patricia Taylor, the ghost of Charles' first wife, Elvira wafted here and wafted there with the perfect grace and ease of a champagne bubble, crazily on the loose. Karen Lohr (Madame Arcati) was ineffably and puzzlingly indifferent to everything except her medium, and Dodi Howes developed an impeccably impish voice for Arcati's "Daphne." Robert Thiele and Marypaul Magura (Dr. and Mrs. Bradman), like two balloon salesmen in a storm, held onto the airborne cast members; the Bradmans were the atypical comic foils to everyone in the play. Hope Schweir's "Edith" was derived justifiably from one of Aristophanes's running slaves.

Since Mr. Downing was not replaced (see ref. #18), the theatre was facing a year without a resident technical director. As if by magic, help materialized (courtesy of Mr. Ellertson and President Miller) in the person of David Golden, a graduate student from the Ohio University Theatre, who was hired for *Blithe Spirit*. He created the scene design and supervised the technical work that made all the scenic effects of the séance and shenanigans of the ghosts probable and possible. Cheri Swiss was Production Supervisor, a position she held throughout the year.

Blithe Spirit was the only major production that I directed during the season. I had not gone into early retirement; in fact, I was busier than ever. The theatre had developed a backlog of one-acts, which students must direct if they were to meet their academic requirements. I became active in the instruction of student-directors in the fundamentals of directing, and watching them as a critic while they rehearsed their plays for performance.

The 1974 spring semester began March 13-16 with a set of student-directed one-act plays. A second set was produced on April 17-19. On April 18 and 20, Denise Cox presented the equivalent of a senior seminar with her Honors Project of the famous Salzburg Medieval allegory, *Everyman*, written by Hugo Von Hofmannsthal.[19]

On April 18-19, Marypaul Magura, who was student-teaching at West Muskingum High School, directed Neil Simon's *Star-Spangled Girl* at Ohio University's Olsen Hall in Zanesville, Ohio, for her seminar requirement.[20]

An unusual production concluded the theatre season on April 30 and May 2. To fulfill her seminar requirements in theatre, Jill Giguere, student director and choreographer, presented her dance drama, *Seven Stimulations,* in the Women's Gymnasium.[21]

The program was composed of seven dances: "Chaos and Love," "Search," "Universal Soul," "Good and Evil," "Love II," "You Are Chosen/Task and Attitude," and "Wind." The program was performed by ten dancers: Amy Rozmus, Debbie Deemer, Wendy Prentice, Sue Cook, Tina Stiles, Jeff Schroeder, Betsy Nutting, Gail Tuttle, Jill Giguere, and Chris Gregory.

1974–1975

Tartuffe caused Moliére problems that almost lost him the patronage of Louis XIV. The basic theme of the comedy is a favorite theme of dramatists–illusion versus reality. The subject matter of *Tartuffe* is hypocrisy. Moliére's specific target was the people of Louis's court who were insincere church members. Whether Moliére intended to satirize the Church or not is a moot point. The religious hypocrites couldn't possibly confess their own insincerity; therefore, they convinced Louis that the man they loved to hate was making fun of the Church. Louis couldn't afford to offend the Church, so he banned the play. After five years, the ban was lifted and the play became the most popular of Moliére's comedies.[22]

The Misanthrope had proved successful with the students and the Muskingum audience. Rex McGraw and his students had fun with *The Doctor in Spite of Himself* (1964) and I had success with the same play at the University of Idaho Summer Theatre. Michel St. Denis, lecturing in New York City in the late '50s, indicated that Moliére's achievement in comedy may have been greater than Racine's in tragedy. What we [Americans] needed were good translations. *Voila!* Richard Wilbur, a Pulitzer Prize poet, appeared on the scene with excellent translations of Moliére, not in prose, but in a variety of iambics—usually in rhyming pentameter—that gave the effect of the Alexandrine verse in which Moliére and Racine had composed their plays. Wilbur's translations of Moliére were being done on Broadway, to great acclaim. Shakespeare had a rival in the comedy genre. That was how I rationalized my choice of *Tartuffe* for the 1974-75 theatre season opener.

Tartuffe, 1974. (from the left) Cleante (D. Van Dyke), Dorine (B. Sheil), Orgon (R. Hill), Flipote (C. Foster), Elmire (H. Schwier); (seated) Mme. Pernelle (P. Taylor), Mariane (K. King), Damis (G. Senf). *Theatre file photo courtesy M.C. Public Relations Office.*

After the cast learned to speak the lines according to meaning, instead of poetic meter, everything went well in rehearsals and performances. The students were extraordinarily gifted, and I took advantage of educational theatre to double-cast four roles: Patricia Taylor and Hope Schwier alternated as Mme. Pernelle and Elmire; Kathy King and Cherie Foster alternated as Flipote and Mariane. Ted Sofis was masterful as Tartuffe, the hypocrite, in rehearsals, but when he put on the full-bottom wig for performances, he positively glowed. I never saw anybody enjoy a part so much! Bobbi Sheil as Dorine, the Maid, was always interrupting everybody, as directed. Greg Senf, as Orgon's son, Damis, was always ready to fight; David Van Dyke as Cleante, Elmire's brother, tried to reason with Rick Hill, who, as Orgon, head of the household, was seriously gullible to every whim of Tartuffe. Neil Gartner as Mariane's suitor, Valere, was properly proper, and Rich Werner as M. Loyal, a bailiff, was agreeably traitorous when he presented Orgon with an eviction notice. We all thanked God for Mark Preslan who, as an Officer of Louis's court, true to his part as a perfect *deus ex machina*, resolved the situation. Tartuffe was imprisoned, and Orgon and his family were freed, at last, of the villain.

The play made a useful seminar vehicle for four members of the cast: Kathy King, Hope Schwier, Bobbi Sheil, and Ted Sofis. It also proved to be an excellent way to introduce the public to our new technical director, Jerry Martin, whose scene design and technical expertise served Moliére well.

During the Interim, a class in musical comedy presented two famous musicals. *Flower Drum Song* by Richard Rodgers and Oscar Hammerstein II was directed by James N. Holm, Jr.; Donna Henderson Turner directed Leslie Bricusse's and Anthony Newley's *Stop the World I Want to Get Off!*. The class spent two weeks rehearsing and building the shows. The musicals opened at the Little Theatre on January 21 and 22. They toured to Churchill Area High School in Pittsburgh, Riverview High School in Coshocton, Ohio, the YMCA in Cambridge, and the Municipal Auditorium in Zanesville. The final performances were held at the Little Theatre on February 4-5. Jerry Martin designed the sets and supervised the technical work for both musicals.[23]

The Caretaker, 1975. Davies (A. Patterson) and Aston (R. Hill). *Theatre file photo courtesy M.C. Public Relations Office.*

The Caretaker, written by Harold Pinter, one of England's famous and most prolific dramatists, was the first major production of the spring semester. The play was designed and directed by Jerry Martin. True to the Pinter style, the actors " . . . gave detailed, thoughtful performances."[24] Art Patterson played Davies, a tramp, who nearly succeeds in alienating two brothers–Aston, played by Rick Hill, and Mick, played by John Saylor. The audience enjoyed this Pinter drama, which won the *London Evening Standard* award for the best new play of the year.[25] Beth Sanders, in her review for the *Black and Magenta*, gave the play an excellent rating.[26]

In March, I directed my third production of *A Midsummer Night's Dream*. The company of principals proved to be especially strong: the young lovers, Lysander (Ron Petronio) and Hermia (Bobbi Sheil), Demetrius (Jim Hayes), and Helena (Cherie Foster), were presided over by the Duke of Athens, Theseus (Bruce Leavitt) and the Queen of Amazons, Hippolyta (Ann Milosevich), all of whom were closely watched by the King and Queen of Shadows, Oberon (Rich Werner) and Titania (Linda Hierholzer), as well as the devilish Puck (Debbie Davidson). As usual, the mechanics or rustics, who were rehearsing a play for the Duke, almost stole the show: Quince, a carpenter (David Van Dyke), Bottom, a weaver (Ted Sofis), Snug, a joiner (Sherman Liddell), Flute, a bellows-mender (Greg Senf), Starveling, a tailor (John Rogers), his dog, played by Guest Artist, "Puck," and Snout, a tinker (Jeff Hill). The principals were ably supported by Danny Toops (Philostrate), Bob Bartlett (Egeus), Beth Sanders (Mustardseed), Wendy Cook (Peaseblossom), Judy Gilkerson (Cobweb), Bonita Tacket (Moth), Kathy King and Myra Stanley (Ladies), and Bruce Hare and Bob McCarrell (Attendant Lords). All of the actors were responsible for "One of the happiest productions of the second half of the school year. . . . "[27]

In April, Greg Senf directed *Glass Menagerie* by Tennessee Williams, in partial fulfillment of his theatre major seminar. Greg emphasized the mood of the play, the quiet nostalgia of time remembered. The actors responded to the direction with a subtle and muted style. Cherie Foster was Amanda Wingfield, the mother; Jeff Hill played Tom, her son; Nancy Slack portrayed Laura, her daughter; and the director played Jim O'Connor, The Gentleman Caller. The actors suited their movements and costumes to the emotion inspired by the music. The scene design and staging were executed by Jennifer Baxter; these elements blended well with the production idea and helped the play achieve its impressionistic effects.[28]

Guest Artist Mercedes McCambridge performed on May 1 with student actors in Dylan Thomas's *Under Milk Wood*. (This production is discussed in detail in the section entitled, People and Events.)

The final show of the season was a directing seminar by Rick Hill: Murray Schisgal's comic treatment of the battle of the sexes, *Luv*.

> Although slight in plot, the dialogue and comic action keep the play moving at a fast and funny pace. Underneath all the hilarity flows a serious commentary on male-female relationships more readily seen in "Memorial Day." [In preparation for his seminar, Rick Hill directed that short one-act by Murray Schisgal for the February 20 meeting of Muskingum Players.][29]

The cast of the production consisted of Rick Porter as Milt Manville, Rick Hill as Harry Berlin, and Debbie Davidson as Ellen Manville. Rick Hill not only directed and acted in his own production, but also designed and supervised the construction of the set.

1975–1976

O n September 24, A. A. Milne's *Winnie-the-Pooh* began the 1975-76 theatre season. The show was directed and designed by Jerry Martin. Patricia L. Taylor reported, "The cast . . . performed ably with an infectious enthusiasm . . . . The show was a visual treat–the setting simple, colorful, and functional; the costumes imaginative and appropriate."[30] Members of the cast included Laurel McCamey (Narrator), Amy Brannon (Christopher Robin), Mary Beth Reeves (Pooh), Wendy Cook (Piglet), William Jones (Owl), Bob Bartlett (Eeyore), Linda Hierholzer (Kanga), Jenny Baxter (Roo), Myra Stanley (Rabbit), Leslie Conger (Animal I-small rabbit), Bari Oyler (Animal II-skunk), Teresa Ferris (Animal III-rabbit), and Susan Fellows (Animal IV-rabbit).

Winnie-the-Pooh, 1975. (left to right) Pooh (M. Reeves) ponders the problems of a honey pot, while Rabbit (S. Fellows) and Skunk (B. Oyler) watch. *Theatre file photo courtesy M.C. Public Relations Office.*

Thornton Wilder has long been recognized as one of America's major dramatists. As an American Bicentennial offering on October 22-25, I directed *The Skin of Our Teeth*, a 1943 play which won its author his third Pulitzer Prize. The play is a testament to the indestructibility of Man who has survived the accumulated disasters of the world: fire, famine, flood, and war. The story concerns the Antrobus family, who experience all of these calamities and still hope for the best.[31]

For her acting seminar, Patricia L. Taylor played Lily Sabina, the maid, a role created on Broadway by Tallulah Bankhead. The members of the Antrobus family were portrayed by Jim Hayes (Mr. Antrobus), Debbie Dearing (Mrs. Antrobus), Debbie Davidson (Gladys, their daughter), and Rick Porter (Henry, their son). These were the principals who led a cast of approximately thirty students in the performance of this American classic.

The Wizard of Oz, 1976. (from the left) Hank, the Scarecrow (W. Jones), Jim, the Tin Woodman (S. Shipley), Dorothy (A. Brannon). Creative Playmaking, Wilma Barnett; Musical Director, Catherine Johnson. *Theatre file photo courtesy M.C. Public Relations Office.*

During the January Interim, a theatre class of thirty students presented *The Wizard of Oz*. The script was an original adaptation, formulated by the students under the supervision of Education Specialist, Professor Wilma Barnett. After one week, the script was completed and I began rehearsals. Jerry Martin instructed the students to build the sets and make the costumes, while Professor of Music, Catherine Johnson, supervised the musical elements of the play. During the fourth week of the interim, the musical was performed in Brown Chapel for 3,700 elementary students from surrounding schools. On February 5-7, the play was moved to the Little Theatre for regular campus performances.[32] Amy Brannon played Dorothy. Her lovable companions were Bill Jones (Scarecrow), Larry Overmire (Lion), and Sam Shipley (Tin Man). Perry Alers played the Wizard; Gretchen Hoffman was the Wicked Witch of the West; and Pam Fitch was the Good Witch of the North. They were capably supported by the remaining students in the class. Rex Roseman supplied the piano music.

I thought that the bicentennial year might be a good time to have an all-faculty show. According to Cheri Swiss, during the 1910-11 school year,

> A new and unique piece of theatre appeared at Muskingum that year. It had never happened before nor has it happened since. The Faculty staged a play called *The Servant of the House*. It was done on February 24, 1911, and was such a success that it was brought back in March of 1912.[33]

Over sixty-four years had gone by since the first faculty play. The faculty should certainly have recovered by now, and enough time had elapsed for the local clientele to have forgotten and forgiven! For this enterprise, I chose Clark Gesner's musical adaptation of Charles M. Schulz's "Peanuts" comic strip. I had no particular motive or objective in mind, other than I knew there were faculty interested in doing a show, and I liked "Charlie Brown" because it was light, fun, and firmly within range of the talent pool. Any profit from ticket sales would be used to pay for a *Fine Arts Newsletter* and renovation of the Little Theatre.

You're a Good Man, Charlie Brown, 1976. Schroeder (L. Palmer) directs the "Peanuts" chorus: Patty (L. Porter), Linus (E. Grotzinger), Lucy (E. S. Cook), Charlie Brown (J. Martin), and Snoopy (D. Hill. *Theatre file photo courtesy M.C. Public Relations Office.*

Later, I discovered some old reliable truths beneath the surface of the naive and unpretentious script: we learn more from our failures than from our successes ("low aim, not failure is a crime") and, to hope and to persevere is important ("try, try, try again until you succeed"). Charlie Brown may have a "Failure Face," but it belies his persistence. Much more important are the reasons for which he is loved: he is thoughtful, brave and courteous; he has a sense of honor, a heart of gold; and he is humble and noble.[34]

Taken in its entirety, *You're a Good Man, Charlie Brown* is an affirmative statement about the human experience and the human condition. Similar to Wilder's *The Matchmaker*, it " . . . is about the aspirations of the young (and not only of the young) for a fuller, freer participation in life."[35]

On March 17-21, with Katherine Schnitker at the piano, the following faculty took to the Little Theatre stage with *You're a Good Man, Charlie Brown*: Jerry Martin appeared as Charlie Brown (he also doubled as technical director and designer); Eric Grozinger was Linus; Lorle Porter was Peppermint Patty; Louis Palmer was Schroeder; I was type-cast as a dog, Snoopy (I also doubled as director of the show); and Ms. E. Sue Cook triumphed as Lucy.

The show was a huge success. Quite frankly, I believe the success of the show was due, largely, to a very conscientious cast who missed few, if any, rehearsals. When they came to rehearsals, they REHEARSED! REHEARSED! REHEARSED! The most gratifying comments came from the student newspaper, the *Black and Magenta*, which carried the following notice:

> *You're a Good Man, Charlie Brown* . . . was special in that its cast was composed entirely of faculty members, who would have surprised any theatre critic. The play, to say the least, tickled the funny bone, but the real appreciation lay in the

talent displayed by our faculty members. No matter how entertaining the script, it would have gone nowhere if the characters weren't properly mastered. And well mastered they were.[36]

The second semester of the season, dedicated to the Bicentennial, continued with two seminar productions by theatre majors.

Myra Stanley directed Joseph Kesselring's famous farce, *Arsenic and Old Lace*, on April 14-17. One of the longest running hits of the American theatre, it is the story of two zany aunts, Abby and Martha Brewster (Sue Hitch and Sherry Blackwood) who murder thirteen elderly gentlemen in order to win a contest with their brother, Jonathan Brewster (Tim Campbell), who murders only twelve. Enlivening the play is another brother, Teddy Brewster (Ed Boyce), who thinks he is Teddy Roosevelt. Only the nephew, Mortimer Brewster (Mark Liberatore), can unravel the reason for all the macabre hilarity, as he struggles to win the love of his fair lady, Elaine Harper (Wendy Cook). Other members of the cast were Rev. Harper (Arthur Patterson), Officer Brophy (Allan Brooks), Officer Klein (Bruce Hare), Mr. Gibbs (Mark Thomas), Dr. Einstein (David Briggs), Officer O'Hara (Steve Porter), Lieutenant Rooney (Bob Bartlett), Mr. Witherspoon (Galen Wilson), and The Body (Mark Wentz).[37]

On April 28-May 1, Linda Hierholzer directed *Feiffer's People*, a unique revue by America's famous satirist and cartoonist, Jules Feiffer. The author shows modern America's social and political foibles in a series of short sketches. Webb Stickney, Sandy Rodgers, Bill Wilcoxon, Derrol Waggoner, Rick Porter, Sue Fellows, Debbie

The Effect of Gamma Rays on Man-in-the-Moon Marigolds, 1976. Beatrice (P. Taylor) and Nanny (B. Zellar). *Theatre file photo courtesy M.C. Public Relations Office.*

Dearing, John Rogers, Winnie Wolfe, and Mark Preslan portrayed all the characters in the multi-scene show designed to keep the audience laughing and thinking.[38]

Ending one of the most crowded and productive seasons of the Little Theatre was *The Effect of Gamma Rays on Man-in-the-Moon Marigolds* by Paul Zindel on May 5-8. I directed, and Jerry Martin designed and supervised the technical aspects of the show. This powerful and moving study of an embittered woman and her two daughters won the Pulitzer Prize for 1970, the New York Drama Critics' Circle Award as Best American Play, and the Obie Award. The cast of five women included two acting seminars by Patricia Taylor, who played Beatrice, the mother, and Cherie Foster, who played Tillie, her daughter. Katie

Carothers portrayed the older daughter, Ruth; Becky Zellar enacted the decrepit boarder, Nanny; and Bonita Tackett performed the role of Janice Vickery, a competitive classmate of Tillie.[39]

Cast List for
The Skin of Our Teeth
(Thornton Wilder)

Announcer, Sailor, Actor	Webster Stickney
Sabina	Patricia L. Taylor
Mr. Fitzpatrick	Mark Preslan
Mrs. Antrobus	Debbie Dearing
Dinosaur, Actor	Steve Kropp
Mammoth, Actor	Mark Thomas
Michael Catalano	Telegraph Boy, Chair Pusher, Actor
Gladys	Debbie Davidson
Henry	Rick Porter
Mr. Antrobus	Jim Hayes
Doctor, Conveener, Actor	Bob McCarrell
Professor, Conveener, Actor	Allan Brooks
Judge, Conveener, Actor	Mike Dauka
Homer, Conveener, Actor	Bill Hunneke
Miss E. Muse, Conveener, Actress	Kathy Taylor
Miss T Muse, Conveener, Actress	Jane Yonally
Miss M Muse, Conveener, Actress	Sandy Rodgers
Refugee, Broadcast Official, Actor	Larry Overmire
Refugee, Assistant Broadcaster, Actor	Perry Alers
Refugee, Hester	Beth Potter
Refugee, Ivy	Kate Tennant
Usher	Scot Evans
Usher, Sailor, Fred Bailey	Greg McDermott
Drum Majorette	Judy Kadell
Drum Majorette	Jill Hollinger
Lady Conveener, Actress	Pam Nicholson
Fortune Teller	Sue Hitch
Bingo Caller	Robert Bartlett
Defeated Candidate, Mr. Tremayne	Jeff Hill
Woman in Audience	Myra Stanley
Assistant Stage Manager	Lee Baker
Pianist	Faye McPherson
Act I.	Home: Excelsior, New Jersey; The Ice Age/ Our Beginning
Act II.	Atlantic City Boardwalk; Turn of the Century; Before the Flood
Act III.	Home: Excelsior, New Jersey; Today after the War and before another

The Wizard of Oz
(Original Interim Class Play)

Dorothy	Amy Brannon
Aunt Em	Megan Wills
Uncle Henry	Robert Bartlett

Hank, Scarecrow .... William Jones
Gus, Cowardly Lion .... Larry Overmire
Jim, Tin Woodman .... Samuel Shipley
Miss Gulch, Wicked Witch .... Gretchen Hoffman
Witch of the North .... Pamela Fitch
Niece of the Wicked Witch .... Ruth Neumann
Wizard of Oz .... Perry Alers
Mayor of Munchkin City .... David Briggs
Coroner .... Kathryn Dell
Barrister .... Allan Brooks
Munchkin I .... Erin Collins
Munchkin II .... Patricia Jenkins
Munchkin III .... Amy Reitzer
Munchkin IV .... Barbara Kerr
Guard of Emerald City .... Robert McCarrell
General of the Witch's Guard .... Mark Thomas
Voice of Toto .... Lisa Rykowski
Chorus, Munchkins, Citizens of Emerald
City, and Witch's Army: .... Robert Bartlett, Barbara Bauer, Phyllis Berghorn,
        David Briggs, Allan Brooks, Erin Collins, Kathryn Dell, Martha
        Frankel, Patricia Jenkins, Barbara Kerr, Jennifer LeSuer, Robert
        McBurney, Lisa Oakley, Lorna Palmer, Amy Reitzel, Kate Tennant,
        Mark Thomas, Melanie Warren, Megan Wills
Piano .... Rex Roseman

PROLOGUE: A Farm in Kansas
       Scene I: Land of the Munchkins
       Scene II: Follow the Yellow Brick Road
       Scene III: Emerald City
       Scene IV: Witch's Castle
       Scene V: Emerald City
EPILOGUE: A Farm in Kansas

1976–1977

While I was in Minneapolis finishing the details on my doctor's degree, the fall semester of the 1976-77 theatre season got off to a roaring start with two major productions that lit up the Little Theatre stage.

I Do! I Do!, a Tom Jones and Harvey Schmidt musical, based on Jan de Hartog's gentle comedy, *The Fourposter*, opened the theatre season. The play was double cast. Amy Brannon and Bill Jones played the married couple (on campus, October 6 through Parents Weekend, October 9). Pam Fitch and David Diamond opened on campus, November 4, toured to Roscoe Village, November 5-6, and returned on November 7 to perform at a dinner theatre at the Top of the Center. Jerry Martin directed both casts and designed the show. Cheryl May and Faye McPherson were at the piano, and Al Brooks was on percussion. The famed musical begins on the wedding night of a young couple, and traces the high and low points of their lives for thirty-five years. It ends happily, as it began, much to the delight of the cast, crew, and audience.[40]

During Homecoming Week, Gay Manifold directed *The Misogynist*, her own adaptation of Aristophanes' *Thesmophoriazusea*. The plot centers on the tragic dramatist and poet, Euripides, whom the women of Athens accuse of being a woman-hater. Eileen McComb wrote a favorable review, which appeared in the *Black and Magenta* under the headline, "*Misogynist* Hit on Campus."[41] Donald W. Jones of the Cambridge *Daily Jeffersonian* stated, " . . . Gay Manifold's adaptation and direction of the play carried it off beautifully and explicitly." He continued:

> Other credits that cannot be omitted are Jerry Martin for design and technical direction and choreography by Joyce Krumpe. A chorus of six and a college of matrons of eight, fine supporting players and an efficient stage crew helped make this a finished production.[42]

Margi Van Demark of the Zanesville *Times Recorder* called the production " . . . witty, bright, and downright funny,"[43]

The Misogynist, 1976. Hippolyta (D. Fox, at right) presents her case against Melissa (D. Dearing) before the college of Matrons: (seated, left to right) V. Townsend and S. Leindecker; (standing) B. Gepford, R. Story, and R. Montgomery. *Theatre file photo courtesy M.C. Public Relations Office.*

During the January Interim, senior theatre major, Mary Beth Reeves, directed Neil Simon's *Plaza Suite* for her seminar. Two other students used the play for special projects for individual study: Bruce Hare designed the lighting and Jennifer Wilkes executed the costumes. The comedy was performed January 26-29 during the Interim, and was repeated for the campus during the second semester, February 2-5.

Plaza Suite is a series of three plays which can be played as an ensemble piece, as it was on Broadway in 1968, when George C. Scott and Maureen Stapleton headlined the show, or it can be played as three one-acts. In either case, the play is unified by the same subject matter: marital or extra-marital situations. All three acts take place in the same suite of rooms at the New York Plaza Hotel.

Act I, titled "Visitor from Mamaroneck," involves a married couple who have taken the suite while their home is being painted; it happens to be the same room they occupied on their wedding night, twenty-three years previous. Their marriage now is in tatters. The question as to whether or not the problem is resolved is left to the imagination of the audience. Lee Donoho played the wife, Larry Triplett was her husband, and Gretchen Hoffman was the problem–the husband's secretary. Randy Bardonner portrayed a Bellhop and Bruce Jones, a Waiter.

Act II, titled "Visitor from Hollywood," is a lesson in seduction. A Hollywood producer (Dave Diamond) invites an old sweetheart (Donalee Bowser) up to his room to revisit their affair from the past. He succeeds, in spite of the defenses that she summons as a suburban housewife. Randy Bardonner played the Waiter.

Act III, titled "Visitor from Forest Hills," is generally agreed to be the most hilarious of the three acts. On her wedding day, the bride-to-be locks herself in the bathroom. There is not one thing that her parents (Steve Hostettler and LouAnne Sellers) can do or say to get their recalcitrant daughter (Leanne Olson) to come out. Her fiancé (Chris Pegenelli) is summoned. He arrives, goes to the bathroom door, and says, "Cool it!" Immediately the bathroom door opens and the wedding goes on![44]

On March 9-13, the Muskingum College Theatre presented the most popular of Shakespeare's tragedies, *Hamlet*, under my direction, with design and technical supervision by Jerry Martin. On March 11, matinees were held at 9:00 a.m. and 1:00 p.m. for high school students. For these matinees, Jerry Martin designed twelve successful workshop sessions that gave students background information on the Elizabethan period and the production. A special performance was given for patrons of the theatre on March 13 at 9:00 p.m.[45]

Larry Overmire gave an outstanding performance as Hamlet. He received excellent support from Tim Campbell, Claudius; Stephen Hostettler, Laertes; Sue Hitch, Gertrude; and Wendy Cook Ophelia. The remaining members of the hard-working ensemble shared in the success of the play.

On April 13-16 Gay Manifold directed, and Jerry Martin supervised the technical aspects of the popular Faculty-Alumni production. Oscar Wilde's *The Importance of Being Earnest*, one of the most perfect farces in the English language, served as the vehicle for the following cast: Louis Palmer, Lane; Jerry Martin, Algernon Moncrieff; James Manifold, Jack Worthing; Pat Watson, Lady Bracknell; Linda Hierholzer, Gwendolen Fairfax; Sue Leiendecker, Miss Prism; Debby Fox, Cecily Cardew; Art Johnson, Doctor Chasuble; and Charles Pepper, Merriman.

Linda Hierholzer summarized her observations on the play:

> The culmination of six weeks of fun, hard work, exhaustion, learning experiences, and growing friendships resulted in the well-received production of *The Importance of Being Earnest* on April 13-16, 1977.[46]

Alice in Wonderland concluded the 1976-77 theatre season.

Twenty-three students in the Children's Theatre class, which was team-taught by Jerry Martin and me, completed all phases of the theatrical production. After finishing research, the students experimented with improvisations, and composed eight scenes from Lewis Carroll's *Alice in Wonderland* and *Through the Looking Glass*. These scenes, which were condensed into an hour's entertainment included (1) Alice's room where she falls asleep and, in her dreams, follows the White Rabbit to, (2) a field of mushrooms, (3) the Duchess's kitchen, (4) a Mad Hatter's tea party, (5) the Red Queen's croquet court, (6) the trial of the Knave of Hearts, (7) a banquet, and (8) back home again to her own room. Becky Zellar designed the set (which the students built and painted) and the costumes (which the students sewed). Then, they acted in five performances.[47]

Before each performance, the audience got to see the cast do warm-up exercises and make-up demonstrations. These activities were popular with both audience members and actors. They relaxed the actors, oriented the audience to the play, and created the atmosphere of fun that was to follow at the three matinees for school children on May 4, 5, and 6, and at the two evening performances on May 4 and 5 for the general public.[48]

Cast for
The Misogynist
(Gay Manifold's adaptation of Aristophanes' Thesmophoriazusae)

MUSICIANS:	Guitar, Judy Falcsik
	Flute, Laurel McCamey
	Recorder, Mark Liberatore
Demeter	Wendy Cook
Dionysus	Ken Fouts
Euripides	Larry Overmire
Menes	Dave Briggs
Agathon	Art Patterson
Grake	Pam Nicholson
Priestess	Nancy Jacoby
Herald	Erin Collins
Hippolyta	Debby Fox
Melissa	Debbie Dearing
CHORUS:	Donalee Bowser, Luanne Cavalier, Dawn Fuller, Carrie Huffman, Karen Markley, Joan Riggle
COLLEGE OF MATRONS:	Nancy Brown, Barbara Gepford, Ruth Harris, Sue Leiendecker, Ruth Montgomery, Birgetta Nelson, Ruth Story, Vicki Townsend
Scythos	Jeff Flynn
Twinkle Toes	Carrie Huffman
WRESTLERS:	Robert Hach, Bruce Hulme
OLYMPIANS:	Webster Stickney, Jr., Foreman, Ken Fouts, Art Patterson
Scene:	City of Athens, ancient Greece
Time:	Classical Age, 410 B.C.

Hamlet
(William Shakespeare)

Claudius, King of Denmark	Tim Campbell
Hamlet, nephew to the King	Larry Overmire
Polonius, counselor to the King	David Briggs
Horatio, friend to Hamlet	Ken Fouts

Laertes, son to Polonius .... Stephen Hostettler
Voltemand, ambassador .... John Rogers
Cornelius, ambassador .... Vaughn Rasor
Rosencrantz, courtier .... John Cover
Guildenstern, courtier .... Dave Reinhold
Marcellus, soldier .... Jeff Flynn
Bernardo, soldier .... Bruce Hare
Francisco, soldier .... Mike Mason
Osric, courtier .... Galen Wilson
Fortinbras, Prince of Norway .... John Howell
Ghost of Hamlet's Father .... Vance Elderkin
Lord, courtier .... Martin Cook
Gravedigger No. 1 .... Allan Brooks
Gravedigger No. 2 .... Mark Thomas
Player King .... Dave Diamond
Player Queen .... Lee Donoho
Lucianus .... Larry Triplett
Prologue .... Joan Riggle
Priest .... Phil Soergel
Sailor .... Bill Allison
Gertrude, Queen of Denmark .... Sue Hitch
Ophelia, daughter to Polonius .... Wendy Cook
Ladies in Waiting .... Leanne Olson, Amy Marshall, Sherry Blackwood
Norwegian Captain to Fortinbras .... Webb Stickney
Scene: .... Twelfth Century Denmark, Elsinor Castle

Alice in Wonderland
(An Original Class Play based on
Lewis Carroll's *Alice in Wonderland* and
Through the Looking Glass)

Alice .... Kathleen Bare
White Rabbit .... David Briggs
Flowers .... Sherrie Eick, Joanne Stevens, Alison Hand,
Martha Frankel
Humpty Dumpty .... Rob McBurney
Caterpillar .... Randy Okey
Card Footman .... Donalee Bowser
Frog Footman .... Amy Brannon
Duchess .... Gretchen Hoffman
Cook .... Mary Beth Reeves
Cheshire Cat .... Pam Nicholson
March Hare .... Jill Hank
Mad Hatter .... Erin Collins
Doormouse .... Bill Hunneke
Gardener #1 .... Amy Brannon
Gardener #2 .... Donalee Bowser
Red Queen .... Susan Hitch
Red King .... David Spillman
Executioner .... Stephen Watters
Knave of Hearts .... Allan Brooks
Tweedledum .... Amy Brannon
Tweedledee .... Donalee Bowser
Playing Cards .... Sherrie Eick, Joanne Stevens, Rob McBurney,
Randy Okey

Mutton .... Becky Zellar
Soup .... Martha Frankel
Ladle .... Jennifer Wilkes
Mother .... Alison Hand

1977–1978

The Fantasticks, an intimate musical with words by Tom Jones and music by Harvey Schmidt, opened Off-Broadway in 1960, playing at the 149-seat Sullivan Street Playhouse. It won the 1992 Tony Award for Excellence in Theatre.[49] Known as the longest running Off-Broadway hit, there was always a rumor that it was about to close, but through the year 2001, it had been going for forty years and showed no sign of weakening. On January 11, 2002, a news release by CNN disclosed that the longest running musical in American theatre history was giving its last performance on Sunday, January 13, at the Sullivan Street Playhouse. Tom Jones and Harvey Schmidt were interviewed during the announcement.

A photograph of the "Abduction-cum-Rape" scene, which was taken during one of the Little Theatre rehearsals, clearly shows some of the story of the play. The central focus of the picture is El Gallo (Larry Overmire) and his two henchmen, Mortimer, dressed as an Indian (Doug Switzer), and the old actor, Henry (Tracy Summers), being held at bay by the boy, Matt (Paul T. Couch), who is protecting the girl, Luisa (Amy Brannon). Overseeing the contest are the philosophic Mute (Larry Triplett) and the two fathers, Hucklebee, the boy's father (Sam Shipley), and Bellomy, the girl's father (Phil Soergel), who have paid El Gallo to stage the abduction so that no one gets hurt. Although saved from the frightening ordeal, the lovers quarrel and the boy

The Fantasticks, 1977. The fraudulent "rape" scene. The attackers: (from the left) Mortimer as an Indian (D. Switzer), El Gallo (L. Overmire), Henry, the Old Actor (T. Summers); the Watchers: The Mute (L. Triplett), Hucklebee (S. Shipley), Bellomy (P. Soergel); those being attacked: The Boy, Matt (P. Couch), and The Girl, Louisa (A. Brannon). *Theatre file photo courtesy M.C. Public Relations Office.*

leaves with El Gallo on a tour of life. The cruelties of the world are so great that the boy returns to his beloved.

The musical is a splendid mix of fantasy and reality which has been adapted from Edmund Rostand's play, *The Romancers*. It is made totally irresistible by Harvey Schmidt's musical score that includes the delicate poetry of "Try to Remember." The Little Theatre arena, designed with a few platforms and props, was just the right place for this audience-pleaser. I directed the show, Brent Fleming (the Theatre's new technical director) designed and executed the technical elements, Deann Fleming costumed the production, and Faye McPherson accompanied brilliantly on the piano. *The Fantasticks* entertained Homecoming audiences from October 12-15.

During the January 1978 Children's Theatre Interim, thirty-two students busied themselves preparing for a production of *Tom Sawyer,* a play with music. The theatre facilities in three buildings were utilized. The first week of the course was spent developing a script based upon Mark Twain's famous novel; four films and a number of

Tom Sawyer, 1978. Huck Finn (R. Hoagland) and Tom Sawyer (L. Overmire). *Theatre file photo courtesy M.C. Public Relations Office.*

dramatic adaptations of the novel were studied. Miss Wilma Barnett guided the students through the phases of writing and adapting the script. Every morning during the second and third weeks, the students met in Johnson Hall and at the Little Theatre, to construct the set and costumes designed by Brent Fleming. From 1:00 p.m. until 2:00 p.m., the students gathered in Brown Chapel for music rehearsal with Miss Catherine Johnson, who arranged and adapted folk tunes for the various songs included in the script. Music for the production was supplied by three guitars, played by Shawna Hixson, Tim Tipple, and Barbara Howell; a banjo played by Vaughn Rasor; and piano played by Rex Roseman and Anna Kritselis completed the ensemble. Every afternoon from 3:00 p.m. until 5:00 p.m., students rehearsed the play under my supervision.

After three weeks of work, the cast and crew were ready to perform the three matinees scheduled for the last week in January. Without warning, disaster struck!

One of the largest snowfalls of the decade forced postponement of the show until February. How humiliating! Nevertheless, the class performed the play on three evenings (February 8-10) in Brown Chapel, and gave a special morning performance for the school children on Thursday, February 9. The run-of-show concluded on Saturday, February 11 at a 2:00 p.m. matinee.[50]

On March 8-11, Pat Van De Voort directed the annual faculty show, *The Good Doctor* by Neil Simon, which is based on the short stories of Anton Chekhov. Brent Fleming provided the lighting and technical direction, and Deann Fleming designed the scenery and costumes for the Layton Theatre production.

Lacking a continuous plot, the play took the form of a series of sketches which featured Dave Van De Voort, Vicki Townsend, Scott Dittman, Lynn Flannery, Richard Leimbach, Sue Leiendecker, Deann Fleming, Bob Adams, Art Johnson, Marcy Remer, Russell Brown, Linda Hierholzer, Pat Van De Voort, Mary Gates Dewey, and Brent Fleming. The Neil Simon adaptation of the various Chekhov stories proved entertaining to the attentive audiences.

On April 19-23 student-seminar director, Pam Nicholson, a theatre and religion major, presented a beautiful and rousing production of *Godspell* at the Little Theatre. The final performance (Sunday, April 23) was held as a dinner theatre. Becky Zellar, technical director, designed the set, and Jennifer Wilkes designed the costumes, each for their respective seminars in theatre. Carla Bunfill, a senior music major, served as musical director.

The musical *Godspell* is based on the gospel, according to St. Matthew, and it combines song, dance, and story with the words of the scripture. Conceived and originally directed by John-Michael Tebelak, with music and lyrics by Stephen Schwartz, the show won national acclaim when it was first produced and it has remained a favorite of theatre audiences.

Under the headline, "'*Godspell*' Sellout Success," a staff writer for the *Black and Magenta* praised the production as " . . . an overall success . . . room for movement, dance and creative effects are what help to make '*Godspell*' such a dynamic production."[51] Specific numbers were singled out as being well-performed: "Oh, Bless the Lord," "Prepare Ye the Way of the Lord," "All for the Best," and "You Are the Light of the World." The student newspaper devoted an entire page to the review, and illustrated the article with photos by Dave Stults.[52]

The 1977-78 theatre season ended May 10-13, at the Layton Theatre, with a rollicking burlesque type farce, Moliére's *The Doctor in Spite of Himself.* I moved the seventeenth century French farce to our contemporary American Southwest, and it was billed as "A liberal interpretation of Moliére's *Le Medecin Malgre Lue.* Brent Fleming (theatre technical director) designed a clever country-western theme that dominated the scenery and costuming.

The farce concerns a poor farmer who, cursed with a nagging wife, is unwillingly forced to play the part of a doctor who has encounters with a wealthy landowner's daughter and her suitors, a buxom nurse, zany cowhands, nosey neighbors, and a couple of hicks.

Cast in the play were David Briggs, who played the farmer/doctor; Sherry

Blackwood, his shrewish wife; Bill Allison was Mr. Roberts, a neighbor; Larry Overmire was Gerald, a rich rancher; Amy Brannon was his "dumb" daughter; Larry Triplett was her lover; Web Stickney and John Sweeney were two ranch-hands, Duke and Luke; Eileen McComb was Luke's wife; and Joanna Grey and Leanne Olson were two hicks from the sticks looking for a cure. Added to the original cast was a guitarist, Clarence, played by Paul T. Couch (the man Gerald wanted his daughter to marry).[53]

Although the regular season was over, the Alumni Office needed some entertainment for Alumni Weekend, June 14-17. I already had it in mind to re-cast and re-stage a production of *You're a Good Man, Charlie Brown*, and I felt that this occasion might provide me with a good opportunity to "test the waters" with a preview performance. To this end, I approached members of the original production (1976) who

You're a Good Man, Charlie Brown, 1978. Faculty/Alumni production of the musical shows Lucy (Mary Ann Spitznagel DeVolld) threatening Linus (E. Grotzinger), who clutches his blanket for support. *Theatre file photo courtesy M.C. Public Relations Office.*

were still on campus. Eric Grotzinger (Linus), Lorle Porter (Peppermint Patty), Louis Palmer (Schroeder), and me (Snoopy) agreed that it would be a good idea. I then approached Bob Thiele for the part of Charlie Brown (which Jerry Martin had originally played), and I asked Mary Ann Spitznagel DeVolld if she would play Lucy, played by the late E. Sue Cook. They, too, were agreeable to the production. Since Kay Schnitker was unavailable, Jack Peterson generously stepped into that important post. Brent and Deann Fleming agreed to do the scenery and costumes, and we were off and running with rehearsals.

Everyone was very pleased with the results when we performed the Alumni-Faculty Show, *You're a Good Man, Charlie Brown*, on Alumni Weekend in the Layton Theatre in June, 1978. Prospects for a revival of the show for the September Homecoming looked very good, indeed!

Cast for

Tom Sawyer

(An original play by the Children's Theatre Class
based on Mark Twain's novel and its various dramatizations)

Miss Dobbins ....Jo Gray
School Children: ....Sue Harnick, Barb Howell, Roberta Janotta, Molly Moorehead, Martha Jackson, David M. Diamond, F. Sylver Pondolfino, David Spillman
Huck Finn..Rusty Hoagland
Tom Sawyer ....Larry Overmire
Muff Potter ....Vaughn Hrycanous Rasor
Injun Joe ....William Allison
Aunt Polly ....Lori Opatrny
Mary Sawyer ....Sandy Noyes
Sid Sawyer ....Tim Tipple
Widow Douglas...Kathy Wingerter
Joe Harper ....Doug Wheat
Amy Lawrence ....Amy Couch
Becky Thatcher ....Julie Higgins
Judge Thatcher ....Dave Stults
Doc Robinson ....David Spillman
Suzie Harper ....Sue Harnick
Gracie Miller...Molly Moorehead
Mrs. Harper ....Sue Huffman
Mrs. Thatcher ....Rebecca Dearing
Minister's Wife ....Mary Ann Evans
Townspeople: ....Jan Honaker, Cindy Funk, Ginny Nash, Julie Cooper
Defense Attorney ....David Spillman
Prosecuting Attorney ....David M. Diamond, Sylver Pondolfino
Mrs. Johnson ....Sherry Blackwood
Mrs. Babcock ....Janet Morris
Nettie Edwards..Shawna L. Hixson
Piano: ....Rex Roseman and Anna Kritselis
Time: ....Turn of the Century
Scene: ....Hannibal, Missouri and environs: The River, Aunt Polly's House, The Schoolhouse, The Graveyard, Jackson's Island, Aunt Polly's, The Church, The Courtroom, The Haunted House, Picnic Grounds, and McDougal's Cave.

Godspell
(John-Michael Tebelak)

Dave, Jesus..Dave Diamond
T. C., John the Baptist, Judas ....Tom Carroll
Dana ....Dana LeVan
Scott ....Scott Farhart
Sam...Sam Shipley
Sandy ....Sandy Noyes
Mary ....Mary Regula
Tammy ....Tammy Kuhn

Lori	Lori Opatrny
Diana	Diane Heiskell
MUSICIANS:	
Piano	Barb Howell, Rex Roseman
Guitar	Becky Stevens
Bass	Steve Foster
Drums	Carla Bunfill
Recorder	Mark Wentz
Trombone	Michele Kuhar
Student Seminar Director	Pam Nicholson
Student Seminar Technical Director	Becky Zellar
Student Seminar Costume Designer	Jenny Wilkes
Music Director	Carla Bunfill
Choreographer	Bruce Hare

The Department: 1978–1980

In the summer of 1977, I completed my doctorate at the University of Minnesota. My sigh of relief was cut short by a request from the administration to assume the chairmanship of the department when Mr. Ellertson went on leave. My desire to be free in order to concentrate on theatre classes and productions was frustrated by the request. I accepted the appointment with the understanding that it was temporary.

The climate of the college at the end of the decade was disheartening. In 1978, an Institutional Evaluation Committee report particularized Muskingum's plight:

> Instability has been an overriding problem at the college for more than a decade. Led for three-fifths of a century (1904–1963) by two presidents, Muskingum over the last fourteen years has been organized and directed, reorganized and redirected by six presidents (interim, acting, and otherwise). During the same interval, four deans have influenced the course of academic affairs . . . in recent years the only constant has been curricular and calendrical [sic] change.[1]

Student enrollment in the college had become a problem. The large enrollments of the 1960's peaked in 1969 at fourteen hundred. From 1970 on, enrollments began to slip, until 1975, when they fell below the one thousand mark.[2] In 1978, they took another sharp decline. Tuition money from enrollment is crucial to the operating finances of a small private school. As an example of how enrollment can affect one aspect of college life, read President Miller's response to my request (1973) for a replacement for our technical director:

> I appreciate your desire to have the position of theater technician filled for the 1973-1974 year. The basic fact of economics is that the number of faculty must be reduced as the enrollment drops. When the decision was made to employ a technical person in the theater program, we had hopes of not only stopping the downward trend in enrollment, but reversing the trend. The record of the past two years does not substantiate that optimism. In fact, at the present time both our applications and our admissions are running 25% below the figures of a corresponding date last year.
>
> Therefore, I agree with the recommendation that the specific position [of Technical Director] not be filled for 1973-1974. I only wish it could be otherwise.[3]

To make matters worse, President John Anthony Brown, who had been in office barely three years, died suddenly in 1978. Professor Russell Hutchison was immediately appointed Acting President until a replacement could be found. The Board of Trustees and Administration realized that income and expenditures must be brought under control. The College declared "Financial Exigency" in 1978.

An Institutional Evaluation Committee of faculty from each academic division was formed to analyze the situation and make recommendations for improvement. They decided that student-to-teacher ratio must be changed from 12:1 to 14:1. By 1980, the eighty-one full-time faculty should be reduced to sixty-five, and the fifteen part-time members should be sharply curtailed. As a result of these deliberations, some full-time positions were eliminated and some programs were stopped; some faculty were transferred to administrative positions; and professors nearing retirement were encouraged to take early retirement. Tenured professors, who found their positions terminated, sought positions elsewhere, and some began legal action until a settlement was reached with the college. Other measures included canceling sabbaticals and refusing to replace a professor if he left for other employment. The latter moratorium on hiring was a particular hardship on departments where courses were well-enrolled.[4]

In response to a need for faculty consolidation, reorganization, and development, the Institutional Evaluation Committee recommended that Speech be dropped as a Basic Education requirement. This recommendation, supported by a Basic Education Task Force, required further reductions and reorganization of the department. Another recommendation of the Committee eliminated the Division of Fine Arts, moved art, music, and theatre into one department, and placed all three in a Fine Arts Department in the Division of Humanities.[5]

In the midst of the gloom, a flame of light burst forth. It had been sparked by the late President John Anthony Brown, in the fall of 1977, when he had gained the Board of Trustees approval for a Performing Arts Complex. The site was to be the Old Campus, and the first step of the project was to be the renovation of Johnson and Paul Halls.[6]

The renovation of Johnson Hall included the remodeling of the Old Chapel into a "jewel box" of a theatre.[7] When President Brown died, the responsibility for completing the project passed to Paul Morris, vice-president for Resources and Public Affairs.[8] The Johnson Hall Theatre was completed in the spring of 1978. In March, the new theatre was dedicated as the Layton Theatre, in ceremonies involving Dr. Charles Rush Layton and guest-artist Mercedes McCambridge.[9] In the fall of 1979, Theatre moved into the Department of Fine Arts (later re-christened the Creative and Performing Arts Department), where it remained for two years. In the fall of 1981, Theatre was re-united with Speech in the Speech Communication and Theatre Department.

Note: Events beyond control had conspired to separate Theatre from Speech. When I realized that the autonomy and identity of Theatre was being threatened, I wrote a position paper, "Theatre at Muskingum College: 1980." The paper included background material on the nature, history, and purpose of theatre at Muskingum. I made it clear that I had no objection to Theatre's membership in the Fine Arts Department. (Theatre is a complex art involving all arts, "fine" and otherwise.) What I objected to was the loss of freedom. Theatre is an academic discipline and a performance-oriented skill subject; therefore, the best theatre occurs when it is operated by people educated in theatre. The theatre should have autonomy which gives it freedom to pursue policies and procedures true to the nature of theatre; thus, theatre may better serve the needs of students and benefit the community. Theatre has a history, a common heritage with classical oratory and rhetoric and, as this history has shown, a close relationship with nineteenth century elocution. Theatre in the twentieth century is related to the communication arts: radio, film, and television. In my considered opinion, theatre is served better as a member of the Speech Communication and Theatre Department.

The administration looked upon my argument favorably and paved the way for Theatre's return to Speech.

A similar restorative action occurred in the mid-nineties, at which time the collective faculty requested that Fundamentals of Speech be returned to the Basic Education Core curriculum.

REFERENCES

1   Institutional Evaluation Committee, "Report of the Institutional Evaluation Committee." (New Concord, Ohio, Muskingum College), December 15, 1978, n.p.
2   William L. Fisk, *A History of Muskingum College.* (New Concord, Ohio: Muskingum College, 1978), pp. 254-255.
3   William P. Miller in a letter to the author, February 5, 1973.
4   Institutional Evaluation Committee, "Report."
5   Institutional Evaluation Committee, "Report."
6   John Anthony Brown in a letter to the author, February 23, 1977.
7   "The Muskingum College Creative and Performing Arts Complex," a brochure published by Muskingum College, New Concord, Ohio, n.d., n.p.
8   Paul Morris in a letter to Mercedes McCambridge, April 4, 1978.
9   "Fern P. and Charles R. Layton Theatre Dedication," original program, Muskingum College, New Concord, Ohio, March 28, 1978.

 # The Plays: 1978–1980

1978–1979

The 1978-79 theatre season opened officially with the Homecoming production of *You're a Good Man, Charlie Brown,* September 20-23. The cast, which previewed the production for Alumni Weekend, performed well, according to Leanne Olson's review, "Faculty Recital: *'Peanuts'* Comes Alive."[54]

Tennessee Williams's popular play, *The Glass Menagerie,* received its fourth campus production on October 25-28, in the Layton Theatre. I had directed it in 1960, Elizabeth Wills had directed it again in 1968, and Greg Senf had done it for his theatre seminar in 1975. This time, it was co-directed by Greg Senf (who was doing postgraduate study) and me. The play featured Larry Overmire as Tom Wingfield, Amy Brannon as Laura, Sherry Blackwood as their mother, Amanda, and Greg Senf as Jim

Romeo and Juliet, 1978. The Nurse (L. Opatrny) and Juliet (L. Olson). *Theatre file photo courtesy M.C. Public Relations Office.*

O'Connor. Both Overmire and Brannon used the play as their acting seminars. Warren Shaull, the Theatre's new technical director, designed the set and costumes; he also served as technical director of the show. The play was well acted and designed; Leanne Olson gave the play a favorable review in the *Black and Magenta* article, "Season Breaks with *'Menagerie.'*"[55]

December 12-16 saw William Shakespeare's *Romeo and Juliet* on stage at the Little Theatre. Warren Shaull designed and did the "tech" work for the production, and I directed.

Our "star-crossed" lovers were played by Larry Overmire and Leanne Olson. The school newspaper, *Black and Magenta,* acclaimed the tragedy as " . . . one of the finest productions . . . " of the year.[56] Nevertheless, there was a big jolt during the run-of-show. Besides the five evening performances, there were three matinees scheduled for local high schools: Tuesday, December 12; Thursday, December 14; and Friday, December 15. Early in the morning on December 14, I learned that our Romeo was not only "star-crossed," but that he had also been "double-crossed" by a twenty-four-hour virus that was making the rounds. Luckily, I had asked Ted Hissam, who had directed *Romeo and Juliet* at Zanesville High School in 1970, to act as consultant for our show. I contacted Ted and asked him if he could read the part of Romeo for the matinee, and he said he would be right over to begin rehearsals. Then I called the nearby high school, which had booked the afternoon's performance, and told the person in charge what had happened. I told him that he could cancel his booking if someone reading the part would be too distracting or disappointing for his students. He replied that it would be much too disappointing to cancel; knowing the circumstances, his students could adjust. Ted knew his part better than I could imagine. By the time the first act was over, he had thrown away the book and was acting the role on his own with a modicum of aid from the prompter. (Our Juliet complained, however, that Ted held his kisses longer than Larry!) We all felt lucky to have avoided disappointing an audience, an audience that was not only well-behaved, but also appreciative. That night, Larry returned to the show and delivered his usual fine performance.

The last week in March of 1979 was designated as Inauguration Week, in order to celebrate the installation of the new president, Arthur De Jong; it was also a week in which a Renaissance Festival was scheduled. The Speech Communication and Theatre Department and Muskingum Players co-sponsored two plays as part of the celebrations. The Neil Simon comedy, *The Odd Couple,* was directed by Amy Brannon for her seminar in theatre, and Sherman Liddell directed his seminar, "The Second Shepherd's Play," which was anonymously written.

The Odd Couple proved to be excellent fare for the Muskingum audience. The odd couple in the play were Larry Overmire and Gregory Adams, who portrayed

The Odd Couple, 1979. (left) Oscar Madison (L. Overmire) tries to reason with Felix Unger (G. Adams) on some philosophical point of housekeeping. *Theatre file photo courtesy M.C. Public Relations Office.*

Oscar Madison and Felix Unger, respectively. John Sweeney was Speed; Mike Swanner was Murray; Sam Shipley played Roy; and John Shipley played Vinnie. The Pigeon sisters were played by Eileen McComb (Cecily) and Joanna Gray (Gwendolyn). I supervised the directing and Warren Shaull provided design and technical expertise. The play ran to good reviews March 28-31 at the Layton Theatre.[57]

On March 31, Sherman Liddell presented "The Second Shepherd's Play" on the College Quadrangle. The play is a combination of farcical horseplay involving English shepherds, and a nativity drama. Part of the Medieval play cycles, it has proven popular with both professionals and amateurs. Sherman's decision to use the play for his seminar in theatre was particularly appropriate for the Renaissance Festival and Inauguration festivities. The cast of the play included Greg Senf, Vaughn Rasor, Vijit Ramchandani, Andre Neoto, Kerry Burke, and Kim Smith.[58]

Another directing seminar was staged on April 25-28, when David Briggs presented Leonard Gershe's *Butterflies Are Free,* at the Little Theatre. I supervised the directing and Warren Shaull supervised Bill Allison, who designed the sets and did the technical work for the production. Scott Lemon was the leading man, Don Baker, and Leanne Olson was the leading lady, Jill Tanner. Sharon Johns portrayed Don's mother,

Mrs. Baker, and Mark Preslan played Ralph Austin.

This comedy is not only well written, it also has a strong social conscience that appeals to both young and old. The younger generation can understand Don's desire to be independent and the older generation can understand the mother's desire to help her son. Both age groups sympathize with the handicap of blindness imposed upon the young man. The production was especially well-directed and well-acted. It was an excellent play with which to end the season.[59]

Section Note

The cast and crew of *Romeo and Juliet* appreciated the following note from Nancy Duling of English I at John Glenn High School, after seeing the special performance on December 15, 1978.

> . . . They [her ninth graders] appreciated every role, and each had his favorite. The girls (14 and 15 years old) developed a "crush" on the handsome Romeo, and the guys liked Leanne as Juliet. The most frequent comment was, "This was really good–it's so much more real than reading it from the book."

Cast for
Romeo and Juliet
(William Shakespeare)

Sampson, Servant to Capulet	M. Maurice Swanner
Gregory, Servant to Capulet	David McCann
Abraham, Servant to Montague	Mark Wentz
Balthasar, Servant to Montague	Marty Cook
Benvolio, Montague's nephew	Larry Triplett
Tybalt, Capulet's nephew	Gregory Adams
Officer	Kenneth E. Perkins III
Chief Officer	Andrew Beery
Citizens of Verona:	Sharon Miller, Sylver Pondolfino, Beth Larimer, Jim Campbell, Sheff Webb, Ed Oliver
Servants to Capulet	Kathleen O'Brien, Ginger Rathbone, B. J. Newcome
Lord Capulet	Greg Senf
Lady Capulet	Joanna M. Gray
Lord Montague	Rob Van Heyde
Lady Montague	Eileen Jennifer McComb
Escalus, Prince of Verona	Vaughn Hyrcanous Rasor
Romeo, Son to Lord Montague	Larry Overmire
Paris, a Count and kinsman to the Prince	Sage Cutler
Peter, Servant to Juliet's nurse	Mark Thomas
Angelica, Nurse to Juliet	Lori Opatrny, Sherry Blackwood
Juliet, daughter to Capulet	Leanne Olson
Mercutio, kinsman to the Prince	Mark Preslan
Friar Laurence	Norman W. Ferguson
Apothecary	Vijit Ramchandani
Friar John	Mark Wentz
Scene:	Italy (Verona and Mantua)

1979–1980

Shakespeare feels at home on the Muskingum College campus. The earliest recorded date of a Shakespearean production on campus is 1910, when the newly-formed Dramatic Club produced *A Midsummer Night's Dream*. In 1961, the same play served to seed the beginning of a repertory company of over a hundred students. I revived that play the following year, and added *Hamlet* to the bill. The two plays alternated for six evening performances and two matinees. Student fascination with Shakespeare led directors, Muriel Bain and me, to institute an annual trip to Stratford, Ontario, Canada, to the most famous Shakespearean Festival in this hemisphere. Beginning in the late '60s, these tours became a highlight of the theatre season. Naturally, with such a continuing tradition, associations were formed, and it was not at all surprising to find two of Stratford's actors migrating to our campus for a visit in 1977. Marti Maraden and Nicholas Pennell not only presented their program, "Rogues and Vagabonds," in November of that year, but also gave workshops to aspiring actors.

In 1979 Muskingum Players and the Theatre offered a multifaceted program, consisting of three parts. On September 11-16, students went to Stratford to see *The Taming of the Shrew, Othello, Henry IV, Part I,* and *Henry IV, Part II.* In connection with the Stratford trip, I offered a special four-week course titled "Shakespeare on Stage." Dr. Lorle Porter, Dr. William Fisk, Dr. Alan Chaffee, and the Theatre's new technical director, Ms. Diane Rock, gave lectures on different aspects of Shakespeare and his world. A third phase of the course in Shakespeare was a production of *The Merry Wives of Windsor.*[60]

The Muskingum College Theatre presented *The Merry Wives of Windsor* at the Little Theatre during Homecoming Week (October 3-6) for four evening performances and three high school matinees. I directed and Diane Rock served as technical director of the play.

Rehearsals for *"Merry Wives"* ran smoothly, because many people in the cast had also performed in *Romeo and Juliet.* As was expected, the familiarity of the players with Shakespearean verse and movement assured the audience a good level of playing. Rehearsals were not without incident, however. We were within one week of performance when we discovered that the antlers that Falstaff wears, in a very important scene toward the end of the play, were missing from the prop room. Had they been misplaced? No. Had they been stolen? Who knows. We never found out. I was dumbfounded, angry, and completely frustrated. Finally, toward the end of the week, Greg Adams arrived with a second pair of antlers and everybody heaved a sigh of relief.

Greg not only had to wear antlers, but also he had to carry a vest loaded with padding, in order to achieve the girth for which Falstaff was famous. In this leading role, Greg tries in vain to trick Mistress Page (Joanna Gray) and Mistress Ford (Leanne Olson) into handing over part of their husband's fortunes. The two merry wives, in turn, carry out elaborate plans for revenge against Falstaff. Cast in the roles of their jealous husbands, Masters Page and Ford, were Marty Cook and Scott Lemon. Suzanne Albrecht and Kathleen O'Brien were doublecast in the part of the town busybody and go-between, Mistress Quickly.

The role of Anne Page was also doublecast, with Eileen McComb and Lauren Jones, and the role of her suitor, Fenton, was played by Kevin McCaffrey. Other suitors of Anne included Vaughn Rasor as Abraham Slender and Norman Ferguson as Dr. Caius. Townspeople included Charles Whitt as Justice Shallow, Larry Triplett as Sir Hugh Evans, and Randy Bardonner as Host of the Garter Inn. Servants to Falstaff were Jeffrey Swartz, Nym; William J. Allison, Pistol; and Patricia Bartley, Robin, a page; Servant to Dr. Caius was Barbara Padgett, Rugby; servant to Slender was Thomas Bressoud, Simple; and Servants to Ford were Mark Killorin, John; and Art McMinn, Robert.

Having completed a successful run, the play was performed the following week (October 12-13) for two evenings and two afternoons, as entertainment for Parents Weekend.

The Studio Productions that played in Layton Theatre (December 12-15) were the result of three seminars in directing. Joanna Gray directed "Overruled" by George B. Shaw, Eileen McComb directed "The Fisherman," written by Jonathan Tree, and Leanne Olson directed "Two Crooks and a Lady" by Eugene Pillot. All three plays were later videotaped at the college radio station, WMCO.

The faculty/staff production for the year was *East Lynne*, adapted by Brian J. Burton from Mrs. Henry Wood's famous novel of the same title.* Diane Rock directed, designed, and supervised the technical aspects of the production, which was performed at the Layton Theatre, January 30-31 and February 1-2.

The specifics of the story of *East Lynne* differ according to which dramatic version is used. An article in the *Black and Magenta* summarized the script used for the Muskingum production.

> Described as a sad tale of jealousy, mistrust and villainy, the winsome young heroine Isabel Vane finds herself penniless when her father dies. Left to live with her aunt and uncle, she also eventually loses her home, East Lynne. She marries Archibald Carlyle, but a former lover, Francis Levison tricks her into leaving her husband. Will Isabelle ever be returned to her sick child little Willy? Will Richard Hair ever be cleared of the murder of Amy Halijohns father? Will John Dill ever get Cornelia Carlysle? *East Lynne* will answer all of these questions and more.[61]

The cast of faculty and staff included Scott Dittman, Leslie Haskins, Mark Haskins, Dick Leimbach, Dr. James Nichols, Dr. Lorle Porter, Kim Ronald, Becky Skeen, Vicki Townsend, Nancy Truitt, Winnie Wolfe, and Larry Zettle. Howard Frye

---

* *East Lynne* (1861) was the first novel of Mrs. Henry Wood. She wrote some forty novels in the latter part of the nineteenth century. Her " . . . ingenuous plots about murders, thefts, and forgeries . . . . her numerous courtroom scenes and well-planned clues . . . make her one of the forerunners of the modern detective story . . . many of her novels were world best-sellers, outstripping even Dickens in Australian sales. *East Lynn* was repeatedly dramatized and filmed and translated into many languages, from Welsh to Hindustani. (*The Oxford Companion to English Literature,* Fifth Edition, p. 1081.)
East Lynne was first performed in this country at the Brooklyn Academy of Music, on January 26, 1862, with Lawrence Barrett as Sir Frances Levison and Lucille Western as Lady Isabel. (*S.R.O. The Most Successful Plays of the American Stage,* Compiled by Bennett Cerf and Van H. Cartmell, p. 60.)
Thereafter, the many dramatic versions of the novel became so prevalent in nineteenth century repertories that, whenever someone asked an actor what the next play on the bill was going to be, the answer was usually, "Next week, *East Lynne.*" That reply became the hue and cry of every actor in every company throughout the land.

assisted the director and Dr. David Murchison was the stage manager.[62]

Senior theatre major, Vaughn Rasor, liked to combine theatre with his church work. While fulfilling requisites for his seminar, he directed two one-act plays for the Methodist Church in New Concord. For his senior seminar, Vaughn chose Archibald MacLeish's verse-play, *J. B.* He presented the play at the Little Theatre on February 20-23, and at the Zanesville Central Presbyterian Church on February 24. Two other theatre majors assisted Vaughn by using aspects of *J. B.* for their seminars: Bill Allison designed and executed the set, and Tracy Carter designed the lighting.

MacLeish's Pulitzer Prize-winning play brings the Old Testament story of *Job* into the present. He writes, " . . . the structure of the poem of *Job* is the only one I know into which our modern history will fit."[63] J. B., a successful businessman is the centerpiece of MacLeish's play. J. B. loses everything: his wealth, health, and his wife's love. When J. B. begs for death, God restores his possessions and family.

Vaughn selected the following students for his cast: David Jarrett played the title role, and Lori Opatrny and Suzanne Albrecht alternated in the part of his wife, Sarah. Scott Lemon played Mr. Zuss, and Norman W. Ferguson, Mr. Nickles. J. B.'s children were played by Beth Larimer, Rebecca; Mary Sykes, Ruth; Mary Ann Evans, Mary; Robert Reinhold, David; and Mike Swanner, Jonathon. Tom Bressoud and Marty Cook were the 1st and 2nd Messengers respectively and Molly Hoffman played the Girl. Valerie Ackley, Patricia Bartley, Ruth Montgomery, and Donna Snyder were the Ladies. The Comforters were played by Toshlo Maruo, Bildad; John Blyth, Zophar; and Debu Purohit, Elphaz. Lisa Garraux composed incidental music for the play. Diane Rock and I were advisors for the production.

Two student-directed one-act plays followed *J. B.* on March 31-April 1. Kathleen O'Brien directed Glenn Hughes's comedy, "Red Carnations;" and Randy Bardonner directed scenes from *A Thurber Carnival* by James Thurber.[64]

The official theatre season for 1979-80 concluded with a Children's Theatre production of J. R. R. Tolkein's novel, *The Hobbit,* dramatized by Allan Jay Friedman, David Rogers, and Ruth Perry. Assisting me as director, were Wilma Barnett, script consultant; Catherine Johnson, vocal coach; Diane Rock, technical director; Sue Carpenter, student designer; and a production staff of some thirty students.

Beginning on March 10, over seventy students started preparing for the opening of *The Hobbit,* a term project for the Children's Theatre class. The play was scheduled to open April 22 and commence with four midday performances for the New Concord Middle School; evening performances for the general public began April 23 and ran through April 26. All performances were in the Layton Theatre. Willard K. Starks reported for the *Black and Magenta* on April 25:

> The . . . grease paint roars with the realization of a rare magic as the Children's Theatre Class and Theatre Arts Production Company breathe life into the stage version of J. R. R. Tolkien's modern literary classic, *The Hobbit.*
>
> Winner of resounding critical acclaim from a vast and varied audience, *The Hobbit* is a prelude to *The Lord of the Rings* trilogy. Although written specifically for children, the story has intrigued the imagination and intellect of generations of readers, both young and old.
>
> Dr. Donald Hill, director of the production, suggested that the selection of the

play is both appropriate and timely. "Everybody knows Tolkien—they've all read him. There's something about today's world that gives fantasy enormous appeal. People seem to require a temporary escape. Look at the Peter Pan revival on Broadway and how successful it has been. Tolkien speaks to the same need."[65]

The story of the play deals with the battle of the Dwarves and their Hobbit hero, Bilbo Baggins, who encounter many adventures on their way to slay the dragon, Smaug.

Cast for *The Hobbit*
(A. J. Friedman, David Rogers, and Ruth Perry)

Bilbo Baggins, a Hobbit	Kevin McCaffrey
His Nephew	Lauren E. Jones
Gandalf, a Wizard	Debu Purohit

DWARVES:

Thorin	Greg Adams
Dori	Alisa Reese
Nori	Patricia Bartley
Dwalin	Eileen McComb
Balin	Ken Perkins
Gloin	Kathleen O'Brien
Fili	Sue Huffman
Bifur	Andrew Beery
Bofur	Valerie Ackley
Bombur	Vaughn Rasor

TROLLS:

Bert	Doug Walker
Tom	Bill Allison
William	Randy Bardonner

GOBLINS:

The Great Goblin	Mike Swanner
First Councilor	Thomas Bressoud
Second Councilor	John Blyth
Patrol Leader	Norman W. Ferguson
Goblins on Patrol	Lauren Jones, Donna Snyder, Greg Letizia
Standard Bearers	Paul Couch, Dwight Bowman
Gollum, a Creature	Mary Sykes

ELVES:

Elvin King	Paul Couch
Elvin Queen	Lori Opatrny
Elvin Councilor	Ginny Nash
Turnkey	John Blyth
Galion	Thomas Bressoud
Ladies in Waiting	Barbara Anderson, Wendy Curran
Elvin Gentleman	Dwight Bowman

SPIDERS:

Arachne	Susan Litt
Arachnius	Molly Hoffman
Helper number one	Alicia Gratz
Helper number two	Terri Forner
Smaug, the Dragon	Randy Bardonner

HOBBITS:

Auctioneer	Norman W. Ferguson
Mrs. Sackeville-Baggins	Lori Opatrny
Two Friends	Donna Snyder, Terri Forner
Elderly Hobbit	Charles Whitt

Bilbo's Sister	Kat Whitt

Pianists:	Dinah DiCocco, Melanie Jeffers
Time:	Long ago in the quiet of the world
Place:	From the Shire to the Lonely Mountain and back again

The Alumni Office inquired if the Theatre could supply the entertainment for the June 13-14 Alumni Weekend. I replied with another idea that I had in mind for the next Homecoming Weekend. My dissertation on Noel Coward was languishing on my book shelf. Perhaps this would be an opportunity to put some of his biography together with some of his words and music for an evening's entertainment. For this, I needed help from alumni and friends of the Theatre. I sent out an SOS. Greg Adams, Eileen McComb (Adams), Julie Adams, Mary Ann Spitznagel DeVolld, Vicki Townsend, Larry Triplett, and Evan Stults (pianist) answered my call for help. After a few weeks of rehearsal at the Little Theatre, the entertainment came together nicely and *An Evening of (with) Noel Coward* was born.

REFERENCES (The Plays: 1970–1980)

1 Bob Bielecki, "Parents to View *Summertree,*" *B&M,* October 16, 1970, p. 3.
2 Patty Madigan, "Comedy Plays Two More Nights," *B&M,* March 19, 1971, p. 1.
3 Pris Bentley, "Three Senior Seminar Presentations Close Year at Little Theatre," *B&M,* May 14, 1971, p. 6.
4 Laurel Fais, "*'Matchmaker'* Packs Playhouse," *B&M,* October 29, 1971, p. 6.
5 "*Matchmaker* Review Draws Double Fire," Letters to the Editor from Mary Ann Spitznagel and R.V., *B&M,* November 5, 1971.
6 David Hall, "Little Theatre Productions Win Reviewer Acclaim," *B&M,* March 24, 1972, p. 6.
7 Marypaul Magura, "Alums Sparkle in Absurd Play," *B&M,* March 24, 1972, p. 6.
8 Bob Good, "Little Peanuts: Big Production," *B&M,"* April 21, 1972, p. 10.
9 "Reviewers Find Happiness in *'Charlie Brown,'"* *B&M,* May 5, 1972, p. 8.
10 Nancy Bain, "Muskie *'Peanuts'* a Delightful Treat," *B&M,* May 19, 1972, p. 7.
11 Bev Puckett, "*Antigone* Judged Excellent," *B&M,* November 3, 1972, p. 4.
12 Dee Dee Verley, "Expression Is Key to Satire," *B&M,* October 27, 1972, p. 9.
13 "UHURU Produces Pride," *B&M,* February 23, 1973, p. 1.
14 Lee Anne Smith, "*'Twelfth Night'* Superb," *B&M,* March 23, 1973, p. 8.
15 Debra Chaffin, "Analysis of Beckett's Writing," *B&M,* April 20, 1973, p. 6.
16 Donald Hill, "The Selected Comedies of Noel Coward: An Analysis of Comic Techniques," (A Thesis Submitted to the Faculty of the Graduate School of the University of Minnesota in Partial Fulfillment of the Requirements for the Degree of Doctor of Philosophy, July 1977), p. 217.
17 Becky Englert, "Excellent Show Is Season Opener," *Black and Magenta,* November 9, 1973, p. 8.
18 See President William Miller's letter to the author, February 5, 1973 on page 247 of "The Department: 1978-1980."
19 Kathy Knurek, "One-Act Plays Well-Received," April 26, 1974, p. 12.
20 "Seminars of '74," *Cue,* Muskingum College, New Concord, Ohio, 1975, p. 6.
21 Nancy Stewart, "New Drama Experienced in *'Seven Stimulations,'"* May 10, 1974, p. 8.
22 Donald Hill, "Historical Notes," *Tartuffe,* Original Program, Muskingum College Little Theatre, October 16-19, 1974, n.p.
23 "Musical Comedy Interim," *Cue,* 1975, p. 4.
24 "*The Caretaker,*" *Cue,* p. 4.
25 "*The Caretaker.*"
26 Beth Sanders, "*'The Caretaker'* Introspective and Enlightening," March 19, 1975, p. 14.
27 "*A Midsummer Night's Dream,*" *Cue,* p. 5.
28 *"The Glass Menagerie,"* *Cue,* p. 5.
29 *"Luv,"* *Cue,* p. 5.

30   Patricia Taylor, "*'Winnie'*: a Visual Treat," *Fine Arts Newsletter* (from the Old Campus), Muskingum College, New Concord, Ohio, April, 1976, p. 4.

31   *"The Skin of Our Teeth," Fine Arts Newsletter*, p. 4.

32   *"The Wizard of Oz," Fine Arts Newsletter,* p. 4.

33   Cheryl D. Swiss, "A History of Theatre at Muskingum College" (a thesis presented to the faculty of the Graduate College of Ohio University in partial fulfillment of the requirements for the Degree of Master of Arts, Athens, Ohio, June, 1972), p. 12.

34   Clark Gesner, Music and Lyrics, *You're a Good Man, Charlie Brown!* Based on the comic strip "Peanuts" by Charles M. Schulz (Greenwich, Connecticut: A Fawcett Crest Book, Fawcett Publications, Inc., 1967), pp. 54-55.

35   Thornton Wilder, "Preface," *Three Plays by Thornton Wilder: Our Town, The Skin of Our Teeth, The Matchmaker,* Illustrated by Alex Tsao (New York: Bantam Books, 1972), xi-xii.

36   The *Black and Magenta* Review of *"You're a Good Man, Charlie Brown,"* March 24, 1976, p. 4, quoted in "Faculty Takes the Stage," *Fine Arts Newsletter*, p. 1.

37   "*'Lace,' 'People,'* and *'Marigolds'.*" *Fine Arts Newsletter,* p. 3.

38   "*'Lace,' 'People,'* and *'Marigolds'.*"

39   "*'Lace,' 'People,'* and *'Marigolds'.*"

40   "*I Do! I Do!* Double Cast at Home and Away," *Cue*, Summer, 1977, p. 4.

41   Eileen McComb, "*Misogynist* Hit on Campus," October 29, 1976, p. 5.

42   Donald W. Jones, "*'The Misogynist'* Opens at College Theatre, a Finished Production," *The Daily Jeffersonian,* Cambridge, Ohio, October 21, 1976, n.p.

43   Margi Van Demark, "College Production Proves Entertaining," *Zanesville Times-Recorder,* Zanesville, Ohio, October 23, 1976, n.p.

44   "Neil Simon Comedy Staged for Interim," *Cue,* Summer, 1977, p. 3.

45   William M. Laing, "The History of Theatre at Muskingum College from 1971-1983," (a seminar presented to the faculty of the Speech Communication and Theatre Department at Muskingum College in partial fulfillment of the requirements for the Degree Bachelor of Arts, May, 1983), p. 31.

46   Linda Hierholzer, "Faculty-Alumni Show: *The Importance of Being Earnest,*" *Cue,* Summer, 1977, p. 3.

47   Donald Hill, "Alice is At It Again!", Notes from the original program *Alice in Wonderland,* Muskingum College Little Theatre, May 4-6, 1977, n.p.

48   Ibid.

49   Facts confirmed by Carnegie Library of Pittsburgh and the Muskingum College Library.

50   "Children's Theatre: Supply and Demand, *Tom Sawyer,*" *Cue,* Fall, 1980, p. 3.

51   "*Godspell* Sellout Success," April 28, 1978, p. 8.

52   "Godspell."

53   "Two Classics with a Punch," *Cue,* Fall, 1980, p. 4.

54   Leanne Olson, "Faculty Recital: *'Peanuts'* Comes Alive," *B&M,* September 29, 1978, p. 8.

55   Leanne Olson, "Season Breaks with *'Menagerie'*," *B&M,* October 20, 1978, p. 8.

56   "*Romeo and Juliet* Holds Final Theatre Performances," *B&M,* December 15, 1978, p. 11.

57   Leanne Olson, "Adams Co-stars as Felix," *B&M,* March 20, 1979, p. 15.

58   "Religious Plays Favored by Students," *Cue,* Fall, 1980, p. 4.

59   Leanne Olson, "Final Production: *Butterflies Are Free,*" *B&M,* April 27, 1979, p. 8.

60   "Tours and Productions of 'Bard' Prove Popular: Shakespeare On and Off Campus," *Cue,* Fall, 1980, p. 1.

61   "Only Two Nights Left," *B&M,* February 1, 1980, p. 8.

62   "Only Two Nights Left."

63   "Religious Plays Favored by Students." *Cue,* p. 4.

64   "One-Acts Highlight Spring," *B&M,* March 28, 1980, p. 4.

65   Willard K. Starks, "Tolkien's *'The Hobbit'* Recreated," *B&M,* April 25, 1980, p. 4.

Dr. Charles Rush Layton

D r. Charles Rush Layton died on June 22, 1980, at the age of ninety.[1] Forty-four of those years were spent in the service of Muskingum College (1914-1958), as dean and chairman of the Speech Department, coach of Debate and Oratory, and dean of the college (1943-1949). He maintained the duties of these offices while still working on advanced degrees, which culminated in his doctorate at the University of Michigan in 1952. After his retirement in 1958, he continued to serve as a resource person for the debate teams, even accompanying them to scheduled debates.

Although his expertise lay in the areas of public address and forensics, his interest was in the entire field of speech. He was a perfect helpmate to his wife, Ferne Parsons Layton, who came with him to Muskingum in 1914. Although her main interest was in the areas of interpretation and theatre, she reciprocated with her help in the areas of oratory and forensics. Together they built a department that was respected by their colleagues and favored by students.

Dr. Layton's interest in speech was not confined to the Muskingum campus. Dr. James L. Golden (who succeeded Dr. Layton as chairman of the Department of Speech at Muskingum in 1958) recounts Layton's interest in furthering speech education at other institutions. In 1970, his article, "The Rhetorical Thrust of the Laytons," Dr. Golden (then chairman of Speech Communication at Ohio State University) wrote:

> Apart from their personal impact on students and on the Muskingum College community, in general the Laytons, through active participation in state and national professional associations, influenced speech pedagogy on other campuses. While serving as an officer in the Ohio Speech Association, for example, Dr. Layton made frequent visits to Ohio State University, in the 1930's for the purpose of persuading the president to separate Speech from English. The success of his efforts prompted Earl Wiley to regard Layton as the major contributing force responsible for creating a Department of Speech at Ohio State in 1936.[2]

Five months after Dr. Layton died, a letter from Dr. Loren Reid (Professor Emeritus of Speech at the University of Missouri-Columbia) was relayed to me. Dr. Reid was writing a short history of the Central States Speech Association, an organization which had elected Layton as their first executive secretary (1931-1936) and their third president (1938-1939). Over the years, Dr. Reid had lost touch with Dr. Layton, and was now in need of some information about his career. Dr. Reid recalled the following incident:

> He must have been one of the first teachers of speech to go to England. I believe he was interested in John Bright [Layton's dissertation topic]. Once he observed how differences in personality were shown by comparing libraries; he had recently visited those of Bright and W. E. Gladstone. I thought of his reflection when, a few years ago, I had a chance to compare both.

The letter, which was addressed to our Office of Public Information [Relations], continued,

> You might send a copy of this letter to his family and to Donald Hill. I remember

Charley Layton with great affection.

Many thanks for any information you can send me.[3]

Two months later (January 15, 1981), I received a letter of thanks from Loren Reid and the wish, "I cannot help thinking that if he had lived another year, he would have known that CSSA, which he helped found, was celebrating its Golden Anniversary."[4] About a year later, I received a pamphlet in the mail. The cover bore the title, "Fanfare for Fifty: A Brief History of the Central States Speech Association 50th Year 1931-1981." It was written by Loren Reid and published by the CSSA. In his account of the CSSA, Dr. Reid (Executive Secretary of CSSA, 1937-1939) tells of the difficulties encountered by the organization when it first started, and of Layton's unflagging support for its survival. The CSSA was no sooner on its legs than World War II came along. Then there was the post-war struggle to continue the organization. Finally, the CSSA was revitalized, and it prospered throughout the 1970's.[5]

Dr. William Fisk knew the Laytons well because he had been one of Dr. Layton's debaters, and he had also participated in Mrs. Layton's area of theatre. Five years after his graduation (1941), Dr. Fisk returned to Muskingum as a Professor of History. He followed closely the progress of the debate teams, and he was also an ardent audience member at the plays. In his book, *A History of Muskingum College,* Dr. Fisk weighs in on the career of the Laytons:

> Together the Laytons alternated years of dedicated teaching with interludes of advanced study at the University of Michigan and at the same time shoved Muskingum into national recognition in speech circles. Repeatedly Muskingum debate teams won state and national tournaments, their members having acquired in the course of the regimen of work imposed upon them knowledge and research techniques in many areas of economics, public law, and international relations. Work in theatre, first begun in 1906, and oral interpretation of literature advanced abreast of that in debate and oratory, and the Speech department became the first department in the college to win a national reputation.[6]

Ground Breaking Ceremonies for the renovation of Johnson Hall (1977) shows Dr. Charles Layton, Professor Emeritus of Speech, turning over the earth to signify the beginning of reconstruction of the West Wing, which would house a theatre. Joseph Myers, president of Stanley Works and chairman of the Board of Trustees, looks on. *Theatre file photo courtesy M.C. Public Relations Office.*

My favorite picture of Dr. Layton was taken at the Ground Breaking Ceremonies for the renovation of Johnson Hall. Here, we see this gray-haired patriarch of speech, shovel in hand.

REFERENCES

1   Ronald F. Mazeroski, Director of Alumni Relations, from files in the Alumni Office, Muskingum College, New Concord, Ohio, January, 2000.
2   James L. Golden, "The Rhetorical Thrust of the Laytons," *Muskingum College Bulletin,* Summer, 1970, Muskingum College, New Concord, Ohio, p. 16.
3   Loren Reid in a letter to Director of Office of Information at Muskingum College with a re-direct to Donald Hill, November 10, 1980.
4   Loren Reid in a letter to Donald Hill, January 15, 1981.
5   Loren Reid, "Fanfare for Fifty: A Brief History of the Central States Speech Association 50th Year, 1931-1981," Columbia, Missouri: Central States Speech Association, 1981.
6   William L. Fisk, *A History of Muskingum College* (New Concord, Ohio, Muskingum College, 1978), p. 122.

Mercedes McCambridge

Certainly one of the highlights of the 1980's was the fourth appearance of Mercedes McCambridge on Scholarship Day, March 27, 1981. The college news media heralded her arrival with an invitation encouraging all parents to attend the afternoon convocation so that " . . . they might learn why Mercedes McCambridge is one of Muskingum's very favorite people."[1]

The *McWeek* of March 23 published a beautiful tribute to the Academy Award-winning actress, who " . . . cares deeply about many things, but especially about young people and the world they'll create." The article continued,

> There's one certainty about Mercedes McCambridge. To hear her is to be moved, quickened, and on occasion transported. This unusual woman has many dimensions. She is by profession an actress, by self-definition an alcoholic, by commitment a fighter for causes not yet lost but needing help. Among those causes are the liberal arts and alcohol rehabilitation. She puts her total effort behind her words. She's president of Livengrin Foundation, a rehabilitation facility in Pennsylvania; she's often on campuses as artist-in-residence, pleading the cause of liberal arts.
>   . . . It's appropriate that this tiny woman with enormous talent is our Scholarship Convocation speaker . . . Forty-seven of our students will be designated as distinguished scholars, and a doctor of humane letters will be conferred on Miss McCambridge in recognition of her remarkable career and commitment.[2]

On the afternoon of March 27, Mercy addressed the scholarship audience on "The Futility of Flight." She told the honor students, "This day belongs to you, use it well, remember it well." She continued with, "You are young men and women of singular achievement. I congratulate each and every one of you." Then, by reviewing some of the events of her past life, she urged the students, "Don't back down—don't run away—that's what happened in my life. I managed to survive by backward flight."[3] She electrified her audience by warning them not to retreat in the days to come from the excellence they now display. "Every life you touch will be desolate if the glow goes out."[4]

After her address, I presented Mercy for an honorary degree. I was requested to be brief, at least not to go beyond the time it would take to read what could be put on a 4"x 6" note-card! I began by connecting Mercy to the mission of our college, which is to develop whole persons—uncommon men and women who lead vocationally-productive, personally-satisfying, and socially-responsible lives. Mercedes McCambridge is such a person. I cited her award-winning career as an actress in radio, theatre, film, and television, and her contributions to education and society–clear evidence of an exceptional, as well as an uncommon, woman.

For the reader and for the record, the Faculty Affairs Committee recommended that the honorary degree of Doctor of Humane Letters (LHD) be granted to Miss Mercedes McCambridge in consideration for the following:

> Having served three residencies at Muskingum College, the Planning Committee for Scholarship Day, 1981 is delighted that Miss McCambridge has accepted an invitation to be our guest lecturer; and, in response to her remarkable professional career, her humanitarian contributions to the rehabilitation of alcoholics for which she has been honored at the White House and in Congress, and her devotion to higher education, this committee has nominated a true friend of Muskingum College for the Honorary Degree Doctor of Humane Letters (L.H.D.).[5]

President Arthur De Jong responded to the Presentation of the Candidate with,

> Mercedes McCambridge, you have had an unusually broad professional career covering radio, stage and film displaying your depth of talent and your adaptability, through hard work, skill and self-discipline you have risen to the top of your profession. You have handled your success with grace—a rare attribute in contemporary life.
>
> In your personal life you have displayed the necessary level of self-acceptance, courage and integrity to be a significant leader in our society. You have given time and direction to the troubled, particularly alcoholics, rising above the narcissism which abounds in our society. We especially note your work with college and university students, including our own.[6]

At the Scholarship Day Convocation on Friday, March 27, 1981, D. Hill (right) presented Mercedes McCambridge (center) for an honorary degree. President Arthur DeJong (left) conferred the Honorary Degree of Doctor of Humane Letters (LHD) on Mercedes. *Theatre file photo courtesy M.C. Public Relations Office.*

And with that, Acting Dean David Quinn placed the appropriate hood of honor on Mercy's shoulders.

I could end the McCambridge story here, but there is more. When a person such as Mercy touches one's life, there is always more to tell. I call it "Goodness and Wisdom from an Award-Winning Actress."

The goodness of Mercy is shown in the many workshops that she conducts while visiting campuses in America. Her patience for, and advice to, young people are inexhaustible as she coaches, challenges, and guides students toward the path of creativity, spontaneity, and imaginative response to situations. Without reserve or hesitation, she gives wholeheartedly of her talent. It is an inspiration to watch her. After one such session, she told me confidentially that she could not possibly be a full-time teacher, because she gives so much of herself that she would be dead at the end of a semester!

Mercy spends much of her time doing good works for other people and charitable organizations. For her help with the National United Jewish Welfare, she received a special citation. She has been cited by the National Hemophilia Foundation, for having enlisted Richard Burton and Elizabeth Taylor as members, who have been enormously generous toward that charity. She has received the Golden Award three times from the City of Hope hospitals for work on their behalf. She is a member of the Advisory Council of the National Institute of Alcohol Abuse and Alcoholism and, in the '70s, she was president of Livengrin Foundation. (During this period, I had occasion to speak with her on the telephone. When I asked her what the work was like, she said that they (the people there for treatment) sat around in the basement and read plays by other alcoholics, such as Eugene O'Neill and Tennessee Williams! She has received the Gold Key Award from the National Council of Alcoholism.[7]

Mercy shows her wisdom by the resiliency with which she accepts what she cannot control. Adversity and misfortune have dogged her most of her adult life. After her first marriage and the birth of her son, John, came a divorce, remarriage, two still-born children, another divorce, and her fight against alcoholism. Then in 1987, her son took his own life and those of his wife and two children. Any one of these incidents would have been enough to defeat a less daunting individual, but not Mercy, who bravely faced them all. As she told Ed Blank in an interview, during the tour of *Lost in Yonkers*, "If you go through rough times and sweat it out, it can make you a better person, but you can't let the bitterness take over. I believe that anything that happens to you that doesn't kill you will be for the good."[8]

In 1985, Mercy was on tour in Marsha Norman's Pulitzer Prize play, *'Night, Mother*. It is an emotionally-draining play about a young daughter trying to make her mother understand why she is planning suicide. The play came to Columbus as part of the Ohio University Performing Arts Series. Lorle Porter and I braved the Ohio January weather for our drive to and from Mershon Auditorium to see the play. The play was as Mercy described it, only two people who never leave the stage; there was no intermission, as the fated daughter tries to make her mother understand the reason for her actions, and to prepare her for a future alone.

> It is . . . about raw truth, and that is hard to play. It should be hard to watch. Theater should assault the senses. I think that's what this play does.
>
> How can any person get inside the agony of an individual who is finding life so absolutely intolerable that there is no other option? McCambridge asks. According to Scripture, even Christ felt despair on the cross.[9]

The depth of emotion displayed grew in intensity and was enhanced by the lack of an intermission. The two actresses and the audience shared a death struggle which was always concentrated at "trigger point." The drama took on the aspect of a Greek tragedy that reached ritual proportions and religious significance.

Mercy shared with me two personal experiences that helped me understand more about theatre and acting. She said that actor training is something that never stops. It is a continuing element of life and the professional work of an actor. She told me of an experience she'd had when she was artist-in-residence at Catholic University in Washington, D.C. She was walking on campus one night, when she looked up at the lights of the hall in which drama students were studying. She knew that inside those rooms, minute by minute, hour by hour, day and night, every day, week, month, and all year long, student actors were laying the foundations for careers. That training must be continued for as long as they act. Much the same dedication is expected of music and art students, but it is not commonly accepted or known to be part of actor training. Nevertheless, it is true.

On another occasion, Mercy and I were discussing the emotional life of the actor. Because Mercy was so good at displaying emotions vocally and physically, I asked her about the training of emotions. Surprisingly, she said that everyone is born with the full range of emotions on board. As an example, she cited the time when she and her first husband were playing with John in his crib. They were dangling a watch in front of him, and when he reached for it, they quickly drew it away. The play took on a form of teasing which can be fun for young babies, up to a point. Suddenly, the baby became red in the face and began to squall. The doctor, who happened to be there at the time, or who was told about it, explained that the baby was angry, so angry that if he had it in his physical power, he would have obliterated both of them on the spot. The technique of revealing emotion is something that can be taught and learned by an actor; however, for emotion in and of itself, Mercy said, we are born with all human emotions intact.

I point to two other bits of wisdom that Mercy conveys in her autobiography. One is a saying that came from Seneca, who said, "There is a great difference between a man who does not want to sin and one who doesn't know how to!"[10] Another wise comment came from Robert Penn Warren (who wrote *All the King's Men*): "Imagination is only the lie we learn to live by, if we are going to live at all."[11]

In 1981, when Mercy urged our scholarship students to keep the flame of achievement burning, she was affirming not only a philosophy of life, but also a motto for daily living. In 1992, at the age of 74, Mercy was in Columbus touring Neil Simon's *Lost in Yonkers*. During an interview with Tony Mastroianni, he asked her about retirement. Mercy replied, "I don't believe in retirement. Retirement is what you do when they put you in the ground."[12]

At 74, Mercy showed no signs of slowing down. She loved touring and described the arrival at a new theater " . . . as an almost mystical experience."

> There's the marvelous thing–the miraculous thing–of getting over to the theater and going through the stage door. And then you walk onto the set that is already up, and you sit down in a chair, which is in exactly the same spot it was in 1,800

miles ago night before last. That's miraculous, it really is. It never fails to delight me. I like to arrive 15 minutes before I have to and sit in the empty house. It's like going to church.[13]

Early in 1973, I received a newspaper clipping via college mail, with the following handwritten message in the top margin, "she would be a safe bet for a workshop—M.B." The initials and penmanship I recognized as those of Muriel Bain. The article was an interview of Mercedes McCambridge by Joan Hanauer, with the headlines "Alcoholism Arrested: Star Wins Over Adversity." Above the headlines was a picture of Mercedes, holding a picture of herself with the Oscar she won for Best Supporting Actress in the film, *All the King's Men* ((1949).[14] After Mercedes had received her Oscar on that night in March of 1950, presenter Ray Milland congratulated her for a very "distinguished" acceptance speech which ended with " . . . never get discouraged. Hold on! Just look—look what can happen."[15] Those words became very pertinent to her life and to ours.

I'm glad I pursued Muriel's suggestion. Mercy turned out to be more than a "safe" bet; I would call her the Fort Knox of the theatrical profession! The college, the faculty, the students, and I personally have been enriched by her presence. Thank you, Muriel. Thank you, Mercy.

One of the last times I saw Mercy, she was at the Academy Awards Celebration for 1995. The Academy had invited back all the past winners of Oscar. As the camera panned around the stage, I saw this little woman dressed in black, sitting just like the nuns of Mundelein College had taught her, very prim and proper. However, I had the feeling she was on steel springs, ready to leap into action against the enemy in *Johnny Guitar*.

I saw Mercy again more recently (January 2000) on a re-run of *Magnum P.I.* The sequence was called "Never Say Goodbye." She was playing Agatha Kimball, a rich, blind widow whom Ted Danson was trying to murder. She was all pink and frilly, with her hair a frizzle of curls. That sequence must have been shot in the late '60s or '70s. I remember her telling me how much she enjoyed Hawaii and making the film with Tom Selleck. Film is a wonderful keeper. May it keep you always, Carlotta Mercedes Agnes McCambridge, and may you keep yourself well, wherever you are.

REFERENCES

1   "A Favorite Muskie Returns," *Parents Newsletter*, Muskingum College, New Concord, Ohio, March, 1981, p. 4.
2   "Scholarship Day Friday Brings Family, Friends and an Honorary Muskie to the Campus," *The McWeek*, Muskingum College, New Concord, Ohio, March 23, 1981, p. 1.
3   "Scholars Feted at Muskingum," *The Times Recorder*, Zanesville, Ohio, March 28, 1981, n.p.
4   "Spring Unites Campus Families," *Black and Magenta*, Muskingum College, New Concord, Ohio, Spring, 1981, p. 3.
5   "Honorary Degree Recommendation," Faculty Affairs Committee, January 7 and 14, passed by full faculty in February for presentation March, 1981, Muskingum College, New Concord, Ohio.
6   Arthur J. De Jong, President of Muskingum College, "Presentation of Honorary Degree to Mercedes McCambridge," Scholarship Day, Friday, March 27, 1981, Brown Chapel.
7   "Mercedes McCambridge," *Current Biography, 1964* (New York: The H. W. Wilson Company, 1964), pp. 262-264.
8   Ed Blank, "McCambridge tackles her life, characters: Oscar-winning star challenges adversity," *Columbus Dispatch*, Columbus, Ohio, Sunday, May 17, 1992, p. 3-C.

9   Mary Cambell, "Play's tour draining for McCambridge," *Columbus Dispatch*, Sunday, October 28, 1984, n.p.

10   Mercedes McCambridge, *The Quality of Mercy, An Autobiography* (New York: Times Books, 1981), p. 8.

11   Ibid, p. 22.

12   Tony Mastroianni, "Acting is what drives Mercedes: McCambridge, 74, is the star of *'Lost in Yonkers'* at Palace," *The Beacon Journal*, Akron, Ohio, Wednesday, October 21, 1992.

13   Ibid.

14   Joan Hanauer, "Alcoholism Arrested: Star Wins Over Adversity," *Columbus Dispatch,* Columbus, Ohio, n.d., n.p.

15   Mason Wiley & Damien Bona, *Inside Oscar: The Unofficial History of the Academy Awards.* Ed. Gail MacColl (New York: Ballantine Books, 1987), p. 198.

The Department: 1981–1987

In the fall of 1981, Dr. Jerry Martin had returned from Texas Tech University, with a newly-won doctorate, to become the chairman of the reconstituted Speech Communication and Theatre Department. Theatre's two-year absence had not dimmed the rapport which tradition and history had forged over decades of association. Theatre slipped easily into the berth it had occupied before the separation. My position paper proved valuable as a reference point and storehouse of information for the administration, but there was little new in it for members of a department, all of whom shared subject matter and skills in common. Without exception, everyone in the department knew the fundamentals, not only of speech, but also of theatre. Like the other areas of concentration in speech, theatre is mainly a communication art. Theatre is closely related to film, radio and television; they are all collaborative and collective arts.

With this latter fact in mind, the new theatre curriculum of 1982-83 reflected its brotherhood with the mass media. Courses in acting and directing were designed not only for the stage, but also for film, radio, and television. Film, which had always relied heavily on plays for story material, was easily combined with dramatic literature in course work. A new course, History of Film, was added to the curriculum as an introductory study. This curriculum remained in effect through 1985. (See the Section Note at the end of this section for specific courses and information on the theatre major.)

Staffing presented its problems for the department. Dr. Martin convinced the administration that the department needed teaching staff to further develop the radio and television area, and to re-vitalize the debate/forensic program. He was encouraged, in 1984, with the appointment of Jeffrey Harman as Director of Radio/Television; however, it took three more years to find Gene Alesandrini, who rebuilt the Debate/

Dr. Martin's Winning Debate Team, 1983. (from the left) the debaters are L. Uhlenbrock, K. McNenny, S. Steve (holding trophy), and T. Jones. *Photo courtesy Sharon Walker, M.C. Public Relations Office.*

Forensic area, along with Interpersonal Communication. Dr. Martin was discouraged when we lost, never to regain (as yet), the area of speech audiology and pathology. Besides teaching his own classes, Dr. Martin helped to cover other areas that needed teaching power. He directed one play a year, and acted as technical director when there was no appointment in that area.

In addition to his other commitments, Dr. Martin accepted the chairmanship of the Artist-Lecture Series. Having done that job myself, I know that he spent a considerable amount of time resolving miscommunications between visiting artists, contracts, and administrative obligations. When the administration decided to move speech faculty offices from Montgomery Hall to Cambridge Hall, there was a considerable amount of time spent on niggling details. Nevertheless, in 1984, he published *Henry L. Brunk and Brunk's Comedians: Tent Repertoire Empire of the Southwest*, which was based on his doctoral dissertation. A much-deserved reward came in 1985, when he received the William Oxley Thompson Faculty Award for Excellence in Teaching.[1]

Before mid-decade (1982), Muskingum had put the traumatic days of Financial Exigency behind. The Development and Admissions Offices helped turn the worst of times into better times. A Challenge Campaign was successful and a new Recreation Center was built. Enrollment reached one thousand students in the 1985-86 school year. The Speech Communication and Theatre Department stood united with a staff of five full-time professors: Miss Moore, Dr. Martin, Jeffrey Harman, Donald Lillie (technical director), and myself. The department ranked third in the number of majors studying in its collective areas.

The year 1986 is memorable for a significant loss in teaching staff. Martha Moore retired after thirty-eight years of service. She graduated from Muskingum in 1940 and, after teaching in high school, joined the speech faculty in 1948. She had an M.A. from Ohio State, and taught interpretation, general speech, and directed plays. Martha had strong ties to Muskingum; her brother, the late Charles L. Moore, was a 1935 alumnus who held a law degree and was chairman of the board of trustees; her father was C. Ellis Moore, a 1907 alumnus who served fourteen years in the United States Congress. Martha herself is vice-chairman of the Republican Party in Ohio and National Committee Woman. She was inducted into the Ohio Women's Hall of Fame in 1991.[2] The department would miss the personal charm, sly sense of humor, and gracious manner of this affable lady. Dr. Martin arranged a special dinner, in Martha's honor, at the famous Granville Inn. After she had been dutifully toasted, Dr. Martin presented her with a brass elephant, as a memento of her political affiliations. (For more information on Martha Moore see the note at the end of the chapter.)

In the fall of 1986, the theatre gained a significant member in the person of Mr. Ronald N. Lauck, who joined the staff as technical director. Technical directors are a welcome addition to any theatre staff. We had been averaging a technical director nearly every year since Dr. Martin had left in 1977. Mr. Lauck was unusually qualified because of his experience and skill in all phases of technical theatre. He had the added advantage of being a good director. His gifts in that area lent variety to the directing staff. Mr. Lauck improved the curriculum when he addressed the neglected area of stage lighting.

Meanwhile, Dr. Martin increased the visibility of the college and the department. He became active in statewide theatre affairs through membership in the Ohio Theatre Alliance, an organization of which he served as president. He must have doubled theatre attendance in southeastern Ohio by organizing several children's theatre activities. In 1985, under the auspices of our department and a grant from the Ohio Arts Council, he established a "Children's Theatre Saturday Showcase Series," a continuing program of professional children's theatre shows that were scheduled for two productions each semester.[3] In 1987, Dr. Martin also organized the Appalachian Children's Theatre sponsored by Rio Grande College, Ironton Council for the Arts, and our department.[4] (See the note at the end of this chapter.) In the fall of 1986, he arranged a special performance of *Smircus* by the Fairmont Theatre of the Deaf, in which newly-devised equipment made Audio Description for the Blind possible. Grants from the Ohio Arts Council and the Ohio Theatre Alliance made the performance available to the public.[5] Dr. Martin's interest in children's theatre impacted favorably on the youth and parents of southeastern Ohio. The shows were well-attended and created a desire for more theatre that resulted in a better understanding of theatre and, thereby, assured an educated audience for the future.

Dr. Martin was also instrumental in designing Muskingum's drama curriculum for teacher certification in theatre for the public schools of Ohio. This was a program that the Ohio Theatre Alliance had been advocating for years.

During the 1980's, my interest in theatre expanded. In the '60s and '70s, my energies were devoted to directing and producing plays. My teaching was channeled toward production. Knowledge and theory remained important, if useful and practical in the light of production. In the '80s I was still interested in production, but I became concerned about teaching and the content of what I was teaching. I had always used a variety of teaching aids, especially recordings and film. I took a closer look at these teaching aids. It dawned on me that students in southeastern Ohio have few opportunities to witness professional stage productions; however, a supply of good films was readily accessible, not only in movie theatres, but also on television and video tapes.

Film as an academic subject had steadily increased in colleges since 1920. I remembered that Denison University had a Cinema and Theatre Department when I first came to Muskingum in the late 1950's. Film and cinema departments in colleges, large and small, had been graduating film majors with bachelor, master, and doctor degrees for four decades. Film courses were being taught in the larger urban high schools. Through experimentation, I found that the deliberate use of film in appropriate theatre courses provided added interest and stimulation for me and my students.

Mr. Ellertson had recognized the importance of film as an academic discipline in the 1970's, when he introduced courses in The Movies, Photographic Communication, and Film History in Action.[6] While these courses approached film as a tool of communication or social reform, I was interested in the narrative aspects: the history, theory, and criticism of film—the theatrical aspects. Dr. Martin and President DeJong both agreed that film would be a welcome addition to the curriculum; however President DeJong indicated that there were would be no money for film production courses.

I began taking film courses in the evening at Ohio State University. (Dr. James Golden, our former department chairman (now head of the Speech Communication Department at Ohio State) became my advisor!) Although I had used film in classes to illustrate certain aspects of theatre, I realized that I had never looked upon film as an art form. I also discovered that, since I grew up in the 1930's–the Golden Age of movies–first-hand acquaintance with what are now known as the "classics" of film had its advantages.

As my graduate studies progressed and I neared the completion of a master's degree, I placed more emphasis on teaching narrative film in classes that were ordinarily devoted to drama and theatre only. This dual handling of film and dramatic literature revealed some very interesting methods of presenting course content, and deepened the meaning of the lecture and discussion.

My experiments with the coupling of film and theatre continued throughout the 1980's and 1990's. As textbooks, I used Martin Esslin's *Anatomy of Drama* and Bernard F. Dick's *Anatomy of Film.* These two texts addressed my way of looking at film: it was a form of theatre in a different medium. I felt good about the use of film along with theatre, because I knew that students were getting to know an area not dealt with before (at least not in this way) in any other department.

As a result, film was added to the titles and descriptions of some of the courses already in the curriculum; for example, in course 352. "The Contemporary Theatre and Drama: Avant Garde and Film," attention also centered on the film as it has emerged in the last half of the nineteenth century; in course 381. "Selected Studies in Theatre," the "Musical Theatre" section touched on the Hollywood musical, as well as the Broadway musical. The course title of 451. "Dramatic Theory and Criticism" was changed to "Prize Plays and Famous Films."[7]

Students in rural areas have few opportunities to see live professional theatre, but film, allowing for the differences in medium, can recreate a semblance of the staged play. Many versions of Shakespeare's plays on film or video can illuminate the text in a manner that a mere reading of the plays cannot. A comparative study of the plays or roles of *Hamlet, Macbeth,* or *Lear,* together with articles written on the matter, can yield a wealth of information and knowledge. Similarly, a comparative study of different art forms, such as Christopher Isherwood's novel, *The Berlin Diaries,* compared to John van Druten's play, *I Am a Camera*, and the stage and film versions of *Cabaret,* can provide a valuable learning experience, because they make students aware of changes in content, form, and style when the same materials are transformed from one medium to another. Historical, theoretical, and critical studies are also possible and they, too, present interesting and valid areas for research.

Students were another factor that always played an important part in my teaching. These students had a keen interest in theatre. They were good at taking the initiative in wanting to direct and in knowing what they wanted to direct. I noticed this element, especially toward the end of the decade. Talented students had earned the right and deserved the chance to direct full-length plays. I took this fact as a good sign. It was to make my last few years of teaching a fitting climax to my career.

In the spring of 1987, Dr. Martin applied for, and received, permission to take a sabbatical during the 1987-88 school year.

Section Notes

Course offerings for Theatre at the top of the 1980's reflected the relationship to the electronic media:

102:    203: 303: 303: 404. Projects in Theatre (1–4 hours)
151.   Introduction to Theatre (3)
175.   Movement and Voice (3)
245.   Technical Production (3)
251.   The Classical Theatre and Drama (3)
252.   A History of Film (3)
275.   Acting for Stage, Screen, and Radio (3)
345.   Scenic Design (3)
346.   Scenic Arts: Costume and Makeup (3)
351.   Modern Drama
352.   The Contemporary Theatre and Drama: Avant Garde and Film (3)
375.   Directing for Stage, Screen, and Radio (3)
381.   Selected Studies in Theatre (3-12)
        Children's Theatre (3)
        Musical Theatre (3)
        Religious Theatre (3)
382.   Special Studies in Theatre (3-6)
        Theatre Management (3)
        Playwriting (3)
451.   Dramatic Theory and Criticism (3)
475.   Advanced Acting and Directing (3)
495.   Seminar in Research (2)
496.   Seminar in Performance (2)

A major in Theatre consists of 30 hours which must include 151, 495, 496; one course selected from 245, 275 or 375; one course selected from 251, 351, or 352; one course selected from 345 or 346; and one hour of Projects in Theatre. The student would select courses from departmental offerings to complete a 30-hour major. A student may include up to six hours in Speech Communication on a Theatre major, with approval of the department. A minor in Theatre consists of 15 hours selected from those courses required of the major.

Course offerings for the Speech Communication major were as follows:

101; 201; 301; 401. Communication Practica (14 hours)
105.   Fundamentals of Speech Communication (3)
205.   Extemporaneous Speaking (3)
206.   Voice and Diction (2)
211.   Radio Programming and Production (4)
235.   Interviewing (3)
260.   Oral Interpretation of Literature (3)
310.   Mass Media (3)
311.   Television Programming and Production (4)
315.   Argumentation (3)
325.   Persuasion (3)
335.   Discussion (3)

360.	Advanced Interpretation (3)
411.	Program Generation (2)
425.	Persuasion in Media (3)
495.	Seminar in Research (2)
496.	Seminar in Performance (2)

A major in Speech Communication consists of 30 hours, which must include 105, 260, 325, 495, and 496; one course selected from 235, 315, or 335. The major may include up to four hours of Communication Practica. Up to six hours in Theatre may be counted toward a Speech Communication major, with the approval of the department. A minor in Speech Communication consists of 15 hours, which must include 105, 260, 325, and one course selected from 235, 315, or 335.

(The above curricula and information on Theatre and Speech Communication major requirements are taken from a departmental communication issued for the 1981-82 school year.)

The body of work offered by the department and the major requirements remained essentially the same through my tenure at Muskingum. There was always some fine-tuning going on, with altering course levels and course titles and, once in awhile, a new course would be added and another course dropped. For example, in the 1992-1994 *Muskingum College Bulletin,* there were two new theatre courses: 383. Professional Studies in Theatre, which offered on demand "A. Shakespeare on Stage, B. Professional Stage and Study, and C. Summer Theatre"; and 494. Methods of Teaching Drama/Theatre. There were two changes in course titles: 451. Dramatic Theory and Criticism was changed to Prize Plays and Famous Films, and 495, 496. Seminar in Research and Performance were changed to 495, 496. Independent Study in Research and Performance.

In the Speech Communication area, there were some new courses: 111. Broadcast Writing and Announcing, 295. Introduction to Communication Research, Intercollegiate Forensics and Debate, and 446. Interpersonal Communication.

Martha Moore

The program for the "1991 Ohio Women's Hall of Fame Awards Ceremony and Dinner," held on Thursday, November 7, at the Hyatt Regency in Columbus, offers more biographical information:

[Martha] has served as a member of the Republican State Central and Executive Committee since 1950 and has been the elected vice-chair of the committee since 1968. At her suggestion, the position of county chairwoman was created within the local Republican Party organizations, thus giving women expanded leadership roles.

Martha Moore ('40) at her retirement reception in 1986. Doing the "schmoozing" is choral director Robert O. Jones (left) and religion professor, William McClelland. *Photo courtesy Sharon Walker, M.C. Public Relations Office.*

Gaining national prominence for the role she has played in Ohio Politics, Miss Moore has represented Ohio on the Republican

National Committee since 1968. She was highly honored by the Ohio delegation with her selection as second choice for president of the United States at the 1972, 1976, and 1984 Republican national conventions. In addition, she was elected regional vice-chair of the Republican National Committee by the Midwest States Association in 1984.

Other inductees into the Ohio Women's Hall of Fame include: Doris Day, Ruby Dee, Phyllis Diller, Lillian Gish, Carol Kane, Margaret "Marge" Schott, Gloria Steinem, Nancy Wilson, and our own Dr. Lorle Porter (2000), to name a few.

The year in which Martha retired, she was the recipient of the Muskingum College Distinguished Service Award. She was also an inductee of the Guernsey County Hall of Fame.

Appalachian Children's Theatre

Kathleen O'Brien ('81) chronicled the origin and early history of the Appalachian Children's Theatre for her master's thesis at the University of Akron in 1991. The title of the thesis is "The Appalachian Children's Theatre Service's Role in Increasing Arts Education in Economically Depressed Appalachia Ohio." A copy is on file in the Muskingum College Library. (Kathleen O'Brien in conversation with the author, March 12, 2001.)

REFERENCES

1   Dr. Jerry Martin and Margaret Adams, Assistant to the Vice President for Academic Affairs, in conversation with the author.
2   Miss Martha C. Moore in conversation with the author.
3   "Children's Theatre Showcase," *Cue,* Sesquicentennial Issue, Muskingum College, New Concord, Ohio, Fall, 1986, p. 1.
4   Dr. Jerry Martin, "Children's Theatre Showcase," *Cue.*
5   Rose Kessing, "Audio Description for the Blind," *Cue,* Fall, 1987, p. 1.
6   *Muskingum College Bulletin: 1972 through 1977,* "Courses of Instruction" for the Speech Communication and Theatre Department.
7   *Muskingum College Bulletin: 1984-1986,* "Courses of Instruction" for the Speech Communication and Theatre Department. pp. 96-99.

 The Plays: 1980–1987

1980–1981

The first major production of the 1980-81 theatre season was *An Evening with Noel Coward*, an original entertainment which I drew from my University of Minnesota dissertation, "The Selected Comedies of Noel Coward: An Analysis of Comic Techniques." It was very similar to the presentation that was given on Alumni Weekend; however, I had learned much from that production. I reworked the material and, in general, tightened the script, eliminating one cast member. The final cast included Greg Adams, Mary Ann DeVolld, Kim Ronald, Vicki Townsend, Larry Triplett, and me. Katherine Schnitker was featured at the piano. The production was designed by the new technical director, Sharon (Shari) Taylor.[1]

An Evening with Noel Coward was staged in the Layton Theatre during

An Evening with Noel Coward, 1980. Donald Hill and Vicki Townsend perform "We're a Couple of Swells." *Theatre file photo courtesy M.C. Public Relations Office.*

Homecoming Weekend, October 3-5.

The Corn is Green by Emlyn Williams was directed by Kathleen O'Brien for her senior seminar, and followed closely on the heels of the Noel Coward entertainment, October 8-11. Shari Taylor designed the show and served as technical director for performances at the Little Theatre.

The story, as well as the characters in the play, has made *The Corn is Green* a favorite of amateur and professional theatres. Miss Moffat finds in one student, Morgan Evans, a brilliant young man, destined for greatness. By overcoming local opposition, and coping with a foolish mistake made by Evans himself, she achieves her goal: getting him a scholarship to Oxford.

Kathleen O'Brien had a very good cast that included Norman W. Ferguson (John Goronwy Jones), E. Molly Hoffman (Sarah Pugh), Suzanne Albrecht (Miss Ronberry), Donna Snyder (Mary Morris), Michael M. Swanner (the Squire), Linda Koehler (Bessie Watty), Lori Lynn Opatrny (Miss Moffat), Thomas C. Bressoud (Morgan Evans), Chip Stalter (Robbart Robbatch), Debra Congleton (Glyn Thomas), and Jim Johnston (John Owen).

The Corn is Green was well received by the Muskingum audience. The Ohio Regional Conference of Danforth Associates (an educational organization) requested that the play be staged for their meeting at Salt Fork Lodge. Kathleen and Shari, with the help of the cast and crew, packed up the show and moved it to the Lodge for a performance on October 17.

The Corn is Green, 1980. An English school teacher, Miss Moffat (L. Opatrny) brings education and inspiration to a Welsh miner, Morgan Evans (T. Bressoud). *Photo courtesy Kathleen O'Brien.*

The Danforth audience found the play entertaining and especially pertinent to the purpose of their organization.[2] (See letter in Section Note.)

The next major production of the theatre season was a translation of the Titus Maccius Plautus farce, *The Twins (Menaechmi)*, on February 4-7. This play is the progenitor of Shakespeare's *The Comedy of Errors* and the Rodgers and Hart musical, *The Boys from Syracuse.*

The Twins concerns a Sicilian merchant, the father of twins, who dies when one son is stolen. The paternal grandfather gives the remaining boy at home in Syracuse the name of the stolen twin, Menaechmus (played by Forrest Poston). When this boy grows up, he begins to search for his twin in every land. At last he comes to Epidamnus, the place where his stolen twin brother (Andrew Beery) has been reared. Everyone in Epidamnus thinks that the stranger is Menaechmus, their own fellow citizen; his brother's mistress, Lovey (Suzanne Albrecht), wife (Sherri A. Rose), and father-in-law (Norman W. Ferguson) address him as such. Finally, the two brothers meet and recognize each other, and the chaos is resolved! Other members of the cast include a parasite, Sponge (Charles Whitt), Lovey's cook, Roll (Linda Koehler), Lovey's Maid (Carol Ann Lewandowski), and a Doctor (Scott T. Buckley). I directed and Shari Taylor was technical director and designer of the show for the Layton Theatre.

The final production of the season was *A Little Night Music* by Stephen Sondheim, with book by Hugh Wheeler. It played in the Layton Theatre from April 30 through May 2, and on May 8-9. The production staff for the show included Guest-Director Dona D. Vaughn; Casting Director Mitchell Weiss; Executive Producer and Associate Director Richard Probert; Production Designer and Technical Director Shari Taylor; Musical Director Dr. Jack Peterson; and Choreographer Marilyn Gardner.

The musical was originally inspired by Ingmar Bergman's film, *Smiles of a Summer Night.* It takes place in turn-of-the-century Sweden, and concerns marital infidelities of the continental lifestyle.[3]

The cast, in order of appearance, was as follows: James Clausing (Mr. Lindquist), Joy Rose (Mrs. Nordstrom), Patricia Cline (Mrs. Anderssen), John Krauss (Mr. Erlanson), Julie Whetstone (Mrs. Segstrom), Allison Robertson (Fredrika Armfeldt), Lauren Jones (Madame Armfeldt), Norman W. Ferguson (Frid, her butler), Douglas Smith (Henrik Egerman), Gretchen Anaple (Anne Egerman), James Whetstone (Fredrik Egerman), Elaine Yakubisin (Petra), Barbara Schock (Desireé Armfeldt), Sharon K. Johns (Malla, her maid), Brockton Hefflin (Bertrand, a page), Michael Reiter (Count Carl-Magnus Malcom), Linda Koehler (Countess Charlotte Malcom), and Ruth Crawford (Osa).

Jack and Doris Peterson, professors of music at Muskingum College, played duo piano throughout the production. Douglas Lyle played the cello, while Richard Probert did the vocal coaching.

The production received an excellent review from Guest Reviewer Deron Mikal in the *Daily Jeffersonian*.

> The Ingmar Bergman-inspired play is directed by New York professional Dona Vaughan, and it shows. Blocking, staging, pace, scene changes, music and choreography go smoothly and with the grace and simplicity of professional production. . . .

And if that is not enough, set to all that music and dance, for a spectacle that is alive with pageantry in an overlay that reinforces the beauty and sophisticated splendor of this production and you will go home satisfied that you have had an experience that matters.[4]

Section Note

Dayton, Ohio, 45435
Department of History
Wright State University
October 24, 1980

Ms. Kathleen O'Brien
Department of Theatre and Speech
Muskingum College
New Concord, OH 43762

Dear Kathy:
Your production of *The Corn is Green* for the opening of our Ohio Danforth conference last weekend was outstanding. No words can tell just how much those in attendance enjoyed and appreciated your contribution to the success of the conference. Over and over again, we heard animated and enthusiastic comments about the quality of the performance, the interaction of the cast members in the discussion, and the usefulness of the play in defining themes that could be developed in later parts of the conference.

Your own mastery of the situation especially impressed us. We know how threatening it can be to face last-minute problems—such as those you faced when we found the ballroom in use when you expected to have it for set-up and rehearsal. The calmness and adaptability that all of you exhibited in that situation were remarkable.

You deserve special recognition for your role in this production, and we hope that you will receive it on your campus.
Sincerely,
Carole and Jake Dorn
Copy: President Arthur DeJong

 **1981–1982**
(*indicates alumni and/or guest actors)

The Prisoner of Second Avenue by Neil Simon led the 1981-82 Theatre Season, October 7-10 in the Layton Theatre. The Homecoming Week production was directed and designed by Technical Director Shari Taylor.

(The story of the play sounds very much like the forerunner of a future Simon play, *God's Favorite,* a modern version of the Biblical *Job.*) Mel Edison loses his job; his wife goes to work and then loses her job. The polluted air of New York City is killing his terrace garden; the walls of the apartment are so thin that the lives of the two German stewardesses who live next door, keep him awake; and his apartment is burglarized. As if this weren't enough, his psychiatrist dies with $23,000 of Mel's money, and he has a nervous breakdown. Only Simon could tell all of this with the talent that he has for turning a neat phrase, and the wit that enables him to turn tragedy into comedy. Mel and his family, however, do show the resiliency of the human race and the ability to endure

The comedy was well-directed, well-designed, and well-acted.[5] The cast included Thomas Bressoud (Mel Edison), Suzanne Albrecht, his wife (Edna), Randall J. Smith (Harry), Sherri A. Rose (Pearl), Meredith Grogoza (Jessie), Terrie A. Labella (Pauline), and Susan Brockman, Ruth Montgomery, and Doug Comin (Thieves). Voices were supplied by Christopher Seibert, Mariann Babnis, Jerry Martin, and Michael Murphy.

Never Too Late, the Broadway hit comedy written by Sumner Arthur Long, played the Layton Theatre, February 10-13. This hilarious play was directed by Jerry Martin, who also designed and served as technical director, for the annual faculty/staff production.

The story concerns a fifty-year-old husband who discovers that his wife is pregnant again. The fact that his first and only child, a daughter who is now twenty-four years old and married, but still living with him at home, conjures up a foreboding future. Furthermore, his wife, who is usually easy to get along with, suddenly begins to demand such luxuries as a new bath, a nursery, and her own checking account!

The play received excellent reviews.[6] The cast members of the swift-moving comedy were Sue Leiendecker (Grace Kimbrough), Richard Leimbach (Harry Lambert), Rhoda Van Tassel (Edith Lambert), Roger Robinette (Dr. James Kimbrough), Scott Dittman (Charlie), Kim Ronald (Kate), Russ Brown (Mr. Foley), David Skeen (Mayor Crane), and Richard Kilgore (Policeman).

For the production of *The Merchant of Venice* on February 24-27, I directed and designed the set; Shari Taylor executed the set and designed the lighting for the Little Theatre performances.

The time of the play is 1400; the place of the action is Venice and Belmont, Italy.

Antonio (Michael Swanner), a merchant, borrows money for his friend Bassanio (Steve McFarlane), in order to further Bassanio's courtship of the heiress, Portia (Karen Anderson). Antonio borrows the money from Shylock (Clark Kapelka), who nurses a grudge against Antonio for the many slights the gentleman has made against him and the Jewish nation. Shylock foregoes his usual interest and asks for a pound of flesh, in the event that the 3,000 ducats are not repaid in three months.

Outfitted with the borrowed money, Bassanio sets off in the company of his friend, Gratiano (Dave Jarrett), to press his courtship of Portia. This lady is protected from fortune-hunters by three caskets—one of gold, one of silver, and one of lead. Her father's will has decreed that she shall marry whoever chooses the right casket. Although she declares her love for Bassanio before he chooses, Bassanio shows his worthiness by distrusting outward splendor and choosing the lead casket. However, their happiness is short-lived. Antonio loses his fortune when his ships are lost, and his bond is forfeited. Shylock's hatred, fed by the elopement of his daughter, Jessica (Terrie Labella), (who has run off with the Christian suitor, Lorenzo played by Doug Comin), prepares to take his pound of flesh. In reality, this means the death of Antonio, because Shylock intends to take it from over the heart.

The Duke of Venice (Larry Triplett*) and Portia (who comes before the court disguised as a lawyer) beg Shylock to be merciful, but he is adamant. Portia then forbids Shylock to spill one drop of blood in exacting his pound of flesh. Frustrated by the decree, Shylock gives up his bond. Other members of the cast include Salerio, a friend of Antonio (Jeff Lord), and Solanio, another friend (Scott Buckley); Leonardo, Bassanio's servant (Scott Mackey); Launcelot, Shylock's servant (Frank Gurnick); Old Gobbo, Laucelot's father (Bill Laing); Magnificoes of the Court (Scott Mackey and Drew Robbins); Tubal, friend to Shylock (Bill Emling); a Jailer (Scott Mackey); Nerissa, Portia's Lady in Waiting (Tina Bowling); Stephanie, Portia's Page (Sally Miller); Ladies in Waiting to Portia (Lisa Wolf, Meredith Grogoza, and Linda Koehler); Prince of Morocco, suitor to Portia (Greg Adams*); and Prince of Aragon, another suitor to Portia (Bill Emling).

According to A. L. Rowse, from the time it was first performed (1596), the play was referred to as "The Jew of Venice." Shylock overpowers all the other characters because

> . . . the play relates to the theme that has had so terrible a resonance in our time: the Jew in Europe and the evil phenomenon of anti-Semetism.[7]

To many generations of the twentieth century, the memory of the Holocaust makes it impossible to see much humor in the treatment of Shylock.

Although Shakespeare made Shylock an individual, he could not help but know that the Elizabethans did not, and would not, look upon him as a sympathetic character. Their dislike would have been fueled by the fact that, in 1594, Roderigo Lopez, a Jew and Queen Elizabeth's personal physician, was hanged for treason.[8] Nevertheless, the play speaks in favor of Shylock.

I realized that Shylock was not the only person in the play. He must have his share of the stage, but there are Antonio, and his happy-go-lucky friends, who may not be as interesting as Shylock, but who are on the road to romance. As in many Shakespearean comedies, there is a big wedding scene at the end of the play, in which three sets of lovers are joined.

The Merchant of Venice is a mixture of genres: tragedy and comedy. The play is also a mixture of styles: romanticism and realism. The character of Shylock is a mixture of complex humanity: neither clown nor villain. The action of the play begins with prospects of a happy future and moves through the sad reality of a frustrating present, to an ending of wedded bliss. Ambivalence is an ingrained quality of the *Merchant*. I decided to let Shakespeare speak for himself. I played the script according to the actions involved. I divided the characters of the play into three groups: Antonio and his friends, Shylock, and Portia and her court.

From Antonio's actions would flow the emotions of the carefree attitude of Antonio and his friends, the tragedy of the failed bond, the happiness of the returning ships, and the ensuing weddings. From Shylock would flow the anger and hatred for Antonio, the sorrow of the loss of Jessica, the triumph of the forfeited bond, and the frustration of the court's decision. From Portia and her court would flow the expectation of marital bliss, the joy of the rescue of Antonio, and the happiness of the nuptials.

The Thwarting of Baron Bolligrew is an adventure story for people of all ages. It is not only good theatre, but also good literature. Robert Bolt is the author–the same man who wrote *A Man for All Seasons*. Jerry Martin directed and designed the production for the Children's Theatre class. It played in the Layton Theatre, March 31 through April 3, during Parents Weekend.

Long ago and far away in the days and lands where dragons were common, a Duke (Rob Davenport) and his Knights–Sir Digby Vayne-Trumpington (Chip Stalter), Sir Graceless Strongbody (Scott Roller), Sir Percival Smoothely Smoothe (Scott Burkholder and Steven McFarlane), and Sir Oblong Fitz Oblong (Michael M. Swanner)–look forward to a rest after having killed the last dragon in the realm. However, Sir Oblong Fitz Oblong declares that they must seek to do further good works; therefore, Sir Oblong is sent alone on a one-man mission to overcome the dragon in the Bolligrew Islands. There he meets the wicked Jasper, 15th Baron Bolligrew (Todd Rice), and his blundering Squire Blackheart (Clark Kapelka). After many adventures, Sir Oblong finally meets the Dragon (Scott Roller).

Other members of the cast were the Storyteller (Lisa Zuber), Juniper (Carey Vance), Captain (William Laing), Guards (Sally Miller, Lorri Schmidt), Lord Mayor (Dwight Bowman), Obidiah (Dee Warren), Obidiah's Child (Christopher Martin), Magpie (Gena Varhola), Secretary (Crystal Metzger), Moloch (Lauren Jones), Mazeppa (Rhonda Warner), A Corporal (Sally Miller), Orchestra Leader/Musician (Linda Koehler), and Peasants: #1 (Dwight Bowman), #2 (Deb Freeman), #3 (Wendy Curran), #4 (Teresa Mikus), and #5 (Chip Stalter).

The last play of the 1981-82 theatre season was *Spoon River Anthology* by Edgar Lee Masters, adapted for the stage by Charles Aidman. Mary Sykes directed the play for her seminar, and it was designed by technical director Shari Taylor for the Little Theatre. Music and songs were provided by Linda Koehler and Doug Smith.

Mary supplied the following notes on the play:

> In May of 1914, Edgar Lee Masters began writing a series of poems which were collected into the book *Spoon River Anthology*. Charles Aidman adapted the poems for UCLA's professional company, The Theatre Group, in 1963. Spoon River Anthology remains a favorite play of amateur and college theatre groups.
>
> All of the characters in Spoon River are dead. Each takes this chance to come alive and recount his story. The characters are people we have all met and know. They still live today, but with different names and faces. Certainly, the inhabitants of Spoon River will live on forever.
>
> All of the characters listed are played by only two actors and two actresses; each player playing approximately twenty separate characters.[9]

The players in *Spoon River Anthology* were David B. Aldridge, Forrest Poston, Meredith Grogoza, and Suzanne C. Albrecht.

Although *Spoon River Anthology* officially ended the 1981-82 theatre season, the Alumni Office needed entertainment for returning Muskies during Alumni Weekend, June 11-12. Jerry Martin responded with a revival of the hilarious comedy, *Never Too Late.*

1982–1983

The 1982-83 theatre season began when student director, Mary Sykes, and I revised and rearranged the 1982 production of the Masters-Aidman *Spoon River Anthology* for the Little Theatre. Presented first for Muskingum Players Open Theatre, September 30, it continued through Homecoming Weekend, October 1-2. Guest Artists David and Linda Taylor and Bob Mason provided folk music for the revival. The cast of two actors (David Aldridge and Forrest Poston) and two actresses (Meredith Grogoza and Susan Albrecht) remained the same. Clifford Wiltshire in the *Black and Magenta* labeled the play a "success."[10]

Spoon River Anthology, 1982. Curtain Call. (from the left) S. Albrecht, F. Poston, M. Grogoza, and D. Aldridge. *Theatre file photo courtesy M.C. Public Relations Office.*

On December 3-4, a class in Religious Theatre performed an original production, *The Nativity Cycle,* in the Little Theatre. I directed the play and received special assistance for the production from Dr. Jerry Martin and the Technical Production class. Music for the play came through the courtesy of the College Drive Presbyterian Chancel Choir, under the direction of Mrs. Robert Adams, pianist, Diane Reinhold, flutist, and Reverend C. Wood, pastor.

The plays included on the program were studied, discussed, and adapted for performance by the class in Religious Theatre. The class chose the plays from the most prolific period of religious drama-the Mediaeval Period–when the church clergy used theatre to teach religion, philosophy, and morality to their parishioners. Originating in church liturgy, Mediaeval play production was eventually taken over by cities and guilds, which produced the plays for religious holidays, such as Christmas and Easter. The five plays comprising *The Nativity Cycle* describe the birth of Christ and his adoration.[11]

The first play of the cycle was "The Parliament of Heaven with the Annunciation."

The cast members included Sharon K. Johns (Contemplation), Janet Allen (Truth), Lorri Schmidt (Mercy), Carey Vance Lohman (Peace), Mary A. Sykes (Justice), Scott Roller (Voice of The Father), Henry Wilcox (Voice of The Son), Ed Sahli, III (Voice of The Holy Ghost), Jeannine Fabian (Mary), and Rick Jarrett (Gabriel).

The Nativity Cycle, 1982. Three Kings (D. Comin, R. Jarrett, S. Roller) and Mary (J. Fabian). *Theatre file photo courtesy M.C. Public Relations Office.*

The second play of the cycle was "The Birth of Christ," performed by Jeannine Fabian (Mary) and Gunnar Palm (Joseph).

The third play of the cycle was "The Adoration of the Shepherds." Cast in the play were Rob Davenport as the First Shepherd, Chris Seibert as the Second Shepherd, John MacAleese as the Third Shepherd, and Janet Allen as the Angel.

The fourth play of the cycle was "The Three Kings and Herod." The actors for this play included Scott Roller (First King), Rick Jarrett (Second King), Doug Comin (Third King), Janet Allen (Angel), Mary A. Sykes (Messenger), Todd Rice (Herod), and Lorri Schmidt (Clerk).

The fifth and final play of the cycle was titled "The Gifts of the Magi." The dramatic personnel featured Scott Roller as the First King, Rick Jarrett as the Second King, Doug Comin as the Third King, and Carey Vance Lohman as the Angel.

On December 5, *The Nativity Cycle* was repeated for Morning Worship at the College Drive United Presbyterian Church.

The second semester of the 1982-83 theatre season began on February 9-12, with the Faculty-Staff Production of the Mary Chase fantasy-comedy, *Mrs. McThing,* in the Layton Theatre. Jerry Martin directed and served as his own designer and technical director. He wrote the following "Director's Note" for the performances:

> Regular Faculty/Staff productions at Muskingum began in 1976 with the production of *You're a Good Man, Charlie Brown!* Since that time, Faculty and Staff members from virtually all disciplines have crawled from their offices at the end of long, tiring days to attend rehearsals. The effort is, however, more than the

production of a play. It provides an opportunity for camaraderie, to exchange views and ideas, to become aware of the problems and concerns of others, and, perhaps, most important, to have fun together. We have, indeed, had fun putting the production together.[12]

This comic fantasy, by the author of *Harvey,* was another hit on Broadway and on tour with Helen Hayes as the star. The story involves a real witch and her daughter, who is treated badly by a snobbish lady, Mrs. Howard V. Larue, III. That nasty lady will not let her son play with the witch's little girl. Therefore, the witch pulls the old "switcher-oo," by stealing the little boy away and replacing him with a do-gooder likeness. When Mrs. Larue discovers her real son is in a pool hall, consorting with criminals, she gets knocked about a bit, until she appreciates the sterling qualities of her roughneck son. She takes him back on his own terms and adopts the little witch girl as part of the bargain.

The cast for the production included Rhoda Van Tassel as Mrs. Howard V. Larue, III; Diane Moffett as Carrie, a nurse maid; Kim Ronald as Sybil, a parlor maid; Sue Kokovich as a friend, Evva Lewis; Peggy Adams as a friend, Maude Lewis; and Anne Smith as a friend, Grace Lewis; Bill Tereshko as Nelson, a bodyguard; Steven McFarlane as Boy (Howay); Judith Knight as Ellsworth, the Chef; Kip Howard as Virgil, a waiter; John Griffin as Dirty Joe, a gangster; David Skeen as Stinker, a gangster; Richard Leimbach as Poison Eddie Schellenbach; Lorle Porter as Ma Schellenbach; Abby Van Tassel as Mimi, a little girl; Jim Smith as a Policeman; Katherine Schnitker as Mrs. McThing #1; and Vicki Townsend as Mrs. McThing #2.

Mrs. McThing was an unqualified success. The audience loved it. The production was dedicated to the memory of Marilyn Gleason ('61) and Nancy Gleason Gavola ('70), the two sisters who had died in a plane crash in 1979. All proceeds from the faculty/staff play were contributed to the Gleason Memorial Theatre Scholarship Fund.[13]

On April 19-23, the Little Theatre housed a production of *The Taming of the Shrew.* It was an all-student cast and crew production, headed by Guest Director, Ted Hissam.

Ted Hissam ('69) appeared at the Little Theatre, during his student years, in *Death of a Salesman, Waiting for Godot, Lion in Winter,* and *Taming of the Shrew.* Following graduation, he studied acting and directing at Ohio State University, and Shakespearean drama in England and Canada.[14]

The cast for this well-known bumpy love affair between Katharine and Petruchio contains inventive and imaginative distribution of parts: Tina Bowling (Katharine, Servant, Biondello), Douglas Comin (Lucentio), Jeannine Fabian (Biondello, Bianca), Randy Gedeon (Hortensio), Frank Gurnick (Grumio), Deb Kester (Bianca, Servant), Steven McFarlane (Gremio), Sally Miller (Tranio), Kristin Mollenauer (Katharine, Servant), Todd Rice (Petruchio), Melinda Schwertzer (Curtis, Tailor, Pedant, Widow), Chip Stalter (Baptista), Lauren Jones (Servant to Baptista), Matt Wyscarver (Servant to Baptista), and Mary A. Sykes (Servant).

Needless to say, this was not a traditional or conventional interpretation of The Bard. As I recall, Petruchio arrived on a motorcycle and Grumio made at least one entrance swinging from a rope. The production updates were exciting, and the audience appreciated the departure from the usual performances one sees of this Shakespearean comedy/farce.

Although the official season was over, the Layton Theatre saw another faculty/staff production by the cast and crew of *Mrs. McThing*. The comic fantasy was revived by Dr. Martin for Alumni Weekend, June 10-11. The cast remained the same, except for two replacements: Frank Gurnick took the part of Nelson, a bodyguard, originally played by Bill Tereshko; and Matt Wyscarver played the Boy (Howay), originally performed by Steven McFarlane.

Special Attraction
Page 1 Players

Every once in awhile, something wonderful happens. One of those times was the summer of 1983, when Robert F. Adams and his wife, Norma Jean, announced the premiere summer season of Page 1 Players, which would be housed in the Little Theatre. I directed *A Thurber Carnival* on the last weekend in June and the first weekend in July. Jerry Martin staged Neil Simon's *The Star-Spangled Girl* on July 8-10 and 15-17. Julie Adams (a recent Miami University Theatre graduate) directed Tom Jones's and Harvey Schmidt's musical, *The Fantasticks*, on August 5-7 and 12-14.

I'll never forget the opening night of "*Carnival.*" The day had been an unusual June day; however, as time for the curtain drew near, storm clouds also drew nearer, and lightning struck the college generator minutes before curtain. Poof! We had no lights, and the college had no way of repairing the damage in time to salvage the performance. The box office issued rain checks for disappointed patrons, and I cast one of my acrid spells on all weathermen. Bad cess to the lot!!!

In spite of that inauspicious beginning, Page I Players supplied the community with some very relaxing and enjoyable entertainment for the next two summers.

 1983-1984

Neil Simon's play, *The Star-Spangled Girl,* opened the 1983-84 theatre season in the Little Theatre. It was directed and designed by Dr. Jerry Martin for the Homecoming Week of October 13-15.

Matt Wyscarver and Frank Gurnick portrayed the two journalists, Andy Hobart and Norman Cornell, respectively. In their weekly magazine, *Fallout*, they published the anti-administration sentiments of the 1960's. All went well for the pair until an All-American "Star-Spangled cornpone" blonde moved into the apartment next door. This girl, Sophie Rauschmeyer, played by Sally Miller, threw the characters' lives into a romantic tangle. Neil Simon invented mind-boggling complications as the characters worked out their problems.[15]

Dr. Martin provided further information in his "Director's Note":
> The 1960's were filled with student unrest and protest. Andy Hobart and Norman
> Cornell were doing what was accepted as "the American way" for their generation,

protesting against "the American way." *The Star-Spangled Girl* first appeared on Broadway in 1966. It was the first successful production with an anti-protest theme.[16]

Susan Ransom wrote an excellent review of the show for the *Black and Magenta.*[17]

On November 16-19, my class in Musical Theatre produced and performed *A Musical Revue of the American Musical Theatre: Past and Present.* I supervised the original production in the Layton Theatre; Sunny Boulet performed the duties of assistant director for her senior seminar; and Catherine Johnson served as vocal coach.

Starting with early outside influences, such as Gilbert and Sullivan's *Pirates of Penzance*, on our native musicals, the revue passed from uniquely American influences in minstrelsy and vaudeville to the first modern musical, Jerome Kern's *Showboat.* The revue then skimmed through many popular musicals, such as *Porgy and Bess, Babes in Arms, Oklahoma!, South Pacific, Fiddler on the Roof, Hair,* and *A Chorus Line.* The performances of hit songs–complete with solos, duets, dances, and choruses from each musical–were accompanied by pianists, Sheri Mathes and Lori Shields.

The presentation, narrated by Melinda Polk and Todd Rice, involved not only students, but also faculty and talented individuals from surrounding communities, as well. Musical medleys were performed by the "Rags to Riches" duo, which was composed of Dick Pavlov and Ruth Cyanovich, and Marshall Onofrio, who conducted the College Jazz Band composed of Ann Duff, Laura Huff, Jim Kleefield, Keith Logan, Deb Olsen, Pete Sutherland, and Marcy Zeszotek.

Scott Dittman, registrar of the college, performed "A Modern Major-General" from *Pirates of Penzance,* and Jerry Martin, Lorle Porter, Louis Palmer, Judy Woodard, and Tom Drabick (faculty and staff) sang "A Book Report on Peter Rabbit," from *You're a Good Man, Charlie Brown.*

Other students who performed in *A Musical Review* included Amy Anglin, Sheryl Shaw, Robert Green, De Ann Campbell, Becky Fountain, Randy Smith, Lorrie Templeton, and Deborah Kester (Singers); Jeannine Fabian, Linda Higgs, Deborah Kester, and Lorrie Templeton (Chorus); Gail Hawkenberry, Beth Luteyn, Gunnar Palm, Jerry Van Renesse, Salil Singh, and Lorrie Templeton (Dancers).[18]

Many members of the audience congratulated the class and complimented them on their informative and entertaining performances.

Rashomon, a dramatic adaptation by Fay and Michael Kanin of the Oscar winning film (1951) by Akira Kurosawa, began the second semester of the season of plays in the Layton Theatre, February 22-25. I directed, and Guest Artist Roger Drake designed the costumes and set. Mr. Drake also taught a course in scene design. Mr. Drake and his student crew transformed the Layton Theatre into an elaborate ancient Japanese setting, complete with police court, Rashomon Gate, and forest. This setting provided the environment for the play and enveloped the audience in its mood and atmosphere.

The play itself concerns the retelling of a crime by a Priest (David Stewart), a Woodcutter (Chip Stalter), and a cynical Wigmaker (Salil Singh). The crime committed involved the murder of a Samurai (Steve McFarlane) and the rape of his wife

(Deborah Kester). The chief suspect of the crime is the notorious bandit, Tajomaru (Frank Gurnik).

Each of the main characters who were involved in the incident—the Bandit, the Wife, the ghost of the dead husband, evoked by a Medium (Linda Higgs), and an eyewitness Woodcutter—tells his or her version of what happened. Using flashback techniques, the stories, each of which is different, are presented to the audience. In the end, the play expresses concern for the truth and for Man's pride, which sometimes shapes the truth to fit circumstances.

Other students in the production included Matt Wyscarver as the Police Deputy, and Jeannine Fabian as the Wife's Mother. Brilliant sword fights between the Samurai and the Bandit were built into the production and added an extra touch of realism, thanks to David Lee, who provided stage combat techniques.[19]

Gina Thompson reviewed *Rashomon* for the *Black and Magenta*.[20]

(More information on the preceding three productions can be found in "An Irish Faustus," where they are briefly mentioned in another context. A discussion of *Rashomon* is also found in the section titled, "University of Iowa: 1962-1964.")

The final production of the season is discussed in the next article, "An Irish Faustus." A staff writer for the *Black and Magenta* also wrote a review of the production.[21]

An Irish Faustus
1984

Some plays end before they begin. This would appear to be the destiny of our production of *An Irish Faustus* by Lawrence Durrell. In this case, appearances were deceiving; in fact, the play seemed to have a life of its own: it became the story of the play that would not die. (The play had a sub-theme of vampirism equals everlasting life.)

There are all kinds of hazards in play production. One of them is beginning a production without adequate staff. Every theatre needs at least two staff members: a director and a technical director. Expecting a single person to stage a play is like expecting a single coach to field a football team.

Muskingum finally hired its first technical director in 1971; however, the position did not become permanent until 1986. Until that time, it was always a matter of speculation as to whether or not the administration agreed on the necessity of this position. (Over the years, I spent a lot of time and a lot of ink arguing for a technical director)

The 1982-83 school year was another one of those seasons without a technical director, and it appeared that the same situation would exist for 1983-84.

Indeed, the '83-'84 fall semester began without a technical director, but with Neil Simon's *The Star-Spangled Girl*, which Dr. Martin had designed and directed for the 1983 premier season of Page 1 Players Summer Theatre. He refurbished the set (which he had preserved) and, using the same cast, revived the play for the October Homecoming production. I followed in November with an original script, *A Musical*

Revue, which came from my class in Musical Theatre. That concluded the first semester.

The spring semester was more ambitious, because by that time, the administration had decided to finance technical help. I began the season in February with *Rashomon* by Fay and Michael Kanin, which featured a professional United Scenic Artist, Roger Drake from Zanesville, Ohio, as guest designer and technical director.

Roger (who also held an MFA from Ohio University) created a highly imaginative Kabuki setting for this Japanese classic drama of murder and rape. I was free to devote my time to directing the students through a difficult script. They turned in very commendable performances. I was pleased, because the play was part of the Fine Arts Asian Emphasis Series.

Rashomon was followed in March by one-act plays which the directing class produced. *An Irish Faustus,* which was scheduled for April, featured another guest-artist-designer, John Newton White. The production was offered as a courtesy to the Lawrence Durrell International Conference held on campus April 13-14. The Durrell Conference came to Muskingum under the auspices of our English Department professor, Dr. James Nichols, a ranking member of the International Lawrence Durrell Society.

John Newton White, whose family home is in Cambridge, Ohio, is a 1952 alumnus of Muskingum. He lives and works in New York City as a free lance designer, and he had wanted to return to his alma mater to do a show. When he agreed to design *Dracula* for the Cambridge Performing Arts Center in the spring of 1984, it was convenient for him to prolong his stay and do *An Irish Faustus* for us.

John wanted to do the costumes, as well as the scene design for the production; Dr. Martin supervised the technical aspects of the production; and I directed. I thought we were off and running when I unexpectedly hit a brick wall. Casting became a problem. I opened try-outs to students, faculty, and the community. When I did find a cast, their schedules were so diverse, and their free times so negligible, that I despaired of ever finding the requisite rehearsal time.

I gave the casting problem considerable thought. Casting is of utmost importance to any play; it is a major part of the directorial image. For this drama, I could not only see the characters move, but also hear them speak. The sound of the voices was operatic in nature, as they delivered the meaning and emotion behind the verse. I really wanted to do this play because it was a creative version of a classic drama. I knew that it would stretch the imagination of both the student and adult members of the cast and audience. The play had been performed only twice in America and once in Germany. To my knowledge, no Faustus story had ever been performed on our stage, and I believed that our community might never have another chance to see such a play.

When John presented me with designs and costume sketches that were truly magnificent, I was determined to see them materialize on our stage. I found it impossible to give up the production.

We had a crisis meeting. John indicated that he had seen a play done with large puppets. That idea struck a responsive chord in my thinking. John offered to transfer his costume designs to 4x8-foot sheets of 3/4-inch plywood, include faces of the characters as he imagined them, and cut the figures out with a band-saw. I, in turn, agreed to rehearse the play by scenes and record the voices of the actors on tapes. Faustus would be the only live character on stage. The part was long and difficult; it would require someone really in love with the stage–someone tireless and indomitable. I knew just the person: Ted Hissam, a 1969 graduate. When I contacted him, he was free. With his commitment as guest actor, production was under way.

Since the characters in the play would be only heard, not seen, rehearsals with the actors took on the semblance of a radio show. They had to be coached to produce the right tone and inflection of voice in order to convey meaning, evoke emotion, and suggest movement. (See Section Note A for a list of the actors who supplied the voices for the characters.)

In addition, stage hands–important as they were–must not be seen or heard! They must be dressed in black and taught to keep out of sight behind the huge plywood figures they were moving. Large handles were attached to the backs of the wooden cut-out characters, and glides were put on the lower edges of the wood to make them move easily. The stage hands were rehearsed to move the heavy characters so that they appeared to float on cue through entrances, about the stage, and out the exits. (See Section Note B for a list of personnel who supplied the scenic invention.)

The stage itself was wrapped in black duvetine to make a soft black box. Dr. Martin set the lights and, with the help of Carleton Underwood, light cues were recorded for the crew. Under the light, the black duvetine could have passed for velvet. When the giant eight-foot figures appeared, the intense colors in which they were painted glowed like jewels on black velvet.

An Irish Faustus, 1984. Puppets of Mephisto and his split personalities (Voice of D. Lee), Faustus (Guest Actor, Ted Hissam). *Theatre file photo courtesy M.C. Public Relations Office.*

It was my task to coordinate the actors' recorded voices with movement, and to synchronize the recorded cues with those of the live Faustus that Ted had created. This was done in a few rehearsals and the production was ready as scheduled.

On opening night, I held my breath. The response from the audience was encouraging. The response from the Durrell Conference members was overwhelming. The beautiful imagery of the poetry came through clearly, and the wooden figures took on a life of their own, as they glided about the stage in a seemingly dream-like state. Ted kept the language flowing, and the production moved forward without a flaw.

Ian W. MacNiven, president of the Durrell Society, published the following notice in the Society's *Herald:*

> The production by Donald Hill and J. Newton White of *An Irish Faustus* marked only the second staging of the play in the United States and, so far as I know, the first anywhere to employ heroic sized two-dimensional puppets for all the characters but Faustus himself, played with considerable skill by the professional actor Ted Hissam. Dr. Hill's conception of Faustus was very true to Durrell: a dualistic figure, capable of both good and evil, alternately active and passive, old and young (in that order). The breakdown of the discrete ego, a theme in Durrell's writing for many decades, was emphasized by this production both in the character of Faustus and in the presentation of Mephisto, who is once made to separate into triple images of himself on stage.[22]

Durrell's treatment of the Faust legend deals with man's greed and the Devil's temptation. In this instance, Faustus wins because he realizes his imagination can make him free. The message is delivered to the audience by the story-line, which involves the theft of a magic alchemist's ring and Faustus's recovery and destruction of it.[23]

Meanwhile, Durrell, in Europe, was kept informed of the unusual aspects of this production of his play. He was eager to have his plays performed and agreed with the unique way in which we had adapted *Faustus* to our particular situation. Penelope Durrell Hope recounted to her father a phone conversation she had with me, and she also passed our correspondence on to him. Evidently, other members of the American Durrell Society notified Durrell of our success with his play. Pictures of the production were requested and posted to him.

In a personal letter to Dr. Hill, Ian MacNiven wrote, "Your production of *An Irish Faustus* alone would have made a trip to New Concord more than worthwhile."[24]

According to a letter he wrote to Dr. James Nichols, Durrell felt that the Muskingum production was inspired. He liked the presentation in the form of a soliloquy, with voices and puppets using the existing text, and he wished that he had seen it played that way. If it were to be presented again, he would insist on the American textual approach as essential.[25]

The international attention being paid to our theatrical work was very flattering. However, the attention did not end with the final curtain.

Almost simultaneous with our production, Durrell's daughter was preparing for the Delos Press, a new edition (the first was in 1963) of *An Irish Faustus,* with a new preface by her father. The 1987 edition was limited to four hundred-thirty-one copies, seventy-five of which were numbered and signed by the author. It is worthwhile to quote from the short preface of that edition, in order to understand Durrell's pleasure with our production.

What little I know about theatre I learned from him [the great German actor and impresario, Gustav Grundgens]. It was he moreover who, one day asked me whether I could not build him a Faustus which could be played light-heartedly without betraying Goethe. Unfortunately he died before I could deliver him my text. The play worked well, however, in a full scale production by O. F. Schuh at the Deutsches Schauspielhaus in Hamburg (December, 1926) and was duly published in England. For this edition the text has been further cut and finalized but I must mention a brilliant American adaptation of the text which resulted in transforming the structure into a prolonged soliloquy passing through the head of a single protagonist–making Faustus a one-man play, and carrying out the rest of the action with the aid of beautiful big mobiles, different voices and special effects of lighting. For this production the American producer used the existing text with very few changes and the results proved strikingly dramatic and highly successful. He adapted the present version so that it could be played by one live actor. In other words, I can now offer it to a star as a suitable vehicle. [26]

Subsequent to the Muskingum production of *An Irish Faustus,* Dr. Nichols moved to Georgia Southern University, where he housed another Durrell Conference, with a production of another Durrell play, *Acte.* He asked me to attend the conference (April 1990) and speak on a panel about the experiences we had in producing *An Irish Faustus.* I was able to do just that.

I knew that the panel was being recorded, but I did not know that five years later, I would receive an entire transcript of the panel's discussion from Professor F. K. Sanders of the Georgia Southern English Department. He was preparing it for publication, along with six other essays and an introduction by Dr. Nichols. He wanted me to go over my portion of the panel carefully to prevent any mistakes and to make any additional comments I might wish to add. I did so and returned the copy with my good wishes.

Requiescant in pace, Faustus.

Section Note A

Actors who supplied the voices for the characters were:

Eileen Adams	Princess Margaret
Catherine Johnson	Queen Katherine
Dan Toomey	Paul, Servant to Faustus
Richard Leimbach	Martin, the Pardoner
Fred List	Bubo, his Assistant
Steven McFarlane	An Elderly Man
David Lee	Mephisto
James Nichols	Anselm, Chaplain to Katherine
Robert Jones	Matthew, a Hermit

Section Note B

The scenic invention which was so vital to the success of the play was provided by the following people:

Character Movement

Bill Adams	Erik Goldstrom
Michael Bait	Joel McNenny
James Daly	Todd Rice
Glenn Yoho	

Michael Bait   Tim Miller
David Duncan   Dan Watson
James Johnston   Glenn Yoho

 1984–1985

During the 1984-85 theatre season the administration granted Departmental requests for a technical director, and Donald Lillie was appointed to the position. Once more into the breach, dear friends. I directed the first two shows of the year, *Our Town* and *My Three Angels*. Dr. Martin directed the final two shows, *Arsenic and Old Lace* and *Hans Christian Andersen*. Donald Lillie served as technical director for all four major productions.

Our Town won the Pulitzer Prize in 1938 for its author, Thornton Wilder, and has since become a classic of American theatre repertory. I'll wager that it has been performed by high schools, colleges, and community theatres more than any other play.

In my "Director's Notes" for the program, I wrote,

> A play has meaning over and above the entertainment supplied by the story. Each person gets his own meaning out of a play. Whether it is the meaning intended by the playwright is another matter. Quite obviously, one meaning is stated by Emily and the Dead in the final moments of the play: human beings don't realize life while they live it. The method of staging reflects the meaning of the play: only a few tables and chairs and props are seen because our joys and fears are not in things but in the mind. "The climax of the play needs only five square feet of boarding and the passion to know what life means to us."[27]

In 1901, in Grover's Corners, New Hampshire, live George Gibbs (John Jackson) and Emily Webb (A'dora Phillips). Their lives are woven together from adolescence through adulthood, marriage, and death. The story is told in an episodic fashion by a "stage manager" (George Branyan). He introduces the villagers, whose lives reveal specific social, philosophical, and religious traditions. The "stage manager" says, "This is the way we were in our growing-up and in our marrying and in our doctoring and in our living and in our dying." And so it was, as the play was performed on October 3-6, in the Little Theatre on the Muskingum College campus.[28]

Other than the three characters already mentioned, members of the cast were Pete Sutherland (Dr. Gibbs), Chris Jones (Jo and Si Crowell), Bill Bayer (Howie Newsome), Kathy McGinnis (Mrs. Gibbs), Ginny Massenburg (Mrs. Webb), Sally Miller (Rebecca Gibbs), Chris Jones (Wally Webb), Brian Brake (Mr. Webb), Alyssa Unger (Mrs. Soames), Matt Wyscarver (Constable Warren), Kristine Engle, Becky Fountain, Rose Kessing, Sheryl Shaw, and Holly Hyer (Choir and Townspeople).

T. W. Rickard, critic for the *Daily Jeffersonian*, commented that the cast succeeded in putting across the play's simple message: " . . . that most people go through life and are so worried about what's going to happen next that they don't really see what's going on around them. Then, too soon, it's over." Mr. Rickard continued, "Since the play contains no physical substance in the way of sets or props, that idea is the only substance the players have to work with. Thursday, through their unforced and moving performances, the Muskingum Theatre troupe brought that idea to life, just the way Wilder intended. The results were just this side of brilliant."[29]

Gina Thompson, in her review for the *Black and Magenta,* also found *Our Town* "entertaining."[30] President De Jong was among the audience members who agreed with Gina.

> From the Desk of . . .
> ARTHUR J. DEJONG
> TO: Don Hill
> DATE: October 10, 1984
>
> Don, Joyce and I want to tell you how much we enjoyed the play "Our Town" last week. It was a delightful performance of a play that many of us have seen periodically in the past. The skill involved was among the best performances that I have seen.
> Continued best wishes!
> AJD/ch   Art

Perhaps the first event of the 1984 holiday season occurred on November 14-17, with the Layton Theatre production of Sam and Bella Spewack's comedy, *My Three Angels.* The play had a successful run on Broadway in 1953 before being made into the film, *We're No Angels*, featuring Humphrey Bogart.

My Three Angels is distinguished by its characters and a whimsical, if weird, sense of humor. Three convicts in the French Guiana penal colony of 1910, played by Frederick Frank (Joseph), Brian Brake (Jules), and Mark McDaniel (Alfred) help a family in distress. At Christmas-time, a French store owner, Felix Ducotel (Frank Gurnick), is about to be put out of his home by a stingy, cheating relative, Henri Trochard (Chris Jones). Felix's daughter, Marie Louise (Kristine Engle), is also about to lose her boyfriend, Paul Trochard (George Dickson), the nephew of the relative. The convicts take a hand in righting the wrongs of business affairs and playing cupid by loosing a lethal pet snake, "Adolphe," on the two Scrooges. As a result, the crooked and unfaithful are disposed of, and the honest and true are rewarded![31]

Other talented members of the cast who helped spread Yuletide joy were Kathy Pilcher, Felix Ducotel's wife, Emilie; Sheryl Shaw, a gossipy customer, Mme. Parole; and Robert Zwick, a handsome Naval Lieutenant and future beau of Marie Louise.

In the *Black and Magenta*, Kathy Hovis nodded her approval of *My Three Angels* in her review entitled "Convicts are Committed to Comic Christmas."[32]

In the *Daily Jeffersonian,* critic, T. W. Rickard called *My Three Angels* " . . . no ordinary holiday play . . . not exactly your traditional holiday fare. . . . " He further commented in his review:

> On the whole the play comes off well. The players capitalized on most comedy opportunities and were at least somewhat believable throughout. And the set design was especially impressive, with its bamboo-like walls and tasteful furnishings.
> *My Three Angels* is a non-traditional Christmas story that is refreshingly different. You won't find Scrooge or Tiny Tim or even the Grinch in this play. What you will find, however, is a healthy mixture of laughter and warmth, with a good measure of absurdity thrown in.[33]

Arsenic and Old Lace, 1985. The Reverend Dr. Harper (David Skeen) cannot resist the charm radiated by the Brewster sisters: (seated) Abby (Lorle Porter) and Martha (Judy Woodard). Courtesy Sharon Walker, Public Relations Office.

There are few people in the United States who have not seen *Arsenic and Old Lace,* and I think that anyone who has seen it once would never object to viewing it a second time. It was a smash hit on Broadway in the 1940's and it has continued to keep America laughing in almost every theatre in the country. There are many elements of this comedy-farce that would explain its popularity, but the one I think of immediately is the novel way in which the author, Joseph Kesselring, makes fun of murder.

Who would have thought of creating two elderly, dotty sisters, who have two slightly off-center brothers, and putting them at odds with one another in a contest to see how many innocent people they can kill? Kesselring did, and he gets away with it because of the fascinatingly sweet, although devilish, characters he invents and the expertly funny dialogue he puts in their mouths.

The Muskingum College Theatre presented *Arsenic and Old Lace* as a College-Community Production on February 6-9 at the Little Theatre.

In his "Director's Note" to the production, Dr. Martin reminded the audience,

> Since the first modern-day college-community production of *You're a Good Man, Charlie Brown* in 1976, Muskingum's faculty, staff, and students along with members of the community have taken to the stage regularly to raise money for scholarships. This year the Speech Communication and Theatre Department has established a new fund in honor of long-time faculty members, Charles R. and Ferne Parsons Layton. All proceeds of this production will go to that fund.[34]

The cast (in order of appearance) for *Arsenic and Old Lace* consisted of Dr. Lorle Porter (Abby Brewster), Dr. David Skeen (The Reverend Dr. Harper), Jeff Harman (Teddy Brewster), Scott Krupinski (Officer Brophy), Jay Jackson (Officer Klein), Judy Woodward (Martha Brewster), Kristin Mollenauer (Elaine Harper), Steve Smith (Mortimer Brewster), Dr. Jerry Martin (Mr. Gibbs), Dr. James Nichols (Jonathan Brewster), Dr. Robert Burk (Dr. Einstein), Brian Brake (Officer O'Hara), Richard Leimbach (Lieutenant Rooney), Rev. Harold Kaser (Mr. Witherspoon), James Nichols, Jr. and Chris Martin (doublecast as Mr. Spinalzo).

Ginny Schuster, in her review for the *Black and Magenta*, commented that the performance of the actors resulted in "... controlled chaos that makes this such a good comedy." She explained that, while Mortimer Brewster generally panned the plays he reviewed, "I think he might be a little more generous with *Arsenic and Old Lace*. This delightfully funny play kept the audience laughing as Mortimer and his bizarre family and friends plunged through two very strange days."[35]

On April 24-27, the Theatre and Music Department combined forces to produce the final show of the school year, *Hans Christian Andersen*. The popular musical featured Frank Loesser's music and lyrics, with a book by John Fearnley, Beverly Cross, and Tommy Steele. Dr. Jerry Martin was production director; Robert Owen Jones was the musical director; Donald E. Lillie supplied the design and technical direction; and Dr. Jack Peterson and Joe Perorazio accompanied on two pianos.

According to the program,

> The children's story is based on the true story of a Danish Cobbler who was awarded a royal pension from the King for his undisputed talents in story telling. Hans is a young talented cobbler who journeys to the town of Copenhagen where he sees Doro, the prima ballerina of the Copenhagen ballet. He is completely taken back by her stunning beauty and immediately falls in love with the dancer. He eventually comes to be employed to fix her dance slippers. After witnessing a bitter argument between Doro and her husband, Niels, he mistakenly believes that she is unhappily married. He writes a story about the situation to show Doro that he wants to help her leave her husband.
>
> Touched by the tender story, Doro is inspired. The ballet company turns the tale into a ballet which Hans narrates. Hans eventually realizes that she is happy in her marriage. At the end of the play Hans tells the story of the King's clothes. The King awards Hans a medal and Doro places it around his neck.[36]

The cast acted, sang, and danced their way through the production, which was performed on the stage in Brown Chapel. Kathy Hovis wrote in the *Black and Magenta*, "The cast and crew of *Hans Christian Andersen* are to be commended for a fine show. The quality of the performance was indicative of the time and hard work put into the production."[37]

Cast for
Hans Christian Andersen

Hans	George Branyan
Peter	Chris Jones/Jeannine Fabian
Madam Doro	Becky Fountain
Niels	Andy Wilton
Otto	Thomas Kelley
In Odense:	
Schoolmaster	Jerry Widenhofer
Burgomaster	Homer Baker
Dr. Foss	Ryan Harvey
Mrs. Pfeiffer	Deb Kester
Villagers	Jim Buhrmester, Mark McDaniel, Gerald Widenhofer, Deshon Dillard, Susan Barclay, Sondra Perkins, Beth Bell, Penny Bryan, Sabine Duchemin, Vicki Everett, Kathy Hovis, Shelley Roberts, Deanna Shinn, Jennifer Wilkinson, Teresa Willibey, Marcy Zeszotek, Angela Wilber
Ingrid	Amy Smith
Karia	Missy Starrett

Gudrun ....Lisa Remmert
Arne ....Jeannine Fabian
Anna ....Alyssa Unger
Laura ....Susan Susedik
Finn ....Linda Brown
George ....Tracy Davis
Karen ....Jennifer Loos
In Copenhagen:
Truls ....Robert Robinson
Fishmongers ....Susan Barclay
Meat Vendors ....Janice Thompson
Milkman ....Ed Mitchell
Mrs. Arboe ....Jenn Wilkinson
Vegetable Vendors ....Sondra Perkins
Celine ....Velynda Crewdson
Policeman ....Jim Buhrmester
Haida ....Connie Garces
Mrs. Olson ....Judith Knight
Mrs. Holm ....Kathy Pilcher
Mrs. Hofgaard ....Deborah S. Kester
Editor Holm...Mark McDaniel, David Hoffman
      Townspeople of Copenhagen:

Susan Barclay	Beth Bell	Homer Baker
Sabine Duchemin	Penny Bryan	Kristine Engle
Kathy Hovis	Vicki Everett	Sondra Perkins
Deanna Shinn	Shelley Roberts	Connie Garces
Teresa Willibey	Jenn Wilkinson	Ryan Harvey
David Hoffman	Marcy Zeszotek	

Newsboy ....George Dickson
Matchgirl ....Bonnie D. Long
Elsa ....Amy Smith
Chimneysweeps ....Carolyn Young, A. Thomas Perkins, IV
Ludwig ....Kevin Dunn
Lars ....Alyssa Unger
Anna ....Susan Susedik
Other School Kids ....Jennifer Loos, Lisa Remmert, Missy Starrett, Susan Susedik
Mermaid Ballet:
Narrator ....George Branyan
Mermaid ....Tracy Davis/Linda Brown
Sea Witch ....Kristine Engle
Prince ....Gerald Widenhofer
Foreign Princess ....Angela Wilber
Dancers ....Deshon Dillard, Linda Brown, Beth Bell, Velynda Crewdson
Nobility ....A. Thomas Perkins, IV, David Hoffman, Ed Mitchell, George
                Dickson
        Director....................................Dr. Jerry Martin
        Musical Director ....Robert Owen Jones
        Technical Designer/Director ....Donald E. Lillie
        Pianists ....Dr. Jack Peterson & Joe Perorazio

Most of the plays in the 1985-86 theatre season were connected with classes. *God's Favorite* came out of the class in Religious Theatre. "Studio Productions: II" featured a repertory of *Agnes of God,* (another production by students from the class in Religious Theatre) and *Mass Appeal*, a seminar by senior Peter Sutherland. The "Evening of Gilbert and Sullivan" and *Trial by Jury* were jointly produced by classes in Music and Theatre. *The School for Wives* came from the class in Classic Theatre. *The Passion of Dracula*, presented by a mixed cast of faculty, staff, and students, was the only production not specifically connected to classes.[38]

During Homecoming Week, October 9-12, *God's Favorite* by Neil Simon turned the Biblical Book of Job into a weird and wacky comedy that lost none of its serious message. In this Simon version, a rich box manufacturer loses everything, but he doesn't renounce God; that, of course, saves him and he wins everything back.

The cast for the production, which I directed, included Peter Sutherland (Joe Benjamin), Virginia Massenburg (his wife, Rose), Brian Wagner and Deborah Wolfert (their twin children, Ben and Sarah), Douglas Hess (the older son, David), Kristine Engle (Mady), Steven McFarlane (Morris), and Christopher Jones (a messenger from God, Sidney Lipton), who brings both good and bad news.

In an article for the *Black and Magenta*, Alyssa Unger " . . . noted how important the stage setting was for the play since at one point part of the house falls down around the Benjamin family." The designer and technical director, Donald Lillie explained, "The stage has a personality all its own."[39]

 "Studio Productions II" presented two recent Broadway successes with religious themes: *Agnes of God* and *Mass Appeal*. They appeared in repertory, December 4-7, in the Layton Theatre.

According to *Cue,* "*Agnes of God*, written by John Pielmeier, is a modern mystery and miracle play involving a young nun accused of murdering her baby. The drama appeared on Broadway in 1982 with Elizabeth Ashley, Geraldine Page, and Amanda Plummer . . . it was later filmed with Jane Fonda, Anne Bancroft, and Meg Tilley."[40]

The cast for the Muskingum production, scheduled for December 4 and 6 in the Layton Theatre, included Leilani Joven as the psychiatrist, Dr. Martha Livingstone; Deborah Kester as Mother Miriam Ruth, and Tracy Davis as Agnes. I directed the tense melodrama, and Donald Lillie designed and "teched" the production. Catherine Johnson was the vocal coach and Jeffrey Risner was the organist.

Bill C. Davis's *Mass Appeal* "also appeared successfully on Broadway in 1982, and it was filmed later with Jack Lemon and Charles Durning. The drama concerns the tense conflict between an established cleric and a young seminarian."[41]

The Muskingum production, performed December 5 and 7 in the Layton Theatre, featured Steve McFarlane as Father Tim Farley, and Christopher Jones as Mark Dolson. "Muskingum audiences found the production by Peter Sutherland, who directed for his theatre seminar, exceptionally well-done, with humor designed to point up the important differences in generations."[42] Dr. Jerry Martin supervised the production and Donald Lillie served as designer and technical director. April Kuhr was organist for the drama.

The Passion of Dracula version of the Bram Stoker novel, written by Bob Hall and David Richmond, continues the enjoyment that generations of playgoers have had with the "tongue-in-cheek" chill and charm of the "teeth-in-the-neck" thriller. It was a new and wryly comic point of view of the Dracula legend, presented by a combined Faculty-Staff-Student company on February 19-22 at the Little Theatre.

Eileen McComb Adams, alumna and former Muskingum Player, directed the drama and Donald Lillie assisted with design and technical work. The director found an enthusiastic cast to portray the well-known characters of the Dracula story: Dr. Cedric Seward (Greg Adams), Jameson (Doug Hess), Professor Van Helsing (Tom Petersen), Dr. Helga Van Zandt (Rhoda Van Tassel), Lord Godalming (Jerry Martin), Mr. Renfield (Brian Wagner), Wilhelmina Murray (Martha Wilson), Jonathan Harker (Chris Jones), and Count Dracula (Matthew Elli).

Ginny Massenburg wrote the following review:

> No need to smother those giggles or hide those guffaws. Even lighthearted tittering "he hees" are welcome as the Little Theatre's student-faculty production *The Passion of Dracula*, directed by Eileen Adams, concludes its dynamic four-day run this Friday and Saturday. . . .
>
> With stage personalities ranging from a mentally-institutionalized man who habitually eats flies and spiders to a blood-sucking vampire who has been hanging around for four hundred years, it may be hard for even the most socially-proper dilettante to hold back the laughter.
>
> But do not be misled—characters are not the sole attraction of this show. Mr. Lillie "Muskingum's Merlin of set design and technical wizardry," believes that this particular set, full of unexpected tricks, becomes a multidimensional actor/actress in its own right.[43]

Director Eileen Adams summarized *The Passion of Dracula* experience with, "The students and faculty work well together and give this theatre production its strangely subtle and slightly bizarre sense of humor."[44]

On March 13-15, the Speech Communication and Theatre Department joined forces with the Music Department to produce the comic opera, *Trial by Jury (*words by William S. Gilbert and Music by Arthur S. Sullivan). Student Jerry Widenhofer directed the opera, supervised by Dr. Jerry Martin, and Robert Owen Jones was the musical director. Donald Lillie supplied scenery and technical direction.

The story concerns the heroine, Angelina, who sues Edwin for breach of promise, because he has forsaken her for another. Confusion and complication abound, until the Judge solves the problem by marrying Angelina himself. Additional songs from other favorite Gilbert and Sullivan operas combined with the one-act opera to make a very entertaining evening.[45]

The School for Wives, translated by Richard Wilbur, was first produced by the Phoenix Theatre in New York, February 16, 1971. Joan Van Ark played Agnes, David Dukes was Horace, and Brian Bedford portrayed Arnolphe. Bedford won the Tony Award for Best Actor for his performance in the comedy. *The School for Wives* was written by Moliére in 1662, his first full length comedy.[46]

The School for Wives, 1986. The Young Lady, Agnes (K. Engle) and the Old Man, Arnolphe (F. Frank). *Theatre file photo courtesy M.C. Public Relations Office.*

The story of the play is one that Moliére told more than once; it is also one that he lived in real life. Arnolphe is a typical Moliére comic character who is consumed by one passion: to educate a young woman (Agnes) to be his one and only wife, by keeping her so innocent that she won't shame him by infidelity. The theme is the old one that love conquers all, that youth has a life of its own, and that nature permits hearts that belong together to get together.

In the Muskingum production, which played the Little Theatre on April 9-12, Frederick Frank played the jealous old man, Arnolphe; Kristine Engle was the young bride-to-be, Agnes; William Bayer played the trespassing young man, Horace; Brian T. Wagner and Stephanie Olson portrayed Arnolphe's servants, Alain and Georgette; Greg Files was Chrysalde; Patrick Burke played Enrique; and Steven Marvin was Oronte. I directed and Donald Lillie designed the colorful and practical setting and supervised the technical aspects of the production.

In his review of the play, John Lowe of the *Daily Jeffersonian* declared,

> See Moliére's *The School for Wives* at the Little Theatre. If you do not see this Muskingum College production, you indeed will have missed an entertaining evening.
>
> Forget that the setting of the play is 17th century France. Forget that the lines are in verse. This comedy will have you laughing within ten minutes.
>
> This production is excellent. The casting, especially of the servants, is discriminating. The interpretation of the text by the actors and the director, Dr. Donald Hill, is insightful. The performance by the actors is excellent.[47]

The Saturday Showcase Children's Theatre Series

In the 1985-86 theatre season, the Saturday Showcase Children's Theatre Series was inaugurated by Dr. Jerry Martin, chairman of the Speech and Communication and Theatre Departments, in conjunction with the Ohio Arts Council. Performances were presented twice, at 10:00 a.m. and 2 p.m., in Brown Chapel on each of the Saturdays indicated:

Johnny Appleseed by Hank Fincken .... October 19
Pinocchio by the Hip-Squeak Puppets .... October 26
The Ransom of Red Chief by the Akron Children's Theatre .... March 8
Everything Under the Rainbow by the Child's Play Touring Theatre .... May 10

Cast for
Trial by Jury
(William S. Gilbert and Arthur S. Sullivan)

The Judge	Robert Robinson
Angelina	Ashley Turner
Edwin	Jeffrey Marston
Plaintiff's Counsel	Thomas Kelley
Usher	Thomas Brubaker
Foreman of the Jury	George Dickson
Bridesmaids	Victoria Rundels, Jennifer Loos, Mary Ann Hoopingarner, Brooke Byrd, Charlene Legge, Linda Brown, Carolyn Young, Gweneth Bruner
Jury persons	Trent Cubbison, David Freihofer, Richard Roos, Trevor Walker, James Buhrmester, Kevin Dunn, Roger Terrell, Brian Wagner, D. Marie Campbell, Elizabeth Cullan, Homer Baker
Barristers	Janiece Bigler, Colleen Martin, Beth Rowley
The Public	Catherine Coss, Velynda Crewdson, Mary Halpin, Annette Lothes, Lisa Randles, Michelle Rohrback, Kristin Smalley, Beth Bell, Sherri Wingard, Bonnie Long, Alyssa Unger, Teresa Willibey, Marian Lenhart, Deanne Snedeker, Rebecca Fountain, Michelle Moore, Sondra Perkins, Melissa Starrett, Lee Nixon, Dr. Judith Knight.
Pianists:	Dr. Jack Peterson, Joe Perorazio
Director	Jerry Widenhofer (seminar)

 1986–1987
Indicates Alumni Guest Actors

Founded in 1837, Muskingum College marked its 150th birthday in 1987, the year which also marked the sixty-first anniversary of Muskingum Players, a strong student support organization founded in 1925-26. With the dedication of the Little Theatre in 1939 (a gift of alumni and Muskingum Players in honor of Dr. and Mrs. Charles Layton), the Theatre had a home. In 1978, the Layton Theatre in Johnson Hall was added to the production facilities.[48]

Chris Jones, president of Muskingum Players for the Sesquicentennial, wrote an excellent editorial, which appeared on the front page of *Cue*.

SESQUICENTENNIAL GREETINGS
Since its founding in 1925 [1925-'26], Muskingum Players Dramatic Society has encouraged participation and the maintenance of high standards in theatre production on campus. This Sesquicentennial year for the College makes our goal even more important.

Our current membership will strive to uphold the motto of Muskingum Players by participating in the many special campus events as well as sponsoring some of our own.

The participation of our organization is designed to make everyone aware of our past history and events and to invite you to enjoy the fun and learning experiences scheduled for the future.

Inspiration for high standards and quality in theatre come from alumna Agnes Moorehead, internationally acclaimed actress. Help us pay tribute to the college and to this dynamic actress by attending the Agnes Moorehead Film Festival September 15-19.[49]

Muskingum Players hosted a series of films for which Miss Moorehead received nominations for Academy Awards for Best Supporting Actress. There were four such nominations. The film for which she received her first nomination was *The Magnificent Ambersons* (RKO, 1942); our festival screening was scheduled for Monday, September 15, at 8:00 p.m. in the Science Center Auditorium. (All the following films adhered to the same time and place.) Two years later, she received a nomination for her role in *Mrs. Parkington* (MGM, 1944). That film was shown Tuesday, September 16. The next film was *Johnny Belinda* (Warner Bros., 1948), which was shown on Wednesday, September 17. Contrary to some authorities, Miss Moorehead (however deservedly) did not receive a nomination for *All That Heaven Allows* (U., 1955), but the film was shown anyway on Thursday, September 18. The fourth and final nomination for Best Supporting Actress was *Hush, Hush, Sweet Charlotte* (20th Century Fox, 1965), which was scheduled for Friday, September 19.[50]

The theme which united the theatre season for this anniversary year was the conflict between illusion and reality.

Keats wrote,

"Beauty is truth, truth beauty—that is all
Ye know on earth, and all ye need to know."

However, distinguishing between truth and that which appears to be the truth, or between reality and illusion, is not always easy. Shakespeare's comedy, *A Midsummer Night's Dream,* which began the season of five productions, explores reality through a dream. In "Studio Productions," student directors examined a variety of themes based on reality and illusion. Mary Chase's award winning *Harvey* presented the audience with an imaginary six-foot bunny, in order to urge us not to take life too literally. *Painting Churches,* a new play by Tina Howe, concerns a painter's image of reality which leads to real understanding. The final play of the season, Sr. James Barrie's *Dear Brutus,* returns to the Midsummer Eve scene of the first play, during which a magic wood converts wishes into facts.

One of the values of theatre is that it enables us to see reality and illusion on stage side by side, so that we might better understand the importance of each to our daily lives.[51]

A Midsummer Night's Dream was a good choice to start the 1986-87 theatre season because it presents the theme which generated the selection of the entire season: the conflict between illusion and reality. In this comedy, the author announces that the world of sense in which we live is only the surface facade of a greater, unseen world that gives meaning and beauty to the human condition. It is not by chance that the play is crowded by people in disguise, is haunted by ghosts and witches and supernatural beings, and is filled with such words as "sleep," "dream," and "vision." Central to the meaning is the technique of using a play within a play, because that device is like a mirror in which Man may see himself and his true, rather than his affected, value. Four sets of lovers crisscross in this highly imaginative treatment of love. Shakespeare weaves a magic spell of midsummer madness, chance, and misadventure; but in the end, all seems a dream and the reality is, that

> Jack shall have Jill;
> Naught shall go ill;
> The man shall have his mare again, and all
> shall be well.[52]

Another reason *A Midsummer Night's Dream* was chosen to start the season was the fact that it had been produced more times than any other play at Muskingum–five times to be exact: 1910, 1930, 1961, 1962, and 1975. Since this year marked the Sesquicentennial for the college, it seemed appropriate to revive the play that had proven so popular.[53] I directed the play for the fourth time, and Ronald Lauck, the Theatre's new technical director, designed the lighting. The play was staged in the Layton Theatre on October 15-18 for two matinees and four evening performances.

In connection with the event, alumni who had been in past productions of the play were invited to return to perform in it, and to enjoy a special reception in their honor after the final performance on Saturday, October 18.

The addition of alumni to the production made the occasion especially gratifying and pleasant. Greg Adams ('81), past president of Muskingum Players, played the role of Egeus (Father to Hermia), as a permanent member of the company. While Greg was not in previous productions of *Midsummer*, he had played Tybalt in *Romeo and Juliet,* and Falstaff in *The Merry Wives of Windsor*. Rich Werner ('75), an attorney from Pittsburgh who had played Oberon in 1975, returned to play Quince (a carpenter) for the Thursday and Saturday evening performances. The role was doublecast with Brian T. Wagner, who played Quince on Wednesday and Friday evenings, and at the matinees Wednesday and Thursday. Alan Dawson ('64), who had played Bottom, the Weaver in the 1961 and 1962 productions, returned to play the same role at the Wednesday matinee, and Thursday and Saturday evening performances. This role was also doublecast with Phillip Albaugh, who played Bottom on Wednesday and Friday evenings and for the Thursday matinee.

I could not possibly name all the alumni who saw this particular production, because they came on different evenings. On Saturday, I introduced the following people to the audience: Miriam Caldwell ('61), who had been a Lady of the Court and had also worked on costumes for the 1961 *Midsummer* show; Pat Koster Caudill ('62), who had worked on costumes for the 1961 and 1962 shows and box office on *Hamlet* (1962); and Ted Sofis ('75), who had played Bottom in the 1975 *Midsummer.* Colleen Hawkins Heacock, Director of Alumni Relations, was present to greet the alumni.[54]

Mary Chase's celebrated comic success, *Harvey,* first appeared on Broadway in 1944 with Josephine Hull and Frank Fay in the parts of Veta Louise Simmons and Elwood P. Dowd. When Fay took a vacation from the role, Jimmy Stewart took his place. The critics panned Stewart in the part; however, when Stewart played the same role in the film of *Harvey*, he received a nomination for an Academy Award for Best Actor![55]

Harvey played the Layton Theatre on February 25-28, directed and designed by Jerry Martin. Dr. Martin had never directed the production before, but he had worked extensively in graduate school with an educator who was a close friend of Mary Chase, and who was the first to direct the comedy when it went under the title of *The White Rabbit*.[56] The story of Elwood P. Dowd and his best friend, Harvey, won the Pulitzer Prize for 1944. Although Harvey's presence is very upsetting for the less imaginative and affable members of the Dowd family, they really can't prove that Harvey isn't real. After all, no one can deny that doors mysteriously open and close by themselves in the Dowd home.[57]

The story (and cast) of the play centers around Elwood P. Dowd (Christopher Jones), who has an unusual friend–a six-foot white rabbit who can be seen only by himself and a select few. Veta Louise Simmons (Judy Woodard) and Myrtle Mae Simmons (Deborah Wolfert), Elwood's sisters, try to have their brother committed to Chumley's Rest, in order to rid themselves of Harvey. When Veta is committed by mistake, the sisters are foiled in their attempt to gain control of the estate. Dr. Chumley (William Adams) wants to learn the powers of the rabbit so that he can have a two-week fling under the grove of maple trees outside Akron, Ohio. Dr. Sanderson (Greg Files), Chumley's able assistant, and Ruth Kelly, R.N. (Alisha Lenning) are more interested in each other than in the success of Dr. Chumley's clinic.[58]

Other members of the cast who helped resolve the plot were Christine Slater (Miss Johnson), Deanne Snedeker (Mrs. Ethel Chauvenet), David Tarbert (Duane Wilson), Wendy Pattison (Betty Chumley), Dr. David Skeen (Judge Omar Gaffney), and Philip Albaugh (E. J. Lofgren).

Ginny Massenburg wrote a favorable review of the play for the *Black and Magenta*.[59]

Painting Churches, a comic drama by Tina Howe, was staged at the Little Theatre, March 25-28, under the direction of Ronald Lauck, who also did the scenography, with costumes coordinated by Rene Wallace.

The Churches are a talented family, the father is a poet and his daughter is a painter. However, whether they have ever really understood each other is questionable. As the father and mother prepare for their retirement, the daughter returns home to help. By painting her parents, the daughter comes to terms with them.[60]

According to Mr. Lauck, *Painting Churches* was first staged in New York in February of 1983 at the South Street Theatre. From this Off-Off Broadway location, the play moved to the Lambs Theatre Off Broadway. The work never made the final jump to Broadway, but it has been well-received in many theatres across the United States. This may be because *Painting Churches* is a rich, skillfully-crafted script. It very much followed Ms. Howe's philosophy, as she stated it in an interview with *Contemporary Authors*: "I go out of my way to look for unlikely settings and situations . . . places that are basically predictable and uneventful. Nothing is more theatrical than putting the unexpected on stage. Because the theatre is a place of dreams,

Painting Churches, 1986. Tina Howe's serio-comic domestic drama about family relationships, aging, and artistic promise. The Churches, left to right, Gardner (F. Frank), Fanny (G. Massenberg), and Margaret "Mags" (K. Engle). *Photo courtesy Ronald N. Lauck.*

the more original the spectacle, the better. I'm hopelessly drawn to digging out the flamboyant in everyday life."[61]

The thought of sitting for a portrait seems tedious. It also involves work, but so does the theatre. Through the skill of the playwright, such an event becomes the theatrical medium through which age-old rituals and conflicts of generations are explored with wit, humor, and sensitivity.

The story of *Painting Churches* takes place in the Beacon Hill district of Boston. The Churches–Fanny (Ginny Massenburg) and Gardner (Frederick Frank)–have sold their house and are in the process of moving to their Cape Cod summer home to live the year 'round, as Fanny puts it, " . . . with gulls, the oysters and us." Old age, failing health, and falling income are some of the problems facing the elder Churches. As they struggle with these changes, Margaret "Mags" (Kristine Engle), arrives to paint their portrait and help with the final details of moving. Mags is the family's rising star. When memories of past struggles and delights swirl to the surface, new insights are discovered and the result is, as Clive Barnes of the *New York Post* describes it, "A bittersweet portrait."[62] (The remaining cast member was "Toots" who played himself.)

Kathy Hovis wrote a fine review of the production for the *Black and Magenta*.[63]

Dear Brutus, a comedy by Sir James Barrie, concluded the 1986-87 theatre season. I directed and designed the show and received technical assistance from Ronald Lauck. The play was staged in the Layton Theatre on April 22-25.

Rose Kessing wrote the following article for the *Cue:*

"The fault, Dear Brutus, is not in our stars, But in ourselves, that we are underlings." Taken from the speech of Cassius in Julius Caesar, this quote is a direct source for the title and theme for the upcoming play *Dear Brutus*. [At its first] opening in October 17, 1917, with Gerald Du Maurier, the play ran for 365 performances.

The characters of the play are gathered together for midsummer week "because they all have one thing in common." What that something is they are not aware of. Their host, Lob (Chris Jones), is a queer, old creature of unknown age. Although not human there is a mischievousness about him. He appears amiable but treats humans with a puck-like contempt.

As the play progresses, we discover that what these people have in common is the feeling that if they had another chance they would make a better life for themselves. Lob has the power to give them this chance and to teach them that they probably would have still remained the same.

There is a magic and tenderness in *Dear Brutus* which is easily yielded to. Like the entrancing spell of Peter Pan [also by Sir James Barrie], *Dear Brutus* works an unbreakable spell. Lob, like Peter Pan, is eternal youth.[64]

Dear Brutus, 1987. Fantasy mixed with reality has Mr. Purdie (K. Snyder) dream of loving another woman, but in reality he is in love with Mrs. Purdie (L. Joven). *Courtesy Ronald N. Lauck.*

The characters and cast for this "be-careful-what-you-wish-for" fantasy were: Mr. & Mrs. Purdie (K. Snyder and L. Joven), Mr. & Mrs. Coade (P. Albaugh and K. Green), Mr. & Mrs. Dearth (B. Ewing and C. Slater), Lady Caroline Laney (A. Lenning), Joanna Trout (D. Wolfert), Matey (E. Green), Lob (C. Jones), Margaret (K. Engle), and Household Staff (T. Norris and D. Hill).

In retrospect, this theatre season may have been the most satisfying of the decade. The theme of reality versus illusion (or vice versa) resulted in a choice of excellent plays. The use of a single theme for an entire season served as a unifying force. The Sesquicentennial celebration was another unifying factor. For the most part, the plays embraced life with its highs and lows within the charmed circle of comedy.

The Saturday Showcase Children's Theatre Series

In the 1986-87 theatre season, the Saturday Showcase Children's Theatre Series was held in the Layton Theatre twice, at 10:00 a.m. and 2:00 p.m. on each of the Saturdays indicated. A grant from the Ohio Arts Council made the series possible.

The Lion, the Witch, and the Wardrobe (The Art Reach Touring Company) September 27
Raise the Roof (The Little Miami Theatre works) .... October 25
Victorian Vignettes (Columbus Junior Theatre of the Arts) .... March 21
Smircus (Fairmount Theatre of the Deaf) .... May 9

Cast for
A Midsummer Night's Dream

Theseus, Duke of Athens	Douglas Hess
Hippolyta, his betrothed	Lani Joven
Philostrate, Chamberlain	Paul S. Becker
Lords and Ladies of the Court	Joe Cooper, Tom McNancy, Suzanne Miller, Christine Slater, Mary Jo Williams
Egeus, Father to Hermia	Greg Adams*
Hermia, in love with Lysander	Lori Keller
Lysander, Gentleman in love with Hermia	Christopher Jones
Demetrius, Gentleman in love with Hermia	Gregory Files
Helena, in love with Demetrius	Alisha Lenning
Quince, a carpenter	Brian T. Wagner, Richard Werner*
Bottom, a weaver	Philip Albaugh, Alan Dawson*
Flute, a bellows mender	Brian Ewing
Snout, a tinker	Bill Adams
Snug, a joiner	Toby Arebalo
Starveling, a tailor	Mike Troyer
First Fairy	Sarah Kilbane
Puck, Oberon's messenger	Kristine Engle
Oberon, King of Shadows	Victor Miller
Titania, Queen of Shadows	Deborah Wolfert
Peaseblossom, Titania's Attendant	Angela Howell
Cobweb, Titania's Attendant	Rose Kessing
Moth, Titania's Attendant	Mary Ann G. Hoopingarner
Mustardseed, Titania's Attendant	Janice Thompson
Scene:	Athens, and a wood nearby
Time:	The Past

The Department: 1987-1990

In the spring of 1987, Dean Daniel Van Tassle requested that I take the chairmanship of the Speech Communication and Theatre Department. In view of Dr. Martin's leave, I acceded to his wishes with the understanding that the appointment would last no longer than two years. To accept a longer term of office would put me too far behind in my theatre work.

My outward consent was just the opposite of my inner monologue, which went something like this: "I can't believe it! Ten years ago (1977), my duty prompted me to accept the same post, and it was a prelude to disaster–Financial Exigency and the Fine Arts Department. The responsibilities of office do not look more wonderful the second time around."

As I walked away from the dean's office, my mind was filled with reasons why I should have refused the request. In the first place, I took a dim view of any activity that stood between me and my work in the theatre. The theatre was a time-consuming area and I did not want to spend time on anything except teaching theatre courses and directing plays. In the second place, being the chairman of a department was a busy job with a lot of busy, albeit important, work attached to it. Furthermore, I had no training or ambitions as an administrator, and I certainly was not a visionary who had ideas about the direction in which to move a department.

My view was that any member of the teaching staff was capable of chairing the department. The chair is ultimately a coordinator and a communication conduit for information and ideas from other departments, divisions, and the administration. In fact, it is a job that every member of the department should experience. If each member of the department served a two- or three-year term as chairperson, it would give everybody a better understanding of the problems of management, provide insight into all the areas of governance of the college, and instill confidence and cooperation among the members of the staff. Another benefit of this arrangement is that no one faculty member would be taken away from his or her area of expertise for too long a time.

The school years moved on; I continued to hold my breath, but there was no recurrence of the discombobulating events of my previous term of office. In the spring of 1989, I walked into the dean's office, reminded him that my term as chairman of the department was over, and exhaled. He encouraged me to stay another year, but I diplomatically declined. I suggested he try my idea of a revolving chairmanship, and I recommended Jeff Harman as a likely candidate. Jeff relieved me of my duties in the fall of 1989.

The Plays: 1987–1990

1987–1988

The 1987-88 theatre season was almost "a classic Greek season." The first three major productions originated with ancient Greek authors: Aristophanes's *The Frogs,* Aesop's *Androcles and the Lion,* and Sophocles's *Antigone.* The fourth production was *The Glass Menagerie,* written by Tennessee Williams. That play is considered a classic of the American Theatre; therefore, we still can call the season "classical."

The season opened at the Little Theatre on October 14-17 with *The Frogs.* Ronald Lauck directed the play and supervised the technical aspects of the production. The setting resembled a Greek amphitheatre, costumes were modeled after the Greek style, and, although no masks were used, the choruses sang, chanted, and presented choreographed movements–an important element of Greek comedy.[65]

Mr. Lauck's "Director's Notes" explained,

> Aristophanes (446-385? B.C.) is the best known writer of Old Comedy. Old Comedy is characterized by a festive spirit and a choral format that seems to be the culmination of religious ceremony and ritual. This is rooted in "Komos," a ritual of Dionysian worship characterized by dressing as animals, dancing and singing and general merry making. Additional material is supplied by ritual fights or conflicts presented in the form of Agons [debates]. All of this is rooted in the phallic worship associated with the worship of Dionysus.

> Aristophanes has taken this history and combined it into over forty scripts of which only eleven remain extant. These scripts are characterized by the humor of burlesque and slapstick, sprinkled with critical social commentary and presented through the discipline of a poet.

Of these scripts, "The Frogs" deserves some special note. The production of "The Frogs" in 405 B.C. took first place at the Lenean Festival. The parabasis [choral ode in which the audience is directly addressed] is considered to be one of the best written and is a very patriotic plea. This may have been the reason that "The Frogs" was given the unique privilege of being performed again just a few days after the festival was completed. According to Gassner, "The Frogs" is also the first literary satire written. He also contends that it is the best, but one should perhaps leave that judgement to the audience. Is Gassner right?[66]

Carla Stalder's article, "*The Frogs* Hops to a Muskie Success," appeared in the year's *Muscoljuan.* In re-telling the story, she identified some of the cast members.

> It begins with the not-so-like appearance of Zeus' son, Dionysus (Gregg Suddeth) in a slapstick situation with his slave Zanthias (Rich Tremaglio). They have a continuing superiority contest throughout the first act.
> Then Dionysus takes a jaunt on the River Styx [possibly with the boatman Charon (Jon Jordan)] and there meets with the frogs and continues into Hades where he has many scrapes with disaster. In Hades he is searching for the poet to save his land. This leads to an overly melodramatic, yet quite humorous, contest between Euripides (Eric Green) and Aeschylus (Jon Jordan).
> While this play is very entertaining, the decision to do a Greek comedy did not come without expected difficulties. Student [assistant] director, Toby Arebalo, feels the cast " . . . had a lot of work to establish and understand their characters. They have to act and think as if they are back in ancient Greece." He also seems sure in stating that the actors are now very confident about their characters. "They do their job well."[67]

To complete the cast list for *The Frogs*, the following characters and members of the two choruses must be acknowledged: High Priest (Brian Wagner), Heracles (Phil Albaugh), Corpse (Eric Schwarzreich), Aeacus (Joe Rath), Maid (Wendy Pattison), Landlady (Diane Bourne), Plathane (Randi Porter), Pluto (Eric Schwarzreich), and Porters (Sam Hook and Rob Dauber). The Frog Chorus was represented by Colleen Karpac, Amy Brown, Bonnie King, Deborah Wolfert, and Shelly Coss. The Initiates Chorus included Alisha Lenning, Kristen Green, Vicki Vandenbark, Allison Kimmich, and Shelly Coss.

In one of the first plays dealing with literary criticism, Aristophanes has fun mocking playwrights, Aeschylus and Euripides, but he is oddly quiet about Sophocles, who was considered by the Greeks (and by most modern critics) to be the premiere writer of tragedy. Only at the end, after Aeschylus wins the debate about authorship, does he offer the chair magnanimously to Sophocles.[68]

The second Greek play to be performed was *Androcles and the Lion,* taken from an ancient story told by Aesop. It was modernized and adapted by Aurand Harris for audiences of all ages. Dr. Jerry Martin directed the play and supervised the technical aspects of the production, which played the Layton Theatre on November 18-21, in the evenings, and on Saturday, November 21, at 10:00 a.m. and 2:00 p.m., for the Children's Theatre Showcase.

Aesop, the writer of Greek fables, who lived from 620-560 B.C., told several stories about lions, and there have been countless renditions of his stories. One of the most famous is George Bernard Shaw's play, *Androcles and the Lion*. The Aurand Harris version, staged in the Layton Theatre by Dr. Martin, was a delightful and colorful version told in the style of *commedia dell'arte*. The stock characters, such as Pantalone, Isabella, Lelio, and the bragging Captain, get involved in their usual intrigue of the *commedia* art form. The ferocious-friendly Lion provides an unusual twist.[69]

Carla Stalder wrote the article, "'Androcles and the Lion' Goes Modern," which was published in the 1988 *Muscoljuan*. She delineated the plot and some of the characters. A set of lovers, Lilio (Rich Tremaglio) and Isabella (Alisha Lenning and Diane Bourne are doublecast), run away to be married because Isabella's uncle, Pantalone (Jon Jordan), will not agree to the marriage or give a dowry. Androcles (Brian Wagner), a slave whom Pantalone has hired to protect his niece and his gold, assists the young couple. It is on this journey that Androcles meets the Lion (Gregg Suddeth), who has a thorn in his paw. Androcles removes the thorn and the Lion is deeply indebted to him. When Pantalone finally catches Androcles, he has him thrown into the lion's den. There, Androcles again meets the Lion, who returns the kindness paid to him earlier by Androcles. Both are eventually freed.[70]

Cast and crew members not already mentioned included Gregg Suddeth, who also played the Prologue, and Rob Dauber, who played the Captain. Movement for the play was choreographed by Kristine Engle, Alisha Lenning, Diane Bourne, Philip Albaugh, and Kristen Green. Piano and keyboard music was supplied by Kathleen Wasil. Kristen Green assisted the director and Philip Albaugh was the stage manager and production manager.

Only the theater could actually bring to life the comedy and wonderful sense of humor that permeates *The Frogs* and *Androcles and the Lion*. Nevertheless, the photo essays in the *Muscoljuan* that accompany Miss Stalder's articles do convey some idea of the hilarious good time that the actors and audience experienced. Carla Stalder's review of *Androcles and the Lion* appeared in the *Black and Magenta*: "Modern Adaptation of Fable Appeals to Adults as Well as Kids."[71]

The third classic Greek play of the season was Jean Anouilh's version of *Antigone*. I directed and designed the tragedy, with technical direction by Ronald Lauck; the drama was performed in the Layton Theatre on February 24-27.

The original *Antigone* was written by the Greek author, Sophocles, in 441 B.C., as part of the Theban Legend of Oedipus. Oedipus, King of Thebes, was the most unfortunate of men. He unknowingly killed his father, married his mother, and had two sons and two daughters by her: Eteocles, Polyneices, Antigone, and Ismene. Upon discovering the incest, Oedipus blinded himself. Guided by his two daughters, he was doomed to walk the earth. Oedipus eventually gained sainthood through his penitence, endurance, and stoicism. The two sons fought over the control of Thebes, until both were killed; then their uncle, Creon, took the throne.

The story of *Antigone* begins after the civil war in which the two brothers killed each other, permitting Creon to rule the kingdom. Eteocles is given a state funeral, but the rebel, Polyneices, is left unburied because he was considered a traitor who had attacked his own city. Antigone, in spite of the edict against Polyneices's interment, buries him. Creon could not have predicted the chain of events that quickly follows: Creon has Antigone sealed in a cave as punishment; she hangs herself rather than die a slow death from starvation; Creon's son, Haemon, who loves Antigone, finds her body and stabs himself to death; Eurydice, Creon's wife and mother of Haemon, kills herself after learning of her son's suicide. Creon becomes the most miserable of men.[72]

Allardyce Nicoll sheds further light on Anouilh's *Antigone:*

> Antigone goes, as in the Sophoclean drama, to bury her brother, Polyneices, but this she does not so much because of devotion to his memory, but because of her dissatisfaction with the crass, timorous, unadventuresome society around her. Even when she is offered mercy by Creon, she refuses it; for her, too, death alone can hold inviolate the serenity of spirit that has come to her from her daring. She goes, as she tells Creon, to "a realm which you cannot enter with all your wrinkled wisdom."[73]

Antigone's defiance of the King and of the State placed her in the role of a rebel with a cause. She practiced what Thoreau called civil disobedience, and what is today known as civil rights advocacy. Jean Anouilh found the story intriguing and adapted it to the situation of Paris under Nazi control in 1943. To register his dissatisfaction with the government of South Africa in 1973, Athol Fugard used *Antigone* in the play titled *The Island.* Every age has its Antigone.[74]

In her *Muscoljuan* article, "Muskie Production of Greek Play Offers Moral Lesson with Story," Colleen Karpac quoted Deborah Wolfert (Antigone) as saying,

> This story is important to me because there is more to it than just Antigone's desire to keep her brothers buried. It has to do with standing up for what you think regardless of your position and your relationship with the person you are up against.

Antigone (Anouilh), 1988. Set in Nazi-occupied Paris. When friendly persuasion fails, physical force is worth a try. Antigone (D. Wolfert) and Creon (V. Miller). *Theatre file photo courtesy M.C. Public Relations Office.*

[Since Colleen doesn't quote me (Dr. Hill) directly, I can take the liberty of interpolating and interpreting some of my own remarks.]

"According to the director, Dr. Hill, the play provided students taking Civilization [and other classes] the opportunity to see the actual work [play] that was being discussed in their classes." It also gave students an opportunity to experience a play from another age, re-interpreted in a modern format. I hope it will help create more culturally aware individuals.

The article continued, "The actors who ranged from freshmen to senior[s], and from communication majors to chemistry majors, are all talented." The play gave them a chance to stretch their imaginations and challenge their creativity. "One actor, Rich Tremaglio, reported, "' . . . it [the play] went along by leaps and bounds and everyone got into the production.'"[75]

A review of the production appeared in the *Black and Magenta* under the title "Greek Play *Antigone* Adapts to Setting of Nazi Occupation of World War II."[76]

The cast for Anouilh's interpretation of this play included the following: Chorus (R. Tremaglio), Antigone (D. Wolfert), Nurse (Catherine Coss), Ismene (A. Lenning), Haemon (B. Dalton), Creon (V. Miller), Page (C. Koetting), First Guard (D. Nemeth), Second Guard (P. Albaugh), Third Guard (J. Ransom), Messenger (C. Jones), and Eurydice (J. Suschil).

It's hard to believe, but it may have been as long as ten years since our theatre had been involved in a dinner theatre. At any rate, the last one that immediately comes to my mind occurred when the cast and crew of *Godspell* offered the public a dinner and a show, in April of 1978. So, once again, (April 1988) the Muskingum Players Dramatic Society offered visitors for Parents Weekend the opportunity of attending a dinner and a show! Carla Stalder broke the news with her article in the *Black and Magenta:* "Dinner Theatre Planned for 1988 Parents Weekend"[77]

The players chose an American classic, one that had, as its core, the relationship between a parent and her offspring. *The Glass Menagerie* by Tennessee Williams was directed by Kristine Engle and Deborah Wolfert, who were assisted by Alisha Lenning. The set design was done by Christopher Jones, and the technical aspects were supervised by Ronald Lauck, who was the Players' advisor.

Under the watchful eye of Mr. Lauck, the main basketball court in the John Glenn Gymnasium was turned into a dinner theatre. A platform stage was erected on the north end, and the dining tables were placed facing it. As I recall, there were a lot of tables because the reservations came flooding in. On April 15, the audience sat down to dinner at 6:00 p.m., and at 8:15 p.m., the lights dimmed and the audience grew silent as Tom Wingfield (Christopher Jones) introduced the play with his first monologue. Then his mother, Amanda Wingfield (Deborah Wolfert), appeared with Laura, her daughter (Kristine Engle). Kelly Snyder played the Gentleman Caller, Jim O'Connor.

After the first performance, the set and all the stage appurtenances were moved to the Little Theatre for the usual four-night run on April 20-23. Carla Stalder grabbed her pen again and wrote another favorable review, entitled "Muskingum College Players Perform Classic."[78]

Tennessee Williams has long been recognized as one of the century's great American playwrights. His drama *The Glass Menagerie* has been popular with the American public since its first production on Broadway in 1945. The story, which involves the clashes among a mother, daughter, son, and a Gentleman Caller, strikes a familiar chord in American culture. The themes these people illustrate are illusions of the past, dreams of the present, and hopes for the future; these themes are favorites of college audiences. The play was an excellent choice for Parents Weekend, and a fine note on which to end the season.[79]

It had been a good year for the theatre, but it had been a bad year for me. In November of 1987, I was on my way back from a film class at Ohio State University. I stopped by the farm in Crooksville to visit my mother and brother.

When I entered the house, my brother Gene was watching television. Mother took me aside to say, "All I ask is that I be able to live until your brother is sixty-five." (That would be in February, I thought.) She continued, "Then he will be able to get his Social Security, and that should give him enough to live on." (My mind went racing. The farm had not been worked for years, and she and my brother were living on her Social Security. During her entire youth, my mother had worked in Grandpa's hotel, until she graduated from high school and married. She remained a housewife until her three sons were grown. During World War II, we lived in Grand Rapids, Michigan, where she sewed parachutes in a defense factory, while her two older sons were in the service. After the war, the family moved to Zanesville, and she went to work at Timken Roller Bearing plant in order to help me (her youngest son) through Muskingum. I looked at my mother closely. She looked lonely and worn. I recalled what Agnes Moorehead had said the last year of her life, "I'm tired into the future." Mother looked tired.

At that moment, Mother broke into my thoughts. "This year, Christmas will not be like the Christmases we've had before." She put her hand on my cheek and looked at me knowingly. Less than a month later, on December 22, she had a stroke. On the way to Bethesda Hospital, she stopped breathing and the emergency squad revived her. Although hospitalized, she never fully recovered and, on February 10, 1988, she died. That day was my brother's sixty-fifth birthday. She had timed it to the day! She was right about Christmases, too. They have never been the same.

I was very fortunate to have the support of the full department during this period. Mr. Lauck stepped in and took some rehearsals, and the cast and crew of *Antigone* played beautifully for him. When I returned several days later for the final rehearsals, the play had continued to grow. I thank God for that cast. I had chosen well! They were strong–Wolfert and Miller especially–but also Tremaglio, Lenning, and Jones. All of them possessed a quality of steel that gave the play a sense of endurance under duress.

The Saturday Showcase Children's Theatre Series

During the 1987-88 theatre season, the Saturday Showcase Children's Theatre Series became part of the Appalachian Children's Theatre Series, which was sponsored by Rio Grande College, Ironton Council for the Arts, and the Speech Communication and Theatre Department. Performances were held in the Layton Theatre at 10:00 a.m. and 2:00 p.m. on each of the Saturdays indicated:

Mummerstock by Stromberg and Cooper .... November 7
Androcles and the Lion by Muskingum College Theatre .... November 21
Writings by Children by Child's Play Touring Theatre of Chicago .... March 26
Pinocchio by the Columbus Junior Theatre of the Arts .... April 30

 1988–1989

A R. Gurney's, *The Dining Room,* was director-designer Ronald Lauck's choice to open the 1988-89 theatre season on October 5-8 in the Layton Theatre. It was a unique choice, because the main character was an "inanimate object." Nevertheless, this inanimate object had the ability to speak through the generations that passed in and out of the environs of its formal and former "elegant" space.

In his "Director's Note," Mr. Lauck explained how the audience concentrates, not on a single set of characters at any one time, or even on one event, but on the dining room itself; " . . . we see the dining room as the single unity of the play and interpret its melancholy as we call on our own memories to discover the truth for us in the dining room."[80]

The dining room, carefully designed by Mr. Lauck, changed over the years, just as the generations of people who passed through it changed. The dining room which the audience saw was a typical upper-middle-class room in which the family gathered for breakfast, lunch, and dinner, or for special occasions. The action which took place in the room was not the traditional plot of connected incidents. It was a series of scenes–vignettes in which single situations clarified character interaction and the passage of time. Instead of the usual cast of individual actors, there was an ensemble peopling the room. The actors also changed roles and personalities. Seven actors played the roles of more than fifty characters, in various scenes that portrayed events of family life: Youth coming-of-age, Middle-Age compromising ideals, and Old Age struggling with Death. The human condition was exposed in all its strengths and weaknesses—youthful defiance, adult equivocation, and elderly resignation. All of these events and attendant emotions came together in sadness and joy to form a touching, humorous theatrical experience.

The articles by Abgela Neff[81] and Kathy Lacey[82] for the *Black and Magenta* pointed out the "nostalgia" and the "extraordinary" values of the production. They also praised the acting ensemble, which included Rob Dauber, Kristen Green, Jon E. Jordan, II, Allison Kimmich, John Molino, Joseph Rath, and Deborah Wolfert.

For her senior seminar, Deborah Wolfert directed Jean Genet's, *The Maids*. Genet (1910-1986), a French novelist and playwright, was also a convicted criminal and thief. He was released from a term of life imprisonment in 1947, through the intervention of some of France's leading writers. He is best known for his plays which have achieved popular success: *The Maids* (1949), *Deathwatch* (1954), *The Balcony* 1959), and *The Screens* (1962). Because his subjects concern conflicts between reality and illusion, and his belief in the relative nature of good and evil, his work is classified as Theatre of the Absurd, along with that of such authors as Samuel Beckett, Eugene Ionesco, Harold Pinter, and Edward Albee.[83] Theatre of the Absurd is a theatre of extremes, iconoclastic in nature. It is a theatre of alienation rather than of identification. The absurdist theatre alienates the audience *from*, rather than permits it to identify *with*, its characters. The characters are designed to shock, irritate, antagonize or anger the audience in order to keep it in a state of suspended objectivity. The absurdists claim that they make it easier to understand the absurdity of the world in which we live: an unfriendly world of repression and hypocrisy, against which we are helpless in our attempts to gain freedom. Genet, more than most, knew the repressions of society and the illusion of freedom that could be gained in prison, through the use of role-playing and drugs.

Deborah commented on her play:

> The maids know that to rebel is the only way to free themselves from oppression. Due to their subservient position, however, they can only act out their passionate jealousies amongst themselves in "the ceremony," as they call it. Within this play-acting, reality becomes confused with illusion, and the maids only inflict destruction upon themselves.
>
> For example, during one of the "ceremonies" before the start of the play, the play-acting maids had written and sent falsely incriminating letters to the police, naming Madame's lover as a thief. This action, which happened as part of the maids' illusion caused the very real action of Madame's lover being thrown in jail. The action which unfolds in the play shows the results of their game.[84]

The Maids was performed in the Layton Theatre on November 22-25. The action of the drama was set in Paris, an evening in the late 1930's in Madame's bedroom. In this confined space, the two maids, Claire (Tracy Moreau) and Solange (Suzanne Miller), served the wealthy Madame (Leilani Joven) tea and bowed to her every wish. When the phone rang, Madame had to rush to the jail to be by her lover's side. Then the maids took turns dressing in Madame's elegant clothes and serving her. Their charades grew more and more elaborate and grotesque. The tension grew to equal that of a psychological thriller. At the end, there was no way out of the illusion, except death.

Derek Whitehead did the scenography, and Mr. Lauck was the production supervisor. Allison Kimmich wrote a penetrating article on "*The Maids*: Genet's Web of Illusion," for the *Black and Magenta*.[85]

The 1988-89 theatre season ended with Neil Simon's, *The Star-Spangled Girl,* a sure-fire comic hit. It was directed and costumed by Alisha Lenning; she was assisted with scene design by Ronald Lauck, and lighting design by Philip Albaugh. The production was sponsored by Muskingum Players as a dinner theatre for Parents Weekend. *The Glass Menagerie* had worked out so well the previous year, that the Parents Weekend Committee wanted to repeat the same type of entertainment. The Muskingum Players were delighted to oblige and had hopes that the event might become a tradition.

Alisha Lenning responded to the spirit of the play in her "Director's Notes":

> *The Star-Spangled Girl* takes us back to 1966, a time when it was "hip" to be politically radical, and when the Stars and Stripes, Motherhood, and Apple Pie seemed to be out dated. *The Star-Spangled Girl* was Neil Simon's answer to this prevalent attitude. His star-spangled girl next door and the variation of the girl gets boy theme are as patriotically American as . . . well, "Chicken Chow Mein."[86]

The cast, composed of John E. Jordan, II (Andrew Hobart), Eric Green (Norman Cornell), and Shelly Peters (Sophie Rauschmeyer), responded in kind for a successful production. The regular run-of-show for the comedy was held at the Little Theatre on March 8-11. The play was then transported to the John Glenn Gymnasium on April 14 for the dinner theatre performance of Parents Weekend. The same formula that proved amenable last year was followed. Dinner was served at 6:00 p.m. and the curtain rose at 8:15 p.m.

The play proved so successful that the actors were requested to perform it again for Alumni Weekend, in the Layton Theatre on June 9-10.

The Saturday Showcase Children's Theatre Series

During the 1988-1989 theatre season, the Saturday Showcase Children's Theatre Series, part of the Appalachian Children's Theatre Series, was funded in part by grants from the Ohio Arts Council, the Martha Holden Jennings Foundation, and GTE North. GTE North, the Ohio Theatre Alliance and Ohio Reading Service provided audio description. Performances were held in the Layton Theatre at 10:00 a.m. and 2:00 p.m. on the Saturdays indicated:

 1989–1990

The 1989-90 theatre season was a season of infinite variety in one sense, yet remarkably unified in another. Each of the five plays that were produced represented a different genre, place, and time. Moliére's *The Learned Ladies,* a comic satire, is set in a wealthy, middle-class home of late seventeenth century Paris. *A Doll's House,* a problem play written by Henrik Ibsen, takes place in the Helmer's apartment, somewhere in Scandinavia at the end of the nineteenth century. Ugo Betti's *Summertime*, an idyllic romantic comedy, represents the Italian Alps in the early 1900's. *You're a Good Man, Charlie Brown,* a cartoon musical, is a product of the USA in the middle of the twentieth century. *The Secret Princess,* an original children's theatre play, written by senior theatre major, Alisha Lenning, is set in a China of the past, but it is " . . . not limited to the past nor to that part of the world."

All of the plays are related, in some way, to social problems. *The Learned Ladies* ridicules false and useless learning; it was aimed specifically at a certain group in Louis XIV's court. *A Doll's House* concerns individual human rights or women's rights; the interpretation is a matter of choice. *Summertime* deals with the redemptive quality of love. *You're a Good Man, Charlie Brown* is a shot-gun approach to character, social situations, power, and politics. *The Secret Princess* provides social commentary on human rights by giving specific attention to women's rights.

Moliére's *The Learned Ladies* (1672) opened the season. This verse comedy was first performed by Moliére's *Troupe du Roi* on March 11, 1672, at the *Theatre du Palais-Royal* in Paris. Moliére played Chrysale, and his wife played Henriette. The play was well-received.

The Muskingum production was directed and designed by me, assisted by Ronald Lauck as technical director. It was staged in-the-round on October 11-14, 1989, at the Little Theatre. The production used the version of Moliére's comedy, which Richard Wilbur had translated into English rhyming verse. The Muskingum audience was already familiar with Moliére's work, having witnessed *The Misanthrope*, (1972), *Tartuffe*, (1974), and *The School for Wives,* (1986). All of these plays attacked some aberrant social characteristic of Louis XIV's court. *The Learned Ladies* criticized a clique of men and women courtiers who had grown obsessed with learning for learning's sake; some of them had taken learning to another level: for the prestige inherent in knowledge. Moliére decided to let the hot air out of their pedantry.

The Learned Ladies deals with a subject close to the lives of college students who are directly concerned with education. Moliére's comedy mocks the pseudo-intellectual who pretends to know everything, but really knows little; who learns only from books, if at all; and who knows nothing of real knowledge and of its practical relationship to successful living.

The performance of the students cast in the play made Moliére's intent clear to the audience. The plot concerns Chrysale (Matthew Hiner), a middle-class philistine "who uses a book to press his neckcloth." His wife, Philaminte (Suzanne Miller), wishes to create a *salon*, or school, for learning, in order to advance herself in society and use learning as a means to "avenge her sex." Philaminte's sister-in-law, Belise (Alisha Lenning), is a grotesque eccentric who joins the *salon*; she is under the delusion that every man is in love with her, but he is too proud to let it be made public. Philaminte's daughter, Armande (Tracie Moreau), another pseudo-scholar, becomes a neurotic *poseur*. Two men who become trapped by the lure of false knowledge are Trissotin (Joseph Rath), a wit, and Vadius (Robert Grow), a pedant.[88]

The Learned Ladies, 1988. The Notary (D. Clever) who is to make out the marriage license for the wedding of Henriette (B. Hammer) becomes the center of a quarrel between Chrysale, her father (M. Hiner) and her mother, Philaminte (S. Miller). *Theatre file photo courtesy Ronald N. Lauck.*

Ariste (Philip Albaugh), Chrysale's brother, tries to reason with Chrysale and criticizes him for giving Philaminte too much freedom. However, Ariste's attempts to bring order into the household are unsuccessful. In the midst of all this affectation, Henriette (Beth Hammer), the younger daughter of Chrysale and Philaminte, clearly understands the difference between real learning and affectation. She is in love with

Clitandre (Thomas Perorazio), who also realizes the problems created by the false school of learning. He refuses to have anything to do with the school's impractical interpretation of books. A direct contrast to the *salon* appears in the ungrammatical, but practical maid, Martine (Shelly Peters). Two other members of the household who maintain their distance from the school are Lepine (Samuel Hook), a servant, and A Notary (Daniel Clever).

Moliére's comic characters have such exaggerated obsessions, that usually an outside force is required to resolve the plot.[89] In this instance, someone must prevent the false marriage of Henriette to Trissotin. Ariste becomes the instrument of resolution by presenting false letters to indicate that Chrysale has lost all of his money. Trissotin, who had hoped that a wealthy dowry would come with his bride-to-be (Henriette) drops his suit and Clitandre wins his true love.

Two reviews of *The Learned Ladies* appeared in the *Black and Magenta*: one by J. LaRue[90] and the other by Kevin Moreau.[91]

Henrik Ibsen is a playwright who had a great deal of influence on the style and content of plays. To many authorities, he is regarded as the father of modern drama. If I am not mistaken, the last time an Ibsen play was performed at Muskingum was in 1929, when *Pillars of Society* appeared on the production calendar. The same play had been produced ten years earlier in 1919, and in the interim, one other Ibsen play, *The Lady from the Sea,* was performed in 1927. *An Enemy of the People*, another Ibsen play, adapted by Arthur Miller, was produced in 1963. *A Doll's House* (1879) had never received a full-scale production at the college, nor has its counterpart, *Ghosts* (1881). Both of these plays are considered landmarks in the formation of the modern problem play (a play which deals with controversial social issues). In the case of *A Doll's House,* the problem which some call "women's rights" is, in Ibsen's words, " . . . a question of human rights." In the words of the heroine, Nora, the play is about what a marriage must be—"a true and lasting relationship that allows both partners their human rights."[92]

In an historical sense, the production of *A Doll('s) House* on November 15-18, 1989, at the Layton Theatre, was an important occasion. Ronald Lauck, the director, designed the set and supervised the technical elements of the play. The costume design and lighting design were done by Alisha Lenning and Susan Murphy, respectively.

The action for *A Doll House* (the director preferred to use "Doll" as an adjective, instead of a possessive noun, for his interpretation) takes place in the Helmer's apartment, somewhere in Scandinavia toward the end of the nineteenth century. The story of the play and its student cast follows. "Towald," or Torvald, Helmer (Tom Perorazio) is about to become the head of a bank. He treats his wife, Nora (Alisha Lenning), as if she were a little doll who lives in a doll's house. The duties of the wife are carried out by the servants, who include a maid, Helene (Beth Belanger), and a nurse, Anne-Marie (Lynn Blood). The nurse has charge of the three Helmer children: Yvonne (Erin Blood), Elsa (Jennie Blood), and Emma (Emily Blood). Nora has always been cared for in this way. Even in her father's house, she was like a pet, pampered and spoiled. During the Victorian era, women were not supposed to concern themselves with affairs of this world. Their world was in the home, where they were to make the surroundings pleasant for the husband.

However, Nora is more than a doll. Secretly, she has a mind of her own, and she has desires which are unknown to her husband. Early in their marriage, previous to the action of the play, Nora ventured into the world. Her husband was ill and the doctor ordered him to take a vacation to sunny Italy, in order to cure the malady. Since they did not have the money, Nora borrowed money from a lawyer, Nils Krogstadt (Sam Hook), unaware of the law that women couldn't borrow money under their own signature. The lawyer let her sign her father's name as bond. Later, during the action of the play, Krogstadt desperately needs a job. He threatens to reveal Nora's forgery unless she influences her husband to give him a position in the bank. When Torvald discovers the forgery, he angrily denounces Nora and her indiscretion, because she has jeopardized his position. Her criminal action makes her an unfit mother for the children.

A Doll's House, 1989. Nils Krogstadt (S. Hook) and Nora Helmer (A. Lenning). *Photo courtesy Ronald N. Lauck.*

Torvald's violent reaction to the discovery forces Nora into a realization of the truth: her life has been spent in a false situation. She has only been playing at being a dutiful daughter and a submissive wife. Her husband does not recognize her as a real person, who is his wife and the mother of his children. She cannot continue to live a lie. She leaves her husband and the doll house to live in the real world, to learn what it is like to have thoughts of her own, and to manage her own existence.

The play contains two very important scientific theories of the nineteenth century: the importance of environment and the role of heredity in shaping a person's character. Nora has been a puppet in a world that her father and her husband created for their own pleasure and comfort, without regard for her desires and needs as a fellow human being. Nora's innocent and loving act of borrowing the money is looked upon as a result of a deceitful nature which has kept the forgery a secret. Since Torvald believes Nora's deceitful nature, might be inherited by the children, he must watch the children carefully for signs of a similar tendency, and he must keep Nora away from the children.[93]

In the light of our modern world, all of the husband's actions seem melodramatic, however, the way in which Ibsen manages to convey the story, Torvald's actions are naturally motivated by his character and milieu of the period. Working with the old Scribean model of the well-made play, which was obviously constructed to have a climax at the end of each act, Ibsen created three dimensional characters with individualized and highly motivated reasons for their actions.[94] Mr. Lauck speaks specifically about Ibsen's writing skills in his "Director's Notes."

> As one directs *A Doll House* the skill of Ibsen as a playwright becomes apparent. He very carefully knits his story and message together into a cohesive script that takes advantage of the tools of a playwright.
>
> For instance, we begin to see how many different levels of communication are at work at the point of attack. Krogstadt appears briefly and nonchalantly. Nora engages in a symbolic act, she stokes the fireplace just as Ibsen stokes the action of the story. By watching and listening carefully, the audience can see this skill showing again and again.
>
> Besides working with a skilled playwright, a director is always pleased to work with dedicated students who are learning skills in theatre. The two student designers, the cast, and the student technicians listed all have helped greatly to make this show possible.
>
> With your participation as audience members, our work becomes complete. Enjoy the show![95]

The remaining three members of the cast were A Porter (Jeff Porter), Kristine Linde, Nora's confidante (Nancy Miller), and Dr. Rank, a family friend (Rob Dauber).

The production of *A Doll House* was beautifully designed, well-directed, and well-acted. Susan Murphy wrote an informative article about the play for the November issue of the *Black and Magenta: "A Doll's House* to Open Wednesday.[96]

The second semester of the 1989-90 theatre season opened on February 21-24 with a production of Ugo Betti's *Summertime*, which was staged in the Layton Theatre. I directed and designed the scenery; Ronald Lauck served as technical director of the production.

I had wanted to do *Summertime* for some time. There were several elements of the production which came together in 1990 that made the production feasible. First of all, I had the right people for the various cast members. It is a play that requires principals *and* supporting cast members who possess a certain quality of what Stanislavsky called "charm." *Summertime* is a charming play that must be told by charming people. Even the "blocking characters," who are sometimes called "villains," have to possess an element of charm. Secondly, I could design the show and direct it, but I knew I would never have time to execute the three different sets. I needed a technical director for that task. With Mr. Lauck on board, the play became feasible.

After Pirandello, Ugo Betti, is recognized as the most popular modern Italian playwright. Betti was trained in law, and after the First World War, he became a magistrate in the Italian justice system. His occupation had a permanent influence on the substance of his plays, which usually present individuals facing alternatives to evil. His most popular dramas, *Corruption in the Palace of Justice* (1944), *The Queen*

Summertime, 1990. Francesca (B. Hammer) and Alberto (J. Shade) in the Italian Alps. *Photo courtesy Ronald N. Lauck.*

and the Rebels (1949), and *Crime on Goat Island* (1950), try to determine responsibility for some incident. The search continues in ever-widening circles of people until society, as a whole, shares in the responsibility.[97]

Betti must have been on vacation when he wrote *Summertime* (1937), which he calls "An Idyll in Three Acts," and which is literally translated, "Land of Holidays." It is a lovely pastoral of a young girl and boy who fall in love, and of their two aunts who help their niece and nephew along the way. In many ways, the play has the tone and atmosphere of Edmund Rostand's *The Romancers* and of the American musical, *The Fantasticks*, which is based on the Rostand play. *Summertime* reveals a less taxed and more relaxed Betti, as he illustrates another theme: " . . . the redemptive and transforming power of love, and a belief in the power of the human imagination to transform the quality of life."[98]

A summary of the plot discloses the romantic comedy genre, but it cannot recapture the tender simplicity of the style, nor the gentle capriciousness of the dialogue and actions of the characters.

It is the early 1900's, in a rural district of the Italian Alps. Aunt Cleofe (Susan Murphy) and her niece, Francesca (Beth Hammer), live in a cottage next door to Aunt Ofelia (Shelly Peters) and her nephew, Alberto (Jerry Shade). They are preparing for the annual summer picnic to the mountains. Ofelia and Alberto are ostensibly preparing for the picnic, but it is not known whether Alberto will go along. This fact upsets Francesca, because she has been in love with Alberto since the first grade. Aunt Cleofe tells Francesca two ways in which she can get Alberto to propose: make him jealous by pretending to love someone else, or sprain her ankle so Alberto will have to carry her. Francesca says it will be safer if she proposes to Alberto. At this point, the maid, Adelaide (Amy Brown), brings out the tarts, and the smell of the sweets attracts Alberto. The Postman (Mike Whicker) brings Alberto two telegrams notifying him that Naomi (Tracie Moreau) and her brother, Consalvo (Dan Clever), are on their way to see him. Then the Doctor (Matt Hiner), who loves Francesca, arrives to drive them to the picnic.

Knowing of the embarrassment he will face upon the arrival of Naomi and Consalvo, Alberto springs into action when the Doctor arrives. He rushes the others off to the mountains just prior to the arrival of Naomi and Consalvo. They, too, follow in haste.

When Francesca and Alberto are alone at their favorite spot in the mountains, he describes himself accurately, "I trail disaster with me wherever I go."[99] This is Alberto's way of introducing the series of accidents that occurred earlier in the week when he went job hunting in the city. When he was interviewing for a job with Consalvo, who owns a bank, he met Naomi, Consalvo's sister, a young widow. They got on famously together and they all went on an outing to the beach. Alberto took Naomi rowing on the water, and a storm caused them to wreck the boat. They spent the night in a hut, where the owner found them trespassing and called the police. When the newspaper reporters published pictures of them in their bathing suits, they became the topic of a comic song which was sung in a revue. Naomi felt compromised and wanted Alberto to marry her. So does Consalvo because Naomi's relatives threatened to withdraw all their money from his bank if the two don't marry. This would cause Consalvo's bank to fail.

When Francesca hears this story, she tries to rescue Alberto as she has always done. She proposes to him, but he misunderstands. He thinks she wants him to marry Naomi! Frustrated, Francesca inadvertently pushes Alberto off a cliff, but he is caught by some nettles. Just then, Naomi catches up to them and denounces Francesca as a jealous hypocrite. This makes Alberto angry and he rebukes Naomi.

Embarrassed and angry, Francesca runs away. Alberto catches up with her at a farmhouse in the valley. Naomi and Consalvo arrive shortly thereafter. When Francesca believes Alberto is about to accept Naomi, she pretends to be pregnant. When this trick does not work, she pretends to favor the Doctor. This pretense does work! Alberto becomes jealous. Naomi and Consalvo give up and go back to the city. The Farmer (Ryan Miller) brings them coffee, and Francesca makes Alberto comfortable in front of the fire.

Muskingum Players chose *You're a Good Man, Charlie Brown* for their spring production and Parents Weekend dinner theatre. The show is based on the comic strip "Peanuts," as conceived by Charles W. Schulz, with music, lyrics, and stage adaptation by Clark Gesner. Ronald Lauck, advisor of the Players, directed and supervised the technical work for the production. He made the show extremely portable because, on April 4 and 5, it opened at the Little Theatre, then on Friday, April 6, the set was moved to John Glenn Gymnasium for the dinner theatre, and on April 7, it was moved back to the Little Theatre for a Saturday afternoon matinee. There were four designers for the show: Mr. Lauck, Shelly Peters, Tracy Early, and me. Mary Ryan accompanied the cast on the piano. The cast of "Peanuts" characters consisted of Charlie Brown (Michael Sickle), Linus (Jon Jordan), Schroeder (Joseph B. Rath), Lucy (Diane Bourne), Patty (Beth Belanger), and Snoopy (Christine Slater).

Since the time the comic strip first appeared in October of 1950, Schulz's creations have delighted and puzzled their audiences. Every character is so highly individualized, that it is difficult to fashion a meaning that fits all. Tony Norman, a *Post-Gazette* staff writer, explains.

As the neurotic heirs of a psychoanalytic age, we're more than willing to acknowledge a part of Lucy's narcissism as our own. What choice do we have? We'll
even own up to Linus' cosmic insecurity if we're cornered. You'd be hard pressed to
find anyone who doesn't admire Snoopy's pragmatism and the ruthless efficiency
of his fantasy life as he "battles" the Red Baron, only to be "shot down" over the
neighborhood pumpkin patch, his doghouse trailing smoke.[100]

The experts have all had a turn at dissecting "Peanuts" for meaning and understanding. Norman continues,

Psychologist, philosophers and social scientists fall over themselves trying to
explain the appeal of "Peanuts" according to the biases of their particular disciplines. During the Cold War, the Soviets and the Chinese Communist Party under
Chairman Mao denounced Snoopy and the gang as shock troops of a "capitalistic
reactionary ideology."[101]

Charles Schulz was the only person who could speak with any authority on the
subject of the meaning of "Peanuts." Unfortunately Mr. Schulz died in February of
2000, leaving no successor to continue the strip. Nevertheless, the *Pittsburgh Post-
Gazette* ran the final and farewell "Peanuts" cartoon on February 13, a two-and-one-
half page spread of various articles about Schulz and his cartoon life, and a promise to
run a series of "Peanuts" reprints everyday.

After my experience with *You're a Good Man, Charlie Brown,* I feel as qualified
as any to offer a few remarks on the stage presentation. There is something very true
about every character and every incident that occurs in the story. Every time any
character believes that he or she has found the answer to some puzzlement, it back-
fires. I believe it has something to do with the fallibility of the infallible. It is also
apparent that no matter what happens, all the characters end up in the same boat.
Perhaps *togetherness* is the one word that epitomizes the continuing story of Charlie
and his friends, and of "Peanuts."

The Secret Princess, an original script written, directed and designed by Alisha
Lenning, heralded the end of the 1989-90 season, and my third decade as Director of
Theatre at Muskingum College. This production was Alisha's senior seminar presen-
tation. Dr. Martin was the faculty supervisor, and Mr. Lauck was the lighting designer.
Lynn Blood designed the make-up, and Jim Whitehair and Diane Bourne supplied the
music.

The cast members for the show are listed in order of appearance: Props personnel
and assistant directors (Nancy Miller and Stephanie Rankin), Chong, stage manager
(Shun Lai Yang), Kiri (Jessica Hazard), Han (Jeremy Morrow), Empress (Kathy
Wallace), Machi (Sarah Pauley), U-Chin (Jacklyn Hazard), Maid (Leah Pauley),
Emperor (Joshua Freker), Executioner (Trina Crosland), and Eiken (Katie Bush).

Alisha made the following comments on the play in her "Director's Note":

In the orient women once held so low a position in society that the killing of
girl babies was acceptable and not uncommon. This attitude toward women in the
East is unfortunately not limited to the past nor to that part of the world. Although a
girl is not put to death, she is often restricted by traditional attitudes even in modern
society. The major purpose of this production is to encourage all children, both boys
and girls, to see that members of both sexes can be whatever they want to be.

Many costumes in this production are authentic, direct from Hong Kong. I would
like to offer a special thanks to Kwai Fong Ng, Maria Lee, and Delia Poon for their
contributions in this effort.[102]

The Secret Princess played the Layton Theatre, April 18-21, with a 3:00 p.m. matinee April 21 for Saturday Showcase. Allison Kimmich wrote an articulate feature story on *The Secret Princess* and Lenning's direction of the play.[103]

The Saturday Showcase Children's Theatre Series

During the 1989-90 theatre season, the Saturday Showcase Children's Theatre Series, part of the Appalachian Children's Theatre Series, was funded in part by grants from the Ohio Arts Council and GTE. The performances included a third showing; therefore, curtain times were arranged for 10:00 a.m. 1:00 p.m. and 3:00 p.m. in the Layton Theatre on the Saturdays indicated:

REFERENCES (The Plays: 1980–1990)

1   "Two Productions Open '80-'81 Theatre Season: An Original Revue, *An Evening of Noel Coward*," *Cue,* Muskingum College, New Concord, Ohio, Fall, 1980, p. 1.

2   Carole and Jake Dorn, Department of History, Wright State University, Dayton, Ohio, October 24, 1980 in a letter to Kathleen O'Brien, found in her Production Book for *The Corn is Green* A Directing Seminar, October 1980.

3   Stanley Green, *The World of Musical Comedy: The Story of the American Musical Stage as Told Through the Careers of Its Foremost Composers and Lyricists,* Fourth Edition, Revised and Enlarged (New York: DeCapo Press, Inc., 1980), pp. 290-291.

4   Deron Mikal, Guest Reviewer, "One of the Most Significant Productions in Years," *The Daily Jeffersonian,* Cambridge, Ohio, Friday, May 1, 1981.

5   Jeanne Fierstos, "The '*Prisoner*' in Review," *Black and Magenta,* October 16, 1981, p. 4.

6   Kelly Clevenger, "Faculty Play Enjoyed," *B&M,* February 19, 1982, p. 8.

7   A. L. Rowse, *The Annotated Shakespeare, Vol. I, The Comedies* (New York: Clarkson N. Potter, Inc., Publishers, 1978), p. 278.

8   Ibid., pp. 278-279.

9   Mary Sykes, "Spoon River: A Director's Note," Original Program for *Spoon River Anthology,* a seminar production, April 14-17, 1982, Little Theatre.

10 Clifford Wiltshire, *"Spoon River Anthology* a Success," *B&M,* October 8, 1982, p. 8.

11 Donald Hill, "Director's Note," Original Program for *The Nativity Cycle,* December 3-4, 1982, Little Theatre, n.p.

12 Jerry Martin, "Director's Note," Original Program for *Mrs. McThing,* February 9-12, 1983, Layton Theatre, n.p.

13 Ibid.

14 "Guest Director Mr. Ted Hissam," Original Program for *The Taming of the Shrew*, April 20-23, 1983, Little Theatre, n.p.

15 *"Star-Spangled Girl," Cue,* Muskingum College, Fall, 1984, p. 2.

16 Jerry Martin, "Director's Note," Original Program for *The Star-Spangled Girl,* October 13-15, 1983, Little Theatre, n.p.

17 Susan Ransom, "Simon Play Presented," *B&M,* October 14, 1983, p. 4.

18 "A Musical Revue," *Cue*, Fall, 1984, p. 2.

19 "Rashomon," *Cue,* Fall, 1984, p. 2.

20 Gina Thompson, "*Rashomon* a Taste of the Orient," *B&M,,* February 17, 1984, p. 7.

21 "A Hell of a Show," *B&M,* April 6, 1984, p. 4.

22 Ian S. MacNiven, *The Lawrence Durrell Society Herald,* May 15, 1984, p. 1.

23 "Muskingum Theatre Goes International," *Cue,* Fall, 1984, p. 3.

24 Ian S. MacNiven in a letter to Professor Hill, April, 20, 1984.

25 Lawrence Durrell in a letter to James Nichols, paraphrased by Donald Hill, May 24, 1984.

26 Lawrence Durrell, *An Irish Faustus: A Modern Morality in Nine Scenes,* "Preface," (Birmingham, England: The Delos Press, Peter Baldwin, 1987), n.p.

27   Donald Hill, "Director's Note," Original Program for *Our Town*, October 3-6, Little Theatre, n.p.

28   "Our Town," *Cue,* Fall, 1984, p. 1.

29   T. W. Rickard, quoted in "Our Town," *Cue,* Sesquicentennial Issue, Fall, 1986, p. 4.

30   Gina Thompson, "*Our Town* Entertaining," *B&M,* October 12, 1984, p. 8.

31   "My Three Angels," *Cue,* Fall, 1986, p. 4.

32   Kathy Hovis, "Convicts Are Committed to Comic Christmas," *B&M,* November 9, 1984, p. 8.

33   T. W. Rickard, quoted in *"My Three Angels," Cue,* Fall, 1986, p. 4.

34   Jerry Martin, "Director's Note," Original Program for *Arsenic and Old Lace,* February 6-9, 1985, Little Theatre, n.p.

35   Ginny Schuster, quoted in *"Arsenic and Old Lace," Cue,* Fall, 1986, p. 3.

36   *Hans Christian Andersen*, Description from Original Program, April 24-27, 1985, Brown Chapel, n.p.

37   Kathy Hovis, quoted in *"Hans Christian Andersen," Cue,* Fall, 1986, p. 4.

38   "The Muskingum College Theatre," an Introduction to the Season of Plays, "The Muskingum College Theatre Season: 1985-1986," Muskingum College Theatre, Muskingum College, New Concord, Ohio, 1985, n.p.

39   Alyssa Unger, quoted in *"God's Favorite," Cue,* Fall, 1986, p. 3.

40   *"Agnes of God," Cue,* Fall, 1986, p. 3.

41   *"Mass Appeal," Cue*, Fall, 1986, p. 3.

42   Ibid.

43   Ginny Massenburg, quoted in *"The Passion of Dracula," Cue,* Fall, 1986, p. 4.

44   Eileen Adams, quoted in *"The Passion of Dracula," Cue,* Fall, 1986, p. 4.

45   *"Trial by Jury," Cue,* Fall, 1986, p. 4.

46   "The Production," Jean Baptiste Poquelin De Moliére's *The School for Wives,* Translated into English Verse by Richard Wilbur, "Curtain Time," April, 1972 Selection, (New York: Fireside Theatre Book Club Edition, Harcourt, Brace, Jovanovich, Inc., 1971), p. 6.

47   John Lowe, quoted in "The School for Wives," *Cue,* Fall, 1986, p. 4.

48   "The Muskingum College Theatre," an Introduction to the Season of Plays, "The Muskingum College Theatre Season: 1986-1987," Muskingum College Theatre, Muskingum College, New Concord, Ohio, 1986, n.p.

49   Christopher Jones, "Sesquicentennial Greetings," *Cue,* Fall, 1986, p. 1.

50   "Agnes Moorehead Film Festival," *Cue,* Fall, 1986, p. 1.

51   "The Muskingum College Theatre," Season: 1986-1987, 1986, n.p.

52   *"A Midsummer Night's Dream,"* Season: 1986-1987, 1986, n.p.

53   *"A Midsummer Night's Dream," Cue*, Fall, 1986, p. 2.

54   Donald Hill, "A Midsummer Night's Dream," *Cue,* Fall, 1987, p. 4.

55   Jerry Martin, *"Harvey," Cue,* Fall, 1987, p. 3.

56   Ibid.

57   *"Harvey,"* Season: 1986-1987, 1986, n.p.

58   Martin, "Harvey," p. 3.

59   Ginny Massenburg, *"Harvey* Opens in Comic Style, *B&M,* February 20, 1987, p. 8.

60   *"Painting Churches,"* Season: 1986-1987, 1986, n.p.

61   Tina Howe, quoted by Ronald Lauck in *"Painting Churches," Cue*, Fall, 1987, p. 2.

62   Ronald Lauck, *"Painting Churches," Cue*, Fall, 1987, p. 2.

63   Kathy Hovis, "Fame Falls, Rises in *Painting Churches," B&M,* February 27, 1987, p. 8.

64   Rose Kessing, *"Dear Brutus," Cue,* Fall, 1987, p. 4.

65   "Greek Comedy a Hit," *Cue,* Fall, 1988, p. 7.

66   Ronald Lauck, "Director's Notes," Original Program for *The Frogs,* October 14-17, 1987, Little Theatre, n.p.

67   Carla Stalder, *"The Frogs* Hops to a Muskie Success," *Muscoljuan*, Vol. 82, "Pathways to Success," Muskingum College Junior Annual (New Concord, Ohio: Muskingum College, 1988), p. 38.

68   Donald Hill, "Classical Season Reviewed," *Cue,* Fall, 1988, p. 4.

69   Ibid.

70   Carla Stalder, *"Androcles and the Lion* Goes Modern," *Muscoljuan,* vol. 82, p. 40.

71   Carla Stalder, "Modern Adaptation of Fable Appeals to Adults as Well as Kids," *B&M,* October 23, 1987, p. 8.

72   Donald Hill, *"Antigone* by Jean Anouilh," Notes in Original Program, February 24-27, 1988, Layton Theatre, n.p.

73   Allardyce Nicoll, *World Drama: From Aeschylus to Anouilh,* (New York: Harcourt, Brace and Company, 1950), p. 916.

74   Hill, "Antigone,"

75   Colleen Karpac, "Muskie Production of Greek Play Offers Moral Lesson with Story," *Muscoljuan,* Vol. 82, p. 46.

76   "Greek Play *Antigone* Adapts to Setting of Nazi Occupation of World War II," *B&M,* February 26, 1988, p. 8.

77   Carla Stalder, "Dinner Theatre Planned for 1988 Parents Weekend," *B&M,* February 26, 1988, p. 8.

78   Carla Stalder, "Muskingum College Players Perform Classic," *B&M,* April 22, 1988, p. 8.

79   Hill, "Classical Season Reviewed".

80 Ronald Lauck, "Director's Note," Original Program for *The Dining Room,* October 5-8, 1988, Layton Theatre, n.p.

81 Angela Neff, "*The Dining Room* Serves Up Tastes of Nostalgia," *B&M,* September 30, 1988, p. 8.

82 Kathy Lacey, "*The Dining Room* an Extraordinary Production," *B&M,* October 14, 1988, p. 8.

83 "Jean Genet," and "Theatre of the Absurd," *Benet's Reader's Encyclopedia,* Third Edition, Carol Cohen Editorial Director (New York: Harper & Row, Publishers, 1987), pp. 737, 969.

84 Deborah Wolfert, "Director's Note," Original Program for *The Maids,* February 22-25, 1989, Layton Theatre, n.p.

85 Allison Kimmich, "*The Maids*: Genet's Web of Illusion," *B&M,* February 17, 1989, p. 12.

86 Alisha Lenning, "Director's Note," Original Program for *The Star-Spangled Girl,* March 8-11 and April 14, Layton Theatre and John Glenn Gymnasium, n.p.

87 "Saturday Showcase Programs," *Cue,* Fall, 1988, p. 6.

88 Richard Wilbur, " A Note from the Translator," *Moliére's The Learned Ladies,* in a New Translation by Richard Wilbur (New York: Dramatists Play Service, Inc., 1977), p. 82.

89 "Moliére, Jean Baptiste Poquelin," *The Reader's Encyclopedia of World Drama,* Edited by John Gassner and Edward Quinn (New York: Collier Books, 1967), p. 170.

90 J. LaRue, "Review of *Learned Ladies*," *B&M,* October 13, 1989, pp. 9, 13.

91 Kevin R. Moreau, "*Learned Ladies* Review Misses Point," *B&M,* October 27, 1989, p. 3.

92 "Henrik Ibsen," *Stages of Drama, Classical to Contemporary Masterpieces of the Theatre,* Second Edition, Carl H. Klaus, Miriam Gilbert, and Bradford S. Field, Jr. (New York: St. Martin's Press, 1991), pp. 538-539.

93 John Gassner, *Masters of the Drama,* Third Revised and Enlarged Edition, XIX "Ibsen, The Viking of the Drama," (New York: Dover Publications, Inc., 1954), pp. 366-373.

94 "Henry Ibsen," *Reader's Encyclopedia of World Drama,* p. 446.

95 Ronald Lauck, "Director's Note," Original Program for *A Doll House,* November 15-18, 1989, Layton Theatre, n.p.

96 Susan Murphy, "*A Doll's House* to Open Wednesday," *B&M,* November 10, 1989, p. 12.

97 "Ugo Betti," *Reader's Encyclopedia of World Drama,* p. 67.

98 "Ugo Betti," *Masterpieces of the Modern Italian Theatre,* Edited by Robert W., Corrigan (New York: Collier Books, 1967), p. 170.

99 "*Summertime,* An Idyll in Three Acts (1937)," *Three Plays by Ugo Betti: The Queen and the Rebels, The Burnt Flower Bed, and Summertime,* Translated and with a Foreword by Henry Reed (New York: Grove Press, Inc., 1958), p. 247.

100 Tony Norman, *Post Gazette* Staff Writer, "No One More Surprised by Fame Than Schulz Himself," *Pittsburgh Post-Gazette,* Sunday, February 13, 2000, p. A-11.

101 Ibid.

102 Alisha Lenning, "Director's Note," Original Program for *The Secret Princess,* April 18-21, 1990, Layton Theatre, n.p.

103 Allison Kimmich, "Lenning Directs *The Secret Princess*," *B&M,* March 30, 1990, p. 8.

Theatre in the '90s
People and Events

Ruth and Agnes

Dr. Robert N. Montgomery, Ruth Montgomery, Agnes Moorehead, and a trustee, Mr. Griffin, 1954. Agnes was on the Board of Trustees at the this time, and performed *That Fabulous Redhead* for Homecoming. *Theatre file photo courtesy M.C. Public Relations Office.*

In the mid-eighties I agreed to do several articles about Agnes Moorehead for the *Daily Jeffersonian*.[1] The college archives supplied me with important biographical information. I also remembered stories about Agnes which I had heard in my student days, stories which came from professors who had known Agnes when she was a student at Muskingum. Although she was very young at the time, Agnes was sensitive about her age. One day the page of the family Bible on which her birth had been recorded mysteriously disappeared. Nevertheless, she was born Agnes Robertson Moorehead on December 6, 1901 (also Ruth's birth year) in Clinton, Massachusetts to the Reverend John Moorehead and Mary McCauley Moorehead.[2] On her audition report for the American Academy of Dramatic Arts which was dated August 14, 1926, she listed her age as twenty-three.[3]

While at Muskingum, Agnes majored in biology and related sciences and minored in English and Speech. She took four courses in Speech.[4] She was a good student but she was not a trend follower. She scandalized the professors by wearing lipstick, and she upset the neighborhood when she danced barefoot on the lawn at a May Day festivity.

I had enough information for maybe one article for the *Daily Jeffersonian*, but hardly a series. I felt the need for more background information and anecdotal history, some first-hand knowledge about Agnes to add depth and familiarity to my writing. I called Mrs. Montgomery and she graciously agreed to an interview.

Mrs. Ruth Kelley Montgomery was the wife of the former President of Muskingum College, Dr. Robert N. Montgomery. "Doc Bob," as he was affectionately called, was a pleasant man, very sociable and amenable; no less could be said of his wife, Ruth. During his presidency, they lived in the Manse, which was always open and available to the campus community. Ruth loved to entertain and there were many receptions for students. Each class was honored with a reception, and there were special ones for entering freshmen and departing seniors. Visiting celebrities, guest professors, and artist-performers all found a home at the Montgomery Manse which exuded the warmth of an open hearth. In my memory the glow still emanates from there whenever I pass.

While I was a faculty member, I knew Ruth as a patron of the arts. She was a permanent member of the audience at concerts, gallery openings, and plays. Students waited for her appearance at the theatre; the curtain seldom rose without their eager anticipation being satisfied that Ruth was in her seat. Her attendance went beyond the usual duties of a president's wife. She genuinely enjoyed the performances and appeared on stage in *The Misogynist* (1976) as one of the College of Matrons. Muskingum's "art scene" lost one of its best friends when Ruth died in 1995.[5]

Agnes Moorehead and the Montgomerys were good friends. Whenever Agnes was in the neighborhood, she always dropped by; and whenever the Montgomerys were in California, they visited Agnes at her home in Beverly Hills. Her home, the Villa Agnese, was formerly owned by the composer Sigmund Romberg. When Agnes decided to build a retreat on the family farm near Rix Mills, her visits to the Montgomerys became more frequent and ceased only when Agnes's illness led to her confinement.

At the appointed time for my interview with Ruth, several days later, I drove through the severe Ohio winter to her ranch-style home on Lakeside Drive. The driveway was clear and the walks swept. Almost forty years had passed since I, as a student, visited a Montgomery residence, but the welcome mat was still out. It was impossible for me to enter without feeling the old familiar warmth of a homecoming.

A Reagan sign was on the door and one of the young men students who lived in the basement apartment greeted me at the door. I was ushered into the hallway where a picture of President Reagan smiled down on me.

Ruth greeted me in a lavender housecoat—a favorite color of both her and Agnes. She informed me that we were having apple juice in glasses given to her by Agnes, and there were also raisin cookies. As I remembered, the graciousness was still there, as was the atmosphere of a tastefully done interior. We went into the study and the talk flowed. There was no sense of a real interview. I was glad I had left my pen in my overcoat and the tape recorder at home.

Ruth and Agnes were part of the same generation and a particular climate. Besides the importance attributed to each individual, there was a sense of concern for the immediate problems facing the health and future of the whole country, of which Muskingum was an important part. Both ladies expressed this concern through different channels: Ruth, for thirty years as wife of a college president and later as his widow; Agnes, through a lifetime of devotion to her art. For example, when speaking of her role in the staging of Shaw's *Don Juan in Hell*, she said,

> ...it was a happy marriage of four personalities [the cast consisted of Charles Laughton, Charles Boyer, Sir Cedric Hardwicke, and Agnes]. We respected each other personally and professionally. No one was playing a solo performance. We knew that a certain percentage of people came to see personalities—that they were curious to see how we looked, how we talked—we were vain as all actors, in thinking this. But may I say that after the first twenty minutes that curiosity was satisfied and the audience could have yawned and left, but they stayed to listen to Shaw. That was what we wanted. That was what we believed: that audiences were hungry for good theatre, that they were far above the low average mental level generally credited them by theatrical managers and producers, and that great circles of culture were to be found all over this vast country of ours. This was exciting to me, for all along the tour I reveled in the museums. What wonderful things are being done in the smallest towns! What fresh new perspectives in the arts! What hunger to learn! And how gratifying to the actor to be instrumental in some small way in satisfying that hunger.[6]

Mrs. Montgomery, an Oberlin graduate, taught piano for years and continued to do so long after Doc Bob's retirement, the move from the Manse, and her husband's death. It was a matter of keeping her "hand in." Ruth was attending Oberlin at the same time that Doc Bob and Agnes were students at Muskingum in the early twenties. In fact, he used to date Agnes. After their marriage, Ruth used to twit him with, "You see what you missed? You could have been Mr. Agnes Moorehead instead of the husband of Ruth Montgomery!"[7]

There was regret that Muskingum did not come off better in the Moorehead legacy, but that was because the social code of the college had deteriorated: the permissiveness toward alcohol and drinking. Agnes had very strong views about alcohol. As a person she disapproved of its use, and as a performer she couldn't tolerate its effects. Her disapproval had been intensified when it became the major reason for the divorce in one of her two marriages. (There is a letter in the files of the Development Office in which Agnes dissociates herself from the alcohol policies adopted by the college administration.)

Besides serving as a retreat for herself, Agnes built 'New Place' at the Rix Mills farm for her mother, Mary Moorehead. Her mother was in good health and quite "peppy." (I believe that Agnes at this time must have been in her late sixties, which would have made her mother close to ninety years of age.) One day a phone call from Agnes brought the request for Ruth to find a young male student to stay at 'New Place' with her mother. She knew that Mrs. Montgomery kept a basement apartment for such students to help her about the house and drive her places. There was no mistaking the kind of young man Agnes wanted: he must like the farm and its relative seclusion; he must be clean-cut and wholesome with no bad habits such as swearing, smoking, or drinking. After considerable search, Mrs. Montgomery found a young man and he was taken in.

Some time later, the young man, rather puzzled, appeared at Mrs. Montgomery's door to tell her that Mrs. Moorehead had dismissed him because he was no longer needed; she could take care of herself. Ruth told the young man to invite Mrs. Moorehead to her home for dinner; and while she was there, they would call Agnes and have a talk. This was done. While Agnes was on the phone, she sympathized with the young man; she appreciated all that he had done for her mother; however, she reluctantly told him that if her mother had said she didn't need him...he would have to go.[8]

There is an apocryphal story about Agnes's mother, her agility and uncharacteristic stamina for her age. It evolved from the popularity created by Agnes's role as Endora, the witch, in the "Bewitched" television series. According to a local wag, when the news was released about Agnes's illness, some one asked, "Who is taking care of Agnes?" The response was, "Her mother." The questioner then asked thoughtfully, "Oh, who takes care of Agnes's mother if and when she gets ill?" The reply came quickly, "Why, *her* mother, of course!"

Agnes Moorehead was an established actress long before she created the character of Endora in the *Bewitched* series (1964-1972). Although Agnes received five Emmy nominations for her creation of Endora, and had become known to millions of viewers through the "Bewitched" television series, she didn't care to be remembered as that character. Her contribution to the theatre ran deeper than that: there were the multiple Academy Award nominations for Best Supporting Actress;[9] radio's Golden Mike Award (1953) for the solo performance of Lucille Fletcher's, "Sorry, Wrong Number," and a Gold Record for the Decca recording of the same performance;[10] and the 1967 Emmy for an appearance on the "Wild, Wild West" series episode, "The Night of the Vicious Valentine."[11] Agnes considered the highlight of her career to be the role of Donna Anna in the First Drama Quartette production of G. B. Shaw's, *Don Juan in Hell* (1951). It was a smash hit, played on Broadway, Carnegie Hall, and toured England and the United States for four years.[12]

A certain amount of mystery surrounds Agnes's illness. In 1955 Agnes played the part of "Hunlun" mother of Genghis Khan (John Wayne) in Howard Hughes's multi-million dollar epic *The Conquerer*. The film was shot in Utah near a nuclear test site. Many members of the cast and crew eventually developed cancer. The film featured Susan Hayward, William Conrad, and Thomas Gomez. It was directed by Dick Powell.[13]

Agnes inadvertently contributed to the mystery by keeping her illness a secret and requesting her doctors to withhold medical information. Agnes believed that actors should have and should keep some distance from their audience in order to maintain the magic and illusion of the theatre.[14]

Agnes Moorehead died on April 30, 1974 and interred at Dayton, Ohio, Memorial Park's Mausoleum next to her father.[15]

Both ladies, patron and performer, are well remembered.

REFERENCES

1   Donald Hill, "Musings from the Hill," a series of articles on Agnes Moorehead, *Jeffersonian,* August 9, 16, 25, 1986, p. 4.
2   "The Agnes Moorehead Papers" and "Biography," courtesy the Wisconsin Center for Film and Theatre Research, University of Wisconsin, Madison, 1976, E. McKay and C. Swiss, Inventory;
    "Agnes Moorehead," *Current Biography: Who's News and Why, 1952*, Edited by Anna Rothe and Evelyn Lohr (New York: The H. W. Wilson Company, 1952), p. 437.
3   "Agnes R. Moorehead Audition Report—American Academy of Dramatic Arts," reproduced by Dr. Warren Serk in *Agnes Moorehead A Very Private Person* (Philadelphia: Drone & Company, 1974), p. 24.
4   Scott Dittman, Office of the Registrar, Muskingum College, July 1985, New concord, Ohio.
5   Susan Dannemann, Development Office, Muskingum College, February 7, 2002.

6   Agnes Moorehead, "Staging *Don Juan in Hell*," Speech given at the Convention of Western Speech Association, Fresno, California, n.d.
7   Mrs. Robert N. Montgomery (Ruth), in an interview with the author Donald Hill, Winter, 1986.
8   Mrs. Montgomery (Ruth).
9   "Biography," Agnes Moorehead Papers.
10 "Biography," Agnes Moorehead Papers, "Awards," p. 6.
11 "Biography," Agnes Moorehead Papers, pp. 1-2.
12 "Biography," Agnes Moorehead Papers. and
    "Agnes Moorehead," *Current Biography, 1952,* p. 439.
13 "The Conqueror," *Video Hound's Golden Movie Retriever, 1995* (Detroit, Michigan: Visible Ink Press, 1995), Editors: Martin Connors, Julia Furtaw, p. 287.
14 "Agnes Moorehead," *The Lavender Lady,* Produced by Quint Benedetti for Quinto Records, Toluca Lake, California; A Memorial Album of Excerpts from a performance taped at the University of Wisconsin, River Falls, Wisconsin, 1976.
15 "Agnes Moorehead Will Be Buried in Dayton," *The Journal Herald,* Dayton, Ohio, Thursday, May 2, 1974, p. 42.

The Department: 1990–1993

In the spring of 1992, I took my last sabbatical. Since I had accumulated almost enough hours for a master's degree in film at Ohio State University, the logical step was to finish the degree there. However, the Photography and Cinema Department at OSU was being phased out! Photography became part of the Art Department and Cinema was moved into the Theatre Department. Since a degree was not all that important to me, I decided to indulge myself by attending the University of Southern California, one of the top-ranked film schools in the nation. At the same time, I could enjoy the sunny climate of California.

The University of Southern California School of Cinema and Television began in 1929, through the concerted efforts of the Academy of Motion Pictures Arts and Sciences and USC. The first course was entitled "Introduction to Photoplay," with guest lecturers such as Irving Thalberg, Douglas Fairbanks, Sr., Ernst Lubitsch, Darryl F. Zannuck, and D. W. Griffith. In 1932, it was the first film school to offer a B.A.; a Masters Degree was added in the late 1940's and a Doctor of Philosophy in 1959.[1]

Spring in California is very different from Ohio. There was no snow; the flowers were blooming (in January, yet!); and the temperature was in the 70's. However, there was a down-side to all this glamour. In that one spring, California greeted me with the usual rain and mudslides, then the tremors that preceded the earthquakes, and, as a fitting climax, the Rodney King episode that ended in the burning of some parts of Los Angeles. The police didn't seem too effective in stopping the riots or fires, until they began to close in on Beverly Hills. At that point, everything suddenly came under control and things returned to normal.

As I became more familiar with the facilities of the school of Cinema-Television, I became more and more convinced that I had made a good choice in schools. The George Lucas Instructional Building, the Marcia Lucas Post-Production Building, the Steven Spielberg Music Scoring Stage, the Carson Television Stage, the Harold Lloyd Motion Picture Sound Stage, the Eileen Norris Theatre, the Cinema-Television Library and Archives of Performing Arts, and the Louis B. Mayer Film and Television Study Center all informed me that I had landed on a campus seriously concerned with my chosen field of study.[2]

The 1992 spring semester at the University of Southern California began in January. There were so many graduate courses to choose from that I had difficulty selecting just three—ten hours was the usual course load for graduates. The courses for which I registered seemed particularly pertinent to my program in history of film, film theory, and criticism: Film Genres—the Western, Film Theories, and History of the International Cinema. The courses were excellent, the professors superb, and the academic climate conducive to learning. It was a great way to end the sabbatical experience.

Before I returned to Muskingum, I taught a Musical Theatre course during the '92 Summer Session at the University of Lethbridge in Alberta, Canada. When I arrived home for the 1992-1993 school-year, Dr. Martin had followed Jeff Harman as chairman of the department. Jeff was working on his doctorate at Bowling Green State University from which he has since received his Ph.D. Ronald Lauck was in his first year of a two-year special leave, during which time he completed requirements for the MFA in Scene Design at the University of South Dakota.

1   *The University of Southern California Bulletin: 1900-1991, School of Cinema/Television*, (USC, University Park, Los Angeles, 1990), p. 10.
2   Ibid., pp. 13-14.

The Plays: 1990–1993

1990–1991

The 1990-91 theatre season opened on October 10-13, when Ronald Lauck directed and created the scenography for a production of *The Romancers* by Edmond Rostand.

In his "Director's Note" Mr. Lauck introduced the audience to his production:

> Muskingum College Theatre is pleased to be able to present *The Romancers* as an important work in the history of theatre and in recognition to the role it has played in the history of American musical theatre. It also offers several challenging roles to performers as well as the opportunity for the audience to see a little of time gone by.[1]

For the first time in the history of the Muskingum College Theatre, the audience was privileged to see the complete play which had inspired three previous productions. *The Fantasticks*, based on *The Romancers*, is the ever-popular musical written by Tom Jones and Harvey Schmidt. In the fall of 1963, Rex McGraw directed *The Fantasticks* for Homecoming Week. In the spring of 1971, Amanda Roberts directed a one-act version of *The Romancers* for her seminar in theatre. Again, for Homecoming Week in 1977, I directed *The Fantasticks*. How refreshing to see, at last, the seminal work!

Mr. Lauck comments in his "Director's Note":

> . . . Rostand's work exhibits the idealistic, poetic, and flamboyant nature of his personality. From this beginning rose a craftsman whose best characters rest in the ideals of the Romantic Period of some fifty years before his birth.[2]

The Romancers, 1990. Percinet (T. Perorazio) and Sylvette (T. Dabb). *Photo courtesy Ronald N. Lauck.*

The Romancers was beautifully costumed and staged in the Layton Theatre production. The romancers of the story are Sylvette and Percinet, whose parents wish them to marry. They have other ideas and leave home independently to find their place in the world. They both return home disillusioned. This time, their parents pretend to hate each other and to disapprove of the match. True love wins over all obstacles, as the young boy and girl discover that they love each other after all.

In her review, "*The Romancers* Showcases Good Acting," Kimberly Masteller noted,

> *The Romancers* succeeds thanks to its strong leading performances.
> The Edmond Rostand play, which runs tonight and tomorrow night at the Layton Theatre, also offers an interwoven plot that makes for an interesting evening at the theatre.[3]

At the beginning of the 1990's, I found myself reaffirming the importance of the student-directed one-act play. It is a good and easy way to introduce students to the life of the theatre, not only those in theatre classes, but also every and any student interested in theatre. It gives hands-on experience to students interested in directing, by placing them in charge of a production. It gives students who are interested in acting, or in technical aspects of theatre, a chance to learn from their peer group. It supplies experience and knowledge for students who are planning to teach in high school, and it may be the best and only way for a teacher to determine a student's ability to continue toward a seminar situation.

The importance of the task that lay ahead was firmly in mind when I entered my class in Play Direction to discuss the fundamentals of directing and the elements of production, such as play selection, casting, and rehearsals. As a result, I supervised six students who produced two sets of one-act plays on November 14-17 and November 28-December 1.

A group of three directors chose Neil Simon's *Plaza Suite,* and decided that each one would direct one of three playlets. Tracie Moreau directed Act One: "Visitor from Mamaroneck," Susan Murphy directed Act Two: "Visitor from Hollywood," and Shelly Peters directed Act Three: "Visitor from Forest Hills."

The second set of one-act plays consisted of "The Lesson," by Eugene Ionesco, directed by Joseph B. Rath, "Adaptation," by Elaine May, directed by Samuel G. Hook, and an adaptation of "The Diary of Adam and Eve," by Mark Twain, directed by Beth A. Hammer.

On February 20-23, the second semester of the season began with Alan Ayckbourn's, *Woman in Mind*; direction and scenography was by Ronald Lauck. Mr. Lauck explained in the program notes "About the Play":

> One of Britain's most prolific current playwrights, Alan Ayckbourn, has been called the Neil Simon of Britain, having written more than twenty-six works. *Woman in Mind* is a recent work, first performed in 1985 in Britain and then at the Manhattan Theatre Club in 1989. Many of Ayckbourn's works deal with relationships that turn out to have a comic and a tragic edge.
> As one studies the role of "Susan," this dualism is clear. In order to cope, she has created an alter family who, for a while, seemingly allow her dreams to come

true. But this family has a dark side, too. Although her real family is not one of the most pleasant ones with which to deal, this skewed mix is handled skillfully with a comic effect as all of the real characters bring their individual, discrete worlds into the final haven in Susan's life, her garden. As she struggles to come to terms with the implosion of these worlds upon her, the audience ends up eating "supper from the ceiling" with her. We laugh and we face tragedy.[4]

Traci Dabb reviewed the play in her article for the *Black and Magenta*, entitled "*Woman in Mind*: a Provocative Mind Play Runs This Week." She remarked,

> The play . . . focuses on the descent of an unhappy British housewife into the depths of her troubled mind.
> . . . The entire cast does an excellent job of handling the very serious theme of insanity, flecked with the side elements of sexual repression and various other neuroses dealt with in the play.
> Mention also needs to be made of the play's director, Ronald Lauck, who adapted this very powerful, thoughtful production.[5]

The final production of the season was Leonard Gershe's *Butterflies Are Free,* directed by student, Susan Murphy, with the set and costume designs by seminar student, Shelly Peters, and technical direction by Ronald Lauck. The play was produced by Muskingum Players, April 10-13. Mr. Lauck remembers the production vividly, because it was probably moved more times and played in more theatre spaces than any other show in his memory. I might add that the show was also probably presented under the sponsorship of more organizations for more occasions than any other show in my memory.

Butterflies Are Free was first presented on April 10 and 11 at the Little Theatre. On April 12, it was moved to the John Glenn Gymnasium for the Parents Weekend Dinner Theatre. The show was then returned to the Little Theatre to complete its original run on April 13. These performances were sponsored by Muskingum Players. On June 14 and 15, the play was revived for Alumni Weekend. Under the joint auspices of Muskingum Players, the Alumni Office, and the Speech Communication and Theatre Department, it was moved to the Layton Theatre for the occasion. During the 1991-92 fall semester, it was presented on September 2 for two performances, 1:30 p.m. and 7:00 p.m. in the Layton Theatre. This time, the performances were under the auspices of the Muskingum Players, the Dean of Students, and the Speech Communication and Theatre Department. The occasion for the performances was Freshman Orientation Weekend. Although, admittedly, the director, cast, and crew grew tired of moving, they learned more about the show by playing it in different theatre spaces, for different audiences, than they could have learned by playing in one theatre. It is also to their credit that they kept the show fresh and lively.

Susan Murphy had this to say in her "Director's Notes":

> *Butterflies Are Free* was first performed on October 21, 1969, at the Booth Theatre in New York City. Critic Richard Watts of The New York Post claimed that "the play's most striking quality is its capacity for being warm and touching." This play is about relationships, growing up, and the difficulty of letting go of the ones you love in order to let them be free.[6]

In her review of the show, Kimberly Masteller wrote,

> This was a terrific script . . . but I believe that a great deal of the credit goes to the director. Susan Murphy, a junior, did an excellent job in directing. The play is tight, organized, and has a constant flow of momentum from start to finish.

> . . . This play is . . . uplifting. The strong performances by the whole cast and a solid crew helped make this one of the best plays I've seen at Muskingum. The Muskie Players should be proud because *Butterflies Are Free* is a keeper.[7]

Cast for
The Romancers
(Edmond Rostand)

Sylvette	Traci Dabb
Percinet	Tom Perorazio
Straforel	Dan Clever
Madame Bergamin	Shelly Longwell
Madame Pasquinot	Diane Bourne
Blaise	Trevor Hatcher
Wall	Anji Dunn, Tracie Thompson
Supernumeraries	Beth Belanger, Judy Blank, Vicki Costanzo, Trevor Hatcher, Nancy Miller
Scene:	Neighboring Gardens. The locale is nowhere in particular "provided the costumes are pretty."
Director:	Ronald N. Lauck
Scenographer:	Ronald N. Lauck
Technical Director:	Ronald N. Lauck

Woman in Mind
(Alan Ayckbourn)

Susan Gannet	Beth Hammer
Bill	Jerry Shade
Lucy	Tera Hunsucker
Tony	Bill Connick
Andy	Mike Foster
Reverend Gerald Gannet	Tom Perorazio
Muriel	Shelly Peters
Rick	Amir Attaie
Time:	The Present
Scene:	A small backyard garden in the suburbs of London
Director:	Ronald N. Lauck
Scenography:	Ronald N. Lauck
Technical Director:	Ronald N. Lauck

Butterflies Are Free
(Leonard Gershe)

Don Baker	Thomas E. Perorazio
Jill Tanner Benson	Victoria A. Paul
Mrs. Baker	Tracie L. Moreau
Ralph Austin	Matthew Sembrat and Joseph Rath
Period:	1980
Scene:	The apartment of Don Baker
Director:	Susan Murphy
Scene/Costume Designer:	Shelly Peters
Technical Director:	Ronald N. Lauck

Steel Magnolias, 1991. Truuvy Jones (J. Porter), Shelby (A. Mitchell), Ouiser Boudeaux (S. Peters), Annelle Desoto (J. Johnson), M'Lynn Eatonton (T. Hunt). *Photo courtesy Ronald N. Lauck.*

 1991-1992

S tudent director, Susan Murphy, dominated the first part of the 1991-92 theatre season. Susan had earned much deserved applause for her direction of *Butterflies Are Free*, which closed the last season of plays, and opened the new season on Freshman Orientation Weekend, September 2. On October 16-19, for her theatre seminar, Susan directed Robert Harling's *Steel Magnolias.*

The scene of the action is Truvy Jones's beauty salon in Chinquapin, Louisiana, where a group of steady customers meet frequently to have their hair "done" and exchange friendly repartee, as well as some scathing gossip. When one of the women's daughter, Shelby Eatonton Latcherie, who is a diabetic, forfeits her life in order to have a child, the group draws even closer to shield each other in the face of their fragile mortality.

In her program notes concerning the play, Susan stated,

> *Steel Magnolias* was originally performed at the WPA Theatre in New York City on March 22, 1987. It is a delightful play detailing the lives and experiences of six very strong women. Harling sheds new light on the meanings of friendship, courage and strength.[8]

The Muskingum College Theatre production of *Steel Magnolias* was staged in the Little Theatre arena, under the technical direction of Mr. Lauck. Susan Murphy not only directed but also contributed the scene and costume designs. The arena staging complemented the closeness of the group of women whose friendships were being tested by the tragic loss of Shelby. Susan could not help but be aware of this fact. In an interview with Kimberly Masteller, Susan mentioned how working with a cast of all women made them "more natural," and how the "camaraderie of the actresses will accentuate the play, which revolves around the interactions of several women friends in a small southern town." Susan explained how the play deals with the roles that women play, " . . . not just the feminine, but the strong ones, able to take control of a situation."[9] The arena stage, which accentuated the character and kept character the focus of attention, maximized the dramatic impact of the play. Susan added another hit to her career at Muskingum.

On November 20-23, the Layton Theatre was the scene of the musical comedy, *Ernest in Love,* which was based on Oscar Wilde's *The Importance of Being Earnest,* and written by Anne Croswell, with music by Lee Pockriss. Ronald N. Lauck directed and designed the show.

According to Mr. Lauck's "Program Notes,"

> *Ernest in Love* has been updated from its Victorian origins to reflect some of the social problems of the period in which Croswell and Pockriss conceived the adaptation: the turbulent 1960s. However, it is certainly not the caustic satire of the much later *Hair.* The music is properly gentle and tunefully popular as it rises out of the situations from the various characters.[10]

Mr. Lauck coined the correct phrases to typify the musical comedy and the effect of the play: it is "properly gentle and tunefully popular." Having had several close associations with the source of the musical, Wilde's famous farce, I believe the Muskingum College Theatre's production to be one of the more amiable and pleasant evenings in the theatre that I had enjoyed for some time. The actors and the Music Department, whose chairman, Dr. William Schlacks, served as conductor of a group of very talented musicians, deserved congratulations.

During the second semester of the 1991-92 season, I was on a sabbatical at the University of California studying film. Taking my place was Artist-in-Residence Svetlana Efremova. A short biography was included in *The Seagull* program.

> Born in Novosibirk in Siberia, Efremova was educated in the best Russian schools. Through classes in art, music, and theatre during her elementary school years, the actress developed a sense of pride in and love for her nation's culture. Her talent gained her entry into the Leningrad State Institute of Theatre where she graduated with distinction.
>
> Efremova's directing experience includes the Leningrad State Theatre of Young Spectators and the Children's Theatre Studio of Leningrad, which she organized. The actress taught stage, voice and acting in Leningrad and supervised a theatre studio at the Leningrad Polytechnic Institute, where she won first place in directing at the city's annual festival.
>
> In 1984 she was named outstanding female actress at the Prague Festival of Higher European School of Actors' Craft.
>
> As a member of the Leningrad Salon Theatre, Efremova appeared off Broadway in productions of *Uncle Vanya*. . . . staged alternately in English and Russian! The company appeared at Muskingum in the fall of 1990 and endeared themselves to local audiences both on campus and in area schools with their charm and virtuosity.[11]

For her directing premier at Muskingum College, Svetlana chose one of the most historic dramas, not only of the Russian theatre, but also of the world theatre: Anton Chekhov's, *The Seagull.*

The major plot of *The Seagull* concerns the lives of four artists in Moscow at the turn of the century: Madame Arcadina, Trigorin, Treplev, and Nina. Madame Arcadina, an actress of nineteenth century drama, is trying to preserve her career. She is having an affair with a mediocre writer, Trigorin. Treplev, her son, is a young playwright trying to make a reputation for himself. He is in love with Nina, an aspiring actress. Nina acts in a production of Treplev's play, but the performance is received so badly that Treplev wantonly kills a seagull and places it at Nina's feet as a symbol of his ruined hopes. After Nina runs away with Trigorin, Treplev, in despair, unsuccessfully tries to commit suicide. Two years later, Treplev receives some reputation as a playwright, and Nina returns, having been deserted by Trigorin and having failed as an actress. She re-unites with Treplev. Madame Arcadina has maintained Trigorin as her lover. Nina compares herself to the dead seagull that was wantonly destroyed by a man's whim. When Nina leaves him a second time to try again as an actress, Treplev succeeds in killing himself.[12]

The Seagull, 1992. In rehearsal (from the left) A. Gardner, Svetlana Efremova (Director and Artist-in-Residence), L. Jackson, and B. Connick. *Theatre file photo courtesy Public Relations Office.*

Under the careful direction of Svetlana Efremova, *The Seagull* was successfully performed by a talented Muskingum College Theatre cast on March 4-7 in the Layton Theatre. Ronald N. Lauck was the lighting designer and technical director; Svetlana was the costume designer; and Shelly Peters was the set designer.

For Parents Weekend performances on April 8-11, Muskingum Players presented the longest running hit in theatre history, Agatha Christie's, *The Mousetrap.*

Senior theatre major, Tracie Moreau, directed the mystery, which involves a group of strangers stranded in a boarding house during a snowstorm; one of them is a murderer. The plot unravels to one of Christie's surprise endings. Ronald N. Lauck designed the set and served as technical director; Jennifer Zornow designed the lighting; and Stacie Tennant designed the costumes. The popular reception of the play assured its revival in the fall for Freshman Orientation Weekend on August 30-31.

The final production for the season consisted of two short plays presented on Commencement Weekend, May 8 and 9 in the Layton Theatre. The Muskingum College

Theatre presented "A Pushkin Fairy Tale," directed by Svetlana Efremova, with lighting design and technical direction by Ronald N. Lauck; and The Appalachian Children's Theatre presented "Three Little Pigs," composed and directed by Svetlana Efremova, who also appeared in the play, along with another member of the Leningrad Theatre Salon, Olga Tchainikova.

Cast for
Steel Magnolias
(Robert Harling)

Annelle Dupuy Desoto	Juliet Johnson
Truvy Jones	Jeannine Porter
Clarilee Belcher	Anne Gardner
Shelby Eatonton Latcherie	Amy Mitchell
M'Lynn Eatonton	Tricia Hunt
Ouiser Boudreaux	Shelly Peters
D. J.	J. D. Kimple
Time:	The Present
Scene:	Chinquapin, Louisiana, Truvy's Beauty Parlor
Director:	Susan Murphy (seminar)
Scene/Costume Designer:	Susan Murphy
Lighting:	Ronald N. Lauck
Technical Director:	Ronald N. Lauck

Ernest in Love
(A musical comedy based on Oscar Wilde's *The Importance of Being Earnest*)
(Book and lyrics by Anne Croswell Music by Lee Pockriss)

Jack Worthing	Joseph B. Rath
Perkins	Nick Zakov
Gwendolen Fairfax	Beth Belanger
Alice	Trina Naegle
Algernon Moncrieff	Bob Gordon
Lane	Bill Connick
Lady Bracknell	Tara Phillis
Miss Prism	Traci Weiss
Cecily Cardew	Amy Good
Effie	Erin Graham
Rev. Dr. Chausuble	Tom Perorazio

Musicians

Conductor	Dr. William Schlacks
Clarinet	Kathy German
Clarinet	Tiffiny Pennington
Bassoon	Joyce Alesandrini
Electric Bass	Shawna Weisgerber
Piano	Cecilia Lin
Setting:	England, 1912
Director:	Ronald N. Lauck
Scenic Designer:	Ronald N. Lauck
Lighting:	Jennifer Zornow
Costumes:	Susan Murphy, Stacie Tennant
Choreographer:	Erin Graham
Technical Director:	Ronald N. Lauck

The Seagull
(Anton Checkhov)

Madame Arcadina .... Anne Gardner
Constantine Treplev .... Lloyd Jackson
Sorin .... Tom Perorazio
Nina .... Tera Hunsucker
Shamrayef .... Jerry Shade
Pauline .... Beth Hammer
Masha .... Victoria Costanzo
Trigorin.. Joseph B. Rath
Dorn .... Dan Clever
Medvedenko .... William Connick
Yakov .... Dan Grime
Scene: .... Moscow, 1901; The Sorin estate
Director: .... Svetlana Efremova
Costume Designer: .... Svetlana Efremova
Lighting Designer: .... Ronald N. Lauck
Scenic Designer: .... Shelly Peters
Technical Director: .... Ronald N. Lauck

The Mousetrap
(Agatha Christie)

Mollie Ralston .... Kim Hawkins
Giles Ralston .... Dan Vorhies
Christopher Wren .... Anji Dunn
Mrs. Boyle .... Jeannine Porter
Major Metcalf .... Gwendy Diener
Miss Casewell .... Traci Weiss
Mr. Paravicini .... Bob Gordon
Detective Sergeant Trotter .... George McKendree
Setting: .... England, the present day, The Great Hall at Monkswell Manor
Director: .... Tracie L. Moreau
Scenic Designer: .... Ronald N. Lauck
Lighting Designer: .... Jennifer A. Zornow
Costume Designer: .... Stacie Tennant
Technical Director: .... Ronald N. Lauck

"A Pushkin Fairy Tale"

Pope .... Dan Clever
Balda .... Doug King
Devil .... Joseph B. Rath
Imp .... Jennifer Jones
Popess .... Beatriz Good
People .... Anne Gardner, Vicky Costanzo, Cynthia Mihok, Denise Yniquez
Horse .... Chris Chilson, Juliet Johnson
Director: .... Svetlana Efremova
Lighting Director: .... Ronald N. Lauck
Technical Director: .... Ronald N. Lauck

"Three Little Pigs"
(Composed by Svetlana Efremova)

Nyff-Nyff .... Olga Tchainikova
Nuff-Nuff .... Kirby Statler
Niff-Niff .... Svetlana Efremova

Wolf ....Bob Irvin
Mushroom & Musician ....Alan Daugherty
Director: ....Svetlana Efremova

 1992–1993

The 1992-93 theatre season began on August 30-31 with a revival of *The Mousetrap,* at the Little Theatre on Freshman Orientation Weekend.

While technical director Ronald N. Lauck was studying for his Master of Fine Arts in scene design at the University of South Dakota. Artists-in-Residence, Svetlana Efremova and Olga Tchainikova, assumed some of his duties. Like Svetlana, Olga Tchainikova had also been a member of the Leningrad Salon Theatre which had visited Muskingum two years previously.

In an article in the *Black and Magenta*, Laura Yoder reported on the theatrical and artistic background of Olga.

> While living in Russia, Tchainikova was a professional actress with a long list of performances under her belt. Among these are the Leningrad Comedy Theater, in which she performed for eleven years, her five motion pictures, and three television shows.
>
> According to artist-in-residence Svetlana Efremova, it is hard for people here to understand how famous Tchainikova is in Russia.
>
> "People come to watch Olga, not just the Comedy Theatre. She had her own audience, her own make-up artist, her own hairstylist, and her own group of professionals to collaborate with," said Efremova.
>
> "It's hard to understand," said Tchainikova. "The culture aspect is much stronger in Russia. Actors and actresses are extremely respected and supported by the government. Among the intellectual class, so much attention is given to theater, art and music. Here, it is much different."
>
> In the United States, she said, actors and actresses cannot get by just by acting. They are waitresses or have some other job so that they have enough money to live. In Russia, working under a government company is hard, but it is an honor. The government pays the salaries, and actors get extra, especially those who are in movies.
>
> Although theater plays an extremely important role for her here, Tchainikova is also very much involved in painting and graphics as well. . . .
>
> In Russia, she said she was known as an actress, but in the United States, she finds that people are really taking her art work seriously and she enjoys the success and independence it brings her. Presently, a number of Tchainikova's paintings are on exhibit at the Zanesville Art Center. . . .
>
> Currently, Tchainikova is teaching costume design, and next semester she will teach technical production.
>
> "I enjoy my classes and students very much. In costume design, some students could not draw before, and now they are doing excellent work," she said.[13]

The 1992-93 theatre season officially opened on October 7-10, Homecoming Weekend, with Vasili Shukshin "Characters," translated and adapted for the stage and directed by Svetlana Efremova. The scenic and costume designs were by Olga Tchainikova; lighting design was by Jennifer Zornow, and the head costumer was Stacie Tennant.

Vasili Shukshin was a short-story writer, novelist, and film-writer who was born in Russian Siberia in 1929 and died in 1974 at the age of forty-five.

Shukshin's work always mirrored the land of his birth. Siberian themes and the country life of its people are integral to his stories.[14] Svetlana, who was also born in Siberia, must have felt very close to the four short stories which she presented for the Muskingum audience. The playlets are as direct and simple as the lives of the characters. In "Microscope," the father of a struggling Russian family buys a microscope. Since the object serves no practical purpose, the wife convinces him to sell it. In "Country Dwellers," a grandmother and her grandson debate flying to Moscow to visit relatives. At the end of the play, they are still undecided. In "Stefan," a young man escapes prison in order to visit his family and his mute sister. As the family celebrates, the police arrive to return him to his cell. The only one who seems to notice is his mute sister. In the final one-act play, "Boots," a poor man buys an expensive pair of boots for his wife. They are too small for his wife, but they just fit their daughter. They decide to let her keep the boots. A very unique way of introducing each play consisted of an actress appearing on stage to hang some washing out to dry. On the washing was written the title of the next play.[15]

As a member of the Muskingum audience, although I could not presume to speak for them, I was fascinated and charmed by the production. Svetlana's direction and Olga's designs captured the very essence of the country life, and the hearts and souls of the people who lived in the works of Vasili Shukshin's "Characters." In their artistry, the director and designer were able to convey these intangible elements to the actors and actresses, and they, in turn, conveyed them to the audience. It was a very warm and gratifying theatrical experience.

The tradition of student directed one-act plays continued that year with two sets of one-acts on November 18-21 and December 2-5. My class in Play Direction produced the plays and I supervised the productions.

The first set of one-acts consisted of plays that have a long and time-tested career in American theatre history. All three of the plays had been directed by different generations of students over the years, a fact which bears testimony to their popularity and endurance. Victoria Paul chose to direct "Trifles" by Susan Glaspell. Glaspell founded the Provincetown Playhouse,* which nurtured Eugene O'Neill's early playwriting skills. Her play is a murder mystery, in which a search for the truth overlooks some very important "trifles." Anne Gardner directed William Saroyan's "Hello Out There," which was first produced in the Belasco Theater in 1942. This tender love story, set in a Texas jail, ends in tragedy. Jennifer Zornow directed "Red Carnations" by Glenn Hughes, a farcical love story involving a man, a boy, and a girl. Hughes was a University of Washington professor who pioneered the development of arena theatre in the United States. The comedy was quite at home in the Little Theatre arena.[16]

The second set of one-acts had also proved popular with previous Muskingum audiences; however, they are plays which belong to the American theatre after 1950. Their authors break the illusion of theatre by using such techniques as role-playing,

---

*The Provincetown Playhouse is a small playhouse on MacDougal Street in New York's Greenwich Village. In 1915, a group of amateurs formed the Provincetown Players while vacationing in the Massachusetts coastal village. They moved their operation to New York the next year, where they were joined by their most famous playwright, Eugene O'Neill.

speaking directly to the audience, referring to disturbing political events, and destroying the aesthetic distance. Anji Dunn directed "The Acting Lesson," by Willard Simms a serious play in which actors assume various roles symbolic of life itself. Eddie Martin directed David Fulk's "The Potman Spoke Sooth," a comedy mystery that spoofs Agatha Christie, and makes theatrical use of Pirandello's devices for breaking the illusion of dramatic form. In order to make a complete evening in the theatre, I cast my acting students in Jules Feiffer's "Excerpts from *Feiffer's People*," which is known for its insights into human eccentricities and its attacks on an establishment which caused civil rights riots, sit-ins, and protests against the Vietnam War.[17]

Although too close for an entirely objective point of view, I thought the series of plays went very well. Kelli Coleman, in her review, found the plays "spectacular" and even "stunning."[18]

On March 3-6, the Muskingum College Departments of Music and Speech Communication and Theatre presented Richard Rodgers's and Oscar Hammerstein II's *Oklahoma!* in Brown Chapel. Carol Wilcox-Jones directed; Robert Owen Jones conducted; Marilyn McKelvey choreographed; and Jerry Martin produced the musical.

According to Stanley Green, author of *The World of Musical Comedy,*

> Apart from the charm and inventiveness of the individual songs, what was unique about *Oklahoma!* was the synthesis of its component parts into a complete theatrical entity of great beauty and imagination. Everything fit into place. For the first time, not only were songs and story inseparable, but the dances devised by Agnes de Mille heightened the drama by revealing the subconscious fears and desires of the leading characters.[19]

Oklahoma! ran for over five years on Broadway, and held the record for a long run by a musical until it was surpassed by *My Fair Lady* (1956), which ran for over nine years.[20]

At the time of Muskingum's production, *Oklahoma!* was celebrating its fiftieth anniversary. The College revealed a special relationship to the musical when it noted that 1939 alumna, Jean Snider, had joined the singing chorus of the show when it was about a year old. She was a student at Julliard School of Music and a script typist at CBS when *Oklahoma!* opened on Broadway. She is now Mrs. Bisceglia of Fresno, California, and still active in community musical circles. She sent a note extending her "best wishes to the cast and directors of the Muskingum production."[21]

In her appraisal of *Oklahoma!,* Lynda Tolbert wrote:

> Over one thousand people were in attendance for Muskingum College Departments of Music and Theater's presentation of *Oklahoma!* throughout the show's four performances. . . . According to Dan Vorhies, who attended Friday evening's performance, "*Oklahoma!* was a well put together musical, with shining performances by everyone involved."[22]

The final production of the 1992-93 theatre season was John Pielmeier's *Agnes of God*, presented by Muskingum Players for Parents Weekend on March 31-April 3. The tense drama was directed by a student member of Muskingum Players, Anne Gardner, and I was the supervising advisor. I had directed the play in December 1985, because I had seen it on Broadway and was fascinated by the religious fervor of the play, and by its possibilities for student actors. Anne Gardner impressed me with her talent and serious attitude toward the theatre. I thought it would make a good vehicle for her to direct. I suggested it to her, she read the play, and agreed with me; together we put it into production.

Based on a true incident, *Agnes of God* is a story of a young nun who is on trial for murdering her baby. A court psychologist is employed to determine if she is sane enough to face a trial for manslaughter. A question, which no one succeeds in answering convincingly, is "Who is the father of the murdered child?" According to the court psychologist (played by Victoria Paul) it could be a case of hysterical parthenogenesis, or a local field hand. The Mother Superior (played by Jeannine Porter) prefers to believe the birth was an immaculate conception or a

Agnes of God, 1993. (foreground) Agnes (J. Crumley) and Mother Miriam Ruth (J. Porter). *Theatre file photo courtesy M.C. Public Relations Office.*

miracle, in which case Agnes is a saint. Agnes (played by Jennifer Crumley) believes the baby was God's will, and by murdering it she sent it back to God.

Anne lived up to my expectations. She piloted the production to an unqualified success. She had been so successful with this serious drama that I told her she should try her hand at directing a comedy, if for no other reason than to balance the serious side of her nature with the lighter side.

The Muskingum Players Dramatic Society, which sponsored the Parents Weekend production of *Agnes of God,* is chartered by Student Life, supported by funds from Student Senate and its own volunteer services, and advised by the faculty of the Muskingum College Theatre.[23]

The *Black and Magenta* honored the work of Muskingum Players in the April 23, 1993, issue, with a centerfold article and pictures entitled, "The Play's the Thing: Muskingum Players Spend the Year on Stage."[24]

Cast for
Vasili Shukshin "Characters"
(Vasili Shukshin translated and adapted by
Artist-in-Residence Svetlana Efremova)

"Microscope"
Andrei .... Marc Schodorf
Zoya, his wife .... Amy Mitchell

Masha, his daughter ....Julie Johnson
Sergei, his friend ....Terry Hatcher

"Country Dwellers"
Malanya, the grandmother ....Judy Woodard
Shurka, the grandson ....Chris Jones
Misha, neighbor ....Jerry Shade

"Stefan"
Stefan ....Matt Jordan
Yermolay, his father ....Michael Seiler
Mother ....Judy Woodard
Sister...Anne Gardner
Nura, neighbor ....Shandra Carson
Policemen ....Jerry Thompson

"Boots"
Sergei..Jerry Shade
Klavdia, his wife ....Svetlana Efremova
Grusha, his daughter ....Shandra Carson
Bootseller ....Amy Mitchell
Woman [who introduces the plays] ....Victoria A. Paul.
Director: ....Svetlana Efremova
Scenic/Costume Designer: Olga Tchainikova
Lighting Designer: ....Jennifer Zornow
Head Costumer:................Stacie Tennant

Oklahoma!
(Music by Richard Rodgers
Book and lyrics by Oscar Hammerstein II)
Based on the play *Green Grow the Lilacs* by Lynn Riggs

Aunt Eller ....Gwendolyn Diener
Curly ....Jon Black
Laurey ....Julianna Brackman (Th/S), Melissa Pangle (W/F)
Will Parker ....Mark Kackstetter
Ike Skidmore ....Burt Chappelear
Jud Fry..Daniel Reyes
Ado Annie Carnes ....Erin Graham (Th/S), Traci Weiss (W/F)
Ali Hakim..William Connick
Gertie Cummings ....Shandra Carson
Andrew Carnes..Marcus Schodorf
Cord Elam ....Bob Gordon
Ladies of the Ensemble .... Stacie, Baillie, Julie Denges, Melissa Diener, Becky Ellis, Stacy Evans, Juliet Johnson, Amy Leiendecker, Melissa Marius, Susan Meyer, Julie Montgomery, Kari Naegele, Amy Palmer, Melissa Pierce, Heather Rataiczak, Deborah Risko, Andrea Seckman, Jennifer Urich, Heather Worthen
Men of the Ensemble .... Homer Baker, Edward Barrett, Jeff Conklin, Dave Gass, Scott Goldy, Shawn Miller, Jeff Schmid
Dancers................................... Tina S. Connick, Victoria Constanzo, Lauren Mowry, Venae Mueller
Instrumentalists .... Doris Peterson, Keyboard; Jack L. Peterson, Keyboard; Shawna Weisgerber, Synthesizer
Director: ....Carol Wilcox-Jones
Conductor: ....Robert Owen Jones

Choreographer: .... Marilyn McKelvey
Producer: .... Jerry Martin
Scene Painting: .... Olga Tchainikova
Lighting Designer: .... Jennifer Zornow
Head Costumer: .... Stacie Tennant

The Department: 1993–1995

B y the time of my designated retirement, I began to have a good feeling about the future of the department. Dr. Martin has time and again given considerable gifts of time and energy for which he was recognized in 1991, when the Sears Foundation presented him with an award for teaching excellence and campus leadership.[1]

Dr. Jeff Harman, in his quiet, methodical way, has constantly and consistently improved the courses, the enrollments, and the technology of the radio and television stations. He was recognized in 1995 with the Cora I. Orr Award for Faculty Service for Involvement in leadership in campus programs and meritorious activities in the wider community.[2]

George Alfman, the Broadcast Engineer, is deeply committed to improving the technical standards of radio and television.

Gene Alesandrini who joined the faculty in 1987, has continued to improve, expand, and develop the forensic and interpersonal areas of the department. On leave in 1999-2000, he completed all but his dissertation at Oklahoma State University.

Ronald Lauck is dedicated to the task of Technical Director of the Theatre. His sense of order and discipline is a definite asset in an area that could quickly get chaotic. His skill in all technical areas is enhanced by his knowledge of computer programming, which he has introduced into the areas of design and graphics.

1995 Speech Communication and Theatre Department Staff. (sitting) Jerry Martin, Diane Rao Harman, Jeffrey Harman, Gene Alesandrini. (standing) Ronald N. Lauck, Deborah Phillips, Sonny (George) Alfman. *Photo courtesy Sharon Walker, M.C. Public Relations.*

Dr. Deborah Phillips, who was added to the staff in 1993, puts her multi-faceted talents to use in three areas: public address, interpretation, and film.

Dr. Diane Rao Harman, who replaced me in 1995, has continued the theatre program with a variety of classic, modern, and avant-garde productions.

The department seems to have a nucleus of teachers who have an air of permanence about them. It is difficult for a department to grow when the faculty is in a constant state of flux. This staff seems to be settled and willing to stay in one place long enough to make significant contributions to the history of the department and to the life of the academic community.

REFERENCES
1   Margaret C. Adams, VPAA Office, in conversation with the author, October 10, 2000.
2   Ibid.

The Plays: 1993–1995

1993–1994

*T*he Matchmaker, written by Thornton Wilder and directed by seminar student Anne Gardner, opened the 1993-1994 theatre season on October 13-16, Homecoming Week. I served as Anne's advisor and supervised the technical work for the production, which took place in the Little Theatre arena.

Because of its popularity as the musical, *Hello Dolly!,* there are few people who do not know the plot of *The Matchmaker.* However, let me recount the bare bones of the story. Horace Vandergelder, a middle-aged merchant of Yonkers, New York, decides to get married. He hires Dolly Levi, a matchmaker, to find him a wife. Dolly decides to marry Vandergelder herself, and after some finagling, she finally succeeds. While Vandergelder wants to get married, he won't let his niece marry her artist beau, Ambrose Kemper. When he leaves Yonkers to go to New York to meet a prospective bride, the niece and Ambrose pack their bags and head for the big city. Vandergelder's two hardware clerks decide they will also take a holiday in New York, just for the "adventure" of it. Complications ensue when they all meet in New York. With swift and clever maneuvering, Dolly captures Vandergelder, wins his approval of the niece's marriage to Kemper, and saves the jobs and budding romances of his two clerks.

In a joint venture with the Muskingum Players, the Muskingum College Theatre production played to full houses during the four night run. Anne Gardner's direction was precise and true to the style and genre of the play. The acting ensemble responded well to her direction and grew

The Matchmaker, 1993. Mrs. Levi (J. Dimitt) and Horace Vandergelder (D. Howell). *Theatre file photo courtesy M.C. Public Relations Office.*

confident in their roles. In her review of the play for the *Black and Magenta,* Cynthia Mihok complimented Anne for her directing, and the actors for their confidence and stage energy.[25] In his review for the *Daily Jeffersonian*, Matthew Gladman reported that

> The show . . . provides more than its share of laughs . . .
>
> The players bring energetic and bubbling performances to their characters, which come shining through in their interaction with the audience at the intimate surrounding of the Little Theatre.[26]

The second major production of the season was Murray Schisgal's comedy, *Luv,* performed on November 10-13, and directed by Gene Alesandrini, an assistant professor of speech communication and theatre. Muskingum's audience first saw this play in May 1975, when Rick Hill directed it for his theatre seminar. It was funny then and it was just as funny in 1993.

Luv takes place on a bridge in New York City and involves Milt Manvill's plan to marry his wife, Ellen, to a down-and-out college friend, Harry Berlin, so that Milt can marry the girl he loves. Ellen arrives on the bridge and falls for Harry. The second, and final, act takes place on the same bridge four months later. All three characters have gotten what they thought they wanted, except for Milt and Ellen, who discover that they really love each other and must find a way to undo what has been done. The personalities of the characters, the fast-paced comic dialogue, and the slapstick antics which occur on the bridge, as the characters try to turn their destinies around, supply enough laughs for three acts. Schisgal, however, is wisely resolute as he limits the hilarity to two acts; the audience must be satisfied with the fact that, no matter what he does, Milt ends up falling off the bridge twice in the second act. Strangely enough, the misadventures and misunderstandings which create unhappiness for the trio of mismatched lovers only make the audience laugh harder!

Matt Jones, who wrote the review of the play for the *Black and Magenta*, considered the play excellent and praised both the director and his cast, which included Dan Vorhies as Milt, Marc Schodorf as Harry, and Cindy Mihok, doublecast with Jeannine Porter, as Ellen.[27]

On February 23-26, *Going to See the Elephant*, a drama about four pioneer women on the American frontier, opened the second semester of the 1993-94 season. Guest Director Frederick Frank held tryouts for the play in December, and on January 13, began rehearsals with Violet Taylor as Belle ("Maw") Wheeler; Traci Dabb as her daughter-in-law, Sara Wheeler; Heather O'Brien as Etta; Jennifer Crumley as Mrs. Nichols; and Chris Lewis as her husband. Mr. Nichols is never seen on stage; he is an off-stage voice, only because the play's focus is on the four women in the play. In fact, the play was written for women and created by the unusual number of six women writers: Karen Hensel, Patti Johns, Elana Kent, Sylvia Meredith, Elizabeth Lloyd Shaw, and Laura Toffenetti. Matt Jordan designed the show. The production staff included Juliet Johnson and Robin Hatcher, assistant directors; Patrick Jones, stage manager; Robin Hatcher, lighting and sound; and Carmella Braniger and Laura Reinhart, costumes. Dr. Jerry Martin assumed the duties of technical director for the production, which was held in the Layton Theatre.

Guest Director Frank is a 1987 graduate of Muskingum who majored in Theatre and English, and minored in Speech. He also earned a Master of Arts in Education from Muskingum in 1991. He is now a member of the John Glenn High School teaching staff. In talking with Michelle Ingram, copy editor for the *Black and Magenta*, Mr. Frank commented on the "physical, mental, and psychological survival of four women in the old west," as " . . . not depressing, but rather, 'in many points, uplifting.'"[28]

The American frontier challenged the spiritual and physical strength of the pioneers. Women, as well as men, faced those challenges. *Going to See the Elephant*

Going to See the Elephant, 1994. Traci Dabb as Sara Wheeler. *Theatre file photo courtesy M.C. Public Relations Office.*

concerns the lives of four pioneer women in the Kansas wilderness of the 1870's. "Maw" Wheeler is a rugged survivor and matriarch of the group. Her daughter-in-law, Sara, is a hard worker who accepts things as they are. Etta is a young girl who was once kidnapped by the Cheyenne; she is still hoping for happiness and eventually marriage. Mrs. Nichols is a refined Easterner, waiting for her husband to recover from an illness. They have lost everything and are returning to the East. While the women deal with the fear of Indian attacks and the wild animals of the plains, they talk of "going to see the elephant," which is interpreted here as crossing the next hill to see what lies on the other side. This desire for adventure, and the willingness to face an unknown future, convey a determination to survive that lends significance to their lives and to the drama.[29]

The respect which Guest-Director Frank had for the drama, and for the hardships of women on the frontier, was communicated to the cast. Mr. Frank rehearsed his cast well. The cast became a closely knit ensemble which concentrated on the details of characters and the realistic problems of their day to day existence. The actors conveyed their struggles to the audience, who became absorbed with the lives of the characters.

The realistic set, designed by Matt Jordan helped create the atmosphere of the frontier for the audience and aided the actors in maintaining character. The action takes place on the rustic Wheeler homestead. In his review of the play, Jeff Beitzer discussed the scene design.

> An impressive part about the play was the set design created by sophomore Matt Jordan. Jordan said that the design took about three weeks to create, and about a month and a half to build. He added that to make the set, he used his imagination, historical

research, and then modified some of the ideas used by the original theater group that performed this play first.[30]

The actors sustained the " . . . physical, mental, and psychological [fight for] survival of four women in the old west, . . . " and held the interest of the audience from curtain rise to curtain fall. As Mr. Frank indicated earlier, " . . . the play is not depressing, but rather, 'in many points, uplifting.'"[31]

During February and March, both the Little Theatre and the Layton Theatre were humming with activity. The occasion was the production of six student-directed one-act plays, sponsored jointly by Muskingum Players and the Muskingum College Theatre. The enterprise involved over fifty students and three theatre classes: Play Direction, Technical Production, and Introduction to Theatre. The plays were being prepared to celebrate Parents Weekend in April.

The choice of plays was interesting and accidental, because each student in the Play Directing class chose the play he or she wanted to direct. As it happened, three young men chose plays modern and experimental in nature. They were scheduled to be performed at the Little Theatre, because that facility has a flexible performing space suitable to such plays. Matt Jordan and Nick Zakov each chose to direct four sketches from Jon Jory's *University*. Jory wrote the plays for the Actors Theatre of Louisville, in order to provide young actors with challenging roles. Present-day students relate well to the stories, which come from shared experiences of campus life, such as registration, pledging, sports, and graduation. Jordan cast four actors, each of whom played at least two parts: Marcus Schodorf, Erin Shepard, Kerry Malblanc, and Jill Dimitt. Zakov cast eight actors for his plays: Travis Passaro, David McCarty, Himmat Rana, Kevin Kimmell, Violet Taylor, Jennifer Collins, Missy Kiger, and Beth Lovell. The third one-act play was "The Fifteen Minute Hamlet," which was written by Tom Stoppard and directed by Barrett Hileman. Stoppard, a prize-winning playwright, has outdone himself in condensing a four-to-five-hour Shakespearean tragedy into a neat capsule. The fifteen minute "pill" not only plays well in this version but also is speeded up at the end for a two-minute reprise. The action is fast and furious; there is no waiting around for Hamlet to make up his mind; in fact, the audience is warned not to blink or they will miss half the show. Hileman chose six actors to play a multitude of characters, with hectic doubling: David Howell, Chris Lewis, Carmella Braniger, Heather O'Brien, Nathan Gault, and Barrett Hileman.

These plays were produced April 5, 7, 9 at the Little Theatre. The second set of three one-acts were produced on alternate dates: April 6 & 8 and on April 9 at a matinee. They consisted of three traditional theatre pieces directed by women. They were staged in a traditional manner in the setting provided by the Layton Theatre.

Amy Mitchell directed Robert Anderson's "The Footsteps of the Doves." It is part of a longer work of four one-acts which was performed on Broadway under the title, *You Know I Can't Hear You When the Water's Running*. "Footsteps" is a comedy which concerns a married couple who are trying to decide on twin beds, instead of keeping the regular bed they have become used to. The play featured Melanie Morgan, Nathan Lennon, Tracy Kocinski, and Kyle Harrington.

Kim Hawkins chose to direct "The Happy Journey from Camden to Trenton," by Thornton Wilder Typical of the author's Pulitzer Prize play, *Our Town*, "The Happy Journey" is about a family taking a trip to see the older sister. The conversations and incidents along the way result in changes in perceptions of life and living. Cast in this play were Chris Lewis, Amina Amid, Scott Davis, Mary Long, Bob Gordon, and Kelly Kackley.

Juliet Johnson directed "The Case of the Crushed Petunias," written by Tennessee Williams. Originally written for Helen Hayes, this play concerns a change in character for a young woman who has barricaded herself, and her life, behind a double row of petunias. The petunia fortress is besieged by a young man who changes her mind about living alone and hiding from the world. The cast for this play consisted of Joy Weyand, Kyle Harrington, Barrett Hileman, and Robin Hatcher.

I supervised the production of the six one-acts and Dr. Jerry Martin assigned members of his Technical Production class to work with the directors on the technical aspects of their plays.

Through the generosity of the actors, two of the one-acts were repeated for Alumni Weekend, June 10 and 11: "The Footsteps of the Doves" and "The Happy Journey to Camden and Trenton."

The Matchmaker
(Thornton Wilder)

Horace Vandergelder	David Howell
Ambrose Kemper	Adam Secor
Joe Scanlon	Patrick Jones
Gertrude	Amina Amid
Cornelius Hackl	Scott Davis
Ermengarde	Amy Mitchell
Malachi Stack	David Batteiger
Mrs. Levi	Jill Dimitt
Barnaby Tucker	Barrett Hileman
Mrs. Molloy	Laura Reinhart
Minnie Fay	Jennifer Collins
Rudolph	Chris Lewis
Augusta	Erin Shepard
Miss Flora Van Huysen	Kimberly Hawkins
Her Cook	Robin Hatcher
Scene: Act I:	Vandergelder's house in Yonkers, New York
Act II:	Mrs. Molloy's hat shop in New York City
Act III:	Harmonia Gardens Restaurant, Battery New York City
Act IV:	Miss Van Huysen's house, New York City
Time:	Turn of the century
Director:	Anne Gardner (seminar)
Advisor:	Donald Hill

 1994-1995

Homecoming audiences watched one of the world's most famous farces, when Muskingum College Theatre presented *Charley's Aunt* on October 19-22 at the Little Theatre. This production marked the first time the play had been performed on campus.

Anne Gardner, senior theatre and history major, directed, and Ronald N. Lauck, who had returned from a two-year leave of absence to the University of South Dakota, designed the set and the lights, and served as technical director. I was supervising director and vocal coach, and Gail Monica designed the logo.

Written in 1892 by Brandon Thomas, *Charley's Aunt* was the product of the "gay nineties" in England, at a time when Queen Victoria ruled over an empire that

Charley's Aunt, 1994. All's well that ends well! (from the left) Donna Lucia D'Alvadorez (J. Sinatra), Lord Fancourt Babberly (N. C. Barta); (seated) Ela Delahay (H. Wilt). *Photo courtesy Ronald N. Lauck.*

stretched around the globe. It was the decade in which some of the most witty and delightful theatre pieces of the English language were conceived. George Bernard Shaw, Oscar Wilde, and Gilbert and Sullivan were all writing at the same time that Thomas penned his story of three Oxford students, whose love affairs cannot proceed until Charley's aunt arrives. Their attempts to pass off one of their classmates as the missing aunt sets in motion a series of wild and hilarious events that have been pleasing audiences for over a century.

A summary of the unrestrained merry-making, as acted by the Muskingum cast, may help explain some of the comic elements of the farce.

Donna Lucia D'Alvadorez (Jennifer Sinatra), is on her way from Brazil to visit her nephew, Charles Wykeham (John Nelson), a student at St. Olde's College in Oxford. Charley is in love with Amy Spettigue (Mary Long), and his college chum, Jack Chesney (Michael Bell), is enamoured of Kitty Verdun (Traci Kocinski). They invite the two young ladies to their rooms for luncheon and to meet Charley's aunt. They hope they will have a chance to propose to the girls; the presence of Donna Lucia as chaperone will assure the sanctity which Victorian society requires. Unfortunately, Donna Lucia sends a telegram that her visit is unavoidably detained. At odds as to how they should proceed, the two young men pressure another Oxford undergraduate, Lord Fancourt Babberley (Nathaniel Barta), to don a disguise and pose as Charley's aunt. They introduce the disguised Babberley to the girls, to Jack's father, Sir Francis Chesney (David Mitchell), and to Amy's guardian, Stephen Spettigue (Scott Davis), as Donna Lucia D'Alvadorez, Charley's aunt from Brazil ("where the nuts come from"). When Sir Francis and Stephen Spettigue propose marriage to the impostor Babberley, all hilarity breaks loose. The real Donna Lucia and her companion, Ela Delahay (Heather Wilt), arrive unexpectedly. Sensing the game afoot, she quickly assumes another name to further the confusion. Eventually, all complications are resolved: Charley and Jack, and also Babberley, win the girls of their dreams, and Sir Francis marries the millionairess, Donna Lucia.[32] Brasset, a College Scout (Barrett Hileman) is the one person in the plot who diplomatically manages to stay clear of the shenanigans.

As reported by Jodie Royer in the *Black and Magenta*, the farce was a huge success; the house " . . . was sold out three of its four nights, . . . "[33]

On February 22-25, Wendy Wasserstein's *Heidi Chronicles* was seen in performance at Muskingum College Little Theatre. The play won the 1989 Pulitzer Prize for Dramatic Literature, the Tony Award, the New York Drama Critics Circle Award, the Outer Critics Circle Award, the Drama Desk Award, the Hull-Warriner Award, and the Susan Smith Blackburn Prize.[34] One of the most celebrated successes in many years, *The Heidi Chronicles* speaks to the head, as well as the heart. It is possible to have it both ways and Wasserstein does just that. For the Muskingum production, the direction, scene, and lighting design were done by Ronald N. Lauck; scene bridges were by Anne Gardner; costumes were by Missy Pangle; sound was by Amy Mitchell; and poster and program design were by Gail Modica.

Playwright Wasserstein is a thinker, and her play is an historical journey of the heroine, Heidi Holland, through the radical idealism of the sixties, the rough and tumble feminism of the seventies, and the materialistic cop-out of the eighties. However, the play is not a lecture or a sympathy bath for feminists. The observations are far too perceptive, the dialogue too witty, and the characters too human for sermonizing. Heidi " . . . stands alone in realizing that liberation comes from being true to oneself, basing her goals on need rather than circumstances, and avoiding traps of self-concern, self-involvement, and materialism."[35]

All of the awards that the play won testify to the success with which Wasserstein conveys her heartfelt message. The review that Kelly Streeter wrote for the *Black and Magenta* is further testimony of the play's impact on the human conscience. Kelly writes about the "cyclical journey individuals face through life."[36] Bravo for Kelly; she got the head and the heart of the play.

In his "Director's Notes," Ronald N. Lauck asks some very important questions.

> We have wrestled with the intricacies of the vision of Wendy Wasserstein's *Heidi Chronicles*. It is our hope that our work does both the *Heidi Chronicles* and the idea of theatre justice. However, the final decision rests with you, the audience. So, what is theatre to you? Do you celebrate theatre for its complexity or its singularity?[37]

As a member of the audience, I can say that the director and the cast did honor to Wasserstein's play. Had it been otherwise, Kelly Streeter could not have written such a stirring and perceptive review.

Amy Mitchell chose Neil Simon's *Rumors* for her directing seminar. Muskingum

Players presented the comedy on April 5-8, as part of Parents Weekend festivities. Technical Director Ronald N. Lauck organized the production unit to include Matt

Rumors, 1995. (down left) Claire Ganz (M. Morgan) and Chris Gorman (E. Stock) collide with the rumor mill. *Photo courtesy Ronald N. Lauck.*

Jordan, scene designer; Ronald N. Lauck, lighting designer; Scott Davis, costume designer; Anne Gardner, sound designer; and Robin Hatcher, make-up designer. I served as advisor to Amy Mitchell.

Rumors is not a serious comedy; it is a wild farce, stemming from Harry Brock's attempted suicide on the eve of his tenth wedding anniversary. To celebrate their anniversary, Harry and his wife, Myra, have invited eight of their best friends (four married couples) to dinner. The first to arrive is his lawyer, Ken Gorman, and his wife, Chris, who find Harry bleeding in his upstairs bedroom. He has missed his head and shot his earlobe. Ken and Chris try to keep the incident quiet, because Harry is Deputy Mayor of New York City, and an attempted suicide is a criminal offense. There is also an election looming in the not too distant future. A quick search of the house reveals that Myra and Mai Li, the Chinese cook, are missing. These facts are the shifting sands on which Simon bases his two-act farce.

The cast which Amy chose for the comedy did an excellent job in conveying the plot to attentive audiences. Chris and Ken Gorman (Eva Stock and Barrett Hileman) try to give Harry's attempted suicide the appearance of an accident, and pass it on as such to the next couple to arrive, Claire and Lenny Ganz (Melanie Morgan and Scott Davis). However, the new arrivals have their own ideas as to what happened, and they add their version to the original story when the third couple arrive, Ernie and Cookie Cusack (John Nelson and Violet Taylor). The three couples become part of a very complicated incident by the time Glenn and Cassie Cooper (David Hendrix and Jill Dimitt arrive).

Simon compounds the humor of *Rumors* by multiplying Harry's accident with those of the guests. On their way to the party, Lenny totals his new BMW; by the time they arrive Lenny is suffering from a whiplash and Claire has a bruised lip. The Steuben glass, which they had intended as a gift to Harry and Myra, is completely shattered by the accident. Cookie Cusack arrives with a bad back and, when she and Ernie try to cook dinner, Ernie burns his fingers and Cookie cuts her arm on a broken pitcher. At one point, Chris trips over a phone wire and falls flat on her face, and Ken accidentally fires a revolver so close to his ear that he is deaf for the rest of the evening. Cassie loses a one hundred-year-old crystal down the toilet.

A report of Lenny's car accident brings two policemen: Officer Welch (Robin Hatcher) and Officer Pudney (Phil Black). While asking questions about the BMW, the police stumble onto another accident, when Glenn lets it slip about the gunshots. Lenny pretends to be Harry and explains everything by telling another fantastic story. The police are not convinced, but they are satisfied and leave. Everyone heaves a sigh of relief and the four couples start upstairs to be with Harry. There is a sudden loud knocking at the basement door. It is Myra! The curtain falls.

The play was well-acted, well-directed, and well-attended. It played to full houses, two nights out of the four-night run. Jennifer Laughman, in her review for the *Black and Magenta*, wrote, "*Rumors* . . . was received well, and drew numerous laughs from those in attendance."[38]

A fitting ending to the 1994-95 season was provided by the executive producer of *Rumors* and president of Muskingum Players, Barrett Hileman. In a salute to the Theatre and to Muskingum Players, Barrett wrote,

> Now . . . A Word From the Sponsor!
> Within the majesty, grandeur, and magic of the great institution we have come to know as theatre an element of truth is sought to be conveyed in every production. Whether the medium is a romantic love story, a tragic period play, a nail biting suspense drama, or an uproarious farce, theatre is a powerful provider of life's education. We, as human beings, are afforded an opportunity through the great mirror called theatre to observe, reflect upon, and laugh at ourselves. When we take the time to incorporate these lessons into our lives, a truth has been presented on stage that affects us in a personal way, and a major production goal has been accomplished.
> In the never-ending quest to produce and promote the best in dramatic literature, the Muskingum Players Dramatic Society is pleased to bring to you our very own rendition of Neil Simon's *Rumors*. Muskie Players was founded in 1925 [1925-26] and dedicated itself to serving the college campus and community. We are the oldest organization on campus existing in a service capacity. We take great pride in the tradition established and are pleased to announce that plans are currently underway for the celebration of our 70th year commitment to excellence in theatre. It is our sincere desire that some aspect of truth will be revealed as you witness tonight's production, and most of all, we hope you enjoy yourself immensely!![39]

Cast for
The Heidi Chronicles
(Wendy Wasserstein)

Heidi Holland	Jennifer Sinatra
Susan Johnston	Anne Gardner
Chris, Mark, Waiter	John Nelson
Peter Patrone	Barrett Hileman
Scoop Rosenbaum	David Howell
Jill, Debbie, Molly	Jennifer Crumley
Fran, Lisa, April	Amy Hendrickson
Becky, Clara, Denise	Heather O'Brien

In this play, there are two acts.
In Act I, there is a Prologue and five different scenes: Columbia University; Chicago; Manchester, New Hampshire; Ann Arbor, Michigan; and New York.

In Act II, all scenes take place in New York: Columbia University, an apartment, a
   TV studio, a restaurant, the Plaza Hotel, a pediatric ward, and an apartment.
The time span is not chronologically arranged, but moves back and forth between
   1965-1989.

Director: ....Ronald N. Lauck
Technical Director: ....Ronald N. Lauck
Scene & Lighting Design: Ronald N. Lauck
Scene Bridges: ....Anne Gardner
Costumes: ....Missy Pangle
Sound: ....Amy Mitchell
Poster & Program Design: Gail Modica

REFERENCES (The Plays: 1990–1995)

1   Ronald Lauck, "Director's Note," Original Program, *The Romancers*, October 10-13, 1990, Layton Theatre,
     n.p.
2   Lauck, "Director's Note," n.p.
3   Kimberly Masteller, "The Romancers Showcases Good Acting," *Black and Magenta*, October 12, 1990, p.
     11.
4   Ronald Lauck, "About the Play," Original Program, *Woman in Mind,* February 20-23, 1991, Layton Theatre,
     n.p.
5   Traci Dabb, *"Woman in Mind*: a Provocative Mind Play Runs This Week," *B&M,* February 22, 1991, p. 10.
6   Susan Murphy, "Director's Notes," Original Program, *Butterflies Are Free,* April 10-13, 1991, Little Theatre,
     n.p.
7   Kimberly Masteller, "Student Production of *Butterflies Are Free* Soars," *B&M,* April 12, 1991, pp. 6, 10.
8   Susan Murphy, "Director's Notes," Original Program, *Steel Magnolias,* October 16-19, 1991, Little Theatre,
     n.p.
9   Kimberly Masteller quoting Susan Murphy, *"Steel Magnolias* Comes Into Bloom Wednesday," Photographs:
     Traci Dabb, *B&M,* October 11, 1991, pp. 6-7.
10   Ronald N. Lauck, "Program Notes," Original Program, *Ernest in Love,* November 20-23, 1991, Layton The-
     ater, n.p.
11   "Svetlana Efremova," Original Program, *The Seagull,* March 4-7, 1992, Layton Theatre, n.p.
12   "The Sea Gull," *Benet's Reader's Encyclopedia*, Third Edition (New York: Harper & Row, Publishers, 1987),
     p. 879.
13   Laura Yoder, "Famous Russian Actress Teaches Costume Design at Muskingum," *B&M,* November 20, 1992,
     p. 1.
14   "Vasily Makarovich Shukshin (1929-1974)," *Reader's Encyclopedia,* p. 897.
15   Lynda Tolbert, "Theatre Season Opens with Russian One-Acts," *B&M,* October 16, 1922, p. 3.
16   Donald Hill, a paraphrase of "About the One-Acts," Original Program, *A Night of One-Acts I,* November 18-
     21, 1992, Little Theatre, n.p.
17   Donald Hill, a paraphrase of "About the One-Acts," Original Program, *A Night of One-Acts II,* December 2-
     5, 1992, Little Theatre, n.p.
18   Kelli Coleman, "One Acts Provide Entertainment, *B&M,* December 4, 1992, p. 3.
19   Stanley Green, *The World of Musical Comedy:* "The Story of the American musical stage as told through the
     careers of its foremost composers and lyricists," Fourth Edition, Revised and Enlarged (New York: A Da
     Capo Paperback, 1980), p. 209.
20   Stanley Green, *Broadway Musicals, Show by Show,* Third Edition (Milwaukee, Wisconsin: Hal Leonard
     Publishing Corporation, 1990), pp. 119, 168.
21   "Muskingum College Graduate appeared in *Oklahoma!* during its first Broadway run," Insert in Original
     Program, *Oklahoma!,* March 3-6, 1993, Brown Chapel, n.p.
22   Lynda Tolbert, *"Oklahoma!* Packs Brown Chapel," *B&M,* March 12, 1993, p. 9.
23   Donald Hill, "Muskingum Players," Original Program *Agnes of God,* March 31-April 1-3, Layton Theatre,
     n.p.
24   "The Play's the Thing: Muskingum Players Spend the Year on Stage," *B&M,* April 23, 1993, pp. 6-7.
25   Cynthia Mihok, "Actors Confident in *The Matchmaker, B&M,* October 29, 1993, p. 9.
26   Matthew J. Gladman, "'*Matchmaker'* Provides Ample Laughs," *The Daily Jeffersonian,* Thursday, October
     14, 1992, p. 10.
27   Matt Jones, "*Luv* Receives 'Excellent' Review," *B&M,* November 19, 1993, p. 9.
28   Michelle Ingram, "*Going to See the Elephant* Revolves Around Four Women Surviving Pain and Hardship in
     the Old West," *B&M,* February 4, 1994, p. 8.
29   *"Going to See the Elephant," Complete Catalogue of Plays:* Dramatists Play Service, 1992, p. 129.

30   Jeff Beitzel, *"Going to See the Elephant* Deals with Struggle of Pioneer Women,"* B&M,* March 4, 1994, p. 8.

31   Michelle Ingram, *"Going to See the Elephant . . .".*

32   Brandon Thomas, "Charley's Aunt, Story of the Play," *Charley's Aunt,* A play in Three Acts (New York: Samuel French Inc., 1962), p. 3.

33   Jodie Royer, "Muskie Players Present *Charley's Aunt,*" *B&M,* October 28, 1994, p. 3.

34   *"The Heidi Chronicles," Complete Catalogue of Plays: 1992-1993,* p. 74.

35   Ibid.

36   Kelly Streeter, *"Heidi Chronicles* Comes to Muskingum," *B&M,* March 3, 1995, pp. 3, 8.

37   Ronald N. Lauck, "Director's Notes," Original Program *The Heidi Chronicles,* February 22-25, 1995, Little Theatre, n.p.

38   Jennifer Laughman, Editor-in-Chief, "Comedic Farce Abounds with *Rumors,*" *B&M,* April 14, 1995, p. 1.

39   Barrett Hileman, "Now . . . a Word from the Sponsor!" Original Program, *Rumors,* April 5-8, 1995, Layton Theatre, n.p.

Epilogue
The Plays: 1995–1999

1995–1996

For Homecoming Week, October 11-14, 1995, the Muskingum College Theatre presented Moliére's *Tartuffe*, directed by Dr. Diane Rao, with scenography and technical direction by Ronald N. Lauck.

Dr. Rao's production clarified the universality of Moliére's criticism of hypocrisy and idolatry in two ways: (1) women were cast in two important male roles; and (2) the blind adherents of Tartuffe were dressed in period costumes, while the detractors of Tartuffe were dressed in modern attire. Jennifer Sinatra played Tartuffe and Sabrina Tyus enacted Damis, the disaffected son of Orgon. Followers of Tartuffe, who were dressed in period costumes, were the gullible master of the house, Orgon (Scott Davis), and his mother, Mme. Pernelle (Mary Long). The family and friends of Orgon, who saw through the hypocritical machinations of Tartuffe, wore modern dress, and included Orgon's wife, Elmire (Heather O'Brien); the maid, Dorine (Jennifer Collins); Damis (Sabrina Tyus); Orgon's daughter, Mariane (Jessica A. Kinsbach); Elmire's brother, Cleante (John P. Nelson); a suitor to Mariane, Valere (Phillip W. Black); and a bailiff, M. Loyal (Viren Gilani).

The *deus ex machina*, who "untangled" the "entangled" and resolved the complications of the plot, was The Angel of God, played by Barrett

Tartuffe, 1995. Tartuffe (J. Sinatra) and Orgon (S. Davis). *Photo courtesy Sharon Walker, M.C. Public Relations Office.*

Hileman, who unmasked Tartuffe to all as a fraud and a criminal, and sent him to prison.

Much to the credit of Muskingum audiences, the play proved popular and sold out three performances of the four night run. The director, cast, and crew were congratulated on their performances by Kimberly West in her review, "Cast Performs Moliére's *Tartuffe* to Sell-Out Crowd for Homecoming," which appeared in the *Black and Magenta*,[1] and by Scott Davis in his follow-up, "95-96 Season in Review: *Tartuffe*," in *Cue*.[2]

Love Letters, written by A. R. Gurney, provided interesting and unique evenings of theatre, November 15-18. The power of written language interested the audience, as the actors read letters which two people had exchanged over a lifetime. Andrew Makepeace Ladd III and Melissa Gardner grow up together as schoolmates, then go their separate ways. However, they continue to exchange letters which reveal their closest thoughts and desires. This lifetime of confidences is sometimes touching and sometimes funny, but always a " . . . telling pair of character studies, in which what is implied is as revealing and meaningful as what is actually written down."[3]

The play was directed by Guest-Artist Bob Belfance, formerly director of the Weathervane Playhouse. Ronald N. Lauck was technical director and lighting designer. A unique feature of the play was the casting. Director Belfance chose a different set of actors for three of the four performances. Dr. Daniel Van Tassel and Rhoda Van Tassel, professors in the English Department, performed on November 15; John Nelson and Jen Crumley read the letters on November 16; and Scott Davis and Traci Kocinski finished the run on November 17 and 18 in the Layton Theatre.

The play was well-received at Muskingum. The audience was especially intrigued by the casting: some members of the audience came back a second night in order to see how different actors handled the parts. In her review of the production for the *Black and Magenta*, Kelly Streeter recommended it as enjoyable, with an " . . . interesting plot and good acting."[4] In his follow-up of *"Love Letters"* in *Cue*, John Nelson remarked that "From the viewpoint of both an actor and audience member, I felt watching these plays was a very rewarding experience."[5]

The *1959 Pink Thunderbird* is just one subject of conversation in two one-act plays written by James McClure: "Lone Star," and "Laundry and Bourbon." The significance of the classic car lies in the nostalgia evoked by the model. This fact is easily understood by most "baby-boomers," and especially by the Ford Motor Company, which revived the model in 2000, for just that reason. The two comedies were directed by Dr. Diane Rao; light and set design was by Ronald N. Lauck, Costume

1959 Pink Thunderbird, 1996. (left to right) E. Cochran, D. Hendrix (the Fullernoys), L. Thomas, D. Mitchell (the Caulders), S. Davis (Ray Caulder), and V. Taylor (Hattie Dealing). *Photo courtesy Ronald N. Lauck.*

Design was by Scott K. Davis, and Stage Management was by Robin Hatcher. The plays were presented by the Muskingum College Theatre on February 21-24 at the Little Theatre.

Although the two comedies concern the same family and friends, each play is composed of a single gender: "Lone Star" is devoted to three males: Roy Caulder (David Mitchell), a Vietnam War veteran; Ray Caulder (Scott Davis), his brother; and Cletis Fullernoy (David Hendrix), a newly-wed. "Laundry and Bourbon" is composed of three females: Elizabeth Caulder (Lori Thomas), Roy's Wife; Hattie Dealing (Violet Taylor), a friend; and Amy Lee Fullernoy (Elaine Cochran), a busybody. Both plays take place in Maynard, a small town in Texas; the time is summer. As an aid to continuity, Dr. Rao kept all actors on stage for both plays.

Heather Sernka's review for the *Black and Magenta* praised the cast members: " . . . the actors put on an outstanding performance, and I believe that the play's success was largely due to this aspect."[6]

In her summary of the experience, Violet Taylor wrote,

> In both plays, the Thunderbird illustrated pleasant nostalgia and an escape from the present problems. And even though the play tackled some pretty strong emotional issues, it also contained comical elements that kept it from getting weighed down. The audience enjoyed the dose of comedy that came along with emotional tidal waves.[7]

The actors were not the only ones in the limelight for this production. Mr. Lauck mentioned that congratulations were due to the publicity team for *1959 Pink Thunderbird.*

> Heidi Fought, Emily Mowry, Emonde Prosper, and Elaine Cochran. . . . entered their poster work for *1959 Pink Thunderbird* in the Juried Art Show and received Best of Show for graphic arts work.[8]

Parents Weekenders enjoyed Susan Sandler's *Crossing Delancey*, April 10-13 in the Layton Theatre. The play was produced by Muskingum Players and directed by senior, Barrett Hileman.

As dramatized by the Muskingum cast, *Crossing Delancey* shows how tradition clashes with modern culture. A young Jewish girl, Isabelle (Mary Long), who clerks in a New York City book store, is a frequent visitor to her grandmother, Bubbie (Carmella Braniger), who lives in the old Jewish neighborhood in Manhattan's Lower East Side. Isabelle believes she is in love with a young writer, Tyler (Viren Gilani). However, Bubbie senses a mismatch in the combination and asks her matchmaker friend, Hannah (Jennifer Sinatra), to find a man more suited to her grand-daughter's temperament and heritage. The matchmaker finds a pickle salesman, Sam (Nathan Gault), who falls in love with Isabelle. After some soul-searching by Isabelle and honest courting by Sam, Isabelle decides that Sam is her man.

The design team for the production included Robin Hatcher, technical director; Michele Sheets, Stage Manager; Kathryn Arnold, Assistant Stage Manager; Scott K. Davis, Costume Designer; Mary Margaret Long, Make-up Designer; Heidi Fought and Emily Mowry, Publicity Designers; Ronald N. Lauck, Light and Set Designer; Barrett Hileman and Scott Davis, Sound Designers. Scott Davis was also Assistant Director. Dr. Diane Rao was advisor to the director and Ronald N. Lauck was production

Crossing Delancey, 1996. Student Director, Barrett Hileman, for Muskingum Players. Setting by Ronald N. Lauck, 1996. *Photo courtesy Ronald N. Lauck.*

advisor.

A Saturday matinee, which was added to the usual four-night run, proved highly successful. Virginia Black's review in the *Black and Magenta* quoted Julie Griffith, a junior, as stating that " . . . the reason the play was so well-received was because 'the cast did a fantastic job and Barrett was a great director.'"[9] In her summation of the play for *Cue*, Carmella Braniger wrote, "Many appreciative parents came to see the show over the weekend and walked away with a strong sense of family and tradition."[10] Mr. Lauck, in his "Advisor's Notes," commented:

> . . . congratulations and thanks to all the people who helped make *Crossing Delancey* one of the best Muskie Players productions in recent history. Many people who have experienced New York commented that the production really captured the flavor of the old Lower East Side.[11]

Although the official 1995-96 theatre season was over, A. R. Gurney's *Love Letters* was revived for Alumni Weekend on June 14 and 15 in the Layton Theatre. The cast included Rhoda Van Tassel as Melissa Gardner, and Daniel E. Van Tassel as Andrew Makepeace Ladd III.

 1996–1997

On October 23-27, the Muskingum College Theatre presented William Shakespeare's comedy, *Twelfth Night,* directed by Diane Rao, with lighting design and technical direction by Ronald N. Lauck. The play was performed for four nights and a Sunday matinee at the Little Theatre.

The plot of *Twelfth Night* centers on the love interests of Duke Orsino and the Lady Olivia. A sub-plot consists of the self-love of Olivia's steward, Malvolio. The ship-wrecked twins, Viola and Sebastian, solve the problems of Orsino and Olivia, but it takes Sir Toby Belch and Olivia's entire serving staff to bring Malvolio to heel.

The complications provided by mistaken identities and the conniving of servants make a hilarious entertainment for the audience. A summary of the play is found in the details of the March 14-17, 1973 production.

A cast of fifteen students (four of them double-cast) played the following roles: Orsino, Scott K. Davis; Sir Toby Belch, Nelson Chimilio; Sir Andrew, Sarah Young; Malvolio, Kevin Schmidt; Sebastian, Donny Pritt; Antonio, Mary M. Long; Curio and Officer, Libby Selyak; Priest and Servant, Elizabeth Crabtree; Fabian and Valentine, Tonya Shipley; Captain and Officer, Amanda Murray; Musician, Kerry Malblanc; Feste, the Jester, Violet Taylor; Olivia, Jennifer Sinatra; Maria, Allyson Swinehart; Viola-Cesario, Kate Landis.

Something new and important was added to this production when it was announced that it had been entered in the Kennedy Center American College Theater Festival (KC/ACTF). The Festival is presented and produced by the John F. Kennedy Center for the Performing Arts, supported in part by The Kennedy Center Corporate Fund, The U.S. Department of Education, and the Ryder System.

> . . . The aims of this national theater education program are to identify and promote quality in college-level theater production. To this end, each production entered is eligible for a response by a regional KC/ACTF representative, and certain students are selected to participate in KC/ACTF programs involving awards, scholarships, and special grants for actors, playwrights, designers, and critics at both the regional and national levels. Productions entered on the Participating level are eligible for inclusion at the KC/ACTF regional festival and can also be considered for invitation to the KC/ACTF national festival at the John F. Kennedy Center for the Performing Arts in Washington, DC, in the spring of 1997.
>
> Last year more than 900 productions and 18,000 students participated in the American College Theater Festival nationwide. By entering this production, our department is sharing in the KC/ACTF goals to help college theater grow and to focus attention on the exemplary work produced in college and university theaters across the nation.[12]

News Editor Missy Mann reviewed the play for the *Black and Magenta*. According to her, "Junior Aimee Knupsky expressed her enjoyment of the play by saying, "'I was very impressed with the actors' abilities to handle a play at a very difficult Shakespearian level. I was also surprised at how entertaining the students made this play.'"[13]

Student design and production credits were awarded to Carmella Braniger, dramaturgé; Chris Carter, Sound Design; Andy King, Stage Manager; Poster Design, Elaine Cochran; and Portrait Design, Traci Shipley.

Kathryn Schultz wrote *Blue Horses* about ten years ago, when she was still associated with ArtReach, a touring theatre based in Cincinnati, Ohio. On November 14-17, the play was presented in the Layton Theatre, under the direction of Dr. Jerry Martin. Although the play is typed as a children's theatre fantasy, the play promotes originality and creativity, a theme that is universally accepted and understood.[14]

According to Dr. Diane Rao, "The play presents the idea that kids who color outside the lines are okay too. . . . The theme is a life-affirming message. It has an appeal for all ages."[15]

Blue Horses, "An Imagination Play," takes place in Tracy's Backyard at dusk.

Here an ensemble of four students create the magic of the play: Sean Clark, Christine Shine, Adam Tilton, and Sabrina Tyus. Jill Dimitt created the choreography for the play, and Ronald N. Lauck was the technical director. The play was given five performances: two at 7:30 p.m. on November 14 and 15, two on November 16 at 10:00 a.m. and 2:00 p.m., and one on Sunday, November 17 at 2:00 p.m.

For four nights and one Sunday matinee, February 12-16, 1997, the Muskingum College Faculty took to the Layton Theatre stage in James Thurber's *A Thurber Carnival*. The show was presented by the Muskingum College Theatre and co-directed by Jerry Martin and Gene Alesandrini. Design and production credits were extended to Jerry Martin, Set Design; Ronald N. Lauck, Light Design and Technical Direction; Elaine Cochran, Poster Design; Jeff Harman, Video Engineer; and Joyce Alesandrini, Keyboard Player.

A Thurber Carnival was called a "Revue" by Thurber himself, because it consists of a series of unconnected short sketches taken from his various books of stories, essays, and "one-liners" from his many cartoons.

The seventeen-member acting ensemble included Peggy Adams, Gene Alesandrini, Joyce Alesandrini, Frederick Frank, Andy Frese, Jeff Harman, Carolyn Higginbotham, Marie Jones, Jerry Martin, Joe Nowakoski, Debbie Phillips, Diane Rao, David Skeen, Russ Smucker, Rhoda Van Tassel, Richard Williamson, and Vicki Wilson.

The student review typified *A Thurber Carnival* as enjoyable and appreciated. Steph Mann, a Staff Writer for the *Black and Magenta,* obviously mesmerized by the Thurberesque style and sense of humor, recounted all " . . . fourteen different little stories . . . " that made up the evening's entertainment, and finalized the event with, "The play then ends the same way it began with the entire cast dancing around and acting crazy."[16]

Ayn Rand's *Night of January 16th*, a clever combination of courtroom melo-drama and improvisational happening, devised to exploit her "objectivist philosophy," was presented by the Muskingum College Theatre nightly (March 12-15) and for a Sunday matinee (March 16) at the campus Little Theatre. An explanation of the production, directed by Diane Rao, scene and lighting design by Technical Director Ronald N. Lauck, costume design by Heather Sernka, poster design by Elaine Cochran, and program by Amanda Murray, is contained in the original program published as the *Muskingum College Theatre Times/Week of March 10, 1997.*

> "Audience Participation: The Power of One"
> This play is a murder trial without a prearranged verdict. The jurors will be selected from the audience. They will witness the play as real jurors and bring in a verdict at the end of the last act. The play is built in such a way that the evidence of the defendant's guilt or innocence is evenly balanced and the decision will have to be based upon the jurors' own values and characters. This play, like the American judicial system itself, truly represents "the power of one."[17]

The final production of the 1996-97 theatre season was a set of one-act plays directed by students. The catchy title for the event, "5 Nights and a Pair of Shorts," caught the public's attention. When spoken, the title sounded like five knights errant (or errant knights) running around in their briefs. When seen, the title was easily understood to mean that two short plays were to be performed on five nights.

Carmella Braniger, senior theatre minor, directed Alice Gerstenberg's "Overtones," and Robin Hatcher, senior double-major in Theatre/English, directed Neil Simon's "Visitor from Forest Hills," April 9-13 in the Layton Theatre.

Carmella summarized "Overtones," as being " . . . about two women who want what they don't have and can't have what they want."[18] Gerstenberg splits each of her two characters in half; one is the social self that society accepts and the other is the secret self which society rejects. In "Overtones," Harriet (Elaine Cochran) and Margaret (Susan Jackson) pretend to get along, but their other selves, Hetty (Jennifer Sinatra) and Maggie (Mary M. Long) "go at it" tooth and nail. Psychologically interpreted, it is the battle between the conscious and the subconscious.

Neil Simon is the Mozart of the theatrical world; no matter where one happens to be, someone is playing one of his pieces. This time it was Muskingum College and Robin Hatcher (who admitted, "I love Neil Simon."),[19] who chose to direct "A Visitor from Forest Hills." This playlet is the most popular of three that comprise *Plaza Suite.*[20] The scene is a suite in the New York City Plaza Hotel, and the time is Mimsey Hubley's (Michele L. Sheets) wedding day. Her mother, Norma (Tracy Kocinski), and her father, Roy (Scott K. Davis), are nearing the end of their tether because Mimsey, for some unknown reason, has locked herself in the wedding party's bathroom, and she will not come out. THE WEDDING IS OFF! After Mom and Dad have completely and irretrievably "lost it," they send for the groom, Borden Eisler (Chris Tucci Carter). This young man enters, crosses to the bathroom door, and says, "Mimsey? . . . This is Borden . . . Cool it!" He then leaves the room, saying to the Hubleys, "See you downstairs!"[21] The bathroom door opens and Mimsey appears all smiles. THE WEDDING IS ON!

"5 Nights and a Pair of Shorts" was presented by Muskingum Players. Sarah Young designed the set, Elaine Cochran designed the posters, and Dr. Jerry Martin, Dr. Diane Rao, and Mr. Lauck watched from the wings. The audience watched from the auditorium and enjoyed this production.

Cast for
The Night of January 16th

District Attorney Flint	Chris Tucci Carter
Defense Attorney Stevens	Leslie Jeffries
Karen Andre	Jennifer Sinatra
Nancy Lee Faulkner	Katy Cahill
John Graham Whitfield	Viren Gilani
"Guts" Regan	Sean Clark
Dr. Kirkland	Michele Sheets
Jonna Hutchins	Robin Hatcher
Helen Van Fleet	Tracy Kocinski
Elmer Sweeney	Jim Gill
Magda Svenson	Larina Waite
Jane Chandler	Michele Myers
Siergurd Jungquist	Brian Scarpino
Ingrid Jungquist (March 15 only)	Li Hsu

Clerk	Erin Shepard
Bailiff	Adam Tilton
Stenographer	Teresa Wang
Judge Heath (March 12th)	Steve McGuire
Judge Heath (March 13th)	Mary Long
Judge Heath (March 14th)	Scott Davis
Judge Heath (March 15th)	Nelson Chimilio
Judge Heath (March 16th)	Tom Taylor

 1997–1998

T he Muskingum College Theatre presented the premiere production of *In Search of the Red River Dog* by Sandra Perlman, October 15-19 at the Little Theatre. The play was directed by Dr. Jerry Martin, who also designed the set and costumes; Technical Director Ronald N. Lauck designed the lighting; Elaine Cochran designed the program.

The story takes place in Deerfield, an old town in southeastern Ohio, where mining companies have taken a toll on the local population by dumping toxic waste. Paulette, played by Jennifer Sinatra, is the young wife of a jobless steel worker, Denny, played by Christopher Tucci Carter. Paulette is an affectionate wife, who blames the death of her child on water pollution caused by chemical dumping. She is an enlightened woman who is interested in the welfare of others. Her husband is interested only in creature comforts; he loves his wife, but ignores her needs. Paulette's mother, Bertie, played by Violet Taylor, is a good woman who fails to recognize her daughter's marital problems. Paulette's father, John, Sr., played by Nelson Chimilio, is a dispirited old miner and steel worker who has turned to alcohol for comfort.

Paulette is the only family member who understands the urgency for action, if tragedy is to be avoided. She wants to leave the area in which she was born and raised. When Denny reacts to her desire to leave by killing her dog and raping her, Paulette tears herself away from her home, her family, and her husband.[22]

In describing her play, Perlman said:

> it follows a young Ohio girl's journey which ends when her search for her lost dog leads her to confront her husband's fear, her mother's manipulation, and her father's lost dreams. From the deserted mines of her childhood to the poisoned landscapes of her marriage, this character follows a trail of choices.[23]

In his "Director's Notes," Dr. Martin wrote,

> It is the first time in recent history that the college has produced an unpublished full-length script. . . .
> The play was selected for production by a play reading group of students and faculty during the spring of 1997. A total of 67 new play scripts were submitted from Ohio playwrights to be read and considered for inclusion in the production season. All who read the play agreed that the subject matter was important for our community.[24]

In Search of the Red River Dog, 1997. (from the left) Bertie (V. Taylor), Paulette (J. Sinatra), Denny (C. Tucci). *Photo courtesy Sharon Walker, M.C. Public Relations Office.*

Dr. Martin went on to describe how, in the first part of the twentieth century, the Ohio River Valley rivers and back yards became polluted with waste from the mines. Finally, by the 1970's, legislators created the Ohio Reclamation Act that forced mining companies to handle the Southeastern Ohio hill country more responsibly. "With this performance, we not only remember the days of industrial blight, but are given an opportunity to study the human conditions of those caught in the socio-economic decline of the late 1960s and 1970s."[25]

As a result of its entry into the Kennedy Center American College Theatre Festival, *In Search of the Red River Dog* was selected by two festival adjudicators to be performed at the Region III KC/ACTF at the Pike Performing Arts Center in Indianapolis on Friday, January 9, 1998. Muskingum College was the only college from Ohio chosen to perform with five other colleges and universities, representing other states which comprise Region III: Illinois, Indiana, Michigan, and Wisconsin. Those colleges also participating were the University of Wisconsin at Green Bay, Oakland University, University of Evansville, Adrian College, and Valparaiso University.[26]

"'This was a truly great honor for us.' said Dr. Jerry Martin, professor of communication and theater. He added, 'In spite of the facilities we have, we showed that we can still produce a great show.'"[27]

The second production of the 1997-98 theatre season was *Cotton Patch Gospel*, a musical presented by the Muskingum College Theatre, and co-sponsored by Muskingum Players Dramatic Society. Based upon Clarence Jordan's translation of the Gospels of Matthew and John, Harry Chapin composed the music and lyrics, and Tom Key and Russell Treyez wrote the book. Ronald N. Lauck directed, served as technical director, and designed the lighting. Other members of the design team included Emily Mowry, choreography, Alicia Bridwell, set, and Heather Sernka, costumes.

Members of the acting ensemble who performed the play on November 19-23, in the Layton Theatre, included Sean Clark, Kevin Bowers, Amanda Bintz, Meredith

Gariglio, Sean Staneart, Katy Cahill, Krista Lance, Kate Landis, Emily Pieratt, Anne Elise Alesandrini, Amanda Broadway, Jen Hajny, Carissa Griffith, and Melanie Weisgerber. The musicians who accompanied the singers were Dr. Betsy Nichols, Piano; Sean Clark, Guitar, Krista Lance, Fiddle and Flute; and Matt Coombs, String Bass.

The familiar story of the birth of Jesus with the inn, the stable, and the manger, " . . . are replaced with the 'Dixie-Delite Motor Lodge, an abandoned trailer, and an apple crate."[28] The location of the story is Gainesville, Georgia, and it is here that the familiar incidents of Jesus's birth, life of ministry, death, reappearance, and Ascension are retold in the contemporary South.[29]

The 1997-98 season for the second semester began with *A Ride with Huey the Engineer*, February 18-22 in the Layton Theatre. Written by Jesse Stuart and adapted for the stage by the Appalachian Children's Theatre Series, the play was presented by the Muskingum College Theatre and directed by Dr. Jerry Martin. Technical Director Ronald N. Lauck designed the lighting, Heather Sernka was costumer, and Danielle Baisden was stage manager.

> Jesse Stuart (1906-1984) [the original author] was one of America's best known and best loved writers. During his lifetime he published more than 2,000 poems and 460 short stories, and, in addition, he produced more than 60 books of fiction, essays, biography, autobiography, poetry, and juvenile work books which have immortalized his native hill country. [Kentucky]
>
> Stuart wrote eight books for young people. The Jesse Stuart Foundation, a nonprofit organization devoted to preserving the legacy of Jesse Stuart, is making these works available to a new generation of readers.[30]

The story of the play concerns Huey, who was engineer on train Number 5, and the children who ride the train. Huey was played by Chris Tucci Carter; Sunny Logan was played by Christine Shine; Ma Logan, Kate Landis; Mrs. Clarke, Nadine Miller; Ed Webb, Sean Clark; Erin, Wray Withers; and Mrs. Wheeler, Sarah Young. Cathy Compton and Shannon Torch provided "Bells, Whistles, and Percussion," and Gene Alesandrini and Sean Clark played guitar.

According to Adam Tilton's article, cast member Sarah Young "' . . . learned that there is a difference between children's theatre and theatre for college students.'" Young added that children's theatre "' . . . is a lot more fun to perform.'" Another member of the ensemble, Kate Landis, agreed that she enjoyed working on *Huey* "' . . . because the audience was very responsive.'"[31]

The final production of the 1997-98 season was *Fefu and Her Friends*, written by Cuban-born playwright, Maria Irene Fornés, and directed by Dr. Diane Rao, with Ronald N. Lauck in charge of technical aspects of the play.

Fornés is among a number of women playwrights, such as Marsha Norman, Beth Henley, and Wendy Wasserstein who achieved acceptance after 1968. *Fefu and Her Friends* (1977) is set in 1935 at a New England retreat. During a weekend, eight women discuss their past lives and try to understand how they operate within a patriarchal society. Although set in 1935, the issues they discuss have a frightening relevance to contemporary problems.

"'College is a time in which people should explore alternative viewpoints and other perspectives. Theater, and particularly this play is one way in which we can do these things,' said Rao."[32]

The all-female cast for the Muskingum production featured Kate Landis as Cindy; Katy Cahill, Fefu; Michele Sheets, Christina; Michele Meyers, Julia; Heather Kubli, Emma; Cathy Compton, Paula; Stacey Dragosin, Sue, and Violet Taylor, Cecilia.[33]

Fefu and Her Friends was performed April 1-5 as part of Parents Weekend. According to the review written by Adam Hennessey, "For those college students who enjoy experimental theatre, *Fefu and Her Friends* delivered."[34] The Little Theatre, which was the scene of the performances, recorded high attendance during the five day run.

 1998–1999

Zara Spook and Other Lures, by Joan Ackermann, opened the 1998-1999 Muskingum College theatre season on October 7-11 in the Little Theatre. The comedy was entered in the Kennedy Center American College Theatre Festival XXXI, and was Guest-Directed by Maureen Ryan. Technical Director Ronald N. Lauck designed the set and lights, Heather Sernka designed the costumes, and Sean Clark designed the sound for the production. Amy Little created the poster and program image, which was based on Georgia O'Keefe's "Ladder to the Moon" (1958).

The plot and characters of this comedy, which have been called alternately "wacky" and "wonderful," stole the spotlight at the Humana Festival of the Actor's Theatre in Louisville. The action takes place in West Virginia, *Truth or Consequences*, New Mexico, and on the road in between. Evelyn is a young woman who wants to win the women's national bass fishing championship tournament sponsored by "Bassin' Gal Magazine." Two obstacles stand in her way: Talmadge, her boyfriend, who keeps after her to marry him, and Ramona, the competitor, who is the very best. If Talmadge will just let her concentrate, Evelyn believes she can win at least, "Rookie of the Year" honors. Ramona is not without her problems: her macho husband, Mel, has been shut out of her life because he is "insensitive"; however, Mel believes it is because Ramona is seeing Talmadge. When the two men meet, they like each other, and Mel's suspicions are put to rest. Ramona is bitten by a rattler and Mel carries her to safety. Evelyn lands the biggest bass of the tournament and is proclaimed "Rookie of the Year." All is well that ends well.[35]

In the Muskingum production, the cast included Chip Barr (Talmadge), Annie Alesandrini (Evelyn), Michelle Beatty (Teale), Larina Waite (Margery), Chris Tucci (Mel), and Lisa Powers (Ramona).

On November 18-22, *The Menaechmi* by Plautus, edited and translated by Lionel Casson, was performed in the Layton Theatre, under the direction of Dr. Diane Rao. The play was entered in the Kennedy Center American College Theatre Festival. (For a discussion of plot see the February '81 production of *The Twins*.)

The cast for the Muskingum production was as follows: Matt Sullivan and Corrie

Williams (Prologue); Jason Larson (Sponge); Chris Tucci (Menaechmus of Epidamnus); Carissa N. Griffith (Wife of Menaechmus); Christine Shine (Lovey); Joshua Melvin (Roll, the Cook); Chip Barr (Menaechmus of Syracuse); Kate Milligan (Messenio); Carlos Domenech, Justin Moore, Adam R. Tilton (Slaves, Baggage Porters, and Decio); Katy Cahill (Lovey's Maid); Kurt Hall (Father of Menaechmus's Wife); Dustin Jasinski (Doctor).

The Menaechmi, 1998. Chip Barr and Chris Tucci Carter as the twin brothers. *Theatre file photo courtesy Dr. Jerry Martin.*

Technical Director Ronald N. Lauck designed the set; Robin Stock designed the lights; Stacey Dragosin and Michelle Sheets designed the costumes, Kate Landis designed the sound, and Amy Little designed the posters.

In her review of the play for the *Black and Magenta*, Leah Allen quoted Dr. Richard Williamson (English professor) as saying, "'The performances were very good, and the set and costumes captured the mood of the play well. . . . ' 'This performance clearly demonstrates the talents of our theatre students, both on and off stage. I am looking forward to next season.'"[36]

On February 10-14, the Muskingum College Theatre presented the Annual Faculty-Staff Show in the Little Theatre. *The Rat Trap*, an original murder mystery, was written by James and Bronwyn Jameson, and directed by

The Rat Trap, 1999. Father Mellon (B. Kerrigan) tends his flock: (at the table from the left) Susan (C. Higginbotham), Cassandra Deerhound (R. Van Tassel), and Wendy Spencer (A. Darnell); (kneeling) Otto (D. Skeen). *Photo courtesy Dr. Jerry Martin.*

Dr. Jerry Martin. Light Design and Technical Direction were by Ronald N. Lauck; Music and Sound Effects were by Joyce Alesandrini; make-up was by Margaret Adams and Becky Skeen; and the Back Stage Assistant was Robin Hanson. The production of *The Rat Trap* was sponsored, in part, by a grant from the Ohio Theatre Alliance Playwright's Project.

In an article for the *Black & Magenta*, Stacey Dragosin interviewed the cast and crew. English professor, Dr. Andre DeCuir, who played the role of Dr. McNebb, said, "'It has been a positive experience and it all came together nicely.'" History professor, Dr. William Kerrigan, who played Father Mellon, said, "'It gave me an opportunity to get to know my colleagues in a different setting.'" Dr. Martin, the director, thought that the audience was responsive. "'I think the audience responded pretty well, but it's hard to tell if they are responding to the play or to the characters,'" he said. Patty Murphy, a senior, said, "'I think that even if the play itself hadn't been entertaining, I still would have enjoyed it just because of the faculty cast.'"[37]

March 3-7 was devoted to "Two one-act plays by Caryl Churchill: 'Seagulls' and 'Three More Sleepless Nights'." The plays were directed by Dr. Diane Rao; technical director was Ronald N. Lauck; and light designer was Elizabeth Snyder.

The plays were presented at the Little Theatre with students Annie Alesandrini, Candace Miller, and Jeff Strausbaugh cast in "Seagulls," and Wray Withers, Dustin Jasinski, Kurt Hall, and Rebekah Ellis cast in "Three More Sleepless Nights."

According to Stacey Dragosin, staff writer for the *Black and Magenta*,

> Both plays . . . are set in London and work to address specific social problems. "Three More Sleepless Nights" presents three scenes of three different troubled relationships. "Seagulls" is a play about not getting what you want and learning to be happy with what you have.[38]

"Seagulls" and "Three More Sleepless Nights" continue Churchill's exploration of life from a feminist point of view. Andrea Laine Finken, who reviewed the plays, expressed her enjoyment and approval: "In all, both short plays were well performed and interesting. I feel that all involved deserve an extra round of applause for a job well done."[39]

The final production of the 1998-99 season was a series of student-directed works presented on April 8-11, in the Layton Theatre. On April 8 and 11, Adam Tilton directed "Afterglow," a new play by Eric C. Peterson; and Nadine Miller directed "The Way We Live Now," a short story written by Susan Sontag, and arranged for reader's theatre by Edward Parone. On April 9 and 10, Tricia English directed "Landscape with Waitress," written by Robert Pine; and Nelson Chimilio directed "Reflections," an original play written by himself.

The plays were advertised under the title, "Will Work for Food." Admission was $2 per person or canned goods. All proceeds were donated to Christ's Table.

Cast for "The Faculty/Staff Show
The Rat Trap, A Comedy in Two Acts"
Wendy Spencer, The proprietor of the Cardigan-Spencer House .... Amy Darnell
Susan, Wendy's cousin .... Carolyn Higginbotham

Otto, Susan's husband, mayor of the small town where
he and Susan live .... David Skeen
Dr. McNebb, quite elderly, a retired history professor .... Andre DeCuir
Tina Delafemina, McNebb's attractive companion .... Vicki Wilson
Robert Woodford, a restaurant critic for a major New York paper .... Gene Alesandrini
Cassandra Deerhound, a playwright and actress on the
verge of emotional collapse .... Rhoda Van Tassel
Koussa, a secretive, surly man with a thick foreign accent .... Debbie Phillips
Father Mellon, a Catholic priest .... Bill Kerrigan

"Into the Next Century: 1999–2000"
by Dr. Diane Rao Harman

D r. Diane Rao Harman downloaded the following information from her computer and gave it to me when I requested information concerning the 1999-2000 theatre season. I received her permission to present it in the same format here. Her summation of the 1999-2000 season reveals how theatre has remained student-centered at Muskingum College. (Cast lists for some of the events are found at the end of this section.)

"So what's Muskingum College Theatre like?"

We usually do four mainstage productions a year—one in each theatre each semester. The Little Theatre is a black box theatre housed in an historical building which seats 120 in a moveable arrangement. Built in 1900, it was constructed as a gymnasium and remodeled in 1939 as a theatre. The Layton Theatre, located in Johnson Hall, seats 160 and features a proscenium stage space.

One of our most famous alumnae, Annie Glenn, was the subject of the first show of our 1999-2000 season. Wife of former Senator and astronaut John Glenn, Mrs. Glenn is a member of the Muskingum College Board of Trustees. A music major from the class of 1942, Annie suffered from a severe stuttering problem until the 1970s, when successful speech therapy finally permitted her to speak publicly and participate more fully in her husband's political campaigns. *The Annie Glenn Story*, which chronicled the challenges and successes of her life as a stutterer, was performed in Layton Theatre during National Stuttering Awareness Week. This show, an Associate entry in the American College Theatre Festival, was written for Muskingum College by Cincinnati playwright Mary Tensing. The cast and crew featured many theatre scholarship students. For her performance as Annie Glenn, sophomore Michelle Beatty was nominated to participate in the ACTF Irene Ryan Acting Competition.

Eric Bogosian's *SubUrbia* packed the Little Theatre in November. This gritty drama followed a group of misguided Generation-Xers whose only escape from their deteriorating suburban world is through alcohol and drug abuse, promiscuous sex, and fantasies of fame. The cast included first-time actors as well as more seasoned veterans. Senior theatre major Tricia English directed and designed the set for the show, while Robin Stock, senior theatre and psychology major, created the light design. *SubUrbia* was entered as an Associate entry in the American College Theatre Festival. For her performance as BeeBee, junior theatre major Annie Alesandrini was nominated

SubUrbia, 1999. Life is not easy for these young adults behind the Shop and Go Convenient Store. Caught between two gunmen (from the top): Tim (Jimmy Sharp) and Norman (Rohit Radhakrishnan) is Jeff (Chip Barr). *Photo courtesy Dr. Jerry Martin.*

to participate in the ACTF Irene Ryan Acting Competition.

Ever played an alligator who dies when sprinkled with salt? Or a band of opera-singing Taco Bell employees? How about a caveman nurturing a Magic 8-Ball baby? Not exactly your typical theatre fare. But then again, the twenty Muskies who enrolled in Improvisational Theatre class aren't exactly your typical theatre folk. At the beginning of each month, the Improvisational Theatre class invited the Muskingum community to observe their progress at "Muskie Night at the Improv," held in the Thomas Hall Dining Room. Performances included such audience favorites as "Three Minute Musicals," "What's in the Box?" scenes, and Abbreviated Fairy Tales. As an extension of that class, students are planning to start a Muskie Improv Troupe to continue the practice and public performance of this challenging theatre style.

In December, students from the Introduction to Theatre Classes collaborated to write, design, and perform *The New Concord Christmas Cycle Play.* Performed in Brown Chapel, the play was organized in the fashion of a medieval cycle play, with multiple settings and simultaneous scenes. Students performed their scenes 8-10 times throughout the performance, leaving audiences with the cumulative (if not always chronological) vision of the Christmas Story.

Milwaukee, Wisconsin was the site of the 2000 ACTF Region III festival, and as usual, Muskies were in attendance. In addition to the Irene Ryan competitors (Annie Alesandrini, Michelle Beatty), and their scene partners, Muskies participated in the ACTF scene design competition (senior majors Tricia English, Robin Stock) and the National Critics Institute competition (Chris Tucci Carter, Kurt Hall). Students are already making plans to attend next year's festival!

For the past three years, Muskingum has included in our season a play written by an Ohio playwright. This year, if you come to campus in mid-February, you might catch the production *Three the Hard Way,* by Ohio playwright Linda Eisenstein, (Feb.

9-13; Layton Theatre) directed by Jerry Martin. This four member cast (junior Annie Alesandrini, faculty member Amy Darnell, sophomore Jason Larson, and first-year student Natalie Rader) play offers audiences a challenging examination of family dynamics as the complex characters face one of life's most difficult moments: loss of a parent. On Friday, February 11, Ms. Eisenstein will be on campus, addressing theatre students and discussing her play with audiences after the show.

April is a full month for Theatre students. On Parents Weekend, theatre students

Three the Hard Way, 2000. Three sisters (from the left) played by N. Rader, A. Alesandrini, and A. Darnell, come together to bury their father, the over-all presence in the play, enacted by J. Larson. *Photo courtesy Dr. Jerry Martin.*

will offer their parents, classmates, and the public at large a "Showcase of Student Artistry." This show will feature an eclectic mix of student works, ranging from Senior theatre Major Chris Tucci Carter's performance of "An American Player in Pyramus and Thisbe," a work of his own creation, to the performances of original choreography by the dance students in Rick Early's Movement and Voice class. Additional scenes of contemporary drama will be contributed by members of Diane Rao's Directing class. The student showcase—with its more unusual and avant garde fare—is an annual favorite for Muskingum audiences.

You've probably heard of "The Lone Ranger," "The Green Hornet," or "The Edgar Bergen-Charlie McCarthy Show," but you probably have never heard of "A Spy Story," "Sea of Blood," or "Half-Cocked." While you may recognize the first three as classic radio dramas from the 1930's and '40s, you would have to be listening to WMCO (90.7)—the Muskingum College radio station—to have encountered the radio dramas created by Muskingum students over the past several years. In April, the students of THEA 395 and SPCO 395 (Special Topics classes in Radio Drama) will collaborate to create a live radio drama extravaganza. The live performance will transform Muskingum's Brown Chapel into a sound stage reminiscent of the Golden Age of Radio. Simultaneously broadcast on WMCO and performed in front of a live audience, the Radio Drama Showcase will feature student actors, producers and foley crews creating three original radio dramas written by the class.

"The New Concord Passion Play" is the final production of the spring semester. Students from the Introduction to Theatre class will collaborate to tell the story of the Easter Passion. Performed in Brown Chapel, the Passion Play will include scenes from the Gospel stories which relate to Jesus' death and Resurrection. A project which has special meaning for both actors and audience members, the Passion Play project is an unique opportunity for students to synthesize the skills and concepts introduced in the course with an application of Muskingum's Christian mission."[40]

Cast for
The Annie Glenn Story
(Mary Tensing)

THE GLENN FAMILY
Annie in 1998 .... Eileen Adams
Young Annie .... Michelle Beatty
Lyn Glenn .... Kate Ryder
John Glenn .... Chip Barr
David Glenn .... Kurt Hall
THE ENSEMBLE
1930 Student, Tom Miller, Fred .... Paul Gledhill
1930 Student, Ida Mai Miller, Therapist .... Kate Landis
Loudon Wainwright, Dr. Webster .... Jason Larson
Mrs. Castor, Elizabeth .... Jennifer Noble
Technician, Bellgirl, Rene Carpenter .... Lisa Powers
1930 Teacher, Marge .... Nicki Somerville
1930 Student, Jean Gilruth, Elsie .... Missie Thouvenin
Frank Erwin, Joe .... Adam Robert Tilton
Dr. Castor, Herb .... Joshua L. Wasson
SPECIAL GUESTS:
TV Interviewer .... Jamie Kosinski
TV Launch Announcer .... Scott Sellins
Director: .... Diane Rao
Technical Director: .... Ronald N. Lauck
Light Designer: .... Ronald N. Lauck

SubUrbia
(Eric Bogosian)

Jeff .... Chip Barr
Tim .... Jimmy Sharp
Norman .... Rohit Radhakrishnan
Buff .... Chris Tucci
Sooze .... Corrie Williams
Bee-Bee .... Annie Alesandrini
Pony .... Jeff Strausbaugh
Erica .... Amanda Turner
Pakeeza.. Dena Warmuth
Scene: .... Behind The Shop and Go Convenient Store
Time: .... 6:00 p.m. – 7:00 a.m.
Director: .... Tricia English
Technical Director: .... Ronald N. Lauck
Lighting Designer: .... Robin Stock
Set Designer: .... Tricia English
Costume Designer: .... Erynn Wheatley
Sound Designer: .... Christine Shine

The Student Showcase
Scenes from THEA 395 (Directing):
A Coupla White Chicks Sitting Around Talking
by John Ford Noonan

Maude .... Kate Milligan
Hanna Mae .... Jessica L. Taylor
Director: .... Elizabeth F. Snyder

The Dutchman
by LeRoi Jones (Imiri Baraka)

Clay .... Jason Woolley
Lula .... Heather Glaser
Director: .... Larina Waite

The Fourposter
by Jan de Hartog

He .... David Skeen
She .... Becky Skeen
Director: .... Robin Stock

Speech events from SPCO 316 (Intercollegiate Forensics)
Andy Yenchochic
Christy Wampler
Becky Wilson
Michelle Beatty
Melissa Thouvenin
Kurt Hall

Dancers from THEA 175 (Movement and Voice)

Annie Alesandrini	Cassie Fairchild
Danielle Baisden	Tonya Isaacs
Larina Waite	Meter Mi-ren
Michelle Beatty	Jennifer Phillips
Amy Chia-Lu	Amy Richardson
Jinnie Choi	Larina Waite

Original Work from THEA 496 (Independent Study in Performance):
"An American Player in Pyramus and Thisbe,"
adapted by Chris Tucci Carter
from William Shakespeare's *A Midsummer Night's Dream*

Player 1 .... Chris Tucci Carter
Player 2 .... Jason Larson
Player 3 .... Chris Jones
Player 4 .... Larina Waite
Director: .... Chris Tucci Carter

REFERENCES (The Plays: 1995–2000)

1. Kimberly West, "Cast Performs Moliére's *Tartuffe* to Sell-out Crowd for Homecoming," *Black and Magenta*, October 20, 1995, p. 1.

2. Scott Davis, "95-96 Season in Review: *Tartuffe*," *Cue*, Muskingum Players Dramatic Society, Muskingum College, New Concord, Ohio, Summer, 1996, p. 3.

3. *"Love Letters," Complete Catalogue of Plays: 1992-1993* (New York: Dramatists Play Service, Inc., 1992), p. 76.

4. Kelly Streeter, *"Love Letters* Tells Tale of Love, Friendship, and Sorrow," *B&M*, December 1, 1995, p. 3.

5. John Nelson, *"Love Letters," Cue,* Summer, 1996, p. 4.

6. Heather Sernka, "Players Present *Thunderbird*," *B&M*, March 1, 1996, p. 6.

7. Violet Taylor, *"1959 Pink Thunderbird," Cue,* Summer, 1996, p. 4-5.

8. Ronald N. Lauck, "Advisor's Notes," *Cue,* Summer, 1996, p. 6.

9. Virginia Black, "Parents, Students and Faculty Attend *Crossing Delancey*," *B&M*, April 19, 1996, p. 1.

10. Carmella Braniger, *"Crossing Delancey," Cue,* Summer, 1996, pp. 5, 6.

11. Ronald N. Lauck, "Advisor's Notes," *Cue,* Summer, 1996, p. 6.

12. "The Kennedy Center American College Theater Festival," Original Program, *Twelfth Night*." *B&M,* November 1, 1996, p. 2.

13. Missy Mann, "Muskingum Theatre Season Opens with Shakespeare's *Twelfth Night*." *B&M*, November 1, 1996, p. 2.

14. Dr. Richard Williamson, *"Blue Horses* Places Emphasis on Imagination," *B&M*, November 15, 1996, p. 2.

15. Dr. Diane Rao, quoted by Dr. Williamson, *B&M*, November 15, 1996, p. 2.

16. Steph Mann, "Muskingum Faculty Display Theatrical Talents in a Play by James Thurber," *B&M,* February 21, 1997, p. 1.

17. Amanda Murray, Original Program, *Night of January 16th*, March 12-16, 1997, Little Theatre, p. 4.

18. Carmella Braniger, "Director's Notes: 'Overtones,'" Original Program, "5 Nights and a Pair of Shorts," April 9-13, 1997, Layton Theatre, n.p.

19. Robin Hatcher quoted by Jennie Shin, "Muskie Seniors Obtain Experiences Directing," *B&M,* April 18, 1997, p. 2.

20. Robin Hatcher, "Director's Notes: 'A Visitor from Forest Hills,'" Original Program, "5 Nights and a Pair of Shorts," April 9-13, 1997, n.p.

21. Neil Simon, "Visitor from Forest Hills," in *Plaza Suite* (New York: Random House, Inc., 1969), p. 113.

22. Udit Gandhi, "Theater Department Presents *'In Search of the Red River Dog,'* *B&M*, October 24, 1997, p. 1.

23. Janice Tucker quotes Sandra Perlman, *"In Search of the Red River Dog* Performed at Theatre Festival," *Muskingum College Bulletin,* Vol. 89, No. 2, Spring, 1998, p. 6.

24. Jerry Martin, "Director's Notes, *In Search of the Red River Dog,* October, 1997," Original Program, *In Search of the Red River Dog,* October 15-19, Little Theatre, n.p.

25. Ibid.

26. "Muskingum College Theatre Production Headed for American College Theatre Festival in Indianapolis," News Release, Office of Public Relations, Muskingum College, New Concord, Ohio, December 15, 1997.

27. Todd Fusner quotes Jerry Martin, "Muskies Perform *'In Search of the Red River Dog'* at the American College Theater Festival," *B&M,* January 30, 1998, p. 1.

28. Lisa Mourer, *"Cotton Patch Gospel* Cast Announced; College Anticipating Performance," *B&M,* September 19, 1997, p. 3.

29. Steph Mann and Andy King, "Muskingum Theatre Department Presents *Cotton Patch Gospel* Musical," *B&M,* December 5, 1997, p. 2.

30. "About the Author," Original Program, *A Ride with Huey the Engineer,* February 18-22, Layton Theatre, n.p.

31. Adam Tilton quotrd Sarah Young and Kate Landis, "Muskingum Theatre Department Presents Children's Play," *B&M,* February 27, 1998, p. 1.

32. Eric Fowler quotes Diane Rao, "Theatre Department Prepares for Upcoming Production," *B&M,* March 6, 1998, p. 2.

33. Ibid.

34. Adam Hennessey, "Theatre Department Presents All-Female Production of *Fefu and Her Friends*," *B&M,* April 10, 1998, p. 2.

35. *"Zara Spook and Other Lures," Basic Catalogue of Plays and Musicals, 1994 Edition* (New York: Samuel French, Inc., 1994), p. 56.

36. Leah Allen, "Theatre Dept. Puts on Plautus Play in Layton Theatre," *B&M,* December 4, 1998, p. 2.

37. Stacey Dragosin quotes Professors DeCuir, Kerrigan, and Martin and Senior Patty Murphy, "Faculty and Staff Members Entertain Audiences with *The Rat Trap*," *B&M,* February 19. 1999, p. 1.

38. Stacey Dragosin, "Muskingum Theatre Department to Present One-Act Plays in Little Theatre," *B&M,* February 26, 1999, p. 3.

39. Andrea Laine Finken, "Muskie Short Plays," *B&M,* March 12, 1999, p. 5.

40. Dr. Diane Rao, "So What's Muskingum College Theatre Like?" Muskingum College Theatre, Muskingum College, New Concord, Ohio, Fall, 1999.

The Forty-Niners' Fiftieth Reunion

I was right about the nucleus of faculty in the department. They remained steady through the year 2001. When I retired, the department had been forming another plan, among many that had never been realized. This time, it was for a Communication Arts Building which would house, not just a theatre, but all the activities of the department: a campus-wide need for classrooms and facilities for forensics, radio, television, *and* theatre.

With the appointment of Dr. Anne C. Steele as the new–and first woman–president of the college, there was an air of optimism as we faced the new century. The miracle which failed to occur during my tenure (a deep personal disappointment) was a new theatre. Now, even that seemed possible. And during Homecoming week, I accepted an invitation to attend the unveiling of the plans for the new Communication Arts Building on October 6, 2001. How did all this happen! For an explanation, let me return to the Forty-Niners Fiftieth Reunion.

In December 1996, Jim White, chairman of the Class of 1949, wrote to alumni requesting ideas for doing something special for the reunion.[1] I replied with the suggestion that the class gift be designated as seed money for a new theatre. Jim wrote back that the college did not want such gifts to be for particular purposes.[2]

The response did not surprise me. Since the Layton years, the college had received requests and made plans for a new theatre, but they had never materialized. I thought that if our class designated our gift for a new theatre, it would, indeed, be something special, even spectacular! However, the refusal did not stop me. I went to Plan B.

I remembered what classmate, Helen Baird Branyan, had suggested to me even before Jim wrote his letter. She had suggested that the Speech majors who gave recitals in our senior year give a program in which each of us would present a scene from the plays that had constituted those recitals.

I went to my phone and to my typewriter and began the process of communicating with the people most concerned. Surprisingly, three recitalists out of five were available for that Alumni Weekend of June 18-20, 1999, and they all agreed to the idea. I then contacted Ron Mazeroski, our director of Alumni Relations, and he liked the idea. When I notified Jim White that it was going to happen, he was delighted, too. In March of 1999, he wrote to all the recitalists:

> What a wonderful idea you folks have hit upon! It is great! I have attended Alumni Weekends for some years now and, to my recollection, this is the first original idea put forth by a class having a reunion. . . .
>
> I do want you to know that this fits in perfectly with the plans for the weekend. As you may know the College is in preliminary discussions relative to a campaign to raise funds for some sort of an arts center. At this time no details are available but it appears that something is going to happen. Maybe an event such as you folks will put on and our Reunion can give the powers that be a little nudge.[3]

In a June letter Jim wrote:

> . . . I am so pleased that you folks are going to put on the program. It is a bit

unusual for the "arts" to have a place on such a program. Incidentally, Don, did you notice in the announcement about the search for the next Muskingum President the reference to a fine arts building? Not only a statement about it but that a major challenge for the new person will be in 'Executing a major capital campaign for constructing new facilities, with Fine Arts being the first priority.' A few weeks ago at Commencement Dave Skeen, the interim President, made the same statement publicly at a news conference. It all may happen yet![4]

God bless you, Jim White, for your enthusiastic remarks. It certainly would be nice if the college followed through with plans for a new theatre! Three Forty-Niners did follow through with their program, "Senior Speech Recitals Revisited" on Saturday, June 19, 1999. Helen Baird Branyan, gave her interpretation of a section of *Peer Gynt* by Henrik Ibsen, Helen Reskovac Goulet presented scenes from Anouilh's *Antigone*; and I gave a scene from Oscar Wilde's *The Importance of Being Earnest*.

CODA

. . . and then (I'll never forget it) on June 15, 2001, it happened. Nancy Wheeley ('66) had stopped by my house on her way from Mississippi to visit me on her way to her 35th Alumni Reunion at Muskingum.

It was between 9:00 and 9:30 in the morning when I waved good-bye. Around 10:00 a.m. the phone rang and I answered it to hear a soft but excited voice telling me the wonderful news . . . it was Laura Wingfield, from the 1960 cast of *The Glass Menagerie,* announcing the gift of a theatre to Muskingum. At first, I couldn't believe it. After several days of thinking about it, I thought that I had better call Sandy Wolfe Thompson to verify what I thought I heard.

All of this was made abundantly clear to me at the 2001 Homecoming, with the unveiling of the new Communications Arts Complex. I sat with Martha Moore, and before us, on a raised platform in the John Glenn gymnasium, were Anne C. Steele, president of the college, and three of our former students: Harold W. Burlingam ('62), chairman of the Board of Trustees, Anne Marshal Saunier ('68), chairperson of the Academic Affairs Committee of the Board of Trustees, and Sandra Wolfe Thompson ('61), president of Kennett Travel, Inc. Each one announced gifts that identified various areas of their field in which they had studied at Muskingum. When Sandy rose to speak, she announced the gift of a new theatre! She made a believer of me that dreams really do come true. It may take time, but never give up hope. Just look what can happen! ! !

Proposed Muskingum College Communication Arts Complex, 2001. This state-of-the-art 32,000 square foot complex will house the speech, journalism, and theatre programs, as well as the new graphic arts initiative. *Illustration courtesy M.C. Public Relations Office.*

REFERENCES

1   James W. White, Class of 1949 chairperson, in a letter to Forty-niners, December 1966.

2   Jim White in a letter to Donald Hill, September 20, 1997.

3   Jim White in a letter to Don Hill, Helen Baird Branyan, Connie Boyd Cross, Helen Reskovac Goulet, and Dorothy Chapman Flanagan, March 1, 1999.

4   Jim White in a letter to Helen Baird Branyan, Connie Boyd Cross, Dorothy Chapman Flanagan, Don Hill, and Helen Reskovac Goulet, June 9, 1999.

The Muskingum College Theatre Production History: 1944–2000
Introduction

Theatre at Muskingum College has always been student centered. In the earliest days of the college, theatre originated in the activities of student literary societies before there were any classes or instruction in Theatre. In the late nineteenth century, student demand brought the first teacher of "elocution" (dramatic reading) to the campus. Before there was a department, each class of the college, especially the juniors and seniors, engaged in theatrical production. It was student alumni who were the driving force behind the renovation of the Alumni Gymnasium, which resulted in The Little Theatre of 1939. Finally, it was student pressure that enabled the Speech Department to institute a theatre major. The same force helped the renovation of Johnson Hall Chapel into the Layton Theatre.

Commentary on the Listings

Author/Director: After the title of the play, the name of the author is listed, followed by the name of the director. Full-length plays were usually directed by faculty or guest directors. When the theatre major was instituted in 1970, qualified students directed full-length plays as seminars. One-act plays were directed by both faculty and students. From the fall of 1945 to the fall of 1959, students who directed one-acts were junior or senior students with sufficient classroom training and experience to warrant directing a play under faculty supervision. In such cases, the faculty director is noted along with student directors. After 1959, classes in directing and advanced directing offered students a platform for their talents. Supervision continued in the person of a production supervisor, who was a theatre staff member or a technical director.

Technical Director and/or Designer: Until 1971, the theatre had no technical director; aided by students from theatre classes, the director of the play was also the technical director and designer. In the fall of 1971, the college agreed to hire a technical director, and that important post has been recognized as generic to a full season of plays. Nevertheless, there were times when a vacancy in that position was not filled with full-time personnel; luckily, qualified adjuncts were found to serve as guest artists or part-time instructors. (Notably, such years were 1973-74, 1982-84, and 1992-94.) The lack of a technical director doubled the work of a director and the student staff, and had a direct effect on the plays chosen for a particular season. Even with a technical director on the staff, there were times when the director wished to design his or her own set. Likewise, the technical director at Muskingum had the option of directing one or two plays a year.

Producers and/or Sponsors: The present Speech Communication and Theatre Department and Muskingum Players have been the two major producers/sponsors of plays at Muskingum. Theatre grew out of a "Department of Speech," which changed its title in the fall of 1971 to a "Department of Speech and Theatre," in order to reflect the new theatre major. In the fall of 1976, the department became known as the "Speech Communication and Theatre Department" to acknowledge the modern trend in communication. In the fall of 1979, Theatre was housed with Art and Music in a newly created "Fine Arts Department," which changed its name the next year to the "Department of Creative and Performing Arts," or 'CAPA' as it became known. In the fall of 1981, Theatre was reunited with Speech Communication.

Muskingum Players, 1950. First Row: M. Sims, B. Slocum, D. Bolton, L. Knight, M. Hutchens. Second Row: R. Diebel, B. J. Marshall, M. Dias, M. J. Ready, Miss Johnson, R. Zerger, H. Alexasaht, J. Yolton. Third Row: K. Grice, C. Gouyd, R. Chambers, L. Buchanan. *Photo courtesy M. E. Johnson theatre file.*

Muskingum Players, founded in 1925-1926, has always been an entity in itself, with a budget and organization made up of students from all departments of the college–students who may be majors in speech or theatre, but who are more likely to have only an avocational interest. The constitution of the organization provides for an advisor from the Speech Communication and Theatre Department, as a means of providing professional guidance, convenience of scheduling, and general student support for theatre on campus. From 1945–1955 Muskingum Players presented all the major productions. From 1956 to 1959, the Play Production Class of the department assumed that role. With the advent of a theatre major in 1970–71, Muskingum Players deferred to the department, which assumed control of most production activities. Muskingum Players still produced Open Theatre and co-sponsored some events with the department, and continued as a support organization for all theatre events. In the spring of 1988, Muskingum Players sponsored a production of *The Glass Menagerie* for Parents Weekend; they continued to produce a play for that event through 1995. (See Section Notes on Muskingum Players and National Collegiate Players.)

Short plays, billed simply as "One-Acts," or as "Freshman-Sophomore Plays," were produced by a Freshman-Sophomore Dramatics Class for the department until 1949; then, the class was supplanted by an Introduction to Theatre Class, also emanating from the department. Beginning in 1960, one-acts, sometimes called "Studio Productions," became the province of classes in Play Direction and Advanced Acting and Directing. Occasionally, there were faculty-directed one-acts; nevertheless, they were considered the training tool for students.

Place of Production: There is no theatre building at Muskingum College. However, there are buildings, originally intended for other functions, that have been renovated or adapted for theatre use. The primary production facility has been the Little Theatre, which was built in 1900 as a gymnasium. It was renovated in 1939 by Muskingum alumni and rededicated to Professors Charles and Ferne Layton. From 1939 to 1978, the Little Theatre continued as the home of departmental plays. In the spring of 1978, the chapel in Johnson Hall (which was built in 1899), was renovated for additional performance space, and rededicated as the Layton Theatre. Other spaces utilized for productions in newer buildings, as they have appeared on campus, are Brown Chapel, John Glenn Gymnasium, and the lecture hall in the Boyd Science Center.

Section Notes

History of Muskingum Players

The first student dramatic club was formed by E. R. Moses in 1907-08. The club planned to present plays of excellent quality. It produced *A Midsummer Night's Dream* by Shakespeare, and *The Rivals* and *The School for Scandal* before it disbanded in 1913.

The Laytons' program of plays created interest in theatre campus-wide and, in 1923, a notice appeared in the *Black and Magenta*, requesting the formation of another dramatics organization, open to all students, not just to those in theatre classes. The organization was officially born in 1925-26 at commencement, when seniors inducted members of the junior class into Muskingum Players.

One very practical purpose of the club was to oversee and care for theatre properties, costumes, sets, and stage tools and equipment. Besides sponsoring junior and senior play productions, the membership discussed and reviewed new plays, held workshops for one-act plays, and experimented with writing and producing original plays. (See Cheri Swiss, "A History of Theatre at Muskingum College," pp. 30-31.)

The constitution of the organization promised that its members would " . . . promote interest on Muskingum's campus in the best dramatic literature and production." (Preamble to the Muskingum Players Constitution, p. 1.)

National Collegiate Players

In 1927, the national theatre honorary, Pi Epsilon Delta (National Collegiate Players) granted Muskingum a chapter. This organization promoted theatre on a national scale by allying itself with the American National Theatre Association (ANTA) and sponsoring international events such as International Theatre Month.

Similar to most national honorary organizations, there were strict requirements for membership: a student must have excellent character, be totally committed to theatrical events, and maintain a fine scholastic record. Finally, a student must present a number of points by being in major productions. Few small colleges could afford the number of theatre classes and exhibit the number of productions which would qualify students for membership. Muskingum was among a few of those schools.

National Collegiate Players remained an energetic organization throughout the Layton's tenure and well into the sixties and early seventies. However, when some of the founding officers of the national organization began to retire, its prominence and stature began to dwindle. Finally, it faded out of the national picture. It was never replaced at Muskingum. There were several attempts to find another national theatre honorary; I led several investigations of theatre honorary organizations, but they never seemed to be as inviting as that we had lost.

Faculty, Guest Directors and Designers

(chronologically arranged)

1944—1972   Mary Elizabeth Johnson, B.A., Diploma in Oratory, Muskingum College; M.A., University of Michigan

1946—1947   Dorothy Myers Gage, B.A., Diploma in Speech, Muskingum College

1948—1949   Pressley McCoy, B.A., Diploma in Speech, Muskingum College

1948—1986   Martha C. Moore, B.A., Muskingum College; M.A., Ohio State University

1949—1950   Wilma McCague, B.S., M.A., Ohio State University

1957—1959   Gail Joseph Sinclair, B.A., Diploma in Speech, Muskingum College; M.A., Northwestern University

1958—1959   Arthur Sinclair, B.A., New Jersey State Teachers College; M.A., Northwestern University

1959—1995   Donald P. Hill, B.A., Diploma in Speech, Muskingum College; M. A., Western Reserve University; M.F.A., University of Iowa; Ph.D. University of Minnesota

1962—1966   Stanley Schutz, B.A., Otterbein College; B.S., M.A., Ph.D., Michigan State University

1962—1964   Rex T. McGraw, Jr., B.A., M.A., Bowling Green State University; Ph.D., Indiana University

1964   Edith Miller, B.A., Wheaton College; M.A., Radcliffe; Ph.D., Columbia University

1966, 1967   Barry Baughman, Guest Lighting Designer; B.A. Muskingum College, M.A. Kent State University

1966—1971   Muriel Bain, B.A., Muskingum College; M.A., University of Michigan

1970, 1975   E. Sue Cook, B.S., Bowling Green State University; M.A., Miami University

1968—1969   Elizabeth Wills, B.A., Washington State University; M.A., University of Denver

1971—1973   Richard Downing, B.S., Wisconsin State University; M.A., University of Michigan

1972—1974   Cheryl Swiss, B.A., Muskingum College; M.A., Ohio University; Ph.D. University of Wisconsin

1973   David Golden, Guest Designer and Technical Director

1974—1977   Jerry Martin, B.S. Ed., M.A., Kansas State Teachers College; Ph.D., Texas

1981—   Tech University

1975   James Holm, Jr., B.A., College of Wooster; M.A., Kent State University; Ph.D., University of Michigan

1976—1978, 1980 Catherine A. Johnson, B.A., Ohio Wesleyan University; M.M., Northwestern University

1976—1977 Gay Manifold, B.A., M.A., University of Hawaii

1977—1978 Brent Fleming, B.S. Ed., Emporia Kansas State College; M.A., Texas Tech University

1977—1978 Deann Fleming, B.S. Ed., Emporia Kansas State College

1978 Pat Van De Voort, B.S., M.S., Illinois State University

1978—1979 Warren Shaull, B.A., St. Mary of the Plains; M.F.A., Memphis State University

1979—1980 Diane Rock, B.S., Ohio State University; M.S., University of Denver

1979, 1983, 1984 Theodore Hissam, Consultant, Guest Director, Guest Actor; B.A. Muskingum College

1980—1984 Sharon Taylor, B.A., Hiram College; M.F.A., Ohio University

1981 Dona Vaughn, Guest Director

1981 Richard Probert, B.S., Wilkes College; M.M.E., Indiana University

1981 Jack Lee Peterson B.M., M.M., Cincinnati Conservatory; D.M., Florida State University

1982 Richard Henzel, Guest Director, Artist-in-Residence

1984 Roger Drake, B.A., Ohio Wesleyan University; M.F.A., Ohio University; United Scenic Artists

1984 John Newton White, Guest Designer; B.A. Muskingum College

1984—1986 Donald Lillie, B.A., M.A., Moorehead State University

1985, 1986, 1993 Robert Owen Jones, B.S., Muskingum College; M.S., Julliard School of Music

1986 Eileen McComb Adams, Guest Director; B.A. Muskingum College

1986 Ronald N. Lauck, B.S., Bluffton College; M.S., Bowling Green State University; M.F.A., University of South Dakota

1992—1993 Svetlana Efremova, Guest Director, Artist-in-Residence

1992—1993 Olga Tchainikova, Guest Designer

1993 Carol Wilcox-Jones, B.A., University of Kansas; M.A., Ohio State University

1993, 1997 Gene Alesandrini, B.S., Bradley University; M.A., Eastern Michigan University

1994 Frederick Frank, Guest Director; B.A., M.A. (Education) Muskingum College

1995 Bob Belfance, Guest Director

1995— Diane Rao Harman, B.A., Gannon University; M.A., Ph.D., Bowling Green State University

1998 Maureen Ryan, B.A., Kenyon College; M.F.A., Indiana University

A Production History
Prologue
1944–1960

1944–1945

<u>1944</u>

[On Thursday, April 20 at 8:00 p.m., Mrs. Ferne Parsons Layton directed three one-act plays open to the public for no charge at the Little Theatre.
The plays were:
The Clouds by Zona Gale
Good Medicine by Jack Arnold
The Burglars by Margaret Cameron.
The plays came from a class meeting once a week in an extra-curricular offering called "The Freshmen Dramatic Club."

<u>1945</u>
January 11–13   **Ladies in Retirement*, by Edward Percy and Reginald Denham; Faculty Director, Mary Elizabeth Johnson

May 7   **Sophomore Dramatics**; Faculty Director, Mrs. Layton
Scenes from *Watch on the Rhine,* by Lillian Hellman
The Admirable Crichton, by James M. Barrie

May 17–19   *Quality Street*, by James M. Barrie; Faculty Director Johnson

1945–1946

<u>1945</u>
October 16   The Freshman-Sophomore Dramatics Class was organized under Mary Elizabeth Johnson in connection with a communication course laboratory.

<u>1946</u>
Jan 31– Feb 1   **The Freshman-Sophomore Plays**; Faculty Director Johnson
The Summons of Sariel, by Magdalene Kessie; student directors Colleen Banford and Norma Richards
The Travelers, by Booth Tarkington; student directors Frances Covault and Betty Jo McDaniel

February 23   **Drama and Poetry Reading Clinic** (First Annual)
The Summons of Sariel, by Magdalene Kessie; Faculty Director Johnson

May 9–11   *Strangers at Home*, by Charles Divine; Faculty Director Johnson

1946–1947

<u>1946</u>   [No plays identified]

<u>1947</u>
January 14–17   *Deep Are the Roots*, by Arnaud D'Usseau and James Gow; Faculty Director Johnson

February 21   **The Freshman-Sophomore Plays**; Faculty Director Dorothy Myers
The Bracelet of Doom, by Vivian Mayo; student director Beverly Sohn
Parted on Her Wedding Morn or More To Be Pitied Than Scorned, by Leland Price; student director Helen Haley

February 27   **The Freshman-Sophomore Plays**; Faculty Director Myers
Happy Journey, by Thornton Wilder; student director Nancy Maurer
The Dweller in the Darkness, by Reginald Berkeley; student director Pauline Coleman
Let's Make Up, by Esther E. Olson; student director Ruth Lang

---

**Ladies in Retirement* was Mary Elizabeth Johnson's directorial debut of a major production at Muskingum. Her tenure was to span the next twenty-eight years, 1944–1972.

May 21–24   *Idiot's Delight*, Robert E. Sherwood; Faculty Director Johnson

1947–1948

1947
November 13   **The Freshman-Sophomore Plays**; Faculty Director Dorothy Myers Gage
                   The Invisible Clue, by William M. Sloane; student director LaVonne Hartman
                   The Valiant, by Holworthy Hall and Robert Middlemass; student director
                   Louise McCarty
                   Night Club, Dan Totheroh; student directors Connie Boyd and Janet Becker
November 20   **The Freshman-Sophomore Plays;** Faculty Director Gage
                   Heritage of Wimpole Street, Robert Knipe; student director Eleanor
                   MacMichael with Pressley McCoy
                   His Jewels, Bernice K. Harris; student director Marian Ausherman
                   Lady Unknown, W. Massey; student director Christine Alter
November 22   **Drama and Poetry Reading Clinic** (Second Annual); Chairperson Mary
                   Elizabeth Johnson

1948
January 14–17   *The Little Foxes*, Lillian Hellman; Faculty Director Johnson; Senior Play
May 19–22   *Berkeley Square*, John L. Balderston; Faculty Director Johnson; Junior Play

1948–1949

1948
November 6   **Drama and Poetry Reading Clinic** (Third Annual); Chairperson Mary Eliza-
                   beth Johnson
                   Thank You, Doctor, Gilbert Emery; Faculty Director Pressley McCoy
November 12–13   **The Freshman-Sophomore Plays**; Faculty Director McCoy
                   What Never Dies, Percival Wilde
                   Thank You, Doctor, Gilbert Emery
                   Blackout, Essex Dane
November 18–19   **The Freshman-Sophomore Plays**; Faculty Director McCoy
                   The Finger of God, Percival Wilde
                   The Tangled Web, Cecil G. Stephens
                   Our Dearest Possession, Robert Middlemass

1949
January 12–15   *The Great Big Doorstep*, Francis Goodrich and Albert Hackett; Faculty Di-
                   rector Johnson
March 17–18   **The Freshman-Sophomore Plays**; Faculty Director McCoy
                   Station YYY, Booth Tarkington
                   Rehearsal, Christopher Morley
                   Undertow, Anne Weatherly
March 25–26   **The Freshman-Sophomore Plays**; Faculty Director McCoy
                   A Mad Breakfast, Isabel McReynolds Gray
                   The Examination, Fred Eastman
                   Four Hundred Nights, Jack Stuart Knapp
April 9   **Drama and Poetry Reading Festival**: The Muskingum College Speech
                   Department in conjunction with the Ohio High School Speech League spon-
                   sored the District 5 contest.
May 18-21   *Dark Victory*, George Brewer, Jr. and Bertram Bloch; Faculty Director Johnson

1949–1950

1949
November 10–12   **The Freshman-Sophomore Plays**; Faculty Director Mrs. Wilma McCague
                   Three by George Kelly
                   The Flattering Word, student director Marilyn Resler
                   Finders Keepers, student director Jim Parrish

Poor Aubrey, student director Bill Berlin

November 19   **Drama and Poetry Reading Clinic** (Fourth Annual): Chairperson Johnson
The Monkey's Paw, W. W. Jacobs; Faculty Director McCague

1950
January 18–21   *Children of the Moon*, Martin Flavin; Faculty Director Johnson
March 16–18   **The Freshman-Sophomore Plays**; Faculty Director McCague
An Evening of Folk Plays:
Fixin's, Paul and Erma Green; student director Al Deal
Sparkin', Ellsworth P. Conkle; student director Bob Walker
White Dresses, Paul Green; student director Gerry Bowdler
May 24–27   *The Young Idea*, Noel Coward; Faculty Director Johnson

1950–1951

1950
November 15–17   **The Freshman-Sophomore Plays**; Faculty Director Martha C. Moore
An Evening of Fun
The Professor Roars, Betty Smith and Robert Finch; student director Annette Monroe
Box and Cox, John Madison Morton; student director Susan Stanchina
Permanent, James Reach; student director Mitzie Cottle
November 18   **Drama and Poetry Reading Clinic** (Fifth Annual): Chairperson Johnson
The Professor Roars, Betty Smith and Robert Finch; student director Annette Monroe; Faculty Director Moore

1951
January 17–20   *Papa Is All*, Patterson Greene; Faculty Director Johnson
April 18–19   **The Freshman-Sophomore Plays**; Faculty Director Moore
Love-Laughter-Tears
The Right Answer, Lucy Kennedy Brown; student directors Gail Joseph and Nancy Nolin
Balcony Scene, Donald Elser; student director Annette Monroe
A Night in the Country, Betty Smith and Robert Finch; student director Betty Sherwood
April 28   **High School Guest Day**; Faculty Director Moore
Balcony Scene, Donald Elser; student director Annette Monroe
May 23–26   *The Late Christopher Bean*, Sidney Howard; Faculty Director Johnson

1951–1952

1951
November 3   **Drama and Poetry Reading Clinic** (Sixth Annual): Chairperson Johnson
Balcony Scene, Donald Elser
Fog on the Valley, Verne Powers (scenes only); Faculty Director Moore
November 14–16   **The Freshman-Sophomore Plays**; student directors (not listed by play) Jack White, Peggy Culp, Frances Henderson, Gail Joseph, and Gene Mast; Faculty Director Moore
A Night of Drama
Everybody's Doing It, Elise West Quaife
The Neighbors, Zona Gale
Fog on the Valley, Verne Powers

1952
January 16–19   *The Silver Whistle*, Robert E. McEnroe; Faculty Director Johnson
April 14–16   **The Freshman-Sophomore Plays**; student directors (not listed by play) Peggy Culp, Shorty Ruth, Bill Scheuerle; Faculty Director Moore
Lily, Nan Bagby Stephens
The Love of Allah, Phil Milhous
Hello, Out There, William Saroyan

April 26	**High School Guest Day**
	The Love of Allah, Phil Milhous; Faculty Director Moore
May 21–24	*Harvey*, Mary Coyle Chase; Faculty Director Johnson

1952–1953

<u>1952</u>
November 8	**Drama and Poetry Reading Clinic** (Seventh Annual): Chairperson Johnson
	Gloria Mundi, Patricia Brown; Faculty Director Moore
November 20–21	**One-Act Plays**; student directors (not listed by play) Lois Cheney and Gail Joseph; Faculty Director Moore
	Cabbages, Edward Staadt
	Rehearsal, Christopher Morley
	Gloria Mundi, Patricia Brown

<u>1953</u>
January 14–17	*All My Sons*, Arthur Miller; Faculty Director Johnson
March 20	**One-Act Play**
	Cathleen ni Houlihan, William Butler Yeats
March 24–25	**One-Act Plays**; student directors (not listed by play) Lois Cheney, John Hickox, Gail Joseph; Faculty Director Moore
	No! Not the Russians!, Osmond Molarsky
	Hung Jury, David O. Woodbury
	Antic Spring, Robert Nail
May 20–23	*Blithe Spirit*, Noel Coward; Faculty Director Johnson

1953–1954

<u>1953</u>
November 19–20	**One-Act Plays**; Faculty Director Moore
	Air Tight Alibi, Walter Hackett
	The Dark Corner, Lyda Nagel
	The Lost Elevator, Percival Wilde
November 21	**Drama and Poetry Reading Clinic** (Eighth Annual): Chairperson Johnson; Faculty Director Moore
	Air Tight Alibi, Walter Hackett
	The Dark Corner, Lyda Nagel
	The Lost Elevator, Percival Wilde

<u>1954</u>
January 13–16	*Cry Havoc*, Allan R. Kenward; Faculty Director Johnson
March 24–25	**One-Act Plays**
	Opening Night, Cornelia Otis Skinner
	One of Us, Charles Emery; student director Dick Shaw; Faculty Director Moore
May 19–22	*Death Takes a Holiday*, Alberto Cassella and Walter Ferris; Faculty Director Johnson

1954–1955

<u>1954</u>
November 20	**Drama and Poetry Reading Clinic** (Ninth Annual): Chairperson Johnson
	Two one-act plays; Faculty Director Moore
December 1–2	**One-Act Plays**; Faculty Director Moore
	Balcony Scene, Donald Elser
	The Best There Is, Marion Wefer
	Before Breakfast, Eugene O'Neill
	A Night in the Country, Betty Smith and Robert Finch

<u>1955</u>
| January 12–15 | *Guest in the House*, Hagar Wilde and Dale Eunson; Faculty Director Johnson |
| April 20–21 | **One-Act Plays**; student directors (not listed by play) Roberta Dietrich, Yvonne Heath, Bruce Henderson; Faculty Director Moore |

	Sorry, Wrong Number, Lucille Fletcher
	Sisters Under the Skin, Mae Howley Barry
	Submerged, H. Stuart Cottman and Levergne Shaw
	The Case of the Crushed Petunias, Tennessee Williams
May 18–21	The Rivals, Richard Brinsley Sheridan; Faculty Director Johnson

1955–1956

<u>1955</u>

October 13	**Open Theatre**, Broadway Once-Removed
	Scenes from *Teahouse of the August Moon*, John Patrick and *Anastasia*, Guy Bolton
November 12	**Drama and Poetry Reading Clinic** (Tenth Annual): Chairperson Johnson
December 7–8	**One-Act Plays**; Faculty Director Moore
	Church Street, Lennox Robinson; student director Roberta Dietrich
	Footfalls, Brainard Duffield; student director Carol Morrow
	John Turner Davis, Horton Foote; student director Carol Arter

<u>1956</u>

January 18–21	*Goodbye, My Fancy*, Fay Kanin; Faculty Director Johnson
May 23–26	*The Shrike*, Joseph Kramm; Faculty Director Moore

1956–1957

<u>1956</u>

October 11	**Open Theatre**
	Curses, the Villain Is Foiled or *Hearts and Flowers*, Henry Rowland
November 3	**Drama and Poetry Reading Clinic** (Eleventh Annual): Chairperson Johnson; Faculty Director Johnson
	Scenes from *Hearts and Flowers*, Henry Rowland
	Have You Anything to Declare?, Gertrude Jennings
November 15–16	**One-Act Plays**; student directors (not listed by play) Mary Jane Campbell, Audrey Herman, Harry Coffield, Barbara Wharton, Barbara Sittig; Faculty Director Johnson
	Have You Anything to Declare?, Gertrude Jennings
	Undertow, Anne Weatherly
	The Travelers, Booth Tarkington

<u>1957</u>

January 16–19	*The Crucible*, Arthur Miller; Faculty Director Moore
May 22–25	*The Torchbearers*, George Kelly; Faculty Director Johnson

1957–1958

<u>1957</u>

November 9	**Drama and Poetry Reading Clinic** (Twelfth Annual): Chairperson Johnson
November 20–21	**One-Act Plays**; Faculty Director Gail Joseph
	The Boor, Anton Chekov; student director Sonya Mugnani
	The Long Christmas Dinner, Thornton Wilder; student director June Browning
	The Hitch Hiker, Lucille Fletcher; student director Patty Jo Davidson

<u>1958</u>

January 15–18	*The Madwoman of Chaillot*, Jean Giraudoux, translated by Maurice Valency; Faculty Director Joseph
April 16–17	**One-Act Plays**; Faculty Director Joseph
	The Neighbors, Zona Gale; student director Jackie Montgomery
	The Old Lady Shows Her Medals, James M. Barrie; student director Janet Click
	Riders to the Sea, J. M. Synge; student director Sue Cross
May 21–24	*Berkeley Square*, John L. Balderston; Faculty Director Joseph

1958–1959

<u>1958</u>

October 23   **Open Theatre**: *A Sunny Morning,* Serafin and Joaquin Quintero; student director Sunny Mugnani

November 12–14   **One-Act Plays**; Faculty Director Arthur Sinclair
Everyman, Anonymous; student director Beth McKelvey
The Stolen Prince, Dan Totheroh; student director Al Beal

November 15   **Drama and Poetry Reading Clinic** (Thirteenth Annual): Chairperson Johnson; Faculty Director Sinclair
The Stolen Prince, Dan Totheroh; student director Al Beal

December 7, 10 & 17   **One-Act Play**: *A Child Is Born,* Stephen Vincent Benet; Faculty Director Gail Joseph Sinclair

<u>1959</u>

January 14, 15 & 17   *The Skin of Our Teeth*, Thornton Wilder; Faculty Director Sinclair

March 18–20   **2 One-Act Plays**; Faculty Director Sinclair
The High-Brow Ladies, Moliére; student director Charles Ransom
Where the Cross is Made, Eugene O'Neill; student director Don Gilbert

April 16   *As You Like It* (scenes), William Shakespeare; Faculty Director Gail Joseph Sinclair

May 20–23   *Night Must Fall*, Emlyn Williams; Sinclair; Play Production Class; 8:15 p.m., Little Theatre (*B&M*, May 19, 1959, p. 1)

1959–1960

<u>1959</u>

October 22   **Open Theatre**: *The Flattering Word,* George Kelly; student director Beth McKelvey

November 7   **Drama and Poetry Reading Clinic** (Fourteenth Annual): Chairperson Johnson; Faculty Director Donald Hill
Never the Time and the Place, Lennox Robinson; student director Marilyn Gleason
The Marriage Proposal, Anton Chekov; student director Sandra Wolfe

November 18–20   **Love and Marriage**, An Evening of One-Act Comedies; Faculty Director Hill
Never the Time and the Place, Lennox Robinson; student director Marilyn Gleason
The Marriage Proposal, Anton Chekov; student director Sandra Wolfe
These Cornfields, Georges Courteline; student director Judy Johnson

<u>1960</u>

January 13–16   *The Glass Menagerie*, Tennessee Williams; Faculty Director Hill

March 29–31   **Two Plays by George Bernard Shaw**: *The Shewing-Up of Blanco Posnet,* and *The Dark Lady of the Sonnets,* George Bernard Shaw; Faculty Director Hill

May 18–21   *The Playboy of the Western World*, John Millington Synge; Faculty Director Hill

A Production History
1960–1970
Indicates special projects or seminars

1960–1961

<u>1960</u>
October 19–22	*Private Lives*, by Noel Coward; director, Donald Hill
November 5	**Drama and Poetry Reading Conference (Fifteenth Annual)**
	The Long Stay Cut Short, by Tennessee Williams; student director, David Kafer
December 7–10	*The House of Bernarda Alba*, by Federico Garcia Lorca; director Hill

<u>1961</u>
January 7	**Two One-Act Studio Productions**
	Fumed Oak, by Noel Coward; student director, Marilyn Gleason
	Joint Owners in Spain, by Alice Brown; student director, Barbara Kukura
January 14	**Two One-Act Studio Productions**
	Rehearsal, by Christopher Morley; student director, Judy Johnson
	Another Way Out, by Lawrence Langner; student director, Claren Branch
March 8–11	*Under Milkwood*, by Dylan Thomas; director Hill
April 22	**Two One-Act Plays**
	He Said and She Said, by Alice Gerstenberg; student director, Edward Tate
	Soldadera, by Josephina Niggly; student director, John Wilkins
May 10–13	*A Mid-Summer Night's Dream*, by William Shakespeare; director Hill, *Costume Design, Barbara Kukura

1961–1962

<u>1961</u>
October 26–28	**Open Theatre, *Two by Ionesco:***
	The Lesson and *The Bald Soprano,* by Eugene Ionesco; director, Donald Hill
November 11	**Drama and Poetry Reading Conference (Sixteenth Annual):**
	The Lesson, by Eugene Ionesco; director, Donald Hill
December 6–9	*Bad Seed*, by Maxwell Anderson; director, Donald Hill

<u>1962</u>
January 6	*Egad, What A Cad!* or *Virtue Triumphs Over Villainy*, by Anita Bell; student director, Rebecca Gillis
March 7–10	*Inherit the Wind*, by Jerome Lawrence and Robert E. Lee; director, Stanley Schutz
March 17	*Under Milkwood*, by Dylan Thomas; director, Donald Hill
May 7–12	**Shakespearean Repertory:**
	Hamlet, by William Shakespeare; director, Donald Hill
	A Mid-Summer Night's Dream, by William Shakespeare; director, Donald Hill
May 26	*The Measures Taken*, by Bertolt Brecht; student director, Robert Layton

1962–1963

<u>1962</u>
October 24–27 (Homecoming)	*The Male Animal*, by James Thurber & Elliott Nugent; director, Stanley Schutz
November	**Drama and Poetry Reading Conference (Seventeenth Annual)**
December 12–15	*J. B.*, by Archibald MacLeish; director, Rex McGraw

<u>1963</u>
January 12	***One-Act Plays**
	The Long Christmas Dinner, by Thornton Wilder; student director, Donald Kelm
	The Maker of Dreams, by Oliphant Downs; student director, Sherran Reynolds

	The Sandbox, by Edward Albee; student director, Bing Bills
	The Informer, by Bertolt Brecht; student director, Carol McFarland Gable
January 19	***One-Act Plays**
	The Happy Journey to Camden and Trenton, by Thornton Wilder; student director, Carolyn Aiken
	Waiting for Lefty, by Clifford Odets; student director, Paul Alvarez
	Pantaloon, by James M. Barrie; student director, Lorraine Commeret
March 13–16	*The Little Foxes,* by Lillian Hellman; director, Rex McGraw
May 8–11	*Twelfth Night* or *What You Will,* by William Shakespeare; director, Rex McGraw

1963–1964

1963

October 15–19 *(Homecoming)*	*The Fantasticks,* by Tom Jones and Harvey Schmidt; director, Rex McGraw
October 26	**Drama and Poetry Reading Conference (Eighteenth Annual)**
	Scenes from *The Fantasticks,* by Jones & Schmidt; director, Rex McGraw
December 11–14	*An Enemy of the People,* by Henrik Ibsen, adapted for the American stage by Arthur Miller; director, Stanley Schutz

1964

February 21–22	*The Doctor in Spite of Himself,* by Moliére; director, Rex McGraw; Readers Theatre English version followed by the acted French version, *Le Medecin Malgre Lui,* by Moliére; director, Edith Miller
March 10–14	*Antigone*: Two Versions, One by Sophocles and the other by Jean Anouilh; director, Rex McGraw
April 26	*Spirits of Shakespeare,* In honor of Shakespeare's 400th Birthday, Readers Theatre; director, Rex McGraw
May 5–9	*The Merry Wives of Windsor,* by William Shakespeare; director, Rex McGraw
May 16	**Two One-Act Plays**
	The Zoo Story, by Edward Albee; student director, Janet Small
	The Hour Glass, by William Butler Yeats; student director, Sally McCracken
May 23	**Two One-Act Plays**
	Aria da Capo, by Edna St. Vincent Millay; student director, Judy Sjoberg

1964–1965

1964

October 21–24 *(Homecoming)*	*Androcles and the Lion,* by George Bernard Shaw; director, Stanley Schutz
November 7	**Drama and Poetry Reading Conference (Nineteenth Annual)**
	Spirits of Shakespeare; director, Rex McGraw
December 9–12	*The Importance of Being Earnest,* by Oscar Wilde; director, Donald Hill

1965

March 17–20	*Dinny and the Witches,* by William Gibson; director, Donald Hill
April 9–10	**Beauty and the Beast,* by Nora MacAlvay; student director, Janet Small
May 15	**Two One-Act Plays**
	The Apollo of Bellac, by Jean Giraudoux; student director, Judy Moore
	Sorry, Wrong Number, by Lucille Fletcher; student director, Carol Link
May 22	**Two One-Act Comedies**
	The Workhouse Ward, by Lady Gregory; student director, Sandy Wilkins
	Another Way Out, by Lawrence Langner; student director, Judy Ross

1965–1966

1965

October 13–16 *(Homecoming)*	*Death of a Salesman,* by Arthur Miller; director, Donald Hill

October 30	**Drama and Poetry Reading Conference (Twentieth Annual)**
	Scenes from *Death of a Salesman*
December 8–11	*Stalag 17*, by Donald Bevan and Edmund Trzcinski; director, Stanley Schutz
December 14	*Stalag 17*

1966

January 8	**One-Act Plays**
	Trifles, by Susan Glaspell; student director, Sally Schenck
	The Boor, by Anton Chekhov; student director, Barbara Drake
January 13–15	**One-Act Plays**
	*The Adventures of Harlequin; student director, Judy Moore
	Through a Glass Darkly, by Stanley Richards; student director, Mary Ellen Matson
	The Flattering Word, by George Kelly; student director, Nancy Wheeley
March 16–19	*Doña Rosita (The Spinster),* by Federico Garcia Lorca; director, Donald Hill
May 4–7	*Hay Fever*, by Noel Coward; director, Donald Hill, *scene design, Sally Schenck
May 21	**One-Act Plays**
	Puss in Boots, by Madge Miller, student director, Saralynn Wingard
	The Room, by Harold Pinter; student director, Mike Naas

1966–1967

1966

October 19-22 *(Homecoming)*	*A Thurber Carnival*, by James Thurber; director, Donald Hill
November 5	**Drama and Poetry Reading Conference (Twenty-First Annual)**
	Scenes from *A Thurber Carnival*
November 9, 11–12	*The Swampdwellers,* by Wole Soyinka; director, Muriel Bain
December 14–17	*Medea*, by Robinson Jeffers, freely adapted from the *Medea* of Euripides; director, Donald Hill *costumes, Peggy Basnett

1967

January 14	**Two One-Act Plays**
	Glory in the Flower, by William Inge; student director, Lillian Kestner
	Riders to the Sea, by John M. Synge; student director, Suzanne Fontaine
January 20	**The Play Within a Play*, an original one-act by student director, Susan Rau
January 21	**Two One-Act Plays**
	The Ugly Duckling, by A. A. Milne; student director, Alma Perry
	Orphé, by Jean Cocteau; student director, Tom Forgrave
March 8–11	*The Amorous Flea*, by Jerry Devine and Bruce Montgomery; director, Donald Hill
March 15	**The Zoo Story*, by Edward Albee; student director, Lillian Kestner
March 20–21	**The Flies*, by Jean-Paul Sartre; A Readers Theatre by student director, Thomas Forgrave
May 10–13	*Waiting for Godot*, by Samuel Beckett; director, Donald Hill
May 20	**Two One-Act Plays**
	The Case of the Crushed Petunias, by Tennessee Williams; student director, Peggy Basnett
	Way Down East, (Anonymous); student director, Carol Beth Boyer

1967–1968

1967

September 29	**Open Theatre**
	The Case of the Crushed Petunias, by Tennessee Williams; student director, Cheri Swiss
October 18–21 *(Homecoming)*	*Little Mary Sunshine*, by Rick Besoyan; director, Donald Hill

October 28	**Drama and Poetry Reading Conference (Twenty-Second Annual)**
	Scenes from *Little Mary Sunshine*
November 18	**Bertolt Brecht, A Readers Theatre**
	The Jewish Wife, The Informer, and *Threepenny Opera*
December 6–9	*Mother Courage and Her Children*, by Bertolt Brecht, adapted by Eric Bentley; director, Donald Hill

1968

January 13	**One-Act Plays**
	Sotoba Komachi, by Kwanami Kiyotsugu
	Kayoi Komachi, by Ka'nami Metsukaze (two Noh plays); student director, Sheila Williams
	Red Carnations, by Glenn Hughes; student director, Penny Heacock
	The Marriage Proposal, by Anton Chekhov; student director, Beth Brown
March 6–9	*Our Town*, by Thornton Wilder; director, Muriel Bain
March 20	**Two One-Act Plays**
	Hello, Out There, by William Saroyan; student director, Robert Barrows
	The Death of Bessie Smith, by Edward Albee; student director, Linda Weber Enstrom
May 8–11	*The Taming of the Shrew*, by William Shakespeare; director, Donald Hill

1968–1969

1968

October 16–19 *(Homecoming)*	*The Glass Menagerie*, by Tennessee Williams; director, Elizabeth Wills
October 26	**Drama and Poetry Reading Conference (Twenty-Third Annual)**
	Scenes from *The Glass Menagerie*
November (no dates)	**Muskingum Players Touring Theatre**
	Scenes from *The Fantasticks, Little Mary Sunshine, The Amorous Flea, Lysistrata, A Thurber Carnival,* and *The Taming of the Shrew* toured to Meadowbrook, Cambridge, John Glenn, and West Muskingum High Schools; coordinator, Muriel Bain
December 5	**Two One-Act Plays**
	Snowangel, by John Carlino; student director, Charles W. Clark
	The Flattering Word, by George Kelly; student director, Larry Ledford
December 7	**Two One-Act Plays**
	The Dark Lady of the Sonnets, by George Bernard Shaw; student director, Theodore W. Hissam
	Carrie of the Carnival, by Helen M. Stuart; student director, David Beall
December 8	*The Contrite Spirit,* by Alberta Hause; student director, Richard Jackson

1969

January 29	*Journey into Everyman*, A "Winterim" Readers Theatre; director, Mary Elizabeth Johnson
March 19–22	*The Lion in Winter*, by James Goldman; director, Muriel Bain
May 14–17	*The Time of Your Life*, by William Saroyan; director, director, Elizabeth Wills

1969–1970

1969

September 19	**Open Theatre**
	Scenes from *Spoon River Anthology*, by Edgar Lee Masters, adapted and arranged by Charles Aidman
October 1–4 *(Homecoming)*	*Ten Nights in a Bar Room*, An original Musical by Al Evans and Darryl Bojanowski based on the temperance melodrama by William Pratt; director, Donald Hill

October 18	**Drama and Poetry Reading Conference (Twenty-Fourth Annual)**
	Scenes from *Spoon River Anthology*
	Selections from *Journey into Everyman;* "Winterim" Readers Theatre
December 4	**Studio One-Acts**
	The Whiteshop, by Garrett Robinson (A Midwest Premiere for the Columbus [Ohio] Playwright); student director, Rozelle Hill
	The Ghost of Mr. Penny, by Rosemary Gabbert Musil; student director, Bette McMuldren
December 5	**Studio One-Acts**
	The Whiteshop, by Garrett Robinson; student director, Rozelle Hill
	The Public Eye, by Peter Shaffer; student director, Nancy Gleason
	Bedtime Story, by Sean O'Casey; student director, Cheri Swiss
December 6	**Studio One-Act**:
	The Ghost of Mr. Penny, by Rosemary Gabbert Musil; student director, Bette McMuldren
1970	
January 13, February 5	**Theatre of Involvement**: A series of *avante garde* theatre
	The American Dream and *The Zoo Story,* by Edward Albee
	A Happening Graffiti
	Chartreuse: a Protest Theatre Piece
	Comings and Goings, by Megan Terry
	Triple Play; supervisors, Ms. Sue Cook and Mr. Donald Hill
January 28	Every Face Tells a Story, an Interim Readers Theatre; director, Mary Elizabeth Johnson
March 18–21	*The Birds*, by Aristophanes, adapted by Walter Kerr; director, Donald Hill
April 16-17	*****Two One-Act Plays**
	The Relatives, or *The Best Part of Us Is Underground,* a new script by student playwright, Sally Stinson; student director, Rozelle Hill
	Something Unspoken: student director, Cheri Swiss
May13–16	*The Firebugs*, by Max Frisch; director, Muriel Bain

A Production History
1970–1980
Indicates special projects or seminars

1970–1971

<u>1970</u>
October 8–10 *(Homecoming)* *Summertree*, by Ron Cowen; director Donald Hill

Oct 16–17 *(Parents Weekend)* *Summertree*

December 2 & 4   **Studio One-Acts**: *The Clod,* by Lewis Beach; student director, Amanda Roberts
Impromptu, by Tad Mosel; student director, Margaret Leta Harris
This Property Is Condemned, by Tennessee Williams; student director, Susan Simerka
December 3 & 5   **Studio One-Acts**: *A Slight Ache,* by Harold Pinter; student director, Rick Hamilton
A Pound on Demand, by Sean O'Casey; student director, Wayne Morrison
December 7 & 13   *Dust of the Road,* by Kenneth Sawyer Goodman; directed by Muriel Bain

<u>1971</u>
January 27   **Theatre of the Mind**, Readers Theatre, and *The Bald Soprano,* by Eugene Ionesco; student directors, Jeffrey Schroeder and Joanna McDonald; production supervisors Russell Hutchison and Donald Hill
March 17—20   *The Comedy of Errors*, by William Shakespeare; directed by Muriel Bain
May 5 & 7   ***Two Seminars**: *Suddenly Last Summer,* by Tennessee Williams; student director, Susan Simerka
The Romancers, (a one-act version) by Edmond Rostand; student director, Amanda Roberts
May 6 & 8   **Tiny Alice*, by Edward Albee; student director, George Richard Hamilton
No Date or Time Given   *The Diary of Adam and Eve,* by Mark Twain; directed by Muriel Bain

1971–1972

<u>1971</u>
Oct 20–23 *(Parents Weekend)* *The Matchmaker*, by Thornton Wilder; directed by Donald Hill
November   **Modern Language Series**: *La Lecon,* by Eugene Ionesco; student director, Priscilla Bentley
Don Dimas De La Tijereta, by Ricardo Palma; student director, Margaret Leta Harris
Threepenny Opera (scenes), by Bertolt Brecht; student director, Mary Ann Spitznagel
December 1 & 3   **An Evening of One-Acts**: *In the Shadow of the Glen,* by John M. Synge; student director, Jeff Clark
Scene from *Threepenny Opera,* by Bertolt Brecht; student director, Mary Ann Spitznagel, music by Vroni Sigrist
No Exit, by Jean-Paul Sartre; student director, Debra Chaffin
December 2 & 4   *Plaza Suite*, by Neil Simon: Act I *Visitor from Mamaroneck;* student director, Jeff Schroeder
Act II *Visitor from Hollywood;* student director, Mark Weingart
Act III *Visitor from Forest Hills;* student director, Jeff Hillyer
<u>1972</u>
January 21–23   *Spoon River Anthology*, Edgar Lee Masters adapted by Charles Aidman; directed by Richard Downing
January 26   *People Will Be People*, Readers Theatre; directed by Mary Elizabeth Johnson

January 28	*Under Milkwood*, by Dylan Thomas; directed by Donald Hill
February 3 & 6	*The Contribution,* by Ted Shine; student director, Ray Valentine
February 23–April 25	**Muskingum Players Touring Theatre**:
	Threepenny Opera (scenes), by Bertolt Brecht; student director, Mary Ann Spitznagel
	A Sunny Morning, by Joaquin and Serafin Quintero; student director, Margaret Leta Harris
	The Lesson, by Eugene Ionesco; student director, Priscilla Bentley
March 13–18	**Repertory**: *Macbeth*, by William Shakespeare; directed by Donald Hill
	King Ubu, by Alfred Jarry; Guest director Cheri Swiss
May 10–13	**You're a Good Man, Charlie Brown*, by Clark Gesner; student director, Margaret Leta Harris, *scene design by Jeff Hillyer

1972–1973

<u>1972</u>

September 8	*The Apes Shall Inherit the Earth,* by Werner Aspenstrom; directed by Donald Hill
September 10	**Open Theatre**: Scenes from *You're a Good Man, Charlie Brown*, by Clark Gesner; directed by Mary Ann Spitznagel
Oct 17–28*(Homecoming)*	**Repertory**: *Antigone*, by Sophocles; directed by Richard Downing
	The Misanthrope, by Molíere; directed by Donald Hill
Nov 8 & 10*(Parents Weekend)*	**Studio One-Acts**: *The Jewish Wife,* by Bertolt Brecht; student director, Debra Chaffin
	The Chairs, by Eugene Ionesco; student director, Donna Turner; Advanced Play Direction Class; 8:00 p.m., Little Theatre *(B&M,* Nov. 3, 1972, p. 12)
Nov 9 & 11*(Parents Weekend)*	**An Evening of One-Acts**
	Overruled, by George Bernard Shaw; student director, Mary Ann Spitznagel
	The Footsteps of Doves, by Robert Anderson; student director, Mark Weingart
	I'm Herbert, by Robert Anderson; student director, Jane O'Brien
Nov 29 & Dec 1	**Studio One-Acts**
	Love and How to Cure It, by Thornton Wilder; student director, Gary Crissman
	Red Carnations, by Glenn Hughes; student director, Ray Valentine
	The Valiant, by Holworthy Hall and Robert Middlemass; student director, Ann Wagner
Nov 30 & Dec 2	**Studio One-Acts**
	Sorry, Wrong Number, by Lucille Fletcher; student director, Bernice Steinberg
	Crawling Arnold, by Jules Feiffer; student director, Terry Haschke
	Feiffer's People (scenes), by Jules Feiffer; student director, Denise Cox

<u>1973</u>

January 19–20	*The Silence of Life*, An original Pantomime; directed by Richard Downing
February 7–10	*Purlie Victorious*, by Ossie Davis; student director, Ray Valentine
March 14–17	*Twelfth Night*, by William Shakespeare; directed by Donald Hill
April 25–28	*Endgame, by Samuel Beckett; student director, Debra Chaffin
May 9	**Two One-Act Plays**
	I'm Herbert, by Robert Anderson; student director, Jane O'Brien
	The Seven Ages of Women, by Toledo Repertoire Armchair Theatre Committee
May 9–12	**Last of the Red-Hot Lovers*, by Neil Simon; student director, Mark Weingart
April 25–28	*Carousel, by Richard Rodgers & Oscar Hammerstein II; directed by Betty Ward, assisted by student director, Mary Ann Spitznagel

1973–1974

<u>1973</u>

Oct 31–Nov 3*(Parents Weekend) Blithe Spirit*, by Noel Coward; directed by Donald Hill

November 16 & 17	**Student-Directed One-Acts**
	The Boor, by Anton Chekhov; student director, Ted Sofis
	The Typists, by Murray Schisgal; student director, Greg Senf
December 5 & 7	**Student-Directed One-Acts**
	The Dumb Waiter, by Harold Pinter; student director, Marypaul Magura
	A Message from Cougar, by Jean Raymond Maljean; student director, Richard Werner
December 6 & 8	**Student-Directed One-Acts**
	Something I'll Tell You Tuesday, by John Guare; student director, Robert Thiele
	The Lady of Larkspur Lotion, by Tennessee Williams; student director, David Van Dyke
	The Tape Recorder, by Pat Flowers; student director, Hope Schwier

1974

March 13–16	**One-Act Plays**
	The Chronicle, An Original Script written and directed by Matt Elli
	The Harmful Effects of Tobacco, by Anton Chekhov; directed by Donald Hill
	Something Unspoken, by Tennessee Williams; directed by Donald Hill
April 17 & 19	**One-Act Plays**
	Overtones, by Alice Gerstenberg; student director, Karen Lohr
	Krapp's Last Tape, by Samuel Beckett; student director and actor, Rick Hill
	A Day for Surprises, by John Guare; student director, Greg Senf
April 18 & 20	*Everyman,* by Hugo Von Hofmannsthal; student director, Denise Cox for an Honor's Project
April 30 & May 2	**Seven Stimulations*, a Dance Drama by student director and choreographer, Jill Giguere
April 18–19	**The Star-Spangled Girl*, by Neil Simon; student director, Marypaul Magura

1974–1975

1974

September*(no date given)*	**Open Theatre**: *The Boor,* by Anton Chekhov; student director, Ted Sofis
October 16–19	*Tartuffe,* by Moliére; directed by Donald Hill
November 13–16	**Studio One-Acts Repertory**
	The Ugly Duckling, by A. A. Milne; student director, Sharon Thorpe
	Nobody Sleeps, by Guernsey Le Pelley; student director, Linda Hierholzer
	Hello, Out There, by William Saroyan; student director, Sharon Gruenschlager
	The Sandbox, by Edward Albee; student director, Patricia Taylor
	Repertory Schedule:
November 13	*The Ugly Duckling*
	Hello, Out There
	Nobody Sleeps
November 14	*Hello, Out There*
	Nobody Sleeps
	The Sandbox
November 15	*The Ugly Duckling*
	Hello, Out There
	Nobody Sleeps
	The Sandbox
November 16	*The Ugly Duckling*
	Hello, Out There
	The Sandbox

December 4 & 5	**Studio One-Acts** *A Marriage Proposal,* by Anton Chekhov; student director, Kathy King *Impromptu,* by Tad Mosel; student director, Myra Stanley *Egad, What a Cad!*; student director, Bobbi Sheil
December 6 & 7	**Studio One-Acts** *Suppressed Desires,* by Susan Glaspell; student director, Rick Hill *The End of the Beginning,* by Sean O'Casey; student director, Greg Senf *Egad, What a Cad!*, student director, Bobbi Sheil

1975

January 21–February 5	**Muskingum College Comedy Players Touring Company**: *Flower Drum Song,* by Richard Rodgers and Oscar Hammerstein II; directed by James Holm, Jr. *Stop the World, I Want to Get Off!*, by Anthony Newley and Leslie Bricusse; directed by Donna Henderson Turner, *costume design, Linda Hierholzer Performance Schedule:

January 21: *Flower Drum Song* opened at Little Theatre
January 22: *Stop the World, I Want to Get Off!* opened at Little Theatre
January 24-25: Churchill Area High School, Pittsburgh
January 27: Riverview High School, Coshocton, Ohio
January 29: YMCA, Cambridge, Ohio
January 31: Municipal Auditorium, Zanesville, Ohio
February 4–5: Final performances at Little Theatre (*Cue,* 1975, p. 4)

February 20	*Memorial Day,* by Murray Schisgal, student director, Rick Hill
February 28	*Impromptu,* by Tad Mosel; student director, Myra Stanley
March 12–15	*The Caretaker*, by Harold Pinter; directed by Jerry Martin
March 19–22	*A Midsummer Night's Dream*, by William Shakespeare; directed by Donald Hill
April 16–19	**The Glass Menagerie*, by Tennessee Williams; student director, Greg Senf
May 1	*Under Milkwood*, by Dylan Thomas; Guest Artist Mercedes McCambridge; directorial supervision, Donald Hill and Ms. Sue Cook
May 7–10	**Luv*, by Murray Schisgal; student director, Rick Hill

1975–1976

1975

September 24–27	*Winnie-the-Pooh*, by A. A. Milne dramatized by Kristin Sergel; directed by Jerry Martin
October 22–25	*The Skin of Our Teeth*, by Thornton Wilder; directed by Hill
November 12–15	**Studio One-Acts Repertory** *The American Dream,* by Edward Albee; student director, Pam Nicholson *The Trysting Place,* by Booth Tarkington; student director, Mary Beth Reeves *The Case of the Crushed Petunias,* by Tennessee Williams; student director, Jennifer Baxter; Play Direction Class *Comings and Goings,* by Megan Terry; student director, Myra Stanley *Trifles,* by Susan Glaspell; student director, Linda Hierholzer Repertory Schedule:

Nov 12	*The American Dream* *Comings and Goings* *Trifles*	Nov 14	*The American Dream* *The Case of the Crushed Petunias* *Trifles*
Nov 13	*The Trysting Place* *Comings and Goings* *Trifles*	Nov 15	*The American Dream* *The Trysting Place* *The Case of the Crushed Petunias*

1976

January 27–29	*The Wizard of Oz*, An Original Script; Creative Playmaking & Audio Development, Wilma Barnett; music director, Catherine Johnson; technical

	director, Jerry Martin; stage director, Donald Hill.
February 5–7	*The Wizard of Oz*
March 17–21	*You're a Good Man, Charlie Brown*, by Clark Gesner; directed by Donald Hill
April 14–17	**Arsenic and Old Lace*, by Joseph Kesselring; student director and designer, Myra Stanley
April 28–May 1	**Feiffer's People*, by Jules Feiffer; student director and designer, Linda Hierholzer
May 5–8	*The Effect of Gamma Rays on Man-in-the-Moon Marigolds*, by Paul Zindel; directed by Donald Hill

1976–1977

<u>1976</u>

Oct 4–9 *(Parents Weekend)*	*I Do! I Do!*, by Tom Jones and Harvey Schmidt based on *The Fourposter* by Jan de Hartog; directed by Jerry Martin
Oct 20–23 *(Homecoming)*	*The Misogynist (Thesmophoriazusea)*, by Aristophanes; adapted and directed by Gay Manifold, designer and technical director, Jerry Martin
November 17–20	**Studio Productions**, One-Act Plays
	Revue Sketches, by Harold Pinter; student director, Susan Hitch
	American Primitive, by William Gibson; student director, Mary Beth Reeves
December 1–4	**Studio Productions**, One-Act Plays
	Triumph of the Egg, by Sherwood Anderson; student director, Tim Campbell
	Quiet Please, by Howard Buermann; student director, Becky Zellar;
	***Dust of the Road, by Kenneth S. Goodman; student director, Bruce Hare

<u>1977</u>

January 27, 28 & Feb 2-5	**Plaza Suite*, by Neil Simon; student director, Mary Beth Reeves
March 9–13	*Hamlet*, by William Shakespeare; directed by Donald Hill
April 13–16	*The Importance of Being Earnest*, by Oscar Wilde; Manifold
May 4–6	*Alice in Wonderland*, An Original Script adapted from Lewis Carroll's *Alice in Wonderland* and *Through the Looking Glass*; directed by Donald Hill and Jerry Martin. *scene design, Becky Zellar

1977–1978

<u>1977</u>

Oct 12–15 *(Homecoming)*	*The Fantasticks*, by Tom Jones and Harvey Schmidt; directed by Donald Hill
October Weekend & 28–29	*The People Versus Christ,* by Albert Johnson; student director, Bruce Hare, *lighting design for one-act play series by Bruce Hare
November 16–19	**One-Act Plays**
	The Anniversary, by Anton Chekhov; student director, Larry Overmire
	The Cave of Salamanca, by Cervantes; bilingual production by student director, Pam Nicholson
December 9–10	**One-Act Play**: *No Exit,* by Jean-Paul Sartre; student director, David Briggs

<u>1978</u>

February 8–11	*Tom Sawyer*, An Original Script from the Mark Twain novel; script advisor, Wilma Barnett; choral director, Catherine Johnson; designer and technical director, Brent Fleming, stage director, Donald Hill
March 8–11	*The Good Doctor*, by Neil Simon based on Anton Chekhov stories; directed by Pat Van De Voort

---

***Dust of the Road toured throughout the year to Alexander United Presbyterian Church, Athens, Ohio; the Bloomfield United Presbyterian Church; vesper services on campus in Brown Chapel; the College Drive United Presbyterian Church, New Concord

March 14–16	**Student-Directed One-Acts**: Two Readers' Theatre Productions
	The Leader, by Eugene Ionesco
	A History of Fingers, by H. Allen Smith; student director, David Briggs
	The Zoo Story, by Edward Albee; student director, Larry Overmire (****Johnson Hall Theatre)
April 19–23	**Godspell*, by John-Michael Tebelak; student director, Pam Nicholson, *technical direction, Becky Zellar, *costume design, by Jenny Wilkes
May 10–13	*The Doctor in Spite of Himself*, by Moliére; directed by Donald Hill
June 14–17	*You're a Good Man, Charlie Brown*, by Clark Gesner; directed by Donald Hill

1978–1979

1978

September 15	**Open Theatre**, Two One-Act Plays
	Still Alarm, by George S. Kaufman; student director, Vaughn Rasor
	Stuffings, by James Prideaux; student director, Kevin Poland
Sept 20–23 *(Homecoming)*	*You're a Good Man, Charlie Brown*, by Clark Gesner; directed by Donald Hill
Sept 27 & 29 *(Parents Weekend)*	**Studio Productions**, Student Directed One-Act Plays
	Riders to the Sea, by John M. Synge; student director, William Allison
	Still Alarm, George S. by Kaufman; student director, Vaughn Rasor
	Smoking Is Bad for You, by Anton Chekhov; student director, Larry Overmire
Sept 28 & 30 *(Parents Weekend)*	**Studio Productions**, Student Directed One-Act Plays
	The Case of the Crushed Petunias, by Tennessee Williams; student director, David Spillman
	Stuffings, by James Prideaux; student director, Kevin Poland
	Ledge, Ledger, and the Legend, by Paul Elliott; student director, Sherman Liddell
Oct 1 *(Parents Weekend)*	**Studio Productions**, Student Directed One-Act Plays
	Riders to the Sea, Smoking Is Bad for You, and *Ledge, Ledger, and the Legend*
October 25–28	*The Glass Menagerie*, by Tennessee Williams; student director, Greg Senf with Donald Hill
December 12–16	*Romeo and Juliet*, William Shakespeare; Hill

1979

March 28–31	**The Odd Couple*, Neil Simon, student director Amy Brannon
March 31	**The Second Shepherd's Play* (Anonymous); student director, Sherman Liddell
April 25–28	**Butterflies Are Free*, by Leonard Gershe; student director, David Briggs

1979–1980

1979

Oct 3–6 *(Homecoming)*	*The Merry Wives of Windsor*, by William Shakespeare; directed by Donald Hill
Oct 10–13 *(Parents Weekend)*	*The Merry Wives of Windsor*, by William Shakespeare
December 12–15	* **Studio Productions** 1979
	Overruled, by George Bernard Shaw; student director, Joanna Gray
	The Fisherman, by Jonathan Tree; student director, Eileen McComb
	Two Crooks and a Lady, by Eugene Pillot; student director, Leanne Olson

1980

| January 30–31 & Feb 1-2 | *East Lynne*, by Ned Albert adapted from Mrs. Henry Wood's novel; directed by Diane Rock |

****The Johnson Hall Theatre became the Layton Theatre when it was officially dedicated on March 28, 1978. Academy award-winning actress, Mercedes McCambridge, was guest artist for the occasion. Other speakers on the program included Dr. Layton, Dr. Russell Hutchison, and Dr. William Fisk.

February 20–23	*J. B., by Archibald MacLeish; student director, Vaughn Rasor, *scene design by William Allison, *lighting design by Tracy Carter
February 24	J. B. toured to the Central Methodist Church, Zanesville, Ohio
March 31–April 1	Red Carnations, by Glenn Hughes; student director, Kathleen O'Brien
April (no date given)	*A Thurber Carnival (scenes), by James Thurber; student director, Randy Bardonner
April 22–26	The Hobbit, dramatized by Allan Jay Friedman, David Rogers, and Ruth Perry, from J. R. R. Tolkien's novel; directed by Donald Hill. Script consultant, Wilma Barnett; vocal coach, Catherine Johnson; technical director, Diane Rock; designer, Sue Carpenter.
June 13–14	An Evening of Noel Coward, An Original Script written and directed by Donald Hill

A Production History
1980–1990
Indicates special projects or seminars

1980–1981

1980
September 18 — **Open Theatre**: Workshops on *An Evening with Noel Coward,* directed by Donald Hill
The Corn Is Green, by Emlyn Williams

Oct 3-5 *(Homecoming)* — *An Evening With Noel Coward*, An original Entertainment arranged and directed by Donald Hill

October 8–11 — **The Corn is Green*, by Emlyn Williams; student director, Kathleen O'Brien
October 17 — *The Corn is Green* for Danforth Foundation at Salt Fork State Lodge.
December 10–13 — **Studio One-Acts**
A Marriage Proposal, by Anton Chekhov
A Sunny Morning, by Serafin & Joaquin Quintero
The Lesson, by Eugene Ionesco; Hill

1981
February 4–7 — *The Twins (The Twin Menaechmi),* by Titus Maccius Plautus; directed by Donald Hill
March 25–26 — **Studio One-Acts**
El Cnisto, by Margaret Larkin; student director, Mary Sykes
I'm Herbert, by Robert Anderson; student director
Mar 28 *(Parents Weekend)* — *A Sunny Morning,* by Serafin & Joaquin Quintero; directed by Donald Hill
April 30, May 1–2, 8–9 — *A Little Night music*, by Stephen Sondheim; Guest Director Dona D. Vaughn

1981–1982

1981
September 11 — **Open Theatre**: *I'm Herbert,* by Robert Anderson; student director, Mike Swanner

Oct 7–10 *(Homecoming)* — *The Prisoner of Second Avenue*, by Neil Simon; directed by Shari Taylor
November 11–14 — **Studio Productions**, An Evening of One-Act Plays
Impromptu, by Tad Mosel; student director, Michael Swanner
How He Lied to Her Husband, by George Bernard Shaw; student director, Mary Sykes
Of Poems, Youth, and Spring, by John Logan; student director, Sharon Johns
The Happy Journey to Camden and Trenton, by Thornton Wilder; student director, Lauren Jones

1982
February 10–13 — *Never Too Late*, by Sumner Arthur Long; directed by Jerry Martin
February 24–27 — *The Merchant of Venice*, by William Shakespeare; Hill
Mar 31-Apr 3 *(Parents Weekend)* — *The Thwarting of Baron Bolligrew*, by Robert Bolt; directed by Jerry Martin
April 14–17 — **Spoon River Anthology*, by Edgar Lee Masters adapted for the stage by Charles Aidman; student director, Mary Sykes
June 11–12 — *Never Too Late*, by Sumner Arthur Long; directed by Jerry Martin

1982–1983

1982
September 30 — **Open Theatre**: *Spoon River Anthology*, by Edgar Lee Masters, adapted for the stage by Charles Aidman; the April 1982 production revised and rearranged by student director, Mary Sykes and Donald Hill.
October 1–2 *(Homecoming)* *Spoon River Anthology*

October 27–30	*You Can't Take It With You*, by George S. Kaufman and Moss Hart; Guest Artistic Director Richard Henzel, for student directors of each act: Suzanne Albrecht, Act I, Lauren Jones, Act II, and Sharon Johns, Act III
December 3–4	*The Nativity Cycle*, An Original Script based on Medieval dramas; Hill
December 5	*The Nativity Cycle*

1983
February 9–12	*Mrs. McThing*, by Mary Chase; directed by Jerry Martin
April 19–23	*The Taming of the Shrew*, by William Shakespeare; Guest Director Ted Hissam
April (no dates)	*The Butcher's Wife,* a *commedia* script by Agna Enters; Hill Acting Class
June 10–11	*Mrs. McThing*, by Mary Chase; directed by Jerry Martin

1983–1984

1983
Oct 13–15 *(Homecoming)*	*The Star-Spangled Girl*, by Neil Simon; directed and designed by Jerry Martin
November 16–19	**A Musical Revue**
	The American musical Theatre Past and Present; An Original Script; directed by Donald Hill, *assistant student director, Sunny Boulet
	Rags to Riches duet with Dick Pavlov and Ruth Cyanovich, Tom Drabick, Jerry Martin, Louis Palmer, Lorle Porter, Judy Woodard, and Marshall Onofrio and the Jazz Band

1984
February 22–25	*Rashomon*, by Fay & Michael Kanin; directed by Donald Hill
March 23–24	**One-Act Plays**
	Rockabilly Nowhere Man, by Ruth Angell Purkey; student director, William Emling
	The Tiny Closet, by William Inge; student director, Jeannine Fabian
	Beauty and the Beast, by Nicholas Stuart Gray; student director, Linda Higgs
	While the Toast Burns, by Mary C. Werts; student director, Sally Miller
April 5 & 11	*Beauty and the Beast* toured several elementary schools.
April 11–14	*An Irish Faustus*, by Lawrence Durrell; directed by Donald Hill

1984–1985

1984
| October 3–6 | *Our Town*, by Thornton Wilder; directed by Donald Hill |
| November 14–17 | *My Three Angels*, by Sam and Bella Spewack; directed by Donald Hill |

1985
| February 6–9 | *Arsenic and Old Lace*, by Joseph Kesselring; directed by Jerry Martin |
| April 24–27 | *Hans Christian Andersen*, by Frank Loesser (music and lyrics), John Fearnley, Beverly Cross, and Tommy Steele (book); directed by Jerry Martin, musical director Robert O. Jones. |

1985–1986

1985
October 9–12 *(Homecoming)*	*God's Favorite*, by Neil Simon; directed by Donald Hill
November 13–16	**One-Acts 1985** (in repertory)
	The Dear Departed, by Stanley Houghton; student director, Jerry Widenhofer
	Egad! What a Cad!, by Anita Bell; student director, Kristine Engle
	Overtones, by Alice Gerstenberg; student director, DeAnn Marie Campbell
	The Zoo Story, by Edward Albee; student director, Kathy McGinnis
	Schedule:
	October 13: *Egad! What a Cad!; Overtones; The Zoo Story*
	October 14: *The Dear Departed; Overtones; The Zoo Story*
	October 15: *The Dear Departed; Egad! What a Cad!; The Zoo Story*
	October 16: *The Dear Departed; Egad! What a Cad!; Overtones*

December 4–7	**Studio Productions** (a repertory of two modern Broadway successes with religious themes)
	Agnes of God, by John Pielmeier; directed by Donald Hill
	*Mass Appeal, by Bill C. Davis; student director, Peter Sutherland

1986

February 19–22	*The Passion of Dracula*, by Bob Hall and David Richmond; Guest Director Eileen McComb Adams
March 13–15	**Trial by Jury*, by William Gilbert and Arthur Sullivan; student director, Jerry Widenhofer
April 9–12	*The School for Wives*, by Moliére, translated by Richard Wilbur; directed by Donald Hill

Saturday Showcase, a Children's Theatre Series featuring different theatre companies, was inaugurated in 1985 by Dr. Jerry Martin, chairman of the Speech Communication and Theatre Department, in conjunction with the Ohio Arts Council

Johnny Appleseed by Hank Fincken (October 19)
Pinocchio by the Hip-Squeak Puppets (October 26)
The Ransom of Red Chief by the Akron Children's Theatre (March 8)
Everthing Under the Rainbow by the Child's Play Touring Theatre (May 10). The series found a more comfortable home in the Layton Theatre the following year, where it remained until 1991, when it moved to the Pritchard-Laughlin Cambridge Civic Center.

1986–1987

1986

September 15–19	**Agnes Moorehead Film Festival**
	Sept. 15, Mon.—*The Magnificent Ambersons* (1942)
	Sept. 16, Tues.—*Mrs. Parkington* (1944)
	Sept. 17, Wed.—*Johnny Belinda* (1948)
	Sept. 18, Thurs.—*All That Heaven Allows* (1956)
	Sept. 19, Fri.—*Hush, Hush, Sweet Charlotte* (1965)
October 15–18	*A Midsummer Night's Dream*, by William Shakespeare; directed by Donald Hill
November 19–22	**Spotlight on Students**, An Evening of Student-Directed One-Act Plays in Repertory
	The Acting Lesson, by Willard Simms; student director, Chris Jones
	The Informer, by Bertolt Brecht adapted by Eric Bentley; student director, Frederick Frank
	A Marriage Proposal, by Anton Chekhov; student director, Brian Wagner
	The Monkey's Paw, by William W. Jacobs; student director, Deborah Wolfert

1987

February 25–28	*Harvey*, by Mary Chase; directed by Jerry Martin
March 25–28	*Painting Churches*, by Tina Brown; directed by Ronald Lauck
April 22–25	*Dear Brutus*, by James M. Barrie; directed and designed by Donald Hill

1987–1988

1987

| October 14–17 | *The Frogs*, by Aristophanes; directed by Ronald Lauck |
| November 18–21 | *Androcles and the Lion*, by Aurand Harris; directed and designed by Jerry Martin |

1988

February 24–27	*Antigone*, by Jean Anouilh; directed and designed by Donald Hill
March 14	**An Evening of Romantic Comedy**
	Red Carnations, by Glenn Hughes
	Here We Are, by Dorothy Parker; student director, Rose Kessing

April 15 *(Parents Weekend)* **Dinner Theatre**: *The Glass Menagerie*, by Tennessee Williams; student directors, Kristine Engle, Chris Jones, and Deborah Wolfert

April 20–23 *The Glass Menagerie*, by Tennessee Williams

1988–1989

<u>1988</u>

October 5–8 *The Dining Room*, by A. R. Gurney; directed by Ronald Lauck

November 16–19 **An Evening of One-Acts**

If Men Played Cards As Women Do, by George S. Kaufman; student director, Victor Miller

Suppressed Desires, by Susan Glaspell; student director, Philip Albaugh

The Exchange, by Althea Thurston; student director, Beth Landis

Ludlow Fair, by Lanford Wilson; student director, Alisha Lenning

Impromptu, by Tad Mosel; student director, Derek Whitehead

<u>1989</u>

February 22–25 **The Maids*, by Jean Genet; student director, Deborah Wolfert; scenography, Derek Whitehead

April 14 *(Parents Weekend)* **Dinner Theatre**: *The Star-Spangled Girl*, by Neil Simon; student director, Alisha Lenning

March 8–11 *The Star-Spangled Girl*, by Neil Simon

June 9–10 *The Star-Spangled Girl*, by Neil Simon

1989–1990

<u>1989</u>

October 11–14 *The Learned Ladies*, by Moliére, translated by Richard Wilbur; directed and designed by Donald Hill

November 15–18 *A Doll's House*, by Henrik Ibsen; directed by Ronald Lauck

<u>1990</u>

February 21–24 *Summertime*, by Ugo Betti; directed by Donald Hill

April 4, 5 & 7 *You're a Good Man, Charlie Brown*, by Clark Gesner; directed by Ronald Lauck

April 6 *(Parents weekend)* **Dinner Theatre**: *You're a Good Man, Charlie Brown*, by Clark Gesner

April 18–21 **The Secret Princess*, An Original Script by student director Alisha Lenning

A Production History
1990–1995
Indicates special projects or seminars

1990–1991

<u>1990</u>

October 10–13   *The Romancers*, by Edmond Rostand; directed by Ronald Lauck

November 14–17   **Student-Directed One-Acts**
Plaza Suite, by Neil Simon; (a student director for each act)
Act I–*Visitor from Mamaroneck*, Tracie Moreau
Act II–*Visitor from Hollywood*, Susan Murphy
Act III–*Visitor from Forest Hills*, Shelly Peters

Nov 28–Dec 1   **Student-Directed One-Acts**: *The Lesson*, by Eugene Ionesco; student director, Joseph Rath; *Adaptation*, by Elaine May; student director, Samuel Hook; *The Diary of Adam and Eve*, by Mark Twain; student director, Beth Hammer

<u>1991</u>

February 20–23   *Woman in Mind*, by Alan Ayckbourn; directed by Ronald Lauck, scenography, Ronald Lauck

April 10, 11, 13   *Butterflies Are Free*, by Leonard Gershe; student director, Susan Murphy, *set and costume design, Shelly Peters

April 12   **Dinner Theatre**: *Butterflies Are Free*

June 14–15   *Butterflies Are Free*

1991–1992

<u>1991</u>

September 2   **Freshman Orientation Weekend**
Butterflies Are Free, by Leonard Gershe; student director, Susan Murphy

October 16–19   **Steel Magnolias*, by Robert Harling; student director, Susan Murphy

November 20–23   *Ernest in Love*, by Anne Croswell and Lee Pockriss; directed by Ronald Lauck

<u>1992</u>

March 4–7   *The Seagull*, by Anton Chekhov; directed by Artist-in-Residence Svetlana Efremova

April 8–11 *(Parents Weekend)*   *The Mousetrap*, by Agatha Christie; Student director, Tracie Moreau

May 8–9
(Commencement Weekend)   *A Pushkin Fairy Tale & Three Little Pigs*, Composed and directed by Artist-in-Residence Svetlana Efremova

1992–1993

<u>1992</u>

August 30–31   **Freshman Orientation Weekend**: *The Mouse Trap*, by Agatha Christie; student director, Tracie Moreau

October 7–10   **The Works of Vasili Shukshin**: *Characters,* arranged and directed by Artist-in-Residence Svetlana Efremova, scenography by Visiting Artist Olga Tchainikova

November 18–21   **A Night of One-Acts I**
Trifles, by Susan Glaspell; student director, Victoria Paul
Hello, Out There, by William Saroyan; student director, Anne Gardner
Red Carnations, by Glenn Hughes; student director, Jennifer Zornow

December 2–5   **A Night of One-Acts II**
Feiffer's People (scenes), directed by Donald Hill
The Acting Lesson, by Willard Simms; student director, Anji Dunn
The Potman Spoke Sooth, by David Fulk; student director, Eddie Martin

1993

March 3–6   *Oklahoma!*, Richard Rodgers and Oscar Hammerstein II; directed by Carol Wilcox-Jones, produced by Jerry Martin.

Mar 31–Apr 3
(Parents Weekend)   *Agnes of God*, by John Pielmeier; student director, Anne Gardner, *lighting design, Jennifer Zornow

1993–1994

1993

Oct 13–16 *(Homecoming)*   **The Matchmaker*, by Thornton Wilder; student director, Anne Gardner

November 10–13   *Luv*, by Murray Schisgal; directed by ,Gene Alesandrini; *stage management Becky Ellis

1994

February 23–26   *Going to See the Elephant*, by Karen Hensel, Patti Johns, Elana Kent, Sylvia Meredith, Elizabeth Lloyd Shaw, Laura Toffenetti; Guest Director Frederick Frank

Apr 5, 7, 9 *(Parents Weekend)* **An Evening of One-Act Plays I**

University (scenes), by Jon Jory; student director, Matt Jordan

University (scenes), by Jon Jory; student director, Nicholas Zakov

The Fifteen Minute Hamlet, by Tom Stoppard; student director, Barrett Hileman

Apr 6, 8, 9 *(Parents Weekend)* **An Evening of One-Act Plays II**

The Foot Steps of Doves, by Robert Anderson; student director, Amy Mitchell

The Happy Journey to Camden and Trenton, by Thornton Wilder; student director, Kimberly Hawkins

The Case of the Crushed Petunias, by Tennessee Williams; student director, Juliet Johnson

June 10–11   *The Footsteps of Doves,* and *The Happy Journey from Camden to Trenton*

1994–1995

1994

September 7–8   **Open Theatre**: *I'm Herbert,* by Robert Anderson; directed by Donald Hill

Oct 19–22 *(Homecoming)*   **Charley's Aunt*, by Brandon Thomas; student director, Anne Gardner

1995

February 22–25   *The Heidi Chronicles*, by Wendy Wasserstein; directed by Ronald Lauck

April 5–8   **Rumors*, by Neil Simon; student director, Amy Mitchell, *scene design, Matt Jordan

Theatre Seminars
Commentary

A seminar is the capstone experience for a student majoring in a specific area. The number of years represented in a seminar may be as many as four, or as few as two. Therefore, as the final and culminating work in a major by the student, the seminar is usually taken in the senior year. In exceptional cases (cases in which it is a matter of scheduling or in which the student may be taking two majors), it may be advisable to start the seminar in the junior year. In any case, a considerable amount of time and work is involved.

Under advisement of the seminar professor, the student, engages in individual study and research which results in a thesis that meets academic standards of the school and the department of origin.

If a student is working in theatre, a paper is required in the areas of history, theory, criticism, or dramatic literature. If the student chooses to work in a performance area, such as directing, acting, designing, playwriting, or theatre management, further work is required in the form of a play analysis, production plan, rehearsals, a portfolio of drawings and elevations, and a live performance.

Students in creative and performance areas of study are well-advised concerning the hazards of production. The writer, the artist, the musician, the director, the designer, and the actor are all subject to frailties of the body, the whims of nature, the accidents of living in the real world, and the scrutiny of the public eye. There is always an added stress on the person who ventures forth creatively into the spotlight, however fleeting and tentative that venture may be.

Although there was no theatre major until 1970-1971, it was still possible for a student to write a seminar in theatre under the rubric of Speech. Students in theatre were encouraged to double major because of the interdisciplinary nature of theatre, and because it made the student more flexible to career choices.

It was a school rule that students did not have to do more than one seminar. Some theatre majors chose to do seminars in other areas; others wrote seminars that were acceptable in both areas, even though they were registered in one only. Some students completed, yet never declared, theatre as a major, because they already had another major to their credit. These are some reasons why the list of seminars below is, at best, a partial list. Nevertheless, there are enough seminars in the following list to suggest to the reader that theatre as an area of knowledge in a liberal arts college is well-represented.

Theatre Seminars

1961	Barbara Kukura, *A Midsummer Night's Dream*, William Shakespeare: Production Book and Costume Design Seminar, May
1962	Robert Layton, *The Measures Taken,* Bertolt Brecht: Directing Seminar, May
1963	Carolyn Aiken, Paul Alvarez, Bing Bills, Lorraine Commeret, Carol McFarland Gable, Donald Kelm, and Sherran Reynolds, One-Act Plays: Projects in Directing Seminars, January

1965   Janet Small, *Beauty and the Beast,* Nora MacAlvay: Directing Seminar, April

1965   Barbara Drake, *Death of a Salesman*, Arthur Miller: Play Analysis and Role Analysis of Linda Loman, Acting Seminar, October

1966   Judy Moore, *The Adventures of Harlequin:* Directing Seminar, January

1966   Barbara Drake, *Hay Fever*, Noel Coward: Play Analysis and Role Analysis of Judith Bliss, Acting Seminar, May

1966   Sally Schenck, *Hay Fever*, Noel Coward: Scene Design Seminar, May

1966   Nancy Wheeley, "A Comparison of *Doña Rosita* with *Mariana Pineda, Yerma,* and *The House of Bernarda Alba,*" Federico Garcia Lorca: Dramatic Literature and Criticism Seminar, May

1966   William McCloskey, *The Glass Menagerie*, Tennessee Williams: Critical Analysis Seminar, May

1966   Margaret Basnett, *Medea*, Robinson Jeffers (adapted from the *Medea* of Euripides): Analysis of the Play and Costume Design Seminar, December

1966   Carol Beth Boyer, *Medea*, Robinson Jeffers: Analysis of the Play and Role Analysis of the Nurse, Acting Seminar, December

1967   Carol Beth Boyer, *The Amorous Flea*, Jerry Devine (Book) and Bruce Montgomery (Music and Lyrics): Play Analysis and Role Analysis of Agnes, Acting Seminar, March

1967   Lillian Kestner, *The Zoo Story,* Edward Albee: Production Book, Directing Seminar, March

1967   Thomas Forgrave, *The Flies*, Jean-Paul Sartre: Production Book, Directing Seminar, March

1970   Rozelle Hill, *The Relatives or The Best Part of Us Is Underground* (a new script), Sally Stinson: Directing Seminar, April

1970   Cheryl Swiss, *Something Unspoken,* Tennessee Williams: Directing Seminar, April

1970   Jack Falcon, *The Firebugs*, Max Frisch: Analysis of Sepp Schmitz, Acting Seminar, May

1971   Susan Simerka, *Suddenly Last Summer*, Tennessee Williams: Directing Seminar, May

1971   Amanda Roberts, *The Romancers* (one-act version), Edmond Rostand: Directing Seminar, May

1971   Richard Hamilton, *Tiny Alice*, Edward Albee: Directing Seminar, May

1972   Robert Thiele, *Macbeth*, William Shakespeare: Play Analysis and Role Analysis of Macduff, Acting Seminar, March

1972   Margaret Leta Harris, *You're a Good Man, Charlie Brown*, Clark Gesner: Production Book, Directing Seminar, May

1972   Jeff Hillyer, *You're a Good Man, Charlie Brown*, Clark Gesner: Scenic Design Seminar, May

1972   Priscilla Bentley, "Comedy and Theatre of the Absurd": Theory and Criticism Seminar, May

1972   Robert Thiele, *The Misanthrope*, Moliére: Analysis of the Play and Role Analysis of Philinte, Acting Seminar, October

1972	Terry Haschke, *The Misanthrope*, Moliére: Analysis of the Play and Role Analysis of Celimene, Acting Seminar, October
1973	Debra Chaffin, *Endgame*, Samuel Beckett: Production Book, Directing Seminar, April
1973	Jeffrey Schroeder, *Endgame*, Samuel Beckett: Analysis of the Play and Role Analysis of Hamm, Acting Seminar, April
1973	Mary Ann Spitznagel, *Carousel*, Richard Rodgers and Oscar Hammerstein II: Production Book, Directing Seminar, April
1973	Mark Weingart, *The Last of the Red Hot Lovers*, Neil Simon: Production Book, Directing Seminar, May
1973	Terry Haschke, *The Last of the Red Hot Lovers*, Neil Simon: Analysis of the Play and Role Analysis of Elaine Navazio, Acting Seminar, May
1973	Ann Wagner, "Drama Night: Bellefontaine High School": Seminar in Educational Theatre, May
1973	Denise Cox, *Blithe Spirit*, Noel Coward: Play Analysis and Role Analysis of Ruth, Acting Seminar, October
1973	Karen Lohr, *Blithe Spirit*, Noel Coward: Play Analysis and Role Analysis of Madame Arcati, Acting Seminar, October
1974	Denise Cox, *Something Unspoken,* Tennessee Williams: Analysis of the Play and Role Analysis of Grace, Acting Seminar, March
1974	Karen Lohr, *Something Unspoken,* Tennessee Williams: Analysis of the Play and Role Analysis of Cornelia, Acting Seminar, March
1974	Marypaul Magura, *The Star-Spangled* Girl, Neil Simon: Production Book, Directing Seminar, April
1974	Jill Giguere, *Seven Stimulations*, Jill Giguere: Book and Choreography, Seminar in Dance Drama, April
1974	Wendy Prentice, "Psychodrama and Sensitivity Training, A Comparative Overview": Drama and Psychology Seminar, May
1974	Kathy King, *Tartuffe*, Moliére: Role Analyses of Mariane and Flipote, Acting Seminar, October
1974	Hope Schwier, *Tartuffe*, Moliére, Role Comparison of Elmire and Madame Pernelle: Acting Seminar, October
1974	Bobbi Sheil, *Tartuffe*, Moliére: Analysis of the Play, the Author, and the Role of Dorine: Acting Seminar, October
1974	Ted Sofis, *Tartuffe*, Moliére: Analysis of the Role of Tartuffe: Acting Seminar, October
1975	Linda Hierholzer, *Stop the World I Want to Get Off*, Leslie Bricusse and Anthony Newley: Individual Study in Costume Design Seminar, January-February
1975	Cheryl Foster, *A Midsummer Night's Dream*, William Shakespeare: Play Analysis and Role Analysis of Helena, Acting Seminar, March
1975	Greg Senf, *The Glass Menagerie*, Tennessee Williams: Production Book, Directing Seminar, April

1975	Jennifer Baxter, *The Glass Menagerie,* Tennessee Williams: Scene Design Seminar, April
1975	Richard Hill, *Luv*, Murray Schisgal: Production Book, Directing Seminar, May
1975	Hope Schwier "Planning Three Varied Courses for Theatre": Seminar in Educational Theatre, May
1975	Patricia Taylor, *The Skin of Our Teeth,* Thornton Wilder, the Role of Sabina: Acting Seminar, December.
1976	Myra Stanley, *Arsenic and Old Lace*, Joseph Kesselring: Production Book and Designs, Directing and Design Seminar, April
1976	Linda Hierholzer, *Feiffer's People*, Jules Feiffer: Production Book, Directing Seminar, April
1976	Patricia Taylor, *The Effect of Gamma Rays on Man-in-the-Moon-Marigolds*, Paul Zindel: Individual Study of the Play and Role Analysis of Beatrice, Acting Seminar, May
1976	Cheryl Foster, *The Effect of Gamma Rays on Man-in-the-Moon-Marigolds*, Paul Zindel: Play Analysis and Role Analysis of Tillie, Acting Seminar, May
1976	Myra E. Stanley, "Creative Dramatics for Children:" Seminar in Educational Theatre, May
1977	Mary Beth Reeves, *Plaza Suite*, Neil Simon: Production Book, Directing Seminar, January
1977	Becky Zellar, *Alice in Wonderland*, Original Script for Children's Theatre Class: Scene Designer's Production Book, Design Seminar, May
1977	Bruce Hare, "Lighting One-Acts": Lighting Design Seminar, November-December
1978	Pam Nicholson, *Godspell*, John-Michael Tebelak: Directing Seminar, April
1978	Becky Zellar, *Godspell,* John-Michael Tebelak: Technical Directing Seminar, April
1978	Jenny Wilkes, *Godspell,* John-Michael Tebelak Costume Design Seminar, April
1978	Amy Brannon, *The Glass Menagerie*, Tennessee Williams: Play Analysis and Role Analysis of Laura Wingfield, Acting Seminar, October
1978	Larry Overmire, *The Glass Menagerie*, Tennessee Williams: Actor's Handbook Based on the Role of Tom Wingfield, Acting Seminar, October
1978	Sherry Blackwood, *Romeo and Juliet*, William Shakespeare: Play Analysis in Communication, Theatre Seminar, December
1979	Amy Brannon, *The Odd Couple*, Neil Simon: Production Book, Directing Seminar, March
1979	Larry Overmire, *The Odd Couple*, Neil Simon: Actor's Handbook Based on the Role of Oscar, Acting Seminar, March
1979	Sherman Liddell, *The Second Shepherd's Play* (Anonymous): Production Book, Directing Seminar, March
1979	David Briggs, *Butterflies Are Free*, Leonard Gershe: Production Book, Directing Seminar, April

1979	David Spillman, "Theatre Department Research Project on Theatre Business": Theatre Management Seminar, May
1979	Joanna Gray, *The Merry Wives of Windsor*, William Shakespeare: Analysis of the Play and a Role Analysis of Mistress Page, Acting Seminar, October
1979	Joanna Gray, *Overruled*, George Bernard Shaw: Directing Seminar, December
1979	Eileen McComb, *The Fisherman*, Jonathan Tree: Directing Seminar, December
1979	Leanne Olson, *Two Crooks and a Lady*, Eugene Pillot: Directing Seminar, December
1980	Vaughn Rasor, *J.B.*, Archibald MacLeish: Directing Seminar, February
1980	William Allison, *J.B.*, Archibald MacLeish: Design Seminar, February
1980	Tracy Carter, *J.B.*, Archibald MacLeish: Lighting Design Seminar, February
1980	Randy Bardonner, *A Thurber Carnival* (Scenes), James Thurber: Theatrical Videotaping Seminar, May
1980	Kathleen O'Brien, *The Corn Is Green*, Emlyn Williams: Production Book, Directing Seminar, October
1981	Carey Vance, *Fumed Oak*, Noel Coward: Production Book (no performance) Seminar May
1982	Mary Sykes, *Spoon River Anthology*, Edgar Lee Masters: Analysis of the Play and Production, Directing Seminar, April
1982	Michael Dixon, *Our Town*, Thornton Wilder: Production Book (no performance), Seminar, May
1983	William M. Laing, "The History of Theatre at Muskingum College from 1971-1983": Theatre History Seminar, May
1983	Sunny Boulet, *A Musical Revue of the American Theatre Past and Present*, Original Script by Musical Theatre Class: Assistant Director's Production Book Seminar, November
1984	Linda Higgs, "A Portfolio of Costume Designs for William Shakespeare's The Tempest": May
1985	Matthew Wyscarver, The Living Word Experience: Outdoor Theatre Production Seminar, May
1985	James Daly, "A Definition of 'Capra-esque' Based on an Analysis of Three Films by Frank Capra": Research and Film Presentation Seminar, May
1985	Peter Sutherland, Mass Appeal, Bill Davis: Production Book, Directing Seminar, December
1986	Jerry Widenhofer, Trial by Jury, William Gilbert and Arthur Sullivan: Directing Seminar, March
1987	Frederick S. Frank, "Fate and Character in Eugene O'Neill's Long Day's Journey into Night": Dramatic Literature Seminar, May
1987	Kristine M. Engle, "John Huston: The Man and His Work": Film Theory and Criticism Seminar, May
1988	Deborah Wolfert, "A Study in Effective Publicity Techniques for the Muskingum College Theatre": Theatre Management Seminar, May

1988   Deborah Wolfert, "The Theatre of the Absurd According to Sartre and Beckett": Theory and Criticism Seminar, May

1989   Deborah Wolfert, The Maids, Jean Genet: Production Book, Directing Seminar, February

1989   Alisha Lenning, The Secret Princess, "Developing The Secret Princess": Playwriting Seminar, April

1989   Derek Whitehead, "Adolphe Appia's Lighting Theories Applied to Layton Theatre": Theatre Lighting Theory Seminar, May

1990   Alisha Lenning, The Secret Princess, Original Script by the Director: Directing Seminar, April

1990   Philip D. Albaugh, "Craig's Theories Applied": Theatre Design Theory Seminar, May

1990   John C. Ridenour, "Stage vs. Screen: A Comparative Study of Acting for Theatre and Acting for Film": Acting Theory Seminar, May

1990   Sam Hook, Life with Father, Howard Lindsay and Russell Crouse: Production Book (no performance) Seminar, May

1991   Shelly Peters, Butterflies Are Free, Leonard Gershe: Set and Costume Design Seminar, April

1991   Joseph B. Rath, "'Recognition' in a Few English Tragedies": Dramatic Literature for Oral Interpretation Seminar, May

1991   Amy S. Brown, "Handicapped in the Theatre": Theatre Public Relations Seminar, May

1991   Tracie Moreau, "Analysis of the Play The Belle of Amherst": Dramatic Literature Seminar, May

1991   Beth Hammer, "Theatrical Effectiveness of the Supernatural in Macbeth": Dramatic Theory and Criticism Seminar, May

1991   Susan Murphy, Steel Magnolias, Robert Harling: Production Book, Directing Seminar, October

1993   Jennifer Zornow, Agnes of God, John Pielmeier: Lighting Design Seminar, March

1993   Victoria Costanzo, "The Meaning of Dance in Kiss Me, Kate": Dance-Theatre Seminar, May

1993   Anne Gardner, The Matchmaker, Thornton Wilder, Directing Seminar, October

1993   Becky Ellis, Luv, Murray Schisgal: Stage Manager's Production Book, Stage Management Seminar, November

1994   Angela Dunn, "August Strindberg and Miss Julie": Theatre History and Criticism Seminar, May

1994   Anne Gardner, Charley's Aunt, Brandon Thomas: Production Book, Independent Study in Directing Seminar, October

1995   Amy Mitchell, Rumors, Neil Simon: Production Book, Directing Seminar, April

1995   Matt Jordan, Rumors, Neil Simon: "A Designer's Perspective": Scene Design Seminar, April

Epilogue
A Production History
1995–2000

1995–1996

1995

October 11-14   *Tartuffe*, by Moliére; directed Diane Rao
(Homecoming)

November 15-18   *Love Letters*, by A. R. Gurney; Guest Director Bob Belfance

1996

February 21-24   *1959 Pink Thunderbird,* by James McClure; directed by Diane Rao

April 10-13   *Crossing Delancey*, by Susan Sandler; student director, Barrett Hileman

June 14-15   *Love Letters*, by A. R. Gurney; Guest Director Bob Belfance

1996–1997

1996

October 23-27   *Twelfth Night*, by William Shakespeare; directed by Diane Rao

November 14-17   *Blue Horses*, by Kathryn Schultz Miller; directed by Jerry Martin

1997

February 12-16   *A Thurber Carnival*, by James Thurber; directed by Jerry Martin and Gene Alesandrini

March 12-16   *Night of January 16th*, by Ayn Rand; directed by Diane Rao

April 9-13   **Two Student-Directed One-Acts**: "5 Nights and a Pair of Shorts:" "Overtones," by Alice Gerstenberg, student director, Carmella Braniger "A Visitor from Forest Hills," by Neil Simon, student director, Robin Hatcher

1997–1998

1997

October 15-19   *In Search of the Red River Dog*, by Sandra Perlman (a premier production); directed by Jerry Martin

November 19-23   *Cotton Patch Gospel*, music and lyrics by Harry Chapin, book by Tom Key and Russell Treyez; (Based upon Clarence Jordan's translation of the Gospels of Matthew and John), directed by Ronald Lauck

1998

February 18-22   *A Ride With Huey the Engineer*, by Jesse Stuart (Adapted for the stage by the Appalachian Children's Theatre Series, through the auspices of the Jesse Stuart Foundation Theatre Series); directed by Jerry Martin

April 1-5   *Fefu and Her Friends*, by Maria Irene Fornes; directed by Diane Rao

1998–1999

1998

October 7-11   *Zara Spook and Other Lures*, by Joan Ackerman; Guest Director Maureen Ryan

November 18-22   *The Menaechmi*, by Plautus; directed by Diane Rao

1999

February 10-14   *The Rat Trap*, by James and Bronwyn Jamison; directed by Jerry Martin

March 3-7   **Two One-Act Plays by Caryl Churchill**: "Seagulls," and "Three More Sleepless Nights," by Caryl Churchill; directed by Diane Rao.

April 8-11   "Will Work for Food," Student-Directed Workshop;
(Parents Weekend)   "The Way We Live Now," by Edward Parone, after a short story by Susan Sontag; student director, Nadine Miller "Afterglow," by Eric C. Peterson; student director, Adam R. Tilton

"Landscape with Waitress," by Robert Pine; student director, Tricia English

"Reflections," an original drama by Nelson Chimilio; student director, Nelson Chimilio

1999–2000

1999

October 20-24	*The Annie Glenn Story,* by Mary Tensing; directed by Diane Rao
November 17-21	*SubUrbia,* by Eric Bogosian; student director, Tricia English
December 2	*The New Concord Christmas Cycle Play,* an Original Script by Theatre 151 Introduction to Theatre Students; advisors, Diane Rao and Ronald Lauck
Continuous	*Muskie Night at the Improv!* Students in the Improvisational Theatre Class performed at the beginning of each month in the Thomas Hall Dining Room.

2000

February 9-13	*Three the Hard Way*, by Linda Eisenstein; directed by Jerry Martin
April 5,7,8,9	**The Student Showcase**, featuring creative work of Theatre 395 (Directing):
	"A Coupla White Chicks Sitting Around Talking," by John Ford Noonan; student director, Elizabeth F. Snyder
	"The Dutchman," by LeRoi Jones; student director, Larina Waite
	"The Fourposter," student director, Robin Stock
	Speech Events from SPCO 316 (Intercollegiate Forensics)
	Dancers from Theatre 175 (Movement and Voice) and Original Work from Theatre 496 (Independent Study in performance)
	"An American Player in Pyramus and Thisbe," adapted by Chris Tucci Carter from William Shakespeare's *A Midsummer Night's Dream*
April 13	**The Radio Drama Showcase**, organized by Professors Jeffrey Harman and Diane Rao, the Radio Drama Writing and Production Class performed original dramas in the style of old-time radio dramas the dramas were seen live on stage and simultaneously broadcast over WMCO. (The Showcase was part of the inauguration of President Anne C. Steele.)
April 19	*The New Concord Passion Play,* an original script by students in Theatre 151 Introduction to Theatre Class

Campus Buildings Used for Special Events and Theatre

The Little Theatre • 1900

The Little Theatre was originally the men's gymnasium, and then the women's gym, then a storage area, then a theatre workshop, until it was renovated into a theatre in 1939 by alumni.
Photo courtesy M.C. Public Relations Office.

Brown Chapel • 1912

Brown Chapel was named for college benefactor, J. M. Brown of Wheeling, West Virginia. It has served as a chapel and as an auditorium for musicals and plays since 1913. *Photo courtesy M.C. Public Relations Office.*

John Glenn Gymnasium • 1935

John Glenn Gymnasium, 1935. This building was re-named in 1962 for the distinguished United States astronaut/senator/alumnus. It has served large audiences for athletics, visiting speakers, and theatre productions. *Photo courtesy M.C. Public Relations Office.*

The Muskingum College Little Theatre Gallery

Featuring portraits and posters by William Blakesley
A poster and caricatures by Chab Guthrie

Introduction to The Gallery

From the early years of the Renaissance, the easel artist has been attracted to the theatre. There was ample work for him to do if he wished: scenery to design and paint, and costumes to design and execute. Long before the invention of the camera and the evolution of photography, the artist had become an integral part of many theatres. Among these artists are the Bibiena family, Giacomo Torelli, Antoine Watteau, William Hogarth, Jacques Callot, Jean Berain, Henri de Toulouse Lautrec, Edgar Degas, Leon Bakst, Ernst Stern, Robert Edmond Jones, Lee Simonson, Donald Oenslager, Joel Mielziner, and Tanya Moiseiwitsch.

The Little Theatre was indeed fortunate to have its own artist-in-residence, William Blakesley, a member of the Muskingum College Art Department. The Theatre's need for someone to do posters for advertising, and Mr. Blakesley's love of theatre, brought the two together in the '60s and '70s. He liked to come to rehearsals to learn something about the play and get ideas for sketches. He would sit in one of the audience chairs and scratch furiously with charcoal. The actors were especially enthusiastic about his sketches and portraits.

Chab Guthrie, a student, also did a significant amount of art work for the Theatre. The work of these two artists attracted patrons and admirers, some of whom conned the posters soon after they were distributed. We learned not to put the art work on display too soon because it had a tendency to disappear into private rooms in the dorms and club houses!

The work of these two artists resulted in what I call the Little Theatre Gallery and I present it to you on the following pages.

A Short Survey of William Blakesley's Work

William Blakesley earned his B.S. in Education at Ohio State University in 1947, and became Instructor in Drawing at his alma mater from 1947-1949, during which time he also earned his Master of Fine Arts (1948). He joined the Muskingum College faculty in 1949 as head of the Art Department and, in 1956, was awarded an Associate Professorship.

Art professor William Blakesley hard at work in his studio, creating that particular magic which served the Little Theatre so well in the '60s and '70s. *Photo courtesy M.C. Public Relations Office.*

Mr. Blakesley is nationally known for his oil paintings, water colors, serigraphs, and silk screen prints. He has received a number of prizes, including the Roulet Medal, and First Place Honors in oil and graphics at the Toledo Museum of Art; firsts in oil and graphics at the Columbus Art League shows, Columbus Gallery of Fine Arts; firsts at Ohio State Fair; prizes in Ohio Watercolor Society shows, Ohio Printmakers Exhibition, Boston Printmakers, and the All-Island Art show at Martha's Vineyard, where he owns a gallery.

He has exhibited in the Ohio Valley Oil and Watercolor show, the Massillon Museum Annual show, Bradley University national exhibition of prints; Buffalo Print Club; the Art Association of Newport; Old Northwest Territory Exhibition; the Philadelphia Print Club; National Print Biennial at Albany, New York; Northwest Printmakers in Seattle; the Annual Exhibit of the Society of American Etchers, Engravers, Lithographers and Woodcutters; National Academy of Design; Audubon Artists; National Serigraph Society; Society of Graphic Artists, the National Print Exhibition at Laguna Beach, California; Graphic Arts Exhibit at Wichita, Kansas; and many private galleries.

His works are included in such notable private collections as those of Frank Seiberling, Edward G. Robinson, Josephine and Philip Bruno, Mr. and Mrs. Richard Leahy, Mrs. Tishman, and in the collections of a number of colleges and universities, the Zanesville Art Institute, Columbus Gallery of Fine Arts, and the Toledo Museum of Art.

Mr. Blakesley retired from Muskingum College in 1975 and moved to his gallery at Martha's Vineyard.* (*Supplied by the Muskingum College Library Archives.)

Chab (Clarence) Guthrie

Chab Guthrie as Gottlieb Biederman in *The Fire-bugs*, 1970. *Theatre file photo courtesy M.C. Public Relations Office.*

As a student and alumnus of Muskingum, Chab Guthrie has unselfishly contributed to the Theatre his talents as an actor and as an artist. It is difficult to decide in which of the two arts he excels the better, but I am quite happy that he shares them so liberally with the Theatre.

I have salvaged one of his posters from the ravages of time, the illustrations which he created for the Muskingum College Handbook, and several of the program covers that he designed for plays. To be honest about some of the designs, I never quite understand them, but their styles seem to be a mixture of crazy, witty, sophisticated baroque, rococo, and art-deco.

In a class by themselves are the caricatures he drew of himself and his fellow actors, as they exposed themselves hell-bent for performance in front of the discriminating theatre populace of New Concord, Ohio. Luckily, I preserved a mere handful of those revealing portraits, and I offer them here for the reader's pleasure.

Credits

The William Blakesley portraits and posters are from the author's private collection and are printed here with permission of the artist.

The Chab Guthrie poster and caricatures are from the author's private collection and are printed here with permission of the artist.

The Gallery

Vladimir and Estragon wait
in *Waiting for Godot*
WILLIAM BLAKESLEY, 5/67

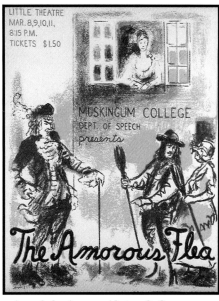

Arnolph, Agnes, Alain, & Georgette
from *The Amorous Flea*
(a musical based on a Moliére play)
WILLIAM BLAKESLEY, 3/67

Judy Sjoberg as Rhoda Penmark
in *The Bad Seed*
WILLIAM BLAKESLEY, 12/61

Captain "Big Jim" Warington
in *Little Mary Sunshine*
as played by Gerry Lefever
CHAB GUTHRIE, 10/67

Alain in *The Amorous Flea*
as played by Chab Guthrie
CHAB GUTHRIE, 3/67

Sheila Williams as "First Ayola"
in *Doña Rosita*
WILLIAM BLAKESLEY, 3/66

Ted Hissam as "Enrique"
in *The Amorous Flea*
WILLIAM BLAKESLEY, 3/67

Mme. Ernestine Von Liebedich
in *Little Mary Sunshine*
as played by Donna Brevak
CHAB GUTHRIE, 10/67

Scenes from
Mother Courage and Her Children
WILLIAM BLAKESLEY, 12/67

Dr. Donald Hill as "Porter"
in *Macbeth*
WILLIAM BLAKESLEY, 3/72

Mercedes McCambridge
in *Under Milk Wood*
WILLIAM BLAKESLEY, 5/75

Epops in *The Birds*
as played by Mr. Gardner
CHAB GUTHRIE, 3/70

Fritz Enstrom as "Pa Ubu"
in *King Ubu*
WILLIAM BLAKESLEY, 3/72

Donna Brevak as Katharine
in *The Taming of the Shrew*
WILLIAM BLAKESLEY, 5/68

Pithetaerus in *The Birds*
as played by Mr. Hamilton
CHAB GUTHRIE, 3/70

Judith Moore as "Mother of the Spinsters"
in *Doña Rosita*
WILLIAM BLAKESLEY, 3/66

Jeffrey Schroeder as "First Murderer"
and Richard Werner as "Macbeth"
in *Macbeth*
WILLIAM BLAKESLEY, 3/72

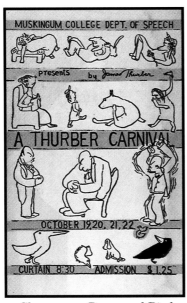

Characters, Dogs, and Birds
from *A Thurber Carnival*
WILLIAM BLAKESLEY, 10/66

Fritz Enstrom as "Pozzo"
in *Waiting for Godot*
WILLIAM BLAKESLEY, 5/67

Georgette in *The Amorous Flea*
as played by Donna Brevak
CHAB GUTHRIE, 3/67

Lyn Webber as "Ma Ubu"
in *King Ubu*
WILLIAM BLAKESLEY, 3/72

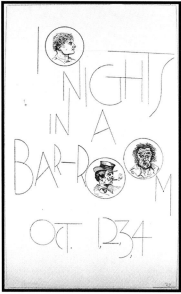

Ten Nights in a Bar-Room
A Musical Melodrama
CHAB GUTHRIE, 10/69

Mercedes McCambridge
during rehearsals for
Under Milk Wood
WILLIAM BLAKESLEY, 5/75

Dr. Donald Hill
as "Dromio of Ephesus"
in *The Comedy of Errors*
WILLIAM BLAKESLEY, 3/71

Horace in *The Amorous Flea*
played by Jim Scott
CHAB GUTHRIE, 3/67

Ted Hissam as "Vladimir"
in *Waiting for Godot*
WILLIAM BLAKESLEY, 5/67

Arnolphe in *The Amorous Flea*
as played by James Hall, Jr.
CHAB GUTHRIE, 3/67

Dr. Donald Hill as "Chrysalde"
in *The Amorous Flea*
WILLIAM BLAKESLEY, 3/67

Robert Adams as
The Stage Manager in *Our Town*
WILLIAM BLAKESLEY, 3/68

General Oscar Fairfax, Retired
in *Little Mary Sunshine*
played by Chab Guthrie
CHAB GUTHRIE, 10/67

Euelpides in *The Birds*
as played by Mr. Spengler
CHAB GUTHRIE, 3/70

FleetFoot
in *Little Mary Sunshine*
played by Mr. Hill
CHAB GUTHRIE, 10/67

Rile, Ida 32
Roberts, Amanda Emily 187, 192, 193, 218, 331, 396, 410
Roberts, Emogene 77
Roberts, O. H. 35
Robinson, Beth 116, 149, 150, 153, 154
Robinson, Rev. Charles H. 18
Rose, Harrison 67
Ross, Edith Isabelle 77
Ross, Judy 157, 392
Roulet Medal 420
Rush, Dr. James 30
Rush, Thelma Auriel 76
Russell, William 15, 30, 34

S

Sargent, Franklin 31
Saroyan, William 186
    plays 186
Schenck, Sally 158, 169, 393, 410
Schofield, Anna Mae 77
school newspaper 185
schools
    acting 31, 201, 325, 328
    oratory 30, 32, 33, 37, 38, 39, 40, 41, 42, 43, 45, 46, 57, 59, 63, 75
Schott, John R. 34
Schreiber, 64, 113
Schroeder, Jeff 192, 219, 221, 225, 396
Schwier, Hope 230, 398, 411, 412
Secrest, Robert ix
seminars
    Acting 410, 411, 412, 413
    Analysis of the Play and Costume Design Seminar 410
    Costume Design 409, 411
    Critical Analysis 410
    Dance Drama 411
    Debate 60, 111
    description 128, 132, 158, 159, 174, 175, 191, 205, 212, 216, 218, 221, 224, 225, 228, 230, 231, 232, 235, 238, 249, 251, 255, 258, 274, 279, 284, 295, 296, 311, 320, 321, 331, 332, 333, 346, 347, 352, 409
    Directing 321, 409, 410, 411, 412, 413
    Drama and Psychology 411
    Dramatic Literature and Criticism 410
    Educational Theatre 411, 412
    Interpretation 60, 76, 111, 116
    Lighting Design 412

seminars (con't)
    Production 409
    Recital 71, 72, 114, 116
    Scene Design 410, 412
    Speech 61, 76, 111, 114, 116
    Theatre 412
    Theatre Management 413
        Seminar Students 409-414
Seneca 16, 264
Senf, Greg 225, 226, 230, 231, 249, 251, 252, 398, 399, 400, 411
set design 33, 45, 46, 54, 68, 80, 82, 91, 99, 102, 105, 108, 110, 115, 116, 119, 120, 125, 127, 129, 130, 132, 135, 136, 138, 139, 141, 142, 144, 147, 148, 151, 152, 155, 156, 157, 163, 168, 169, 173, 174, 178, 180, 181, 182, 185, 189, 191, 203, 204, 217, 220, 223, 224, 225, 228, 230, 231, 232, 238, 239, 240, 243, 244, 245, 250, 251, 255, 264, 276, 277, 285, 286, 287, 291, 293, 295, 296, 297, 305, 307, 309, 311, 312, 313, 315, 317, 319, 332, 333, 335, 337, 338, 340, 341, 345, 348, 349, 351, 352, 353, 358, 359, 360, 361, 362, 363, 364, 365, 366, 367, 368, 369, 370, 371, 379, 393, 420
Shanley 64
Sheil, Bobbi 224, 226, 230, 231, 399, 411
Sheldrew, James 214
Shelton, Jim 186
Sheppard 19
Sheridan, Thomas 16, 29, 30, 33
Shoemaker, J. W. 32, 36, 39, 42, 74
Shonkwiler, Peter 187
Simerka, Susan 193, 218, 396, 410
Simonson, Lee 420
Sittig, Barbara Jean 77
Sjoberg, Judy 129, 134, 148, 149, 154, 194, 392
Skinner, Otis 88
Sklar, George 142
Small, Janet 148, 154, 158, 159, 392, 410
Smith, Catherine 185
Smith, Helen Kathryn 76
Smith, John Coventry 76
Smith, John ix

Smyth, Corinne E. 187
Snodgrass, Jessie Eva 44
Snyder, Elizabeth F. 369, 374, 416
Socratic method 15
Sofis, Ted 209, 221, 222, 224, 226, 230, 231, 300, 398, 411
Sophocles 16, 151, 153, 194, 223, 226, 305, 306, 307, 392, 397
Speck, Samuel W., Jr. xiii, 68, 114
speech
    correction 30, 38, 160, 163, 213, 370
    events 416
    therapy 30, 160, 370
Speech Department 59, 66, 67, 70, 113, 129, 160, 164, 172, 198, 259, 379
Spillman, David 241, 246, 400, 413
Spitznagel, Mary Ann xi, 193, 217, 219, 221, 225, 226, 245, 257, 396, 397, 411
St. Denis, Ruth 31
Stanislavsky 101, 102, 103, 119, 137, 155, 317
Stanley, Myra 204, 225, 231, 232, 235, 236, 399, 400, 412
State Oratorical Contest 25, 41, 43, 45, 68
Steele, Joshua 29
Steinberg, Bernice 222, 397
Stephenson, Gladys Olive 76
Stern, Ernst 420
Stevens, Thomas Wood 88, 93, 197
Stinson, Sally 191, 395, 410
Stock, Robin 368, 370, 371, 373, 374, 416
Sturgeon, J.B. 65
Sturm, Jo Clude 77
Summers, Bessie Mary 44
Sutherland, Peter 295, 405
Swabb, Joel 68, 69, 133
Swanner, Michael 277, 403
Sweigart, Charles 193, 211
Sweitzer, Harry P. 67, 77
Sweitzer, Robert Edward 77
Sykes, Mary 255, 256, 279, 280, 321, 403, 413

T

Tate, Edward 391
Taylor, Jack 171
Taylor, Laurette 169
Taylor, Patricia 226, 228, 230, 235, 258, 398, 412
teacher certification ix, 18, 33, 34, 214, 269
Teener, Alice Adaline 76
Terence 16

About the Author

Donald P. Hill, Ph.D., Professor Emeritus of Speech Communication and Theatre from Muskingum College in New Concord, Ohio, has spent most of his life deeply involved with the theatre.

He received his Bachelor of Arts degree from Muskingum College in 1949, then taught public school for ten years. He received a Masters in Dramatic Art from Western Reserve University in 1956, and returned to his alma mater in 1959 as Director of Theatre. During his tenure at Muskingum, he continued his education in theatre, obtaining a Master of Fine Arts from the University of Iowa, and his Doctorate from the University of Minnesota.

After his retirement from Muskingum in 1995, Don set out to document a lifetime career in the theatre. Forty-six years dedicated to teaching students the skills of acting, directing, and other facets of the theatre have provided him with the vast amounts of information found in *Mostly Theatre*.

"I am totally committed to the amateur and professional theatre, and to theatre as a significant element in a liberal arts education," says Don. "I am pleased to have been a part of the tradition of excellence at Muskingum College, and the rich heritage of speech and theatre which has contributed substance and value to Muskingum's education of 'uncommon men and women.'"

His previous publications include *The Muskingum Theatre Handbook* (1970) and "Honors in Theatre: Bertolt Brecht," published in nationally-recognized industry magazine, *The Speech Teacher* (1968).